ECONOMIC HISTORY

THE AGRICULTURAL REVOLUTION

AGRICULTURE

THE AGRICULTURAL
REVOLUTION

ERIC KERRIDGE

LONDON AND NEW YORK

First published in 1967

Reprinted in 2006 by
Routledge
2 Park Square, Milton Park, Abingdon, Oxon, OX14 4RN
711 Third Avenue, New York, NY 10017

Routledge is an imprint of the Taylor & Francis Group, an informa business

First issued in paperback 2013

British Library Cataloguing in Publication Data
A CIP catalogue record for this book
is available from the British Library

The Agricultural Revolution
ISBN 0-415-38146-0 (volume)
ISBN 0-415-37652-1 (subset)
ISBN 0-415-28619-0 (set)
ISBN 13: 978-0-415-84597-7 (Pbk)
ISBN 13: 978-0-415-38146-8 (Hbk)

Routledge Library Editions: Economic History

THE AGRICULTURAL REVOLUTION

ENGLISH
FARMING
COUNTRIES
in the age of the
Agricultural Revolution

THE AGRICULTURAL REVOLUTION

ERIC KERRIDGE

University College of North Wales

London

GEORGE ALLEN & UNWIN LTD

RUSKIN HOUSE MUSEUM STREET

To Daphne

PREFACE

I wish to express warm thanks to those who have helped me write this book: to Professors Sir John Neale and John U. Nef, who both aided and inspired; to Professors S. T. Bindoff, Duncan Black, F. E. Hyde, S. B. Saul, W. M. Scammell, W. Woodruff, J. D. Chambers, J. Hurstfield, H. R. Trevor-Roper, and H. J. Habakkuk; to Doctors Dorothea Oschinsky and J. R. Harris; to the Trustees of the Houblon-Norman Fund, without whose generous act of faith the work could never have been completed; to the marquesses of Bath and of Lansdowne, the Earl of Pembroke and Montgomery, the Lady Nairne, Mrs Mary Arnold-Forster, and others, who kindly allowed me access to their manuscripts and extended their hospitality to me; to the Misses Joan Wake, Elizabeth Crittall, Carolyn Merion and Susan Flower; to Mrs Margaret Spufford and Joan Thirsk; to Major F. H. T. Jervoise; to Messrs M. Fowle, P. I. King, R. B. Pugh, G. E. Fussell, W. J. Slack, G. Bishop, B. W. Parker, A. S. Wood, and R. H. Adams; to the kingdom's archivists and their assistants, for services and kindnesses; to all my brothers and sisters, and my parents; to the late R. H. Tawney and the late Miss Pinchin of Withington Bassetts, Box; and, above all, to my wife, who joined me in several searches in the archives, and has helped in other ways too numerous to list, too important to forget.

University College of North Wales, Bangor   E.K.

NOTE ON ABBREVIATIONS

not among standard forms in C. C. Matthews,

A Dictionary of Abbreviations

Acc. *Accession*
Acq. *Acquisition*
A/d *Archdeacon(ry)*
Add. *Additional*
A.O. *Augmentation Office*
Art. *Articulus*
B. *Broxborne Bury*
B.A. *Bulk accession*
Bpl. *Birthplace*
Ch. *Chamber, Charter*
Compl. *Complaint*
Cons. *Consistory*
D. *Deed*
Dep. *Deposition*
D.L. *Duchy of Lancaster*
Ecton *Sotheby (Ecton)*
F.-H. *Finch-Hatton*
F.(M.) *Fitzwilliam (Milton)*
G'bury *Gorhambury*
G.S. *General Series*
H. *Holywell*
HEN. *Heneage of Hainton*
H.M. *Hand Morgan*
Hood *Gregory-Hood*
H.R. *Historical (History) Review*
I.(L.) *Isham (Lamport)*
K.R. *King's Remembrancer*
Lans. *Lansdowne*
L.B. *Lennard, Brassey & others*
Leigh *Stoneleigh (Leigh)*
L.P. *Letters & Papers*
L.R. *Land Revenue*
M.,m. *Membrane*
M.B. *Miscellaneous Book(s)*

Mont. *Montagu*
M.R. *Manorial Records*
Mun. *Muniment*
O.(K.) *Ormonde (Kilkenny)*
O.W. *Original Will(s)*
P.&M. *Philip & Mary*
Pec. *Peculiar*
R. *Roll*
R.&S. *Rentals & Surveys*
Recog. *Recognition*
Req. *Court of Requests Proceedings*
R.H. *Rider, Heaton, Meredith & Mills*
R.O. *Record (or Archives) Office*
Rot. *Rotulet*
S.(G.) *Silverman (Geddington)*
Sp. *Special*
S.P. *State Papers*
S.P.D. *State Papers Domestic*
Throckmorton *Coughton (Throckmorton)*
T.R. *Treasury of Receipt*
W.deB. *Willoughby de Broke*
Westmill *Westmill-Wakeley-Buntingford*
Wilts.Mag. *Wiltshire Archaeological & Natural History Magazine*
W.(S.) *Westmorland (Sharlston)*
Y.(O.) *Young (Orlingbury)*
York *Borthwick Institute of Historical Research, York*

NOTE: dates O.S. in references to manuscripts, elsewhere N.S.

CONTENTS

CHAPTER I

INTRODUCTORY

THIS book argues that the agricultural revolution took place in England in the sixteenth and seventeenth centuries and not in the eighteenth and nineteenth.

A far earlier age had seen a transformation of agriculture by the widespread substitution of permanent for temporary cultivation, and the present century has seen another wrought by chemical and mechanical means; but here we shall mean by 'agricultural revolution' that cluster of innovations more usually associated with the period from 1750 to 1850. Although the ramifications of the agricultural revolution stretched far and wide, considerations of space forbid that we should hereinunder attempt more than to answer the questions of what took place and when and how, leaving the whys and wherefores for separate treatment.

The salient features of this revolution are usually held to be the enclosure of common fields by Act of Parliament, the accompanying replacement of bare fallows by root crops and artificial grasses, the institution and dissemination of the Norfolk four-course system, the introduction of drills and other improved implements, the drainage of farmland, the breeding of new and better sheep and cattle and the supersession of draught oxen by horses. The pioneers and heroes of this revolution were formerly conceived to be Tull, Townshend, Coke and Bakewell; and even though their stature may now have been somewhat diminished, the original conception of the agricultural revolution has hardly been changed. Adherence is still given to the view that the agricultural revolution, or the opening stages of it, coincided, by a fortunate chance, with the industrial revolution, which itself commenced with the accession of George III and was more or less complete in time for the Great Reform Bill of 1832. The current statement of this standpoint asserts that by 1760 'in no part of Britain—not even in Norfolk itself—were the innovations adopted on such a scale as to make it possible to speak of an agricultural, or even an agrarian revolution'.[1]

---

[1] Ernle, *Eng. Farming Past & Pres.* 1927; T. S. Ashton, *Ind. Rev. 1760–1830* 1948, pp. 27–8, 60 sqq.

When we come to examine the conventional criteria of the revolution, the first, relating to enclosure, proves unsatisfactory. The simple world in which all land was either common or enclosed turns out to be imaginary. Reality was far more complex. Many often large parcels in common fields were enclosed with quicksets, though no less subject to common rights. These closes were Lammas lands and had to be thrown open to common of pasture at Lammas.[1] Were the gates not left open, the commoners would make no bones about tearing a gap in the hedge.[2] The spread of Lammas closes facilitated the division of common fields.[3] For one thing, it made it easy to take a step towards severalty by persuading the commoners temporarily to forbear from exercising common rights. Thus they might be given ten shillings a year in lieu of common rights in a Lammas croft.[4] A Lammas close in which common rights were entirely forborne was the most attenuated form of common field that could be, for the occupier had only to neglect payment and the land was *de facto* severalty. A court case in 1630 neatly illustrates this. The presentment[5] is that:

'Mr Corbin hath sowed some parte of the Hale Close against the gate on purpose to hinder the tennants . . . of their right of common there, the said Hale Close and Hale Meadowe being both Lammas grounds. . . . If Mr Corbins predecessors or ancesters at any tyme had corne growing uppon the Hale Close which they could not get into theire barne before Lammas eve, they allwayes sent to the tennants of Shuttington to give them satisfaccon for theire forbearance.'

This Corbin had now failed to do. Another farmer, who owed £2 a year compensation for sufferance to plough up some Lammas closes from time to time even if it interfered with the exercise of common rights,

[1] E.g. H. S. Darbyshire & G. D. Lumb, *Hist. Methley* Thoresby Soc. 1937 xxxv, 211; G. F. Farnham, *Quorndon Recs.* 1912, p. 14; J. W. F. Hill, *Med. Lincoln* 1948, p. 336; J. Smyth, *Descron Hund. Berk.* 1885, p. 51; Deene ho. Brudenell b. ii. 15–6; BM, Add. 27535, ff. 37, 45v.; 33453, f. 119v.; Sir Th. Phillips' Tracts: Topog. & Geneal. iii, Wanborough Ct R. pt i, 23–5, 27–8, 30–2, 37, 40, 42 sqq., 51, 53, 55, 57, 60; PRO, D.L., M.B., 109, f. 111; Exch. L.R., M.B. 185, ff. 30–1, 43v.; 192, m. 22(18)d.; Herts. R.O., 7059, 7062; Wilts. R.O., acc. 132 bdl. 10 Ct Bk Bishopstrow 1685; Salt Lib. H.M. (Chetwynd), Ct R. Ingestre 5 Oct. 39 Eliz., 9 Oct. 2 Jas; Cams. R.O., L. 88/3 ct files Caxton 29 Mar. 1 Chas; Glos. R.O., D. 184/M24, p. 134; War. R.O., M.R. 5 Moreton Morrell 9 Oct. 1710; Beds. R.O., A.D. 1060; Oxon. R.O., Eynsham Svy Bk 1650, f. 43; Northants. R.O., F-H 272, ff. 78, 92v.; 2758; Higham Ferrers Du. Ct 12 Apr. 16 Eliz.; Mont. Northants. 10/50 Ct R. Geddington 20 Apr. 5 Eliz.; 14/12 Ct. R. Brigstock 2 May 21 Eliz.; F(M) Misc. 211.

[2] P.R.O., Exch. K.R., Deps. by Commn 20 Eliz. East. 4, ex parte quer. & def.; Trin. 3, dep. by Wm Hutchens; St. Ch. Hy VIII 19/11, comple. & ans.; 18/90.

[3] B'ham Lib. 344741.

[4] Wilton ho. Ditchampton Ct Bk starting 1742, 1755–6 entry.

[5] P.R.O., Exch. A.O., M.B. 380, f. 18.

eventually developed scruples about paying this money into the poor box.[1] Secondly, some none the less common meadows, pastures, hams, crofts and arable fields were enclosed with hedges or walls.[2] Thus a Ryme widow had 'one acre of wheat in common close'.[3] Sometimes this situation arose from an exchange of lands whereby an enclosed severalty field was granted in common in return for common field surrendered elsewhere. At Kenilworth three such common closes contained 300 acres altogether.[4] Other common closes resulted from the commoners' decision to improve their fields by walling or hedging and ditching.[5] Furthermore, many intakes from rough grazing in hilly districts took the form of closes held in common by a group of tenants, and some of these 'improvements' were arable.[6] Thus Rye Croft in Audley is a 'butty field, where there is common of pasture when it is graised and when it is tilled common for tillage'.[7]

Conversely, much open land was free of common rights, as free as the most enclosed of enclosures. Bringing the dispersed properties of each person into fewer pieces, freed from all rights of commonage, was called 'putting the lands in *severalty*', in contradistinction to those subject to common rights, which were called *tenantry* lands. Severalty lands were thus neither common nor enclosed.[8] In the sixteenth and seventeenth centuries more and more land in the Chalk Country was put into severalty by the extinction of common rights. Thus at Chilmark and Ridge the demesne farm acquired three new severalty fields between

[1] P.R.O., L.R., M.B. 198, f. 53; Req. 129/45, compl. & ans.

[2] E. Bateson & al. *Hist. Northumb.* 1893–1940 ii, 422; xii, 157; R. C. Shaw, *Recs. Lancs. Fam. fr. XII to XX cent.* 1940, p. 190; F. S. Colman, *Hist. Barwick-in-Elmet* 1908, p. 285; A. Raistrick, *Malham & Malham Moor* 1947, p. 20; E. Salt, *Hist. Standon* 1888, pp. 106, 109; E. C. K. Gonner, *Com. Land & Inclo.* 1912, p. 17; W. Brown *Yks. Deeds* Yks. Archaeol. Soc. Rec. Ser. 1909 xxxix, 45–6; G. Bradford, *Proc. in Ct St. Ch. in reigns Hy VII & VIII* Soms. Rec. Soc. 1911 xxvii, 56 sqq.; B.M., Add. 33452, f. 134; P.R.O., Sp. Coll. Ct R. G.S. 194/59, m. 2; D.L., M.B. 113, f. 32; 119, f. 51v.; Exch. L.R., M.B. 201, f. 48; 207, f. 20(18); 221, f. 276; T.R., Bk 174, f. 70; Lancs. R.O., DD.X. 160/3; Cartwright Hall, Swinton: Ct R. Newsam 30 May 24 Eliz.; Glouc. Lib. R.F. 30. 3; Northants. R.O., Wmld 4. xvi. 5, Nassington svy c. 1550; Old Par. Recs. fd offrs' bk, 1744; I.(L.) 128 Ct R. Lamport 1 Oct. 9 Eliz.; Mont. Northants. 7/66/12 Ct R. Weekley 22 Oct. 1695; War. 6/14 Ct R. Newbold 23 Oct. 1700.

[3] Wilts. R.O., Dioc. Reg. Sarum. inv. Mary Piddle 1666 Ryme.

[4] P.R.O., Exch. L.R., M.B. 185, ff. 37v., 43, 47; A.O., Parl Svys War. 15, ff. 18–9.

[5] Northants. R.O., Mont. Northants. 7/72 Ct Bk Weekley 18 May 8 Eliz.; Salt Lib. H. M. (Chetwynd): Gt Ct Ingestre & Salt 21 Apr. 27 Eliz.

[6] H. Fishwick, *Svy Manor Rochdale 1626* Chetham S. 1913 lxxi, 106, 119, 126; W. H. Chippindall, *16th-cent. Svy & Yr's A/c Estes Hornby Cas.* id. 1939 cii, 47–9; Bateson, op. cit. ii, 417, 422; T. S. Willan, 'Parl Svys N.R.', *Yks. Archaeol. Jnl* xxxi, 252, 254; Soms. R.O., D.D./C.N. Ct Bk Jn Francis 1573–87, p. 95.

[7] L. M. Midgley, 'Terryar for Audley', *Colls. Hist. Staffs.* 1947, p. 83.

[8] G. Slater, *Eng. Peasantry & Enclo. Com. Fds* 1907, pp. 234–5; T. Davis, *Gen. View Ag. Co. Wilts.* 1794, p. 14; W. Pearce, *id. Berks.* 1794, p. 49.

1567 and 1631.[1] In 1585 the Bulford farmer reached an agreement whereby he exchanged, consolidated and freed from common rights all his open arable, while the tenantry continued theirs in common field.[2] The way for the extinction of common rights was prepared by consolidating parcels hitherto dispersed, and in various townships certain farmers had their land in a few large parcels, so, even if they were not yet in severalty, the transformation would present few difficulties.[3] Sometimes lords of manors intervened to hasten consolidation, as at Hill Deverill, where Edmund Ludlow claimed some tenements had 'ben inbettered to all theyre contentmentes' by having 'theyre groundes placed neere together'.[4] Without some general agreement consolidation might be slow to achieve. It took the Nicholas family of Roundway the best part of the sixteenth century to exchange and consolidate thirty acres of field land.[5] Severalty gained ground steadily, but here quickly and there slowly. Much open land was in severalty and no more than three-quarters, probably much less, was subject to common rights at any time in the early modern period. In many townships tenantry and severalty balanced about evenly and in many more tenantry was less than severalty.[6] The significance of open land in severalty is, however, lost in any general view. Mostly, and increasingly, the large, especially the demesne, farms were in severalty, and family and part-time farms in tenantry. At Winterbourne Bassett, e.g. almost if not all the demesne farm was in severalty in 1567 and nearly all the severalty was part of the demesne farm.[7] In 1548 Pangbourne demesne farm had no common land whatsoever.[8] In 1552 a great part of Collingbourne Ducis demesne farm was in severalty.[9] At North Newton in 1567 only six and a quarter acres of the demesne farm were in common field.[10] All the arable of Fovant manor farm was in severalty.[11] At Amesbury Earls the demesne arable was not dispersed in common field but 'lyinge all together'.[12] Similarly, where there was much enclosure, it was the manorial tenants' land and not

[1] C. R. Straton, *Svy Lands Wm 1st E. Pembroke* 1909 i, 118; Wilton ho. Svys Manors 1632–3.

[2] P.R.O., Exch. L.R., M.B. 191, ff. 126 sqq.; 203, ff. 365 sqq.

[3] R. C. Hoare, *Hist. Mod. Wilts.* 1822–44, Hund. Alderbury 67 sqq.; Straton, op. cit. i, 267; E. J. Bodington, 'Church Svys in Wilts. 1649–50', *Wilts. Mag.* xl, 404–5; Wilts. R.O., Savernake: Svy Burbages 1574, f. 17; acc. 283, Bk Exts. Ct R. Seymour manors.

[4] P.R.O., St. Ch. Eliz. A. 11/8.

[5] B.M., Add. R. 37534.

[6] Inf. 46.

[7] Straton, op. cit. i, 265–7; Davis, op. cit. 15.

[8] P.R.O., Exch. L.R., M.B. 187, f. 400.

[9] P.R.O., D.L., M.B. 108, ff. 55v.–6.

[10] Straton, op. cit. i, 285–6.

[11] Wilton ho. Svys Manors 1631 i, Foffonnt, f. 1(3).

[12] Wilts. R.O., acc. 283, Amesbury Svy Bk 1574.

the demesne that remained in common field.[1] Precisely because of this general coincidence, 'tenantry' became synonymous with 'common'. Where a farmer's arable was in severalty, so usually were his down, pasture and meadow, and then his flock and fold were private. Thus, broadly, there were two classes of farms: severalty with private, and tenantry with common flocks. Open fields in severalty obtained not only in the Chalk Country[2] and in other down, wold and heath countries,[3] where to raise quickset hedges or make walls or fences was often impracticable and seldom advantageous, but also elsewhere.[4]

Two separate distinctions need making, then: between open and enclosed fields; and between common lands and severalty.

The assumption that open fields were old-fashioned and enclosed ones new and improved is unhistorical: whether they were open or enclosed depended primarily upon the terrain. In some places hedges were impossible, in others inevitable. Wherever land had first been brought into cultivation from the wood-pasture state, the numerous separate clearings remained bounded from each other by hedgerows and shaws that were merely the remains of the woods.[5] Whether the fields were open or enclosed has little bearing on the agricultural revolution.

Nor has the extinction of common rights much relevance to our argument, for it was not necessarily accompanied by any considerable improvement in husbandry. To change over from permanent tillage to permanent grass was no technical advance, and nobody could seriously imagine that the enclosure of enormous areas of Exmoor, the High Peak, the Welsh hills and other such tracts ever made them anything better than the rough grazing they have been since time immemorial.[6]

Neither the extinction of common rights nor enclosure can be used as a criterion of agricultural progress. But even if enclosure were such a criterion, it would, in the present state of historical studies, prove a useless one, for its progress has not yet been subjected to mensuration, and

[1] G. W. Kitchin, *Manor Manydown* Hants. Rec. Soc. 1895 x, 179–81; P.R.O., Exch. L.R., M.B. 187, f. 90v.

[2] W. Marshall, *Rev. Reps. to Bd Ag. fr. Midl. Dept* 1815, p. 450; Davis, op. cit. 14; Pearce, loc. cit.; Slater, loc. cit.

[3] W. Marshall, *Rural Econ. S. Cos.* 1798 ii, 39; P. Kalm, A/c *Visit to Engl.* 1892, p. 265; H. C. M. Lambert, *Hist. Banstead* 1912 i, 187–8; J. A. Venn, *Fndns Ag. Econ.* 1933, p. 44, opp. 64; W. G. Clarke, *In Breckland Wilds* 1926, p. 22; J. C. K. Cornwall, 'Agrarian Hist. Suss. 1560–1640', ts. thesis M.A. Ldn Univ. 1953, p. 196; A. Young, *View Ag. Oxon.* 1809, p. 124; P.R.O., D.L., M.B. 108, ff. 27v.–8; 116, f. 36; Exch. A.O., M.B. 421, ff. 33 sqq.

[4] W. Marshall, *On Landed Prop. Engl.* 1804, p. 13; Bateson, op. cit. i, 153; ii, 129; H. R. Thomas, 'Enclo. open fds & coms. in Staffs.', *Colls. Hist. Staffs.* 1933, p. 68; B.M., Add. 27605, f. 96; Harl. 368, f. 14(15); P.R.O., D.L., M.B. 116, f. 11v.; Exch. A.O., Parl. Svys Yks. 28, f. 16; Glos. R.O., D. 184/M24, pp. 199 sqq.

[5] Inf. 123, 129, 132.

[6] Inf. 149 sqq.

provided most of the allotments; but the awards rarely distinguish new severalty from old.[1]

In short, then, the Acts are complete, but give at best only rough estimates of the extent of land to be allotted, while the awards are extant only in samples and rarely allow the acreage of new enclosures to be calculated with any accuracy. With such data no statistical representation can be of much service. Slater was content to use the estimates in the Acts where these were forthcoming and to guess when they were not. Gonner was more scholarly, but even he could not avoid similar makeshifts, for the documents he used lacked the data he required.[2] Differences in method led to markedly discrepant results. Gonner's estimates of the extent of parliamentary enclosures in Norfolk are much lower than Slater's and so more agreeable with Gray's, whereas in Leicestershire and Huntingdonshire Gonner's estimates are higher than Slater's. Gonner's estimate for Oxfordshire is virtually the same as Gray's, with the significant qualification, however, that Gray was firmly convinced his estimates were too high.[3]

What is more interesting than the extent of parliamentary enclosures in general is the extent of common-field land that was enclosed by Act, for it is only this that signifies a clean break in the plan of farm management. Here again the records are unhelpful or misleading. It is usually difficult or impossible to determine from the Acts what proportion of the land to be enclosed was in common field.[4] Mention of common fields in the Acts is all too often merely part of cumbersome legal phraseology intended to comprehend all conceivable contingencies and cannot be taken as an indication that common fields existed. The Bredwardine Act mentions common fields, but the award shows only hills and heaths. Slater's list of enclosures of common fields contains some Acts better omitted, for no common fields were enclosed by them, despite their wording. Even where there was little or no common field, it was customary to ask for the nominal allotment of the entire township in order to obviate any remaining claims to common rights, to establish titles, to consolidate the farms and extinguish fold-courses if any existed.[5]

The best estimates of the extent and progress of parliamentary enclosure—those made by Gonner and in part corrected by Gray[6]—are but a fallible guide to the progress of enclosure in the eighteenth and nineteenth centuries. But even if they were perfect, no comparison could be struck with earlier times, for throughout the eighteenth century and

[1] Gray, op. cit. 112.
[2] Slater, op. cit. app.; Gonner, op. cit. 196–7.
[3] Curtler, op. cit. 182 sqq.; Gray, op. cit 114, 305, 536 sqq.
[4] Ibid. 306; Gonner, op. cit. 195; Riches, op. cit. 50.
[5] Gray, op. cit. 138–41, 305–6.
[6] Ibid. 115; Gonner, op. cit. 270 sqq.

the first half of the nineteenth, parliamentary enclosures were accompanied by divisions and enclosures neither ratified nor authorized by Act of Parliament.[1]

Similar difficulties arise from the study of enclosures ratified in courts other than parliament; but what is most discouraging is that no catalogue of enclosures can ever be exhaustive; nor the extent of its omissions be more than guessed at. In order to obtain adequate ground for generalization it is necessary to have resort also to estate records and analogous documents. Here at least may be found the states of the land at various times, even though it may only be vouchsafed that the field was 'ancient enclosure' or 'newly enclosed'. Estate records, too, permit escape from the conventional categories of enclosed and open land, which ignore both Lammas closes and lands in open severalty, not to speak of common closes.

Assessing the whole body of evidence, no matter what its provenance, it is possible to make broad generalizations concerning the progress of enclosure. In the Vale of Taunton Deane, the High Weald, the Wealden Vales and Romney Marsh, there never were common fields. In the Sandlings, Saltings, South Seacoast and Northdown countries, in High Suffolk, East Norfolk, the Woodland and the Petworth District the areas of common field were insignificant throughout the early modern period. The Cheese, Butter and Cheshire Cheese countries, the Vale of Berkeley and the Lancashire Plain all had some common fields, but they were of small and often decreasing extent. In the West Country, Wales and the North-western Lowlands, what little common field there was had only a temporary character. In the Peak-Forest District, the North Country and the Blackmoors there was slightly more common field in the early modern period, but it was mostly temporary. In the North-eastern Lowlands temporary common fields had originally been numerous and extensive, but were mostly enclosed in the course of the sixteenth and seventeenth centuries. Common fields were not of the first importance in the Vales of Hereford and they were mostly enclosed before 1700. The north-western escarpment apart, the Chiltern Country was mainly in severalty in the sixteenth century. There had been a considerable extent of common field in the Norfolk Heathlands, but it was mostly enclosed by agreement about the last quarter of the seventeenth century. The Vale of Pickering was enclosed in the course of the sixteenth and seventeenth centuries. Although many common fields still remained, the Fen

---

[1] Ibid. 45–6, 188, 190; Hammond, op. cit. i, 36; Gray, op. cit. 116–18; Curtler, op. cit. 251–2; Harrison, art. cit. 118–19; Raistrick, op. cit. 43; Bateson, op. cit. ii, 45; iii, 2–3; xii, 239, 318–19; W. H. Hosford, 'Eye-witness's A/c 17th-cent. Enclo.', *EcHR* 1951 iv, 219; R. Stewart-Brown, *Hist. Manor & Tp Allerton* 1911, p. 126; E. C. Woods and P. C. Brown, *Rise & Prog. Wallasey* 1929, p. 27; Thomas, art. cit. 71, 79–82; L. E. Tavener, *Com. Lands Hants.* 95; A. G. Ruston & D. Witney, *Hooton Pagnell* 1934, p. 90.

Country was mainly enclosed by about 1700. In the Western Water-lands, however, enclosure was less rapid. At the beginning of the eighteenth century perhaps as much as half the tillage was in common field in the vales of Evesham and London. In the Breckland, and in the Blackheath and Poor Soils countries, perhaps as much as a third of the land was divided and enclosed in the eighteenth century. By 1650 about half the Oxford Heights Country was already enclosed. In 1700 the Chalk, Southdown, Cotswold and Northwold countries still had much common-field land, but hardly less severalty. Most of the small farms were in common field, but few of the large ones. By 1650 for example, at least one-quarter of the Chalk Country was in severalty. The Midland Plain, too, was half enclosed by about this time. The vales of Evesham and London were areas of late enclosure. All in all, it might be roughly estimated that in 1700 about one-quarter of the enclosure of England and Wales remained to be undertaken. The hoary fable of the supreme importance of parliamentary enclosures should be relegated to limbo.

It might be suggested that the extension of cultivation be taken as a yardstick to measure the progress of the agricultural revolution; but this would be to misunderstand the nature of economic revolutions and to confuse technological innovation with mere economic growth. If by the extension of cultivation is meant the winning of farmland from the wild, then this had long ceased to be possible. There was much waste land in the legal sense, not being in the particular ownership of any one person, but none, mountain tops excepted, that was not farmed in one way or another. If by the extension of cultivation be meant the subjection of wider areas to the plough, then this was nothing new, but merely keeping on with old ways. It may have signified economic growth, but it could not have been part of an agricultural revolution in the early modern period: the horizontal extension of existing techniques was not revolutionary, it was conservative. Those who try to bolster their case for an agricultural revolution in the period from 1750 to 1850 by alleging a huge extension of the cultivated area then, are really giving their whole case away. But if they assert only that there was a greater extension of cultivation at that time than in the previous 200 years, their case is lost by lack of evidence. They cannot strengthen their hands by pointing simply to the enclosure of wastes—of moors, heaths, hills and downs—for these had largely been subject to the plough in a system of temporary cultivation for ages.[1] Nor can they point to anything in the later period comparable to the disparking movement that swept through England between 1560 and 1673.[2]

[1] Inf. 107. This cat is inadvertently let out of the bag by J. D. Chambers & G. E. Mingay, *Ag. Rev. 1750–1880* 1966, p. 207: 'The agricultural industry responded by taking in new land rather than by developing new practices.'

[2] R. V. Lennard, *Rural Northants. under Comm.* 1916, pp. 75, 82–3; V. Sackville-

Indeed, as far as the downlands are concerned the balance tips the other way. In the Chalk Country, between 1558, when the demesne farmer of Manningford Bohun had 140 acres of arable 'newe enclosed out of the common called the hethe'[1] and 1632, when heathland at West Harting was being marled and improved for tillage,[2] similar grounds were being enclosed and brought into cultivation throughout the Chalk Country.[3] At the same time woodlands were also cleared for the plough.[4] The ploughing-up of downs and heaths was aided by the re-introduction of denshiring. Aubrey says, 'Mr Bishop of Merton first brought into the south of Wiltshire the improvement by burnbeking (denshiring) about 1639. . . . It is very much used in this parish and their neighbours doe imitate them'.[5] This is substantially correct. To overcome the 'extreame barrennes of the land' in part of Horsey Farm in Martin, Bishop was engaged in 1638–40 in 'rooteinge parte of the grounde' and in the 'burning of beete', activities involving an outlay of about £230.[6] Burnbaking was the way to make thin heath and 'redland' soils bear corn. The surface of the turf was skimmed off with a breast-plough, piled loosely in heaps, ignited at the top and left to smoulder away. The resultant ash was scattered and ploughed in. Then the soil was good for four or five crops at the most, after which it had to be laid down.[7] This practice produced corn, but hardly improved the sheep-down. Aubrey notes

---

West, *Knole & Sackvilles* 1923, p. 25; M. E. James, *Este A/cs. E. Northumb. 1562–1637* Surtees S. 1955 clxiii, p. xxviii; W. P. Hedley, 'Manor Simonburn & Warks Pk', *Archaeologia Aeliana* 1952 xxx, 86; C. Jackson, 'N. fr. Ct R. Manor Epworth', *Reliquary* 1882–3 xxiii, 89; J. Cullum, *Hist. & Ant. Hawsted & Hardwick* 1813, p. 246; J. Aubrey, *Wilts. Topog. Colls.* 1862, pp. 204–5; Smyth, op. cit. 36; Dors. R.O., D. 54, Svys &c. manors L. Arundel 1563 Ryme Intrinseca; P.R.O., S.P.D., Chas vol. 95 no 11; Interregnum vol. G58A, ff. 341v.–2; Exch. K.R., Sp. Commn 2395; L.R., M.B. 186, f. 5v.; A.O., Parl. Svys Corn. 18, f. 1; 25, ff. 1–2; 40, f. 3; Hants. 14, ff. 1–4; 25, f. 1; Herts. 7, ff. 3–4, 6 sqq.; 9, ff. 2–5(1–4); Leics. 6, f. 2; War. 20, f. 11; 21–2; Wilts. 36, 41, 47; Cornwall, op. cit. 205; J. L. M. Gulley, 'Wealden Landscape early 17th cent. & antecedents', ts. thesis Ph. D. Ldn Univ. 1960, opp. 61, 71–2, 243–4; A. H. R. Baker, 'Fd Systs. Kent', ts. thesis Ph.D. Ldn Univ. 1963, pp. 129–30; F. Hull, 'Ag. & Rural Soc. Ess. 1560–1640', ts. thesis Ph.D. Ldn Univ. 1950, opp. 54–5; T. Gerard, *Partic. Descron Co. Soms.* Soms. Rec. Soc. 1900 xv, 165, 221.

[1] P.R.O., D.L., R. & S. 9/28.
[2] B.M., Add. 28529, f. 143(132)v.
[3] P.R.O., Exch. K.R., Sp. Commn 2418; D.L., Sp. Commn 871; M.B. 115, f. 50v.; Wilton ho. Svys Manors 1632–3, Barford f. 3; Wilts. R.O., Savernake: svys Shalbourne W'ct 1552, & 1639 ff. 17–18, 24; Chisbury 44 Eliz. f. 34v.
[4] Ibid. acc. 283, Svy Urchfont c. 1640, ff. 76 sqq., 95; P.R.O., Sp. Coll. R. & S.GS 25/14; Exch. T.R., Bk 157, p. 81; Chanc. Proc. ser. ii Chas I, 260/16, ans.
[5] Bodl. Aubrey 2, f. 83; Straton, op. cit. i, 291; ii, 542–3.
[6] P.R.O., Sp. Coll. Shaftesbury Papers 32/7.
[7] Davis, op. cit. 21, 85; Pearce, op. cit. 28; J. Laurence, *New Syst. Ag.* 1726, p. 68; W. Folkingham, *Feudigraphia* 1610, p. 25; Marshall, *S. Cos.* ii, 326–7.

that farmers 'say "T'is good for the father, but naught for the sonne", by reason it does so weare out the heart of the land'. When burnbaked, land could be restored by heavy applications of muck, 'but best of all by the fold'.[1] There would be little advantage in burnbaking the down, if it could not be fed again by sheep; and little in producing corn, if, in order to restore the sheep-down, it was necessary to withdraw the fold from the lower fields, to the detriment of crops there. Hence the beneficial practice of burnbaking depended on a growth of flocks and increased feed and fodder, at a time when the sheep-pastures were being restricted by burnbaking itself. The great extension of denshiring was possible, therefore, only as part and parcel of an agricultural revolution. However, with burnbaking, chalking, grasses and clovers, the ploughing-up of the 'redland' soils could proceed rapidly. Aubrey estimated that at least a quarter of Salisbury Plain was converted to arable at some time between 1660 and 1685.[2] Defoe and Laurence remarked on how much of the downs had recently been brought under the plough,[3] so knowledge of this had become general. By about 1685 most of the 'redland' soils were probably arable.

Then, at the turn of the eighteenth and nineteenth centuries, when corn prices were extremely high, much of the tender 'blackland' on the downs was brought into tillage by burnbaking. The results were disastrous. Once the grass was broken on 'blackland' soils nothing but burnbaking could induce a crop and nothing but famine prices justify it. The usual field-course in 'blackland' was, (1) turnips or rape sown in the ashes and fed off by sheep for (2) oats undersown with rye-grass. At the first burnbaking good crops were obtained, but these merely exhausted the soil. The grass grown under the oats soon gave out and what took its place was not sheep-down grass but black couch and bent. A young tender-mouthed flock of sheep would sooner starve than eat this, so the farmer was forced to put down his ewes in favour of wethers. These fed badly and provided poor fold. Yet without folding or mucking the land would grow nothing. Hence it had to be either folded with sheep fed elsewhere, to the detriment of the other arable, or abandoned altogether. For this reason farming experts were almost unanimous in their opposition to ploughing up 'blacklands', of which the only prominent advocate was Arthur Young. Davis's protests was echoed by other reporters to the Board of Agriculture. Young attempted to refute these writers by arguing that rents had increased by the ploughing of 'blackland', but, as one of them correctly prophesied, as soon as rents and

[1] Bodl. Aubrey 2, f. 83.

[2] Ibid. ff. 86v., 115; Davis, op. cit. 56; W. Marshall, *Rev. Reps. to Bd Ag. fr. S. Dept* 1817, p. 306; M. C. Naish, 'Ag. Landscape Hants. Chalklands 1700–1840', ts. thesis M.A. Ldn Univ. 1960, pp. 126–7, 141–2, 154–5, 158.

[3] Laurence, loc. cit.; D. Defoe, *Tour through E. & W.* Everyman i, 187.

prices fell from their unstable height, the land was thrown out of production altogether.[1] The 'blackland' was natural sheepdown and its plough-up deprived the flocks of their best feed, so that many had to be put down and the sheep that remained contracted goggles, while the staple of the wool was prejudiced.[2] In an attempt to overcome these troubles the Horn sheep were crossed with the new Southdowns to produce the Hampshire Down. But these were not such good folding sheep and were less suited to close-cropping the down pastures, which were allowed slowly to deteriorate.[3] By this and the wasting of the 'blacklands', the sheep-fold itself was jeopardized. As soon as grain prices fell from their war-time peak, great stretches of downland went out of cultivation altogether, and even the best of the swards started to become coarse and tufty, so that when much of the land was later taken over for military training, it was already semi-derelict. In the Northwold Country, too, ploughing up thin and infertile soils on the upper wolds at the turn of the eighteenth and nineteenth centuries led to a few successions of (1) rape, (2) corn, but soon resulted in the complete robbery and destruction of the land itself. Similar crop-mining occurred then in the North-western Lowlands.[4] Thus much land was driven out of cultivation by farmers who were unable to do more than extend existing methods.

The next of the conventional criteria of agricultural revolution is just as unsatisfactory. The extent to which bare fallows have ever been replaced by fallow crops is usually exaggerated. Indeed, the prevalent notion that bare fallows are synonymous with bad, and fallow crops with good, husbandry is without foundation. The truth is, bare fallows continued even in the new husbandry, that is supposed to have abolished them. In the up-and-down farms of the Midland Plain, bare fallows preceded barley occasionally and wheat regularly. In the improved husbandry of the Northdown Country, cleaning fallows were accorded to barley rather than wheat, but this was frequently preceded by a bare fallow for the duration of a summer, a year or eighteen months, it being a principle with the farmers that 'the land must have a holiday' to produce the best wheat. Fallow wheat was, indeed, worth almost twice as much an acre as clover wheat. Similar bare fallows continued also in the Wealden Vales, the South Seacoast and Chiltern countries, the vales of Taunton Deane, London and Pickering, the Lancashire Plain, and the North-eastern Lowlands. Wheat was often preceded by a bare summer fallow in High Suffolk. In the Southdown Country bare fallows con-

[1] Naish, op. cit. 232–4, 282–4; Marshall, op. cit. ii, 326; *S. Dept* 91, 250, 265, 277, 299–300, 325, 347, 352; C. Vancouver, *Gen. View Ag. Hants.* 1813, pp. 74, 266–8, 332, 457–9; W. Mavor, *id. Berks.* 1808, p. 239; Pearce, loc. cit.; Davis, op. cit. 21, 56, 84–5.

[2] Ibid. 26; E. Lisle, *Obs. in Husbandry* 1757, p. 425.

[3] Marshall, op. cit. 58–9.

[4] H. E. Strickland, *Gen. View Ag. E. R. Yks.* 1812, pp. 106–7; E. Hughes, *N. Country Life in 18th cent. ii Cumb. & Wmld 1700–1830* 1965, p. 232.

mon-field farmers when they wanted to lay down the ends of some of their ridges. Sown in March, they would produce a crop of grass by midsummer.[1] In a general remark on the formation of permanent grass, Marshall[2] points to the disadvantages of this method:

' "hayseeds" have been used for that purpose ... for a century past; and a better plan, perhaps, will not be discovered for a century to come: *provided* a well-herbaged hay ground, of a nature similar to the land to be sown, be carefully weeded, in the manner of corn crops, from time to time, during the early stages of its growth; and the swaths carefully looked over after the crop is mown—*provided* also, that different parts of the herbage, so freed from noxious plants, be cut in different stages of ripeness, that the seeds of the nutritious herbs may be saved in a state of maturity; and *provided*, of course, that the several parcels of hay be thrashed, as they become sufficiently dry for the operations (without being heated in bulk);—the different products of seeds be intimately blended by sifting them together;—and carefully stored till the season of use.'

It may be doubted if many farmers complied faithfully with all these instructions, but the better of them exercised some care. Norden, who reflected the best practice, advised the formation of grass by sowing 'in the spring-time some hay seeds, especially the seede of the claver-grasse, or the grass honysuckle, and other seeds that fall out of the finest and purest hay', under a nurse crop of chichling vetches (everlasting pea). Folkingham remarked that the 'sowing of the seed of trefoyle, of clavers, melitot, prunel, milfoyle, ribwort, septfoile, cinque-foyle, etc., mixed with murling mould, doth much inrich meddowes and pastures both in forrage and fenage'.[3] Farmers had at their disposal, indeed, virtually every 'grass' they could use to advantage, including much perennial rye-grass, perennial red and wild white clover, common and creeping bent and trefoil, besides the variety of herbs necessary for healthy live-stock.[4] Thus Folkingham is able to describe a parcel as follows: 'This

---

[1] Marshall, *Glos.* i, 158–60; *Rural Econ. Yks.* 1788 ii, 86–7; *Rev. Reps. to Bd Ag. fr. N. Dept* 1808, p. 483; J. Boys, *Gen. View Ag. Co. Kent* 1796, pp. 107–8; J. Crutchley, *id. Rutland* 1794, p. 14; W. Pomeroy, *id. Worcester* 1794, p. 10; Lisle, op. cit. 32; W. Blith, *Eng. Improver Improved* 1652, p. 60; J. Norden, *Surveiors Dialogue* 1618, p. 208; G. Atwell, *Faithful Surveyour* 1662, p. 100; 'St Ch. Hy VIII & Ed. VI', *Colls. Hist. Staffs.* 1912, p. 113.

[2] Marshall, *S. Dept*, 491–2.

[3] Op. cit. 207–8; op. cit. 25.

[4] Ibid.; Norden, loc. cit.; Pomeroy, loc. cit.; Blith, op. cit. 138; R. Plot, *Nat. Hist. Oxon.* 1676, p. 154; W. Pitt, *Gen. View Ag. Co. Northampton* 1806, pp. 114–16, 118; *id. Leicester* 1809, p. 136; *id. Stafford* 1794, p. 24; J. Gerarde, *Herball* 1597, pp. 1–4, 8, 10, 26, 895 sqq., 888–9, 1017–18, 1021–4, 1030, 1034, 1633, pp. 1185–6, 1190; W. Coles,

pasture is projected in large ridges extending and declining south; the soil is a sandy clay of 18 inches crust, close sworded and well repleate with trefoiles, cinquefoile, ribwort, morfus, yarrow, and other grazing herbes of good growth'.[1] An additional resource in seeding down was the collection of 'seeds' as they grew wild or in grasslands, lanes and woods. The term 'bents' was applied to the seed stems of grasses in general, including perennial rye-grass ('ray-grass'), 'benting' time being when the grass was ripe for picking; and there is some evidence that these 'bents' were collected for seeds as well as for interior decoration, for bye-laws forbade anyone to collect them from other people's land, from amongst corn in the fields, or from common meadows and pastures.[2] Thus all told the farmers did not lack means of seeding down; but even if they took no advantage of these, they could turn tillage to grass merely by leaving things to nature. 'Man, it is true, can now cultivate herbage —can make "artificial grasses"—but if the soil be suffered to remain only a few years, undisturbed, nature will not fail to treat silly man as a bungler, and cover the ground with a valuable assortment of natural plants which are better adapted to the soil, situation and climature.'[3]

Selected clovers were also widely introduced in arable-grass rotations for short leys or hay crops in what still remained essentially permanent tillage, as distinct from up-and-down land. But tares previously answered the same purpose, being grown alone, or with oats for them to climb by, or mixed with peas, beans or lentils. Winter vetches were sown in autumn to be fed off by sheep in spring, and spring varieties, cut when in bloom, made highly nutritious hay. Spring tares were commonly the chief constituent in a mixture called 'horsemeat' in the Chalk Country and 'podware' in the Northdown. Similar crops were grown in all the farming countries destined to adopt clover. Tares, it is true, tended to scour young stock, but this disadvantage was shared by clover. In soils too poor for vetches and tares, lentils served the same purpose and made similar hay. One of the great functions of selected clovers was to replace tares, 'horsemeat' and 'podware', though rarely lentils, for land too poor to grow tares would hardly bear clover. Selected clovers also displaced peas and beans as the chief fodder crops in some plain

---

Adam in Eden 1657, cap. cxxxii, ccxcviii; W. Turner, *Herbal* 1568, f. 110v.; J. Ray, *Historia Plantarum* 1686–1704 i, 345, 347, 611, 617, 943–4, 949–52, 967–8; ii, 1256–8, 1264–7, 1269, 1271–2, 1283–5.

[1] Op. cit. 87.
[2] W. Marshall, *Rural Econ. Midl. Cos.* 1790 ii, 434; *Glos.* i, 160, 164; T. Batchelor, *Gen. View Ag. Co. Bedford* 1808, p. 431; Plot, loc. cit.; Lisle, op. cit. 42; Ray, op. cit. ii, 1283; Gerarde, op. cit. (1597) 5; *E.D.D.*; P.R.O., D.L., Ct R. 81/1117, m. 10; B.M., Add. 36908, f. 8; Shak. Bpl. Leigh: Stoneleigh pains & ords. 1597.
[3] Marshall, *S. Dept*, 140.

country. This implement excelled in fallow stirrings on chalky, stony, gravelly and flinty soils, where it was important not to plough too deep. It had both a land-wheel and a furrow-wheel, the former smaller than the latter and both vertically adjustable. Although more difficult to set up than the plain plough, it was then easier to handle in the conditions in which it was used. Jolting was avoided; it did not matter that the soil was too light to hold the plough down; it was efficient on hillsides; and heavy enough not to be torn to pieces by rough going. This class of plough was usually pulled by two pairs of horses abreast, or by one pair assisted by a lone outrunner, with nothing to do but pull a light harrow and take lateral stresses. Fourthly, special ploughs were employed in fens, marshes and mosses. These had disc coulters and broad-finned shares, both of which had constantly to be filed and sharpened against the rough herbage often encountered. The disc coulter cut through the rank swards of grass and sedge, while the broad fin-shaped share pared them off ready for burning. Fifthly, turnwrest ploughs were used in the Northdown and similarly hilly countries. Like other hill country ploughs the turnwrest rode on two wheels and could be adjusted exactly to the ploughing depth. The peculiar feature of these ploughs, of which the Northdown variety was the heaviest, was that they could turn all the furrow slices downward of a hill without ever having to be jacked up and run back idle. This was achieved by having two shares and mould-boards, one pair of which could be raised while the other was lowered for use. Sixthly, special light ploughs were used in the light soils of East Norfolk, the Sandlings Country and the Vales of Hereford. The East Anglian light-soil plough had a broad, flat share that eventually formed a plough-pan. It was commonly drawn by no more than one pair, sometimes by two pairs, and frequently by only a single horse. Whatever size the team, this plough, unlike most others, was handled by a single ploughman, who could comfortably till two acres a day without the help of a boy. Seventhly, drags and tormentors were employed in some thin, light soils instead of ploughs. These heavy cultivators, which were also used to break down land after the plough and before the light harrows, did not turn over furrow slices, but these could not be cut in the thinnest soils in any event. The West Country tormentor was in the nature of a multi-shared sub-plough, and likewise was a similar im-plement in use in the Northdown Country. Much the same, too, was the drag of the Chalk and Cotswold countries, which had half a dozen large straight tines with chisel points and was equally useful for levelling, down furrows, burying long-straw manure, or preparing hill pastures for corn. Lastly, in the seventeenth century, some double-furrow ploughs came into use. In addition, there were breast or push-ploughs, for skimming off turf in preparation for burning, and special trenching and draining ploughs. Farmers on any substantial scale needed more than one plough, and each with alternative sets of irons, for different tillages in various types and states of soil. In the Chiltern Country, farmers had heavy two-wheelers for fallowing, single-wheel ones for brush crops, and still lighter ones for preparing a wheat tilth. Chalk Country farmers had drags and two-wheel ploughs, but also foot-ploughs for dealing with stiff 'whiteland', not to mention breast-ploughs. Those in the Sandlings Country and High Suffolk used both wheeled- and foot-ploughs. In the Northdown Country, the turnwrest did not answer all needs.[1] Plating wood with iron rendered ploughs lighter and cheaper to use. The all-iron ploughs made in Suffolk about 1766 by Brand and later by Ransome of Ipswich[2] helped further to reduce the numbers of men and horses needed in cultivation. But the lightening of ploughs used in heavy soils was not all advantage, for here the very weight of the plough assisted the tiller; nor the abridgment of labour by dispensing with plough-boys, all gain, for they were training to be plough-men; nor the reduction of teams all saving, for these might be composed either of beasts being exercised to promote appetite, or of horses being inured to labour in preparation for employment elsewhere.[3] It is difficult then, to regard changes in plough design and manufacture as of more than minor importance.

Tumbrels, carts and wains were now mostly being equipped with iron tyres and binding. The old farm wain was a great two-wheeled carriage that could be adapted for harvesting by fitting ladders into

[1] Ibid. 479, 539; *Rev. Reps. to Bd Ag. fr. W. Dept* 1810, p. 280; *id. E. Dept* 1811, p. 210; *Midl. Dept*, 487; *Midl. Cos.* i, 138; ii, 427; *Glos.* ii, 25; *Rural Econ. W. Engl.* 1796 i, 125, 296; *id. Nfk* 1787 i, 12, 53; *S. Cos.* i, 60, 350, 372; ii, 10–11, 277, 322, 368, 405; J. Bailey, *Gen. View Ag. Co. Durh.* 1810, p. 73; J. Bailey & G. Culley, *id. Northumb.* 1805, p. 38; *id. Cumb.* 1805, p. 212; A. Young, *id. Ess.* 1807 i, opp. 142; J. Claridge, *id. Dors.* 1793, p. 16; Mavor, op. cit. 114, 119–20; Pearce, op. cit. 66–7; Pitt, op. cit. 50–3, 55; Davis, op. cit. 67–70; Vancouver, op. cit. 216–5 (recte 7); Boys, op. cit. 56; J. Sinclair, *Ag. Hints*, 5; Plot, op. cit. 247; E. Melling, *Kentish Sources* iii 1961, pp. 29–31; W. Ellis, *Chiltern & V. Farming Expl.* pp. 307, 309, 317, 319–20, 326; J. Mortimer, *Whole Art Husbandry* 1707, pp. 39–40; Laurence, op. cit. 55–6; Kalm, op. cit. 238, 250–1, 263; Lisle, op. cit. 34–5, 71; C. Fiennes, *Jours.* 1947, pp. 32, 164; Folkingham, op. cit. 27; J. Beale, *Herefs. Orchards* 1657, p. 36; Fitzherbert, *Boke of Husbandrie* 1523, f. 1; Blith, op. cit. 193, 198 sqq.; J. Worlidge, *Systema Agriculturae* 1669, pp. 205–6; C. Heresbach, *Husbandry* ed. B. Google 1601, f. 20v; *Arch. Cant.* lxi, 60 sqq., 72–5; *Rep. & Trans. Devon Assoc.* l, 276, 278; Bodl. Hearne's diaries 158, p. 30; B.M., Add. 15559, f. 2v.; R. 18517; invs.:—York, Snaith Pec. Jn Scholes 1690 Balne; Nfk R.O., Cons. Ct 1664:66; 1690–1: 27; E. Sfk R.O., A/d 1685: 27, 61; 1702: 66, 98? (sic), 107; Hants. R.O., Cons. & A/d cts; Wilts. R.O., Preb. Ct Husborne & Burbage 1/14; Dioc. Reg. Sarum. Geo. Noyes 1617 E. Grafton, & pass.; W. Sfk R.O., Episc. Commy Ct Bury St Edm's. 1696: 84; R. V. Lennard, 'Eng. Ag. under Chas II', *EcHR* 1932–4 iv, 31; J. B. Passmore, *Eng. Plough* 1930, pp. 8–9, 13–14, 20.

[2] Ibid. 13–14, 20; D. Hudson & K. W. Lockhart, *R.S.A. 1754–1954* 1954, pp. 81–2; Nfk R.O., Cons. Ct inv. 1665: 26.

[3] Marshall, op. cit. i, 57; Mavor, op. cit. 120–1; Laurence, op. cit. 129.

special sockets. 'Wain' and 'wagon', being doublets, were interchange-able, but the latter was also used to distinguish the four-wheeled road vehicles many farmers were starting to use. Such wagons were first employed by carriers and others for road haulage and were then taken up by farmers about 1580, the farm wagons being built locally as replicas of those used in road services to London and elsewhere. By 1644 farm wagons were common in the Northdown Country, the Wealden Vales and Romney Marsh. They were introduced in the Chalk Country and the main body of the Midland Plain about 1630. In these places, and in the Woodland, the Norfolk Heathlands, the Breckland, the Petworth District and the Chiltern, South Seacoast and Southdown countries, they had been generally adopted by 1655, in High Suffolk, East Nor-folk, the Vale of Evesham and the Fen and Cheshire Cheese countries by 1675, in the vales of Berkeley and York and the Cheese, Cotswold, Oxford Heights and Poor Soils countries by 1690, and in the vales of Pickering and Taunton Deane before 1720.[1] Seed-drills were virtually the only new implements introduced. Jethro Tull was formerly con-sidered a hero of the agricultural revolution because of his system of drilling corn in monoculture and horse-hoeing between the rows. His experiments were, indeed, extraordinary, but Tull was a crank and his system unworkable, and the monoculture of horse-hoed wheat had no advantage over an alternation of wheat and bare fallow. Some of Tull's other ideas were useful, but hardly original. Worlidge had long since described a corn-drill, and by 1706 East Anglian farmers were accustomed to trailing harrows and corn-riddles behind their ploughs. Horse-hoes could have no more than limited application and did not essentially differ from the brake-ploughs of the Northdown Country. All that Tull did was to make drilling an 'infatuating operation' peculiar to 'Tullian husbandry'.[2]

[1] Marshall, *Tks.* ii, 362; *Glos.* ii, 230; Plot, op. cit. 257; J. Mastin, *Hist. & Ant. Naseby* 1792, p. 25; J. Parkes, *Trav. in Eng. in 17th cent.* 1925, p. 7; Melling, op. cit. 22–3; G. H. Kenyon, 'Kirdford Invs. 1611 to 1776', *Suss. Archaeol. Colls.* xcii, 117–18; Bodl. Aubrey 2, f. 89; Oxon. R.O., Bl. I/v/2. f. 12v.; Dors. R.O., D.E. 10/E105 Ct R. Winfrith Newburgh 7 Oct. 1685; invs.:—A/d Ct Dors.; Bodl. Cons. & A/d cts Oxon.; Leics. R.O., A/d; Lichfield Jt R.O., Pecs.; York, Dean & Chap.; Bp Wilton, Selby & Snaith Pecs.; Soms. R.O., Episc. Cons. Ct A/d Taunton; Wilts. R.O., Cons. Ct Sarum, esp. M. 1676–1720; Joan Meriwether 1675 Bps Lavington; Dioc. Reg. Sarum.; Lincs. R.O., Cons. Ct 1674–9; Kent R.O., A/d Ct Cantuar. 1644–5, 1649–50; Cons. Ct Cantuar. 1645–6; Herts. R.O., A/d Ct St Albans; A/d Hunts, Hitchin Div.; Worcs. R.O., Cons. Ct, esp. 1670: 141; 1675: 156; 1680: 201, 219; 1690: 18, 95, 42, 47, 67, 385; Ches. R.O., Cons. Ct 'Supra' 1675; E. Sfk R.O., A/d 1685; Nfk R.O., Cons. Ct, esp. Misc. 1637–68: A/41; Hants. R.O., Cons. & A/d cts; W. Sfk R.O., Episc. Commy Ct Bury St Edm's.; Glouc. Lib. Cons. Ct 1677–1719, W. Suss. R.O., Cons. Ct Bp Cicestr. for A/d Cicestr.

[2] T. H. Marshall, 'J. Tull & New Husbandry', *EcHR* 1929–30 ii; Tull, *Horse-hoeing Husbandry*; Marshall, *S. Dept*, 87, 134; Worlidge, op. cit. 46 sqq.; *Arch. Cant.* lxi, 60 sqq., 75; B.M., Lans. 691, f. 24v.; Kalm, op. cit. 142.

All these implement changes together were an inconsiderable contribution to the agricultural revolution; but even if they were considered, they would not help to assign this revolution to the period 1750–1850 rather than the earlier one, for, while all-iron ploughs would have to be put on one side of the scales, seed-drills and wagons would have to go on the other.

As for field drainage, trench drains were known of old. Their bottoms were filled with bushes, brushwood, stones, or iron-forge cinders, and then covered with straw ropes or turves. Hollow drains were also constructed, of alderwood pipes, which were made by boring out tree trunks, or of 'soughing' bricks. Turf drains with shoulders spread from the mosslands of the north-west to the Midlands.[1] Field drainage made some progress in the early modern period, but much remained to be attempted. Blith noticed a tract of hundreds and thousands of acres near Dunstable, below Chalk Hill, in need of drainage, but his offer to undertake the work was refused.[2] There is little doubt that field drainage could not be perfected until the invention of new methods in the eighteenth and nineteenth centuries and the manufacture of cheap and efficient drainage pipes. The early 'plug' drain (a precursor of the mole-drain), the art of deep draining introduced by Elkington in 1764—he used an auger to locate the spring and then intercepted it by a drain at the highest point of the affected patch—the subsoil trenches devised by James Smith in 1823, the tile drain-pipes produced by John Reade in 1843, their manufacture by Scragg's method shortly after, and Fowler's perfected mole-plough of 1859 all made possible and economic the complete drainage of heavy lands.[3] These improvements, however, were necessarily of limited application: most farmland needed no drainage beyond ridge and furrow, gutters, trenches and ditches. Large-scale pipe drainage was a notable advance, but it did not affect, far less revolutionize, more than a part of English agriculture.[4]

[1] Ibid. 64; Marshall, *W. Dept*, 180; *E. Dept*, 480, 509, 511; *Midl. Cos.* i, 189 sqq.; ii, 256, 265; Griggs, *Gen. View Ag. Co. Ess.* 1794, p. 20; A. Young, *id. Sfk* 1794, p. 22 (recte 27); J. Wedge, *id. Warwick* 1794, p. 19; Vancouver, op. cit. 44, 99, 105, 108, 119, 121, 148, 150, 153; R. Plot, *Nat. Hist. Staffs.* 1686, p. 356; T. Tusser, *Hundreth Good Pointes of Husbandrie* 1931, p. 67; 'Chanc. Proc. Temp. Eliz.', *Colls. Hist. Staffs.* 1926, pp. 67–8; Pitt, *Leics.* 38; Fitzherbert, *Boke of Surveyinge & Improvementes* 1535, ff. 47v.–8; J. Wake, *Q. Sess. Recs. Co. Northampton: files for 6 Chas & Comm.* Northants. Rec. Soc. 1924 i, 128; L. E. Harris, *Vermuyden & Fens* 1953, p. 38; E. Sfk R.O., V. 5/22/1, ff. 21v.–2; B.M., Harl. 7180; P.R.O., Exch. K.R., Deps. by Commn 26–7 Eliz. Mich. 24, dep. by Jn Marsh; Blith, op. cit. 10, 36, 67 sqq.

[2] Ibid. 85–6; W. J. Slack, *Ldp Oswestry* 1951, pp. 56–7, 74–5.

[3] S. Switzer, *Practical Fruit-gardener* 1724, pp. 25–6; Wedge, op. cit. 17; H. H. Nicholson, *Prin. Fd Drainage* 1944, pp. 37–9, 68–9, 74; & v. Shak. Bpl. Leigh: Stoneleigh Ct R. 29 Oct. 1764.

[4] L. Hoelscher, 'Improvemts in Fencing & Drainage in mid-19th cent. Engl.', *Ag. Hist.* xxxvii, 76–9.

The replacement of oxen by horses in draught is sometimes said to be one of the achievements of the supposed agricultural revolution of the eighteenth century, despite the fact that Arthur Young was vainly trying to persuade farmers to abandon horses in favour of oxen. These needed only good grass and hay, whereas horses had to be corned when working. Oxen, too, could eventually make beef. They thus involved less outlay and depreciation, but were less efficient than horses in both field and road work. In consequence, though petty farmers might be satisfied with oxen, or even with dry cows, substantial ones generally preferred horses. But in great cattle countries, where oxen were cheap and rearing beasts often needed to be worked gently, it was economic to inspan some bullocks. In the period 1560–1723 they may even have won some work from horses in the Midland Plain. Yet even where oxen were yoked, they were commonly led by horses. In the later eighteenth century it was estimated that no more than one-sixth of all farm work was performed by oxen.[1] There was, indeed, some changeover, but even at the beginning of the sixteenth century horses were employed much more than oxen.

Livestock improvements should be distinguished from mere changes. The Dishley strain of the New Leicester pasture sheep, for example, did not improve on all the features of the pasture sheep that preceded them, for the sheep bred by Bakewell sacrificed the quantity and quality of the wool and the quality of the mutton to the mere quantity of mutton. It would be absurd to draw comparisons between these pasture sheep and the fallow sheep of the common fields, because each served quite different purposes. Too close a comparison between the Dishley sheep and the old pasture sheep would also be wrong, for their purposes were also somewhat diverse. Much the same may be said of Bakewell's new strain of longhorn cattle, which sacrificed the dairy to the butcher. The New Southdown sheep, similarly, cannot be considered an improvement in all particulars, for they sacrificed folding qualities to the quantity of mutton. And in many countries, folding breeds of sheep were still needed. However fashionable it may have become in the eighteenth century for theoretical agriculturists to deride sheep-folding as barbaric, robbing one part of the farm for the benefit of another, still in all heath and down countries, where the finest corn was produced, where the farms were large and where much of the tillage was too remote to be mucked with farmyard manure, the sheep-fold was the basis of husbandry.[2] What constituted the great improvement was less the new breeds themselves than the making available to farmers of an extended range of breeds.

At no material time was much advance made in veterinary science

[1] Marshall, *S. Dept*, 337; *N. Dept*, 59–61; *S. Cos.* i, 56; & v. inf. 50, 97, 199.
[2] Vancouver, *Hants.* 462–3; Davis, op. cit. 20, 85; T. Stone, *Gen. View Ag. Co. Bedford* 1794, p. 38; Marshall, *Midl. Dept*, 424, 428.

and there is no evidence that livestock losses were reduced in the eighteenth century: they may well have increased. As cattle were kept so much in the open, the incidence of bovine tuberculosis was probably low. Foot-and-mouth disease struck occasionally, but was not incurable, and the slaughter of infected beasts was not adopted as public policy until the eighteenth century. Foot and liver rots broke out frequently in wet or waterlogged pastures, but the tainted sheep were usually fattened up quickly and sold off without much loss to the farmer. Wood-evil was probably as great a menace as rots, but it was rare for any of these diseases to grow into great disasters.[1]

Thus, of the conventional criteria of the agricultural revolution, the spread of the Norfolk four-course system belongs to the realms of mythology; the supersession of oxen by horses is hardly better; the enclosure of common fields by Act of Parliament, a broken yardstick; the improvement of implements, inconsiderable and inconclusive; the replacement of bare fallows, unrealistic; developments in stock-breeding, over-rated; and drainage alone seems a valid criterion. The failure of historians to locate the agricultural revolution has thus arisen, in part at least, from mistaken notions of what form an agricultural revolution could have taken.

More important than the valid conventional criteria are those conventionally ignored. An improvement hitherto overlooked, even in the Midland Plain, is the alternacy of tillage and grass on up-and-down land in a grass-arable rotation. It was not merely the practice of up-and-down husbandry that was the improvement, for this had been established, for centuries, in the Cheshire Cheese Country and the Lancashire Plain, for example; but the substitution of up-and-down husbandry for permanent tillage and permanent grass, as in the Midland Plain, or for shifting cultivation, as in the North-eastern Lowlands, was revolutionary. Such changes have not only greatly increased crops of corn and grass, they also made positive improvements in soil structure and fertility. As much corn was grown as before, and with less labour and cost; the numbers of livestock were multiplied; and the temporary leys made the soil crumbly and loamy. In comparison with this, the bare fallows of the common fields at best arrested soil deterioration at a certain point and lent the soil a semblance of good structure by purely mechanical means. The best possible soil structure for crops of all kinds is that created by a temporary ley, of up to a score or so years' duration composed largely of perennial rye-grass and wild white or perennial red clover, which are the natural components of temporary grazing leys in plain countries. Up-and-down husbandry thus effected cumulative improvement.[2] Another advance ignored by conventional pictures of

[1] Smyth, op. cit. 31; T. S. Ashton, *18th cent.* 1955, pp. 53–4; inf. 204.
[2] Jacks, op. cit. 198.

the agricultural revolution is the floating of water-meadows, which both Blith and Marshall regarded as a cardinal improvement. Indeed, floating, especially by the flowing or ridge and furrow method, is 'the most scientific operation that has entered into the common practice of husbandry'.[1]

The chief criteria to be used in assessing the agricultural revolution, then, must be the floating of water-meadows, the substitution of up-and-down husbandry for permanent tillage and permanent grass or for shifting cultivation, the introduction of new fallow crops and selected grasses, marsh drainage, manuring, and stock-breeding. There were other developments, but some of these belonged equally to all parts of the early modern period; and, in any event, if all the innovations neglected here had been simultaneously introduced into any single farming country, they would not have revolutionized its husbandry. Each of the main criteria will, therefore, be taken in turn and agricultural progress measured against it.

[1] Op. cit. 2–3; *Midl. Cas.* i, 274, 277.

CHAPTER II

THE FARMING COUNTRIES
OF ENGLAND

BEFORE we can do justice to the technical innovations that revolutionized agriculture, it is necessary to describe the farming that was transformed. However, it is no simple scene that has to be set, for farming was
not a single pursuit, but a group of allied and interdependent industries.
It is thus only at a high level of abstraction that any generalization can
be made of the congeries of agricultural industries as a whole. There are,
it is true, some minutiae of agricultural practice, especially relating to
tillage operations, that permit wide generalization, yet as far as farming
practice as a whole is concerned, general statements are applicable only
to particular farming regions or countries.

A farming country may be defined as an imprecisely bounded and
inconstant area in all but the periphery of which there is uniformity or
similarity in a single plan, or in two or more competing plans, of farm
management, sufficient to permit the formulation of general conclusions
on husbandry systems.

Numerous farming countries existed in England and Wales in the
early modern period and the nomenclature adopted for these has, as far
as possible, been based on traditional or contemporary names. The
whole kingdom may be assigned to various of these farming countries or
to their areas of merger save only one, the Bristol quarter, a residual
district where no general plan of management is discernible. Soils, subsoils, bases, terrain, topography, and climatures were all diverse; nor did
the metropolis of Bristol exert sufficient influence to promote any considerable degree of similarity in plans of farm management. The whole
quarter was a vast area of merger and of the confusion of the farming
practices of the neighbouring countries, outlying portions of whose
natural features occurred haphazardly throughout the quarter. In consequence, the only generalization that can be made about the husbandry
of the Bristol quarter is to say that it was highly diversified. With this
exception, however, the whole of England and Wales may be examined
farming country by farming country.

THE CHALK COUNTRY

The Chalk Country comprehended all the chalk mass in, about and radiating from Salisbury Plain, together with forelands at the foot of the down escarpments and in some of the neighbouring vales. The soils were highly diverse. In the easterly parts of the Vale of Wardour there were chalky clay marls, and in the westerly, sandy and shelly loams. To the east of Salisbury Plain the chalk rock was widely disintegrated and the soils were often strong, red, flinty loams, similar to the predominant soil of the Chiltern Country. The Vale of Pewsey had chiefly sandy loams, which were found everywhere immediately below the escarpment. In the valley bottoms there was a calcareous or gravelly loam. On the first ascent of the downs many flints had been lost to the valley bottoms and there was a belt of strong calcareous clay, stiff and adhesive when wet, but otherwise friable enough. This was called 'whiteland', 'malm', or 'tobacco-pipe clay'. Above this, there were, on the slopes and level tops of the downs, calcareous loams, often of moderate depth, but on the steeper slopes and escarpments excessively thin. These were called 'redland'. On the higher downs, there were also light-textured loams, known as 'blackland', mostly shallow, sometimes extremely so. The base was almost universally chalk. In consequence, rain was imbibed almost as fast as it fell. Standing on such a base, even 'whiteland' could not be over-retentive. In spite of local variations, the whole constituted a single farming country, there being no different plan of management on the sandy loams, for instance, than elsewhere.

Sheep-downs formed about half the country. Most townships had each between one and four to five, or even twelve thousand sheep.[1] For centuries sheep had grazed the hills and created downland pastures. Chalky soils suited both grasses and sheep and the sweetness of the feed depended on it being nibbled short. Once sheep were removed, the grass carpet became coarse and clumpy and finally declined into rough pasture.[2] Between hill pastures and bottom meadows lay wide arable lands. The villages, in which the farmsteads crowded, were mostly set snugly in valleys between the arable and the meadows or strung in a girdle along the line of springs below the escarpment. Either way, the townships themselves were long and narrow, running from streams and meadows to topmost downs and including all varieties of land. There

---

[1] V. my 'Agrarian Development Wilts. 1540–1640', ts. thesis Ph.D. Ldn Univ. 1951, p. 111; J. Aubrey, *Nat. Hist. Wilts.* 1847, p. 108; R. Hine, *Hist. Beauminster* 1914, pp. 264, 268; A. & W. Driver, *Gen. View Ag. Co. Hants.* 1794, pp. 23–5; P.R.O., D.L., M.B. 108, ff. 7–8; 116, f. 5; Kent R.O., U. 214/E7/63; Davis, op. cit. 19.

[2] Ibid. 18–19; Vancouver, op. cit. 266; W. H. Hudson, *Shepherd's Life* Everyman 8–9; Bodl. Aubrey 2, f. 111; Marshall, *S. Cos.* ii, 330; *S. Dept,* 347.

were also some upland townships in residual position, but their shape was determined by the same desire for comprehensiveness. Down pastures, arable fields and bottom meadows all formed part of each farm and all were used together in a single farming system.[1]

The arable was maintained by the dung of sheep fed on the downs. The sheep-fold was 'the sheet-anchor of husbandry' and the primary purpose of keeping sheep was the dung of the fold, wool being only a secondary consideration. Folding was the great object in breeding, rearing and feeding.[2] The same breed of horned sheep was stocked throughout the Chalk Country. 'Western', 'Old Wiltshire' or 'Old Hampshire' sheep were bred for folding, i.e. bred to walk, unlike sheep intended for fatting and bred to stand still. Carcass improvement, so far from being the farmer's object, was incompatible with it. All that was looked for was hardiness to enable the sheep to gain a livelihood on close-fed hill pasture, walk two or three miles for food and then carry its dung back to the fold. Ewe lambs were needed to keep up the flocks, but wether lambs lived hard with the ewes during the summer and were then sold to farms that lacked convenience for breeding.[3]

All farmers employed the sheep-fold. Most wealthy ones had private flocks and pastures in severalty able to carry between 400 and 1,400 sheep or more; and a private flock could hardly be less than about 400 as great numbers were needed for close-folding the arable.[4] The man with only a few score sheep could not fold his arable with these alone and it was not worth his while to employ his own shepherd. This was a country in which a small number of large farms existed cheek by jowl with numerous small ones, most of which had pasture for less than 100 sheep.[5] In order to fold their arable, the small farmers of most townships

[1] Ibid.; *S. Cos.* ii, 307; Davis, op. cit. 12; Mavor, op. cit. 165, 169–70; Vancouver, op. cit. 267.

[2] Ibid. 462–3; Davis, op. cit. 20, 27, 85; Mavor, op. cit. 358; Claridge, op. cit. 7; J. Billingsley, *Gen. View Ag. Co. Soms.* 1794, p. 93; Laurence, op. cit. 90; Worlidge, op. cit. 66; Norden, op. cit. 229; Folkingham, op. cit. 23, 29; H. C. Brentnall, 'Longford MS.', *Wilts. Mag.* lii, 18; Bodington, art. cit. xl, 315–6; P.R.O., Req. 105/10; St. Ch. Hy VIII vol. 6, ff. 74, 255; 23/186; Eliz. A. 11/8; Wds, Feodaries' Svys Wilts. unsorted bdl. confessions Th. Hearne/Netheravon, Margery Cooke/Blunsdon; Wilts. R.O., Savernake: Ct Bk Collingbourne Ducis 25 Apr. 1593; Soms. R.O., D.D./T.H., inv. Ric. Draper/N. Perrott; Marshal, op. cit. ii, 318–19; *S. Dept*, 54, 252.

[3] Ibid. 349; *S. Cos.* ii, 370; Marshall, Redhead & Laing, *Obs. on diff. Breeds Sheep* 1792, p. 26; Mavor, op. cit. 381–2; Driver, op. cit. 23; A. Young, *Gen. View Ag. Co. Suss.* 1793, p. 47; W. Ellis, *Compl. Syst. Exper. Improvemts made on Sheep* 1749, p. 42; G. White, *Nat. Hist. Selborne* ed. G. C. Davies, 173; Davis, op. cit. 20, 27.

[4] P.R.O., D.L., M.B. 108, ff. 12v.–13; 116, f. 7v.; Exch. L.R., M.B. 191, f. 129v.; 203, f. 377; B.M., Add. R. 37571 init.; Wilton ho. Svys Manors 1631 i, Chalke ff. 3, 2(6); Svys Manors 1632–3, Alvediston f. 2; Bishopstone f. 2; Barford St Martin f. 1; Wilts. R.O., acc. 283, Lib. sup. Amisburie f. 18; Amesbury Svy Bk 1574; Svy Amesbury 1635 f. 46; Straton, op. cit. i. 69–71, 270–1, 300.

[5] Ibid. pass.; Slater, op. cit. 21; Wilts. R.O., acc. 23, N. on manor Ogbourne St

put all their sheep into a common flock.[1] Whether common or private, the flock's management and routine were much the same. The sheep went on the downs the whole year through. They had the run of stubbles after harvest and of the summer field until ploughed for wheat. They were cotted only in the severest weather and then their dung was carted to the tillage. Otherwise the flock was folded in pens on the arable at night-time. When the ewes, and they were the most favoured stock, were near yeaning, they were taken to meadows or enclosed pastures and by the time they had yeaned, the wet meadows were ready to receive them and their lambs. When the meadow was laid up for hay, the sheep passed to the summer field. The rams were put to the ewes about October, at the date deemed necessary for the couples of ewes and lambs to have the first bite on the wet meadows. Hog sheep were not usually put on the meadows, which at this time were reserved for the couples, but were kept on the higher downs, with hay or straw scattered for their relief in hard weather.[2] Sometimes the sheep were divided into separate ewe, hog and wether flocks, but they were all upon the downs in day-time for the greater part of the year, attended by their shepherds. The dew-ponds were easily exhausted, so that, 'in the tyme of necessity of dryeth the farmors . . . had their sheepe come downe running, being athirst, from the downe to the water, where they would drink by the space of halfe an houre'. Otherwise, however, the sheep remained on the downs all day and descended every night to be folded on the arable. Sometimes, after wheat seed, the fold was put on the downs at night for a time, but more usually on the wheat stubble in preparation for barley. Thus at Bourton the custom was to fold the downs day and night for eight weeks, but otherwise the fields. Here the fold itself was set large, especially for ewes and lambs. One fold could serve for at least 300 couples, with three or four square yards apiece. Usually 1,000 or 1,200 sheep or about 500 couples were allowed per acre per night. The size of the fold was regulated by that of the field, with a view to manuring all the land before sowing, and 500 couples could well fold a customary acre in

---

Geo. p. 10; Soms. R.O., D.D./H.K., Ct N. Perrott m. 3d.; Dors. R.O., D. 54, Svys &c. manors L. Arundel, terriers w. rentals Melbury Abbas 1563, Long Crichel Govis, Fountnell 1564; Davis, op. cit. 15.

[1] Ibid. 17; Worlidge, loc. cit.; Naish, op. cit. 61; Wilts. R.O., acc. 283, Ct Bk Amesbury Erledom 15 Mar. 28 Eliz.; Ct B. Hyde fam. 7 Apr. 1609, 23 Sept 1629; Wilton ho. Ct Bk Var. Pars. 1633–4 ff. 6, 46v.; Berks. R.O., D./E.Bt E28; D./E.C. M151; B.M., Harl. 6006, f. 52; N.S.B. & E. C. Gras, op. cit. 510; F. J. Baigent & J. E. Millard, *Hist. Anc. Tn & Manor Basingstoke* 1889, pp. 323, 325–6, 333, 350; Bennett, 'Ords. Shrewton', *Wilts. Mag.* xxiii, 36–9; Marshall, *S. Cos.* ii, 319, 350–1.

[2] Ibid. 346–9; Straton, op. cit. i, 311–2; G. E. Fussell, *Robt Loder's Fm A/cs.* R. Hist. S. Camd. 3rd ser. 1936 liii, 17, 41; Wilts. R.O., Savernake; svy Collingbourne Kingston 1595 ff. 51–2; Davis, op. cit. 16–17.

a single night. The arable fields lay open and the nightly fold moved over all the acres of a field in turn, spending one night on each. In these nocturnal folds of wattle hurdles the sheep had leisure to digest their food and in the morning, their stomachs empty, they were eager to climb the hills to their daily pasture.[1]

The timing and course of the fold had to be integrated with other farming operations. The fold was the sole way of manuring barley, but the dung-pot (tumbrel) supplemented it in the lower part of the wheat field and in the vetch or hitching ground in the summer field. This was because, although the fold was used throughout the year, sheep manure was at its best in the spring, its quality corresponding to that of the feed. Furthermore, while the wether flock could be folded on barley land before the ewes had weaned, the fold of the couples was better, for the grass nutriment went more to the growth of the wethers than of the ewes, the 'tails' of the lambs were especially rich from the residue of the milk sucked, and ewes made more urine than wethers. One couple gave more than four wethers. The best fold of all was that of couples that began to feed valley meadows just before barleyseed and were thence forth folded unremittingly until the lambs were cut about the end of May. Handled in this way the sheep-fold was proverbially reckoned worth a quarter of barley a ridge. In Patney and perhaps elsewhere in the favoured Vale of Pewsey, barley was sown about May, in other places April, before the couples had left the barley field, folding proceeding even after sowing. This top-folding provided an excellent top-dressing and consolidated the light, loose tilths. Even after shooting, the fold was continued, in order to set the corn firmly in the ground. Wheat, if too rank and forward, was frequently top-folded, promoting a better crop, and providing the sheep with good feed. It was usual to fold the wheat field until about mid-October, when the flock was sometimes withdrawn to the downs for a month. Then the barley fallows were folded. The fold stayed in the barley ground until the earlier part of May, when it passed to the summer field.[2]

This was champion country, but enclosure was making headway. In some places about a tenth, not counting the sheep-down, in others no less than a third or half, was enclosed in the period 1550–1650. In addition, there were a few townships, mostly where flinty loams pre-

[1] Ibid. 61; Aubrey, op. cit. 108; P.R.O., Exch. K.R., Deps. by Commn 2 Jas Hil. 3; St. Ch. Hy VIII 23/186; Lisle, op. cit. 325–6; Laurence, loc. cit.; C. V. Goddard, 'Customs Manor Winterbourne Stoke 1574', *Wilts. Mag.* xxxiv, 215; Marshall, op. cit. ii, 349; *S. Dept*, 86, 253, 281–2.

[2] Ibid. 54; Lisle, op. cit. 13, 21, 119, 140, 306, 308, 315, 321–3, 325–6; Davis, op. cit. 61; Worlidge, loc. cit.; Fussell, op. cit. 41; Norden, loc. cit.; Bodl. Aubrey 2, f. 84; Vancouver, op. cit. 447; B.M., Harl. 6006, ff. 17v., 52; Wilton ho. Ct R. 1666–89 Stoke Verdon 19 Sept. 1677; Ct Bk Var. Pars. 1633–4 f. 47; Hoare, op. cit. Hund. S. Domerham 42.

dominated, where the greatest part of the land had long been enclosed. General enclosure was rarely undertaken, however. Part of the common field might be enclosed,[1] or the common meadow or marsh, the demesne farmer exchange lands with the tenants and consolidate his farm, or small closes be improved from heaths or downs, yet still leaving much or most of the land open.[2]

Many of the open fields were also commonable. Most family farmers sent their sheep to the common flock and had their arable dispersed in common fields, which were largely in a three-field course of (1) winter corn (mostly wheat, but sometimes partly rye), (2) spring corn (more barley than oats), (3) fallow (part hitched for pulse crops, but mostly bare). Some places, however, had a four-field course of (1) winter corn, (2) barley, (3) oats, (4) fallow. In addition, especially on the thinnest soils in permanent tillage, as at Harwell, there was a two-field course of (1) corn, (2) fallow. In this corn field the farmer grew wheat, barley or oats at will, often, like Robert Loder, having more barley than wheat or varying the proportions in different crops according to the state of the market or season.[3] In both common and severalty fields, hitch (catch) crops were grown in the nearer and easily mucked part of the summer (fallow) field, being sown on the stubble crop without a regular tilth, so, even in a three-field course, some parts had three crops in succession. This did not mean the hitching field was not bare fallowed, only that it

[1] Ibid. 40 sqq.; Hund. Alderbury 67 sqq.; W. Money, *Purveyance R. Household in Eliz. Age, 1575* 1901, pp. 63 sqq.; Wilton ho. Svys Manors 1631, 1632–3; Svy Burcombe 1632; Svy Flambston 1631; Wilts. R.O., acc. 7, Enford Ct Bk; acc. 212B, B.H./5b, 8; Wr. 1b; acc. 283, Svy Urchfont c. 1640; Lib. sup. Amisburie; Svy Amesbury 1635; Amesbury Misc. Papers & Docs. Billet land c. alijs, Baicliffe partic.; Savernake: svys.: Barton & Marlboro', Collingbourne Kingston, Chisbury, Shalbourne W.ct 1552, 1638–9; Collingbourne Ducis 1635; Pewsey 1552, 1614; Gt Bedwyn Preb. 1552; Burbages 1574; B.M., Add. 34008 f. 19; R. 37571; Hants. R.O., 5 M53/747,pp. 9 sqq.; P.R.O., S.P.D. Interregnum, vol. G58A, ff. 340–1, 350 sqq.; R. & S. G.S. 20/27; Exch. K.R., Sp. Commn 2409; L.R., M.B. 187, ff. 146–9; 191, ff. 78 sqq. 130 sqq., 173 sqq.; 203, ff. 365 sqq.; A.O., M.B. 420, ff. 7 sqq.; D.L., M.B. 108, ff. 46v. sqq., 70v. sqq., 86 sqq., 115, ff. 37v. sqq., 48v. sqq. 58–61; R. & S. 9/26, 28; Sp. Commn 313; Straton, op. cit. i.

[2] Ibid. 69, 306–8; Wilton ho. Svys Manors 1631 ii, Wylye ff. 10(9) sqq.; Netherhampton; Svys Manors 1632–3, Barford; Svy Flambston 1631; Money, op. cit. 105–8; B.M., Add. 34008, f. 19; R. 5074; Dors. R.O., D. 4, Thornhull fam. ct bk sect. i, Woolland 6 Nov. 4 Ed. VI; D. 10/E103 'Rate for sheepe made 1598 Winfryth'; P.R.O., Exch. K.R., Sp. Commn 2418, 2424; D.L., M.B. 116, f. 7v.; 117, f. 29; R. & S. 9/28; Chanc. Proc. ser. i Jas I, C. 16/59; H. 36/74, m. 1; Slater, op. cit. 21; Wilts. R.O., Savernake: Ct Bk Shalbourne E. ct 1601–14, 20 Apr. 41 Eliz.; svy Shalbourne W. ct 1639, ff. 17–18, 25.

[3] Ibid. Collingbourne Ducis Ct Bk, 25 Apr. 1593; Easton svy c. 1760, p. 2; acc. 283, Lib. sup. Amisburie; Davis, op. cit. 43–4; Bodington, art. cit. xli, 266–7; Lennard, art. cit. 42; Slater, op. cit. 20; Goddard, art. cit. 212; Soms. R.O., D.D./H.K., Ct R. N. Perrott m. 2; Berks. R.O., D./E.Hy M26; P.R.O., Exch. L.R., M.B. 187, f. 226; A.O., Parl. Svys Wilts. 43, ff. 3–6; Fussell, op. cit. ix.

did not have a whole year's bare fallow. When the tares or peas were off the field, the hitching piece was given a bare fallow in late summer or early autumn. The hitching was often a large fraction of the summer field. Robert Loder of Harwell, e.g. hitched about a quarter of his fallow field every year.[1] The usual hitching crop was 'horsemeat', i.e. a dredge of spring tares, peas or lentils, with oats for them to climb by, all being cut together and both pods and hay fed to horses. Vetches were grown as sheep feed, and occasionally for green manure, as well as for hay. On land too poor for peas or tares, lentils were grown.[2] Tares and lentils were mostly spring sown as catch-crops for horsemeat, but if grass and hay were in short supply, winter vetches were sown for the sheep in spring, or, like lentils, to be mown as hay for the horses or lambs. Even after grass and hay had become plentiful in the Chalk Country as a whole, there remained some localities with insufficient meadow, and here, as at Tilshead, the hay of winter vetches continued as a staple winter fodder for sheep. In the strong 'whitelands' of the Vale of Pewsey, beans and lentils were sown on alternate ridges for miles along the escarpment, barley sometimes being grown with the latter to support them. Beans were not widely grown in other soils because only the 'whitelands' were strong enough to bear them without first being left to sward for a year or two.[3] Some soils were too light to be stirred at all in fallowing and instead were left as 'still' fallow for a year or more to gain some sward, which, when ploughed under, would give them strength to bear a crop, though rarely of beans. This practice was common on thin hill soils in preparation for red wheat.[4]

In the flinty-loam districts, which were generally enclosed, convertible husbandry was usually adopted;[5] and elsewhere on the downs some of the 'redland' was in convertible husbandry, being divided into

[1] Ibid. 11, 41, 97–8, 103–4; Goddard, loc. cit.; Slater, loc. cit.; Straton, op. cit. i, 162; Berks. R.O., D./E.Bt E28; D./E.Ah E5/1, 2; Davis, op. cit. 46, 50–1, 62.

[2] Ibid. 50–1, 62; Bennett, art. cit. 39; Wilts. R.O., Savernake: Collingbourne Ducis Ct Bk, 22 Jan. 1593; W. Stevenson, *Gen. View Ag. Co. Dors.* 1812, p. 243; Lisle, op. cit. 23, 172, 174; Mavor, op. cit. 231; J. Parkinson, *Theatrum Botanicum* 1640, p. 1068.

[3] Fussell, op. cit. 96; Worlidge, op. cit. 38; T. Hitt, *Treatise Husbandry* 1760, p. 151; B.M., Egerton 2559, ff. 42–5; invs.:—Wilts. R.O., Dioc. Reg. Sarum.: Jn Piper 1573 Gt Bedwyn, Marg. Golle 1595 Broad Chalke, Jn Pike 1624 L. Bedwyn, Th. Whithorne 1584 Nether Woodford; Hants. R.O., A/d Ct 1597: David Smithe/ Church Oakley; 1614: Robt Lipscome/Weston Patrick; Cons. Ct 1619: Th. Danger-field/E. Dean; Pec. Ct Meonstoke &c.: Th. Collins 1633–4; Lisle, op. cit. 21, 108, 161–2, 332; Davis, op. cit. 51.

[4] Ibid. 58; Lennard, art. cit. 32; Kitchin, op. cit. 184–5; Money, op. cit. 111–12; P.R.O., Wds, Feodaries' Svys Wilts. unsorted bdl. Baskervile confession 19 Jas; St. Ch. Eliz. A. 8/37; A. 11/8; Wilts. R.O., acc. 283, Lib. sup. Amisburie, partic. billet lands; Savernake: Svy Collingbourne Kingston 1595, f. 54.

[5] Ibid. Svy Chisbury 44 Eliz. ff. 6, 19; Dioc. Reg. Sarum. inv. Miles Rumsey 1634 Gt Bedwyn.

shifts or 'laines' ('leynes') for the purpose. At Collingbourne Ducis the demesne farmer 'did yerely newly breake upp and eare a parcell of the downe', which was tilled for four or five years and called 'Shiphouse Layne' from its vicinity to the sheepcote whose compost it received.[1] In 1518 there were amongst the hill-pastures of Boulsbury, Toyd and Allenford, scores of acres of arable 'que indifferenter seminari possint vel pasturam inde facere ad comodum domini'.[2] At Knighton in Chalke in 1567 the demesne farm includes 'in the Middelfeld arrable lands now sowen x acres, and there is that hath been sowen xxx acres, and in the Estfield in the furlong called Prestway xxx acres arrable, another pece upon the hill called Geldknappe iiij acres, another pece above the hill called ix acres; also more lands arrable there which have not been in tillage this manie yeares'.[3] Surveying Fordington in 1607, John Norden says of two adjacent parts of the sheep-down, 'Theis are now arrable'.[4] Similar convertible husbandry was to be found at Horndean, Winter-bourne, Hill Deverill, Chilbolton and West Harting.[5] Leys were formed either by natural swarding, or by sowing hayseeds or hay-dust, or by the cultivation of selected natural grass seeds. Natural grasses gave good results and natural swarding was the best way of restoring the sheep-down grasses.[6] After a crop or two of corn, the land was laid to sheep-pasture again, and the cultivations had, therefore, to be light, in order to preserve the natural grasses in the ground until needed again. In ploughing up, the ley might be raftered, i.e. alternate furrows only be ploughed and the furrow slices turned bottom-side up on the unploughed grass furrows, the whole then receiving a light cultivation. The corn thus grew, so to speak, in the turf itself. These practices were confined to the 'redlands', and even these could be forced to bear crops thanks only to the sheep-fold, which was the best and almost the only way to restore the soil. The land was usually laid to grass under wheat, so it has a fine tilth, good straw for protection and the best possible start, but even then it was about two years before the sward was fully restored. On the thinnest soils only one crop of barley or wheat was taken; on the deepest perhaps a succession of (1) wheat or barley, (2) oats and vetches, (3) wheat; elsewhere a crop of barley or oats might be followed

---

[1] Ibid. Savernake: Ct Bk Collingbourne Ducis, 22 Jan., 25 Apr. 1593; Ct R. Bk 1741–58, pp. 345, 370, 377; Straton, op. cit. i, 119 sqq.; Wilton ho. Svys. Manors 1632–3, Chilmark & Rudge; P.R.O., Exch. L.R., M.B. 187, f. 428.

[2] Hoare, op. cit. Hund. S. Domerham 41.

[3] Straton, op. cit. i, 307–8.

[4] B. M., Add. 6027, ff. 136(126)v.–7.

[5] W. H. Godfrey, *Booke Jn Rowe* Suss. Rec. Soc. 1928 xxxiv, 3; B.M., Harl. 3961, f. 87v.; Add. 28529, f. 162(153)v.; P.R.O., St. Ch. Eliz. A. 11/8; A. 34/10.

[6] Marshall, *S. Cos.* ii, 325; Wilts. R.O., Dioc. Reg. Sarum. invs. Alice Pildren 1593 W. Grinstead, Anne West 1634 Netheravon; Berks. R.O., D./E.C. M114/1; Brentnall, art. cit. 16; Lisle, op. cit. 32, 264.

by one of wheat. The land was then laid to grass for between four and seven years. Thus, at West Harting in 1632, some land that had been sheep-down for two years was being folded to prepare it for tillage, while other land was being laid down under wheat.[1] Apart from sheep-pastures and wet meadows, then, there was little permanent grassland. If landlords forbade or restricted the ploughing up of grasslands by lease covenants, this was only to ensure control and exact woading and corning rents.[2] Enclosures, it is true, were often described as 'closes of pasture' or somesuch, but this wording was, for the most part, merely conventional, and it was only more rarely that other descriptions, such as 'arable or pasture', truly represented the state of the land.[3] The area subject to convertible husbandry was considerable, and in severalty farms, often extensive. Roger Earth, a gentleman farmer of Donington, had 44 acres in up-and-down husbandry and William Jesse of Chilmark almost 120. John Twogood, a gentleman farmer of St James Ugford, had 93 acres in Chapel Farm, which had no less than 60 alternately ploughed up for corn and laid down to grass.[4]

The upshot of all the different field-courses and rotations was that the two main crops were wheat and barley, which were sown about equally. The wheat was mediocre and the barley excellent. Together they were by far the most important market crops and constituted the chief object of farming. The main consumption crops were oats, tares, lentils and peas, and these, with beans, made up about one-quarter of the acreage under crop. There were, in addition, small quantities of winter vetches and of rye, both intended chiefly for sheep.[5]

Oxen were shod and employed, but were inferior to horses in ploughing downside slopes and in traction on hill roads, so much so that every farmer who sent to market needed a team of horses for this alone. For these reasons most farmers of any substance used shire horses, largely to the exclusion of oxen.[6] Sometimes the plough-team was composed of

[1] Ibid. 3–6, 266; Davis, op. cit. 53–5, Pearce, op. cit. 28. Marshall, op. cit. ii, 326–7; S. Dept, 300; B.M., Add. 28529, ff. 166(157)v., 189–90(178–9), 200(190); Bodl. Aubrey 2, f. 83.

[2] R. B. Pugh, Cal. Antrobus Deeds Wilts. Archaeol. & Nat. Hist. Soc. Rec. Br. 1947 iii, 71; Wilts. R.O., acc. 283, Lib. sup. Amisburie, ff. 25–6; Svy Amesbury 1635, f. 43.

[3] Ibid. Savernake: Svy Chisbury 44 Eliz.; Svy Barton & Marlboro' 1638; acc. 212B, Wr. 1b; Berks. R.O., D./E.C. M10B, p. 1; B.M., Add. 28529, ff. 143(132)v., 164(155); R. 37571; P.R.O., Exch. L.R., M.B. 187, f. 106; 203, ff. 365 sqq.; S.P.D., Interregnum, vol. G58A. ff. 350 sqq.; Straton, op. cit. i, 267; Wilton ho. Svys. Manors 1631 i, Foffonnt, Dinton & Teffont, Netherhampton; 1632–3 Chilmark & Rudge.

[4] Ibid. f. 2; 1631 i, Dinton & Teffont, f. 2(3); Bulbridge &c. f. 1(2).

[5] Davis, op. cit. 51, 55; Mavor, op. cit. 180, 203, 207, 209, 212, 214, 217; Marshall, op. cit. 249; S. Cos. i, 327; ii, 324; Bodl. Aubrey 2, f. 83; & inf. 50 n.1.

[6] Fussell, op. cit, 3, 7, 17–18, 21; Davis, op. cit. 73–4, 111; Lisle, op. cit. 67; Stevenson, op. cit. 183; Marshall, op. cit. ii, 320: S. Dept, 55, 337; Bodl. Aubrey 2, f. 89.

one, sometimes of two pairs, but most usually of three horses, two of which pulled abreast, while the third drew a chain fixed to the centre of the whippletree and walked on the unploughed ground hard by the right hand. These teams ('ploughs') are often discernible in the probate inventories, and of all the farmers who kept teams in the early modern period, two-thirds had horse-ploughs, one-seventh ploughs mainly of oxen, with perhaps some steers or dry cows, and the remainder either both horse and ox teams or those of mixed composition. Poor husbandmen often had ox or mixed teams, but the great farmers relied chiefly on horses.[1] These horse teams might appear extravagant, and they were certainly slow; but the horses were reared in the plain countries and sold to Chalk Country farmers, at between two and three years, to be inured to moderate labour before being re-sold at about six years for street and road haulage. While on the farm, therefore, they were not intended to be worked hard; nor had they, indeed, lost the snail's pace acquired where they were bred and reared.[2] Winter fallowing was usually done about October, when the horses were still at grass. After this they could go on a diet of 'horsemeat' and straw until the spring ploughings.[3]

The farmers kept some cows, with up to half a dozen in milk, and made some pale-coloured butter and cheese, but dairy produce had largely to be bought farther afield. Specialist dairymen were virtually unknown, but the domestic dairy was essential and every township had its cow-down, where a common cowherd took charge of the tenantry's beasts. From early May until the fields were rid, the common herd grazed the cow-down, going up in the morning and coming down at night. They fed the stubble field side by side with the sheep and after the hay was cut they had exclusive use of the water-meadows until October or November, when they went into the yards. Here they fed chiefly on straw, which barely sustained them. Whereas everything on the farm was done, so to speak, to please the sheep, the cows were the least considered of all the livestock. As soon as they left the down for the stubble, the former was appropriated for the sheep; and if the cows were allowed

[1] N. S. B. and E. C. Gras, op. cit. 547; Wilts. N. & Q. v, 554, 556; B.M., Sir Th. Phillipp's Tracts, Topog. & Geneal. iii, pt 2, Wanborough Ct R. 1649, pp. 35–6, 50, 58; Add. Ch. 59152; Egerton 2559, ff. 42–5; Bristol Univ. Lib. Shrewton 67/12; P.R.O., Exch. K.R., Invs. goods & chattels, 2/36–7; Wds, Feodaries' Svys Wilts. 268; Berks. R.O., D./E.Ah E5/3; invs.:—Wilts. R.O., Dioc. Reg. Sarum. Cons. Ct Sarum.; A/d Sarum; A/d Wilts.; Pec. Ct Dean Sarum.; Preb. Ct Husborne & Burbage; acc. 283 Ct Bk Amesbury Erledom starting 27 Mar. 25 Eliz.; Savernake: Ct Bk Collingbourne Ducis, 1578–92; Devizes Mus. Jn Sloper 1643 Roundway; Soms. R.O., D.D./T.H., Ric. Draper; Cons. Ct A/d Taunton; Hants. R.O., Cons. & A/d cts; Pec. cts Meonstoke &c., W. Meon, E. Meon, Crawley, Compton, N. Waltham, Wonston, Twyford; O. W., Admins. & Invs.; unclassified.

[2] Marshall, op. cit. 92; Midl. Cas. i, 311–2; inf. 113, 258.

[3] Lisle, op. cit. 50.

on the meadows during late summer and early autumn, this was only because the sheep would not have been safe on them.[1]

Sheep-and-corn farming was almost the universal plan of management. Cast-off ewes fit only for fatting were usually sold away to the neighbouring plain and vale countries, and hardly more than a few rotting kebbs were fed for local consumption.[2] Only where a shortage of meadow compelled farmers to keep flying flocks were wethers stocked in large numbers, and few of these were fatted in the Chalk Country.[3] Most farmers were anxious only to keep good flocks of breeding ewes. Some theaves were retained for replenishing the flocks, but nearly all wether hogs were sold as soon after midsummer as possible to the Chiltern and Northdown countries, the Vale of London and the Midland Plain.[4]

THE SOUTHDOWN COUNTRY

About Chichester and the River Lavant, the Chalk Country ended and the Southdown Country began. Here the chalk hills were in a narrow and elongated formation stretching east-south-eastwards to the sea. Immediately east of Chichester an even smaller ridge of chalk downs branched off in an easterly direction. This was farmed in conjunction with the intervening vale and here the Southdown Country was at its widest. Elsewhere, even though larger than the South Downs themselves, the country was usually less, and often much less, than ten miles wide. The hills themselves had more steepness than those of the Chalk Country, being, so to speak, all escarpment. Most of their soils were light calcareous loams resting on a chalk bed, but generally thinner than those of the Chalk Country. Moreover, flinty clay loams and associated woodlands were almost entirely absent. North of the escarpment lay a narrow belt of chalky clay, provincially 'mawmy' or 'maam' land, and beyond this a vein of sandy loam. There resulted a northern arable foreland that was farmed together with the downs, the villages including lands both above and below the hill. The tops of the downs were sheepwalk, the lower slopes and foreland arable, and the valley bottoms and vale grounds wet meadows, permanent grass and convertible land. The

[1] Bodl. Aubrey 2, f. 103; Davis, op. cit. 17–18; Marshall, *S. Cos.* ii, 324.

[2] Ibid. 349; Wilton ho. Svys Manors 1631 i, Fugglestone, ff. 3(4) sqq.

[3] P.R.O., Exch. A.O., Parl. Svys Wilts. 44; Hants. 25, f. iv.; Wilts. R.O., acc. 3, N. on manor Ogbourne St Geo.; Straton, op. cit. i, 259, 302; Hoare, op. cit. Hund. S. Domerham 42; J. Waylen, 'Wilts. Compounders', *Wilts. Mag.* xxiv, 314; Marshall, op. cit. ii, 348.

[4] Ibid. 346–7; Davis, op. cit. 4, 17; Ellis, op. cit. 294; W. Youatt, *Sheep* 1837, p. 245; R. B. Westerfield, *Middlemen in Eng. Bus.* Trans. Conn. Acad. Arts & Sc. 1915 xix, 188; P.R.O., D.L., M.B. 108, ff. 7–8, 12v.–13; Bodl. Aubrey 2, f. 148; & v. inf. 55, 59, 96, 174.

chalk ridge near Chichester recommenced in the Isle of Wight, where it ran from Culver Cliff in the east to the Needles in the west. In the extreme south of the island rose a further clump of chalk downs and between these and the ridge 'mawmy' and sandy loam soils occurred. Owing to their common plan of management, this southern part may be considered a detached portion of Southdown Country. By the coast, and especially in the Isle of Wight, the winds were of some consequence, for they impeded the growth of trees and hedges. Despite maritime mildness and the shading of the northern slopes, the climature for crops was generally forward and congenial, the rainfall being moderate and rapidly imbibed.

Common fields, sheep-walks, flocks, folds and meadows existed in most townships and were managed almost exactly as in the Chalk Country,[1] and, as there too, the demesne farms were largely in open severalty.[2] The native Southdown sheep were stocked at rates that varied between one and five to an arable acre and averaged about two. One acre of down would keep five couples in summer and two or three in winter. In contrast there were only one or two head of cattle to a score of acres.[3] The general plan of management was to feed ewe and wether flocks on the downs by day and fold them on the arable at night. Folding was continued almost unremittingly throughout the year, in winter for barley, peas and oats; and in summer for wheat and rye. Only in the worst weather were the sheep cotted on the downs at night and only occasionally was the fold put upon them in the summer. Wheat and barley were the two chief objects of farming. Wether sheep were sold off for fattening elsewhere and dairies of 'Sussex' cows were for domestic and local consumption only. Not many oxen were reared and then only to draw wains, for horses were more suited to the hilly fields and roads

[1] Marshall, op. cit. ii, 265, 274, 363, 367; S. Dept, 500, 504; Young, op. cit. 39; Godfry, op. cit. 61–2, 70, 200, 202, 211, 219, 222, 225; E. D. D. & J. Britten, O. Country & Farming Words E. D. S. 1880 s.v. lain(e); P. D. Mundy, Abs. St. Ch. rel. to. Co. Suss. Hy VII to P. & M. Suss. Rec. Soc. 1913 xvi, 97; C. Thomas-Preston, Abs. Ct R. Manor Preston ibid. 1921 xxvii, 7–8; BM, Add. 38487, ff. 49v.–50; R. 28264, 32385; Lans. vol. 784, ff. 35(38) sqq.; P.R.O., Exch. A.O., M.B. 368, ff. 91(pp. 6) sqq.; 421, ff. 16(3) sqq., 33 sqq.; Cornwall, op. cit, 48–51, 101, 111–2, 134, 146; 'Farming in Suss. 1560–1640', Suss. Archaeol. Colls. xcii, 52–3; G. M. Cooper, 'Berwick Par. Recs.', ibid. vi, 229, 232, 240–1; Northants. R.O., Wmld 5. ix.

[2] Ibid.; B.M., Add. 6027, ff. 130(120)v.–132(122); P.R.O., Exch. T.R., Bk 157, ff. 91–2 (pp. 174–6); A.O., M.B. 359, ff. 3 sqq.; 368, ff. 2 sqq., 77(1) sqq.; 421, ff. 2 sqq., 12; Cornwall, art. cit. 49; Marshall, op. cit. 504; Godfrey, op. cit. 57, 62–3, 65, 67, 69, 70, 107. Cf. sup. 17–19.

[3] W. Suss. R.O., Cons. Ct Bp Cicestr. for A/d Cicestr. invs.; Cooper, art. cit. 241; Godfrey, op. cit, 61, 65, 69, 202, 204, 225; Marshall, op. cit. 500; B.M., Add. 6027, f. 119(118); R. 32385; P.R.O., Exch. A.O., M.B. 368, ff. 2 sqq.; 421, ff. 2 sqq.; Northants. R. O., Wmld 5. ix; Cornwall, op. cit. 107; & v. inf. 53 n. 3 Chalk Country sheep fnd in I.W.–J. Childrey, Brit. Baconica 1660, p. 51; Marshall, S. Cos. ii, 284.

and were generally employed in ploughing, mostly in teams of four.[1] Hog sheep were often wintered in neighbouring vales. In the eastern extremity many of the larger farms had out-farms or annexes in Pevensey Level for the maintenance of horses and the fatting of cattle. Thus a 1,200-acre farm at Eastbourne had 200 acres, and a 1,260-acre farm there 300 acres, in the level.[2] The chief market crops remained throughout wheat and barley and the minor ones rye, maslin, wool and store lambs. The chief consumption crops were grass and hay, peas, tares, oats, buckwheat and beans. Peas, tares and 'horsemeat' were grown in the hitching fields, chiefly for horses, but partly for sheep. Oats, tail wheat and occasionally beans were fed to horses also, while hogs sometimes had peas, and poultry barley, as well as buckwheat.[3]

THE NORTHDOWN COUNTRY

As the North Downs formed a relatively narrow ridge, the rivers and bournes that intersected them gave little meadowland, but some compensation was found in the marshlands near the Isle of Thanet and the Thames and Medway estuaries, especially Ash Level and Minster and Monkton marshes, all of which had long since been drained and were a great resource for neighbouring farmers. Northdown Country soils differed considerably from those of either the Southdown or the Chalk countries, for while in the two latter it might be said that the chalk stood above the clay, in the former the clay stood, so to speak, above the chalk, the swells of the downs being generally covered, to a depth of three or four feet, with decomposed chalk, on which lay a reddish, flinty clay loam. Chalky soils were largely confined to the Isle of Thanet, the western extremity, the valleys and the lower parts. The valleys had some light, and some very deep and productive, calcareous sandy loams, or 'coombs', which were especially prevalent in the combes of the Canterbury district, in the vales of Harbledown and Farnham, and along the northern skirts of the downs. In the Maidstone district and the extreme south there were some sandy soils and sandy loams. Between Canterbury, Dover and Deal were some chalk loams of between 3 and 7 inches

[1] Ibid. 267, 274, 276, 278, 280–1, 285–8, 368, 373, 376, 378; S. Dept, 504–5; Northants. R.O., Wmld 5. ix; invs.:—Hants. R.O., A/d & Cons. cts; W. Suss. R.O., Cons. Ct Bp Cicestr. for A/d Cicestr.; B'ham Lib. 370338; B.M., Add. 6027, f. 131 (121); 38634, f. 1; P.R.O., Exch. T.R., Bk 157, f. 92 (p. 175); Cornwall, op. cit. 98; art. cit. 91; L. Mascall, Cattell 1587, p. 236; W. H. Hudson, Nature in Downland 1925, p. 32; Godfrey, op. cit. 61–2; Cooper, art. cit. 232; Suss. Archaeol. Colls. vi, 192 sqq.

[2] Ibid.; Marshall, op. cit. 469.

[3] Ibid. 484, 488; S. Cos. ii, 278–9; Cornwall, op. cit. 146; art. cit. 91; Young, op. cit. 67; Suss. Archaeol. Colls. loc. cit.; N. S. B. Gras, op. cit. 404 sqq.; B.M., Add. 38634, f. 1; invs. ut sup.

in depth, some 'cledge' or flinty clay loams, some 'hazel mould', i.e. rich loam on a clay bottom, and varying mixtures of sandy, gravelly and flinty loams. Between Faversham, Deal and Sandwich the soils were mainly flinty clay loams and sandy loams. In the west, the upper downs had some thin, light-textured soils, best suited to sheep-pasture; but it was the Isle of Thanet that bore the greatest superficial resemblance to the Chalk Country. Its soils were mainly chalk loams, but of an unusually great depth, as much as 18 inches or 2 feet in some parts, especially towards the west, thus being the deepest and richest of their kind in England. In the Northdown Country, the climate approached the Continental, but the Isle of Thanet was swept by strong, cool winds in summer and by bitterly cold ones in winter, making the cultivation of trees and hedges difficult. Rainfall was everywhere moderate and, thanks to the chalk base and the loamy character of most of the soils themselves, the climature was generally excellent for all tillage crops.

Flinty clay loams were associated with trees and woods, especially beech-woods. The higher swells of the downs were generally enclosed from woodlands; and between the enclosures were hedge or coppice rows excepted from the clearance. Only the more elevated of the chalky soils, and the poorer ones in the west that were all too apt to overrun with furze and heath, were left as sheep-downs; but in the Isle of Thanet the whole countryside lay open. In most of the country, common fields had never existed and most townships had detached hamlets or 'streets', such as are associated with woodland settlement. In the Isle of Thanet, however, although several of the capital farms were isolated, nucleated townships generally continued, after the fashion of common-field countries. Long, narrow lands of the open field type, too, persisted into the nineteenth century.[1] Common fields had been general in the deeper chalk loams and many survived, in name at least, in the sixteenth and seventeenth centuries.[2]

Almost all the land was arable, much of which was alternately tilled for up to half a dozen years and then laid down with hay seeds for three or four years.[3] The deepest soils were kept in permanent tillage. Whole-

---

[1] Marshall, op. cit. i, 19, 21; ii, 6, 8, 394; *Yks.* ii, 244; *VCH Kent* iii, 321.

[2] W. James & J. Malcolm, *Gen. View Ag. Co. Sy* 1794, pp. 38–9, 45; J. Aubrey, *Nat. Hist. & Ant. Co. Sy* 1719 iv, 16; *VCH Sy* iv, 430, 438; Marshall, *S. Dept*, 356; Guildford Mun. Rm, Loseley 674; Sy R.O., 10/1, 2, 4 Ct R. Ashstead; acc. 137, f. 12; acc. 169, Ashstead pl. 1638; acc. 344, svy Dorking 1649; 18/13/1 Ct Bk L. Bookham starting 1673; 34/1/2 Ct Bk Gt Bookham, f. 25; 34/1/3a Ct Bk Eastwick, f. 92; 34/3 svy id. 1614, ff. 17, 27; 34/4 svy Fetcham, p. 12; B.M., Add. R. 27886; Stowe 858, ff. 39, 45, 66–7; P.R.O., Exch. K.R., M.B. 40, ff. 2, 6v., 8–11, 15, 20–1, 47; L.R., M.B. 196, ff. 116, 117v., 169, 268v.–9; 197, f. 72v.; 198, ff. 8v.–9, 23, 38, 39v., 44v.; 218, ff. 192, 255, 304; 219, ff. 104, 111, 123, 133, 145, 150, 154, 171, 184, 269, 284, 291, 335, 342, 344, 434–5; A.O., Parl. Svys Kent 26, f. 32; *Sy Archaeol. Colls.* xx, 100, 103, 111, 113; xli, 42, 44; Baker, op. cit. 20; Lambert, op. cit. i, 185; ii, 55–6.

[3] Ibid. i, 199 sqq., 254; Marshall, *S. Cos.* i, 22; ii, 3–4, 34; Boys, op. cit. 107;

year bare fallows were accorded to some wheat crops everywhere, but were only made with any regularity on the chalky clay soils, with the object of rendering the soil crumbly.[1] Otherwise crops were grown in almost all the fallows. Until the latter part of the seventeenth century, the paramount fallow and fodder crop here was 'podware', i.e. mainly tares and peas or a maslin of the two, with a few kidney beans added in deeper soils. Such 'podware' was grown as extensively as wheat. Crop samples show about three-tenths each of wheat and podware and two-fifths of barley, with an inconsiderable quantity of oats.[2] Thus the prevailing fallow crop of the Chalk Country—'horsemeat'—which was there usually grown only on part of the fallow field, was grown in almost all fallows in the Northdown Country. This did not, however, exclude bare fallows altogether, for after the podware was off the ground, fallow ploughings and cleaning cultivations were carried out in preparation for wheat. As in the other down countries, the sheep-fold was the firm foundation of husbandry, horses supplied the teams, and cattle were suffered only in small numbers, except in the marshes. In the absence of extensive down pastures, podware fed the sheep.[3] In the east and about Maidstone, many Romney Marsh sheep were wintered, but Chalk Country horned sheep, largely wethers, bought from Weyhill Fair, were generally stocked elsewhere.[4]

Fruit cultivation developed considerably, especially in the Vale of Farnham, in the Maidstone district, and in the combes along the north of the downs between Crayford and Sandwich, i.e. where there were suitable chalky loams. Cherry gardens were more extensive than orchards of table apples and pears. Orchards and gardens were often kept

Sackville-West, op. cit. 25; A. Savine, *Eng. Mons. on Eve Dissolution* 1909, pp. 175–6; Sy R.O., 34/3 svy Gt Bookham 1614, ff. 3 sqq., 13; Ess. R.O., D/DL M46; P.R.O., Exch. L.R., M.B. 196, ff. 118v., 247, 266, 269; 197, ff. 10, 76; 198, ff. 1, 12–14, 37, 40v.; 218, ff. 81 sqq., 208; 219, ff. 108, 124–6, 128, 133, 206–7, 269, 322, 343–4, 377–8, 400, 409; A.O., Parl. Svys Kent 26, ff. 2–3, 5; Chanc. Proc. ser. i Jas I, B. 1/68; B.M., Stowe 858, ff. 5, 59–60, 62, 67; Harl. 3749, ff. 13–14; G. Markham, *Inrichmt Weald Kent* 1625, p. 7.

[1] Ibid.; Boys, op. cit. 16–17, 55, 57, 62, 65, 69.
[2] Ibid. 97; J. M. Cowper, 'Tudor Prices in Kent', *Trans. R. Hist. S.* 1875 i, 170, 175–6; R. Keen, 'Inv. Ric. Hooker 1601', *Arch. Cant.* lxx, 235–6; ibid. lxi, 60 sqq.; B.M., Add. R. 16280; Ess. R.O., D/DL E61, a/c 1586; Herts. R.O., 22042; Marshall, *S. Dept*, 393; Melling, op. cit. 16 sqq., 22–3; invs.:—Hants. & Kent R.O.s, Cons. & A/d cts.
[3] Ibid.; B.M., Herts. & Ess. R.O.s—as prev. n.; Lennard, art. cit, 31; R. Weston, *Enlargemt Discourse Husbandry used in Brabant and Fland.* ed. S. Hartlib 1651, p. 8; *Arch. Cant.* lxi, 60 sqq., 69–72; Marshall, *S. Cos.* i, 56–7, 69, 320, 322; ii, 10–12, 404, 411.
[4] Ibid. i, 68, 153, 325–7, 378; ii, 11, 35–7, 411–13; *S. Dept*, 408–11; invs., B.M. & Herts. R.O.—as prev. n.; Aubrey, op. cit. i, Evelyn's pref.; ii, 306–7; Boys, op. cit. 110–11, 152, 155.

in grass for pasture and hay.[1] Both they and the hopyards were sometimes big, and a farm of hundreds of acres might have as many as
scores in fruit, or the annual produce of a farmer's orchards and
gardens be sold for £120 in 1592–3; but the chief objects of farming
were, in order of importance, arable crops, fruit and hops, fat sheep,
and fat cattle.[2]

THE CHILTERN COUNTRY

The Chiltern Country was dry, hilly, mainly arable land on a chalk
base. Along the escarpment of the Chiltern Hills and the East Anglian
Heights were beds of chalky loams more extensive than those of the
Northdown Country, save the Isle of Thanet, but few or none as deep,
and some extremely thin. Below the scarp, as elsewhere, lay successive
beds of chalky clay and sandy loams. On the back of the hills were
gravelly and hurlocky or hard chalk soils, chalky clay loams, marls,
loams, and more frequently, especially towards the south and west, red,
gravelly or flinty clay loams. The base being permeable and the climate
much like that of the Chalk Country, the climature for crops was likewise similar. In the thinner soils quick hedges could be raised only with
difficulty and the land usually remained open or bounded only by an
earthen ridge or balk. Along the escarpment, slopes otherwise too steep
to cultivate were laid out in terraces or platforms along the contours,
with greensward linches or balks between them. The flinty clay loams
were associated with woodland, especially with beech-wood, parts of
which had been cleared. The fields were therefore bounded with hedgerows, coppice-rows and hedge-greens that were merely the remains of
the woods. As chalky and flinty clay loams were considerably intermixed,
the landscape was often a chequer-board of champion and woodland.[3]

Most of the land, especially that in demesne, was in severalty, whether

---

[1] T. Fuller, *Hist. Worthies Engl.* 1840 ii, 112; Norden, op. cit. 214–5; Fiennes, op.
cit. 131; Kent R.O., U. 214/E7/10, 21; P.R.O., Req. 61/39; Exch. L.R., M.B., 197,
ff. 11v.–2; 198, f. 1v,; 219, ff. 280–1, 303, 319, 324–5, 327; Melling, op. cit. 15–16,
28–31, 56–9; Marshall, op. cit. 235; *S. Cos.* i, 22, 67.

[2] Ibid. 22, 67–8; Kent R.O., A/d Ct Cantuar. invs.:—1665; Wyatt Chowne/
Boughton Monchelsea; 1678: Wm Charleton/Boughton; 1680: Th. Carter/E.
Sutton; P.R.O., Req. 61/39; Exch. L.R., M.B. 197, ff. 10–13; 198, ff. 1–2; 219, ff.
269 sqq.

[3] Marshall, *S. Dept.* 27; J. Norden, *Desron Harts.* 1598, p. 1; Blith, op. cit. 82; R.
Davis, *Gen. View Ag. Co. Oxf.* 1794, p. 9; W. James & J. Malcolm, id. *Buckingham*
1794, p. 11; C. Vancouver, id. *Ess.* 1795, p. 105; *Cams.* 81; J. Leland, *Itin.* 1906–10 v,
7; E. Sfk R.O., V. 5/23/2. 1, f. 17; Kalm, op. cit, 215, 265; F. Seebohm, *Eng. Vil.
Commun,* 1883, pp. 4–5; Venn, op. cit. frontis. 44, opp. 64; F. Harvey, *Ickworth Suy
Books* pp. 8, 10; M. Spufford, 'Rural Cams. 1520–1680', ts. thesis M.A. Leicester
Univ. 1962, pp. 8–9.

open or enclosed;[1] but common fields, greens, meadows, hills and heaths were widespread. Only along the arable foreland and escarpment, both spanned by each north-western township, did many large common fields or spacious common downs exist,[2] except that a few temporary common fields were created where common heaths were ploughed for two years or so and then left in heath several years, as at Mapledurham in 1720–1.[3] On the northerly aspects of the hills especially, were many parks, some of recent origin, though in the seventeenth century, not a few were disparked and let out to farmers.[4] The typical Chiltern 'pasture' consisted of copses or woods interspersed with grassy glades. Newnham, for instance, had 'one other Chiltorne pasture in severall cauled Newnham Wood'. Clumps of trees were dispersed throughout the greater part of the pasture's 90 acres, but between them a good deal of grazing was to be had.[5] Not much wet meadow was found and the permanent grasslands were largely these Chiltern pastures and the hedge-greens, about 20 feet or more wide, that surrounded the arable fields. When the field was cropped, the hedge-green was mown and the aftermath depastured, and when fallowed, sheep grazed there. Cattle sometimes fed the hedge-greens, or resorted to the coppice-rows for sustenance, shade and shelter, or browsed in the woodlands and woody pastures.[6] About a tenth of the land was permanent grass, between a tenth and a half Chiltern pasture or woodland, of which there was more in the south and less in the north, and the rest mostly arable. Generally, the sunny slopes were arable and the shaded not.[7] Most arable fields were in convertible

[1] B.M., Add. Ch. 35524A; Herts. R.O., 1434; 8154, 1st foliation, 1 sqq.; G'bury xi. 2 svy Gorham & Westwick 1569; V. Bell, L. Gaddesden 1949, p. 46; P.R.O. Exch. L.R., M.B. 224, f. 152.

[2] Ibid. 196, ff. 185v. sqq.; Bell, op. cit. 10; Marshall, op. cit. 8; Spufford, op. cit. 17; W. M. Palmer, Hist. Par. Bor. Green Camb. Ant. S. 8vo pubns 1949 liv, 136–9; R. L. Hine, Hist. Hitchin 1927 i, 59, 64–5; J. A. Tregelles, Hist. Hoddesdon 1908, pp. 330, 336; Aspley Hth Sch. Hist. Soc. Hist. our Dist. 1931, pp. 33–5, 45; Vancouver, op. cit. 14, 16, 19, 21, 25–6, 30–1, 37, 40–3, 46 sqq., 53–4, 56 sqq., 64–6, 68 sqq., 77 sqq.; J. Spratt, 'Agrarian Conditions in Nfk & Sfk 1600–50', ts. thesis M.A. Ldn Univ. 1935, pp. 26, 57, 236; Cams. R.O., L. 1/167, ff. 3–4; R. 51. 29. 1 (a) & (d); Beds. R.O., C. 237 Ct R. Biscot.

[3] A. H. Cooke, Early Hist. Mapledurham Oxon. Rec. Soc. 1925, vii, 198.

[4] Kalm, op. cit, 183; Bucks. R.O., D/M.H. 28. 2; Herts. R.O., 8154, 2nd foliation, 31; P.R.O., S.P.D. Chas vol. 95 no 11; Exch. A.O., Parl. Svys Herts. 7, ff. 5 sqq.; 9, ff. 4(3)–5(4); Sfk 18; T.R., Bk 157, f. 6 (p. 13); L.R., M.B. 207, f. 68(65).

[5] Ibid. 224, f. 152.

[6] Ibid. 197, ff. 247v. sqq.; T.R., Bk 157, f. 6v. (p. 14); A.O., Parl. Svys Herts. 7, f. 12; B.M., Add. 33582, ff. 4–5; Bucks. Mus. Wexham Ct R. bdl. 1, 10 Oct. 15 Jas; Herts. R.O., G'bury xi. 11, f. 199; 8154, 2nd foliation, 3; Marshall, op. cit. 18.

[7] Ibid. 19; Midl. Dept, 448; Blith, loc. cit.; Hervey, op. cit.; Atwell; op. cit, 102; Ellis, Sheep, 51; Kalm, loc. cit.; W. Camden, Brit. ed. E. Gibson 1722 i, 343; P. M. Briers, Hist. Nuffield end papers, map Mays fm 1635; A. Kingston, Hist. Royston 1906, p. 118; Oxon. R.O., Fa. xxi, 1; F. xiv. 1, ff. 2 sqq.; acc. 477; Cams. R.O., L. 58.5;

husbandry. The method in the lighter soils was first to sow wheat, next peas, and then fallow for wheat, or else sow oats after the wheat and lay down to grass. Only chalk marl was available and the soil needed constant applications of farmyard manure or the sheep-fold. When these did not suffice, the land had to be laid to grass to put some heart in it.[1] The heavier soils were mostly fallowed every third year, but sometimes every second or fourth. The chalky clay loams were good for wheat and beans and the flinty clay loams for wheat, barley and peas.[2]

The outline of management was sheep-and-corn husbandry. All the year the sheep fed on heaths, downs, temporary pastures, hedge-greens, stubbles and forage crops by day and were folded by night on the tillage at the rate of between one and three sheep an arable acre, all concentrated on single ridges, acres and half-acres in long rectangular folds of five-slotted hurdles.[3] Sheep were often top-folded, too, on wheat and

---

Bucks. R.O., D/MH 28.2, 3; ST/11; Herts. R.O., 1434; G'bury xi. 2, svys Napsbury, Windridge; P.R.O., Exch. L.R., M.B. 224, f. 152; 258, f. 1, Davis, op. cit. 9.

[1] Ibid.; Marshall, loc. cit.; S. Dept, 8, 15; Hervey, op. cit. 5, 8–11, 13, 16, 19, 36, 69; Hull, op. cit. 322; Lisle, op. cit. 86; Kalm, op. cit. 216; Hine, op. cit. i, 59; Cullum, op. cit. 243–4, 246–7; Camden, op. cit. i, 327; Fitzherbert, Surveyinge, f. 48v.; B.M., Add. 6027, f. 5v.; R. 32971, mm. 1d.–2, 5–6, 9, 11–13, 15d.; P.R.O., S.P.D. Chas vol. 95 no 11; Exch. A.O., Parl. Svys Oxon. 10, f. 2; Sfk 18; T.R., Bk 157, f. 5v. (p. 12); L.R., M.B. 196, ff. 72, 89, 186; 200, f. 66; 207, f. 67(64); 210, f. 278; Herts. R.O., 282; 8154, and foliation, 14, 31; 46325; G'bury x.B.3a, 4 Oct. 98 Eliz.; xi.2 svys Gorham, Westwick; xi. 11, ff. 192, 194; Ess. R.O., D/DB M46, ff. 2 sqq.; E. Sfk R.O., V.5/23/2. 1, f. 17; Norden, Surv's. Dial. 225–6.

[2] Ibid. 290; Blith, op. cit. 82; Hull, op. cit. 90; Cullum, op. cit. 249; Marshall, op. cit. 13; Midl. Dept, 561; James and Malcolm, op. cit. 21–2; Walker, op. cit. 12, 29; Young, Ess. i, 239; Vancouver, Cams. 16, 21, 42–3, 72–3, 82, 87–8; Lisle, op. cit. 147; Ellis, op. cit. 51, 219–20; Chiltern & V. 59, 309; Davis, op. cit. 11–12; R. Reyce, Breviary Sfk 1902, p. 29; Plot, Oxon. 240–1, 243–4; Herts. R.O., 41673; 44467, 65810, pp. 143 sqq.; G'bury xi. 11, ff. 203–5; A/d St Albans, inv. Em. Peckock 1684 Redborne; Cams. R.O., L. 58.5; B'ham Lib. 499037; Beds. R.O., A.D. 1501; B.M., Sloane 3815, f. 141 (p. 319); P.R.O., Exch. A.O., Parl. Svys Herts. 9, f. 5(4); Aspley Hth Sch. op. cit. 33–4.

[3] Ibid.; Marshall, op. cit. 636; S. Dept, 8, 15; Batchelor, op. cit. 560; Walker, op. cit. 29; Vancouver, op. cit. 19, 54, 59; W. Austin, Hist. Luton 1928 ii, 271–3; Spratt, op. cit. 236–7; Tregelles, op. cit. 330, 398–9; Reyce, loc. cit., A. Campling, Hist. Fam. Drury, 72; S. Tymms, Wills & Ints. fr. Regs. Comnty Bury St Edm's & A/d Sudbury Camd. S. 1850 xlix, 121, 152–3; F. G. Emmison, Jac. Household Invs. Beds. Hist. Rec. Soc. 1938 xx, 80; H.M.C., Household & Fm Invs. in Oxon. 1550–90 ed. M. A. Havinden, Jt Pubn 10, 1965, pp. 125–6, 144–5, 177–8, 180–1, 199–201, 226–7, 242–3, 251, 285, 293–4; B.M., Sloane 3815, f. 144 (p. 325); Stowe 847, f. 28 (p. 47); Add. 27977, ff. 9, 358; Ess. R.O., D/DK Fz/6; D/DQi/126; Beds. R.O., C.237; Bucks. Mus. Ct R. Halton, r. 9; Pitstone Ct R. P. 24/1, 3; Herts. R.O., 9442, 10869, 10878, 19477, 22069, 22101, 41673; 41674, f. 13; 44817–9; Westmill 155; invs.:—A/d St Albans & A/d Hunts. Hitchin Div.; E. Sfk R.O., A/d; W. Sfk R.O., Episc. Comny Ct Bury St Edm's.; Ellis, op. cit. 14–7, 381; Sheep, 211, 219–21, 224, 228, 235–7.

barley, consolidating roots and eating down over-rank foliage. This made for later ripening but improved quality.[1] Three breeds of sheep were stocked: in the far north, East Anglians ('Norfolks'); and elsewhere Oxford Height Notts, or more commonly, Chalk Country horned sheep. All were suited to the fold, and Chalk Country wethers, in particular, were highly regarded for soundness of body, for living on short grass, for folding, and for driving from field to field and between fields and commons.[2] Dairying and the fattening of beasts were undertaken for only a strictly local demand. Horses were universally employed. Two abreast made a plough-team on light soils and two or three pairs on heavy. The chief consumption crops were peas, vetches, tares, lentils, rye and oats, with some beans on the heavier soils. Tares, beans, peas, winter vetches and rye were folded off to sheep, and the two first were also used to provender horses. A little buckwheat was grown, mainly for poultry. The chief market crops throughout were barley and wheat, much more the former than the latter, for some lighter lands were unable to bear wheat often.[3] One local speciality was saffron cultivation in the deep sandy loams in the Cam and Granta valleys and in the gap between the Chiltern Hills and the East Anglian Heights, Saffron Walden being the chief market.[4]

[1] Ibid. 232–3; *Chiltern & V.* 15; Plot, op. cit. 255; Kalm, op. cit. 288–9; Marshall, op. cit. 36.

[2] Ibid. 18–19, 41; *Midl. Dept*, 603, 621; *E. Dept*, 465; *Sheep*, 33; J. Luccock, *Essay on Wool* 1809, p. 281; Ellis, *Sheep* 41–4, 51; Tregelles, op. cit. 398–9; E. Sfk R.O., A/d inv. 1583–4: 376/16; Northants. R.O., Cons. Ct Petriburg. Cams. Bds & Invs. 1662: Jn Clerke/L. Wilbraham; Herts. R.O., 7644, 8780, 14594, 14618, 22069, 22101; Bodl. Aubrey 2, f. 148; B.M., Harl. 127, ff. 18(29)v., 22(37); Emmison, loc. cit.

[3] Ibid.; invs.:—Northants. R.O., Cons. Ct Petriburg. Cams. Bds & Invs.; E. Sfk R.O., A/d; W. Sfk R.O., Episc. Commy Ct Bury St Edm's.; Herts. R.O., A/d St Albans, A/d Hunts. Hitchin Div.; 6693, 6718, 7644, 8481, 8483–4, 8579, 8780, 10511–2, 10514, 10517–18, 10520–1, 14594 14618, 20042, 22069–70, 22101; G'bury ii. O. 12A; Westmill 155; Tymms, loc. cit.; Havinden, op. cit. 125–6, 144–5, 177–8, 180–1, 199–201, 209, 226–7, 242–3, 293–4; Beds. R.O. ABP/W. 1613/185; Ess. R.O., D/DK F2/6; D/DQj/126; Ellis, op. cit. 209, 220; *Chiltern & V.* 59, 309; Campling, op. cit. 71–2; James & Malcolm, op. cit, 19; Plot, op. cit. 240–1, 243–4; Tregelles, loc. cit.; *Cal. SP Ven.* xv, 249; Oxon. R.O., F. xiv. 1, f. 2; Aspley Hth Sch. op. cit. 19 sqq.; A. Woodworth, *Purveyance for R. Household in reign Q. Eliz.* Trans. Am. Phil. Soc. 1945 xxxv, pt i, 80; Fuller, op. cit. ii, 37–8.

[4] Ibid. i, 222, 492; Blith, op. cit. 244–5; R. Blome, *Brit.* 1673, p. 95; R. Holinshed and W. Harrison, *Chron.* 1586, pp. 232–3; Laurence, op. cit. 115; Folkingham, op. cit. 30–1, 35; Gerarde, op. cit. 123–4; Hull, op. cit. 20; J. Norden, *Descron Co. Ess.* Camd. S. 1840, p. 8; J. Blagrave, *Epit. Art Husbandry* 1669, pp. 217–9; *VCH Herts.* iv, 214; *Ess.* ii, 359–60, 362, 364; B.M., Add. R. 27170; P.R.O., Exch. K.R., Deps. by Commn 4 Jas Mich. 25; Northants. R.O., Cons. Ct Petriburg. Cams. Bds & Invs. 1662: Jas Bankes/Stapleford, Alice Barber/Fulbourn, Jn Haylocke/Sawston; & v. Spufford, op. cit. 106.

THE NORTHWOLD COUNTRY

The chalk hills had their northernmost and not least magnificent extension in the wolds that lay in two divisions north and south of the
Humber. This discontinuity was more apparent than real: the Northwold Country was an indivisible whole throughout which the same
general plan of management prevailed. The western escarpment arose
abruptly from the Midland Plain, and to the east a marked chalk cliff
overlooked deep, heavy soils and salt-marshes. Everywhere the surface
was billowy, but the slopes were generally more abrupt north than south
of the Humber. The higher wolds were excessively dry, being watered
only by bournes. In the extreme south and east lay many calcareous
clay, sand and gravel loams, along the escarpment some sandy and clay
loams and on the backs of the wolds some flinty clay loams. Most of the
soils were friable and calcareous, their productivity varying directly
with their depth. In some shallow vales, as from Duggleby to Wold
Newton, the soils were rich and deep, making excellent wheat land, but
on the higher wolds mostly much thinner. In the north-east, in particular, the soil was largely thin and infertile, fit only for inferior sheep-
walk or rabbit-warrens and easily overrun with furze or heath. The
subsoil was everywhere chalky rubble and the base a chalk harder than
that of most chalk-down countries. Winters were as cold as in other parts
of eastern England and summers somewhat cooler than those of other
chalk hills. Absorbency, making for a forward climature, was offset by
the naked elevation of the wolds themselves, so the seasons, if earlier than
in the Blackmoors, were nevertheless later than in the Vale of York, hay
not being mown until early July and winter corn cut only in the latter
part of August. The Northwold Country was by no means coterminous
with the wolds themselves, for the larger farms included, in the west,
some vale grass lands as well as the arable foreland; in the east and
south, fens and marshes. Sometimes farms had detached portions or out-
farms of vale or marsh land and, along the border of wold and vale
or marsh, townships were sited to combine both upland and lowland. Such dispositions united the country north and south of the
Humber.[1]

The country was champion and in early modern times largely, but
decreasingly, in common fields of arable lands and grassy leys and
balks, with common sheep-walks and cow-downs, common 'ings' or

[1] Marshall, *E. Dept*, 130; G. Eland, *Shardeloes Papers 17th & 18th cents.* 1947, p. 61;
J. Thirsk, *Eng. Peasant Farming* 1957, pp. 176–7; Lincs. R.O., HEN. 3/2, 3; P.R.O.,
Exch. A.O., Parl. Svys Lincs. 10A, f. 7; M.B. 390, f. 23; L.R., M.B. 229, ff. 74 sqq.;
230, ff. 325 sqq.; 256, f. 14; B.M., Add. R. 37691; H. King & A. Harris, *Svy Manor
Settrington* Yks. Archaeol. Soc. Rec. Ser. 1962 cxxvi, frontis.

bottom meadows and common 'carrs' or marshes, the only enclosures being in the immediate vicinity of the villages, into which most of the farmsteads and cottages were crowded. Even if not commonable, the land was rarely enclosed, except for demesne farms in lower situations, but lay in entire parcels of down or large 'flats' in the fields, in severalty.[1] Field-courses varied chiefly according to soil depth and elevation. The poor, thin soils of the upper wolds were worth, as arable, only a quarter of those under the wold, because they could bear tillage at most one year in three, at least one in twelve. These higher, thinner lands were divided into shifts, called 'falls' or fields. Each year one of these was pared and burned for a single crop of oats or barley. Then the land was left gradually to regain some natural sward. When these 'falls' were commonable, one at a time was selected for tillage by agreement between the various parties and then divided, usually by lot, into the parcels of what was a temporary common field. Neither corn nor herbage in the 'falls' had the benefit of any manure and their crops were all consumed on the farm, so land above the wold was robbed for the sake of that below it, a practice serving to exaggerate disparity between the two. Since the usual crops on outfield shifts above the wolds were oats and barley, these tended to be excluded from successions on 'ardured' land or infield below the hill.[2] Here the lighter soils were in a two-field course of (1) fallow, (2) corn. There were no uniform crop rotations, but one succession was (1) fallow, (2) wheat, rye or maslin, (3) fallow, (4) peas and vetches, (5) fallow, (6) barley.[3] Deeper lands were sometimes divided into four quarters or shifts with a more productive two-field course, in which half the fallow bore a crop instead of being bare as in the thinner soils. The succession might be then (1) bare fallow, (2) barley, (3) vetch or pulse fallow, with cleaning cultivations in late

[1] Ibid. & p. 3; B.M., Add. R. 37691; Lans. vol. 654, ff. 3(6) sqq.; P.R.O., D.L., M.B. 119, ff. 32v., 34, 62–3, 75v.; Exch. L.R., M.B. 229, ff. 74 sqq., 88 sqq., 144 sqq., 163–4, 166 sqq., 172 sqq., 239 sqq.; 230, ff. 193v. sqq., 325 sqq.; 256, ff. 14–15; A.O., M.B. 390, ff. 24 sqq.; Parl. Svys Lincs. 5, ff. 3 sqq.; 10A, ff. 3–5; Yks. 57, ff. 6 sqq.; 59, ff. 2–3; Lincs. R.O., HEN. 3/3; H. Best, *Rural Econ. in Yks in 1641* Surtees S. 1857 xxxiii, 17, 43, 98; C. T. Clay, *Yks. Deeds* Yks. Archaeol. Soc. Rec. Ser. 1926 lxix, 99; J. S. Purvis, *Sel. XVI cent. Causes in Tithe fr. York Dioc. Reg.* id. 1949 cxiv, 18; *Bridlington Ch., Ct R. & Papers* 1926, opp. 209, 244–6; M. W. Barley, *Lincs. & Fens* 1952, p. 81; Gray, op. cit. 75; A. Harris, *Rural Landscape E. R. Yks. 1700–1850* 1961, p. 56; Norden, *Surv's. Dial.* 222 (1st occ.); Marshall, *Yks.* ii, 246.
[2] Ibid. 245; *N. Dept*, 516; Best, op. cit. 56; Lennard, art. cit. 41; King & Harris, op. cit. 14; Harris, op. cit. 24–6; P.R.O., Exch. L.R., M.B. 229, ff. 201, 222; 230, ff. 193v., 214v.; A.O., M.B. 390, f. 23; York invs.:—N. Newbald Preb. 1693: Wm Walkington, Edm. Barfe; M. W. Barley, 'E. Yks. Manorial Bye-laws', *Yks. Archaeol. Jnl* xxxv, 52.
[3] Ibid. 48, 52; Lennard, loc. cit.; Purvis, op. cit. 242–3, 286; Clay, loc. cit.; J. W. Clay, *Yks. Royalist Compo. Papers* Yks. Archaeol. Soc. Rec. Ser. 1895 xviii, 36–8; E. W. Crossley, 'Test. Docs. Yks. Pecs.', in *Miscellanea vol. ii* id. 1929 lxxiv, 87, 94, 101.

summer, (4) winter corn.[1] In the deepest soils three-field courses were even possible, these being (1) fallow, (2) winter corn, (3) spring corn. The chief crops were then wheat, rye, maslin, barley, oats and peas.[2] Finally, the larger, especially the demesne farms, often had a few enclosures of plain or marsh land in convertible husbandry.[3] The people of Barrow-on-Humber, e.g. claim common for the town herd in a close of pasture or marsh called Ham Close, when, as they say, 'their is noone corne upon the said pasture', and it 'lyeth faloo'.[4] All told, barley and wheat were the main market crops.

The outline of management was sheep-and-corn farming: every farmer kept sheep for folding his arable. In the day-time, breeding flocks fed the carpet down or the temporary down-pastures of the 'falls', while at night they were close-folded on the infield, which was sometimes top-folded also, at the rate of between one and three sheep to an acre of tillage. The fold itself, especially nearer the coast, was often of network, i.e. light, small-cord nets stretched on wooden frames. Otherwise hurdles of willow and ash bars were used.[5] Common flocks and folds were almost unknown. Capital farms had private flocks and folds of up to about 2,000 head, and these were swelled by the sheep of the small tenant farmers, under informal joint control.[6] In most places folding could be pursued throughout the year, but in the more retentive soils towards the east it could not start until about the beginning of May and had to stop at the onset of winter rains.[7] Hay could be bought in from the fens and other neighbouring lowlands, but the shortage of spring grass could be overcome only by the occupation of marsh or vale grassland, by delaying lambing until the end of March, and by giving oats and peas to the ewes in late winter. Some wether lambs were fatted, especially if the farm had a lowland annex, but the farmer's prime con-

---

[1] Marshall, op. cit. 515; *Yks.* ii, 253, P.R.O., Exch. A.O., M.B. 390, ff. 23, 27v.; Parl. Svys Lincs. 5, ff. 3 sqq.

[2] Ibid. L.R., M.B. 229, ff. 163–4, 166 sqq.; Lennard, loc. cit.; Best, op. cit. 42–3, 57, 94; Barley, art. cit. 52; Harris, op. cit. 24; invs.:—Lincs. R.O., Cons. Ct; York, Mkt Weighton & N. Newbald Prebs.

[3] B.M., Lans. 654, ff. 4(7), 10(13); P.R.O., Exch. A.O., Parl. Svys Lincs. 10A, ff. 5–6, 8–11; Yks. 57, f. 12.

[4] P.R.O., St. Ch. H. VIII 18/90; 19/11.

[5] Marshall, op. cit. ii, 255, 259; *E. Dept*, 63; Thirsk, op. cit. 85; Best, op. cit. 15–16, 94, 171–3, 175–6; Purvis, *Causes in Tithe*, 24; 'N. on XVI cent. Farming in Yks.', *Yks. Archaeol. Jnl* xxxvi, 453–4; J. W. Clay, loc. cit.; P.R.O., D.L., M.B. 119, ff. 62v., 66; invs.:—Lincs. R.O., Cons Ct; York, Mkt Weighton & N. Newbald Prebs., Prerogative Ct Abp.; I. Leatham, *Gen. View Ag. E. R. Yks.* 1794, p. 42; C. T. Clay, op. cit. 98; Barley, art. cit. 39; Crossley, art. cit. 91–2, 101.

[6] Ibid. 87–8, 101–2; Marshall, *Yks.* ii, 260; *N. Dept*, 515; Leatham, op. cit. 45–6; Purvis, *Bridlington*, 242–3, 251, 286; King & Harris, op. cit. frontis.; Lincs. R.O., HEN. 3/3; M.M. VI/5/24; Best, op. cit. 15–16, 94.

[7] Ibid. 14, 17, 43, 94, 98.

cern was breeding and rearing sheep for the fold. Dairies of shorthorn cattle and swine with them, were maintained for domestic and local consumption only. In earlier times some oxen were occasionally worked, but team and plough were usually supplied by horses. For heavy ploughing four horses were harnessed and for light only three, and then one of them merely pulled a light harrow at the side.[1] A peculiarity of the country was at its great number of extensive cony-warrens on the wolds, where conies and sheep shared the grazing. As parts of the warren became mossy, they were enclosed off, pared and burned for a single crop and then laid down again. Thus of about 1,500 acres in a warren, some 200 might always be in tillage.[2]

THE OXFORD HEIGHTS

Bounding the Vale of White Horse to the north and west and running through the midst of the Cheese Country, was a narrow and barely continuous stretch of sheep-and-corn land. Its hills had an escarpment facing north and west, seldom rose above 300 feet, and were composed of a limestone harder than that of the other downs but softer than that of the Cotswolds. The country's soils were principally loams, chalk loams, sandy loams, and chalky sands and gravels. In addition the farms included some vale lands, chiefly clay loams, clays and strong clays. The hill lands all stood on permeable limestone, but the vale had a retentive base.

In the early sixteenth century about three-quarters of the arable was in common field.[3] On the hills, field-courses resembled those of the Chalk Country, and in the vale those of the Cheese Country. In the former, sheep were folded throughout the year for both wheat and barley, in the latter only in the summer. In the one the fallows were often

---

[1] Ibid. 1 sqq., 12, 20, 27–8, 75–6, 94, 118–19, 133, 171–3, 175–6; C. T. Clay, op. cit. 98–9; Harris, op. cit. 27; J. W. Clay, loc. cit.; Purvis, op. cit. 242 sqq.; art. cit. 453–4; Lennard, art. cit. 30; Crossley, art. cit. 89, 91–4, 100–1; P.R.O., St. Ch. Hy VIII 19/11. D.L., M.B. 119, f. 63; Exch. L.R., M.B. 229, ff. 75 sqq.; invs.:—York, Prerogative Ct Abp, Mkt Weighton & N. Newbald Prebs.; Lincs. R.O., Cons. Ct; HEN. 3/2; W. H. Long, 'Reg. Farming in 17th-cent. Yks.', Ag. HR 1960 viii, 107, 112; Marshall, op. cit. 520; Yks. ii, 252–5 (954 recte 254).

[2] Ibid. 245, 252, 261 sqq. 268.

[3] P.R.O., Exch. L.R., M.B. 191, ff. 145v. sqq., 158v. sqq.; Sp. Coll. R. & S. G.S. 4/2, ff. 2 sqq.; roll 709; S.D.P. Eliz. Add. vol. 12 no. 22, ff. 44 sqq.; Wds, Feodaries' Svys Wilts. 276; Chanc. Proc. ser. i Jas I, E. 1/51; B.M., Harl. 3961, ff. 64 sqq.; Add. 37270, ff. 30v., 105v.; Bowood ho. Svy Bremhill 1629; Basset Down ho. N. Maskelyne's A/c Bk, ff. 61–2, 78–9, 136; Wilts. R.O., acc. 212B, Bm. 01; acc. 40 Sevenhampton Ct Bk 1541–1624; acc. 84 Ct Bk Andr. Baynton, ff. 47, 54v., 63; acc. 122 Svys Bromham, Bremhill, Rowden & Stanley 1612; C. B. Fry, Hannington 1935, pp. 26–8; G. S. & E. A. Fry, op. cit. 92–3, 363–5; Bodington, art. cit. xli, 122–3.

still ones, and in the other they were mostly stirred. Barley was the chief spring corn on the hills, and beans and peas in the vales. Everywhere common flocks and folds were maintained.[1] The chief market crops were wheat and barley, rye being grown but little and then for sheep feed. The consumption crops were pulses, tares in the lighter lands and peas and beans in the heavier. All farms had domestic dairies and some as many as a dozen milkers, but dairy farmers pure and simple were rare. Plough-teams were diverse, some of oxen or of oxen led by horses and some of horses alone. Some of the larger farmers with vale lands fatted both muttons and beeves, and worked some of their feeders gently, while small cultivators often used oxen. All farms stocked sheep at the rate of about one to an acre of tillage and large ones might have up to 1,600 or more folding sheep, chiefly of the native Nott breed.[2]

THE COTSWOLD COUNTRY

The Cotswold Country consisted of the Cotswold and Stroudwater Hills, Edge Hill, Dundry Hill, and the South Wolds or southerly extension of the same range together with some associated lands. Townships were mostly situated in the river valleys and their lands ran in long strips from the meadows through the arable fields to the tops of billowy hills. The prevailing soil was 'stonebrash', i.e. calcareous gravel loam. It was generally good turnip soil, but its fertility depended on its depth, which was not usually much above 4 inches. On the lower easterly slopes 'stonebrash' gave way to 'cornbrash', a calcareous, gravelly clay loam, impervious and tenacious when wet, and, unlike the 'stonebrash', apt for permanent grass. In the Stroudwater Hills most of the soils were thinner and less productive. Nearly all soils rested on hard and almost impervious limestone. Although the air was healthier than in the surrounding vales, the climate was somewhat wet and mild. In consequence, the climature was less suited to wheat and the sheep-fold than that of the chalk-down countries.

[1] Ibid. 28; F. H. Manley, 'Customs Manor Purton', *Wilts. Mag.* xl, 116–17; '1614 Customs Xn Malford', id. xli, 174; Devizes Mus. Wm Gaby His Booke 1656, pp. 30, 42, 60–1, rev. 15, 30; J. G. Nichols, *Unton Invs. rel. to Wadley & Faringdon* Berks. Ashmolean Soc. 1841, pp. 8–10; Havinden, op. cit. 47–8; Wilts. R.O., Keevil & Bulkington Ct Bks 44 Eliz.-2 Chas & 1643–64; invs.:—Cons. Ct Sarum. Tristram Flower 1605 W. Ashton; Dioc. Reg. Sarum. Wm Bridges 1585 Highworth; Bowood ho. Svy Bremhill 1629; B.M., Add. 37270, ff. 114, 121, 136v.; P.R.O., Wds, Feodaries' Svys Wilts. unsorted bdl. Jn Bryan 1620 S. Marston; Exch. L.R., M.B. 191, f. 156; Req. 74/95; G. & E. Fry, op. cit. 92–3.
[2] Ibid.; *Wilts. N. & Q.* v, 393–4; Marshall, *S. Dept*, 94; Mavor, op. cit. 380–2; Aubrey, *Wilts. Topog. Colls.* 127; Nichols, op. cit. 8–10, 13, 30; Havinden, loc. cit.; invs.:—Wilts. R.O., A/d Wilts., Cons. Ct Sarum., Dioc. Reg. Sarum.

Up until the middle of the eighteenth century the country was largely open and partly in common fields, sheep-walks ('sleights') and meadows.[1] The 'cornbrash' districts, however, were largely enclosed from the common-field state in or before the second and third quarters of the seventeenth century,[2] and many townships saw some of their common fields enclosed, partly with the object of providing more pasture and meadow, increasing the numbers of stock, and so improving the tillage. Some enclosures were made also from the hill sheep pastures.[3] In addition, demesnes were often imparked, enclosed or in open severalty, even when the tenantry lands remained common. Some demesnes were perhaps never in common field, or had long ceased to be so, and others were enclosed in the sixteenth and seventeenth centuries by agreements and exchanges of land.[4] The common-field course was almost universally (1) fallow, part hitched, (2) corn,[5] and the fields

[1] Billingsley, op. cit. 93–4; Marshall, *Glos.* ii, 9; J. L. G. Mowat, *16 O. Maps Props. in Oxon.* 1888, pp. 1 sqq.; S. C. Ratcliffe & H. C. Johnson, *War. Co. Recs.* ii, *Q. Sess. Ord. Bk 1637–50* 1936, p. 68.

[2] J. Aubrey, op. cit. 9–10, 131; 'Intro. to Svy & Nat. Hist. N. Div. Co. Wilts.', in *Misc. on Sev. Curious Subjs.* 1714, pp. 31–2; *Nat. Hist. Wilts.* 104; E. M. Leonard, 'Inclo. Com. Fds in 17th cent.', *Trans. R. Hist. S.* 1905 xix, 115; Straton, op. cit. ii, 409 sqq.; M. A. Havinden, 'Rural Econ. Oxon. 1580–1730', ts. thesis B. Litt. Oxon. 1961, p. 183; G. P. Scrope, *Hist. Manor & Anc. Barony Cas. Combe* 1852, p. 321; W. B. Willcox, *Glos.* 1940, pp. 280, 283; P.R.O., Chanc. Proc. ser. i Jas I, S. 39/64; St. Ch. Jas 18/12, m. 9; Exch. L.R., M.B. 202, ff. 169 sqq.; 207, f. 14(12)v.; 224, ff.54–6; B.M., Egerton 3007, ff. 69 sqq., 87, 90, 130; Harl. 6006, ff. 3v., 40v.; Add. 6027, ff. 71–3 (70–2); 34683, f. 4; penes Mr W. Pinchin, Forest Hill, fd maps Hazelbury, Ditteridge & Box; Glouc. Lib. 16526/28; Wilts. R.O., acc. 88 Charlton Este Papers, box B, Svy Bk Charlton, Brinkworth, Hankerton & Brokenborough; Soms. R.O., DD/S/WH, Ct Bk Regilbury 1598–1639, ff. 1, 12v., 21; Ct R. Chew Baber 10 Apr. 1650; DD/X/GNS ct files Kilmersdon 7 Oct. 1656; DD/PO, Ct Bk Farmborough Greville & Rowswell, p. 77; W. P. Phillimore & G. S. Fry, *Glos. Inqs. P.M. in reign K. Chas I* Index Lib. 1893–9 i, 85, 217–18; ii, 34.

[3] Ibid. iii, 38–9; Straton, op. cit. ii, 425; B.M., Harl. 4606, ff. 12 (25) sqq.; Add. 24787, f. 52; Glos. R.O., D. 738 ct files Colne St Dennis 27 Oct. 1710; D. 184/M7, r. 2; D. 444/M1, 1573; P.R.O., Exch. K.R., M.B., 39, f. 15(14)v.; L.R., M.B., 224 f. 76.

[4] Ibid. ff. 55–6; 191, f. 134; 225, f. 43; Sp. Coll. Ct R. G.S. 208/28, f. 39v.; J. Ritchie, *Reps. Cs decided by Bacon in Ct Chanc.* 1932, pp. 183–6; *Trans. Bristol & Glos. Archaeol. Soc.* l, 249; B.M., Add. 23150, f. 4; 6027, ff. 31–3 (30–2); Harl. 3961, f. 190; Glouc. Lib. 16526/28; Bristol R.O., 4490, f. 13v.; Shak. Bpl. Leigh: Ct R. Longborough 16 Mar. 34 Eliz.

[5] Ibid. pass; Ct R. Adlestrop; N. J. Hone, *Manor & Manorial Recs.* 1912, pp. 175, 178; E. S. Lindley, *Wotton under Edge* 1962, p. 147; G. Turner, *Gen. View Ag. Co. Glouc.* 1794, p. 27; Savine, op. cit. 174; Smyth, op. cit. 4; Marshall, op. cit. i, 328; ii, 36; A. Ballard, 'N. on Open Fds', *Oxon. Archaeol. Soc. Rep.* 1908 (1909), p. 31; 'Tackley in 16th & 17th cents.', ibid. 1911 (1912), 31, 38; J. Morton, *Nat. Hist. Northants.* 1712, p. 56; H. M. Colvin, *Hist. Deddington* 1963, p. 89; S. & B. Webb, *Manor & Bor.* 1924 i, 79–81; B.M., Add. 6027, ff. 32(31)v.–33(32), 36(35); 23150, f. 23; 36585, ff. 164, 262, 284v., 300; 36875, ff. 29, 31v.; R. 18517; Plot, *Oxon.* 153,

C

contained a good deal of permanent grass.[1] Stonebrash was seldom ploughed more than once for any crop. The whole secret of cultivation was to reduce it to the minimum. In fallowing for wheat, stirring was occasionally performed in late spring or early summer, if the land were already grassy or swardy; but it could only be done when the soil was wet, lest it blow in the wind or scorch in the sun. If the land were 'scary', i.e. without sward or cover, as often, hayseeds might be sown, or old thatch and straw or the most strawy part of the dung-hills might be spread together with ditch-mould, yard sweepings and other dressings, or even sheep folded in the field all with the same object of encouraging the growth of some herbage. The husbandman could not, indeed, expect a good crop unless there were some sward on the ground when ploughed. Fallowing for barley was in autumn or early winter, according to the degree of moisture and sward obtaining. After only breaking up and without any subsequent stirring, the land was left to weather, so that it worked well on the second 'earth' when ploughed and sown to barley. If the land were still not swardy enough for a winter fallow, it was sometimes streak-fallowed (raftered) in the spring; i.e. alternate furrows only were ploughed, the furrow slices inverted on the unploughed balks between them, and the whole harrowed down; but this expedient could not be resorted to repeatedly.[2]

In the easterly cornbrash soils, where enclosure was accompanied by the development of dairy farming, the practice of the Cheese Country was married to, or mingled with, the sheep-and-corn husbandry of the rest of the country.[3] Generally, the plan of management hinged upon

242-3; B'ham Lib. 168002, 168163; Oxon. R.O., DIL. II/W/75; Dashwood VIII/33 Ct R. Duns Tew; Misc. M. I/t; Glos. R.O., D. 444/M1, 2; D. 745 ct files Disley; P.R.O., St. Ch. Jas 18/12, m. 9; 108/2, mm. 1-2; Exch. K.R., Deps. by Commn 31 Eliz. Hil. 25, ex parte quer.; T.R., Bk 157, p. 61 (f. 32); D.L., M.B, 117, f. 77.

[1] Ibid. ff. 75-6; Exch. L.R. M.B. 185, ff. 183 (3) sqq.; 224, ff. 186 sqq., T.R., Bk 157, pp. 56-7; B.M., Add. 23150, ff. 15, 23; 23151, f. 55; 24787, f. 51; 36585, ff. 163v., 167; R. 9285, m. 11; Harl. 3961, ff. 5v.-6, 8, 56v.; Glos. R.O., D. 184/M7, r. 1, 2, 8; D. 247, Ct R. Longborough 42, 44; Wilts. R.O., acc. 192 Swinton: Thornhill Svy Bk c, 1574, att. partic. Sadler's lands 1587; Northants. R.O., Ct R. Aynho; B'ham Lib. 168124, 168162-3; Shak. Bpl. Leigh: Ct R. Ratley, Longborough; Ct Bk Maugersbury, f. 60; Adlestrop, f. 10v.; Oxon. R.O., DIL. II/W/75; Dashwood VIII/33 Ct R. Duns Tew; Phillimore & Fry, op. cit. i, 117, 119, ii, 61; V.C.H. Glos. ii, 164-5; R. W. Jeffrey, Manors & Advowson Gt Rollright Oxon. Rec. Soc. 1927 ix, 177; Plot, op. cit. 154, 242.

[2] Ibid. 242-3; P.R.O., Req. 39/58; Marshall, op. cit. ii, 41, 43.

[3] Ibid. 27; Plot, loc. cit.; Havinden, op. cit. 44-5, 134-5, 262-4, 289; Wilts. R.O., invs.:—A/d Wilts.: Robt Sargent 1637 Grittleton; Cons. Ct Sarum. Roger Kilbury 1643 & -Naile 1604 id., Th. Lyte 1627 Easton Peirce, Nic. Bp 1634 Nettleton, Jn Barbor 1606 Ashton Keynes; Dioc. Reg. Sarum.: Th. Pheltham 1590 Atworth, Jn Rogers 1542 & Joan Pykeryng 1564 Bradford, Th. Mallard 1605 Gt Sherston,

the manuring of tillage by sheep, which were stocked at the rate of about two to a customary acre; but not as in the chalk-down countries, for the wolds were naturally wetter and rarely safe for sheep in the winter months. Therefore, while folded in summer, they were cotted throughout the winter. Both breeding and wether flocks of Old Cotswolds were stocked, preferably the former if the spring grass sufficed. In the winter months the sheep were foddered on hay and straw in their cotes and the resulting compost was carted to the tillage in the spring. In the summer the sheep fed the sleights and ley lands by day and were folded on the tillage at night, with such regularity that shepherds said the ewes could find their own way to the fold of hurdles that moved across the tillage day by day from acre to acre. Folding was far more beneficial to the crops than compost from the sheep-cotes, was 'allmost the only improvement' for stonebrash soils, but impossible in wet, wintry weather.[1] Hay was scanty and wain-loads had to be imported from the Cheese Country or elsewhere.[2] This shortage limited the livestock that could be over-wintered. Except in the 'cornbrash' district, dairies were perforce merely domestic. Drag ploughs or heavy cultivators were used for some tillage operations, but the ordinary ploughs

---

Dorothy Coffyn 1564 & Anthony Iles 1600 S. Wraxall, Robt Huntley 1625 Winsley, Hy Kyppenges 1641 Wraxall; Aubrey, *Nat. Hist. Wilts.* 105; Turner, op. cit. 8.

[1] Ibid. 9; Marshall, op. cit. ii, 47; *W. Dept.* 409, 416; Straton, op. cit. ii, 417; Wilts. Clothier, *Wool Encouraged*, 53; Phillimore & Fry, op. cit. i, 91; Scrope, op. cit. 344; Davis, *Wilts.* 127–8, 130; Lennard, art. cit. 34; Webb, op. cit. i, 81–2; Ballard, art. cit. 37–8, 47, 73; 'Open Fds', 28–9; C. C. Brookes, *Hist. Steeple Aston & Middle Aston* 1929, p. 131; Jeffrey, op. cit. 25; Hone, loc. cit.; Lindley, loc. cit.; Havinden, *Invs.* 56, 77–9, 122–3, 127, 131–3, 136–7, 140, 145–6, 161–3, 165–6, 169–70, 176–7, 181 sqq., 189, 198–9, 203, 210–1, 215–16, 218, 221–2, 229, 231–2, 259–60, 273–4, 291–3, 296–7, 300–3; *Trans. Bristol & Glos. Archaeol. Soc.* xvi, 91; Wedge, op. cit. 31; B.M., Add. 6027, ff. 29(28)v., 36(35); 23150, ff. 9, 21; 36585, ff. 163–4, 170, 262; 36875, ff. 23, 29v.; R. 9284, 9289, 18513 m. 9d., 18515 m. 2d., 18517; Egerton 3007, ff, 71v., 75, 90; Glouc. Lib. 16064, 16209, 16526/28, 18253 ff. iv., 4v., 7; 28899(4), 28917; Cons. Ct invs.; Glos. R.O., D. 129 ct files Weston Birt; D. 158/M1; D.184/M7, r. 2; M 24, pp. 165 sqq.; D. 247/18, 44, 68; D. 269B/M3; D. 444/M2; D. 445/M4. D. 547a/M29; D. 745 ct files Bisley; D.C. 1; Shak. Bpl. Leigh: Ct R. Longborough, Adlestrop, Ratley; Ct Bk Bledington; Oxon. R.O., DIL. II/W/75, 122; II/a/2; IV/a/78/v; IV/a/89; Misc. M. I/1; Dashwood VIII/33 Ct R. Duns Tew; VIII/34 valn Harrison's fm; Northants. R.O., Ct R. Aynho; Soms. R.O., D.D./P.O. Ct Bk Farmborough Greville & Rowswell, p. 77; invs.:—Cons. cts A/d Taunton, Bath. & Well.; Lichfield Jt R.O., Cons. Ct; Worcs. R.O., Cons. Ct; P.R.O., R. & S. G.S. 2/46, ff. 92 sqq.; Chanc. Proc. ser. i Jas I, B. 17/19, m. 1; H. 8/53; D.L., M.B. 116, ff. 83–4; 117, f. 89; Exch. of Recpt, Recpt Bk 23 Aug. 1610; K.R., Deps. by Commn 31 Eliz. Hil. 25, ex parte quer.; M.B. 39, ff. 19(18) sqq.; A.O., M.B. 394, ff. 16(15) sqq., 21(20) sqq., 48–9(47–8); Parl. Svys Soms. 42, f. 8; L.R., M.B. 185, ff. 181(1), 189(9), 192(18), 196–7(12–13); 224, ff. 73 sqq., 91 sqq., 152 sqq., 171 sqq.; T.R., Bk 157, pp. 61, 89 (ff. 32, 47).

[2] Ibid. p. 61 (f. 32); Basset Down ho. N. Maskelyne's A/c Bk, f. 37.

were long and heavy, requiring a team of about five horses or oxen and never less than four. Oxen and horses were used about equally in the sixteenth century, but horses predominated in the seventeenth and by the eighteenth outnumbered oxen by two to one.[1]

THE SOUTH SEACOAST COUNTRY

Along the coast between Brighton, Southampton and Poole, and in the north of the Isle of Wight, lay a plain from one to six miles wide. Its soils were mostly deep loams, but included also many other varieties. Below the chalk hills were some gravelly loams and some mere gravels and sands. Portsdown was a narrow ridge of chalk down with calcareous soils. To the west of Southampton Water, were many sandy loams, some deep loams, as around New Milton, and some gravel loams as about Beaulieu and Lymington. Much of the base was absorbent. The country as a whole highly suited cultivation, but various parts on the coast were rendered barren by driven sand, and the cliff-side was much eroded. Rainfall was moderate, and under shelter of the downs the winters were mild and the summers warm. A good deal of the country, moreover, inclined towards the sun and the climature was everywhere remarkably forward and favourable.

The townships were usually small and compact, not extending up the slopes of the chalk hills. Some common fields survived in the early modern period, especially in and about Selsey Island, with their sheep-and-corn husbandry and the sheep-fold on the tillage; but most of the land was already enclosed, and common fields and pastures continued to be swallowed up, piecemeal and by agreement.[2] Most of the land was

---

[1] Marshall, op. cit. 403, 407, 451; *Glos.* ii, 29–32, 35; Davis, op. cit. 134; Hone, op. cit. 176; Brookes, op. cit. 110; *Trans. Bristol & Glos. Archaeol. Soc.* xvi, 91; *Trans. B'ham Archaeol. Soc.* 1888 (1890), 79–82; Havinden, op. cit. 44–5, 56, 77–9, 118–19, 122–3, 127, 131 sqq., 140, 145–6, 149–50, 161–3, 165–6, 169–70, 176–7, 181 sqq., 189, 198–9, 203, 210–1, 215–6, 218, 221–2, 231–2, 259 sqq. 273–4, 289, 291–2, 296–7, 301–3, 310–2; Ballard, art. cit. 28; Lindley, loc. cit.; Glouc. Lib. 28917 svy. Tresham 1674; Cons. Ct invs.; Glos. R.O., D. 129 Ct R. Weston Birt; D. 184/M7, r. 2, 18; M24, pp. 165 sqq.; D.C. 1; B.M. Add 6027, f. 36 (35); 36585, f. 164; 36875, f. 29v.; R. 9284, 18517; Egerton 3007, f. 71v.; Oxon. R.O., Misc. MI/1; Shak. Bpl. Leigh: Ct R. Ratley, Adlestrop; invs.:—Wilts. R.O., Cons. Ct Sarum.; Dioc. Reg. Sarum.; Soms. R.O., Cons. Ct A/d Taunton, Cons. Ct Bath. & Well.; Northants. R.O., A/d Ct Northampton; Lichfield Jt R.O., Cons. Ct; Worcs. R.O., Cons. Ct; Kent R.O., U. 269/A. 421; P.R.O., Chanc. Proc. ser. i Jas I, B. 17/19, m. 1; D.L., M.B. 117, f. 89; Exch. T.R., Bk 157, p. 61 (f. 32); K.R., M.B. 39, ff. 19 (18) sqq.; A.O., Parl. Svys Soms. 42, f. 8; L.R., M.B. 185, ff. 181 (1), 183 (3), 189 (9), 196–7 (12–13).

[2] Ibid. 191, ff. 23–4; 203, ff. 20 sqq.; Marshall, *S. Cos.* ii, 230; Leonard, art. cit. 110; Godfrey, op. cit. 102; R. H. D'Elboux, *Svys. Manors Robertsbridge & Michelmarsh & Demesne Lands Halden in Rolvenden 1567–70* Suss. Rec. Soc. 1946 xlvii, 163 sqq.;

arable, but there were many rich grasslands: upland pastures, river-side marshes and meadows, 'stripes' or open salt-marshes, and old salt-marshes embanked and ditched and so made fresh. In the sandy and gravelly soils were found considerable stretches of heath and rough grazing and the townships bordering on the New Forest and the Forest of Bere had rights of common for cattle and horses therein.[1]

The arable was mostly permanent tillage, though the weaker soils were convertible.[2] Much of the country was powerful wheat land and wheat was grown as much as barley and oats put together. The market crops were wheat and barley; and the consumption crops, peas, winter vetches, tares, oats, and rye. There were no regular field-courses or crop rotations and tillage management was in the nature of a continuous round of straw and pulse crops. Some of the successions employed were: wheat, oats, wheat; peas, wheat, barley; wheat, late summer fallow, and wheat again, in two years round; wheat, pulse with late summer fallow, and then wheat again. The land was ploughed deeply for wheat and clean, rank crops resulted, the soil being rich but not given to couch. In the eighteenth century, five quarters an acre was regarded as an ordinary wheat crop in the deep loams and the yields generally were amongst the highest in England. The farms were well stocked with sheep, principally of the 'Dorset' breed. In-lamb ewes were brought in autumn from Dorchester and the Butter Country and fed highly during winter on hay, peas, oats and tares. During this time they suckled the twin lambs born in December. Both ewes and lambs were folded on rye in early spring and then on winter vetches. The lambs were forced to a great size at an early age and then sold fat. When their lambs were removed, the ewes were fattened on grass and forage crops and sold off to make way for the fresh autumn draft. Mutton, ewe-mutton and manure formed useful by-products, and so, to a lesser extent, did wool. Most large farms included estuary or coastal marshes, and the 'stripes' or salt-marshes would carry two ewes an acre and fatten them quickly without danger of rot. They also made excellent fatting grounds for bullocks and the farmers usually fed some of these cheek by jowl with the ewes. Some also produced stall-fed winter beef. The native cattle were of the 'Sussex'

Hants. R.O., 12 M60/64, 5 M53/768; B.M., Add. 6027, ff. 98 (97)v., 103v.–105 (102v.–4); R. 32387, 54238; Wilts. R.O., Heytesbury Hosp.: Svys Pembroke's Manors; Northants. R.O., Wmld 5. ix.

[1] Ibid.; Hants. R.O., Cons. & A/d cts invs.; B.M. Add. 6027, ff. 100 (99) v., 108 (107), 111 (110); P.R.O., Exch. T.R., Bk 157, pp. 138, 144–6 (ff. 72, 75–6); L.R., M.B. 203, ff. 20 sqq.; Vancouver, *Hants.* 82; D'Elboux, op. cit. 164; Marshall, *S. Dept*, 285; S. *Cos.* ii, 231–2.

[2] Ibid. 240; B.M., Harl. 6006, f. 210v.; P.R.O., Exch. L.R., M.B. 203, ff. 23, 25–6; A.O., Parl. Svys Hants. 14, ff. 1–3; Hants. R.O., 12 M60/64; Cornwall, op. cit. 33.

breed, but some 'Devons' were bought from the West Country for feeding also. Oxen were employed for draught often, but the plough-teams
were usually composed of horses, of which four made a team on the deep
loams. Nearly all the farms had domestic dairies, but rarely more.
Farmyard manure was produced in abundance, and in spring the sheep-
fold was no mean asset. Although the majority of farmers, and those with
larger farms, combined the fatting of house or early lamb with cereal
production, there were also a few family farmers and cottagers who
specialized in dairying and pig-meat, or in the cultivation of cereals by
the expedient of allowing the great sheep-masters to eat off their feed
crops gratis, in return for the 'tails' needed for corn.[1]

THE PETWORTH DISTRICT

The Petworth District coincided with a break in the escarpment of the
South Downs. Its lands differed from those of the Wealden Vales and
were formed by a broadening out of the otherwise narrow belts of
calcareous sandy loams, clays and clay loams that ran the length of the
northern skirts of the downs. In the Petworth District these soils were
sufficiently extensive to justify a distinct general plan of management,
whereas elsewhere they were merely part and parcel of the Southdown
Country, receiving special cultivations but being farmed according to a
plan adopted from considerations into which they hardly entered.
Some downland was included in farms in the south of the district.
Sutton had 343 acres of sheep-down, Duncton about 176. Nevertheless,
even here, the down was never fundamental to farm practice. Travelling
from south to north, the first soil encountered below the downs was a
waxy but chalky clay or clay loam. This 'maam' land ran in a mostly
narrow vein, merely a field or furlong wide, but near Sutton, Bignor and
Bury, broadened out to nearly a mile. Although mainly standing on a
chalk rock, this soil was somewhat stiff and retentive and had, as a rule,
to be gathered up into high, narrow ridges for the sake of surface drainage. To the north of the 'maam', there was a wide area of light sandy
loam, resting on a mass of sand, and north of this again a belt of excellent, deep, sandy loam. Finally, the north-western extremity of the
district had some poor sandy soils, and the north and east some strong
clays, providing respectively small areas of barren heath and of per-

[1] Ibid. 72–3, 84, 111–12, 156; art. cit. 50, 64, 73, 91; Marshall, op. cit. ii, 232–5,
238–40, 243, 256, 280–1, 285; Vancouver, op. cit. 81–2, 85–6, 347; Driver, op. cit.
25; Lisle, op. cit. 86; Woodworth, op. cit. 44; Mundy, op. cit. 40; P.R.O., Exch.
L.R., M.B. 203, ff. 20 sqq.; B.M., Add. 6027, f. 97 (96)v.; R. 32387; invs.:—Wilts.
R.O., Dioc. Reg. Sarum.: Hants. R.O., Cons. & A/d cts; Pec. cts Bishopstoke,
Upham, Twyford, Meonstoke &c.; W. Suss. R.O., Cons. Ct Bp Cicestr. for A/d
Cicestr.

manent grass. Apart from these, and from the downs and small areas of 'brookland', marsh and meadow, all the lands were arable. The climature was forward and favourable to tillage crops.

In the seventeenth and eighteenth centuries there were still some common fields, especially towards the south, on the 'maam' land. The district had probably been in a common-field state originally, the townships being elongated and running from down to vale, with contour ploughing; but most of it had been divided in the Middle Ages and now lay in small closes. In early modern times, there was considerable consolidation in the remaining common fields and a great deal of emparkment. At the turn of the sixteenth and seventeenth centuries, however, Petworth Great Park was disparked, divided into smaller enclosures and turned over to ordinary farm cultivation.[1] Even when enclosed, this remained as always a sheep-and-corn country, and in the south there were still extensive sheep-walks. At Sutton in 1574 the customary tenants had downland pastures for 515 sheep.[2] The greatest part of the district, nevertheless, was composed of enclosed arable fields of sandy loam, used in a convertible system. At Petworth itself, for instance, in 1557, some fields were 'sometimes used for pasture and most commonly sown with corn' and others had 'sometime been used for corn and sometime for pasture', the land being 'good for both, according to the soil and nature of the ground of that country'. These descriptions, and other similar ones, give a glimpse of a system of temporary leys of medium duration formed of natural grasses.[3]

The invariable objects of farming were corn and early lamb. The chief market cereals were barley and wheat, much more the former than the latter. As the meadowland was restricted, the tillage was largely sown with consumption crops; and of these by far the most important was rye cultivated to be fed off by sheep. Rye and barley were each grown about four times as much as wheat, which was largely confined to the 'maam' land. Some oats and peas were also cultivated as fodder for the horses and sheep. Oats were the usual first crop on ploughing up the turf, and some buckwheat was grown, principally for folding to sheep. Winter vetches were much sown for the spring feed of sheep and sometimes formed a maslin with rye. Tares were the chief hay crop. Domestic dairies and horses were maintained, but otherwise sheep were the main livestock. 'Dorset' sheep were brought in autumn, and fed on the downs, leys and stubbles until they lambed in or about December. Then the

[1] Petworth ho. Svy Demesne Manor Petworth &c. 1557; svys Petworth, Sutton, Duncton 1574; Leconfield, *Petworth Manor in 17th cent.* 1954, pp. 26, 45–6, 56–9, 62 sqq., maps x, xi; *Sutton & Duncton Manors* 1956, pp. 1, 10–11, 66–7, end maps; Marshall, op. cit. ii, 169.

[2] Ibid. 199; Leconfield, op. cit. 8–10, 68; Cornwall, op. cit. 84, Petworth ho. svys Sutton, Duncton 1574.

[3] Ibid. Svy. Petworth &c. 1557, pp. 1–3; Leconfield, *Petworth*, 46.

ewes and their twins were kept on tare hay and other fodders until they could be folded on the rye that was their mainstay. When the rye was finished, they might pass to winter vetches and then to other pulse crops. Forced to a great size at an early age, the lambs were then sold for the butcher, largely to London. The ewes went to Wealden Vale farmers for fatting, or, in the south, were retained for a while to feed the downs and fold the tillage.[1]

THE NORFOLK HEATHLANDS

North of the Breckland the chalk hill range was continued in the Norfolk Edge and Cromer Ridge. Here the base was overlain sometimes by chalky clay, mostly by sandy and gravelly soils. These latter gave rise to much heath, furze, bracken and thin grassland, which often occupied half a township's land. Along the north coast, from Holme to Cley were many salt-marshes, and, immediately inland from these, tracts of inferior sandy soil. The marshes and the foreland of chalky clay and sandy loams below the western escarpment were the only highly fertile districts. The climate was moister than that of most of East Anglia, and, due to the sea-breezes, also colder. Owing mainly to the land's absorbency, the climature generally favoured tillage crops more than natural grasses.

About half the ground in permanent cultivation, and most demesne land, was enclosed, while the heathlands were largely in severalty or quasi-severalty. Nevertheless, common fields obtained in most townships.[2] The heaths were subjected to temporary cultivation only, being divided into 'brecks', and sometimes subdivided into shifts, one of which was, at long and regular intervals, broken up for a single crop, and then allowed to revert to heath, while cultivation was shifted to another 'breck' or to one or some of its shifts. When its turn came for the plough, one of two courses could be adopted on a 'breck'. Either it could be double-tathed by sheep for a single crop, on two earths, of rye, oats or barley, or it could be marled and sown for several years before being laid down to what must have often been a much-improved sward.

[1] Ibid. 66, 105; *Sutton & Duncton*, 8, 17–18, 56, 59–60, 76; Marshall, op. cit. ii, 167, 171, 173–4, 188, 199–200, 209–10; Cornwall, art. cit. 91; op. cit. 84, 111–12; Woodworth, op. cit. 80; W. Suss. R.O., Cons. Ct Bp Cicestr. for A/d Cicestr. invs.

[2] Spratt, op. cit. 36–7, 39, 47, 50–1, 55–6, 238, 254–5; B.M., Stowe 765, ff. 4v., 9 sqq., 29 sqq.; Add. 14850, ff. 145v.–8; R. 19082, m. 14; 19083–4; 26866; P.R.O., Req. 102/45, compl.; Chanc. Proc. ser. i Jas. I, B. 14/17; C. 16/29, m. 1; Exch. L.R., M.B. 201, ff. 56v.–8, 65 sqq.; 220, ff. 330–2; 255, ff. 35 sqq., 50–1; Slater, op. cit. 331; Marshall, *Nfk* ii, 14–15; Gray, op. cit. 313–15, 319–21, 324; W. J. Corbett, 'Eliz. Vil. Svys', *Trans. R. Hist. S.* 1897 xi, 70–1, 86; R. H. Tawney, *Agrarian Prob. in 16th cent.* 1912, pp. 254–5; Nfk R.O., Dean & Chap. Norvic.: Parl. Svys 1649, ff. 98 sqq.

Sandy and gravelly loams were in permanent cultivation as arable land, in which successions of crops and periods of 'summerley' alternated. 'Summerleys' were still fallows and were adopted because these lands were liable to blow or scorch in the course of fallow stirrings and could only gain heart to bear corn if some vegetation were ploughed in. The rule of thumb was that the 'summerley' continued for one year only, if the succeeding stirrings were to be accompanied by heavy mucking; and was otherwise left for two years, after which it might be broken up by a single ploughing for corn. Around the heaths especially, there were many arable enclosures with soils that were not strong enough for permanent tillage and yet could not lie long in grass before being over-grown with furze and brakes. They were, therefore, alternated between tillage and 'layers', i.e. temporary leys, mostly of short duration. In the deeper and more productive soils, there was often a two-field course of (1) fallow, (2) corn. In this the rotation was usually (1) fallow, (2) wheat, rye or barley, (3) fallow, (4) peas or oats, the precise crops and their succession being determined by immediate circumstances. At Titchwell, and elsewhere, the 'infield' was largely in a six-field course of (1) summerley, later broken up and brought to a tilth, after four ploughings, for (2) rye, (3) barley, (4) peas, (5) barley, (6) summerley. The best of the 'infield', however, the 'wheatlands', underwent a five-field course of (1) summerley, broken up and fallow-stirred, mucked with about twelve loads of farmyard manure an acre, and sown on four or five earths for (2) wheat, (3) barley, (4) peas or vetches, (5) barley. Amongst the other 'infield' courses were: (1) summerley, (2) wheat or rye, (3) barley, (4) peas, (5) oats; and (1) summerley, (2) barley or summer corn, i.e. oats, peas and vetches, (3) summerley, (4) rye or wheat, (5) summer corn. Meanwhile, the 'brecks' were in turn 'double-tathed', i.e. close-folded with sheep twice in rapid succession, and forced to bear a single crop of oats, which might yield only about three or four combs, or between a dozen and sixteen bushels, to the acre.[1] The chief bread and drink corns were barley, rye, wheat and maslin. Not many beans were sown and the chief consumption crops, besides natural grass, were barley, oats, vetches and peas. Vetches were widely grown for hay, to repair the deficiencies of the meadowlands. In the extreme north, with its poor sandy soils, wheat could be grown only after marling and its acreage was but about one-twentieth of the whole, while the proportion of barley was correspondingly higher. Thus at Holkham in the mid-

[1] Ibid. ff. 111, 115–7; City Lib.: 1505, f. 1; N.R.S. 9276; B.M., Sloane 3815, ff. 79, 88, 105, 141, 144 (pp. 173, 191, 245, 319, 325); Add. 14850, ff. 144–7, 148v.; P.R.O., Exch. L.R., M.B. 201, ff. 55–6, 94; Chanc. Proc. ser. i Jas I, C. 1/50, compl.; A. Simpson, 'E. Anglian Foldcourse: Some Q.', Ag. HR vi, 95; R. J. Hammond, 'Soc. & Econ. Circes Ket's Rebellion', ts. thesis M.A. Ldn Univ. 1933, p. 57; Gray, op. cit. 318–21, 325; Slater, op. cit. 78–9; Spratt, op. cit. 253.

seventeenth century, 1,300 acres were sown to barley and 1,000 divided between wheat, rye, oats, peas and vetches. All told, the country's tillage crops were between half and two-thirds barley, one-fifth peas and vetches, one-fifth wheat, rye and maslin, and one-twentieth oats.[1] Sheep-and-barley husbandry reigned supreme. Barley was by far the most important crop, for both market and farm consumption. It was used for malting, for bread, for feeding poultry and doves, for fatting swine and, in a mash, for foddering horses. There were dairies for domestic and local consumption and bullocks were reared and fatted. Some oxen were used in draught, but the plough-teams were almost universally composed of horses, of which three made a team in most soils and two in the sandy ones.[2]

There were some cony-warrens, especially in the poor sandy soils of the north; but the chief application of heathland was to sheep-walk. 'Norfolk' sheep were fed on the heaths by day and folded on the tillage at night. Each township supported great flocks, usually no less than 500 sheep, often more than 1,000 and sometimes 2,000, 3,000 or 4,000. These were mainly breeding, but partly wether flocks, and wethers and crones were much fatted in the northern salt-marshes. The rate of stocking in the sheep-walks was approximately two per acre, i.e. one sheep to every one or two acres of permanent cultivation.[3] In late afternoon and early morning the sheep moved to and from the heaths and fields along green-sward driftways, called 'leys'. In the fields they were folded behind hurdles for the sake of their 'tath' or 'tash'. Two hundred sheep would 'tash' a statute acre in a week, but the folds were usually much larger than this and fertilized a ridge or an acre in a single night. It required two applications, however, to fold a heathland 'breck' for corn. Folding was unremitting from May Day until about a month before Christmas, and then occasional, if the weather were not too wet. A thousand sheep could thus fold about 100 acres a year, more or less according to the soil. The sheep-fold was the basis of husbandry and land that had been

[1] Ibid. 185–6, 193, 230; Gray, op. cit. 318–21; Sinclair, op. cit. 1; Tusser, op. cit. 120; Riches, op. cit. 95–6; B.M., Sloane 3815, ff. 79, 88, 141 (pp. 173, 191, 319); Add. R. 16551; P.R.O., Exch. L.R., M.B. 201, f. 94; 220, ff. 330–2; invs.:—Nfk R.O., A/d & Cons. cts; W. Sfk R.O., Episc. Commy Ct Bury St Edm's.; F. W. Brooks, 'Supp. Stiffkey Papers', Camd. Misc. xvi, Camd. 3rd ser. 1936 lii, 40–1.

[2] Ibid. 42; Blith, op. cit. 207–8; J. Norden, Chorography Nfk 1938, p. 67; B.M., Add. R. 16551; Nfk R.O., N.R.S. 9276; invs. as prev. n.; Spratt, op. cit. 229–30.

[3] Ibid. 242, 265; Camden, op. cit. i, 455; Riches, op. cit. 101; Sinclair, loc. cit.; Hammond, op. cit. 63; K. J. Allison, 'Wool Supply & Worsted Cloth Ind. in Nfk in 16th & 17th cents.', ts. thesis Ph.D. Leeds Univ. 1955, pp. 140 sqq.; Nfk R.O., Cons. Ct inv. 1633: 108; B.M., Stowe 775, ff. 32v. sqq.; Add. 14850, f. 149v.; R. 16551; P.R.O., Chanc. Proc. ser. i Jas I, B. 14/17; C. 1/50, compl.; C. 6/35, compl. & ans.; C. 16/29, mm. 1, 4; Exch. L.R., M.B. 201, ff. 92, 93v.–4; 220, ff. 331v.–2; 255, ff. 47–8, 54v.–5.

'tashed' was thereby about half as valuable again.[1] In the Norfolk Heathlands, as well as in the Breckland and in parts of other neighbouring countries, the sheep-fold was generally organized by means of the fold-course or fold-right. A fold was a small enclosure of hurdles used in 'tashing', and a sheep-course simply a sheep-walk; but a sheep-course could not constitute part of a fold-course unless the sheep were periodically removed from it to 'tash' the tillage. A fold-course thus consisted of four parts: first, folding sheep on the tillage, 'that by treading and dunging the place they make itt more firme and more apt for corne'; secondly, a flock, i.e. a set number of sheep belonging to a particular fold-course; thirdly, the several heath of sheep-walk for the daily feeding of the flock; and, fourthly, the right to feed on common-field land when this was 'shack', i.e. when no corn was growing. Where there was a fold-course, the manorial tenants owed fold-suit, i.e. they were bound to send their sheep to the lord's fold that he might have their 'tash', and to give precedence to the lord's flock in feeding 'shacks' and summerleys.[2]

THE BRECKLAND

Between the Chilterns and the Norfolk Edge a break was made in the range of chalk hills by a tract of about 400 square miles of heathy land. The level base of this Breckland was chalk rock. Most of the soils were sandy, gravelly and thin. The sandy soils were sometimes as much as 15 inches deep, but usually much shallower, tending to become progressively thinner towards the west. There were in addition a few deep, flinty, sandy soils and sandy loams and loams. The subsoils were mostly loft chalk, but occasionally a mixture of sand and flints or, in the east, mild clay. The vast majority of soils and bases were thus highly absorbent, so much so that streams were few and far between. Only heavy rain, which was comparatively infrequent, would moisten the land for any length of time. In consequence, the soils were usually powdery and liable to blow, so that a waggish farmer might say, in reply to the question whether his land stood in Norfolk or Suffolk, it depended which way the wind was blowing. 'Sand-floods' were, indeed, the only ones known. Since so much had been blown, all the soils contained a good deal of sand and most were covered with a pall of it. Turf

[1] Ibid. 201, f. 94; Spratt, op. cit. 247–8; Tusser, op. cit. 63; Allison, op. cit. 248, 264–5; B.M., Sloane 3815, ff. 57, 79, 144 (pp. 127, 173, 325); Hammond, op. cit. 55, 57.

[2] Ibid. 57–8; Eng. Reps. lxxiv, K.B. iii, 10–11; Allison, op. cit. 28–9; Spratt, op. cit. 249; B.M., Add. 27403, marked 'Hist. of Faldcourse—Quere if not written by Sir Hy Spilman whilst Sir Hy Hobert was cheif justice of the Comon Pleas bet. the years 1617 and 1626: it is the handwriting of Gudbon Goddard Esq. recorder of Lenne' (f. 1).

formed with the greatest difficulty and could only be maintained for a limited period, being all too apt to turn to heath. The climate was extreme enough to favour cereals, but the soil was too weak to bear a long succession. No worth-while crops could be obtained without intensive sheep-folding. The less the soil was disturbed, the greater its fertility and retention. Yet if left in still fallow, it did not acquire much sward. Such land would clearly defy the best endeavours of all but the most skilled husbandmen. Nearly treeless, the country's natural produce was heather, bracken, sand-sedge and poor stalky grass; all most of it suited was heath sheep-walk and to this design of Nature it was appropriated. Owing to the shortage of surface water, settlement was impossible in the heart of the heaths, except near a few brooks and meres, and the Breckland was farmed, in the main, from townships sited on the chalky or sandy loams on its margins. It was thus encircled by a girdle of long, narrow townships that shared the heaths between them. The westernmost townships had great tracts of fen, mostly dry in summer even before the drainage of the Great Level, and used as mowing grounds and summer pastures. Most villages had some small meadows, fens, paddocks and grassland closes, and some arable lands, either open or in large enclosures, all of which were 'infields', and not subject to liberty of fold-courses.[1]

Further away lay the common fields, which had field-courses not unlike those of the Chalk Country, but with a far higher proportion of four-field ones and still fallows almost everywhere.[2] Beyond these common fields, the townships extended centripetally into the heart of the heaths, where there were great sheep-walks, as large as common fields, infields and village sites put together, and often, indeed, much larger. Here were fed flocks of hundreds and thousands of sheep, which had, nevertheless, to compete for sustenance with hordes of rabbits and hares and the conies of numerous warrens.[3] The sheep-fold alone enabled the

---

[1] Clarke, op. cit. 24, 99–100; Spratt, op. cit. 254; J. Saltmarsh & H. C. Darby, 'Infield-Outfield Syst. on Nfk Manor', *Econ. Hist.* iii, 39, 35–6; M. R. Postgate, 'Fd. Systs. Breckland', *Ag. HR* x, 91–2; P.R.O., St. Ch. Eliz. A. 22/20; Chanc. Proc. ser. i Jas I, L. 15/7, compl. & ans.; D.L., R. & S. 9/6; Exch. A.O., M.B. 419, ff. 58 sqq.; B.M., Add. 40064, f. 31; R. 63505, 63591; Herts. R.O., 12298; E. Sfk R.O., V. 11/2/1/1.

[2] Ibid; Spufford, op. cit. 93, 95 sqq.; Spratt, op. cit. 39, 258; Postgate, art. cit. 83, 88–91, 93; 'Hist. Geog. Breckland 1600–1850', ts. thesis M.A. Ldn Univ. 1960, pp. 99, 111, 117–18; Gray, op. cit. 311–12; B.M., Add. R. 16549, 63505; E. M. Leonard, *Early Hist. Eng. Poor Relief* 1900, p. 334; P.R.O., Exch. A.O., M.B. 419, f. 59; D.L., R. & S. 9/5–6; Req. 65/52; Chanc. Proc. ser. i Jas I, D. 8/11, m. 1; L. 15/7, compl. & ans.; W. 11/60, compl.

[3] Ibid. W. 26/15; Exch. A.O., M.B. 419, f. 59; D.L., R. & S. 9/6; St. Ch. Eliz. A. 22/20; Req. 65/52; Ess. R.O., D/DP E25, ff. 23, 53–4; Spratt, op. cit. 237–8, 242–3, 246, 258; Clarke, op. cit. 131, 133, 135, 143; Spufford, op. cit. 11; Fuller, op. cit. i, 222; ii, 444–5; Savine, op. cit. 188; Saltmarsh & Darby, art. cit. 97–9.

farmers to subject almost all the heathland to shifting cultivation. Arable tracts, including warrens, were divided into shifts or 'brecks', each between thirty and sixty acres, and enclosed with earthen banks. About once every seven years the breck would be double-tathed for a single crop of barley or oats, before being allowed to revert to heather, moss, lichen, hair-grasses, creeping bent, wild thyme, sand-sedge, and eventually turf. In very dry seasons, too, temporary cultivation could be undertaken in the beds of the meres.[1]

Sheep-folds were organized as in the Norfolk Heathlands: the fold-course system operated equally in both, and the same aboriginal sheep were stocked. Both breeding and wether flocks were kept and the flock-master's shepherds might have charge of two, three and four thousand or more sheep, of which the majority belonged to their employer. Folding was thus intensive and stocking heavy, with perhaps one sheep for every two or three acres of heath. Excellent mutton was produced, especially in the western fens, but breeding and rearing were generally more important.[2] The sheep-fold was paramount, but was supplemented by farmyard manure and marl and by ploughing in buckwheat. The chief crops were rye, barley and some mutton for market; and rye, barley, peas, lentils and tares for consumption. Small amounts of wheat, saffron, and hemp were also grown. Buckwheat served for green manure and sheep and poultry feed. Oats were grown chiefly for the horses that were everywhere used in ploughing, in teams of two or three. What dairies there were, sufficed merely for liquid milk demands.[3]

THE SANDLINGS COUNTRY

Between High Suffolk and the coast, the countryside lay largely in tracts of deep, sandy soils, on a sandy base. These were called sandlings, and the one between the Orwell and the Deben was the Great Sandling. They were watered by lazy rivers with wide tidal estuaries and numerous creeks. By the riversides were gravel soils, marshes and mud-banks, and on the sea-coast not a few saltings and salt-marshes. Further inland, the sandy soils gave rise to many heaths, as those of Danbury, Tiptree,

[1] Ibid. 36, 42; P.R.O., Chanc. Proc. ser. i Jas I, B. 6/57, compl.; Gray, op. cit. 311–12; Clarke, op. cit. 20, 22, 53, 55, 58, 86, 135; R. Somerville, *Hist. DL* 1953 i, 308; Spufford, op. cit. 9–10, 19–20, 93; Simpson, art. cit. 94; Postgate, op. cit. 82, 128–9; art. cit. 91, 93, 97; Spratt, op. cit. 61, 244.

[2] Ibid. 237–8, 242, 244 sqq., 261; Saltmarsh & Darby, art. cit. 37–9, 42; Allison, op. cit. 282, 290; Marshall, op. cit. i, 363–4; *E. Dept*, 465; B.M., Add. R. 16549, 63591; P.R.O., Exch. L.R., M.B. 257, f. 163; Ess. R.O., D/DP E25, f. 23; invs.:— Nfk R. O., Cons. & A/d cts; W. Sfk R.O., Episc. Commy Ct Bury St Edm's.

[3] Eland, op. cit. 23–4; Clarke, op. cit. 23; Leonard, loc. cit.; Postgate, op. cit. 106; Spufford, op. cit. 106; invs. as prev. n.

Weeley, Rushmere, Foxhall, Sutton and Southwold, which produced largely red and purple heather, ferns, gorse, broom and brambles, but, where trodden by sheep, also much short grass. The townships were sited on gravelly and sandy loams, and lay on the estuaries, just inland from the salt-marshes, or along the bounds of the sandlings, which they shared between them. The climate favoured cereal growing, for the summers were hot, the winters hard and the rainfall low.

Many townships had remnants of common fields, but most of the field land was enclosed with hedges and ditches and employed in convertible husbandry.[1] From the more homeward parts of the heaths, too, many rectangular enclosures had been, and were being, taken in.[2] Hawthorn would not grow well in the thin, sandy soils unless planted on high banks. Alternatively, one might set furze hedges, i.e. two or three ranks of gorse bushes. If cut back short for the first few years, the gorse branched out thickly and presented an impenetrable front to cattle.[3] Heath enclosures could not bear lengthy periods of tillage and if left long to graze became broomy, furzy and ferny, so they had perforce to be cultivated in a convertible system.[4] Some salt-marshes on the sea and estuary coasts remained open or even commonable,[5] but most were enclosed with sea-walls and drained with gutters and sluices. Along the banks of the streams and brooks lay drained fresh marshes or fens. Furthest from the villages were the great heaths, of hundreds or thousands of acres. These were used primarily as common or several sheep-walks, but partly also as cattle commons and cony warrens.[6] In addition, most heathland was temporarily enclosed from time to time for shifting cultivation. The lord of Blythburgh and Walberswick manor or his farmer, it is said,[7]

'have used to plow such parte of the . . . walke or heath as they would; and when any parte thereof was sowen with corne, the inhabitants of Walberswick did not put their cattle upon such places soe sowen untill the corn was reaped; but if their cattle did stray and come on the corne,

[1] B.M., Egerton 2789A. ff. 3v. (pp. 2) sqq.; Add. 32134, ff. 24, 26, 29, 76v.–7 (31, 33, 36, 72v.–3); Herts. R.O., G'bury xi. 11, ff. 86–7; E. Sfk R.O., 50/22/12.6; 50/1/74(1), pp. 1, 3, 6–7, 15, 25, 42, 47–8, 51–2; 50/1/74(12), ff. 3–4 (pp. 5, 7), pp. 20–3.

[2] Ibid. f. 4 (p. 7), pp. 20 sqq.; V. 5/22/1, ff. 11v.–2, 13v.–4; B.M., Add. 23956, f. 17; P.R.O., D.L., R. & S. 9/15; S.P.D. Jas vol. 150 no 7.

[3] Norden, Surv's. Dial. 235.

[4] P.R.O., D.L., R.&S. 9/15.

[5] Ibid.; B.M., Egerton 2789A, f. 22v. (p. 40); Spratt, op. cit. 64.

[6] Ibid. 239–40; Norden, Ess. 9; P.R.O., Exch. A.O., Parl. Svys Sfk 17, ff. 1–2; B.M., Add. 23950, f. 98v.; 23956, f. 17; Egerton 2789A, f. 7(5)v.; 2789B; Ess. R.O., D/DRa C5; E. Sfk R.O., V. 5/22/1, ff. 7, 15v.–6, 17v.–9, 21v.–2, 25v.–6, 29v.–30; 50/1/74(12), p. 23; 50/22/3(1).

[7] Ibid.

they were impounded. And that it appeares by the riggs and furrowes on most parte of the heath, that the same have usually byn plowed'.

John Norden indicated on his maps those parts of the heaths near Eyke, Butley, Rendlesham, Wantisden, Sutton, Hollesley and Hatchley Barn newly enclosed for corn, as well as those that were reasonably good rye ground, even though sandy and apt to turn to heath. In Dedham similar shifting cultivation was conducted in temporary common fields.[1] The tread of the sheep consolidated the light sandy soils and sheep and cattle browsed the young gorse, killing or stunting it. Gorse and broom, too, were cut and stubbed for fuel. Breaking the land up for corn also improved the swards; sheep further ameliorated them; and the soil was thus strengthened to bear much rye and some oats and barley.[2]

Between two-thirds and three-quarters of all the grain grown was rye, wheat only about one-seventh or one-eighth, oats one-twentieth, barley one-thirtieth and peas, tares, buckwheat, beans and hemp even less. Nearly all farmers kept sheep of the native East Anglian breed in flocks of up to 700 or more. The larger farms had both breeding and wether flocks and their marshes enabled them to fatten up to 100 wethers and crones in the summer months, some being bought from inland farms. Most farmers had domestic dairies, but where marsh feeding was available, establishments were on a much larger scale, ranging up to forty or more milch kine to a farm. Grass milk was made into both cheese and butter, but more the former than the latter. With these dairies, large numbers of swine were fattened. In spring and summer, too, surplus steers, bullocks and cow-bullocks were grazed on estuary and coastal marshes. Home-breds were joined by North Country steers and altogether a farmer might have fifty or so beasts fatting in the summer months. Poultry were kept in large numbers, as in all cereal countries, but here turkeys were of especial importance, the sandy soils being highly favourable to their rearing. Traction was everywhere provided by the native breed of Suffolk Punch horses. The larger farms often stocked about a dozen of these, which they both bred and reared.[3] In ploughing, one or two punches constituted a full team, able to turn two acres of sandy soil a day.[4] The horses were provendered on peas, oats,

[1] G. H. Rendall, *Dedham in Hist.* 1937, pp. 33–5; E. Sfk R.O., V. 5/22/1, ff. 15v.–6, 17v.–18, 21v.–2.

[2] Ibid. ff. 15v.–6, 17v.–18, 21v.–2; 50/22/3(1); Norden, *Surv's. Dial.* 234; E. D. R. Burrell, 'Hist. Geog. Sandlings Sfk 1600 to 1850', ts. thesis M.Sc. Ldn Univ. 1960, p. 60; Nfk R.O., Cons. Ct inv. 1632:23.

[3] Ibid. Cons. & A/d cts invs.; H. M. Doughty, *Chrons. Theberton* 1910, pp. 94–5, 145; R. Blome, *Brit.* 207; Spratt, loc. cit.; Marshall, op. cit. 430; Norden, op. cit. 213; Allison, op. cit. 293; Ess. R.O., D/DRc F88; B.M., Egerton 2789A, f. 1 (p. 3); Add. 23949, f. 67; 32134, ff. 78 (74)v., 95 (84); E. Sfk R.O., 50/22/3(5) agrt 11 Aug. 1645; 50/22/12(6); A/d invs.

[4] Mortimer, op. cit. 39; Blith, op. cit. 207–8.

straw, chaff and grass and tare hay. Buckwheat was sown for folding off to sheep and for feeding poultry. In winter both sheep and cows had hay and straw only.[1]

THE BLACKHEATH COUNTRY

East of the Chalk Country lies an extensive area of heath and wood-land. The best-known black heaths are those of Bagshot, Ascot and Bexley. Maidenhead Thicket, Windsor and Alice Holt forests and the 'forest district' of woods and heaths towards Kingsclere, all formed part of the same country. The prevailing soils were thin, blackish or grey, sandy and gravelly, amongst the worst in England and including much blowing sand. Their natural produce was mostly dwarfish, stunted red heath, which was the only safeguard against sand-floods. There were also some pale 'woodland' clays, which rarely ameliorated into clay loams. The black heaths themselves were seldom more than five or six miles wide and included, here and there, some clumps of woodland and a few slips of cultivated land, as in the Blackwater Valley.

Townships were sited on the more fertile soils encircling the heaths, and by streams in the woodlands, so that the wastes were shared be-tween them. Near the villages there were common fields, meadows and marshes. Probably two- and three-field courses of the Chalk Country type were employed.[2] A good deal of land lay in enclosures, particularly on demesne farms; and even open demesnes were often in severalty, so altogether possibly no more than half the land was common.[3] Near the heaths themselves many enclosures were convertible, being too poor to be long in either tillage or grass.[4] This practice was already old-

---

[1] Gerarde, op. cit. 1030; E. Sfk R.O., V. 5/18/10(1), p. 29; Nfk R.O., Cons. Ct invs. 1633: 180, 287.

[2] Money, op. cit. 60 sqq.; F. J. Baigent, *Crondal Recs.* iii Hants. Rec. Soc. 1891, pp. 178–9, 258 sqq., 359 sqq., 369 sqq.; B.M., Add. 6027, f. 2 (6); Sy R.O., 29/1/4; Berks. R.O., D/EN M6, M31, M33–4; D/ETh M1, p. 13; M10, p. 39; P.R.O., D.L., M.B. 108, f. 4; Exch. T.R., Bk 157, ff. 1v., 2v. (pp. 4, 6); L.R., M.B. 187, ff. 36v.–40, 45v., 49v., 52, 53v., 101v.–3, 160, 163; 196, ff. 223–5; 197, ff. 192, 193v.–5; 199, ff. 13v.–4, 15v., 17v., 24, 26, 30, 31v., 32v.–3, 36, 39 sqq., 206 sqq.; 203, ff. 32, 90 sqq., 110a sqq.; 209, f. 19; 226, ff. 2, 72 sqq.; A.O., Parl. Svys Sy 55, ff. 3–4; Berks. 28, ff. 5–6; 11, f. 3.

[3] Ibid.; L.R., M.B. 187, ff. 49v., 162; 199, ff. 192 sqq.; 209, ff. 17, 92, 195–8; 226, ff. 72 sqq.; T.R., Bk 157, f. 1 (pp. 3–4); D.L., M.B. 108, f. 3; 116, ff. 9–11; Guildford Mun. Rm, Loseley 937, 959; Wilts. R.O., Dioc. Reg. Sarum. inv. Th. Chapman 1584 Sonning; B.M., Add. 6027, ff. 1 (5)–2 (6); Baigent, op. cit. 203, 211 sqq., 222 sqq., 258 sqq., 330 sqq., 359 sqq.

[4] Ibid. 387; Money, op. cit. 62 sqq.; Berks. R.O., D/EN E1/2; Guildford Mun. Rm, Loseley 937, 959; B.M., Add. 6027, f. 1(5); P.R.O., Exch. L.R., M.B. 196, f. 223; 197, f. 195; 203, f. 103; 209, ff. 17–19, 92, 102; T.R., Bk 157, f. 1 (pp. 3–4).

established in 1519 when land at Greenham and Welhampton was 'summe yeres in tillage and summe yeres in pasture after the custome of the seid countres amongst the husbondmen afore this tyme usid'.[1] Beyond these fields, the townships frequently intercommoned in the heaths. Here went some ponies and small, mean-looking cattle, but chiefly the little, black or brown-faced, thin, long-legged, ill-formed aboriginal sheep, called 'heath-croppers'. Their meagre living was mostly gained from stunted heather, so they had no chance to run to fat and produced small quantities of sweet, lean mutton. They bore small fleeces of clothing wool, thirteen to the tod. The sheep fed the heaths by day and were folded on the arable by night. Generally it was only possible to stock one heath-cropper for each two or three acres of tillage. Common-field farmers usually formed common flocks and prevented unauthorized staff-herding on the heaths, and demesne farms often had their severalty flocks. The largest single aggregation of sheep was on Bagshot Heath; but these were not all folded locally, for it was the practice to hire out flocks, with or without shepherds, for folding on the common fields of Salt Hill, Slough and district in the Vale of London, so depleting the fertility of the heathlands.[2] The poorest heaths, indeed, were of so little value for agriculture, that almost any alternative use was profitable. A good deal had been converted to fish-ponds, and new ones were being made from time to time, so that there were said to be more here than in half the rest of England.[3] Nevertheless, despite the poverty of the black heaths, their best parts were brought into tillage under a system of shifting cultivation. In the east, in Norden's time, these plots were forced to bear single crops of rye by paring and burning the heathy sward.[4] Some of the woodlands, like Maidenhead Thicket, were enclosed; but Windsor and Alice Holt forests included within their bounds parts of the many surrounding townships. One could put in horses (and sometimes sheep), and great cattle, to share the herbage with the red and fallow deer, but this advantage was cancelled out by the deers' liberty to share farm crops.[5]

Farmers were able to keep domestic dairies of small cows, flocks of

[1] P.R.O., Chanc. Com. Law Pleadings bdl. 24, Prior St J's. case; Exch. K.R., Memoranda, Recorda, 11 Hy VIII, rot. 40.

[2] Ibid. L.R., M.B. 187, ff. 103v., 163; 226, f. 11; A.O., Parl. Svys Sy. 55, f. 10; Miscellanea of Exch. 10/11; D.L., M.B. 108, f. 3v.; Berks. R.O., D/EN M6; D/ETh M1, p. 1; invs.:—Wilts. R.O., Dioc. Reg. Sarum.; Hants. R.O., Cons. & A/d cts; B.M., Add. R. 27991; Defoe, op. cit. i, 143; Vancouver, Hants. 81; Marshall, Midl. Dept, 532; S. Dept, 95, 349; Sheep, 30; S. Cos. ii, 85–6.

[3] Ibid. 86; E. Straker, Wealden Iron 1931, p. 447; J. Taverner, Certaine Experiments concerng Fish & Fruite 1600; Norden, op. cit. 225–6 (1st occ.).

[4] Ibid. 224 (2nd occ.); Guildford Mun. Rm, Loseley 959.

[5] Ibid. 1081/41, 43; B.M., Harl. 3749, ff. 4–5; Marshall, Sheep, 30; P.R.O., Exch. A.O., Parl. Svys Berks. 16; 21, ff. 1, 5; Hants. 14–15; L.R., M.B. 199, ff. 13v. sqq.; 187, f. 44.

dwarf sheep, and plough horses, and to grow considerable acreages of
rye, oats, dredge and buckwheat, together with small quantities of
wheat, barley, peas, tares and lentils; but the objects of farming were
confined, on large farms, to sheep, for mutton, wool and the hire of
folds, to rearing beasts, to fat swine, where there were woodlands, to the
cheese and butter dairy, along the Enborne and Blackwater valleys, and
on small farms, merely to subsistence.[1]

THE POOR SOILS DISTRICT

The Poor Soils District had mainly sandy soils, giving rise to many
dreary, barren heaths and rough grazings. Some weak 'woodland' clays
were also found. The Isle of Purbeck was mostly chalk and the Isle of
Portland limestone, both rocks being hard and giving rise to infertile
soils. Only in the Avon Valley was there any considerable extent of
loamy soil.

The villages were situated mostly in river valleys and along the bounds
of the district. Except in the New Forest (from which sheep were
excluded for the sake of the deer), the heaths and rough grazings,
whether in common or in severalty, were used chiefly as sheep-walks.
Some capital farmers kept up to 1,600 sheep and a score or so of beasts
on hundreds of acres of heath and one of the many family farmers
might put perhaps 100 sheep and half a dozen beasts into the common.
In some places there were also cony-warrens. Throughout the year
flocks of small sheep fed the heaths and commons by day and were
close-folded on the tillage at night.[2] Near the villages there were
meadows, and some marshes, which were employed for grazing cattle,
fatting a few culled sheep and cutting turves for fuel and compost.[3]
Common fields were widespread;[4] but manor farms usually had sheep-
walks in severalty and fields, meadows and pastures enclosed.[5] Some

[1] Ibid. f. 163; D.L., M.B. 108, f. 3v.; Guildford Mun. Rm, Loseley 937; Worlidge,
op. cit. 37; Baigent, op. cit. 394; *Sy Archaeol. Colls.* xxiii, 79–80; invs.:—Wilts. R.O.,
Dioc. Reg. Sarum.: Hants. R.O., Cons. & A/d cts, & Pec. Ct E. Woodhay.

[2] Invs.:—Hants. R.O., Cons. & A/d cts; Dors. R.O., Corfe Cas. & Wimborne
Minster Pecs.; B.M., Add. 6027, f. 95 (94); P.R.O., D.L., M.B. 108, ff. 28, 44v.–5;
116, ff. 20–2, 36, 39v., 41v.; Exch. L.R., M.B., 191, f. 32; T.R., Bk 157, ff. 65v., 66v.
(pp. 124, 126); Marshall, *S. Dept,* 245, 253; Stevenson, *Dors.* 394.

[3] Norden, op. cit. 222 (1st occ.), 226 (2nd); P.R.O., D.L., M.B. 108, f. 28; 116,
ff. 20, 38v., 41v.

[4] Ibid. ff. 20, 38v.–40; Exch. L.R., M.B. 214, ff. 99 sqq.; T.R., Bk 157, f. 65v.
(p. 124); A.O., Parl. Svys Dors. 8, ff. 2–4; Hants. R.O., 12 M60/64; Marshall, op.
cit. 268; B.M., Add. 6027, f. 95 (94)v.; Dors. R.O., D. 10/M91; D. 37/1, 3, Mus.
1408.

[5] Ibid. Corfe Cas. Pec. inv. i/30; P.R.O., Exch. L.R., M.B. 191, f. 32; D.L., M.B.
108, ff. 28, 44; 116, ff. 20, 36.

manor lords or farmers had enclosed tracts of field and sheep-walk in earlier times, but general enclosure ensued only in the later eighteenth century,[1] and meanwhile the family farmers continued with their common-field husbandry. Most of the arable was in permanent tillage and was managed in much the same way whether the fields were common or not. By dint of folding there was possible in more favoured situations a three-field course of (1) winter corn, (2) spring corn, (3) fallow. Two-field courses, however, were more usual. The crops were wheat, rye, barley, oats, peas, and tares, including winter vetches. Dairies were maintained for domestic and local needs and draught was usually supplied by horses. In a word, the Poor Soils District was a vastly inferior version of the Chalk Country.[2]

Since sheep were restricted, the New Forest had more woodland than the rest of the country and many more deer. Forest farms put some dairy cows in the clearings, but most cattle in the forest were stores intended to be sold for fatting in the marshes of the South Sea-coast Country. Wild ponies were periodically rounded up. Many swine were fed on acorns and beech-mast to produce excellent, close-grained bacon. Bees were also kept in considerable numbers. All this was small compensation for the lack of sheep-walk, however, and although some farmers grazed a few sheep, they were unable to keep even common flocks. In default of the fold, no more land could be tilled than was mucked with farmyard manure, few farms having more than a dozen acres under the plough and the vast majority much less.[3] In some few enclosures convertible husbandry may have been practised.[4] By these means, the petty farmers who were the usual occupiers were able to keep teams and raise small crops of rye, oats, peas and even a little wheat.[5] The New Forest locality was thus an inferior version even of the Poor Soils District and an indication of what other parts would have been like, had they been deprived of sheep-walk, flocks and folds and exposed to incalculable mischief from deer.[6]

HIGH SUFFOLK

What may be termed the farming country of High Suffolk contained not only a large portion of that county, but also the south-eastern mar-

[1] Ibid. f. 20; Exch. T.R., Bk 157, f. 67 (pp. 127–8); B.M., Add. 6027, ff. 94(93)v.–95(94); Hants. R.O., 12 M60/64; Marshall, op. cit. 245.

[2] Ibid. 268; P.R.O., D.L., M.B. 116, ff. 20, 38v.–40; invs.:—Dors. R.O., Corfe Cas. & Wimborne Minster Pecs.; Hants. R.O., Cons. & A/d cts.

[3] Ibid.; Fuller, op. cit. ii, 3.

[4] P.R.O., S.P.D. Jas vol. 8 no 76, f. 5; Norden, loc. cit.

[5] Hants. R.O., Cons. & A/d cts invs.

[6] Marshall, op. cit. 314.

gin of Norfolk and a small part of Essex. The subsoils were extremely various; ranging between gravel and clay. Nearly all the soils, however, were deep, and centuries of cultivation had reduced them to fertile loams, sufficiently retentive to render adequate a rainfall of 25 inches a year or less, yet never so impermeable as to weep even after the heaviest rains. They were rich enough to be stiff under the plough (often, indeed, being laid in narrow ridges for wheat), yet, under good management, never adhesive or intractable—in short, almost perfect agricultural soil.

The climate, too, was excellent and the farmer could expect more successful wheat and barley harvests here than almost anywhere else in the world. Despite a low rainfall, the grass grew gay and high, this being the sole justification for the country's traditional name, for the landscape undulated only gently.

In the sixteenth and seventeenth centuries, and even in the eighteenth in a few places, there survived remnants of common fields, and a few severely stinted common pastures, marshes and meadows. Exceptionally in the small broadlands, as at Oulton Broad, there were still many cattle 'goings' and 'scythe rights'; and at Bungay, where the Waveney had changed its course, 400 acres of the old river bed were used as a common mowing ground under the management of fen reeves. The serpentine meanderings of lazy, and often calcareous, rivers and streams had resulted in numerous fens, most of which had long been enclosed and ditch-drained or trenched, and many 'aldercarrs', i.e. marshy grounds replete especially with alders. Most of the country was already enclosed in 1500 and the typical township was entirely enclosed. Everywhere closes, crofts and 'pightles' had been withdrawn from commonage piecemeal, leaving small, irregularly shaped enclosures scattered and dispersed about the township in such a way that one farm's fields were intermingled with another's much as parcels were in common fields.[1] So inconvenient was this intermingling that there had already started a movement to consolidate small 'pightles' and closes into large ones. The Thrandeston Field Book of 1579 describes many pieces of land and fen 'inclosed together', and two also 'ploughed cross'. At Grundisburgh a close called Woodfield, formerly in several pieces, was now laid to-

[1] Spratt, op. cit. 40–1, 50, 63–4, 258; *VCH Ess.* ii, 323; Riches, op. cit. 52 sqq.; Corbett, art. cit. 75; Tusser, op. cit. 67; Rendall, op. cit. 21–2; F. G. Davenport, *Econ. Development Nfk Manor 1086–1565* (1906, opp. p. 1, 5; A. Suckling, *Hist. & Ant. Co. Sfk* 1846 i, 131; B.M., Add. 14850, ff. 154, 158v.–60; 21054, ff. 6, 18, 21 sqq., 75v.; 36745, ff. 2 sqq., 40063, ff. 70 sqq.; 40064, f. 4; R. 26339; Ch. 55495; Stowe 870, ff. 3 sqq., 83 sqq., 135–6, 186–8 (pp. 4 sqq., 161 sqq., 271–3, 385 sqq.); P.R.O., Chanc. Proc. ser. i Jas I, C. 7/14, compl.; H. 14/34, compl. & ans.; U. 2/35, compl.; D.L., R.&S. 2/11, f. 40 (p. 80); 2/21; 9/19; Exch. L.R., M.B. 220, ff. 190 (2) sqq.; 221 (2) sqq., 238v. sqq., 334 sqq.; A.O., Parl. Svys Sfk 15, ff. 3–4; E. Sfk R.O., V. 11/5/3; 51/1/13–14; 51/2/12, 26; 51/10/11.5, f. 16; 51/10/17.2.

gether.[1] In short, enclosures were almost complete and consolidation and rearrangement already commenced.

Apart from wet meadows, fens and aldercarrs, most of the land was in a convertible system, for whose alternating courses the enclosures were grouped or divided into shifts.[2] Wheat, rye and maslin formed nearly half the tillage crops, barley one-third, and summer grain (oats, peas and tares) one-fifth, with smaller fractions of flax, hemp, hops and buckwheat. During the tillage period, which was usually three or four years, there was no regular or uniform succession. Oats, hemp, flax and peas were sometimes the first crops on the turf before a summer fallow for wheat or rye. The succession usually included summer grain and one whole year's summerley trifallowed for winter corn. Buckwheat was sown in May on three earths as a fallow crop succeeding winter corn or barley and often preceding barley, and was chiefly for poultry-feed. Finally, the land was laid to grass under barley or oats for six or seven years, the swards being composed largely of annual meadow grass.[3] Hemp was widely grown, particularly in the Waveney and Dove valleys, not only in small plots by cottagers, but also in whole fields by farmers as a smothering crop before wheat.[4] Of all these crops, grass and grass hay were the largest. Just after hay-making farmers had about one-tenth of all their capital stock in their haystacks.[5]

While the proportion of arable was great, that of tillage was hardly more than enough to supply the country itself with market, consumption and industrial crops. In the fens, and so especially in the north, dairy-bred bullocks and dry cows were fattened and much grass beef produced, but feeding never became more than a sideline. Numerous poultry were kept, including ducks, geese, turkeys and pea-fowl; but these were the wife's province. Some farmers grazed no sheep at all, though most had a few feeding in the summer months for domestic provision and to eat down the grass after the cows. Others even overwintered small flocks of the East Anglian breed. Yet a farm's sheep were

[1] Ibid. V. 11/3/3, pp. 40, 50; 51/2/12, f. 25v.

[2] Ibid. 51/2/26, ff. 7, 17; 51/10/17.2; 51/10/17.3, f. 39; Tusser, op. cit. 37 (& v. 16); P.R.O., D.L., R.&S. 2/21; 9/13; Exch. L.R., M.B. 203, ff. 180 sqq., 247 sqq.; 215, vy Witham, m. 1; 225, ff. 212 sqq.; A.O., Parl. Svys Ess. 12, f. 2; Sfk 15, f. 3; B.M., Stowe 870, f. 21v. (p. 38); Add. 14850, ff. 153v., 154v. sqq.; Herts. R.O., G'bury xi. 11, ff. 133, 139, 141, 145, 147.

[3] Ibid. f. 133; Tusser, op. cit. 37, 43, 45, 66–7; Gerarde, op. cit. 82, 1030; Spratt, op. cit. 202; Savine, op. cit. 174; Suckling, op. cit. ii, 355 sqq.; B.M., Add. R. 16549; E. Sfk. R.O., G.B. 1/2/14/33; 51/10/11.5, ff. 10–1, 13–14; invs.:—ibid. A/d; W. Sfk R.O., Episc. Commy Ct Bury St Edm's.; Nfk. R.O., A/d & Cons. cts.

[4] Ibid. Cons. Ct 1598–91; 84; 1611: 109B; 1632: 107; 1633: 34, 308, 315; 1634: 63, 90; Marshall, E. Dept, 442–4; E. Sfk R.O., G.B. 1/2/14/33; A/d invs. 1582–3; 247/15, 249/15; 1583–4: 273/16, 318/16, 321/16; 1589–91: 116/17.

[5] E.g. ibid. 1583–4: 318/16; Nfk R.O., Cons. Ct inv. 1675: 61; B.M., Add. R. 17751.

usually outnumbered by its dairy-cattle and the former's value rarely exceeded one-third the latter's. Draughts was supplied entirely by punches. In summer they helped to crop the grass short and trim and in winter, when not doing much heavy work, they were provendered largely on a chaff that was more straw than hay. Four horses, or five at the most, sufficed for any cultivation in the heaviest of the soils. As the arable was extensive, many horses were maintained, up to two dozen on a single farm.[1]

This was the one eastern country suited to dairying and farmers made it their speciality. Forty, fifty or sixty cows were often kept on a single farm, though some had less and others up to ninety or a hundred. These were amongst the largest dairy herds in England. In conjunction with the dairy, large numbers of swine were reared and fattened, for the pig was 'tied to the cow's tail'.[2] All summer the cows never left the fields even to be milked, for the dairy maids went out to them. In autumn, the cows were removed to yards and houses, where they were fed on straw and hay. Some were brought into milk for the winter and were given chiefly hay, but more were dried off and had mostly straw. The straws were not fed mixed, but separately and in ascending order of quality. First the cows had the rye straw, and when this was all finished, the wheat straw, and so in turn the pea, oat and barley. When this was done, they graduated to hay. The dairy was applied to both butter and cheese, on the self-same farms, and both were light in colour. Cheese was made mostly from grass milk in spring and summer, but also somewhat from hay milk. Two kinds were offered, small cream cheeses and large, hard ones. The former, made of whole milk, was an excellent table cheese, but the latter was made of skimmed milk and was eaten chiefly by work-people. It was called 'bang' and said to be 'so hard that pigs grunt at it, dogs bark at it and none dare bite it', and to mock 'the weak effort of the bending blade'. Butter was made throughout the year from grass and hay milk. A little whey-butter, largely for lubrication, was a by-product of cream cheese. Most of the whey went to the porkers and baconers and helped skimmed milk, buttermilk, beechmast, acorns and barley-meal to produce good pig-meat. Though it was 'bang' that tipped the balance, somewhat more cheese was made than butter.[3] Both were sold

---

[1] Ibid. 16548–9, 17749; P.R.O., Chanc. Proc. ser. i Jas I, E. 28/46, compl. & ans.; E. Sfk R.O., G.B. 1/2/14/33; invs.:—A/d Sfk; Nfk R.O., A/d & Cons. cts; W. Sfk R.O., Episc. Commy Ct Bury St Edm's.; Reyce, op. cit. 29, 38, 42–8; Davenport, op. cit. lxxxiii–iv; Spratt, op. cit. 201, 258; Tusser, op. cit. 29, 53; Suckling, loc cit.

[2] Ibid; Reyce, op. cit. 26, 29, 37, 39; Spratt, op. cit. 199–201, 203–4, 235–6; Hammond, op. cit. 12; Defoe, op. cit. i, 58, 60; invs.:—Nfk R.O., Cons. Ct.; W. Sfk R.O., Episcopal Commy Ct Bury St Edm's.; E. Sfk R.O., A/d Sfk; B.M., Add R. 16548–9, 17749.

[3] Ibid. 17749, 17751; F. de la Rochefoucauld, Frenchman in Engl. 1784 1933, p. 192; R. W. Blencowe, 'Exts Jnl & A/c Bk Rev. G. Moore', Suss. Archaeol. Colls. i, 69; E.

on the butter markets of Ipswich, Clare, Woodbridge, Framlingham and other towns, and distributed further afield chiefly by cheese-mongers.[1]

EAST NORFOLK

East Norfolk displayed a singular degree of uniformity in its soils, which were mostly shallow, sandy loams standing on an absorbent sandy sub-soil and base. Tilling this soil with a broad, flat plough-share formed a marked pan, below which weed seeds accumulated. In addition, a few hungry gravel soils and some rich loams were found. The broadland district, in particular, had many deep, fertile loams and clay loams, but nowhere any intractable clay soils, for marl and muck made even the strongest of them friable and loamy. With the exception of the declivities of the broads, the country was almost uniformly flat. Strong sea-winds sweeping across made it cooler than High Suffolk. The rainfall, too, was higher than in most eastern countries, especially in late summer and autumn. The climature was thus highly favourable to both cereal and root cultivation.

Common fields barely survived into the late eighteenth century and were already few and small in the sixteenth.[2] All the time the slow, piecemeal enclosure of common fields proceeded, much assisted by exchanges of land, but a general agreement for dividing a township's lands was rarely necessary. Since the ownership of land enclosed piece-meal was sometimes intermixed, and often part copyhold and part freehold, the closes themselves were occasionally divided, according to ownership and tenure, by meres and balks surviving from the common fields; and the variously owned, small, irregular fields were much dis-

---

Leigh, *Engl. Described* 1659, p. 184; Fuller, op. cit. iii, 158; Heresbach, op. cit. ff. 139v.–40; Gerarde, loc. cit.; Tusser, op. cit. 33, 40–1, 46; Marshall, *S. Dept*, 164–5; Bodl. Aubrey 2, f. 103; E. Sfk R.O., G.B. 1/2/14/33; S. 1/2/6.7; invs.:—A/d Sfk; Nfk. R.O., Cons. Ct; W. Sfk R.O., Episc. Commy Ct Bury St Edm's.; Reyce, op. cit. 37.

[1] Ibid. 40–1; Fuller, loc. cit.; Leigh, loc. cit.; Defoe, op. cit. i, 53, 253; T. S. Willan, *Eng. Coasting Trade 1600–1750* 1938, pp. 135–6, 139, 207; J. H. Andrews, 'Trade . . . Faversham 1650–70', *Arch. Cant.* lxix, 130; *L.P.* Hy VIII, iv, pt ii, no 3649; R. Steele, *Tudor & Stuart Proclamations* 1910 i, 88, 102; P. L. Hughes & J. F. Larkin, *Tudor R. Proclamations* 1964 i, 359–60; Blome, op. cit. 207, 213–4; Spratt, op. cit. 204–5.

[2] Ibid. 40–1, 51; Riches, op. cit. 53; Marshall, *Nfk* i, 4, 8, 96, 116; Gray, op. cit. 311; C. M. Hoare, *Hist. E. Anglian Soke* 1918, p. 340; B.M., Add. 20745, ff. 1 (pp. 30) sqq.; R. 26569–73; Ess. R.O., D/DL M81 Ct Bk 1, ff. 62, 83, 109v.–10, 133v.; Northants. R.O., Mont. Nfk, box P, pt ii, Ct R. Foxley c. Bawdswell; Corbett, art. cit. opp. 70, 75.

persed and intermingled. Some enclosures, too, were excessively small. These disadvantages were largely overcome, especially in the later eighteenth century, by the exchange of closes between farms, by the erasure of hedges and by the formation of larger fields out of small 'pightles'.[1] Not a few common marshes, meadows and heaths also survived. Much arable had already been improved from the heaths, and in the sixteenth and seventeenth centuries many more commons were divided and freed of common rights and fold-course liberties by agreement, the resulting enclosures being rectangular and compact, in marked contrast to those formedi pecemeal.[2] The remnants of common fields bore much superficial resemblance to the fields of the Norfolk Heathlands and many had formerly been under similar management, with sheep-folds, fold-courses and summerleys; but little distinguished in their cultivation from that of the enclosures, except in the district to the west of the broadlands. On and about the open heaths here, there were still large sheep-flocks and fold-courses as in the Norfolk Heathlands, and with similar field-courses; all of which were dissolved in the sixteenth and seventeenth centuries in sharp conflicts between flockmasters and cultivators and by piecemeal and general enclosures.[3]

The field-courses consisted of irregular variations on the theme of (1) winter corn, (2) spring corn, (3) summer corn, (4) summerleys of varying durations. The chief crops were barley and wheat, slightly more of the former than of the latter, for which rye was sometimes substituted. Vetches were next in importance and then oats; and some peas and buckwheat were also grown. Barley, wheat and rye were market crops. Buckwheat was partly for the poultry, especially for fatting turkeys, partly as a smothering crop, and partly as green manure. The farms had dairies with herds of up to a score or more of cows, and butter and cheese were made. The richest fields were in the broadlands, where there was a danger of the crops being over-rank. In the Halvergate marshes and the swampy margins of the broads were many fen grounds, defended against land and sea floods, but occasionally overflowed, and having a natural produce of reeds, sedge and coarse grasses. In summer

[1] Ibid. opp. 70, 75, 86–7; Marshall, op. cit. i, 8–9, 130; ii, 5 sqq.; E. Dept, 301; B.M., Add. 20745, f. 5 (p. 38); Northants. R.O., Mont. Nfk, box P, pt i, Ct R. Foxley c. Bawdswell 9 Apr. 31 Eliz.

[2] Ibid. 2 Oct. 27 Eliz., 20 Apr. 28 Eliz.; Ess. R.O., D/DL M81, Ct Bk 1, ff. 55, 91v.; P.R.O., Chanc. Proc. ser. i Jas I, B. 13/47, compl.; B.M., Add. R. 26569, 26573-4, 26576; Ch. 14054; Corbett, art. cit. opp. 70, 83–4.

[3] Ibid. opp. 70, 70–1, 83–4; Spratt, op. cit. 55, 243; Allison, op. cit. 64, 238 sqq.; B.M., Add. 20745, ff. 1 (pp. 30) sqq.; R. 26569, St Matt. 10 Eliz.; 26572-3; Ch. 14054; Stowe 775, ff. 32v. sqq.; P.R.O., Chanc. Proc. ser. i Jas I, B. 33/30; C. 6/24, compl. & ans.; Ess. R.O., D/DL M81, Ct Bk 1, p. 7, ff. 42v., 57, 63, 81, 83, 90, 97–8, 109v.–10, 118v., 133v.; Northants. R.O., Mont. Nfk, box P, pt ii, Ct R. Foxley c. Bawdswell: rental demesnes temp. Sir Ed. Coke, partic. 1566; & v. sup. 75.

these fens were used for mowing and for fatting cattle. Beasts reared on farms near the fens or bought in from other parts of the country were fattened in considerable numbers and a score of feeding bullocks was no unusual sight in the summer. Reeds were also cut for thatching and turves dug for fuel which, in localities with heaths or heathlets, was supplied by whin and gorse. Horses were used for team and plough, two or three in tillage according to soil and seasonal requirement. Near some heaths were large breeding flocks, but otherwise not many sheep were stocked and some farmers had none at all. The chief sources of dung were the horses, dairy herds and feeders.[1]

THE WOODLAND

South-west of High Suffolk was a well-wooded country of strong wheatland. The prevailing soil was a marl that owed its calcareosity partly to assiduous chalking. It was stiff and productive, but never highly retentive or intractable even when standing on a clay bottom. The soils were eminently suited to cereals, above all to wheat, and so was the climate, with its hot summers, hard winters and moderate rainfall. In the eastern counties generally, the farmer could rely on harvesting a longer sequence of favourable grain crops than anywhere else; and this climate was combined with soils eminently suited to wheat, which was thus almost the natural product.

Some commonable lands survived in the sixteenth and seventeenth centuries, but only as exceptional remnants in course of abolition by the piecemeal enclosure of common-field parcels and the division of commons by general agreement, for the rest had been enclosed largely from the wood-pasture state.[2] Wet meadows and a few marshes apart, the closes were mostly appropriated to arable in a convertible system, and for this purpose were grouped or divided into shift fields.[3] There was no

[1] Marshall, *Nfk* i, 126, 210–11, 253–4, 319–20, 375–6; ii, 190–2; Folkingham, op. cit. 26; Worlidge, op. cit. 37; Norden, *Nfk*, 67; W. Dugdale, *Hist. Imbanking & Drayning* 1662, p. 297; H. Hall, *Soc. in Eliz. Age* 1887, p. 158; *Nfk Archaeol.* v, 332 sqq.; Gerarde, op. cit. 82, 1030; B.M., Add. R. 17750, 26569, 26573–4, 26576; P.R.O., St. Ch. Jas 3/33, compl.; Nfk R.O., Cons. & A/d cts invs.; Stat. 7 Jas c. 20; Spratt, op. cit. 204.

[2] Ibid. 49–50; P.R.O., Exch. L.R., M.B. 215, f. 1; A.O., Parl. Svys Ess. 15, ff. 2, 4; B.M., Add. 40063, ff. 54 sqq., 92 sqq., 100 sqq., 109 (1) sqq.; 40064, f. 18v.; R. 32901; Sloane 3664, ff. 1 (135) sqq.; Hall, op. cit. 30 sqq., 40–1.

[3] Ibid. 56, 71–2, 92; W. R. Emerson, 'Econ. Develpmt Estes Petre Fam. in Ess. in 16th & 17th cents.', ts. thesis D.Phil. Oxon. 1951, pp. 262, 264 sqq.; Gerarde, op. cit. 1034; B.M., Sloane 3664, ff. 1 (135) sqq.; P.R.O., Exch. L.R., M.B. 203, ff. 299 sqq.; 215, f. 1; Wds, Feodaries' Svys. Ess. bdl. 30 pt ii no 403; E. Sfk R.O., H.A. 12/C9/9, p. 26; Ess. R.O., D/DFa T48/22; D/DPl. 9; D/DP E25, ff. 59v., 61v., 105; E26, ff. 1–2, 18–21, 84; M186, esp. ff. 23, 25 sqq., 33, 49, 51–2, 54; M549, ff. 123;

regular field-course or crop rotation, but grasslands were often broken up in spring by a single ploughing for oats sown on the inverted turf. After these the land might be fallowed, twifallowed and trifallowed, mucked with farmyard manure and sown to wheat, or sometimes to rye or maslin. Next year barley, peas, tares, oats, or a dredge ('bullimong') of any two of them, was sown as an etch crop on a single ploughing of the stubble. Then the land was usually given a whole year's bare fallow as before, in preparation for winter corn. Subsequently there might be another crop on the stubble or a bare fallow preceding a final crop of wheat, but then the land was laid to grass. Lease covenants did not attempt to control successions, but contented themselves with ensuring that the farmers neither ploughed the heart out of the land towards the expiry of their terms nor took more than a certain number of straw crops without a summer fallow. Sometimes two successive straw crops were forbidden, sometimes only four, mostly usually three, according to the strength of the soil. Most land thus had a summer fallow every third year. Since wheat was the crop most desired, great emphasis was placed on thorough fallowing and clean tilths. Sometimes, indeed, even barley was preceded by summer fallow stirrings. After about half a dozen years of tillage in this style, the land was laid in broad, flat, plain ridges for grass, either simply by leaving things to Nature, or by sowing indigenous seeds, mostly perennial rye-grass, meadow grasses and white or perennial red clover. These leys were regarded more for their improving effect on the subsequent tillage than for their own produce and were generally left down three or four years or as long as deemed necessary to perfect soil structure. In this way more than half the arable was in tillage and the remainder being prepared for the plough; and as most farmland was arable, about half the country was tilled at a time. Excellent long leys could have been formed and left down for a greater duration, but here the chief object was wheat. It was sown about twice as much as barley, and the consumption crops—oats, peas, tares and 'bullimong'—were even smaller.[1]

Most farms had at least domestic dairies and some herds of up to a dozen, or occasionally a score, making both cheese and butter; but

[1] Ibid. ff. 6, 108, 111–12; Marshall, op. cit. 429, 436; Griggs, op. cit. 8, 10, 16, 22; Reyce, op. cit. 30; F. W. Steer, *Fm & Cottage Invs. Mid-Ess. 1635–1749* 1950, pp. 52–3, 74 sqq., 82 sqq., 93–4, 96–7, 100–2, 104 sqq., 112–15, 130, 134, 157, 164, 169, 194, 199; W. J. Ashley, *Bread of our Forefathers* 1928, pp. 49–50; invs.:—Nfk R.O., Cons. Ct; E. Sfk R.O., A/d; W. Sfk R.O., Episc. Commy Ct Bury St Edm's.; P.R.O., Wds, Feodaries' Svys Ess. bdl. 30 pt i no 425; B.M., Add. R. 17751; Ess. R.O., D/DFa T48/22; D/DGE. 506; D/DPl. 9; D/DP E25, ff. 61v., 105; E26, ff. 14, 84v.–6; F240; D/DQs. 58/6; Emerson, op. cit. 265–6, 270; Hall, op. cit. 71–2, 92.

dairying was a secondary consideration. Not a few beeves were fatted on spring and summer grass or stall-fed on grain in winter. Some sheep and lambs were bought in to be grazed in summer, but were rarely more than thrice as numerous as the cattle. They were sometimes outnumbered by them and hardly equalled them in value. They kept the pastures conveniently short and added a little to farm income, but were of no great concern. Farmers gave more weight in their plans to cereals than to any kind of livestock (unless horses) and often had wheat and barley crops worth twice or thrice the combined value of all their dairy herds, feeding beasts, sheep and swine. Oxen, shod for the purpose, were occasionally used in cultivations, but plough-teams were usually composed of four, five or six punches, six being sufficient for the heaviest work. All year the horses had oats, peas, and 'bullimong', but in summer they also had ley grass at will, and in winter straw in plenty.[1]

THE MIDLAND PLAIN

The Midland Plain included many vales, such as those of Trent, Belvoir, York, Stockton, Rasen, and Aylesbury; also some hills, like the attenuated limestone range of the Cliff and the Heath alongside Ermine Street; but the country as a whole was in the nature of a disjointed, rolling plain.

In soils the greatest variety was displayed. Large tracts of sandy soil were found towards the north-west and north-east. The more central and southerly districts had some often calcareous gravels and gravel loams. Especially towards the west and north-west, a great deal of deep sandy loam ('redland') obtained. Many 'woodland' or 'whiteland' clay soils, and some strong, heavy clays, occurred. They were adhesive, retentive, and highly glossy when ploughed. Lastly, clay loam ('blackland') was widely distributed, and so was middle loam ('hen-mould'). Subsoils and bases showed hardly less variety. Some sandy loams had a subsoil of sand, some of gravel, some of red or blue clay or marl, and others of brick-earth. Some gravels and gravel loams had a bed of limestone and some of intermixtures of clay and sand. Most clays and clay loams stood on clay, but some on limestone. The thin, sandy soils gave rise to heath and were fit only for sheep-walks or shifting cultivations. Gravelly loams were better suited to rye or maslin than wheat, and to peas rather than beans. The gravels were warm, but infertile. The sandy loams,

[1] Ibid. 537, 545; P.R.O., Wds—as prev. n.; invs.—do; B.M., Harl. 127, ff. 17–18, 22–5, 33, 36v. (28–9, 37–40, 70, 8ov.); Add. 34682, ff. 1 sqq., 16 sqq., 22, 24, 55, 100; R. 17751, 65980; Beeleigh Abb. inv. Th. Wilson 1627 Bocking; Ess. R.O., T/B 65/1; D/DPr. 426; D/DP F240, F311; D/DQs. 58/6; Steer, op. cit. 52–5, 74 sqq., 82 sqq., 96–7, 101–2, 104 sqq., 112–15, 132, 148–9, 163; Reyce, op. cit. 26; Norden, Ess. 9.

being naturally warm and of middling fertility, gave good and safe feeding for sheep, but were inferior to clay loams in finishing off fat stock,
and produced their best crops only in the wettest years. Barley, rye
and peas all grew well in them, but not beans. The clay soils refused to
dry when wetted and when dry could not quickly be wetted. If ploughed
wet, they stuck fast like so much mortar. The clay loams were similarly
glutinous, but often remarkably fertile. Clays, heavy clays and clay
loams, properly cultivated, were good for most years. They were also
the 'fremmest' soils, i.e. they gave good pastures of fast-growing grass,
even in drier years; but in wetter ones were hardly safe for sheep. The
climature for crops varied greatly too. In the sandy loams towards the
west, it was as forward as in the Vale of London and a fortnight earlier
than in East Norfolk, but was much more backward on the clays. One
remarkable feature of the rainfall was that, although generally moderate
and suitable to cereal cultivation, it was considerably higher in July
and August than it was in East Anglia. This meant harvests were less
sure, while pastures rarely dried up in high summer, and were, on the
contrary, given a new lease of life.

At the outset of the early modern period and decreasingly thereafter,
the chief form of management, not only in the champion or 'fielden',
but also in the woodland or 'arden' parts, was common-field husbandry,
with its tillage 'lands', grassy leys or 'ley lands', and common pastures
and meadows.[1] In some less fertile soils, a two-field course was employed,
viz. (1) corn, (2) fallow, mostly bare, but part sown with a catch crop of
pulse and oats.[2] The best clay loams, as in the Vale of Belvoir, were often
in a four-field course of (1) fallow, (2) tilth field, for winter corn or
fallow barley, (3) breach field, for peas and beans, (4) breach field, for
barley or oats.[3] A three-field course, not as in the Chalk Country, but a
distinctly characteristic plain-country course of (1) tilth, (2) breach,
(3) fallow, was, however, the one most frequently met. Each shift in
turn was first sown in a fine tilth, after summer fallow stirrings, and
then, with no thorough working or regular tilth, a breach or etch crop
was harrowed into the rough clods. The tilth field was suitable to, and
reserved for, wheat, rye, maslin, bigg, and fallow spring barley; the
breach field was sown with peas, beans, oats, or feed barley, often called
'brush' barley, because grown on an old stubble. After this, the field
was bare fallowed and then brought once again to a fine tilth. This was

[1] e.g. Marshall, *Midl. Cos.* ii, 225; *E. Dept*, 47–8; *Midl. Dept*, 15, 168, 284, 291;
294, 399, 423, 521–2.

[2] D. M. Barratt, *Eccl. Terriers War. Pars.* Dugdale S. 1955 xxii, 144 sqq.; War.
R.O., M.R. 14; P.R.O., Chanc. Proc. ser. i Jas I, S.29/7, m. 2; Marshall, op. cit.
452; *E. Dept*, 47–8.

[3] Ibid.; *Midl. Dept*, 169, 452; Shak. Bpl. Throckmorton: Ct R. Coughton 13 Oct.
1615, 16 Oct. 1654, 9 Oct. 1662, 23 Oct. 1689, 28 Oct. 1731; P.R.O., Exch. L.R.,
M.B. 231, m. 27d.; Lennard, art. cit. 42; Wedge, op. cit. 15; Plot, *Oxon.* 240.

prepared by twice or thrice gathering the ridges, that the corn might be safe from winter rains, and the wheat or rye was then usually sown under furrow and ploughed in.[1] If the tilth field were too lean for wheat, rye or maslin was grown, and in lighter soils peas were preferred to beans.[2] The cultivators chose what crops they pleased in the tilth and breach fields and could, if they wished, sow both to barley or grow, say, hemp in the breach field.[3] In the tilth field, that part sown to wheat in one year would, when the course came round, be under barley, while oats, peas, barley and beans might be similarly alternated in the breach field. The acreages under these different crops were not necessarily either equal or constant, but the general upshot was in the nature of a sexennial crop rotation of, say, (1) wheat, (2) barley, (3) fallow, (4) barley, (5) peas, (6) fallow.[4] Moreover, in many fields a catch or hitch crop of pulse, usually peas, vetches or lentils, was taken on part of the summer fallow,[5] and small parts were often sown to garden peas as a gathering hitch, for the relief of the poor, on condition they did not pick elsewhere.[6] Two and four-field courses were mere variations on this three-field theme. In the former, the breach field was omitted, and in the latter doubled.

This same inflexible, uniform, three-field course of (1) tilth, (2) breach, (3) fallow, with harmful cross-cropping prevented by manorial courts and lease covenants, may be seen throughout the length and breadth of the plain; in court rolls, manorial surveys and estate documents, by the seasons—'white corn' (tilth), breach ('broke'), fallow

[1] Ibid. 239–40; *Staffs.* 340–1; Lisle, op. cit. 324; W. Ellis, *Mod. Husbandman* 1740 i, 48; ii, 49–50; Marshall, *Midl. Cos.* ii, 225, 227; *E. Dept.* 47–8; *Midl. Dept,* 168–9, 225, 401, 409, 503, 560; Brown, op. cit. iii, 41–3; Purvis, *Causes in Tithe,* 39; Lennard, loc. cit.; Seebohm, op. cit. 11; W. E. Tate, *Par. Chest* 1951, p. 255; Leics. R.O., A/d invs.:—1709:57; 1710:102; Ellen Kilburn 1706 Sileby; Ric. Lowe 1716 Sapcote; Jn Gervis 1730 Hose; Jn Shelton 1773 Syston; Fitzherbert, *Husbandrie,* ff. 6–8; Pitt, *Northants.* 76, 298; *Leics.* 71; Tuke, *Gen. View Ag. N.R. Yks.* 1794, p. 32; T. Stone, *id. Co. Lincoln* 1794, p. 54; *id. Huntingdon* 1793, p. 9; *Beds.* 14; Vancouver, *Cams.* 11–2, 102, 109; Wedge, loc. cit.; James & Malcolm, *Bucks.* 21; Mavor, op. cit. 167 sqq.; Crutchley, op. cit. 8–9.

[2] Ibid. 9; Plot, op. cit. 341; *Oxon.* 240; Mastin, op. cit. 15; P.R.O., Ct R. G.S. 195/79, m. 6; Shak. Bpl. Leigh: Ct R. Stoneleigh 15 Apr. 1574, 30 Sept. 1686, 6 Oct. 1692, 5 Oct. 1693; Hood: Ct R. Wolvey 23 Oct. 1594; War. R.O., M.R. 16/9; Northants. R.O., F.(M.)Misc. 222; Leics. R.O., A/d invs.:—1708:43, 1710:85.

[3] Ibid. 1618:202; 1664:117; Emmison, op. cit. 92–3; & v. inf. 95.

[4] Marshall, op. cit. 401; Fitzherbert, op. cit. f. 11 (recte 9); Stone, loc. cit.; *Hunts.* 9; Vancouver, op. cit. 12.

[5] Emmison, op. cit. 140; Berks. R.O., D/EP2 E2/2; B.M., Add. R. 44654; Shak. Bpl. Ct R. Whitchurch; Throckmorton: Ct R. Upton in Haselor; Ches. R.O., Vernon (Warren) Ct R. 5, 7, 9, 11, 13; Northants. R.O., XYZ: Ct R. Greatworth; Pitt, *Northants.* 64; Plot, *Staffs.* 347.

[6] Ibid. 204; P.R.O., Ct R. G.S. 194/55; Ches. R.O., Vernon (Warren) Ct R. 1; Northants. R.O., Mont. Northants. 18/160 ct ords. Barnwell; 7/66/5, 6 ct files & bk Weekley; 7/72 Ct R. id.

(summer) field—or by the names of the chief crops used to designate the shifts and all that grew in them;[1] and in inventories and accounts, from the crop proportions and groupings.[2] At Little Oakley in 1776, tithes taken from 220 acres of common-field tillage, of which 73 were fallowed, were from 37 acres of wheat, 37 of barley and 73 of beans.[3] An outstanding feature of common-field husbandry was its combination

[1] Ibid. 18/160; War. 6/14; box P, pt 2, X. 890; Misc. Led. 132; 145, pp. 70, 98–9, 183–4; Higham Ferrers Burg. R. fd ords. 1696–1725; I.(L.) 128; Wmld 5. v. 1; F.(M.) Misc. 222; Mastin, op. cit. 15–16; C. S. & C. S. Orwin, *Open Fds* 1938, pp. 47, 161, 163, 165, 173, 176, 180; Gray, op. cit. 76; T. Cave & R. A. Wilson, *Parl. Svy Lands & Possons Dean & Chap. Wigorn.* Worcs. Hist. Soc. 1924, p. 9; J. H. Blundell, *Toddington* 1925, p. 65; F. E. Hyde & S. F. Markham, *Hist. Stony Stratford* 1948, pp. 40, 80; S. P. Potter, *Hist. Wymeswold* 1915, p. 91; T. Lawson-Tancred, '3 17th-cent. Ct R. Manor Aldborough', *Yks. Archaeol. Jnl* xxxv, 201–2; *Recs. Yks. Manor* 1937, p. 96; J. Charlesworth, *Wakefield Manor Bk* Yks. Archaeol. Soc. Rec. Ser. 1939 ci, 89 sqq.; J. W. Clay, op. cit. i, 183–4; N. R. R.O., Z.A.L. ct files Snape & Well; Z.Q. 1; Beds. R.O., L. 26/280–1; O.R. 804; H.A. 5/1, ff. 2 (1) v., 34v.; T.W. 10/2/9; B'ham Lib. 167917, 344742; B.M., Add. 36908, ff. 9, 14v., 80v.; R. 37391; Bucks. Mus. Ct R. Quainton 1–3; Long Crendon 10/48; Weston Turville 38–9/51; Cams. R.O., L. 1/8, 112; L. 19/17, 20; L. 88/4; Shak. Bpl. Leigh: ct files Stoneleigh; Throckmorton: Ct R. Oversley, Upton in Haselor; Hood: Brinklow c. membris, pains c. 1558; W. de B. 1393a, 1654; Leicester Mus. 44/28/902; Deene ho. Brudenell I. v. 61; O. viii. 8; O. xxiv. 1; Ches. R.O., Vernon (Warren) Ct R. 1, 3, 4, 7–9, 11–4; Bucks. R.O., Swanbourne agrt 7 Nov. 22 Geo. II; acq. 35/39 fd byelaws & regs. Padbury 1779; Cartwright Hall, Swinton: svy Monks Kirby 1611; Staffs. R.O., D. 260, 3 (a); Salt Lib. Ct R. Shenstone; H. M. (Chetwynd): Ct R. Ingestre; Leics. R.O., D.E. 10 ct files Barrow-on-Soar; Leire agrt 1689; D.E. 41/1/30.2; A/d invs.:—1660 small: 72; 1708:43; 1693 V.G.:11; 1710:85 & Wm Carter/Leire.

[2] Ibid. 1599:18, 53; 1602:7, 143; 1608:112; 1614:33, 45, 177; 1618:202; 1627:16, 56, 140; 1628:108; 1633:93; 1636:73–4, 132; 1637:159; 1638:144, 238; 1639:16, 79, 125; 1649:21, 63; 1660 gt:318; 1665:75; 1669:14, 207, 216; 1693 V.G.:11; 1705:13; 1706:28 & Ellen Kilburn/Sileby; 1709:53, 81, 88, 115; early 16th-cent.: 8, 14, 65, 105, 128, 143, 154; mid-16th-cent.:14, 22, 51, 59, 71, 93, 100, 102; 18th-cent.: Ric. Marshall 1728 Barkstone, Jn Seagrave 1729 Frisby-on-the-Wreake; Rothley & Evington Commy cts. 1, 13, 15, 17, 23, Hy Wats 1613; invs. Worcs., Northants. & Lichfield Jt R.O.s, & Leeds Lib. & York, as listed App. A; B'ham Lib. 277414, 350221; Herts. R.O., 8435, 8442; B.M., Add. 29609A; 26582, ff. 11, 24, 37, 63–4, 72, 75–7, 85, 92–3, 109, 112, 128; Emmison, op. cit. 56–7, 68–71, 92–3, 97–8, 127, 143; Farnham, op. cit. 200; C. E. Freeman, 'Eliz. Invs.', in *Harrold Priory &c.* Pubns. Beds. Hist. Rec. Soc. 1952 xxxii, 104–5; P. A. Kennedy, *Notts. Household Invs.* Thoroton S. Rec. Ser. 1963 xxii, 26–8, 32–5, 39, 46–9, 77–9, 97–101, 114–6; Havinden, op. cit. 42 sqq.; 49–51, 56–7, 75–7, 90–1, 107–8, 170–1, 173–6, 189–90, 223–6, 228–31, 281; G. E. Kirk, 'Wills, invs. & bds manor cts Temple Newsam 1612–1701', in *Miscellanea* Thoresby S. 1935 xxxiii, 248–9, 257–8, 262–3; *Wills & Invs. N. Cos.* pt i Surtees S. 1835, pp. 156–9, 198–9, 240; *Wills & Invs. fr. Reg. at Durh.* pt ii id. 1860 xxxviii, 77–9, 168–70; pt iii id. 1906 cxii, 136–8, 166–7, 176–7, 184–5; pt iv id. 1929 cxlii, 94; J. Raine, *Wills & Invs. fr. Reg. A/d Richmond* id. 1853 xxvi, 41–2, 57, 161–4; *Wills & Admins. fr. Knaresborough Ct R.* ii id. 1905 cx, 215–17, 246–7; W. E. Preston, *Wills proved in Ct Manor Crosley, Bingley, Cottingley & Pudsey* Bradford Hist. & Ant. Soc. Local Rec. Ser. 1929 i, 109 sqq.

[3] Northants. R.O., Mont. Northants. 16/9.

of inflexibility of field-course with maximum freedom in cropping. The cultivator's liberty to choose what crops he liked in the corn field of a two-field course or in the tilth and breach fields of the Midland three-field course was nothing new and did not indicate that common-field husbandry was progressing or becoming more flexible or adaptable.[1] Wheat, rye and maslin were often sown less than barley, peas, oats and beans; but nothing indicates that the ratio of winter to spring corn in common fields (1:5) appreciably widened in the course of the early modern period.[2] What is significant is less the preponderance of barley over wheat, but that what appears at first sight to be one barley crop, was two distinct crops of fallow and brush barley, which differed in cultivation, quality, purpose, and probably strain. The predominance of spring crops was no inconvenience to the farmer; and even if it had been, he could not have eased matters by sowing crops in mid-winter.[3] In summer the fallow field was stirred and prepared for the tilth, part of which was sown in autumn and the remainder left bare until spring. Peas and beans were cultivated by slitting down the old wheat ridges in winter, ploughing upward in February and sowing as soon as the season would permit, usually in March or early April and never before the middle of February.[4] After his pulse, the farmer had only barley and

---

[1] Pace W. G. Hoskins, *Midl. Peasant* 1957, p. 154; 'Leics. Farmer in 17th cent.', *Ag. Hist.* xxv, 11, 13.

[2] Farnham, loc. cit.; Camden, op. cit. i, 335; Fiennes, op. cit. 73; Emmison, op. cit. 50, 56–7, 60–3, 68–9, 79–80, 92–3, 97–8, 108–10, 117–18, 120–1, 131–3, 137–8, 143; Freeman, art. cit. 60, 104–5; Havinden, loc. cit.; Kennedy, op. cit. 26–8, 32–5, 39, 43–4, 46 sqq., 63–5, 77–9, 97–101, 114–16; W. Cunningham, *Growth Eng. Ind. & Comm.* 1907 iii, 899; B.M., Add. 29609A; B'ham Lib. 277414, 350221; Beds. R.O., ABP/W: 1605:126; 1614:172; 1641:141; G.A. 1732; Herts. R.O., 8435, 8442; invs. Worcs., Northants. & Lichfield Jt R.O.s, & Leeds Lib. & York, as listed App. A; Leics. R.O., A/d invs.:—1602:55, 126, 143; 1608:112; 1614:2, 33, 45, 177; 1616:6; 1618:26, 202; 1627:16, 19, 56, 140; 1628:57, 108; 1631:125; 1632:60; 1633:93; 1636:73–4, 132; 1637:23, 159; 1638:144, 238; 1639:79, 125, 131; 1642–3:19; 1649:21, 32, 63; 1660 gt: 56, 165, 318; 1669:14, 35, 45, 207, 216; 1693 VG:11; 1703:21; 1706: Kilburn ut sup.; 1709:53, 81, 88, 113, 115; 1710:1, 85 & Th. Crane/Gt Dalby; early 16th-cent.: 8, 14, 36, 105, 126, 128, 143, 154–5; mid-16th-cent.: 4, 18, 18A, 22, 51, 59, 71, 78A, 93, 96, 100, 102–3; 18th-cent.: Geo. Fisher 1726 Barrow-on-Soar, Jn Shelton 1773 Syston, Seagrave & Marshall—ut sup.; Rothley & Evington Commy cts. 1, 15, 17 & Hy Wats 1613. Pace Hoskins, art. cit. 12–15; *Essays in Leics. Hist.* 1950, pp. 160–2, 167 sqq.

[3] Pace Hoskins, art. cit. 11; *Midl. Peasant*, 155; & J. Thirsk in *V.C.H. Leics.* ii, 212.

[4] B'ham Lib. 277414; B.M., Add. 29609A; Leics. R.O., A/d invs.:—1608: 112; 1614:33; 1618:202, 1626:141; 1627:140; 1628:79, 108; 1631:125; 1636:23; 1649:63; 1669:35; 1708:1, 1710:57 & Robt Kirkeman/Hemington; mid-16th-cent.: 4, 14, 102–3; 18th-cent.: Jas Crossland 1715 Gt Appleby, Th. Towers 1756 Bottesford, Marshall, Seagrave & Shelton—ut sup.; Rothley & Evington Commy cts. 15; Freeman, art. cit. 104–5; Emmison, op. cit. 50, 60–1, 63–4, 68–71, 79–80, 86–7, 92–3, 97–8, 110, 137–40; Ellis, op. cit. i, 48; Laurence, op. cit. 102; Plot, op. cit. 340; Fitzherbert, op. cit. ff. 6, 8; Lisle, op. cit. 162; Marshall, *Midl. Cos.* ii, 227.

oats to sow. Much the greatest labour load fell in summer and early autumn, when a tilth was being prepared for wheat and barley on four or five ploughings,[1] and whether sowing was in autumn or spring was, in this respect, a matter of indifference. The preference for spring corn was not due to any disintegration of the common fields. Laying more land to grass did not increase the proportions of spring crops, for this affected the whole cycle of the field-course:[2] and neither did any break-down of control, for there is clear evidence that common-field courses continued to be precisely and rigidly regulated right up into the eighteenth century.[3] A free choice of crops within an inflexible field-course rigor-ously enforced—this was the rule in the common fields.

The common-field lands supported cows for the pail, horses for the plough and sheep for the fold, common rights being stinted by the yard-land, the oxgang, and other similar units of assessment. Sheep com-mons were stinted at rates equivalent to between 1,000 and 3,000 to a township.[4] Many homebred sheep were kept in the fields, but in the general absence of a native breed of folding sheep, reinforcements had constantly to be recruited either from local breeding flocks, especially in Cannock Chase, the Lincolnshire Heath and similar districts, or from the Cotswold, Northwold, and Chalk countries. Wethers were usually bought, except in the north-west, where in-lamb ewes were imported from about the Wrekin and Cannock Chase, the surplus lambs being sold back to the same dealers for fatting in the Cheshire Cheese Country. At the end of the summer folding season the sheep might either be over-wintered for a further year's work, or have a little flesh thrown on them for domestic and local consumption, or be sold to graziers to be fatted in enclosures.[5] Corn-growing was the common-field farmers' chief concern and they only stocked sheep and horses for the tillage and

[1] Ibid.; Lisle, op. cit. 42–3.

[2] Pace Hoskins, art. cit. 14.

[3] P.R.O., D.L., Ct R. 106/1529, 1532, 1534–5; Leics. R.O., D.E. 10 Ct R.; D.E. 40/40; B'ham Lib. 167919, 168125; Bucks. Mus. Ct R. Quainton, r. 3; War. R.O., M.R. 16/9; Beds. R.O., X. 69/6; O.R. 816; Northants. R.O., Misc. Led. 129, 132, 145; Higham Ferrers Burg. R. fd ords. 1696–1725; Mont. War. 6/14; box P, pt. 2, X. 890; Grafton 3422; Shak. Bpl. Leigh: Ct R. Stoneleigh; ct files Whitchurch; Throckmorton: Ct R. Upton in Haselor, Coughton, Oversley; Hood: Ct R. Brink-low, Stivichall; W. de B. 1393a; Trevelyan: Ct R. Snitterfield; Potter, op. cit, 89–92; Mastin, op. cit. 15–16.

[4] Ibid. 17; Blundell, op. cit. 64; Hyde & Markham, op. cit. 38, 42; J. E. Stocks, *Mkt. Harborough Par. Recs. 1531–1837* 1926, p. 318; P.R.O., R.&S. G.S. 13/20; C. R. G.S. 195/78, m. 3v.; D.L., M.B. 117, f. 99; Exch. L.R., M.B. 189, f. 13; Beds. R.O., T.W. 10/2/9; Shak. Bpl. Hood: Ct R. Binley; Leigh: Ct R. Stoneleigh, 'Custumes of the Manor of Stoneley'; Ches. R.O., Vernon (Warren) Ct R. 3, 4, 6, 8, 9; Pitt, *Leics.* 72; *Northants.* 67.

[5] Ibid. 128; G. Eland, *Purefoy Letters 1735–53* 1931 i, 162; Bodl. Aubrey 2, f. 148; Barratt, op. cit. i, 7; Marshall, op. cit. i, 376; *Midl. Dept,* 327.

cows for local dairy supplies. Oxen were employed less than horses, and ploughing was done mostly with a string of between three and six shire horses. Eight horses were needed for the heaviest fallowings, but four, five or six sufficed for most purposes even in strong clays. Where oxen were used for ploughing, they were usually yoked in two pairs and led by a single horse.[1] Strong teams were necessitated by the stubbornness of many of the soils and by the great weight of the plain-country swing plough.[2] Most common-field farms had domestic dairies and some up to a score of milkers. As more land was laid to grass, dairy herds tended to increase, for the satisfaction of local demand in the countryside, market towns and growing industrial centres; but dairy farming never developed on a great scale in common-field farms. Towards the north and west, cheese was more important, and towards the south and east butter; but neither ever contributed greatly to the national supply. In the more easterly parts the dairy was somewhat restricted and common-field farmers took rather to fattening a few beasts on their ley lands. Many farmers fattened a few lambs and sheep for themselves and also some calves, steers, bullocks and dry cows, but all could equally well be sold

[1] Ibid. 209, 403, 422–3, 453, 595, 634–5, 637; *Midl. Cos.* i, 133–5; R. Lowe, *Gen. View Ag. Co. Nottm* 1798, p. 130; Pitt, *Leics.* 53, 215, 217; *Staffs.* 102; Parkinson, *Hunts.* 95 sqq.; Tuke, op. cit. 33–4, 61; T. Burton, *Hist. & Ant. Hemingborough* 1888, p. 362; Purvis, art. cit. 453–4; Clay, op. cit. i, 183–4; ii, 21–2, 25–7, 35–6, 41–2, 47, 75–6; *V.C.H. Beds.* ii, 99–100; M. Bloxsom, *Hist. Par. Gilmorton* 1918, pp. 26–7; Hall, op. cit. 157; Colman, op. cit. 216 sqq.; Kirk, loc. cit.; Preston, loc. cit.; *Wills & Invs.* pt i, 156–9, 186–7, 198–9, 205–8, 211–13, 240, 270–1, 428; pt ii, 77–9, 168–70; pt iii, 2–3, 52–3, 122–3, 126–7, 130–1, 136 sqq., 166–7, 176–7, 184–5; *Wills & Admins. Knaresborough* i Surtees S. 1902 civ. 45–6, 148 sqq.; ii, 215–17, 234–5, 246–7; Raine, op. cit. 41–4, 57, 60–1, 88, 161–4, 229–31; Farnham, op. cit. 200, 274–5; Austin, op. cit. ii, 312–14; Havinden, op. cit. 41 sqq.; 56–7, 61, 69 sqq., 79–80, 83–4, 89 sqq., 96 sqq., 115–16, 123–4, 138–9, 148–9, 167 sqq., 187 sqq., 201 sqq., 216 sqq., 223 sqq., 239–42, 248–9, 251–4, 256–9, 269–70, 274 sqq., 281 sqq., 297–300, 307–10; Emmison, op. cit. 50, 54–5, 60, 63–6, 68–70, 72–3, 78–9, 80–3, 86 sqq., 108–9, 114–15, 124, 126, 131–2, 134; Kennedy, op. cit. 6–9, 12–16, 19–20, 24 sqq., 30 sqq., 39, 42 sqq., 56 sqq., 71 sqq., 92 sqq., 114 sqq., 122 sqq.; Freeman, loc. cit.; *Beds. N.&Q.* iii, 252–4, 276–8; *Trans. Salop. Archaeol. & Nat. Hist. Soc.* 1906 vi, 212–15; B.M., Add. 36582, ff. 11, 24, 37, 63–4, 72, 75–7, 85, 92–3, 96, 109, 112, 118; Ch. 54117; R. 49323; P.R.O., Exch. A.O., Parl. Svys Beds. 20, f. 5; St. Ch. Jas 159/16, m. 4; Worcs. R.O., B.A. 824 no 25; B.A. 1176 invs. Th. More 1686 Wootton Wawen, Ed. Hopkins 1681 Budbrook; B'ham Lib. 252320, 281291–2, 335817, 350196–7, 350203, 351983; Bournville Vil. Trust 14; Elford Hall 294; Northants. R.O., F–H 991, 2431–2; I.(L.) 508, 769; F.(M.) Misc. 897; W.(S.) 11/46; L. B. 46; Beds. R.O., A.B.P./W. 1607: 98; 1614: 172; 1616: 78; 1617: 224; G.A. 1732; P.A. 180–1; Herts. R.O., 8435, 8442; Shak. Bpl. W.deB. 898, 1024a, 1651, 1654 'Laings forth in the yeare 1636'; Stratford: Wills & Invs. 22, 59; Leigh: inv. Hy Chambers 1735 Langley; & invs. listed in App. A.

[2] Marshall, op. cit. i, 138; Plot, *Oxon.* 247; Blith, op. cit. 198, 201, 210–13; Crutchley, op. cit. 9; G. Maxwell, *Gen. View Ag. Co. Huntingdon* 1793, p. 18; Pitt, *Northants.* 72.

D

to graziers.[1] For fodder, common-field farmers relied greatly on tillage crops. Horses were not often given oats, but peas, beans, pea straw, tares and tare hay, and wheat and barley chaff. Peas and barley-meal helped to fatten a few sheep, cattle and swine. Other beasts lived through the winter largely on straw. Wheat, rye and maslin were for bread corn and even gentle households consumed some barley bread, which was the poor's staple food. Peas and beans were also used for bread sometimes. Brush barley was mostly destined for stock-feed, but fallow barley provided both bread and drink.[2]

The townships had common meadows and there were wide stretches of rich grass by the larger rivers, especially the Dove, where farmers could agist their horses.[3] Of rough grazing there was a considerable, but unevenly dispersed, area. Some townships had little or none,[4] while others had large heathlands, wolds and hills for sheep-walks and stinted pastures.[5] There were also some greens and 'plains', i.e. land that had

[1] Ibid. 36, 197; Marshall, *E. Dept*, 61; *Midl. Dept*, 208–9, 231, 504–5; Plot, *Staffs.* 108–9; Lowe, op. cit. 29, 42, 44; J. Farey, *Gen. View Ag. & Minerals Derbs.* 1811–17 iii, 30; J. L. & B. Hammond, op. cit. i, 32; *V.C.H. Cams.* ii, 75; *Beds.* ii, 99–100; *Trans. Salop. Archaeol. & Nat. Hist. Soc.* loc. cit.; Freeman, loc. cit.; Austin, loc. cit.; Bloxsom, op. cit. 24–7, 39–41; Farnham, op. cit. 427; T. W. Dowling, *Recs. Knowle* 1914, pp. 377–8; J. W. Ryland, *Recs. Rowington* 87–9; Worcs. R.O., B.A. 824 no 25; B.A. 1176 invs. ut sup.; Herts. R.O., 8435; B'ham Lib. 252320, 261547, 277414, 335817, 350197, 350252; P.R.O., St. Ch. Jas. 106/20, m. 3; Berks. R.O., D/EP2 E2/2; B.M., Add. 29609A; Ch. 54117, 54127; Northants. R.O., L. B. 46; Beds. R.O., A.B.P./W. 1612: 226; 1624: 172; 1616: 54, 78; 1617: 224; 1641: 192; G.A. 1732; Shak. Bpl. Stratford: Wills & Invs. 22, 59; W.deB. 1654 'Laings forth in the yeare 1636'; invs. listed App. A; Kennedy, op. cit. 40–1, 97–8, 120–1; Emmison, op. cit. 56–7, 60, 63–6, 68–9, 83, 86 sqq., 97–8, 108–9, 112, 117–18, 120–1, 124, 126–7, 131–2, 135–6.
[2] Ibid. 140; Marshall, op. cit. 226, 603; Morton, op. cit. 16, 480; Ellis, *Sheep*, 216; Lisle, op. cit. 222, 351; Pitt, op. cit. 93–4, 96; *Leics.* 108–9, 114–15, 126; J. Donaldson, *Gen. View Ag. Co. Northampton* 1794, p. 16; Potter, op. cit. 92; E. of Cardigan, 'Dom. Exes Nobleman's Household', in *Harrold Priory &c.* Pubns Beds. Hist. Rec. Soc. 1952 xxxii, 112–13, 120–1; G. Markham, *Eng. Husbandman* 1635, p. 66; J. Lee, *Vindication Regulated Inclo.* 1656, p. 22; J. Moore, *Crying Sin of Engl.* 1653, p. 9; *Scripture-word agst Inclo.* 1656, p. 7; Shak. Bpl. Stratford: Wills & Invs. 22; Berks. R.O., D/EP2 E2/2; P.R.O., Exch. K.R., Deps. by Commn 8 Chas East. 19; Northants. R.O., Aynho Ct R.; F-H 3712A; Mont. Northants. 18/160; Leics. R.O., A/d invs.:— 1599; 40; 1602: 7, 55; 1636: 49; 1668 A/d 49.
[3] P. Kynder, 'Historie Darbs.', *Reliquary* xxii, 119; C. Leigh, *Nat. Hist. Lancs., Ches. & Peak in Derbs.* 1700 bk i, 23.
[4] P.R.O., Exch. K.R., M.B. 41, f. 41v.; L.R., M.B. 185, f. 68v.; D.L., M.B. 109, f. 54.
[5] Morton, op. cit. 9, 14, 42; Lowe, op. cit. 44; Pitt, *Northants.* 164; Anon. 'Descron Weston', *Gent's. Mag.* xxxiii, 446; Marshall, *Midl. Cos.* i, 3; 'Chanc. Proc. temp. Eliz.', *Colls. Hist. Staffs.* 1926, pp. 90–2; 'Eliz. Chanc. Proc. ser. ii: 1558–79', ibid. 1931, pp. 186–7; 'St. Ch. Hy VIII & Ed. VI', ibid. 1912, pp. 36–9; 'Rowley Regis Rent R. 1556', ibid. 1936, p. 222; B'ham Lib. 378173; Beds. R.O., A.D. 2007–8; Northants-R.O., I.(L.) 29; F-H 272, ff. 69v., 73; Wmld 5. v. 1 Ct R. Tansor; Mont. Northants.

never been thrown into ridge and furrow, like Rockingham Plain.[1] Lastly, common woods and the numerous forests, such as Galtres, Knaresborough, Feckenham, Rockingham, Sapley, Charnwood, Barnwood, Needwood, Salcey, Leicester, Whittlewood and Leighfield, and several chases, provided rough grazing for the beasts and horses from neighbouring townships and common of escape for their sheep in inclement weather.[2] The area of such rough grazings was, however, declining, for, in the course of the early modern period, extensive clearances were made from forests, woodlands, heaths, wolds, and wastes.[3] Still further grassland was found in the balks ('greenfurrows') that bounded acres, parcels and furlongs in the fields themselves.[4]

18/160; Maps 1385, 1388, 1392; Misc. Led. 132; Shak. Bpl. W.deB. 1386; Throckmorton: Ct R. Sambourn; Leigh: Stoneleigh Ct R.; svy. 1597, p. [33]; Leics. R.O., A/d invs.:—1660 small: 125; 1708: 95; 1709: 11; Staffs. R.O., D. 260, iii (b) Walsall ct recog. & svy 15 Jas, f. 34; Salt Lib. H.M. (Chetwynd): Ct R. Ingestre & Salt; P.R.O., R. & S. G.S. roll 909; Ct R. G.S. 183/44; D.L., M.B. 113, f. 32; Exch. A.O., Parl. Svys Beds. 9, ff. 6, 14; 20. ff. 4–5; Oxon. 13, f. 4; Worcs. 7, ff. 5–6; L.R., M.B. 185, f. 79v.; 187, f. 271v.; 221, ff. 63 sqq. 320; 224, ff. 44 sqq.; 228, f. 4; 255, ff. 148, 150; K.R., M.B. 41, f. 35; Deps. by Commn 33–4 Eliz. Mich. 42; 3 Chas East. 1; 11 Chas II Trin. 9, mm. 2d–3.

[1] Ibid. 21–2 Eliz. Mich. 28; 29 Eliz. Trin. 5; 10 Jas East. 10; 10 Chas Mich. 11, arts. 3–4; Mich. 61, m. 2d.; Sp. Commn 5553, deps. mm. 2, 18; Ct R. G.S. 195/82, mm, 1, 3; Northants. R.O., F-H 3839; Deene ho. Brudenell A.S.R. 562, p. 16; Leics. R.O., D.E. 10 partic. Beaumanor 1594; Morton, op. cit. 11.

[2] Ibid. 10–12; Leonard, art. cit. 112; B.M., Add. 27534, f. 20; Leics. R.O., D.E. 10, Ct Bk 'Mr Robt Pilkington Stwd', f. 8; partic. Beaumanor 1594; Ct R. id.; A/d invs. 1632: 160; Worcs. R.O., B.A. 2358 no 86a; Shak. Bpl. Leigh: Ct R. Stoneleigh, Kenilworth; Northants. R.O., Wmld 4. xvi. 5; 5. v. 1 Ct R. Yarwell; 5. vi Ct R. Duddington; P.R.O., Exch. A.O., Parl. Svys Oxon. 13, f. 7; Yks. 15, f. 14; K.R., Deps. by Commn 17 Eliz. East. 1; 12 Chas East. 34, ex parte def.; 1650 East. 9; L.R., M.B. 193, mm. 72, 87–9 (4, 19–21); 201, f. 37; 221, f. 8; 229, ff. 2 sqq., 105 sqq.; 230, f. 44; D.L., M.B. 124, f. 121; Sp. Commn 679–80; Ct R. 81/1120; 82/1122; S.P.D. Jas vol. 191 no. 18; 194 no 3; Deene ho. Brudenell A.S.R. 562, pp. 16, 39.

[3] Ibid. 19; Blith, op. cit. 82; W. Burton, *Descron Leics.* 2; H. Stocks, *Recs. Bor. Leicester 1603–88*, 1923, pp. 239, 370; 'St. Ch. Hy VIII & Ed. VI' (1912), 169–70; B.M., Harl. 71, f. 6; Shak. Bpl. Leigh: Stoneleigh svy 1597, p. 14; Leics. R.O., A/d invs.:—1639: 85; 1641: 57, Northants. R.O., F-H, 1723, 2859, 3524; Mont. Northants. 18/160; P.R.O., Req. 106/60; Exch. A.O., Parl. Svys Beds. 9, f. 6; L.R., M.B. 222, f. 296; K.R., Sp. Commn 4684; Deps. by Commn 17 Eliz. East. 1; 33–4 Eliz. Mich. 42; 3 Chas East. 1; 6 Chas Mich. 12, art. 11; 11 Chas Trin. 9, mm. 1–3; Mich. 13, m. 1; 12 Chas East. 34, ex parte def.; 1650 East. 9; Morton, op. cit. 10–13.

[4] Ibid. 14; Corbett, art. cit. 72; Laurence, op. cit. 60; St J. Priest, *Gen. View Ag. Bucks.* 1813, pp. 131–4; W. Cooper, *Wootton Wawen* 1936, App.12; Marshall, *Midl. Cos.* ii, 225; my 'Reconson some form. Husbandry Practices', *Ag.HR* iii, 37–9; Lawson-Tancred, art. cit. 202; Colman, op. cit. 137; Ruston and Witney, op. cit. 59, 61; B.M., Add. 36584, f. 118; 36908, f. 3v.; R. 54166; Leics. R.O., Leire agrt 1689; War. R.O., M.R. 14, 16/9; Beds. R.O., B.S. 1276 Ct R. Tempsford; T.W. 10/2/9; B'ham Lib. 344742; Salt Lib. Ct R. Shenstone; H.M. (Chetwynd); Ct R. Ingestre

Quite apart from balks, the common fields were composed not merely of tillage ridges, provincially 'lands', but also of ridges that were left to sward over and called 'leys'. In addition, many headlands were laid down as 'headleys'. Ridges and headlands of permanent grass formed a marked, but not a distinctive feature of early modern Midland common fields.[1] Frequently whole ridges were laid to grass singly, but sometimes part of a ridge might be in tillage and part in grass, or all be in tillage except the end, which had been laid to grass; and often there were pieces, or even complete furlongs or fields of contiguous 'leys'. Such large blocks might be common sheep-walks, or meadows, in which the various lots could conveniently be distinguished by ridge and furrow; but more usually they were cow-pastures and were laid down for this purpose from the worst, exhausted or most distant parts of the tillage.[2] The 'leys' laid down individually were treated just the same as the balks, being fed first by the common herd and then by the sheep-flocks when the field was fallow or stubble, and mown for hay and tethered to horses when it was in corn.[3] It was left to individuals to lay

---

c. membris; Shak. Bpl. Whitchurch pains & ords.; Leigh; Stoneleigh Ct Bk p. 23; ct files Sowe; Hood: Ct R. Stivichall; Trevelyan: Ct R. Snitterfield; Throckmorton: Ct R. Coughton, Oversley; W.deB. 1194, 1393a; Deene ho. Brudenell O. x. 14; Northants. R.O., F-H 937, 1626; I.(L.) 12, 128; Daventry: 532–3, 540, 542; O.(K.) 295; Mont. box P, pt 2, X. 890; Northants. 25/51; 7/66/9-10; 20/32, mm. 16–17; Misc. Led. 129; 145, pp. 71, 157–8, 236, 460, 469, 510; P.R.O., Ct R. G.S. 207/42; D.L., R.&S. 8/6a, pp. 3–4; Ct R. 82/1133, m. 29; 106/1529, m. 9d.; 106/1534, m. 6; 106/1535, mm. 1, 5; Exch. K.R., Deps. by Commn 21–2 Eliz. Mich. 8; 26 Eliz. Trin. 8; Blith, op. cit. 80.

[1] Ibid. 80–1; Fitzherbert, *Surveyinge*, f. 52; Marshall, *Midl. Dept*, 201–2; *Midl. Cos.* ii, 225.

[2] Ibid.; Morton, loc. cit.; G. N. Clark, 'Enclo. by Agrt at Marston', *E.H.R.* xlii, 88; C. M. Ingleby, *Shak. & Enclo. Com. Fds at Welcombe* 1885, map; A. Gooder, *Plague & Enclo.* 1965, p. 12; Rylands Lib. Eng. 216, f. 35; Salt Lib. Ct R. Eccleshall 26 Mar. 41 Eliz.; Shak. Bpl. Throckmorton: Ct R. Upton in Haselor 20 Oct. 1692; Northants. R.O., Geddington terrier 1687; F-H 272, esp. ff. 8v., 10, 16–17, 29, 36v., 55, 57, 79v., 82–3, 89–90; 296, pp. 28, 31; 298, esp. ff. iv., 21, 68, 84 sqq.; 982; F.(M.) Misc. Vol. 71, Helpston; O.(K.) 289; Wmld 5. v. 1 Ct R. Wadenhoe 4 Oct. 1660; Mont. Hunts. 26/22; Northants. 18/160, 9 Dec. 5 Chas.; 25/55; Misc. Led. 123, esp. pp. 19–20, 45–6, 68 sqq., 88–90; 124, esp. pp. 6, 32, 65; 125, esp. pp. 23–5, 39–40, 51, 61–3, 75, 84–5, 124–5; 126, esp. pp. 14, 68–70; B'ham Lib. 167919, 508624; Beds. R.O., H.A. 13/6a, 11; P.R.O., Chanc. Proc. ser. i, Jas I, 7/4, compl.; D.L., Sp. Commn 363; M.B. 115, f. 6v.; Exch. A.O., Parl. Svys Northants. 21, f. 22; Deene ho. Brudenell A.S.R. 562, p. 35; A. xii. 10; O. xxiv. 1 Stonton Wyville 15 Apr. 33 Eliz.

[3] Ibid. Cranoe 6 Apr. 15 Eliz., 28 Apr. 16 Eliz.; Deene Oct. 18 Eliz.; Marshall, loc. cit.; *Midl. Dept*, 603; Pitt, op. cit. 256; Laurence, op. cit. 60; Fitzherbert, *Husbandrie*, f. 6; Farnham, op. cit. 14; B.M., Add. 36908, ff. 9, 65v.; R. 37391, 3 Apr. 10 Jas; Bucks. Mus. 38/51 Weston Turville Ct R. Pittenham ords. 17th cent.; Cams. R.O., L. 19/17; Ches. R.O., Vernon (Warren) Ct R. 1, 9; Leics. R.O., D.E. 40/40,

down what land they wished and this mostly sufficed for sheep commons. Those who laid down land for the partial benefit of the common flock were usually rewarded by being allowed to keep about two extra sheep for every ridge turned to grass, or indirectly by the imposition of extra charges for the flock and fold on men who had not laid down any land.[1] Furlongs or fields of 'leys' intended for cow-pastures were, however, wholly under public management. Laid to grass by common agreement, they were neither parts of the various holdings, nor waste (in which no one had property but the manorial lord), but belonged to the township.[2] Since such cow-pastures were in nobody's individual occupation, they were not usually mentioned in probate inventories or terriers; and since they were not waste in which the lord could rightfully claim any interest, there was no reason to include them in manorial surveys. They were, nevertheless, noted occasionally and incidentally in survey books and frequently in field-books and records of courts baron. Great significance attached to these common pastures. If common-field farmers wanted to increase the size of their dairies or keep more beasts, they would agree to lay more land down to grass and it would be ordered in the manor court that so many acres a yardland be laid to grass when the field was next fallowed, or that a stretch at the ends of the ridges be turned to grass to augment the 'headleys'. At Whitchurch in 1636 four acres in every twenty were to be laid to grass.[3]

---

1 Oct. 1690; A/d invs.:—1710: 99; 1706: Ellen Kilburn/Sileby; Salt Lib. H.M. (Chetwynd) Ct R. Ingestre 15 Aug. 23 Eliz., 9 Oct. 2 Jas; Cartwright Hall, Swinton: svy Monks Kirby 1611; P.R.O., Chanc. Proc. ser. i Jas. I, S. 29/7, m. 1; St. Ch. Jas 55/29, mm. 2, 4, 8; D.L., M.B. 117, f. 136v.; Ct R. 105/1506, m. 1; Ct R. G.S. 195/79, m. 7; 194/77; Exch. K.R., Deps. by Commn 8 Chas East. 11; 10 Chas Mich. 61, m. 2; L.R., M.B. 221, f. 320; Northants. R.O., Ecton 1201; Daventry 540, 4 Oct. 16 Chas. II; 573a; X.Y.Z. 985, 10 Oct. 1618; 988, 12 Jan. 1628; O.(K.) 305; L.B.48, Oct. 20 Jas; I.(L.) 1491; 128, 13 Apr. 13 Eliz.; Wmld 5. ii. 3 Ct R. Duddington 6 May 1731; 5. v. 1, Wadenhoe 4 Oct. 1660; 5. iii. 2, id. 14 Sept. 11 Jas; Mont. Northants. 16/98 Ct R. L. Oakley, St Andr. 37 Hy VIII; 18/160, 9 Dec. 5 Chas; 24/52, 25 May 16 Eliz.; 7/66/5, 18 Apr. 22 Eliz.; 17/160, 5 Apr. 6 Ed. VI; Misc. Led. 129 L. Oakley 13 Oct. 1721; 145, pp. 184, 214, 469; Long Buckby Ct R. 6 Apr. 12 Eliz.; Shak. Bpl. W.deB. 703a, 30 Sept. 1 Jas; 1393a; 1194.

1 Ibid. 6 Apr. 11 Chas; Northants. R.O., Grafton 3450a; I.(L.) 110; Misc. Led. 145, pp. 214, 451, 543.

2 Ibid. Mont. Northants. 25/55; P.R.O., D.L., M.B. 113, f. 74v.; Exch. A.O., Parl. Svys War. 25, ff. 3, 5.

3 Marshall, op. cit. 402; Shak. Bpl. Throckmorton: Ct R. Oversley 13 Oct. 1762; W.deB. 1194, 6 Apr. 11 Chas; P.R.O., St. Ch. Jas 55/29, mm. 2, 4, 8; Northants. R.O., Higham Ferrers Burg. R. fd ords. 1696–1725: 2 Apr. 1725; Daventry 540, 16 Oct. 1660; 542, 20 Oct. 1684; Grafton 3422, 31 Oct. 1732, 27 Oct. 1733; Wmld 5. v. 1 Wadenhoe 9 Sept. 1622; Mont. Northants. 18/160, 25 May 1613, 1 Dec. 1614; Bucks. Mus. 219/35 Wing Ct R. 8 Chas; 15/51 Whitchurch Ct R. 14 Jan. 11 Chas.

That common-field lands were being thus continually laid to grass in the sixteenth and seventeenth centuries is shown not only by specific references,[1] but also by allusions to 'bastard leys', i.e. ridges that resembled 'leys', although not swarded over completely.[2] By 1610 the tenants of Cublington had already laid to grass at least 250 acres.[3] In the seventh and eighth decades of the sixteenth century there were newly laid down in Kineton common fields, from which the demesnes were excluded, no less than 140 ridges, scores of headlands and two whole furlongs, not to mention the ends of some 500 ridges.[4] Some fields, it is true, had fewer 'leys' than did others. Some were two-thirds grass, others less than a third, most about half.[5]

The common fields thus contained both permanent tillage and permanent grass, but what they could not have was temporary tillage and temporary grass in grass-arable rotation in convertible or up-and-down husbandry. Gray correctly took the 'leys' in the common fields of plain countries as evidence that farmers were turning land to permanent grass.[6] They were leys in the modern sense, but permanent, not temporary. Fitzherbert, Blith, and Marshall, the leading experts in Midland agriculture in the sixteenth, seventeenth and eighteenth centuries respectively, all regarded common-field 'leys' or 'ley lands' as permanent grass.[7] 'Lands' or 'leys' were usually given the same valuation[8] not because they alternated, but because 'leys' were tenant's grass and ploughable without the landlord's permission. There is evidence that 'leys' were occasionally ploughed up; but this consists almost entirely in by-laws forbidding the ploughing up of balks, 'leys' and other old greensward used for common pasture and meadow,[9] or imposing fines

[1] 'St. Ch. Hy VIII & Ed. VI', (1912) p. 113; Northants. R.O., F-H 1145; F.(M.) Misc. Vol. 71.

[2] Ibid.; P.R.O., Exch. K.R., Deps. by Commn 18 Jas East. 3; D.L., Sp. Commn 363; Deene ho Brudenell A. iv. 16(a).

[3] P.R.O., Chanc. Proc. ser. i Jas I, M. 7/4.

[4] P.R.O., Exch. K.R., Deps. by Commn 21–2 Eliz. Mich. 28.

[5] Leicester Mus. 35/29/415; B.M., Add. 27535, ff. 37 sqq.; 33582, f. 221; 34683, ff. 9v.–11; R. 54166; Northants. R.O., Misc. Led. 125, esp. pp. 100 sqq.; I.(L.) 1491 Faxton A/c Bk, ydland terrier c. 1582; F-H 2758; Deene ho. Brudenell B. ii. 15; E. vii. 1; O. viii. 8; O. x. 14; O. xxii. 4, ff. 125v.–6; P.R.O., Chanc. Deps. Jas F. 13/16, art. 8; Bucks. R.O., S.T./1; D/MH/28/1; Oxon. R.O., Eynsham fd bk 1650; Blith, op. cit. 80–1; Pitt, op. cit. 65; Leics. 78–9; Mastin, op. cit. 14–15; W. Cooper, Hist. Lillington 1940, p. 118.

[6] Gray, op. cit. 35, 106–7, 408; Spufford, op. cit. 19. Pace Hoskins, art. cit. 15; Midl. Peasant, 162, 164, 233–4.

[7] Blith, loc. cit.; Marshall, Midl. Cos. ii, 225, 439; Fitzherbert, Surveyinge, ff. 52–3.

[8] Lennard, op. cit. 59.

[9] Beds. R.O., T.W. 10/2/9, 14 Apr. 8 Chas; B.S. 1276 Ct. R. Tempsford 30 Apr. 1617; L. 26/563, 2 May 1633; B'ham Lib. 167919; B.M., Add. 36908, f. 3v.; Northants. R.O., Ecton 1183, 1204; F-H 834, 1626; Mont. Northants. 18/160, 9 Dec. 5 Chas; Gretton Ct R. 4 Nov. 1658; Shak. Bpl. Whitchurch pains & ords. 12 Oct.

for this offence, or ordering the return to grass of land converted to tillage. The farmer who ploughed up one of his 'leys', by virtue of which he had enjoyed extra sheep commons, did not escape rustic jurisdiction.[1] When the Harpole farmers laid down 'leys' for a common cow-pasture, they entered bonds against ploughing up without the township's consent and went to law against a transgressor. Ploughing common 'leys' without consent was usually an offence, yet some old greensward could be broken up with impunity and John Rolfe of Harpole asserted that some people there 'have plowed or broken up and still doe plowe and breake up greenesworde and pasture grounde within the common feilds'.[2] Perhaps he was right, for it was usually only boundary balks whose plough-up was unconditionally and absolutely prohibited.[3] Balks between an occupier's 'middle lands', which did not form a boundary, were often specifically permitted to be ploughed up, though frequently only on condition that as much land was laid to grass elsewhere in the field. Likewise, by-laws usually allowed a man to plough up his own 'leys', provided no extra sheep commons had been taken for them and provided, sometimes, that as much land was laid down elsewhere.[4]

We cannot, then, be surprised to find that some 'leys' were ploughed up. At Ravensthorpe, in 1760, ten acres were to be ploughed in the old greensward on the hills.[5] In Brafield-on-the-Green, it was said, 'there was twice as much grasse ground plowed up for corne there' as had been laid to grass. Yet nothing suggests a convertible system in the common fields. Six 'leys' had been ploughed up twenty-four years before and had been in tillage ever since, i.e. they had been converted to permanent tillage.[6] Some 'leys' were ploughed up in a few places; but the court presentments to this effect imply they were made into permanent

---

1711; W.deB. 1393a, 6 Apr. 8 Geo.; Hood: Ct R. Stivichall 3 Oct. 1724; Trevelyan: Ct R. Snitterfield 27 Oct. 1713 (erron. 1715), 26 Oct. 1725; Leigh: ct files Sowe 23 Apr. 1663.

[1] Ibid. Stoneleigh Ct Bk p. 23; W.deB. 703b, 12 Apr. 1616; Hill, op. cit. 336; Hone, op. cit. 191; H. Stocks, op. cit. xxxvii, 201–2, 214; P.R.O., D.L., Ct R. 105/1507, m. 2; B.M., Add. 36904, f. 28v.; War. R.O., M.R. 14; Deene ho. Brudenell I. v. 75; Northants. R.O., Grafton 3422, 27 Oct. 1733; I.(L.) 21, 30 Apr. 1655; Daventry 573a, 573c; 585 23 Oct. 1730; Wmld 7. lxxi, f. 2, 5; F.(M.) Misc. 222; Misc. Led. 145, pp. 236, 451, 510.

[2] P.R.O., Req. 86/61.

[3] Salt Lib. Ct R. Shenstone 1 May 9 Chas; War. R.O., M.R. 16/9; Leics. R.O., Leire agrt 1689; P.R.O., Exch. K.R., Deps. by Commn 26 Eliz. Trin. 8; Shak. Bpl. Hood; Ct R. Stivichall 3 Oct. 1724; Northants. R.O., Daventry 533, 20 Oct. 29 Chas II.

[4] Ibid. 549b, 27 Oct. 1740; Misc. Led 146, p. 105; P.R.O., Req. 86/61.

[5] Northants. R.O., Daventry 573c.

[6] P.R.O., Exch. K.R., Deps. by Commn 6 Chas Trin. 2, Mich. 48.

tillage.[1] Another reference to newly-broken arable likewise suggests the extension of permanent tillage.[2] In 1640 Wootton Wawen court ordered that[3]

'Stubfeild pasture shalbe kept in pasture as it was att the first incloseinge after one cropp . . . by the space of tenn yeeres next comeing and noe longer and that dureing that time noe man to till any parte thereof . . . upon paine that every one who tilleth any parte of the said pasture contrary to the order to forfeite five pounds'.

This concerned a common close and the ten years might have referred to the duration of the order rather than of the ley. Some occasional and infrequent alternation of corn and grass is nevertheless suggested. A survey of Luddington-in-the-Brook describes ninety 'leys' containing twenty-five acres 'alwaies used and occupied for neits pasture', but also 'lxiiij leis together containing xix acres called the neitts pasture, where dyvers of the tenantes have eared parte thereof and knowe their occupyinges'. In Little Oakley half the common cow-pasture and one single 'ley' had been ploughed up about 1727.[4] Possibly the clearest example of an individual practising an alternacy of corn and grass in a Midland common field is provided by Walter Blith. He says he had himself fifteen or sixteen short 'lands' lying all together, in a 'common field', as an annex to an enclosed farm. This piece was very gravelly and had lain in grass for at least nineteen or twenty years on end until he ploughed it up, marled it and tilled it for nine years. Blith, however, was no ordinary common-field farmer, his 'lands' were probably in severalty, and, as he says, marling itself was an unusual practice in common fields, which were normally only mucked or folded.[5] There was thus some alternation of corn and grass in the common fields, but no system of convertible husbandry, at least not before about 1690.[6]

It might be expected that collating terriers of the same common fields at different dates would reveal the alternation of 'lands' and 'leys', but it does not. Collations of Irthlingborough terriers of 1739 and 1771 and a field-book of 1791, of surveys with terriers for Great Weldon in 1584 and 1648, and of similar documents for Lamport, Higham Ferrers and

---

[1] B.M., Add. 29611, f. 26; 36908, f. 85v.; R. 49700; Deene ho. Brudenell E. x. 33b, I. xi. 8; o. xxiv. 1, Thistleton 8 Apr. 34 Eliz.; Leicester Mus. 11. D. 53/VI/1; Northants. R.O., Mont. Hunts. 26/28, 18 Apr. 2 & 3 P. & M.; Northants. 7/72, Ct R. Weekley 31 Mar. 2 & 3 P. & M.; 7/66/4, even date; 25/52, 10 Oct. 2 Eliz.

[2] W. N. Henham, 'Newnham Priory: Bedford Rental 1506–7', *Pubns Beds. Hist. Rec. Soc.* 1947 xxv, 61–2, 77.

[3] Cooper, *Wootton Wawen*, App.34.

[4] Northants. R.O., Mont. Northants. 16/101, ff. 26, 31; 25/55.

[5] Blith, op. cit. 136–7.

[6] V. inf. 289.

Geddington all fail to disclose anything in the nature of convertible husbandry.[1] However, these documents would be unlikely to show such practices in any event. Terriers were compiled or supplied by the tenants themselves and delivered to the estate officers under court order or on demand. Lessees covenanted to supply their landlords with terriers. Customary and other tenants brought their terriers to courts of survey together with their other deeds and writings.[2] It is still possible to come across files of these terriers just as they were made four centuries ago, when some of them were used in the compilation of field-books.[3] Similar terriers accompanied conveyances of common-field lands and are still often filed with them in the archives.[4] Tenants, conveyancers, surveyors, landlords, and purchasers were immediately concerned only with areas and bounds. The practice of conveyancing clerks, except only where newly constituted premises were concerned, was to copy the parcels from the vendor's deeds. The occupiers of little common-field farms were concerned above all to ensure nothing was omitted from their tenements. The easiest, cheapest and safest way to prepare a terrier for handing in at court was to copy the previous one. An old yeoman gives a good description of how common-field farmers dealt with this business. He himself used a terrier found amongst the deeds his father left seven years before, and how old his father's terrier was he would not venture to guess.[5] A royal commissioner in 1603 thought nothing of returning a terrier copied from one made, or transcribed, nearly a century before.[6] Lamport glebe terrier made in 1711 was faithfully transcribed in 1720, 1723, 1726, 1733, 1749 and 1752, when it once again served on the occasion of the bishop's visitation; and this was a common way with glebe terriers. Terriers, then, can neither prove nor disprove the alternation of 'lands' and 'leys' in the common fields.[7]

In some localities shifting cultivation was practised. The cliff and

---

[1] Northants. R.O., F.(M.) Misc. Vols. 47–8, 77, 93; F-H 272, ff. 16 sqq.; 298, ff. 64 sqq.; I.(L.) 35, 811–2, 865; Mont. Northants. 10/50; ex box 14, terrier Geddington 1687; P.R.O., Exch. L.R., M.B. 221, ff. 83 sqq.

[2] Ibid. K.R., Deps. by Commn 35 Eliz. East. 11; A.O., Parl. Svys Berks. 22, f. 5; 29, f. 6; 35, f. 5; Worcs. 2, f. 5; R. H. Gretton, *Burford Recs.* 1920, pp. 673, 679; R. L. Rickard, *Progr. N. Wdn Woodward round Oxon. Estes New Coll. Oxf. 1659–1675* Oxon. Rec. Soc. xxvii, 35; P.R.O., Exch. K.R., Deps. by Commn 35 Eliz East. 11; A.O., Parl. Svys Berks. 22, f. 5; 29, f. 6; 35, f. 5; Worcs. 2, f. 5; Northants. R.O., F-H 1626, att.; O.(K.) 295; Mont. Hunts. 26/28, 10 Apr. 7 Ed. VI; Northants. 25/51, 12 May 11 Eliz.; 24/52, 6 Apr. 10 Eliz., 6 May 26 Eliz.; I.(L.) 812.

[3] Ibid. 812, 865; B.M., Add. 36903, ff. 1 sqq.

[4] E.g. Deene ho. Brudenell J. xx. 9a, 11a–b.

[5] P.R.O., Exch. K.R., Deps. by Commn 21 Jas Mich. 12, ex parte quer.

[6] P.R.O., D.L., Sp. Commn 645.

[7] Doughty, op. cit. 217, 230–1; Barratt, op. cit. i, 121; M. W. Barley, 'Fmhos. & Cottages 1550–1725', *EcHR* 1955 vii, 301; Northants. R.O., I.(L.) 50, 812, 859, 865.

heath were divided almost equally between the bounder townships of the Midland Plain and those of the Fen Country. These uplands, soiled with chalky, silver sands, and gravels, and towards the east almost waterless, gave rise to heath, bracken and gorse, and were used as sheep-walk for folding flocks and as cony-warrens;[1] but were also temporarily subjected to shifting cultivation. In the eighteenth century, it is reported, 'the tenants divide and plough up the commons, and then lay them down to become common again; and shift the open fields from hand to hand in such a manner that no man has the same land two years together'.[2] When the heathlands were 'plowed or eared upp' in this way, it was by 'the consent of the major part of the owners', just as in other temporary common fields. Much the same husbandry was employed in enclosures.[3] It is explained that 'twoe hundred acres of ground at the least within the . . . towne of Honington is of its owne nature soe barren that it hath accustomabile bene used to lie leye and unsowen for diverse yeares to recover hart againe, as the use all over the countrie is for grounds of like nature and qualitie'.[4] When the heaths were finally enclosed in the eighteenth century, shifting cultivation continued much as before.[5] In the west, near Cannock Chase, parts of the heath were enclosed for two or three years of tillage and then laid open to the common again.[6] At Bearley seventy-two ridges were ploughed up in a waste called Henthill, by common agreement, with the intention that the land should be 'tilled for nyne yeares, and at the end of the said nyne yeares it should bee laid downe and used as wast land, as formerly it had byne'.[7] Sutton Coldfield township was wont to enclose and allot to its members different parts of the waste in turn, these lot acres being 'cast open agayne after twoe or three cropps of corne' or after about five years of tillage.[8] Similar shifting cultivation was practised at Hopton, Chartley and elsewhere.[9] Three main methods were employed to bring the hot, sandy soils of these sheep-walks into temporary cultivation; burn-baking, liming and marling. Some land was beat-burned,

[1] P.R.O., D.L., M.B. 119, ff. 14v., 49v.; Rylands Lib. Eng. 216, ff. 9, 12, 19, 61; Barley, *Lincs. & Fens*, 83; Hosford, art. cit. 217, 219; Marshall, *E. Dept*, 10–11.

[2] Ibid. 102.

[3] Hosford, art. cit. 219; P.R.O., St. Ch. Jas. 10/4, mm. 4, 7.

[4] Ibid. 17/24, m. 3.

[5] Hosford, loc. cit.; Marshall, op. cit. 51; S. A. Johnson, 'Enclo. & Changing Ag. Landscape in Lindsey', *Ag. H.R.* xi, 96.

[6] 'Chanc. Proc. temp. Eliz.', *Colls. Hist. Staffs.* 1926, pp. 90–2; Staffs. R.O., D. 260 A. (f) Otherton ct recog. (erron. 'svy') 1657, f. 3; 16 (b) Penkridge svy 1660, f. 25; Lichfield Jt R.O., invs.:—Cons. Ct: Robt Gregg 1633 Lynn; Pec.: Nic. Adey 1698 Chorley; Salt Lib. H.M. (Chetwynd): ct files Ingestre, exts. Mar. 23 Eliz.

[7] P.R.O., Exch. K.R., Deps. by Commn 6 Chas Mich. 12, art. 11.

[8] Ibid. Sp. Commn 4684; M. W. Beresford, 'Lot Ac.', *EcHR* 1941–3, xiii, 75.

[9] 'St. Ch. Hy VIII & Ed. VI' (1912), pp. 169–70; Longleat ho. Devereux MSS. vol. 5—ex inf. Miss Carolyn Merion.

the rubbishy turf, bushes, fern, broom and gorse all being grubbed up, piled in heaps and burned, so that seeds could be sown in the scattered ashes. Some temporary cultivations were prepared simply by heavy liming. When marling was undertaken the whole plot was stocked up, broom and gorse removed for fuel and then marl laid on and left to break down during the winter. In the following year a succession of crops might be commenced. If this could be prolonged for seven or eight crops, the broom and gorse might be killed off altogether and the sheep-walk be improved for some time afterwards; otherwise the gorse at least would soon reappear when the land was thrown open to the common again.[1]

From the viewpoint of the whole plain these practices were quite exceptional, almost exotic; and such shifting cultivation had little in common with convertible husbandry. Ley farming may be conducted in an arable-grass rotation, with short leys between the corn crops of what remains nevertheless essentially permanent tillage or quasi-tillage; or in a grass-arable rotation, with long leys, in a system of up-and-down husbandry; but either way it forms permanent cultivation. This is quite distinct from shifting or nomadic cultivation in which plots are tilled occasionally and otherwise revert to the wild, and often to waste, in which no particular person has property. In this shifting cultivation it is not with meadow and pasture that the tillage is alternated, but, at the best, with rough grazing; the alternacy is between cultivation and wilderness.

In short, in the permanent common fields there was some casual alteration of 'lands' and 'leys', but before about 1700, no ley farming, no up-and-down husbandry, no convertible system. Had there been convertible husbandry in common fields, the advantage attaching to enclosure would have been much less or even non-existent. Not common rights themselves, but Midland common-field practice precluded any up-and-down husbandry. Up-and-down husbandry would have demanded that the ploughed turf, especially its radical particles, remain in the ground throughout the whole period of tillage, that a new turf might form in the ruins of the old when the land was laid down again. The ground would have had always 'to have some turf in it'. 'Turf' could survive winter fallow stirrings, but was injured by even a still fallow in summer and extirpated by summer fallow stirrings. In up-and-down land, therefore, summer stirrings would have to have been eschewed. In the common fields, however, winter fallow stirring was avoided lest the pulverized soil should run. Instead, summer fallow stirrings were the universal rule. The fallow field was broken up just after barley-seed, the furrow slices being thrown downward from the ridges. In June or thereabouts the fallows received their first stirring,

[1] Plot, op. cit. 334, 344; Blome, op. cit. 201; Fitzherbert, op. cit. ff. 46v.–7; P.R.O., Exch. K.R., Sp. Commn 4684; Marshall, *Midl. Dept*, 51.

when the furrows were ploughed upwards and ridges elevated. Then, in August, followed a second stirring, omitted only by slovens, sometimes downward, sometimes upward of the ridge. During these fallow ploughings grass particles were exposed and scorched and any remaining couch was picked out of the soil with three-pronged forks. Even if there had been turf in the land to start with, it could not have survived this treatment. One of the chief objects of the summer fallow in common fields was, it need hardly be said, to extirpate all the weeds, including grass, and summer stirrings were the sovereign remedy for the presence of grass.[1]

In fine, Midland common fields consisted of permanent tillage and permanent grass. The permanent tillage was subject to regular, inflexible and rigorously enforced field-courses, of which the chief was the three-field one of fallow, tilth and breach. Sheep were folded only in summer for winter corn, while the spring corn land was mucked with farmyard manure. The permanent grass was for sheep for the fold, cows for the pail, and horses for the plough; and the object of husbandry was domestic and local consumption.

There had been considerable enclosure before 1500 and much more followed, so that by about 1670 over half the farmland was enclosed,[2] though the exact age of the closes cannot always be determined.[3] Similar enclosures continued also in later times.[4] The conventional view is that these closes were formed by the conversion of common-field tillage into sheep pastures for the sake of wool; and contrary views have seldom been proffered, still less accepted.[5]

[1] Ibid. 534; *Midl. Cos.* i, 195; ii, 29, 40–3, 46, 226–7; Plot, *Oxon.* 239; Fitzherbert, *Husbandrie*, ff. 8–9, 13v., 18; & v. sup. 92.

[2] E.g. *V.C.H. Derbs.* ii, 171 sqq.; *Ruts.* i, 223; *Leics.* ii, 254 sqq.; Gray, op. cit. 117–18; Barratt, op. cit. i, 1–2, 4–5, 24, 38; 'Inclo. Manor Wasperton in 1664', *B'ham Univ. Hist. Jnl* iii, 144–5; D. R. Mills, 'Enclo. in Kesteven', *Ag. H.R.* vii, 85–6; J. C. Wall, *Kelmarsh* 1927, pp. 84–7, 89–90; Leonard, art. cit. 110–12, 119; Ryland, op. cit. 55–6; M. E. Finch, *Wealth 5 Northants. Fams 1540-1640* Northants. Rec. Soc. 1956 xix, 15–17, 74, 87, 116, 146–7, 154–6; Hyde & Markham, op. cit. 38, 41; Hosford, art. cit. 217, 219; C. Gill, *Studies in Midl. Hist.* 1930, p. 113; E. Young, *Hist. Colston Bassett* Thoroton S. Rec. Ser. 1942, ix, 57; T. M. Blagg, *Misc. Notts. Recs.* id. 1945, xi, 111 sqq.; Cave and Wilson, op. cit. 3–4, 15, 55–6, 60, 64, 66, 72, 92, 129, 142, 159–60; Rec. Commn, *Cals. Proc. in Chanc. in reign Q. Eliz.* 1827–32, i, 109; iii, 180; Ritchie, op. cit. 63; Johnson, art. cit. 95; Spufford, op. cit. 23–4; Hoskins, *Essays*, 43; Priv. Act 4 W.&M. no 31; *Wills & Admins. Knaresborough* i, p. xi; Somerville, op. cit. i, 307; Lawson-Tancred, op. cit. 95–6, 98; art. cit. 202; T. Burton, loc. cit.; Bailey, *Durh.* 86; Willan, art. cit. 263; Brown, op. cit. iii, 41–3; Clay, id. iv, 100–2; Charlesworth, op. cit. 61 sqq., 175–7; Thomas, art. cit. 66–7, 69–70, 73–4, 83.

[3] E.g. ibid. 70–2; B.M., Add. 34683, ff. 6v.–8; Leicester Mus. 35/29/317–18; Deene ho. Brudenell Map 6; Shak. Bpl. partic. 'Parke Hall w. the demesnes'; Leigh: partic. Dunton in Curdworth demesnes 1687.

[4] Gonner, op. cit. bk ii.

[5] H. Bradley, *Enclos. in Engl.* 1918.

Landowners had parks to produce venison and other meat for their households, to hold fat stock pending consumption, to accommodate horses and domestic dairy herds and as nurseries of timber trees, as well as for pleasure and grandeur. Portions of these parks might also be agisted by the beasts of neighbouring farmers or leased out as grazing grounds. Some parks, too, were entirely leased out to farmers or cultivated by their owners.[1] There was, then, no sharp distinction between the management of parks and of other enclosures, many of which were largely in permanent grass: partly for dairy-farming, especially near market towns and cities and in some river valleys, such as those of the Soar, Trent and Dove;[2] partly, too, in suburbs and along the great highways, for accommodation closes, paddocks, and pastures for grazing butchers, carriers, drovers and the like;[3] but mostly for fatting stock, and more frequently so in the district of Leicester, Rugby, Market Harborough, Melton Mowbray and the Vales of Catmose and Belvoir.[4]

[1] Morton, op. cit. 12; Norden, *Northants.* 24–5, 301; H.M.C., *Middleton MSS.* 319–20, 393; P.R.O., R. & S. G.S. 10/11; Exch. A.O., Parl. Svys Beds. 10, ff. 1–4; 14, ff. 1–2; 17, ff. 1–2; Bucks. 14, ff. 1, 6; Northants. 34, ff. 1–3; Oxon. 12, ff. 22–5; Staffs. 44, ff. 1–2, 7–8, 22–3, 25, 28, 40; War. 10, f. 3; 11, ff. 5–6; L.R., M.B. 185, f. 67; K.R. Deps. by Commn 17 Chas East. 16; B.M., Add. 38065, sheet P; Beds. R.O., L. 4/310; Deene ho. Brudenell A. iv. 1; Northants. R.O., F-H 272, ff. 1, 62; Wmld 4. xx. 3. f. 6; Leics. R.O., D.E. 40/22/2; D.E. 10 partic. Beaumanor 1594; Leicester Mus. B.R. II. p. 8a. 1963.

[2] Emmison, op. cit. 104, 110–11; B'ham Lib. 373943; Beds. R.O., ABP/W. 1611–2/144; invs.:—Worcs. R.O., Cons. Ct 1615: 93b; Lichfield Jt R.O., Cons. Ct: Th. Byrche 1566 Pilleton, Th. Warde 1594–5 Dodslye; Leics. R.O., A/d:—1638: 129; 1673: 9; 1696: 7, 1709: 73, 93 & H. More/Barwell; 1710: 49, 50; 18th-cent.: Th. Highton 1714 Barwell, Jn Sutton 1714 Kegworth, Ed. Moore 1716 Sewstern; mid-16th-cent.: Jn Houghton c. 1550 & Wm Smyth 1557 Leicester; Jn Whitby 1551 Abb. Gate, Jn Whyte 1561 Abb. Pk.

[3] Ibid. Th. Flemynge 1564, Jn Thompson 1571, Jn Abbatt 1556 Leicester; 1628: 199; 1662 A/d: 1; 1671: 31, 1678: 116; Preb. St Marg.: The Blunt 1663; P.R.O., Exch. K.R., Deps. by Commn 1655–6 Hil. 23.

[4] P. A. Kennedy, 'Gent's. Home in reign Hy VIII', *Northants. Past & Pres.* 1954, ii, no 1, pp. 22, 26; Wilts. R.O., acc. 88, A. 1/17a; Deene ho. Brudenell A. xv. 4; Boughton ho. Sir Ed. Montagu's A/cs.; B.M., Add. 36582, ff. 26v.–7, 130; R. 44459; Leics. R.O., D.E. 53/104; A/d invs.:—1617: Sir Wm Turpin/Knaptoft; 1625: 77; 1628: 199; 1631: 124; 1633: 6; 1636: 120; 1639: 85; 1641: 57; 1647: 76; 1662 A/d: 1, 1662 Commy: 157; 1663 Bp's Visitation: 5; 1664: 3, 150; 1667: 1; 1668 A/d: 143; 1669: 15, 22, 118, 156; 1670: 92; 1671: 31, 65; 1676: 107; 1677: 2; 1678: 116; 1696: 67; 1697: 9, 46; 1702: 27, 29, 38; 1705: 5; 1706: 81; 1709: 36, 110, 114; 1710: 8, 100 & Wm Rowe/Bellesdon; 18th-cent.: Jas Spell 1744 Burton Lazars, Anthony Pick 1751 Cold Newton, Th. Woodcock 1755 Burton Overy; & Blunt, Flemynge, Thompson, Abbatt—as prev. n.; Morton, op. cit. 15; Crutchley, op. cit. 12, 16; Lowe, op. cit. 29; A. Murray, *Gen. View Ag. Co. Warwick* 1813, p. 128; *Wills & Admins. Knaresborough* i, 93 sqq.; Leeds Lib. RD/AP 1, invs. Ric. Medcalf 1611 Wilstrop & Wm Coulson 1616 Whitwell; Kirk, op. cit. 163–6; *Wills & Invs.* pt iii, 143; pt iv, 15; Raine, op. cit. 30–1, 54–5, 107–9, 223–4, 248–9; Marshall, op. cit. i, 361, 440–1; *Midl. Dept*, 219; Hoskins, op. ct. 117 sqq.

Sheer graziers were few in number and employed great capitals on large farms. Some were great landowners operating on their home and estate farms, but even humbler men might have sheep and beasts in pastures in several different townships.[1] Graziers had some pure meadow or pure pasture, but most of their grounds were fed and mown in alternate years. Chiefly spring and summer grass was fed, but some pastures were preserved for use in late winter. If oats, peas, barley and straw were needed for dairy cows, sheep, horses, poultry and pigs, they had to be brought in. In particular, it was usual to buy peas from common-field farmers for fatting wethers in winter.[2] Many graziers had harrows for their grasslands, some had ploughs for opening drainage furrows, but few had enough working horses to make up a team. Cultivations were confined to harrowing or furrow draining or to stubbing anthills, which were sometimes cast down, harrowed and sown to oats in a small plot amidst the grass. The other field work consisted of mucking out, spreading manure, killing moles, making and cleansing ponds, mowing down rushes, nettles and thistles, cutting, carrying and making hay, hedging and ditching, and the like. Livestock needed little attendance in closes, but branding, washing and clipping sheep provided some seasonal work. Agriculture proper was altogether eschewed. The skill of grazing resided in meticulous grassland management, in acute judgment of stock, and in watching the market.[3]

Grazing on permanent grass was agriculture only in the widest sense of the word, but was, nevertheless, a necessary adjunct to common fields, where farmers were unable to fatten many sheep or beasts. Until husbandry was improved, grass meat could be produced only on permanent grass. Common-field farmers, with their excessive tillage had, therefore, the inescapable companionship of graziers who abhorred the very sight of a plough. The monoculture of cereals was necessarily accompanied by the monoculture of grass. The two supported each other. Common-field farmers bought in hay just as graziers did grain.

---

[1] Ibid. 121–2; Savine, op. cit. 193; Leics. R.O., A/d invs.:—1617: Wm Turpin/ Knaptoft; 1631: 124; 1633: 6; 1667: 1, 1706: 81; 1710: 8; Pitt, *Northants*, 37; Marshall, *Midl. Cos.* i, 114.

[2] Ibid. 271–2, 362; Morton, op. cit. 16; H. McCall, *Yks. St. Ch.* Yks. Archaeol. Soc. Rec. Ser. 1911 xlv, 151–2; M. Bateson, *Recs. Bor. Leicester* 1905 iii, 321; *A.P.C.* N.S. xxv, 7; A. Bland, P. Brown & R. H. Tawney, *Eng. Econ. Hist.: Sel. Docs.* 1925, p. 273; Salt Lib. D1734/4/1/6; 4/1/8, f. 22; 4/1/9, f. 32v.; P.R.O., St. Ch. Jas. 159/16, m. 9; Exch. K.R., Deps. by Commn 1655–6 Hil. 23; Leics. R.O., A/d invs.:—1617: Turpin ut sup.; 1636: 120; 1639: 85; 1664: 3; 1669: 15, 118; 1697: 46; 1706: 81; 1709: 110, 114; Preb. St Marg.: Blunt ut sup.

[3] Ibid. A/d: 1633: 6; 1647: 76; 1662 Commy: 157; 1669: 22; 1676: 107; 1706: 81; Boughton ho. Sir Ed. Montagu's A/cs. bk ii, f. 29; B.M., Harl. 7180; P.R.O., Exch. A.O., Parl. Svys Bucks. 11, f. 6; Salt Lib. D1734/4/1/6; Folkingham, op. cit. 22; Blith, op. cit. 71–4, 95; Donaldson, op. cit. 25; Pitt, op. cit. 179; Marshall, op. cit. i, 372, 374; ii, 221.

Both employed fundamentally the same technique, that of permanency. Grazing on permanent grass in enclosures was neither new nor improved husbandry. It had been going on for hundreds of years. Nothing new was contained in rigid division between permanent tillage and permanent grassland. This was a legacy of the past and an integral part of common-field husbandry. Nor was permanent grass a more efficient way of using the land than permanent tillage. A well-managed piece of permanent grass on rich soil became deeply rooted and produced a good flush of grass in spring and early summer; but its produce was far from insurpassable and its excellent soil structure could have been produced at least as well by the alternation of long grazing leys and temporary tillage. Some permanent grass was, moreover, markedly poor, deficient in clovers, and infested with thistles, rushes, nettles, docks, moss, mushrooms, coarse, tufty grass, anthills and all manner of rubbish up to and including scrub. It was because of the poor quality of much of their permanent grass that the graziers needed to occupy so much land, and it was this wasteful method of production that excited the indignation of farmers and state alike.[1]

The graziers bred many or most of their sheep, and bought others, mainly wethers of two or three years, in autumn, from local markets and fairs, to depasture throughout the winter months together with the breeding and hog flocks. In late winter or in spring, cattle were bought in, chiefly steers and bullocks of two or three years of age. Brought from a distance by drovers and put on sale at the numerous cattle markets and fairs, these beasts came from the Vales of Hereford, Wales, the Vale of Evesham, the Cheshire Cheese, Peak-Forest, North, and Fen countries, the Lancashire Plain, the North-eastern Lowlands—in short, from most of the neighbouring and many of the stock-breeding and rearing countries. The main breeds were longhorns from the Lancashire Plain, shorthorns from the North-eastern Lowlands and middlehorns from the Vales of Hereford. In spring these stores joined the resident dairy herd and the homebreds in the pastures. Then both wethers and bullocks and some others, were fatted on spring and summer grass. By May, when the sheep were sheared, the first lamb and beef would be ready and thenceforward the sale of fat stock steadily increased until the August peak. The grazier was still busy selling fat stock and buying in sheep until about October. In November most of the dairy cows would be dried off and fatting discontinued, except that a few fat cows might be finished off on preserved pasture and hay or a few thriving sheep put into the warmest pastures for a time and then finished off on peas and beans for sale in early spring. While feeding, sheep were not

[1] Ibid. 219; *Midl. Dept*, 600–1; Blith, op. cit. 73; Pitt, op. cit. 37, 114, 136, 138–9, 179; Crutchley, op. cit. 13; J. Monk, *Gen. View Ag. Co. Leicester* 1794, p. 57; P.R.O., Exch. A.O., Parl. Svys Staffs. 44, ff. 17–18; Salt Lib. D1734/4/1/7, f. 7; 4/1/6.

folded nor bullocks worked; they had but to put on flesh, ready to be sold fat either to local butchers or to London, Rotherham or Birmingham.[1] By the beginning of winter the fat stock had gone, leaving only the dairy herd, the breeding flock, and perhaps a few sheep and beasts being over-wintered in the hope of better prices next year. Thus many sheep were stocked throughout the year, but most beasts were only in the grounds in spring and summer, and many were on the way to market by high summer, when the period of fastest grass growth was over. Most of the stock was not over-wintered, but sent to the butcher by autumn at the latest, and disposals were on so large a scale that a priory has been suspected of making its assets liquid in the face of approaching dissolution, when innocently engaged in routine stock sales.[2] The conventional picture of the slaughter of livestock before the onset of winter is thus roughly true of the Midland Plain and of all grass beef

---

[1] Ibid.; 4/1/7, ff. 6, 14v.; 4/1/8, ff. 9–10; 4/1/9, ff. 5v., 39; Hall, op. cit. 153; Marshall, *Midl. Cos.* i, 315–16, 362, 370, 379; ii, 220–4; *Nfk* i, 351; *Yks.* ii, 271–2; *N. Dept*, 403, 406; Lisle, op. cit. 228; Morton, loc. cit.; Pitt, op. cit. 128–30, 194–5, 270; Crutchley, op. cit. 16; Hammond, op. cit. i, 32; Finch, op. cit. 41 sqq.; 75, 117, 122, 171–2, 193–5; H.M.C., *Middleton MSS.* 393; 'Eliz. Chanc. Proc.', *Colls. Hist. Staffs.* 1938, p. 129; 'E. R. & Purveyance Contt R. Household temp. Jas I', *Trans. E. R. Ant. Soc.* i, 78, 80–1; Raine, op. cit. 19–21, 98 sqq., 107–9, 132 sqq., 200 sqq., 243 sqq.; Lawson-Tancred, op. cit. 175 sqq.; Fiennes, op. cit. 216; Defoe, op. cit. ii, 219; Kirk, op. cit. 251–2; *Yks. Archaeol. Jnl* xi, 279 sqq.; E. W. Crossley, 'Temple Newsam Inv.', ibid. xxv, 94 sqq.; Purvis, art. cit. 449–52; *Wills & Invs.* pt i, 109–10, 161–4, 271–2; pt ii, 77–9, 96–8, 237 sqq.; *Wills & Admins. Knaresborough* i, 129 sqq.; T. B. Franklin, *Brit. Grasslands* 1953, p. 90; I. S. Leadam, *Domesday Inclos.* 1897 ii, 487–8; B.M., Add. 25079, ff. 55, 107; 36582, ff. 39–40, 81v., 86, 107–8, 127; R. 44459; Kent R. O., U. 269/A413; P.R.O., Chanc. Proc. ser. ii, 376/70 compl.; Exch. K.R., Deps. by Commn 8 Chas Mich. 37; 9 Chas East. 19; invs.:—Leeds Lib. TN/M7/1; RD/AP 1, Geo. Barrows 1562 Knaresborough, Robt Constable 1566 Langthorne, Jn Garth 1595 E. Layton, Francis Askwith 1631 Mowton, Robt Stannel 1634 Ellingthorpe, Hy Earle 1637 Rockcliffe, Th. Smithson 1638 Melsonby, Wm Nicholson 1638 Akebar, Th. Squire 1639 Anderby Steeple, Chris. Nicholson 1640 Bedale; Lichfield Jt R. O., Pec. cts.: Hy Agarde 1661 Brereton, Jn Creswell 1662 Barnhurst, Jn Alcocke 1620–1 Fauld, Wm Griniley 1666 Fisherwick, Jn Eardley 1724 Eccleshall, Jn Morris 1663 Whittington, Humphrey Arkoll 1695 Penkridge, Wm Averne 1694 Rugeley; Cons. Ct: Wm Bowyer 1541 Knypersley; A1560: Jas Austen/Normcott Grange; T-V1569: Jn Tailor/Burton Extra; York, Dean & Chap. 1488–1691: Isabel Parkinson/Beaumont Hill; Bp Wilton Pec.: Wm Blanchard 1721 Bolton; Selby Pec.: Jn Harland 1666 Newand, Wm Knowles 1729–30 Hambleton; Worcs. R.O., Cons. Ct: 1563: 83; Lincs. R.O., Cons. Ct 1632–3: 204; Leics. R.O., A/d: 1617: Turpin ut sup.; 1625: 74; 1631: 124; 1636: 120; 1639: 85; 1647: 76; 1662 Commy: 157; 1663 Bp's Visitation: 5; 1664: 3, 150; 1667: 1, 1668 A/d: 143; 1669: 15, 22, 118, 156; 1671: 65; 1676: 107; 1696: 67; 1697: 9, 46; 1700 stamped: 73; 1702: 27, 29; 1703: 38; 1705: 5; 1706: 81; 1709: 36, 110, 114; 1710: 8, 100; 18th-cent.; Spell, Pick, Woodcock—ut sup.; Preb. St Marg.: Blunt ut sup.; D.E. 10 Sir Wm Herrick's A/c Bk 1610–36, pp. 37, 39, 41, 59, 61, 237, 240–3; D.E. 53/104.

[2] Savine, loc. cit.

and mutton.[1] Fat stock was not the graziers' sole interest. Most had domestic dairies and some sent cheese to market. Some also had pigs, poultry or bees.[2] Next in importance to sheep and cattle, however, were their horses. Graziers usually had riding and cart horses, and specialized in rearing shires. They bought yearlings mainly from the Fen Country, kept them until two years and a half, and then sent them to markets and fairs, whence they were purchased by farmers far afield, in the Chalk and Northdown countries, for example. In the vales of York and Stockton, firm-footed Cleveland Bay horses were reared for farm and road work, and were sold far afield as riding, coach and stud horses.[3]

THE VALE OF EVESHAM

What are variously known as the vales of Gloucester, Tewkesbury, Evesham and Red Horse, constituted one farming country. The soils were chiefly deep, fertile loams and clay loams based on retentive marl and clay, although the main towns stood on absorbent soils. The vale had the warm summers and medium rainfall of the Midland Plain, but prolonged autumns and milder winters.

In both common fields and enclosures, farming objects were four: corn, and breeding, fatting and milking cattle. Some small men specialized in one of these, but most substantial farms pursued all four. The chief crops were wheat, barley, beans and natural herbage, with some oats and peas. Sheep were kept for shortening the grass, folding on permanent tillage, and fatting, for which some lambs were purchased from Midland common fields; but the vale was notorious for rot and many farmers did not over-winter sheep, but bought in during spring and sold off in autumn, or wintered sheep away, or merely took summer agistments. The natural stock of an essentially dairy country was the old Gloucester breed of cattle. Since milking was the great consideration, only their strong preference for this race induced farmers to breed

[1] Pace Hoskins in *Assoc. Ag. Rev.* 1954, no 22, p. 3.

[2] Leics. R.O., A/d invs.:—1631: 124; 1633: 6; 1636: 120; 1639: 85; 1647: 76; 1662 Commy: 157; 1663 Bp's Visitation: 5; 1664: 3; 1669: 15, 22, 118; 1671: 65; 1676: 107; 1697: 9, 46; 1702: 29; 1703: 38; 1709: 110, 114; 1710: 8, 100; 18th-cent.: Spell ut sup.

[3] Ibid. 1617: Turpin ut sup.; 1662 Commy: 157; 1664: 150; 1668 A/d: 143; 1669: 22, 118; Leeds Lib. RD/AP 1, York, & Lichfield Jt R.O., ut sup.; Kennedy, art. cit. 26; Pitt, op. cit. 215; J. Granger, *Gen. View Ag. Co. Durh.* 1794, p. 42; Long, art. cit. 107; Fuller, op. cit. iii, 394–5; Defoe, op. cit. ii, 219, 221; T. Burton, loc. cit.; Purvis, art. cit. 451–2; Raine, op. cit. 98 sqq., 132 sqq., 243 sqq.; *Wills & Admins. Knaresborough* i, 129 sqq.; *Wills & Invs.* pt i, 109–10; pt ii, 96–8; pt iii, 41–4; B.M., Add. 36582, ff. 39–40, 81v., 107–8; Marshall, *S. Dept,* 92; *S. Cos.* i, 320; *Yks.* ii, 272–4; *Midl. Cos.* i, 306, 311.

from their best homebreds, which they did with excellent results. Herds were not large, twenty or thirty cows making a full dairy; and only a few farmers had as many as forty. The milk was applied to calves, to both whey and milk butter, and above all to cheese. Some cattle were fattened, but this was no specialist meat country. Butter was principally for local consumption, being sold no further afield than Gloucester, Cheltenham, Tewkesbury and Evesham. Cheese was sold thrice a year, in spring, July and late September, largely to factors who sent much to London, where it was known as 'Warwickshire'. Tall, white, native swine were fatted on whey, buttermilk, beans and peas. Homebred shires provided draught, between four and seven forming the strong teams necessitated by heavy soils and ploughs.[1] Most farms had apple and pear orchards and cherry gardens. Orchards were conducted much as those in the Vales of Hereford, except that their ground was permanent grass. The apples were generally inferior, the pears superior, to those of that country. Both were made into liquor and some table fruit was also sold.[2]

Common fields were exceptionally long-lived here, and were found in half the townships even in the late eighteenth century. Plain-country courses were followed in them, chiefly the four-field one of (1) fallow, (2) tilth, (3) and (4) breach; and as in other similar situations, sheep-folding was restricted to the summer.[3] The general excellence of common-

---

[1] Ibid. 138, 376; *Glos.* i, 49, 54, 62–3, 207, 209 sqq., 215 sqq.; 221, 227, 262, 283, 313–4, 316–18; Markham, *Wealth* pt i, 89; Barratt, op. cit. i, 7, 55; J. Maclean, 'Hist. Manor & Advowson Clifford Chambers', *Trans. Bristol & Glos. Archaeol. Soc.* xiv, 62; ibid. xlvi, 188 sqq.; *Eng. Reps.* cxxiii, C.P. i, 57; J. M. Martin, 'Soc. & Econ. Trends in Rural W. Midls. 1785–1825', ts. thesis M. Comm. B'ham Univ. 1960, pp. 55–6; Shak. Bpl. Stratford: Wheeler Papers i, f. 67; Misc. Docs. i, nos. 11, 17, 19, 26, 30–1, 42, 65, 75–7; v, no 32; vii, no 144; Wills & Invs. 43; B'ham Lib. 350198, 350276, 572721; Worcs R.O., B.A. 855 inv. Jn Sebright 1592 Moore; B.A. 950, 9/183; B.A. 1097, 2/2; B.A. 104, parcel 37, inv. Hy Bromley 1667 Upton-on-Severn; Cons. Ct invs.; Glouc. Lib. R.Z. 152. 1 (38); Cons. Ct invs.

[2] Ibid. 1633: 9, 20; Bodl. Hearne's diaries 158, p. 170 (180); 159, p. 173; Norden, *Surv's. Dial.* 214; Beale, op. cit. 10; Childrey, op. cit. 114; Worcs. R.O., Cons. Ct invs.:—1615: 29, 238; 1617: 134; 1638: 21, 150, 156; B.A. 494, partic. Gt Comberton; B.A. 104, parcel 6, partic. Upton-on-Severn Southend c. 1655; B.A. 385 parcel 74, Kempsey indre 28 Apr. 41 Eliz.; B.A. 54, Ct R. id.

[3] Ibid. 31 Mar. 1656; B.A. 104 parcel 37 inv. Bromley ut sup.; B.A. 351, 8/1; B.A. 494 partic. Morton Underhill 1648; B.A. 950, 6/131; B.A. 1097, 2/2; B.A. 2358, no 131a; invs. Cons. Ct:—1545: 285, 300; 1546: 37, 103, 105; 1563: 18, 42; 1566: 118; 1592: 28; 1596: 61, 74; 1612: 1, 6; 1615: 236; 1617: 134; 1633: 105; 1638: 151; Glouc. Lib. Cons. Ct:—1615: 1, 1633: 9; Glos. R.O., D. 184/M1, f. 2; M9, ff. iv. sqq.; M18, mm. 1, 12, 14, 19; M19, m. 12; M20, m. 14; M24, pp. 30 sqq., 58 sqq., 69 sqq., 79 sqq., 111 sqq., 135 sqq., 188 sqq., 200 sqq.; D. 326/E1, ff. 8v.–9, 14v. sqq., 48v.; P.R.O., D.L., M.B. 116, ff. 81v.–2; Exch. K.R., Deps. by Commn 4 Chas Mich. 6; L.R., M.B. 228, ff. 291 (3) sqq.; A.O., M.B. 379, ff. 30 sqq., 42 sqq.; R. & S. G.S. 2/46, ff. 112 sqq.; Req. 394/70, deps. m. 1; Chanc. Proc. ser. i Jas I, B. 12/68, m. 3; B. 27/59; Shak. Bpl. Ct Bk & R. Alveston & Tiddington; Ct R.

field practice tended to discourage enclosure. Nevertheless, demesnes were often enclosed when the townships at large were not;[1] and enclosures were made from common fields in the 100 years after 1560, frequently, as at Cropthorne in 1585, for the express purpose of providing more meadow and pasture to support the tillage.[2]

THE VALE OF TAUNTON DEANE

Bounded by the Blackdown Hills, Exmoor, the rising grounds about Curry Mallet, the Western Waterlands, and the sea, the Vale of Taunton Deane was only small, but its farming differed radically from that of any of its neighbours. The country was enclosed and common fields unknown. On the north side of the vale and in the coastal plain, the soils were largely deep sandy loams, natural carrot land; and on the south side, red clay loams or middle loams. Ages of good husbandry had greatly assimilated these soils. The climate was mild and serene, without undue rain. Autumns were prolonged and springs backward, but as the climature was favourable and the soil productive, the vale became the granary of the south-west.

The lowest lands were mostly meadow, the higher permanent tillage, and the middle convertible. Well laid down, the middle lands spontaneously formed good temporary leys of natural herbage, chiefly perennial rye-grass and red or white clover. Wheat was usually the first crop on newly ploughed leys, and the main tillage crops were wheat, barley, oats, peas, beans and vetches, there being more beans in the south and more peas in the north.[3] Malting barley was produced, but cider apples were widely grown and cider was the popular beverage. The orchards were, for the most part, merely enclosures, often of up-and-down land, with many fruit trees set in the hedgerows.[4] The vale was a

Shottery; Throckmorton: Ct R. Throckmorton; Stratford: Misc. Docs. i, nos. 11, 17, 19, 26, 30–1, 42, 65, 75–7; v, no 32; vii, no 144; Wheeler Papers i, f. 67; Wills & Invs. 43; W.deB. 1253; B'ham Lib. 572721; Maclean, loc. cit.; Cave & Wilson, op. cit. 29–32, 41, 44, 49, 79–80, 125, 147; Turner, *Glos.* 35, 41–2; Marshall, op. cit. i, 16, 64–5, 68–9, 98–9, 113, 118–19, 121–2, 140–2, 147, 209; *W. Dept,* 398, 417–18; Pomeroy, op. cit. 12, 16; Gray, op. cit. 88–9; Phillimore & Fry, op. cit. i, 44–5, 105–7; Barratt, op. cit. i, 9–10, 21, 48 sqq., 73–4, 96 sqq., 115 sqq.

[1] Ibid. 7, 21, 73–4.

[2] Ibid. 10, 75, 125; Leonard, art. cit. 114–15; J. Smythe, *Lives Berkeleys* 1883 ii, 114; P.R.O., Chanc. Proc. ser. i Jas I, B. 27/59.

[3] Ashley, op. cit. 180; Billingsley, op. cit. 157; Marshall, *W. Engl.* ii, 170; Soms. R.O., D.D. N.N.F. Ct R. W. Bagborough 24 Sept. 8 Eliz.; P.R.O., Exch. L.R., M.B. 202, ff. 271 sqq., 280 sqq.; 255, ff. 175 sqq.; A.O., Parl. Svys Soms. 13, f. 2; 35; K.R.; Deps. by Commn 6 Jas East. 16; 31–2 Eliz. East. 10, ex parte quer.

[4] Ibid.; 6 Jas East. 16; Soms. R.O., invs. Cons. Ct Bath. & Well., & Cons. Ct

'land of Canaan' and the 'paradise of England', partly owing to the great pains bestowed on tillage, especially for wheat. In ploughing for wheat, the land was gathered up into narrow ridges of six furrows width. Between each pair of ridges was left a green, unploughed furrow called 'a comb'. This done, three or four workers went along the combs with mattocks to chop down the furrows, break up the clods, and draw part of the earth against the comb's side. After the seed was sown, the land was harrowed by two horses drawing abreast, one horse proceeding along each of the combs flanking the ridge. Then the combs themselves were slit down with a special 'combing' plough that threw furrows right and left. Workers with mattocks thereupon struck and drew the comb soil out of the resulting open furrows, throwing it over the ridge, thus helping to cover the seed, making the land lie round, to secure the seed against winter rains, and leaving ridges and water-furrows as neat as asparagus beds. This was superb practice where trampling would have poached the land and endangered the crop. Careful cultivation gave excellent returns. About 1600, an acre of wheat yielded between thirty-two and eighty bushels; and much seed wheat was sold to farmers in the Chalk and Southdown countries.[1]

Horses provided draught and team. Nearly all farms had domestic dairies and their milk was well suited to butter. Farmers bred their own cattle in part, and reared more. Large, red, West-country oxen, having been worked until five or six, were then imported for fattening. Three breeds of sheep were stocked. Farmers with substantial dairies often imported 'Dorsets' from the Butter Country in autumn and fattened lamb for spring sale. Others fatted forest sheep bought from the West Country at three or four years. There was also a native breed of polled pasture sheep, apt for enclosures and giving a heavy fleece of combing wool. Incidentally, all sheep and cattle bred and reared in the vale were noticeably larger than those of the West Country, owing to their superior feed.[2]

THE VALE OF PICKERING

The Vale of Pickering was a lake left dry by Nature. The escaping waters left behind wide layers of clay, silt and other deposits, making hillocks

---

A/d Taunton; DD/SH, Coll. N. Jn Strachey for proposed Nat. Hist. Soms. sect. 116; J. Norden, *Descron Mx & Harts.* 1593, p. 12; Gerard, op. cit. 55, 61.

[1] Soms. R.O., Cons Ct Bath. & Wells. invs. Jn Porter 1591 Watchet, Simon Aishford 1634 Dunster; Norden, *Surv's. Dial.* 227–9; Billingsley, op. cit. 156–9; Marshall, *S. Dept.* 601.

[2] Ibid. 602–4; Billingsley, op. cit. 158, 160; Soms. R.O., invs. & DD/SH ut sup.

of fat clay amongst the sandy loams of the western vale and amongst the clays and vegetable moulds of the wet meadows, marshes and woodlands to the east. Save on the coast, the entire vale was ringed by a horseshoe of limestone and chalk hills. A chain of upland swells ran from near Scarborough along the foot of the Blackmoors to the Hambleton Hills and then along what William Marshall named the Howardian Hills to Malton, whence the Northwolds completed the horseshoe. Although generally only about a mile wide, this belt gave rise to a distinct set of calcareous, free-working loams. The climature was backward, being, so to speak, more northerly than its latitude, so that summers started three weeks later than in southern England.

Under the old plan of management, most towns were sited on the horseshoe, sometimes less than a mile apart, and strung round the vale like a necklace. Each of the townships possessed a strip of land both above and below the hill, so that, apart from some residual settlements in its bottom, the inner vale was made up of their common meadows and pastures. The calcareous swells the towns stood on were laid out in common fields, of permanent tillage mostly, but with grassy balks and leys. Above these were extensive sheep-walks on the moors, wolds and hills.[1] The predominant field-course was the plain-country one of (1) tilth, (2) breach, (3) fallow. The tilth field was chiefly for wheat, bigg and barley, and the breach for oats, beans and other pulse, often for 'blendings', a mixture of peas and beans.[2] Otherwise common-field husbandry was more like that of a chalk-down than of a plain country. Sheep were depastured on the wolds, hills and moors by day and driven by shepherd and dog to folds on the tillage at night. Throughout the year the sheep-fold was the main fertilizer. The sheep were chiefly of the Northwold breed. For the rest, most farmers had domestic dairies and plough-teams of four oxen led by two horses.[3]

THE BUTTER COUNTRY

The vales of Blackmore, Glastonbury, Ilminster, Wardour, Glamorgan and Marshwood constituted one single farming country devoted to butter-making. On some of the surrounding hill slopes were found

[1] Marshall, *Yks.* i, 12, 256, 290–1; Willan, art. cit. 253, 279; R. W. Jeffery, *Thornton-le-Dale* 1931, pp. 78–9; R. B. Turton, *Honor & Forest Pickering* N. R. Rec. Soc. 1894–5 i, 22, 37, 50–1; Helmsley & Area Gp Yks. Archaeol. Soc. *Hist. Helmsley, Rievaulx & Dist.* 1963, pp. 201, 206; B.M., Harl. 6288, ff. 51 sqq., 57 sqq.; P.R.O., Exch. L.R., M.B. 186, ff. 79v. sqq.; 299, ff. 264 sqq., 272 sqq.; 230, f. 79, A.O., Parl. Svys Yks. 42, ff. 1 sqq.; D.L., M.B. 124, ff. 60–1, 66 sqq.
[2] Ibid. (& 60–1); Exch. L.R., M.B. 186, ff. 79v. sqq.; 229, ff. 265 sqq.; 230, f. 79; Turton, op. cit. i, 37, 50–1, 60, 64, 79; Marshall, op. cit. i, 26, 51, 290.
[3] Ibid. 34; Purvis, *Causes in Tithe*, 80, 88–90.

sandy, calcareous or gravel loams on bases of sand, limestone and flint, but most of the soils were clays, clay loams or loams on retentive clay. Some of the clays were strong and red, some pale, cold 'woodland'; some of the loams shallow, others 16 to 30 inches deep and highly fertile; but all on impervious bases and almost too retentive for tillage. The climate was mild and damp, but the land intrinsically cold.

The valleys and vale bottoms were mostly enclosed directly from wood-pasture, but some common fields, meadows and pastures were found, especially on the higher lands. Sheep were folded in summer and two- and three-field plain country courses followed; but the fields themselves were hardly more than fast-dwindling remnants.[1] Even the unstinted cattle commons in Gillingham and Roche forests were swept away in the second quarter of the seventeenth century. The typical farm, especially on demesne land, was enclosed.[2] About two-thirds of the closes were in grass that was never or rarely ploughed up, and one-third in arable, mostly in an up-and-down system. Many farms, especially the smaller, were 'all-green', but the 'woodland' clays were generally arable, for otherwise they became overrun with moss and it was sometimes necessary to pare and burn their poor swards.[3] The usual tillage crops were wheat, beans and oats, with some peas and barley in warmer soils. Sometimes oats, wheat and barley were all grown together as a dredge. Beans were much favoured in the deeper soils. A first crop on old grasslands in the districts of Lyme, Bridport,

[1] Marshall, *W. Engl.* ii, 136; R. Merrick, *Booke Glam. Ant.* 1887, pp. 10, 148; W. Rees, *S. W. & March 1284–1415* 1924, pp. 139–41; M. Davies, 'Fd Patts. in V. Glam.', *Cardiff Nats.' Soc. Reps. & Trans.* lxxxiv, 6 sqq., *V.C.H. Dors.* iii, 247–8; Straton, op. cit. ii, 505 sqq.; Gerard, op. cit. 142, 165, 180, 221; B.M., Harl. 71, ff. 45 (56) sqq.; 3961, ff. 205–6; 6006, f. 17; Egerton 3007, f. 1; 3034, ff. 9–10, 26v.–8; P.R.O., Exch. A.O., Parl. Svys Dors. 9, ff. 6, 9; Soms. 33, ff. 2 sqq.; 38, ff. 3 (4) sqq.; L.R., M.B. 207, ff. 20–1 (18–19); 214, ff. 6 sqq.; Chanc. Proc. ser. i Jas I, C. 26/36; K. 8/48; N. 1/68, mm. 1–2; Dors. R.O., Mus. 7126 svy Beauminster Secunda 1599; D. 4 Thornhull Ct Bk sect. 3, Allweston & Thornhull, Ham; D. 12, Ct Bk Holnest & Long Burton, ff. 1 sqq., 13 sqq.; D. 54, Svys &c. manors L. Marg. Arundel, terriers & rentals Ryme Intrinseca & Melbury Osmond; Soms. R.O., DD/MI, Ct R. Q. Camel; DD/PE Ct Bk S. Petherton 1661–1841; DD/AB Ct R. Norton-sub-Hamdon; DD/X/GB Combe Svy Bk 1704, pp. 4, 7.

[2] Ibid. p. 4; Dors R.O., D.16 M. 115–26; B.M., Egerton 3007, ff. 2–4; 3134, ff. 112 sqq.; Gerard, op. cit. 180; Merrick, op. cit. 10, 148; Straton, op. cit. ii, 428 sqq.; 502–4; P.R.O., Wds, Feodaries' Svys Wilts. unsorted bdl. cert. improved val. Nic. Goddard 1618: S.P.D., Interregnum, vol. G58A, ff. 312, 337v.–9, 341v.–2, 343 sqq. Exch. L.R., M.B. 207, f. 25; 214, ff. 48 sqq., 72 sqq.; A.O., Parl. Svys Dors. 10, ff. 1–3; 15; Wilts. 43, 40.

[3] Ibid.; Soms. 36B, ff. 1–3; Dors. 6, ff. 1–2; 9, ff. 2–4, 7–10; 10, ff. 2–3; 15, ff. 2 sqq.; L.R., M.B. 207, f. 25; 214, ff. 48 sqq., 72 sqq.; S.P.D. as prev. n.; Chanc. Proc. ser. i Jas I, C. 26/36; Wilton ho. Svy Liquett, Glam. 1560; Dors. R.O., D. 12, Ct Bk Holnest & Long Burton, ff. 1 sqq.; D. 54, ut sup.; B.M., Egerton 3007, ff. 2–3, 15; W. Davies, *Gen. View Ag. & Dom. Econ. S.W.* 1814 i, 161; Claridge, op. cit. 16; Marshall, *W. Dept*, 506; *S. Dept*, 236, 250; *W. Engl.* ii, 133–4, 141, 144, 200–1.

Beaminster, Barpole, South Petherton and Under Hamdon was often woad, hemp or flax. Amongst the irregular successions employed were: (1) beans, (2) summer fallow, (3) wheat, (4) oats, (5) oats and 'seeds'; (1) oats, (2) wheat, (3) beans; and continuous alternations of wheat with peas or beans. Whole-year fallows were rare and cultivation was mostly conducted in the negligent fashion of small dairy farmers whose interests in tillage crops were confined to self-sufficiency in grain and straw.[1] The lack of malting barley was supplied by cider-apple orchards.[2]

Although a few Chalk Country sheep might be fattened in summer, the breed chiefly stocked was the native 'Dorset horn'. Breeding and rearing were conducted mostly in the hills and slopes alongside the vales, and there sheep were still folded in the summer. Flocks hired from the uplands were occasionally folded in the inner vales, but their owners were loath to send them down for this purpose except for a short period after harvest when the stubble was safe, for the country was generally so deep and wet as to put all sheep in imminent danger of rot. The sheep-master's chief purpose was to breed and rear stores and sell couples in autumn to farmers specializing in house-lamb in the lower vales or in other countries.[3] Teams, which were maintained only by the larger farmers and by jobbing ploughmen, were usually composed of oxen. The vales were stocked mainly with the native red, dark brown and pied cattle that were good for both meat and milk. Home-bred steers were worked until about six years and then fattened, perhaps on hay in winter, but usually on summer grass, for sale to Bristol, Salisbury, London and elsewhere. In addition, some dry cows were fattened and stores imported from Wales and the West Country to depasture on the poorer swards. Cow calves were all reared for the dairy, to which the grass was mainly applied. With the dairies numerous swine were fattened. Whole-milk cheese was made, but the farmers specialized more and more in butter, leaving room only for an inferior cheese of

---

[1] Ibid. 129, 144–5; *S. Dept*, 234–5, 249, 258, 268, 276; J. B. Hurry, *Woad Plant & its Dye* 1930, p. 67; Lisle, op. cit. 161–2, 167; Billingsley, op. cit. (1798) 107; Folkingham, op. cit. 42; Fuller, op. cit. i, 452; iii, 86–7; W. G. Hoskins & H. P. R. Finberg, *Devon Studies* 1952, pp. 400–2; M. I. Williams, 'Some Aspects Glam. Farming in Pre-Ind. Times', in Stewart Williams' *Glam. Historian* 1965 ii, 179–80; Claridge, op. cit. 16–17; P.R.O., S.P.D., Interregnum, vol. G58A, ff. 341v.–2; Soms. R.O., DD/SH, Nat. Hist. Soms. sect. 116; DD/X/AR, inv. Th. Ewens 1685 Penselwood; invs.:—Cons. Ct Bath. & Well., & Cons. Ct A/d Taunton; Dors. R.O., A/d Ct Dors.; Wilts. R.O., Dioc. Reg. Sarum.; Laurence, op. cit. 85; M. Cash, *Devon Invs.* 1966, pp. 12–14, 26–7, 29–31, 44–5, 137–8, 146–7, 163–4; Norden, op. cit. 213.

[2] Ibid. 214; Marshall, op. cit. ii, 147; *S. Dept*, 235.

[3] Ibid. 239; Lisle, op. cit. 338; Stevenson, *Dors.* 398, 403; W. Youatt, *Compl. Grazier* 1833, p. 215; *Sheep*, 248–9, H. Rider-Haggard, *Rural Engl.* 1906 i, opp. 257; invs. as next to prev. n.; Hoskins & Finberg, loc. cit.; Williams, loc. cit. *Cals. Proc. Chanc. in reign Q. Eliz.* iii, 141; Straton, op. cit. ii, 440–1.

skimmed milk. Although some butter was made from hay in winter, it mostly came from grass. Butter was the great object of farming and grass butter far and away the chief commodity.[1]

What may be termed the Western Waterlands included extensive areas of water-formed land known as the Brue, Brent and Parrett marshes, the Sedgemoors, Clevedon and Nailsea flats, and Wentlloog and Caldicot levels, together with the upland borders, peninsulas, islands and hills, such as the Isle of Avalon, Brent Knoll, Bleadon Hill and the Polden and Mendip hills, where most of the towns and villages were sited. In the marshes, the soil was chiefly a rich, red loam of great strength and tenacity on a bed of pure clay; but north of the Polden Hills and over the Severn there were also silty loams, strong blue clays and black moory earths or vegetable moulds, part of which was mere turf bog. The whole country was characterized by stagnant or slow-moving water, a low, level surface and unwholesome fenland air. The hill soils, apart from the plateaux and lower slopes, were weak and shallow, yet all able to support some vegetation. Although the climate was mild, the rainfall was substantial and, on retentive soils and in the hills, excessive, so that the climature was cool and backward.

Under commissioners of sewers, banks, sluices, sewers, main drains, and other works were both made and maintained, though least of all in Sedgemoor.[2] Wedmore common moor, for instance, was defended against the Brue by a wall, while ditches and sewers carried off the waters. A wall protected some 600 acres in Salt Moor at Stoke St Gregory from the Parrett, whose waters nevertheless occasionally endangered thousands of acres in Lyng township.[3] Sometimes disaster passed beyond threats, as in 1607, when Burnham banks broke, flooding the Brent Marshes to a depth of several feet and drowning many people

[1] Ibid.; Hoskins & Finberg, loc. cit.; Lisle, op. cit. 228, 268; Davies, op. cit. 230; J. Coker, *Svy Dors.* 1732, p. 4; Marshall, op. cit. 227, 234, 236–8, 241, 250–1, 269, 549; *W. Engl.* ii, 141, 148–9; *W. Dept*, 492; A. H. Dodd, *Studies in Stuart W.*, 24; E. A. Lewis, *W. Pt Bks (1550–1603)* H.S.C. Rec. Ser. 1927 xii, 7, 10, 23–5, 30 sqq., 42–3; Williams, art. cit. 175–6, 179–80; Defoe, op. cit. ii, 55; T. Davis, op. cit. (1794) 28, 119; Markham, op. cit. pt i, 89; W. Notestein & al. *Coms. Debates 1621* 1935 iii, 205; vii, 108–10; Steele, op. cit. i, 203; Woodworth, op. cit. 77–8, 80; Westerfield, op. cit. 190; C. Worthy, *Devon Wills* 1896, p. 204; Bodl. Aubrey 2, f. 101; B.M., Lans. vol. 110, f. 196; Soms. R.O., D.D./S.H., Nat. Hist. Soms. sect. 116; D.D./MI., Ct R. Q. Camel; D.D./X./AR. inv. Th. Ewens 1685; invs. ut sup.

[2] Leland, op. cit. i, 147; Dugdale, op. cit. 104 sqq.; Coleman, 'Manor Allerton & its Tenants 1530–1886', *Proc. Soms. Archaeol. & Nat. Hist. Soc.* xlvi, 80–1; D. Sylvester, 'Com. Fds Coastland Gwent', *Ag. H.R.* vi, 11–12; Gerard, op. cit. 131.

[3] Bradford, op. cit. 56 sqq., 170–1, 173.

and beasts.[1] Even without such catastrophes, all the works sufficed only to drain dry most of the land in summer and a little of it in winter. Sedgemoor was under water most of the winter and even in summer afforded largely rushes, reeds and sedge. Parts of some other moors were frequently flooded all the year and much of their land was only fit for turf-cutting, fishing and fowling; but most of the Brue and Parrett marshes were dry in summer and used as stinted mowing grounds or unstinted common pastures. Although it may occasionally have been flooded even in summer, Aller Moor was famed as one of the best grasslands in England. Summer-grounds like this were fed and mown in common by the neighbouring townships, which moved their stock to and from the marshes along droveways that radiated from them to all the country roundabout. Some parts of the marshes, moreover, were dry all through the year. A thousand acres enclosed at Catcott made good winter-ground in 1638 and similar land was found also in Salt Marsh and about Chedzoy and Sutton.[2] In such places up-and-down husbandry was often the practice and drained marshes newly brought under the plough gave a dozen or even a score of abundant wheat crops, not to speak of beans, cole-seed, and some teasels, without any manuring. Indeed, the only manures ever needed in these winter-grounds were the scrapings and scourings of their own drains and ditches, with lime.[3] The majority of farmers remained content to till the islands and uplands, where most townships had their common fields, with plain-country courses and great wheat and bean crops. Sheep were folded on the fallows, at least in summer, and large flocks then shared the ample pastures with herds of cattle.[4] In some townships a

[1] E. Green, 'On some Soms. Chapbks', *Proc. Soms. Archaeol. & Nat. Hist. Soc.* xxiv, pt ii, 53–4; *Gent's. Mag.* xxxii, 306–7.

[2] Gerard, op. cit. 63, 132, 214, 219, 231; Norden, op. cit. 199; Coleman, art. cit. 81; Bradford, op. cit. 60, 171, 173; A. Moore, *Bread for the Poor* 1653, p. 26; Fitz-herbert, *Husbandrie*, f. 16; Straton, op. cit. ii, 443 sqq.; C. D. Curtis, *Sedgemoor & Bloody Assize* 1930, opp. 45; P.R.O., Exch. L.R., M.B. 202, ff. 106 sqq., 203 sqq., 255 sqq.; 207, ff. 4 (2), 22 (20); A.O., Plty Svys Soms. 16, f. 29; R. & S. G.S. roll 566, mm. 4 sqq.; B.M., Egerton 3034, ff. 45 sqq.; 3134, f. 76; Add. R. 28281; Glouc. Lib. 28917; Soms. R.O., D.D./SAS. Aller custumal 1653.

[3] Ibid. invs. Cons. Ct Bath. & Well.; Th. Broke & Ric. Chisman 1590 Draycott; M. Davies, 'Com. Lands in S.E. Mon.', *Cardiff Nats.' Soc. Reps. & Trans.* lxxxv, 7; Billingsley, op. cit. (1794) 69, 86; Bodl. Aubrey 2, f. 152; E. Moir, 'Benedict Webb, Clothier', *EcHR* 1957 x, 264; C. Hassall, *Gen. View. Ag. Co. Mon.* 1812, p. 29; Marshall, *S. Dept*, 588–9; Sylvester, art. cit. 12, 25.

[4] Ibid. 15 sqq.; Fitzherbert, loc. cit.; Coleman, art. cit. 75–6; Davies, art. cit. 8 sqq.; Marshall, *W. Engl.* ii, 196–7, 217–18; Norden, op. cit. 228; Billingsley, op. cit. 61, 83, 131, 138; (1798) 35, 50; Hobhouse, 'On Map Mendip', *Proc. Soms. Archaeol. & Nat. Hist. Soc.* xli, 67–8, 70; Straton, loc. cit.; Bristol R.O., 01235, ff. 2 sqq.; Cart-wright Hall, Swinton: Ct Bk Isle Abbots; B.M., Add. R. 28279, 28281, 28283; Egerton 3034, ff. 45 sqq., 64 sqq., 73 sqq., 94 sqq., 107 sqq., 133v. sqq., 150v. sqq.; 3134, ff. 6 v. sqq., 20 sqq., 37v. sqq., 57v. sqq., 76 sqq., 97 sqq., 104v. sqq., 118v.

considerable part of erstwhile common land or pasture was enclosed; and further exchanges and enclosures continued to be made. As demesne lands were in any event often in severalty, the enclosed proportion was by no means negligible, and many enclosures, especially in the thinner soils, were in an up-and-down system for oats, barley, vetches and wheat and for grass mown or fed in rotation.[1]

Despite good opportunities for tillage, most of the country was appropriated to grass, and even drained marshes were valued chiefly for great crops of hay and grazing rich enough to fatten sheep in winter. From the flocks of the house-lamb breed reared in the uplands and folded on the arable, were drawn in-lamb ewes or dams with their twins destined for winter lamb and summer mutton. Many cattle were fatted, too, and many shire horses bred and reared. In Sedgemoor geese were kept in great numbers, fed on beans in frosty weather and pulled several times a season to provide quills. Above all, it was to the dairy that the grass was applied and dairying was the object farmers preferred to all others. Their chief stock was of red 'Gloucester' cattle and their main products butter and cheese. Most of the country specialized in butter, but cheese was of primary importance in the Brue Marshes, where each township's milk was pooled in a public co-operative dairy to make the great 'Cheddar' cheeses that were perhaps the best, and certainly the dearest, in England.[2]

---

sqq., 146 sqq.; P.R.O., R.&S. G.S. roll 566, mm. 4 sqq.; D.L., M.B. 123; Exch. L.R., M.B. 191, f. 17; 202, ff. 110 sqq., 203 sqq.; 207, ff. 10, 22 (20); 225, ff. 58 sqq., 65 sqq., 82 sqq., 90 sqq.; A.O., Parl. Svys Mon. 1, f. 19; Soms. 16, ff. 2 sqq.; 32, ff. 2 sqq.; 37, ff. 33 sqq.; 39, ff. 3 sqq.; 43, ff. 4–6; Soms. R.O., D.D./X./HO., Ct Bk Tintenhull;; D.D./S./WH. svy Milton juxta Wells 11 July 19 Jas; D.D./S.H. Nat. Hist. Soms. sect. 116; invs. Cons. Ct Bath. & Well., Cons. Ct A/d Taunton; D.D./S.G. no 40, svy c. 1760; nos. 18–19 ct files Shapwick Rectory.

[1] Ibid. no 18 presentmts 29 June 1677; no 36 partic. enclo. ground 1754; D.D./X./N.W., map Mendips c. 1570; D.D./S./WH. as prev. n.; Cons. Ct Bath. & Well. inv. Jn Lane 1633 Worle; Bristol R.O., 4490, ff. 1 sqq.; 01235, ff. 2 sqq.; P.R.O., R.&S. roll 566, mm. 4 sqq.; Exch. L.R., M.B. 191, f. 16; 202, ff. 110 sqq., 203 sqq.; 225, ff. 58 sqq., 65 sqq., 82 sqq., 90 sqq.; A.O., Parl. Svys Soms. 16, ff. 2 sqq.; 39, ff. 3 sqq.; 40, ff. 1 sqq.; 44A; 47, ff. 2 sqq.; B.M., Egerton 3134, f. 51; Add. R. 28281; Straton, loc. cit.; Coleman, art. cit. 74–5; Billingsley, op. cit. (1794) 86; Marshall, *W. Dept*, 514, 521–2.

[2] Ibid. 492, 528–9; *S. Dept*, 239, 588; *W. Eng.* ii, 182–3; Fuller, op. cit. iii, 86; Gerard, op. cit. 232; E. Leigh, op. cit. 165; Markham, op. cit. pt i, 89–90; Fiennes, op. cit. 243; Defoe, op. cit. i, 277–8; Youatt, *Compl. Grazier*, 214; Steele, op. cit. i, 203; J. Fox, *Gen. View Ag. Co. Mon.* 1794, p. 14; Soms. R.O., D.D./S.H., Nat. Hist. Soms. sect. 116; invs. Cons. Ct Bath. & Well., Cons. Ct A/d Taunton; Hassall, op. cit. 34; Lisle, op. cit. 228, 268, 302–3.

THE CHEESE COUNTRY

Between the Cotswold and Chalk countries were two vales, divided along most of their length by a range of low hills. There were gravel loams in the valleys, clay loams, and stiff, retentive 'woodland' clays on the higher lands, especially north-west of the central hills, and elsewhere generally rich, deep, productive loams, all standing on a highly impervious base, despite which the climature was more forward than in the neighbouring sheep-and-corn countries and the grass came a month earlier.

A great deal of the country was enclosed from wood-pasture, partly in the early modern period, and the 'rews' bounding the fields were largely remnants of woodland left for the purpose. Common fields were numerous and widespread, but were generally small and had many balks and leys of permanent grass. Plain-country field-courses were practised, with folding in the summer.[1] Enclosure agreement preambles did not exaggerate in saying the country was unsuited to common fields and sheep-folding.[2] In 1657 Eastcott's tillage would have been better in grass, for the sheep were subject to 'rott and watercore'. Hannington common fields,

'lying in a deep, watrye part of the cuntrye, were subjecte oftentymes to overfloweing with water and thereby to rott and hungerbane suche sheepe and cattle as were put to feede thereon; and by reason of such moystures and rottennes of the soyle . . . were most commonlye soe stocked and trodden downe with the cattle thereon goeing that all the grasse was spoyled.'

About two-thirds of an enclosed farm would be permanent grass and the remainder mostly up-and-down land, where ploughing was regarded primarily as a remedy for poor swards, some of which might only last two or three years.[3] The land was usually sown alternately to

[1] Ibid. 325; Wilts. R.O., acc. 34 Hobhouse Papers A, 25/5; acc. 40; Sevenhampton Ct Bk 1541–1624; acc. 88, Charlton Este Papers, box B, Svy Bk Charlton, Brinkworth, Hankerton & Brokenborough, ff. 60 sqq.; invs.:—Cons. Ct Sarum. Th. Sheppard 1631 Benacre; Dioc. Reg. Sarum. Hy White 1591 Maiden Bradley; Berks. R.O., D./E.Pb. M3, pp. 65, 142, 179; P.R.O., S.P.D. Jas vol. 71 no 107, ff. 10, 21, 23, 44–5, 53–4 (321, 332, 334, 355–6, 364–5); R.&S. G.S. roll 709; Exch. L.R., M.B. 187, ff. 170–3, 176 sqq.; A.O., Parl. Svys Soms. 26, f. 4; 27, f. 4; Wilts. 24, f. 1; T. Davis, op. cit. 130; F. H. Goldney, *Recs. Chippenham* 1889, pp. 2–3; *Wilts.Mag.* v, 32–3; G. & E. Fry, op. cit. 350–1, 399–400; C. B. Fry, op. cit. 26–9.
[2] Ibid. 27; Morris, op. cit. 507–8; L. V. Grinsell & al. *Studies in Hist. Swindon* 1950, pp. 55–6; Berks. R.O., D./E.Pb. E66A.
[3] B.M., Add. 22836, f. 23; Devizes Mus. Wm. Gaby His Booke 1656, pp. 12–13,

fallow wheat and to oats, barley, peas, or beans, and there was some monoculture of barley. If exhausted, the field was occasionally sown down with hay-seed; otherwise the wheat or other stubble was left to turn to grass of itself. There was no uniformity, and little system, in cultivation: the dairymen made slovenly tillage farmers. Oxteams, with up to ten or a dozen beasts in yokes or collars and perhaps a guide-horse or two, did some heavy ploughing, and dry cows, heifers and steers were all pressed into service on occasion, but horses were in increasingly general use.[1] The utmost object of tillage was self-sufficiency in bread and drink corn and in straw, together with grassland improvement, and most of every crop was consumed on the farm. The majority of farmers had only a dozen acres in tillage, or less, or, indeed, none at all; and if some larger men had up to 100 acres, this was because their soils were too clayey to last long in grass. Fallow wheat was a good crop in the heavy soils and winter corn covered half as much land again as either spring corn or pulses. Wheat and maslin were each grown more than barley. There were some tares and beans, but far more peas, and pulses gave more provender than did oats.[2]

The land, then, was appropriated chiefly to natural grass, which was mainly applied to cows, mostly for cheese production. The dairy cattle were of the longhorn breed, partly bred and reared on the farms, partly recruited by the purchase of cows with calves at their feet. Market butter was made only in a small district about Lydiard, where the grounds did not make good cheese, which would heave in hot weather, while those good for cheese were bad for butter, so that otherwise only whey butter, for lubrication and the clothing industry, was produced, and cheese was the main object.[3] Previously all the cheeses were made in thin discs for speedy drying and sale, but after 1680 many were made

---

17, 23, 46, 58–9, 75; rev. 15, 30–1; Bodl. Aubrey 2, f. 87; P.R.O., S.P.D. Jas vol. 71 no 107; Exch. L.R., M.B. 191, f. 132; A.O., Parl. Svys Berks. 13, ff. 2–4; Soms. 27, ff. 2 sqq.; Wilts. 36, 47; Davis, op. cit. 119; Marshall, *Glos.* ii, 142, 151; Lisle, op. cit. 161–2.

[1] Ibid. 42, 86, 268; Davis. op. cit. 134; Marshall, *W. Engl.* ii, 206, 208, 216; A. Young, *Tours in Eng. & W.* 1932, p. 30; Aubrey, *Wilts. Topog. Colls.* 293; Basset Down ho. N. Maskelyne's A/c Bk, ff. 116, 136; Wilts. R.O., acc. 122, Ct Bk, Stanley 16 Oct. 2 Chas, inv. Jn Scott; Bodl. Aubrey 2, f. 89.

[2] Ibid. f. 83; P.R.O., Exch. K.R., Sp. Commn 2450; invs.:—Soms. R.O., Cons. Ct Bath. & Well.; Wilts, R.O., Cons. Ct Sarum., A/d cts Sarum. & Wilts., Dioc. Reg. Sarum.; Lisle, op. cit. 42.

[3] Ibid. 304; Bodl. Aubrey 2, f. 101; Hearne's diaries 158, p. 170 (180); 159, p. 173; Basset Down ho. Maskelyne's A/c Bk, f. 117; invs.:—Wilts. R.O., acc. 122, Ct Bk, Stanley 28 Sept. 16 Jas, Andr. Wilcocks; 16 Oct. 2 Chas, Jn Scott; & Wilts. & Soms. R.O.s, as prev. n.; P.R.O., Exch. K.R., Sp. Commn 2450; R. Atkyns, *New Hist. Glos.* ed. Rudder 1779, p. 548; Marshall, op. cit. ii, 221; *Glos.* ii, 142–3, 152; *S. Dept*, 93, 237.

much thicker. In either form they were known as 'Marlborough' or 'Gloucester', because largely marketed in the one and similar to those from the Vale of Berkeley sold in the other. Factor's cheese was made both from grass milk about May and June, from aftermath milk later, and from hay milk in the winter, all for sale to London and elsewhere. The cows were kept in the fields in summer and through most of the winter, when hay was carried to them and thrown on fresh ground every day, so that it was eaten up clean and all the land received equal benefit. As the beasts were so long in the fields, farmyards were little more than milking places. This meant that pigsties were the chief source of manure, so the judicious dairyman mowed his field the first year after muck-spreading, least the milk be spoilt for cheese. Each cow was reckoned to produce an average of three or four hundredweights of cheese a year and gross production was estimated in thousands of tons, all made on the farms by their womenfolk.[1] The largest farms stocked up to thirty or forty cows, and many a dozen or more, but most, even excluding those with purely domestic dairies, had fewer than twelve cows in milk at a time, and so no more than could be managed by the labour of a single family.[2] When the cheesewoman baled off the whey, she usually poured it straight down a whey-lead to the hogs fattening on barley-meal, pulse and dairy waste. Almost every dairy farmer fed porkers or baconers to the tune of ten, twelve or even thirty, and singed bacon was marketed in some quantity.[3] Calves were bred of necessity and many bull calves fed for veal. Dry cows and old bulls were often fatted and, in the summer, also, a few sheep were drawn from the neighbouring hill countries and stocked at the rate of about one per cow, in order to use the pastures fully, keep the sward short and trim after the cows, and moderate the feed on land too rich for good cheese. Until the mid-seventeenth century, too, some farmers wintered theaves from the sheep-and-corn countries. Thus most of the dairymen had something of the grazier about them.[4]

Wherever the pastures were too rich for cheese, dairying gave way to grazing for meat. Many farms combined dairying and grazing as twin

[1] Ibid. 93; *Glos.* ii, 146, 149, 154, 157 sqq., 181–2; Defoe, op. cit. i, 283–4; Davis, op. cit. 120; Cardigan, art. cit. 112; Devizes Mus. Wilts. MSS. 'C', inv. Stoke ho. 1596, ff. 1, 8; Bodl. Aubrey 2, ff. 100v., 103, 151; Basset Down ho. Maskelyne's A/c Bk, f. 123; Wilts. R.O., Cons. Ct Sarum. inv. B 1678–1700: 41; Lisle, op. cit. 302–4.

[2] Ibid. 298; P.R.O., Exch. K.R., Sp. Commn 2450, 5021; Invs. goods & chattels, 2/37, ff. 16v.–17; Wilts. R.O., acc. 221B, Sd. 1a; acc. 122, Ct Bk, Stanley, invs. engrossed 28 Mar. 14 Jas, 26 May 1616, 28 Sept. 16 Jas, 16 Oct. 2 Chas, 26 Sept. 10 Chas, 2 Oct. 11 Chas; Devizes Mus. cat. no 133, Jn Filkes 1629 Rowde; invs. as next to prev. n.

[3] Id.; Bodl. Aubrey 2, f. 101v.

[4] Invs. ut sup., esp. Dioc. Reg. Sarum. Jn Palmer 1637 Calne; Marshall, op. cit. ii, 154–5, 160; *S. Dept*, 93–4, 237; Davis, op. cit. 119.

objects, and, all told, about a quarter of the country's grassland was given over to meat production. Conversely, fatting beasts depleted soil fertility less than milking cows, and their pastures were therefore the richer. Also, it was the best grasslands that were the least ploughed, at least until the seventeenth century, and the dairymen who had most need of straw, so that grazing tended to coincide with the richer, and dairying with the weaker pastures. Aubrey tells us that

'the pastures of the vale of White Horse, *sc.* the first ascent below the plaine, are as rich a turfe as any in the kingdom of England: *e.g.* the Idovers at Dauntsey, of good note in Smithfield, which sends as fatt cattle to Smythfield as any place in this nation; as also Tytherton, Queenfield, Wroughton, Tokenham, Mudgelt, Lydyard Tregoz, and about Cricklad, are fatting grounds.'

The Idovers were grasslands watered by the Avon, along whose banks were thousands of acres of similar ground.[1] Welsh store cattle were bought in the marches and joined the surplus beasts from dairy farms and other home-breds in pastures and parks. A single grazier might have 100 beasts feeding his grass and some were fatted in winter on hay, with perhaps some pulse or barley meal. As some sheep were needed to maintain the grasslands, the graziers stocked them in spring and summer in numbers ranging up to 200 or more and at rates of about three to one beast.[2]

THE VALE OF BERKELEY

The Vale of Berkeley's soils were mainly deep, rich, clay loams and loams on a retentive base, making excellent grassland. With a climate less sheltered than that of the Cheese Country, the spring came about one week later. The air beside the Severn tended to the unwholesome and the lower vale was said to have wealth but not health.

In the late eighteenth century there was little arable, perhaps hardly more than 1,000 acres in tillage, which was chiefly to provide straw for the dairies. Common-field land was slight in extent, and then lay mostly in the north. Small and numerous fields were grouped into shifts for plain-country courses with wheat and beans as the main crops[3] There

[1] Ibid.; Aubrey, op. cit. 216; *Nat. Hist. Wilts.* 37; P.R.O., D.L., R.&S. 9/26, ff. 6, 8.

[2] Davis, op. cit. 123, 135–6; Woodworth, op. cit. 78; Nichols, op. cit. 9; C. Skeel, 'Cattle Trade bet. W. & Engl. fr. 15th to 19th cents.', *Trans. R. Hist. S.* 1926 ix, 142; P.R.O., Req. 26/63; St. Ch. Hy VIII 26/431; Jas 54/10; Exch. K.R., Sp. Commn 5021; Longleat ho. Misc. Papers Sir Jn Thynne sen. 1561–76 iii/50, ff. 81–4.

[3] Smyth, *Hund. Berk.* 190; Phillimore & Fry, op. cit. ii, 186; iii, 21–2, 29–30;

were also common pastures, meadows and 'warths' (mud-banks in the estuary).[1] Since rights of common were being progressively extinguished, and, in the early seventeenth century especially, many parks and chases were disparked or disforested, broken up into closes, and let out to farmers, enclosed farms more and more overshadowed common-field ones.[2] Marshall observes that 'the principal part . . . of the lands of the vale appear to have been formerly under the plow; lying now in ridge-and-furrow'. This was partly because many closes were up-and-down land.[3] In 1547 Otencroft in Poulton in Awre was 'una clausure terre arrabile sive pasture'. A Whitcliff particular in 1626 records such parcels as 'one close now plowed' and 'one close now sowed', and some land is said to be 'long broken upp and lyes farr from amendment' after being 'soe much worn with long plowinge'.[4] As a rule, up-and-down land was probably tilled as long as it would bear good corn without manure and then turned to grass that was left down until it needed to be broken. The chief tillage crops were wheat, beans and barley. Wheat was sown under furrow after three ploughings, being buried alive, so to speak, and not rising, in a cold season, until December or January, on the maxim that 'when wheat lies longe in bed, it riseth with a heavy head'. Beans were sown between mid-February and early March, in the heaviest clays first and in the loamier ones later, on the principle of 'many seames, many beanes'. Some woad was also grown as a first crop on turf.[5]

The vale's cold pastures were notorious for rotting sheep and although some ran with the cows and fatted in summer, the grass was mainly applied to reddish, middle-horn 'Gloucester' cattle. These were good for both beef and milk, but were stocked primarily for the dairy, for calves, butter, pigmeat and cheese. Dairy farmers who had some rough

Marshall, *Glos.* ii, 87, 90–1, 144; *W. Dept*, 398; B.M., Egerton 2988, ff. 60 sqq., 75v., 78; P.R.O., R.&S. G.S. 2/46, ff. 4 sqq., 44 sqq.; D.L., M.B. 116, ff. 54–6; Exch. K.R., M.B. 39, ff. 41 (39)v.–44 (42), 53 (56) sqq., 75 (67) v. sqq.; Glos. R.O., D. 114, fd bk Bradley 1598; D. 127/608; Glouc. Lib. Cons. Ct inv. 1633; 27; 16526/11; R.F. 30. 3.

[1] Ibid.; P.R.O., Exch. K.R., M.B. 39, ff. 41 (39) v.–44 (42); G. Turner, op. cit. 49; Smyth, *Lives Berkeleys* ii, 227; *Hund. Berk.* 51, 249–50.

[2] Ibid. 36, 51, 89, 152; B.M., Add. 6027, ff. 137–9; Egerton 2988, ff. 60 sqq., 75v. sqq.; P.R.O., D.L., M.B. 116, ff. 54–7; Exch. L.R., M.B. 191, ff. 165–7; A.O., Parl. Svys Glos. 20; B'ham Lib. Fletcher 81; Glouc. Lib. 16526/11; R.F. 30. 3; I.S. Leadam, 'Inq. 1517 Inclos. & Evictions', *Trans. R. Hist. S.* 1892 vi, 189; Phillimore & Fry, op. cit. iii, 19–20.

[3] Ibid. ii, 47–9, 77; Smyth, op. cit. 18; Marshall, *Glos.* ii, 93; Lennard, art. cit. 31; B.M., Egerton 2988, f. 77v.; Glouc. Lib. 28917; P.R.O., R.&S. G.S. 2/46, ff. 122 sqq.

[4] Ibid. f. 125; Glouc. Lib. 16526/11.

[5] Ibid. 16062, pp. 19, 30; invs.:—Cons. Ct; Bristol R.O., Cons. Ct; Blith, op. cit. 226; Smyth, op. cit. 18, 28, 31–3.

grazing reared calves for both themselves and for others, for the cattle were nearly all homebred. Butter was made only for domestic, local and industrial use and cheese-making was all important, the vale producing a large part of commercial 'Gloucester' cheese.[1] Dairy management was closely akin to that of the Cheese Country, differing only in the following particulars. The cows were smaller and were not wintered out in the fields, but withdrawn to yards and houses. As the climature was less forward, the grazing season was shorter; and, since hay was less abundant, little or no cheese was made in winter. There was plenty of grass in spring and summer, but always a shortage of winter fodder. In mid-winter most cows were near calving and all being fed largely on straw, so little milk could be hoped for. The provident husbandman still had nearly all his corn and half his fodder in store, but it was difficult to make this last until the new grass came. The beans were needed for the working horses and the swine. Acorns were a valuable food for hogs and farmers regarded with the same anxiety the fruit of both their oak and apple trees.[2]

'Warths' were a peculiar feature of the vale. The Severn somewhat changed its course every score of years or so, and in so doing cast up banks of silt and sand that remained until the river shifted again in such a way as to remove them. Between about 1628 and 1639, for instance, 300 acres of sands were cast together in Slimbridge, Fretherne and Hurst. These warths had been in Slimbridge at least twice before but the Severn had since removed them to its opposite bank at Awre, and now they were being returned once again to Slimbridge, while by 1660 they had been transported yet again to Awre. After being banked half a dozen years, the sands would begin to bear weeds and aquatic grasses, and the farmers would set about fortifying the warths with walls and building sheep-houses. When fed by sheep for a few years, warths became good fatting grounds for all cattle. Being salt or brackish, they were safe for sheep and excellent for rotten sheep that needed flesh thrown on them rapidly before expiry. These warths were sometimes stinted sheep and cattle commons, hedged and ditched at public expense, sometimes in severalty; but their possession was, not surprisingly, often disputed; and all said and done, the Severn might bear them away again.[3]

[1] Ibid. 4, 31, 89, 249–50; invs. as prev. n.; A. Powell, *Jn Aubrey & Friends* 1948, p. 38; Lindley, op. cit. 149; Woodworth, op. cit. 78, 80; Markham, op. cit. pt i, 89–90; R. Baxter, 'Poor Husbandman's Adv.' *Bull. Jn Rylands Lib.* x, 186; Marshall, op. cit. i, 209; sqq.; ii, 99–100, 103, 107.

[2] Ibid. i, 195, 215 sqq.; ii, 98, 138, 154, 182; Norden, *Surv's. Dial.* 214; Bristol R.O., Cons. Ct inv. 1639: 29; Smyth, op. cit. 30–1, 122.

[3] Ibid. 249–50, 330–1, 337 sqq., 346; S. A. Moore, *Hist. Foreshore* 1888, pp. 285–7, 289, 306–7; Gloc. Lib. R.F. 30. 3; R.F. 274. 12; P.R.O., Exch. K.R., M.B. 39, ff. 41 (39) v.–44 (42); A.O., Parl. Svys Glos. 9, ff. 1–3.

THE CHESHIRE CHEESE COUNTRY

The Cheshire Cheese Country consisted of the Vale Royal, the vales of Warrington, Shrewsbury, Clwyd and Montgomery, and the district of the Wiches. Here the rainfall was higher than in the Midland Plain, and markedly so in winter and spring, while the temperature range was less, so that grass continued to grow late in the year. The climature was generally colder and more backward than the climate, on account of the coolness of the land. Among the highly varied soils, clay loams had the highest incidence, followed by sandy loams, and gravelly, peaty and middle loams also abounded. The Vale of Clwyd had a prevalence of silty loam on a base of pale silt and the Vale of Warrington of sandy loams, while the Wirral had much sandy loam and some sandy soil, not to speak of the blown sand along the coast. In contrast, the sub-soils and bases were usually retentive, consisting largely of clay marl or an inpenetrable 'foxbench', making the land cold and sour and the country a true cheese-dairy one.

Many townships had common, or, as they were called, 'town fields', in which most farms had a few acres as an appendage to their main enclosed bodies. Common-field courses were of the plain-country type.[1] Common pastures and heaths, Delamere and Macclesfield forests, the Frodsham, Peckforton and other hills, provided sheep-walks and rough grazings; numerous marshes, of which Frodsham Marsh, Ince Moss and Chat Moss were the largest, gave good summer pastures, especially for cattle; and mosses, heaths and heathlets furnished an abundance of fuel.[2]

None the less, enclosed fields dominated an essentially woodland landscape. Enclosure was mainly from the wood-pasture state and most hedgerows were merely uncleared woodland left for the purpose. Apart

[1] E.g. Slack, op. cit. 19; Thomas, art. cit. 70–2; H. T. Crofton, 'Relics Com. Fd Syst. in & nr Man.', *Man. Q.* 1887 Jan. 6, 8–9, 11, 14 sqq., 21; D. Sylvester, 'Rural Settlemt in Ches.', *Trans. Hist. Soc. Lancs. & Ches.* ci, 33–4; 'Open Fds Ches.' ibid. cviii, 1 sqq.; V. Chapman, 'Open Fds in W. Ches.', ibid. civ. 35 sqq.; N. L. W. Pitchford Hall 825; Salop, R.O., 167/43, ff. 10v. sqq.; L'pool R.O., Norris Papers 552; F. R. Twemlow, 'Manor Tyrley', *Colls. Hist. Staffs.* 1945–6, p. 139; *Twemlows* 1910, pp. 252–3.

[2] Ibid.; Leland, op. cit. iv, 2; M. C. Hill, 'Wealdmoors 1560–1660', *Trans. Salop. Archaeol. & Nat. Hist. Soc.* liv, 264; Defoe, op. cit. ii, 260; 'Candidus', 'Descron Hanmer in Flints.', *Gent's. Mag.* xxxii, 516; 'Benevolus', 'Nat. Hist. Eastham in Ches.', ibid. 563; Marshall, *W. Dept*, 111; R. Stewart-Brown, *Lancs. & Ches. cs in Ct St. Ch.* Rec. Soc. Lancs. & Ches. 1916 lxxi, 11, 24–5, 67–8; H. Fishwick, *Pleadings & Deps. in Du. Ct Lanc.* ibid. 3 vols. xxxii, xxxv, xl, 1896–9, xxxii, 3–4; J. Harland, *Ho. & Fm A/cs. Shuttleworths, Gawthorpe Hall* Chetham S. 1856–8 xxxv, 52, 104; Man. Lib. Ches. Deeds C. 135; Lancs. R.O., Cons. Ct Cestr. invs.: Geoff. Barnes 1634 & Robt Adamson 1677/Broughton; Th. Hey 1680 Gt Sankey; N. L. W. Pitchford Hall 901; B.M., Add. 27605, ff. 146v., 155v.; W. Smith & W. Webb. *V. Royall* 1656, p. 17.

E

from the wet meadows, which along the Dee and the Severn were large and excellent, most enclosures were treated as up-and-down land 'for pasture and tillage' and described as 'arable pasture' or 'arable or pasture'. It was ordinary to plough up the turf for two, three or four years of tillage and then to lay down to grass for half a dozen years.[1] Oats and barley were the chief crops, followed by wheat, buckwheat, peas, beans, rye, vetches, hemp and flax. The first crops on the turf were usually oats and barley, and, in light soils, rye, which would give a twenty-fold increase and still allow four or five subsequent oat crops. One heavy-land course was (1) oats on turf, (2) fallow, (3) wheat, (4) oats and grass. Barley gave the poorer sort their bread and fattened the swine, and buckwheat, oats, pulse and straw all provided additional winter fodder.[2] After a period of tillage the fields were laid to grass, normally by leaving things to nature, or, if the land had been over-ploughed, by sowing hay-dust under oats, vetches, barley, or wheat. The chief constituents of well-managed leys were perennial rye-grass and white clover. Laid down in heart, level, with plenty of farmyard manure, the field soon swarded again, for the climate was congenial to grass.[3]

The pastures were reserved almost exclusively for longhorn cattle, especially for milking cows, and sheep and horses were confined as far as possible to hills, heaths and aftermaths. In the absence of an indigenous

[1] Ibid. 16–17; Slack, op. cit. 56–7; Leadham, op. cit. ii, 642; Norden, op. cit. 199; R. Stewart-Brown, *Ches. Inqs. P. M.: Stuart Per.* Rec. Soc. Lancs. & Ches. lxxxiv, lxxxvi, xcl 1934–5, 1938 ii, 2–3; iii, 85; Midgley, art. cit. 81–3; B.M., Add. 14415, ff. 1–2; 27605, ff. 142 sqq.; Harl. 2039, ff. 87–8, 106 (91–2, 111); 3696, ff. 57–8, 114; P.R.O., Exch. L.R., M.B. 200, ff. 227 sqq.; 239, ff. 125 sqq.; A.O., Parl. Svys Ches. 11, ff. 2, 4, 10 sqq.; 13A, ff. 19–21; 22, ff. 1 sqq.; Ches. R.O., Nedeham & Killmorey: svy the Hack & Bromall; Chetham Lib. Mun. Rm, Adlington MSS. f. 167; Lancs, R.O., DD.K. 1453/1–2, 1463/1–2, 1464/1, 1470/1, 1471/1–2; Salop. R.O., Bridgwater: svy Ellesmere, Middlehampton & Culmere 1602, f. 63; 167/43, ff. 15 sqq., 84; 320/5, pp. 13, 35; Marshall, op. cit. 23–4, 28–9, 133, 170.

[2] Ibid. 24, 28, 133; Gerarde, op. cit. 82; Smith & Webb, op. cit. 17; Candidus, loc. cit.; Benevolus, art. cit. 563–4; Twemlow, op. cit. 237–8; Camden, op. cit. i, 821; E. G. Jones, 'Plas Cadwgan in 1586', *Trans. Denbighs. Hist. Soc.* vi, 13–15; 'Ingenuus', 'Descron Bromborough', *Gent's. Mag.* xxxii, supp. 616; Stewart-Brown, *Lancs. & Ches. St. Ch.* 116; W. Davies, *Gen. View Ag. & Dom. Econ. N.W.* 1810, p. 170; J. Aikin, *Descron Country fr. 30 to 40 m. round Man.* 1795, p. 44; G. J. Piccope, *Lancs. & Ches. Wills & Invs. fr. Eccl. Ct Chester* Chetham S. 1857, 1860–1, xxxiii, 162 sqq.; li, 28 sqq., 120 sqq.; liv, 91, 100–2, 128, 132 sqq., 210–2; J. P. Earwaker, *Lancs. & Ches Wills & Invs. at Chester* id. 1884 iii, 35–6; 1893, xxviii, 46–8; P.R.O., Exch. A.O., Parl. Svys Ches. 11, ff. 12–13; 13A, f. 20; B.M., Harl. 2039, ff. 55 (60) sqq., 110 (115) sqq.; Man. Lib. Lancs. Deeds L. 36a; L'pool R.O., Norris Papers 656; Lancs. R.O., D.D. Bl. 54/2, 8; invs.:—Lancs. & Ches. R.O.s, Cons. Ct Cestr.; Lichfield Jt R.O., Cons. Ct & Gnossall Pec.; W. J. Smith, '3 Salesbury Mansions in 1601', *Bull. Bd Celtic Studies* xv, 299–300; Harland, op. cit. xxxv, 2, 5, 7, 9, 10, 48, 50, 66, 73 sqq., 117, 119, 133, 150; xli, 245, 255.

[3] Ibid. 146, 223; Salop. R.O., 320/5, p. 35; Norden, op. cit. 208; Marshall, op. cit. 28; T. Wedge, *Gen. View Ag. Co. Palatine Ches.* 1794, pp. 15–16.

breed, the sheep commonly stocked came, either directly or indirectly by way of the Midland common fields, from the neighbouring hill countries, and were mostly the small, polled, speckled, short-wooled 'foresters' from eastern Wales, whose lambs fatted excellently on grass after the cattle had gone over it. In winter the fields were unsafe for sheep and few were stocked.[1] Even in summer the farms carried fewer sheep than cattle. Ox-teams, which were housed through the year, did most of the work, and, until they started to gain ground in the seventeenth century, horses were used on the farm only to lead the plough-oxen and for ploughing sandy soils. Although some beasts were fattened and some full-milk butter made for local consumption, whey butter, pig-meat, fat lamb, veal, and store bullocks were all by-products of cheese, which was the great object in view. The surplus bullocks were sold off to graziers, largely by way of London, whence they were distributed to the Wealden Vales and elsewhere. Many farms had no more than twenty or thirty cows, but herds of forty were common and of eighty, 100 or more not infrequent. The larger dairies, too, might have fifty or more swine with them.[2] Very little hay cheese was made. Kept in the fields day and night, each cow yielded, in spring and summer, about two hundredweights of 'Cheshire' cheese, which was the widest selling in the kingdom. The greatest part of 'Cheshire' cheese was bought up by factors on behalf of cheesemongers in various provincial centres like Carlisle, and in London. They distributed it throughout the length and breadth of the land. Tens of thousands of cows producing thousands of tons of cheese a year—that was the size of the business.[3]

[1] Ibid. 28–9; Smith & Webb, loc. cit.; Blome, op. cit. 52; Marshall, op. cit. 7, 35; *Sheep*, 13; *Midl. Dept*, 50–1; *Midl. Cos* i, 376–7.

[2] Ibid.; *Sheep*, 12; *W. Dept*, 5, 23–4, 41, 134, 159–60; Woodworth, op. cit. 78, 80; Smith & Webb, op. cit. 17–18; Childrey, op. cit. 101; Fuller, op. cit. i, 264; Twemlow, op. cit. 235, 237–8, 248–9, 252–4; art. cit. 120, 278 sqq.; Ingenuus, loc. cit.; Candidus, loc. cit.; Benevolus, loc. cit.; Harland, op. cit. 7, 101, 116, 119; E. C. Lodge, *A/c Bk Kentish Este 1616–1704* 1927, pp. 24, 32; J. U. Nef, *Rise Brit. Coal Ind.* 1931 i, 224; Fishwick, op. cit. 4; Piccope, op. cit. xxxiii, 76 sqq., 105 sqq., 162 sqq.; li, 28 sqq., 71–4, 120 sqq., 275–6; liv, 91, 100–2, 128, 132 sqq., 210–12; Earwaker, op. cit. iii, 35–6, 151–3; xxviii, 46–8; A. F. Pollard & M. Blatcher, 'Hayward Townshend's Jnls', *Bull. I. H. R.* xii, 16; *Trans. Salop. Archaeol. & Nat. Hist. Soc.* 1900 xii, 195; 1902 ii, 296, 410–12; Smith, loc. cit.; E. G. Jones, loc. cit.; B.M., Harl. 2039, ff. 55 (60) sqq.; L'pool R.O., Norris Papers 631, 656; all invs. ut sup.; Blome, loc. cit.

[3] Ibid.; *A.P.C.* xxviii, 372–3; E. Hughes, *Studies in Admin. & Fin. 1558–1825* 1934, p. 9; Fuller, op. cit. i, 263–4; E. Leigh, op. cit. 42; Heresbach, op. cit. f. 139v.; C. R. Hudleston, *Naworth Este & Household A/cs. 1648–60* Surtees S. 1958 clxviii, 104, 129; Boyd, op. cit. 43; Marshall, op. cit. 63, 158–60; Defoe, op. cit. ii, 72, 131; Smith & Webb, op. cit. 17; Blencowe, art. cit. 69; Lancs. R.O., Cons. Ct Cestr. invs.: Th. Beck 1587, Th. Brownsword 1588 & Jn Barnes 1690/Man.; Th. Aspinwall 1690 Highton, Francis Gratix 1700 Reddish. For cheese-making v. Marshall, op. cit. 44 sqq. 'Lancs.' cheese started in late 18th cent. nr Chat Moss & marketed at Leigh as cooking variety.

THE WEALDEN VALES

Although there were some loamier ones in the lowest parts of the north vale, the original soils of the Wealden Vales were almost all pale, weak, adhesive 'woodland' clays or 'marlcope' lands. Exceedingly fleet, deficient in humus, and naturally wet and cold, resting as they did on retentive bases chilled by springs from the hills, these unimproved clays were incapable of bearing above one or two crops successively or of forming leys of any but the briefest duration. Grass, nevertheless, greatly ameliorated soil structure and eventually clay loams and loams ('hazel moulds') were produced. If the townships were mostly nucleated, this was on account of the paucity of healthy sites, for of common fields there was no trace. The country was enclosed directly from woodland simply by making clearings that remained separated from each other by uncleared strips, resulting in a chequered landscape of small hursts, i.e. closes of a dozen or so acres surrounded by 'shaws' or wide hedge and coppice-rows. The hursts were small partly because a close network of drainage ditches was needed in this deep, miry, arable country, and the tall, wide shaws tended to keep wind and sun from the corn, putting it in great danger of rotting in a wet season, so it was fortunate the climate favoured arable farming.[1]

Small areas of wet meadow apart, most of the land was necessarily up-and-down. Although there was little uniformity in cropping, the successions were much as follows. The grass was grazed as hard as possible, to facilitate ploughing and ensure maximum sod impregnation, and ploughed in spring for either (1) summer fallow, (2) wheat, (3) oats, or (1) oats, (2) wheat, (3) oats. Sometimes peas or small tick beans took the place of oats, and if either were sown before the wheat, the turf might be simply skimmed off and inverted. Otherwise wheat was preceded by a fallow thrice stirred. Sometimes woad, flax and hemp were first crops on the turf and barley and tares were occasionally grown, replacing wheat and oats respectively. After such a succession the land was usually laid to grass, but sometimes fallowed again for a last wheat crop. This tended to retard turfing, but provided a better nurse crop. As the period of ploughing was short, the tillage proportion was small, despite most of the land being arable. A farm's tillage rarely exceeded thirty acres, its arable ninety, and its whole acreage 100. After four years of tillage at the most, the land was laid to grass for no longer than six or seven years. If ploughed moderately, so that 'the harte of the grasse' remained unimpaired, dunged, chalked or limed, the field turned spontaneously into a good ley with much perennial rye-grass

[1] Marshall, S. Cos. i, 344–5, 354; ii, 100–1; Markham, Weald, 6–7; B.M., Add. 34155, ff. 1 sqq.

and red and white clover. The chief crops were thus oats, natural grasses, and wheat, in that order.[1]

The leys were stocked chiefly with red 'Sussex' or 'Kent' cattle, a large, hardy, middlehorn breed famed for their ability to 'die well'. Both country and cattle were thus admirably adapted to the farmers' chief object of producing beef from grass. Hay, preserved pasture, pulse and cereals also made some well-grained winter beef. Steers and bullocks were worked gently while feeding, and even when being finished off, for one or two days a week, in fair weather. This kept them healthy and in good appetite. The farmers bought in-calvers and stores from the High Weald and bred and reared many cattle themselves. These homebreds were joined in spring by runts from Wales and longhorns from the Lancashire Plain and the Cheshire Cheese Country. Despite small dairies, the country was deficient in milk products and both 'Suffolk 'and 'Cheshire' cheese were imported. It was necessary to run some sheep with the cattle, especially as fatting beasts did not eat the grass as short as even dairy cows did. Sheep were imported from the High Weald, and extra drafts from the Northdown and Southdown countries in spring, when the grass was growing fastest. Yet even in summer sheep seldom much outnumbered cattle. Mutton and lamb were much less important than beef, and wool brought in less than fat lamb alone. As cultivations were heavy, roads miry, and fatting cattle not to be worked hard, they were made up into teams of between four and eight for the former and six and ten for the latter. Most farmers owned only riding horses, though some larger men had teams of three or four for ploughing and from four to six for road work.[2]

[1] Lodge, op. cit. 8, 13, 23, 32–3, 40, 47, 55, 69, 78, 81, 93, 495; G. H. Kenyon, 'Kirdford Invs. 1611–1776', Suss. Archaeol. Colls. xciii, 93–4, 100, 113 sqq.; C. W. Chalklin, 'Rural Econ. Kentish Wealden Par.', Ag. H.R. x, 37–8, 40; Gulley, op. cit. 69, 71–2; Arch. Cant. lxi, 72–4; Cornwall, op. cit. 111–12, 176, 178; art. cit. 82, 91–2; Lennard, art. cit. 32, 36, 44; Blencowe, art. cit. 69, 75–6, 96; Norden, op. cit. 213; Markham, op. cit. 20; Aubrey, Sy, iv, 176; Boys, op. cit. 77; Marshall, S. Dept, 470; S. Cos. i, 347–8, 355–6; ii, 102, 132, 139–41, 150; Guildford Mun. Rm, Loseley 1965, 1966/3, 4; B.M., Add. 29890; 34162, ff. 15 sqq.; 34164, f. 86; Harl. R. Y19; invs.:—Kent R.O., Cons. & A/d cts Cantuar.; W. Suss. R.O., Cons. Ct Bp Cicestr. for A/d Cicestr.
[2] Invs. ut. sup.; B.M., Add. 29890; 34162, f. 3; 34166, ff. 40v.–1 (pp. 140, 142); Harl. R. Y19; Kenyon, art. cit. 93–4, 113 sqq.; Suss. Archaeol. Colls. vi, 192 sqq.; xiii, 120 sqq.; Chalklin, art. cit. 43–4; Cornwall, art. cit. 82, 91–2; op. cit. 86, 88–9, 96, 161, 163, 168, 177–8; Markham, op. cit. 10; Lennard, art. cit. 31; Blencowe, art. cit. 69, 85; Boys, op. cit. 105, 157; Defoe, op. cit. i, 113–14, 128–9, 131; Marshall, op. cit. i, 347, 350–2; ii, 135, 139; Mascall, op. cit. 61, 70, 72; Arch. Cant. loc. cit.; H.M.C., Middleton MSS, 471–2; Lodge, op. cit. 3, 5, 7, 22, 24, 32.

ROMNEY MARSH

The country here called the Romney Marsh included also Walland and Denge marshes, Broomhill, Rother, Upper, Brede, Wittersham, Guldeford, Mountney, Pett and Pevensey levels, and Shirley Moor, together with the Isle of Oxney and the barren, sandy hillocks standing to the west of the marshlands. The marsh soils were mostly rich clay or silt loams, with some coastal patches of sheer sand and gravelly beach. In winter the marshlands were swept by bleak, unbroken winds and in summer their atmosphere was humid and heavy. They were, indeed, 'evil in winter, grievous in sommer, and never good'.[1]

Apart from some common marshes remaining in the Pevensey Levels until the mid-sixteenth century, and from some worthless patches of gravel and sand, the whole of the reclaimed land was enclosed with fences and railings and with ditches and sewers of almost stagnant water. The fields' sizes and rectangular shapes were determined by drainage considerations. Waters arising in the uplands were carried across the levels in sewers and passed under embankments to the sea by means of sluices that permitted outflow at low tide and debarred entrance at high. Drainage made the land safe for cattle and normally for sheep, though there were occasional outbreaks of rot or 'spearwort'. Despite the absence of springs, droughts were not feared in the marshes, for the drainage was not excessive and every field had its ditch or pond.[2] Townships were few and far between, as every grazier whose establishment was complete had breeding grounds in the uplands as well as fatting grounds in the marshes, and preferred to live high and dry in such places as Tenterden and Battle, leaving the management of both marshes and stock to marshmen or 'lookers', whose cabins were scattered throughout the levels.[3] The sandy hillocks to the west were even more barren than the High Weald and hardly more than healthy residential districts, husbandry being confined to a little tillage and many breeding grounds suited only to store sheep. In other upland parts, however, the farming was assimilated to that of the Wealden Vales, so the complete graziers here were also general farmers on some scale, their stock of corn and cattle in the uplands being worth hardly less than that in the marshes.[4]

[1] W. Lambard, *Perambulation Kent* 1576, pp. 7, 158.

[2] P.R.O., D.L., M.B. 112, ff. 5–6, 33–4; Sp. Coll. Maps & Pls. MP C.11; B.M., Add. 34258, f. 7; Cott. Augustus I/i/24; Kent R.O., U. 214/E12; E7/14; Lodge, op. cit. 4; Marshall, op. cit. i, 360, 366–7, 371, 374.

[3] Ibid. 364; *S. Dept*, 469; Ellis, *Sheep*, 50; J. R. Daniel-Tyssen, 'Parl. Svy Co. Suss.,' *Suss. Archaeol. Colls.* xxiii, 254 sqq.; Kent R.O., A/d Ct Cantuar. inv. 1665: Robt Tilby/Tenterden; Boys, op. cit. 11, 106; Lambard, op. cit. 158; Lodge, op. cit. xxiv.

[4] Ibid. 1, 8–11, 13, 22–3, 32–3, 40, 43, 47, 55, 69; D'Elboux, op. cit. 156 sqq.;

Although the marshlands were mostly in grass, some parts were tilled in an up-and-down system and great crops of wheat, beans, oats and peas grown. The first crop was usually peas, the second peas or beans and the third wheat, which then alternated for a few years with beans or perhaps with oats or peas. Fatting oxen were worked gently in draught and plough-teams. After the first crop, either marl, or, more usually, oozy ditch and sewer sludge was laid on the fields. This 'sleeching', as it was called, was repeated about every third or fourth year during tillage, 300 or 400 loads being put upon an acre. The grasses were entirely natural, but not aboriginal, upland varieties having driven out the saltmarsh ones, probably assisted by the sowing of upland hayseeds, for little or no hay was ever cut in the marshes themselves, their excellent swards being reserved almost wholly for sheep and cattle. The graziers controlled feeding to keep the grass low and level and to prevent coarser varieties gaining ground. Pastures were 'stocked hard' and annually 'brushed', i.e. the stems mown down to leave a lawn of nutritious blades.[1]

In the Pevensey Levels, with their broad streams of running water, fewer sheep were fatted than cattle. Longhorns from the Lancashire Plain and the Cheshire Cheese Country and runts from Wales were bought through London and Canterbury to join the Wealden cattle in fatting on summer grass, or occasionally on hay, and were then sold to butchers in Romney and other nearby towns. Some horses were bred and reared everywhere, but outside the Pevensey Levels the scarcity of running water prohibited great cattle herds. Depasturing some beasts helped to prevent the grass bolting in spring and summer, yet even then there was usually no more than one feeding beast to three or four acres of grass. Although the graziers bought in some 'hillish' sheep from the Northdown and Southdown countries for summer fatting, the pastures were chiefly stocked with breeding, rearing and fatting flocks of the native polled 'Kent' or Romney Marsh breed.[2] Even in winter the sheep were given no hay at all, living solely on rich preserved pastures. If the ground were covered in snow, they could still scratch their way to the grass. The marshlands were too bleak for the lambs' first winter

Melling, op. cit. 13–14; Kent R.O., A/d Cons. cts Cantuar. invs.; Mundy, op. cit. 75–6.

[1] Ibid. 36–8; Marshall, op. cit. 493; S. Cos. i, 372 sqq.; Boys, op. cit. 20, 78–9; Lambard, op. cit. 159; Lodge, op. cit. 8, 22–3, 32–3; P.R.O., Exch. L.R., M.B. 197, ff. 50v.–1; 198, f. 58v.; Chanc. Proc. ser. i Jas I, C. 22/79, mm. 1, 2; Kent R.O., U. 214/E12; E7/14, 44; invs. as prev. n.

[2] Idem; Melling, loc. cit.; B.M., Add. 34258, ff. 5–6; Young, Suss. 47; Cornwall, op. cit. 91; art. cit. 67; Boys, op. cit. 106–7, 110; Mundy, op. cit. 35; Defoe, op. cit. i, 125; Woodworth, op. cit. 78, 80; Marshall, op. cit. i, 372, 384–5; S. Dept. 493; Lodge, op. cit. 1, 3, 5, 7, 21, 24, 32.

and these were sent to the uplands. 'Complete' graziers, i.e. those with upland as well as marsh, despatched the lambs to their own fields; and the 'fatting' graziers, who lacked this convenience, agisted theirs in the Northdown Country or sold them to farmers there. Even upland winters were hard and many lambs failed to survive this transhumance, while the remainder were half-starved when they returned to the marshes in the spring, for they had fed nothing but stubbles and aftermaths. Of the sheep wintered in the marshes, without even the shelter of a hedge, thousands died annually of exposure; but the many more who survived were of the hardiest constitution. Lambs sold at Romney Fair on August 20th by the 'fatting' graziers were retained by the Northdown flock-farmers for two winters, being either fattened in the second or sold back to 'fatting' graziers in the spring. 'Complete' graziers, however, reared their own lambs, which spent their second winter in the marshes. Though they lived hardly then, spring and summer grass soon put weight on them. Twelve two-year sheep were fattened on an acre of marsh in a single season. At this time of year sheep outnumbered cattle about forty to one. A 'complete' grazier might have 1,000 or 2,000 sheep in his breeding, rearing and fatting flocks and over a score of rams to put to 600 ewes in the autumn.[1]

THE SALTINGS COUNTRY

Saltings, or marshes open to tidal flooding, were to be found along the east coast from Westgate-on-Sea to Jaywick and from Walton-on-the-Naze to Dovercourt. Drained or not, these salt-marshes were farmed in conjunction with the neighbouring uplands, where the farmers lived. In the uplands, there were some sandy loams, as on Mersea Island, but strong, glutinous clay soils predominated. In drained salt-marshes, a deep, rich, hazel loam stood on beds of sea-sand, silt or clay. This land trembled underfoot and held impressions made on it. The salt-marshes had an oppressive atmosphere and the retentive uplands were also often under a haze of ground mist. The climate was cold and hard in winter and warm and exceptionally dry in summer, so dry that the retentiveness of the soils was a blessing in disguise.

In the 'highlands', remnants of common fields persisted in the sixteenth century,[2] but almost all the land was enclosed with ditches and quicksets, and much of it directly from the wood-pasture state. Although hamlets and isolated cottages existed in the marshes, these were chiefly for shepherds and stockmen, and the main settlements were in

[1] Ibid. 68, 326, 366–7, 375, 377–8; Boys, op. cit. 111, 151–2; invs. ut sup.; B.M. Add. 34258, ff. 5–6, 19; Lodge, op. cit. 1.
[2] C. W. Chalklin, *17th-cent. Kent* 1965, pp. 15–16; Hull, op. cit. 12–13, 35–6.

the high land, largely just above the apparent cliff that marked its limits. Most farms had thus both upland and marsh. Canvey and Foulness islands were entirely divided up amongst various upland townships and Woodham Ferrers manor included marshes in South Benfleet.[1] Most fields, both above and below the cliff, were treated as up-and-down land. The marshlands were often ploughed from grass in spring and sown to barley or white oats, followed by mustard or cole-seed to be fed off by sheep for wheat. A further crop of oats and one or two of wheat might then precede the summer fallows that marked the beginning of a new succession. Usually no more than two crops were taken without a summer fallow, either bare or cropped. Sometimes cole-seed was grown as the first crop on the turf, fed off to sheep, and suc-ceeded by wheat, oats or barley. After one or two such successions, the marshland was laid to grass, often under wheat, occasionally under black oats. Heavy upland soils were frequently ploughed up, fallowed for wheat, and then sown to wheat and beans alternately for a dozen years, before being laid down in broad ridges under wheat or barley. If the tillage became foul, beans were omitted in favour of a bare fallow with summer stirrings, a cultivation hardly to be avoided in these soils, and so beneficial that the succeeding wheat was often doubled in value. Sometimes, indeed, an eighteen-month fallow was given, the field being broken up after harvest and fallowed until spring twelve month.[2] Flax was often grown for two or three years in newly broken grass-lands.[3] In the marshlands, cole-seed was the usual fallow crop, its seed being merely brushed in on the stubble or sown in a mixture with mustard, whose ample herbage smothered the weeds.[4]

Before 1640, when the practice had almost died out, in the offshore islands, especially in Canvey Island before the reclamations com-menced in 1622, the ewes were milked for cheese and whey-butter,

[1] Ibid. 66; Northants. R.O., F-H 1336; Ess. R.O., D./D.K. F2/10; Stat. 43 Eliz. c. 2 § xvii; F. G. Emmison, 'Svy Manor Woodham Ferrers 1582', *Trans. Ess. Archaeol. Soc.* xxiv, 7.

[2] Hull, op. cit. 322–3; Melling, op. cit. 11–12, 29–31; K. H. Burley, 'Econ. Dev-elopmt Ess. in later 17th & early 18th cents.', ts. thesis Ph.D. Ldn Univ. 1957, p. 99; D. W. Gramolt, 'Coastal Marshlands E. Ess. bet. 17th & mid-19th cents.', ts. thesis M.A. Ldn Univ. 1960, pp. 213, 314 sqq.; Boys, op. cit. 58, 62, 71; Marshall, op. cit. 150, 157–9, 161–2, 433; *E. Dept*, 477; Griggs, op. cit. 10, 16, 22; Lisle, op. cit. 26, 86; Norden, *Ess.* 9; Vancouver, *Ess.* 148–9; Herts. R.O., G'bury xii. 11, ff. 73, 76; Northants. R.O., F-H 1336; B.M., Harl. 6697, ff. 2, 5, 12, 18v.; P.R.O., Chanc. Proc. ser. i Jas I. B. 1/68; Exch. A.O., Parl. Svys Kent 26, ff. 2–5; 42, ff. 2 sqq.; Ess. R.O., D./D.K. E1, pp. 12, 18, 24, 27 sqq., 33, 36, 54, 103, 109; F2/10; D./D.Th M17; D./D.Y.W. 17; D./D.P. E25, f. 70; E26, ff. 6–8, 11, 23–4; D./D.B. 146.

[3] Ibid.; Fuller, op. cit. ii, 14; Kent R.O., A/d Ct Cantuar. invs.:—1671: Wm Whet-land/Murston; 1679: Ric. Marrian/Bobbing; 1680; Jas Tonge, Stephen Hunt/Chislet.

[4] Marshall, *S. Dept*, 150; H. W. Brace, *Hist. Seed Crushing in G.B.* 1960, p. 17; Burley, op. cit. 99; Hull, op. cit. 84, App. 6.

since cows could not be stocked, for they would have to have been watered on the mainland and were unable to pass over the creeks. Otherwise most farmers had up to thirty or so milch cows and produced much cheese and pig-meat and some butter. However, meat was a greater object than the dairy. The rich marshes were excellent for sheep and the saltings kept lean sheep safe from rot in summer. In addition to a native breed, stores were imported in autumn from the Chalk, Chiltern and Sandlings countries, from the Norfolk Heathlands, and especially from Wales. Mountain sheep were eminently suited to the purpose, for they made sweet mutton, fattened well when shown good grass, and were so wild that only ditches and sewers could prevent their escape, whereas arable sheep could be put into upland pastures. After fatting on summer grass, the sheep were often finished off on cole-seed. Feeding sheep, of which a single farmer might have flocks of 1,000 or 2,000, generally outnumbered cattle, though not in the uplands, where the balance was reversed; but a farm's feeding beasts were often more valuable. Calves surplus to the dairies were fattened for veal. In summer, grass beef was produced from long and shorthorn stores, and in winter grass and hay beef from Scots cattle and Welsh runts. Large horse teams were maintained, for the roads were deep and five or six horses were needed to plough the heavy soils.[1]

THE FEN COUNTRY

Flanking the Wash, between the Northwold Country and the sea, in the Welland, Nene and Ouse valleys, and at the confluence of the Humber and the Trent was a great area of water-formed lands of two distinct kinds: towards the coast, silt, and inland, peat on a clay base. Even in the peat fens, however, some silt was deposited; and generally peat and silt merged in a skirt of land that was neither one nor the other. As the drowned lands were unsuitable, settlements were originally sited on isles like Ely, on the ridge between peat fen and salt-marsh, as in Holland and Marshland, or on the country's upland borders.

[1] Ibid. 66–7, 84; Ess. R.O., D./D.K. F2/4, 9 10; D./D.P. A22.6/4 Nov. 1593; A18/24 Dec. 1576, 10 & 14 May & 16 June 1577; F224, m. 5; E25, f. 70; D./D.Q.s.90; D./D.Y.W. 17; T./B. 57/3; Kent R.O., A/d & Cons. cts Cantuar. invs.: Cowper, art. cit. 170 sqq.; Savine, op. cit. 194; Norden, op. cit. 8, 10; Defoe, op. cit. i, 15; *Pl. Eng. Comm.* 1728, p. 283; Emmison, art. cit. 7–8; Boys, op. cit. 156; Fuller, op. cit. i, 492, 497; Heresbach, op. cit. ff. 139v.–40; I. R. in Fitzherbert, *Husbandry* ed. W. W. Skeat E. D. S. 1882 xxvii, 137; Steele, op. cit. i, 40, 49, 88, 102; Ellis, *Sheep,* 50; Woodworth, op. cit. 82; Marshall, *S. Dept,* 150, 161; *S. Cos.* i, 385; Gramolt, op. cit. 303–4, 348–50, 354; Burley, loc. cit.; Melling, op. cit. 11–12, 29–31; J. A. Steers, *Coastline Engl. & W.* 1946, p. 396; J. Houghton, *Coll. Letters for Improvemt Husbandry & Trade* 1681, i, 19.

The peat fens gave rise to highly vegetable loams or fen-moulds. Although some of these marshes were dry enough to graze in winter, they were then mostly flooded, a circumstance much rarer in summer, when they supported reeds, rushes, sedge, coarse hassocks, willows and alders. Osiers were used in basket-work, reeds and rushes were cut for litter and thatching or for baking and malting fuel, and in the peat-hags turves were dug, sometimes discovering the overlain soil. The natural vegetation was thus kept in check and the land somewhat lowered, and so made still more liable to drowning.[1] Much fishing was done in the flooded peat fens, in ditches and sewers, in the many large lakes and meres, and in the 'fields' that were drowned winter and summer alike and served only as fisheries and eelies. In June 1650, e.g. Crowland fishing 'fields' covered some 5,000 acres. Wild fowl, too, abounded in the fens and saltings.[2] In summer more or less wide tracts of peat fen were free of surface water, and parts of them were set out as 'mow-fens', where flags and coarse, rank hay called 'lid' or 'fen-fodder' could be cut and its surplus burned off.[3] Much coarse herbage, too, was grazed by geese, sheep, cattle and horses, usually in common and frequently by

[1] Marshall, *E. Dept*, 21–2, 39, 228–9, 231–2, 239–40; L. E. Harris, op. cit. 15; Morton, op. cit. 8–9, 36; Blith, op. cit. 47, 50; H. C. Darby, *Draining Fens* 1940, pp. 24, 27; J. Thirsk, 'I. Axholme befe Vermuyden', *Ag.H.R.* i, 23–4; C. V. Collier, 'Stovin's MS.', *Trans. E. R. Archaeol. Soc.* xii, 36–8; W. Cunningham, 'Com. Rts at Cottenham & Stretham', *Camd. Misc. xii* Camd. 3rd ser. 1910 xviii, 241; P.R.O., D.L., M.B. 119, ff. 133v., 374; Chanc. Proc. ser. i Jas I, B. 1/37, m. 7; Exch. L.R., M.B. 201, ff. 178, 180; 230, ff. 300 sqq.; 256, ff. 149, 194; A.O., M.B. 380, f. 29; Parl. Svys Cams. 1, ff. 8–9; Lincs. 14, f. 13; B.M., Harl. 368, f. 107 (169); Add. 33452, f. 29v.; 33466, ff. 180, 198, 200v.; 37521, f. 16v.; R. 26836; Rylands Lib. Eng. 216, ff. 38, 40–3, 47, 58, 63; Cams. R.O., L. 1/22; E. Sfk R.O., 50/13/10. 2; Nfk R.O., Cons. Ct invs.:—1593: 44; 1611: 151; 1638: 150; Northants. R.O., Cons. Ct Petriburg. Cams. Bds & Invs. 1669, Jn Parrish/Waterbeach; Wmld 5. v. 1 Ct R. Stanground.

[2] Ibid. Farcet; 5. ii. 2; Nfk. R.O., Cons. Ct invs.:—1633: 362; 1598–9: 143A; Ess. R.O., D./D.L. M65; Cartwright Hall, Swinton: Ct R. Newsam; B.M., Add. R. 26836; P.R.O., Exch. K.R., Deps. by Commn 3–4 Chas Hil. 5, mm. 3, 5; L.R., M.B. 193, mm. 130 (63) sqq., 152 (85)d.; 230, f. 87; 256, ff. 107–8, 194; 285, f. 3; A.O., M.B. 380, ff. 29, 40–2; Parl. Svys Lincs. 14, ff. 1, 4 sqq., 12–14; 15, f. 9; f. 5; Yks. 34, ff. 5–8; 35, ff. 2, 5; Collier, art. cit. 37; Darby, op. cit. 9–10, 23 sqq.; Harris, op. cit. 15; Thirsk, art. cit. 23; *Fenland Farming in 16th cent.* 1953, pp. 25–7; Cardigan, art. cit. 115; J. Tomlinson, *Level Hatfield Chace* 1882, pp. 65–6, 284–7; Cunningham, art. cit. 208–9, 232–3, 265, 272.

[3] Ibid. 208–9, 261, 279; Darby, op. cit. 23–4; Blith, op. cit. 47; Marshall, op. cit. 22, 234–5, 239; Gerarde, op. cit. 2; Atwell, op. cit. 102; *Trans. Cams. & Hunts. Archaeol. Soc.* i, 143; P.R.O., R.&S. G.S. 13/87; Chanc. Proc. ser. i Jas I, B. 1/37, m. 7; Exch. K.R., Deps. by Commn 10 Chas Trin. 4, m. 6; L.R., M.B. 256, ff. 3 sqq.; Ess. R.O., D./D.L. M65; B.M., Add. 14049, ff. 4, 7v.; 24741, f. 13v. (p. 24); 33466, ff. 173, 180, 182–4, 192; Egerton 3003, ff. 136–9, 150v.–2; Nfk R.O., Cons. Ct invs.:—1593: 44; 1611: 16; 1634: 101; 1638: 127, 150, 205–6, 217; Northants. R.O., F.(M.) Misc. 902; Wmld 5. v. 1 Ct R. Farcet, Stanground; Cons. Ct Petriburg. Hunts. Invs. B. 1618–74, Jn Burrowes 1662 Ramsey.

intercommoning townships.[1] These commons were enjoyed not by the vicinage only, for townships for miles around sent their stock down to the fens along grassy droveways radiating from them. In this way, Brandon, King's Lynn and other upland towns sent their beasts into the heart of the peat fens. Thirty or forty towns depastured in Peterborough Fen. Seven intercommoning townships had 30,000 sheep in Tilney Smeeth. Concentric rings of towns fed their stock in Marshland and Farcet fens.[2] As the fens were remote, unhealthy and dangerous, few or no farmers formerly lived in them, only stockmen and shepherds, cottagers and squatters, called 'breedlings' or 'slodgers', who dwelt in cabins on islets amidst the watery wastes. Contemporaries knew these 'slodgers' as 'rude, uncivill, and envious to all others, whom they call "upland men"; who, stalking on high upon stilts, apply their mindes to grasing, fishing, and fowling'.[3] Along the coast the saltings and newly embanked salt-marshes were common pastures, mainly for sheep, which they safeguarded against rot. No one lived in these fens save the shepherds, whose cabins nestling under the sea-walls served also as look-outs. Some marshes were temporarily regained by the sea, as in Marshland in 1613, and sea-floods were especially dangerous in Holderness and thereabouts, where the low clay cliffs were easily eroded.[4]

It would have been little use erecting sea-walls unless other works were made, for the land was liable to sink somewhat as it dried out and

[1] Ibid.: Cams. Bds & Invs. 1669, Parrish ut sup.; Wmld 5. v. 1 Ct R. Farcet; Cams. R.O., L. 1/20, f. 12; 22, 50; B.M., Add. 33452, f. 29v.; 33454, ff. 17–18; 33466, ff. 173, 183, 187, 192; Egerton 3003, f. 150; Tomlinson, op. cit. 84; Darby, op. cit. 7, 9, 10, 23 sqq.; Marshall, op. cit. 21; Blith, op. cit. 50, 60; Webb, op. cit. i, 182; Woodworth, op. cit. 78–9, 82; Vancouver, Cams. 125; W. T. Mellows, Peterboro. Local Admin.; Peterboro' Mon. Northants. Rec. Soc. 1947, xii, 79; Spratt, op. cit. 226; Cunningham, art. cit. 216–17, 219–20, 230 sqq., 259, 261–4, 276 sqq.; 286; P.R.O., Chanc. Proc. ser. i Jas I, W. 11/61, compl.; W. 26/15, compl.; Exch. L.R., M.B. 221, f. 285; 229, ff. 182–3; 256, ff. 15, 194; A.O., M.B. 380, f. 29; 419, f. 59; Parl. Svys Cams. 1, f. 10; Lincs. 15, ff. 34–5; 42, f. 18 (11); 44A, f. 13; Hunts. 7, ff. 2, 5, 37.

[2] Ibid. f. 2; L.R., M.B. 201, f. 181; B.M., Add. 27403, f. 2 (3); 33466, f. 139; Cott. Augustus I/i/78–9; E. Sfk R.O., V. 11/2/1. 1; Northants. R.O., Wmld 5. v.1 Ct R. Farcet 19 Sept. 10 Jas; Nfk R.O., Cons. Ct inv. Misc. 1637–8: file A no 1; H. C. Darby, Med. Fenland 1940, pp. 70–1; Pitt, Northants. 165; R. J. Hammond, op. cit. 86–8; Allison, op. cit. 290; Dugdale, op. cit. 244–5.

[3] H. C. Darby, Hist. Geog. Engl. befe 1800 1948 p. 446; Draining Fens 23–4; B.M., Harl. 368, f. 107 (169); Spratt, op. cit. 209; Thirsk, op. cit. 26.

[4] Ibid. 17; Darby, op. cit. 13, 24–5, 44; Blith, op. cit. 47–8; Somerville, op. cit. i, 308; Spratt, op. cit. 221, 224; Northants. R.O., F-H 119; F.(M.) Misc. 918–19; B.M., Egerton 2994, f. 51; 2999, f. 96v.; Lans. vol. 654, f. 11 (14); Harl. 702, f. 14; P.R.O., D.L., M.B. 119, ff. 85v., 90, 107v., 113, 167, 201, 235, 259v., 375v.–6, 381; Exch. L.R., M.B., 229, ff. 295 sqq.; 230, ff. 18, 33, 87, 182, 187, 208v., 210v., 219–22; 256, ff. 3 sqq., 44–6, 283; 286, f. 82; A.O., M.B. 390, ff. 38–41; Parl. Svys. Lincs. 13A, ff. 1–4; 18, f. 7; 20, ff. 33, 43; 27, ff. 2–4; 35, ff. 1 sqq.; Yks. 34, ff. 7–8; 35, ff. 3, 5, 13.

was thus in peril of flooding by the creeks that ran down to the sea. The walls received a series of sewers that conducted the upland waters to 'choughs' or 'tankard-lid' sluices. Fresh marshes some way behind the sea-walls were usually divided and enclosed with drainage ditches, whose outflow had also to be directed to the sea.[1] Nor could the heavy uplands have been cultivated without surface and ditch-drainage.[2] Wherever fens had been improved to summer or winter-ground, it was by drains, perhaps 12 feet wide and 4 feet deep, with sides thatched with reeds, osiers and sedge. Thus the whole country was 'divided and parted everywhere with ditches, trenches and furrowes to draine and draw the waters away'.[3]

All these waterworks were supervised by dike or fen-reeves elected from the townships and responsible in turn to the sessions of sewers. These reeves had to superintend the maintenance of banks and drains; to call out labourers with spades and shovels and commoners with their teams for day works loading and carting clay, stone and gravel, and building walls; to collect money levied by rate to pay for the drainage; to regulate commoning, impound strays, prevent trespasses – in short, to govern the fens. Their immediate sanction was manorial custom enforced in courts baron and they had powers of distraint.[4] Commissioners of sewers exercised chief supervision of the construction and

[1] Ibid. 35, f. 12; Lincs. 13A, ff. 1–4; 43, f. 4; 44A, f. 8; M.B. 395, ff. 21, 28; L.R., M.B. 256, ff. 44–6; B.M., Egerton 2994, f. 51; 2999, ff. 8ov., 82; 3002, ff. 58, 65, 70; 3003, ff. 38v., 65v.–7, 82, 84, 93; Lans. vol. 654, f. 11 (14); Brown, *Yks. Deeds*, 36–7; Dugdale, op. cit. 165–6; Darby, op. cit. 24; Thirsk, op. cit. 20; B. W. Adkin, *Land Drainage in Brit.* 1933, p. 185; Barley, 'E. Yks. Manorial Byelaws', 48.

[2] B.M., Harl. 2239, f. 106v.; Cams. R.O., L. 64/8, 14; Northants. R.O., Wmld 5. v. 1 Ct R. Stanground, Woodston, Farcet; Vancouver, op. cit. 148, 150, 153; Cunningham, art. cit. 241.

[3] Ibid. 205–6, 270, 273, 279; Tomlinson, op. cit. 83; Darby, loc. cit.; *Med. Fenland*, 147 sqq., 155 sqq., 163–4, 177 sqq.; Dugdale, op. cit. 115 sqq., 142–3, 150–1, 153 sqq., 168–70, 218–19, 244–5, 269 sqq., 288 sqq., 299 sqq., 339 sqq., 356 sqq.; Thirsk, op. cit. 24–5; P.R.O., Exch. L.R., M.B. 211, ff. 97–100; 256, ff. 58, 60, 164, 216 sqq.; A.O., M.B. 380, ff. 21–2; 390, ff. 36–7; Parl. Svys Lincs. 10A, f. 7; K.R., Deps. by Commn 10 Chas Trin. 4, m. 5; R.&S. G.S. roll 857; D.L., M.B. 119, f. 375v.; Chanc. Proc. ser. i Jas I, S. 39/53, compl.; B.M., Cott. Augustus I/i/79; Add. 33454, f. 18; 33466, ff. 1 sqq., 7; Ch. 33101; R. 26836; Egerton 2994, f. 5v.; Cams. R.O., L. 64/8, 14; Northants. R.O., Mont. Hunts. 26/28; Wmld 5 (fd loose) Ct R. Farcet, Stanground temp. Eliz.; 5. ii. 10/4; 5. iii. 1 Ct R. Farcet; 5. v. 1 Ct R. Stanground, Farcet.

[4] Ibid.; 5. iii. 1 Ct R. Woodston; 5 (fd loose) as prev. n.; P.R.O., Exch. A.O., Parl. Svys. Yks. 34, f. 8; D.L., M.B. 119, f. 380; St. Ch. Jas 111/25, m. 1; B.M., Add. 33466, esp. ff. 1 sqq., 7, 119; 33467; Ch. 33101; R. 26836, 27072, 39882; Egerton 2994, f. 75; Harl. 702, f. 14; Cams. R.O., L. 1/182; Mellows, op. cit. 78–9; id. *Feoffees' A/cs.* Northants. Rec. Soc. 1937 x, 13, 47, 55; Cunningham, art. cit. 239–40, 265, 270, 272–4, 279, 281, 284; H. E. Maddock, 'Ct R. Patrington Manors', *Trans. E. R. Archaeol. Soc.* viii, 17–18; Darby, op. cit. 147–8, 162–3; *Draining Fens*, 1–3, 12; *Cals. Proc. Chanc in reign Q. Eliz.* i, 106; Dugdale, op. cit. 269 sqq., 294–7.

reparation of all drainage works. They had wide judicial, legislative and executive powers in their sessions courts and authority to levy sewer rates for both new and existing works on each township benefiting from them, irrespective of whether they were sited within its precincts. A judgment on the equity of the statute in 1609 decided the commissioners' powers did not extend to the cutting of new rivers, but was reversed in 1616.[1]

Farming conditions in the fens or marshes were highly variable; and the stable element in rural economy was provided by the cultivated uplands where the farmers lived and where husbandry practices, though greatly influenced by the proximity of fens, was in some respects assimilated to those of the neighbouring countries.[2]

Along the marches with the Breckland and the Norfolk Heathlands, sheep grazed the heaths in winter, when the fens were flooded, and the fens in summer, when the heaths were brown and parched. Since only the sheep-fold made tillage possible, and this in turn depended on the feed and fodder in the fens, the little common-field farmers took a jaundiced view of further drainage, for this might make their mow-fens and grazings too dry. As it was, thanks to their fens, they were able to practise superior field-courses, such as the Chalk Country three-field one, and even to grow a good deal of wheat.[3] On the borders of the Midland Plain, on the peninsulas such as that on which Soham stood, and in the isles of high land amidst the peat fens, with their cold, heavy soils, there was formerly much common-field land, of which about half was composed of permanent-grass balks, leys and cow-pastures.[4] In

[1] Ibid. 243, 370–1; Stats. 23 Hy VIII c. 5; 13 Eliz. c. 9; *Eng. Reps.* 1907 lxxii K.B. i, 929–30; lxxviii K.B. vi, 1139 sqq., H. W. Saunders, *Offic. Papers Sir Nat. Bacon 1580–1620* Camd. 3rd ser. 1915 xxvi, 106, 120.

[2] Darby, op. cit. 43; Dugdale, op. cit. 374–5; Marshall, op. cit. 130, 229, 231, 238–40; *Yks.* ii, 270; Thirsk, *Eng. Peasant,* 148–50, 177; Parkinson, *Hunts.* 10–11, 14–15; Ess. R.O. D./D.L. M65; P.R.O., Exch. A.O., Parl. Svys Lincs. 10A, f. 7.

[3] Ibid. Cams. I, ff. 1–2, 4, 10; M.B. 519, f. 59; Chanc. Proc. ser. i Jas I, B. 1/37, mm. 1, 4, 7; B.M., Cott. Augustus I/i/78; E. Sfk R.O., V. 11/2/1. 1; invs.: Nfk R.O., Cons. Ct; W. Sfk R.O., Episc. Commy Ct Bury St Edm's.; Vancouver, op. cit. 33–4.

[4] Ibid. 43–4, 123, 125 sqq., 191; Parkinson, op. cit. 9–11, 13–15; *Trans. Cams. & Hunts. Archaeol. Soc.* i, 143, 145, 150 sqq.; Venn, op. cit. 36, 38; P.R.O., Chanc. Proc. ser. i Jas I, S. 39/53, compl.; Exch. K.R., Deps. by Commn 10 Chas Trin. 4, mm. 5, 8; L.R., M.B. 221, ff. 256 sqq.; A.O., Parl. Svys Hunts. 7, ff. 18–19; B.M., Add. 14049, ff. 2 sqq.; 24741, ff. 2 (pp. 1) sqq.; 33452, ff. 17 sqq., 29, 33v. sqq.; 33453, ff. 116–19; 33454, ff. 17–18; 33466, ff. 173, 180–2; R. 26836, 37793–4; Harl. 2239, ff. 2, 4v., 86, 88, 143–4; Egerton 2993, ff. 1 sqq.; 3005, f. 38; Rylands Lib. Eng. 216, ff. 40–2, 44–7, 49, 57 sqq., 68; Cams. R.O., L. 1/20, ff. 4 sqq.; 50, 182; L. 64/9, 14; Northants. R.O., Mont. Hunts. 26/27–8; Wmld 5. iii. 1 Ct R. Woodston; 5. v. 1 Ct R. Stanground, Farcet, Woodston; Map 1389; Cons. Ct Petriburg. Northants. Bds & Invs. 1684; Jn Catlin/Maxey; F.(M.) Misc. 211; Misc. Vols. 71, 86–7, 99; 433, pp. 8 sqq.

these fields, the courses were of the usual plain-country type, most commonly four-field ones.[1] Sheep were folded only in summer for winter corn, cattle went in common herds, and horses did most of the work— all in plain-country fashion.[2] In the 'townland' or settled parts of Hatfield Chase, the Isle of Axholme, Holland and Marshland, the soils included some retentive clays and clay loams, more 'warps' or sandy and silty loams of great depth and fertility on a silt base, and, at the juncture of silt and peat, highly organic silty clay loams known as 'skirt' soils. These districts had many common fields with large meadows and numerous leys. Plain-country courses were practised in the heavy soils, but in the sandy and silty ones the fields were largely every year's ground, where hemp, flax, onions and every kind of grain and pulse were promiscuously cultivated.[3] The formation of Holderness, with its many stiff, cold, weeping clays, some sandy soils and sandy loams, 'moorish' lands or fen-moulds, and warps, resembled that of the rest of the country.[4] Here again there were numerous common fields with much permanent grass in their meadows, leys and balks. Two-field courses of the plain-country type generally obtained, the tilth crops being wheat, rye and barley, and occasionally oats, and the breach ones chiefly peas and beans.[5] All told, wheat, barley and oats were the chief cereals. Much pulse was grown and some rye, as well as smaller quantities of hemp and flax. Fallow sheep were folded in common fields in summer

[1] Ibid. Vol. 99; B.M., Add. 33452, ff. 45, 49, 72v.–3, 92v., 123–4; Sloane 3815, f. 141 (p. 319); Cams. R.O., L. 21/20, ff. 6–7, 9, 35; Morton, op. cit. 14; *Trans. Cams. & Hunts. Archaeol. Soc.* i, 143, 150 sqq.; Vancouver, op. cit. 123, 125, 129, 131, 135 sqq., 142–3, 145–6, 149, 151, 158, 191.

[2] Ibid. 123, 125–7, 131–2, 139, 149; Northants. R.O., F.(M.) Misc. 342, 902, 1097; Misc. Led. 129; Mont. Hunts. 26/28; Wmld 5. v. 1 Ct R. Woodston, Stanground, Farcet; invs.:—Cons. Ct Petriburg; Nfk R.O., Cons. Ct; Cams. R.O., L. 64/8; L. 93/139; P.R.O., Exch. K.R., Deps. by Commn 10 Chas Trin. 4, m. 5; Marshall, *Midl. Dept*, 422–3; Parkinson, op. cit. 116–19, 251; Webb, op. cit. i, 182–4; Mellows, *Chwdns' A/cs.* 64; Cunningham, art. cit. 220, 234, 253, 259, 261–4, 273, 276, 280–1; B.M., Add. 33454, ff. 17–18; R. 26836; Egerton 3005, f. 38.

[3] Ibid. 2994, ff. 4v., 40; 2999, ff. 79 sqq.; Harl. 702, ff. 19, 26; Add. 37521, ff. 30, 38; Lincs. R.O., Cons. Ct invs.; Sinclair, op. cit. 13–15; T. Stone, *Rev. Corrected Ag. Svy Lincs. by A. Young* 1800, p. 96; C. Jackson, art. cit. 90–1; Marshall, *E. Dept*, 4, 6, 48–9; Parkinson, *Ruts.* 60–1; Spratt, op. cit. 39, 56; Collier, art. cit. 50; Norden. op. cit. 213; P.R.O., R.&S. G.S. 11/1; 13/87; D.L., M.B. 119, ff. 229–30; Exch. L.R., M.B. 211, ff. 97 sqq.; 229, ff. 182–3, 230, ff. 300 sqq.; 255, ff. 65–7; 256, ff. 52 sqq.; 217 sqq.; 257, ff. 97 sqq.; A.O., M.B. 395, ff. 2 sqq.; Parl. Svys Lincs. 16, f. 5; 27, f. 37; 42, f. 6; Vancouver, op. cit. 158–60, 166, 217.

[4] Lennard, art. cit. 32, 37, 43; A. Harris, op. cit. 41–2; P.R.O., Exch. L.R., M.B. 230, f. 33.

[5] Ibid. ff. 5 sqq., 14 sqq., 35 sqq., 88 sqq., 99 sqq., 172, 177 sqq., 205–6, 208–10, 219–22, 232–4, 241 sqq.; 229, ff. 55 sqq., 64 sqq., 70–1, 295 sqq.; A.O., Parl. Svys Yks. 23, ff. 4 sqq.; 28, ff. 3, 5, sqq.; 34, ff. 6–7; 41, f. 7; B.M., Harl. 6288, ff. 88–91; C. T. Clay, op. cit. iv, 75; Maddock, art. cit. 16–17; Leonard, art. cit. 109; Barley art. cit. 52.

and pasture sheep fed in the salt-marshes, fens and enclosed pastures. Considerable numbers of cattle were fatted and milked. In ploughing warp and clay soils or heavy loams the team was usually four oxen led by two horses.[1] On the descent from the wolds to the sea south of the Humber, there were first hummocky lands of clay and clay loam soils, followed by fresh and then salt-marshes. The upland common fields, which were being rapidly enclosed, had a two-field plain-country course and much permanent grass.[2] Fresh marshes and upland pastures were reserved for breeding and rearing cattle and for draught oxen and horses, the former salt-marshes for feeders and milkers, and the saltings for sheep.[3] Finally, in all these districts, some demesnes had long been in severalty and enclosures were gaining ground from the common fields.[4]

THE LANCASHIRE PLAIN

The Lancashire Plain's climate resembled that of the Cheshire Cheese Country, being only more maritime. Along the coast lay blown sands, sand-dunes (or 'hawes'), and silty and sandy salt-marshes; and inland of these, peat fens and peaty meres, of which the most extensive were Marton and Martin meres, Pilling, Meols and Tarleton mosses, and Bootle Marsh, where the soil was a black fen-mould. Otherwise the prevailing soils were tender, brown, retentive clays, or, particularly in the Fylde, heavy, well-textured clay loams, aptly and respectively known as

[1] Ibid.; Lennard, art. cit. 30; Purvis, *Causes in Tithe*, 55–7; art. cit. 450–1; Raine, op. cit. 12; P.R.O., Exch. L.R., M.B. 230, ff. 219–22; A.O., Parl. Svys Yks. 35, ff. 5, 13.

[2] Ibid. Lincs. 6, ff. 3 sqq.; 12, ff. 2–4; 20, ff. 2 sqq., 14 sqq., 66; M.B. 390, ff. 38–41; K.R., M.B. 43, ff. 2 (1) sqq.; L.R., M.B. 256, ff. 1 sqq., 15, 272 sqq., 288–9; D.L., M.B. 119, ff. 81 sqq., 98 sqq., 117 sqq., 133v.–4, 136v. sqq., 201v., 205; Lincs. R.O., HEN. 3/3; B.M., Egerton 3002, ff. 58, 65; 3003, ff. 10–11, 38v. sqq., 91–3, 97 sqq., 104–7; Northants. R.O., F-H 119; Thirsk, op. cit. 75–6.

[3] Ibid. 69–71; C. W. Foster, *Lincoln Wills* ii & iii, Lincs. Rec. Soc. 1918 x, 1930 xxiv, vol. ii, 65–6; *V.C.H. Lincs.* ii, 328; Folkingham, op. cit. 9; B.M., Add. R. 44459; Lans. vol. 654, ff. 1 (4), 10–11 (13–14); Egerton 3002, f. 126v.; 3003, f. 150; Northants. R.O., F-H 119; Lincs. R.O., Cons. Ct invs.; P.R.O., D.L., M.B. 119, f. 201v.; Exch. L.R., M.B. 256, ff. 3, 10, 15, 283–4.

[4] Ibid. ff. 52 sqq.; 230, ff. 35 sqq., 87, 172, 177 sqq., 300 sqq.; 229 ff. 295 sqq., 334; A.O., M.B. 390, f. 37v.; Parl. Svys. Lincs. 16, ff. 6, 8–9, 11–12, 14 sqq., 27; Yks. 23, ff. 2–4; 27, ff. 2 sqq.; 28, ff. 2 sqq.; 16; 34, ff. 2 sqq.; 35, ff. 1 sqq.; 41, f. 7; K.R., Deps. by Commn 10 Chas East 19, m. 6; R.&S. G.S. 13/87; S.P.D. Mary vol. 9 no 67; B.M., Harl. 6288, f. 89; 2239, ff. 106v., 112; Add. 33453, f. 119; Leonard, loc. cit.; Clay, op. cit. iv, 74–6; Spratt, op. cit. 46; Jackson, art. cit. 89; Cunningham, art. cit. 193–4, 196–9; Darby, op. cit. 16; Somerville, op. cit. i, 307–8; *V.C.H. Hunts.* ii, 90; Rylands Lib. Eng. 216, ff. 38, 49; Northants. R.O., Mont. Hunts. 26/27–8; *Cals. Proc. Chanc. in reign Q. Eliz.* iii, 292; and sup. last n. but one.

'foxglove' soils and 'rushlands'. Both stood on retentive bases and were naturally cold and wet.

Most townships had town or common fields of permanent tillage and grass, in whose topographical divisions and furlongs, separated by greensward boundary balks, were dispersed the 'lands' and 'leys' of intermingled parcels. The area of common field had always been small, but most farms had their share. In town fields the field-course was (1) winter fallow mucked and stirred for spring barley sown on a fine tilth for bread and drink corn, (2) still winter fallow depastured for a breach crop of spring corn on the brush, partly for feed barley.[1] Most of the plain had never been common field and was enclosed from the wood-pasture state. This great preponderance of enclosures was only slightly increased by the dividing up of town fields, which was not usual before the eighteenth century. The farms might have, then, a little town-field tillage and wet meadow, but mostly closes cultivated in an up-and-down system.[2] The sward was inverted for a crop of oats, which was sometimes preceded by flax or hemp and usually followed by barley, or perhaps by oats again. Oats and barley were the chief crops and the minor ones, in order, wheat, peas, beans, rye, flax, hemp, buckwheat and vetches. Wheat was preceded by a summer, and barley by a winter, fallow. Three or four such crops were taken before the land was laid down again. Sexennial or septennial leys were usually formed by leaving things to Nature, sometimes by sowing hay-seed or hay-dust. The first-year ley could give a crop of hay and in the second year the pasture, largely composed as it was of perennial rye-grass and wild white clover, left little to be desired.[3] All told, then, the arable was extensive, but the

[1] R. Dickson, Gen. View Ag. Lancs. 1815, p 191; J. Holt, id. Co. Lanc. 1794, p. 49; Harrison, art. cit. 118; T. Heywood, Moore Rental Chetham S. 1847 xii, 19, 23; C. W. Sutton, 'Svy Manor Penwortham 1570', Chetham Misc. iii, id. 1915 lxxiii, pp. v. 6–7; Chippindall, op. cit. 36, 84–5; R. C. Shaw, Kirkham in Amounderness 1949, pp. 241, 296; R. Stewart-Brown, 'Townfield L'pool 1207–1807', Trans. Hist. Soc. Lancs. & Ches. lxviii, opp. 24, 43–4, 56–7, 59; J. D. W. Leaver, 'Leyland . . . in 16th & 17th cents.', ts. diss. B.A. Nott'm Univ. 1952, pp. 8 sqq.; W. Farrer, Ct R. Honour Clitheroe 1897, 1912–13 i, 24–5, 32–3, 35, 48, 82, 87, 123; P.R.O., Exch. K.R., M.B. 39, f. iv.; 40, ff. 40, 44v.–5; L'pool R.O., Moore Deeds 190, 511, 552, 716, 757, 923; Lancs. R.O., D.D. Fo. 13/39; D.D. Pt. 39, svy. bk 1698; D.D. F. 52; F. 81, pp. ix, xii, figs. 8, 16; F. 93, 101, 168, 1649; D.D. K. 1454/3; 1455/1–5; 1505/9, 10; 1542/2; D.D. X. 102/66; D.D. Bl. 47/5, 6; 48/39, 40; 54/7, ff. 2, 30.

[2] Ibid. pass.; D.D. K. 1451/1, mm. 2–3, 8, 26; 1452/1, mm. 26–8 & 2nd enumeration 32, 34, 37; 1454/1, m. 2; 1454/2, mm. 13, 28; 1455/1–5; 1456/2, m. 4; 1541/5; D.D. Pt. 39, svy Dunkenhalgh 1657–72; Deene ho. Brudenell H. vii. 6, svy Hornby 1576; P.R.O., Exch. L.R., M.B. 220, f. 12; K.R. M.B. 40, ff. 24v. sqq., 40v.–4; Sutton, op. cit. iv, v; Chippindall, op. cit. 36; Stewart-Brown, art. cit. 36, 61–2; Dickson, op. cit. 254 sqq.

[3] Ibid. 18–19, 232, 254 sqq., 288–9; L'pool R.O., Moore Deeds 1212, 1296; Lancs. R.O., D.D. Bl. 24/13; D.D. F. 2419; D.D. In. 60/26; D.D. K. 1542/2; D.D. Sc. 19/16, 23; D.D. X. 33/69; invs.:—Cons. Ct Cestr.; Cons. Ct A/d Richmond,

tillage modest. Although the best malt was a luxury to be bought through Chester or Halifax, barley and oats, the two main cereals, were both malted; and both provided food, the former bread and the latter clap-bread, bannocks and cakes; but were intended largely for stock-feeding, and oat straw was good cattle fodder. Nevertheless, great mows from the wet meadows and rotation grasslands gave generous supplies of winter feed.[1]

Sheep from the North and Peak-Forest countries were fatted in summer and helped to ensure balanced grazing; but were seldom as numerous as cattle. Road teams were usually of oxen and ploughing ones either of horses or of oxen led by them. Some cattle were fatted on grass or stall-fed. Most farms had dairies, with up to a dozen milkers, and a good deal of cheese was made. The grand object of farming, how-ever, was rearing longhorn cattle, which were the widest-selling of all the breeds. Some calves were bred in the plain, but more bought from the North Country, especially from the Craven district and the upper Ribble valley. Here they had been bred on good but short grass and so responded well to rearing in lush plain pastures. The best of all the cattle reared in the plain were those derived from Craven calves, and the cream of all the cattle raised came from the Fylde, from whose stock-rearing farms longhorns were sold to the Midland Plain and the southerly parts of England. Their great size and sound constitutions were qualities owed to excellent pastures and to the breeders letting the calves suckle to their heart's content. Rearing was conducted on a great scale and many farms had constantly between 100 and 200 head of cattle, not a few between 2,000 and 4,000. The same farms, too, often bred and reared horses, especially for the saddle.[2]

Kendal & Amounderness deaneries; Chippindall, op. cit. 36, 78 sqq.; Holt op. cit. (1795) 23, 57, 72, 74; Harland, op. cit. 2–5, 7, 26, 40, 46, 53, 60–1, 65–6, 68–9, 74–5, 77–8, 100, 102; Shaw, op. cit. 248, 265–8, 712–3, 726, 731–2; *R. Forest Lanc.* 1956, pp. 411–2; Fishwick, *Du. Ct* xl, 224–5; Raine, op. cit. 90–3; Piccope, op. cit. xxxiii, 105 sqq.; li, 52–5, 97 sqq.; liv, 58 sqq.; Earwaker, op. cit. iii, 13–15, 60 sqq.; xxviii, 142 sqq.; T. E. Gibson, *Lydiate Hall & its Assocs.* 1876, pp. 105–6; Fuller, op. cit. ii, 189; J. Weld, *Hist. Leagram* Chetham S. 1913 lxxii, 15–16; Leaver, op. cit. 91 sqq.; Childrey, op. cit. 166; Blome, op. cit. 132; Leeds Lib. R.D./A.P. 1; Dickson, op. cit. 265.

[1] Ibid. 510; Marshall, *N. Dept,* 254; Leaver, op. cit. 35–6; Fishwick, op. cit. xxxv, 153–4; Raine, op. cit. 90–3, 228–9; Piccope, op. cit. liv, 58 sqq.; Gerarde, op. cit. 68; Coles, op. cit. cap. cxliv; Fiennes, op. cit. 188; Lancs. R.O., Cons. Ct Cestr. inv. Humphrey Lock 1601 Litherland; D.D. Pt. 1, A/c Bk starting 1616, a/c 7 Feb. 1617.

[2] Ibid., & 1620, & cattle a/c 1617; invs. as prev. n.; D.D. In. 60/26; D.D. Bl. 24/13; D.D. Sc. 19/16, 23; D.D. X. 33/69; D.D. F. 2419; Leeds Lib. R.D./A.P. 1; L'pool R.O., Moore Deeds 1212, 1296; J. Bankes, *Memo. Bk 1586–1617,* 1935, p. 23; Holt, op. cit. 143; Childrey, loc. cit.; Gibson, loc. cit.; Weld, loc. cit.; Blome,

THE VALES OF HEREFORD

Between the Severn and the mountains of Wales was a great district of vale lands, with no wide, open vale and no big range of hills. Woods on the hills, wet meadows in the valleys and arable fields between the two, gave the country its general form. Towards the east lay some stiff, red, clay loams; towards the west and south, many sandy and gravelly soils, called 'ryelands', because best suited to rye and often refusing wheat, peas and vetches; towards the north, many shallow, hungry, sandy soils; and in the Frome and other valleys, weak, stiff clays and some clay loams. Being sheltered by the mountains, the country's rainfall was no higher than that of the west Midlands, and the summer hardly cooler, while the winter was distinctly milder. The climature was forward enough for harvesting to begin the first week in August.

Small and numerous common fields, with courses of the Chalk Country type, were widespread.[1] Some places had large sheep-pastures and the eligible townships commoned their cattle in the Forest of Dean and in Dorseland and Malvern chases.[2] In a peculiar type of sheep-and-corn husbandry, sheep were not folded on the tillage, but cotted by night and their droppings carted to the fields.[3] Most of the country had been, and was still being, enclosed directly from woodland, heath and rough grazing. Even in common-field townships, the demesnes were

---

loc. cit.; Fuller, op. cit. ii, 190; Shaw, loc. cit.; *Kirkham*, 266, 270, 278, 712–15, 731–2; C. Leigh, op. cit. bk ii, 5; Leaver, op. cit. 21–3, 91 sqq.; Raine, op. cit. 90–3, 215 sqq.; Piccope, op. cit. xxxiii, 105 sqq., 148 sqq.; li, 52–5, 97, 171–4; liv, 58 sqq.; Earwaker, op. cit. iii, 13–15, 35–6, 60 sqq.; xxviii, 156–7; Marshall, *Midl. Cos.* i, 317; *N. Dept*, 324; Savine, op. cit. 194–5; Laurence, op. cit. 130; Woodworth, op. cit. 78, 80; Lodge, op. cit. 32; B.M., Harl. 127, f. 22v.

[1] Ibid. 7369, ff. iv. sqq., 23; Add. 27605, ff. 61 sqq., 96, 97v.–9, 101 sqq., 118 sqq.; R. 27245; Marshall, *W. Dept*, 266–7; *Glos.* ii, 224; Hassall, op. cit. 41; J. Clark, *Gen. View Ag. Co. Hereford* 1794, pp. 18, 69; J. Duncumb, *id.* 1805, p. 51; Gray, op. cit. 37, 145 sqq., 153; Cave & Wilson, op. cit. 12–13, 18, 94–5; Beale, op. cit. 50–1; Berks. R.O., D./E.Bp M4; Hereford Lib. Local: dr. 16 no 480, pp. 7–8; B'ham Lib. Winnington 33; Glos. R.O., D. 326/E1, ff. 73 sqq., 89v., 93 sqq.; N. L. W. invs.:— Conc. Ct Dean Hereford:—1663: 3; 1692: Eliz. Birt/Marden; Episc. Cons. Ct Hereford: 1691–2 Mar.: Nich. Mann/Ross; P.R.O., D.L., M.B., 116, ff. 64 sqq., 73, 78v.; 122; Chanc. Proc. ser. i Jas I, B. 35/66, mm. 1–2; Exch. L.R., M.B. 185, ff. 86v. sqq.; 217, ff. 38 sqq., 49 sqq., 210 sqq., 310 sqq., 328–9, 331, 342 sqq., 362 sqq.; A.O., Parl. Svys Herefs. 19, ff. 6, 9 sqq.; *Trans. Bristol & Glos. Archaeol. Soc.* vii, 251; Glouc. Lib. R. 24. 1.

[2] Ibid.; *V.C.H. Worcs.* iv, 459; Marshall, *W. Dept*, 267; L. E. Harris, op. cit. 118; Glos. R.O., D. 326/E1, f. 89v.; P.R.O., Chanc. Proc. ser. i. Jas I, B. 35/66, m. 1; D.L., M.B. 116, ff. 73v., 78v.; B.M., Add. 27605, ff. 69, 97; Stat. 4 Jas c. 11.

[3] Ibid.; Beale, op. cit. 51, 55.

frequently enclosed and in severalty;[1] and by the mid-seventeenth century most common-fields had been enclosed, either piecemeal or by general agreement.[2] Thus the great and growing majority of fields were what were often called 'closes of pasture'. Most of the grassland had to be broken up periodically and if left too long soon became overgrown with gorse and broom, so up-and-down husbandry was almost the universal practice. Some two-thirds of the enclosed land was arable, half of which was temporary grass.[3] In other words, the land was 'some-tymes errable and sometymes pasture', many 'pastures' were 'att present plowed' and others at present alternately mown and grazed.[4] Hemp and flax were occasionally grown on the turf and outrun ryeland leys were sometimes denshired. Otherwise the course might be, on ryelands, (1) fallow, (2) rye, (3) barley, (4) oats, (5) barley, and so to grass; and on wheatlands, (1) fallow, (2) wheat, (3) peas or oats, (4) fallow, part bare, part sown to tares, (5) wheat, and then ley for four or five years. Variations on these themes were legion and the only rules to give spring corn a winter, and winter corn a summer, fallow.[5] Nearly all farms had arable orchards and fruit trees were also grown in hedgerows and hop-yards. Both cider and perry were made, mostly the former.[6]

If difficulty were experienced in producing spontaneous leys, hay-seed might be sown. Grass seldom needed to be forced by composting and soon established itself. Three or four years after laying down, the grass reached its peak and after half a dozen was ready to plough up. Good swards of perennial rye-grass and wild white and perennial red

---

[1] Marshall, *Glos.* ii, 224; Priv. Act 16 Chas II no. 5; Cave & Wilson, op. cit. 105; Phillimore & Fry, op. cit. i, 61–2; ii, 42–4; N. L. W. Episc. Cons. Ct Hereford 1691–2 Mar. inv. Mich. Mann/Ross; P.R.O., Chanc. Proc. ser. i Jas I, B. 35/66, mm. 1–2; D.L., M.B. 116, f. 78; Exch. L.R., M.B. 185, f. 90v.; A.O., Parl. Svys Worcs. 2, ff. 2–3; 3, ff. 1 sqq.; Glos. R.O., D. 326/E1, ff. 90–2.

[2] Ibid. 67v. sqq., 89v.; Leonard, art. cit. 108; Stat. 4 Jas c. 11; Hereford Lib. Local: dr. 16 no 480; B.M., Add. 27605, ff. 96–7, 105; P.R.O., Chanc. Proc. ser. i Jas I, T. 1/5; Exch. L.R., M.B. 217, ff. 370–2; A.O., Parl. Svys Herefs. 16, ff. 2–5; 19, f. 9.

[3] Ibid. ff. 2 sqq.; Mon. 9, f. 3; 10, ff. 2 sqq.; Worcs. 2, ff. 2–3, 5; L.R., M.B. 185, ff. 85v. sqq.; 217, ff. 342 sqq., 349 sqq.; B'ham Lib. Winnington 52; Glos. R.O., D. 36/P26; D. 326/E1, ff. 63 sqq., 90–2; Fox, *Mon.* 13; Cave & Wilson, op. cit. 1–2, 12, 18, 77, 95, 104, 111; Marshall, *W. Dept*, 267, 278; R. C. Gaut, *Hist. Worcs. Ag.* 1939, p. 87; B.M., Add. 27605, f. 106v.

[4] Ibid. f. 68v.; P.R.O., Exch. A.O., Parl. Svys Worcs. 3, ff. 1 sqq., Worcs. R.O., B.A. 68, Woodmanton le agrt 1612.

[5] Ibid. B.A. 81/1A/23 inv. Milborowe Russel/L. Malvern; B'ham Lib. Winnington 45, 217; Hereford Lib. Local: Deed 4163; Gaut, loc. cit.; Laurence, op. cit. 67; Marshall, op. cit. 279, 282; Beale, op. cit. 51–2.

[6] Ibid. 3–4, 9–11, 32; Norden, *Surv's. Dial.* 214; Marshall, *Glos.* ii, 239–41, 243, 285, 288; *W. Dept*, 277–8; Fiennes, op. cit. 43; Cave & Wilson, op. cit. 13, 18; Gaut, op. cit. 75; Hereford Lib. Local: Deeds 3540, 3682; B'ham Lib. Winnington 52; invs.:—N. L. W. Episc. Cons. Ct Hereford, Cons. Ct Dean Hereford; Glouc. Lib. Cons. Ct; Worcs. R.O., Cons. Ct; B.A. 68, Woodmanton valn 1611.

clover were generally obtained. Hot ryeland leys were short, and so
suited to sheep, and often had a coarse sea-green blade. Elsewhere even
the richest leys frequently contained much crowfoot, which made them
unsuitable for fatting cattle, as the grazing butchers said, for the beef
looked yellow and aged. Except in the ryelands, where sheep were mostly
substituted, the new leys were reserved for breeding cows, coarser ones
for rearing cattle, the highest and rankest for labouring beasts, and the
roughest for saddle-horses.[1] The nature of the grasslands thus dictated
some of the specialized objects of farming, which were breeding and
rearing cattle, or sheep, and cultivating corn and fruit. Sheep were
stocked to manure the tillage, two-fifths of whose crops were winter
corn, mostly rye and maslin outside the 'wheatlands'; one-third oats; and
the rest, barley, peas, vetches and beans. The Hereford cattle bred and
reared were sold as beef stores over much of lowland England, only a few
being fatted in their home vales. Their massive frames made them
excellent in draught and they did most of the farm work. Nearly all
cows were reserved for breeding. Each dam was allowed to raise her
own calf in her own way in rich young leys, thus giving it the best
possible start in life. Rearing heifers and steers went in the older and
poorer leys until time to calve or be sold off as stores.[2] Ryeland sheep
grazed by day on leys unfit for, or already eaten off by, cattle; and at
night, summer and winter alike, were driven to cotes and shut in, with
peas halm, and perhaps some hay and barley straw, for their relief and,
residually, for their litter. Once or twice a year the cote was mucked out
and the proceeds carted to the tillage, which thereupon suddenly
gathered strength. The ryelands where they were reared were so stony
that flocks had to be sold off periodically, for, if retained as long as
two or three years, their mouths would have been worn out.[3]

THE WEST COUNTRY

Mountainous heights restricted permanent cultivation in the West
Country to coastal plains, combes, valleys, the billowy uplands of

[1] Ibid. le agrt 1612; Beale, op. cit. 51, 53–4.

[2] Ibid.; J. Webb. *Memls Civ. War . . . Herefs.* 1879 i, 3; Marshall, op. cit. 277;
Glos. ii, 225–7, 230; Fox, op. cit. 14; Campling, op. cit. 72; Hereford Lib. Local:
Deeds 3540, 3682, 4613; Hopton: Deed box 2 no 57; Biddulph 966; invs.:—Glouc.
Lib. & Worcs. R.O., Cons. cts; N. L. W. Cons. Ct Dean Hereford, Episc. Cons. Ct
Hereford; Pye (Mynd) 193.

[3] Ibid. invs. Cons. Ct Dean Hereford 1663: 28; Episc. Cons Ct Hereford 1667
June: Jas Munn/Tirrells Ct; H.M.C., *Salisbury MSS.* pt xiii 1915, pp. 54–5; Marshall,
op. cit. ii, 233–6; *Sheep*, 20, 23–4; Clark, op. cit. 63; Stat. 4 Jas c. 11; Markham,
Wealth pt i, 107–8; Mortimer, op. cit. 177; Worlidge, op. cit. 150; Pomeroy, op. cit.
10–11; Fuller, op. cit. ii, 68; Beale, op. cit. 51, 54–5.

South Hams and the Vale of Exeter. The chief soils were slaty silt loams and black 'growans'. These latter lay on and near the moors and were either gritty or gravelly or both, being simply the remains of a granite rock. Their fertility depended largely on their depth, which was slight even in the valleys and almost negligible elsewhere. The best growans would winter rearing cattle and bear some rye, barley and oats, but the natural vegetation on most of them was thin, short heath and dwarf furze, and there was hardly any truly grass moor. Where drainage was impeded, many wet moors and peat-bogs were formed; and where it was not, the mountain soil was excessively dry and bore little but sour grass, moss and heath. Exmoor and the Brendon and Blackdown hills had similar soils, only reddish and sometimes giving rise to heaths superior to those of Dartmoor and Bodmin Moor. The slaty silt loams that covered most of the lowlands consisted of perished slate-stone rubble pulverized into its original state of silty mud, with some admixture of vegetable mould. Their fertility partly depended likewise on their depth, which ranged up to 10 inches, and partly on their content of stone and rock fragments, which in some places hindered cultivation. The silty loams were often so shelvy that corn could scarcely take root, but the deeper of them grew good corn and grass. Their impervious slate-stone base turned these soils into quagmires after prolonged rains, though they soon dried off again and were, of themselves, so little retentive that drought frequently threatened. The Vale of Exeter, with its many deep clay loams, red or brown in colour, called 'redlands' and well adapted to wheat and beans, deserved its title of 'the garden of the west'. Some 'redland' was also found south of Bodmin Moor, at the foot of Dartmoor and elsewhere. In South Hams a vein of limestone running along the northern margin gave rise to a belt of calcareous loam. Amongst the other soils were valley gravels and gravel loams, deep, rich, absorbent free-working 'dunstone' land, greyish clay loams on a base of tough yellow clay, light sands, and hazel-moulds. Roughly speaking, the lowlands had silty loams, the uplands growans, the widest vales redlands, and the district about the confluence of the Yeo, the Taw and the Torridge, a mixture of the three. The rainfall was considerable, generally heavy, and on the high moors excessive. The lowlands had an unusually narrow range of temperatures and became progressively milder towards the south-west, but the high moors were much colder. In general the climature was backward. Winters were late and lowland grass went on growing throughout the autumn, while the springs lacked vigour and harvests were tardy. In a very dry year, wheat could be harvested at the end of July, but in most seasons it was still green then. Barley often stood until early October. Hay-making reached its peak only at the beginning of August.

Exceptionally, some of the wider vales and coastal plains boasted small permanent common fields, but temporary ones were far more numerous and widely distributed. Shifting common fields made in the moorland eventually created enormous expanses of ridge and furrow.[1] In the main, enclosure was made directly from the wild, either by way of conversion first to rough grazing and then to temporary tillage plots, which had to be mounded off from the waste, or by emparkment and subsequent disparking.[2] These processes gave rise to large enclosures or 'parks', whose rectangular form resulted from the orderly division of the waste and whose mighty hedgerows flourished on the old moulds.[3] Apart from a few permanent grasslands and some convertible husbandry in the deeper soils, shifting cultivation formed the almost universal outline of management.[4] The plots selected for tillage were broken in spring by 'beat-burning' (burn-baking or denshiring). The sward was removed, either by hand, 'beating' it with an adze or 'spading' it with a turf-spade or breast-plough ('hand-sull'); or by ploughing proper, which might be by one of two methods, viz. either 'velling' or 'skirting' ('skirwinkling'). In velling, a wide plough-share removed all the turf. In skirting, a common share pared off only alternate furrows of sward. The turves were then dried on the surface and pulled to pieces, first by drags or heavy harrows drawn over the lines of turf, and afterwards with light harrows, the horse being walked one way and trotted the other, with the object of shaking the earth from the roots. The fragmented herbage or 'beat' was then gathered in heaps of five or six bushels each called 'beat-burrows' or simply 'burrows'. The windward side of each burrow was ignited with a wisp of rough straw and the beat burned to a fine ash, which was spread over the surface[5] and mixed with the soil in

[1] Marshall, *E. Dept*, 102; *On Appropriation & Inclo. Commonable & Intermixed Lands* 1801, p. 10; *W. Engl.* i, 32, 100; ii, 45–7, 53, 112, 131, 134–5, 196; H. A. Lomas, *Hist. Abbotsham* 1956, p. 7; *Cals. Proc. Chanc. in reign Q. Eliz.* ii, 248; iii, 264; A. L. Rowse, *Tudor Corn.* 1941, pp. 33–5; J. Rowe, *Corn. in Age Ind. Rev.* 1953, pp. 213–14; Venn, op. cit. 45; *Rep. & Trans. Devon Assoc.* xxi, 201–2; B.M., Add. R. 13858, 23 June 17 Jas; Egerton 3134, ff. 217 sqq.; Harl. 71, f. 56 (67); 5827, f. 8v.; P.R.O., Exch. A.O., M.B. 388, pp. 143, 145, 147, 149, 151, 153, 155, 159, 167 (ff. 3 sqq., 11, 15); Parl. Svys Corn. 9, f. 16; L.R., M.B. 207, f. 42 (40)v.; Soms. R.O., D.D./H.P. transcript arts. agrt W. Buckland lds farmers & tenants 1634, art. 4; Hoskins & Finberg, op. cit. 284–6, 330–1. Cf. ibid. 265 sqq.; H. P. R. Finberg. *Tavistock Abb.* 1951, pp. 46 sqq.; 'Open Fd in Devon,' *Ant.* xxiii, 180 sqq.

[2] Soms. R.O., D.D./X./G.B., Combe Svy Bk 1704, pp. 43, 50, 70; P.R.O., Exch. L.R., M.B. 258, f. 125; A.O., Parl. Svys Corn. 18, f. 1; 25, ff. 1–2; 35, f. 4; 40, f. 3; J. Norden, *Descron Corn.* 1728, pp. 20–1; Marshall, op. cit. i, 100, 287. Pace W. G. Hoskins, 'Reclamation Waste in Devon 1550–1800', *EcHR* 1941–3 xiii.

[3] B.M., Harl. 5827, f. 8v.; Marshall, op. cit. i, 65, 288.

[4] Ibid. i, 135; *S. Dept*, 524, 554, 572–3, Fiennes, op. cit. 14; G. L. Apperson, *Gleanings aft. Time* 1907, p. 165; Soms. R.O., D.D./W.O., svys Farway, Seaton, Sherford & Whitewell 1682; Exeter Lib. M.B., 8d Ld Dynham's Svy Bk 1566, ff. 8, 20; B.M., Harl. 71, f. 57 (68).

[5] Ibid. 5827, f. 7v.; Corn. R.O., Cons. Ct A/d Corn. invs.:—P. 1633: Wm Palle-

the process of gathering the land into narrow stitches for winter corn.[1] This first crop was more usually wheat, though rye was grown in poorer lands, especially in earlier times. It might be followed by barley and then by oats. More commonly, two successive crops of wheat preceded one or two of oats. Barley could not be grown after wheat in any but the best lands. Deeper soils, well-manured and bare-fallowed in the penultimate year of tillage, could often be forced to bear four or five crops; but sometimes heavy manuring was needed for only two or three. Thinner soils in furze crofts and moorland enclosures usually gave only a single crop, and that of winter corn, though some farmers tilled them until no more than the seed was returned. Black, or more often naked oats ('pilez', 'pillas') were the usual farewell crop, for the soil would bear nothing better and they served for feed and hay. Beat-burning was a defence against wire-worm and other soil pests and enabled wheat to be grown as a first crop. In the more northerly parts, and occasionally elsewhere, to beat-burning was preferred raftering (rotting the spine'), or even a part-fallow; and as wheat could not then follow, there was substituted an alternative succession of (1) oats, (2) wheat, (3) oats, and so back to grass. Where wheat-and-bean land existed, peas, beans and flax were also cultivated. In the warmest parts, by the coast mostly, was grown a rathe-ripe barley that could be milled eight or nine weeks after sowing. Generally, the barley acreage tended to increase and barley bread and malt to come into wider use. Yet neither barley nor oats became common drink-corns and this restricted the cultivation of hops.[2] Cider was the usual beverage and most farms had apple-orchards

owes/Camborne; P1639: Jn Paskowe/St. Austell; T1616: Bennett Trowusen/St Hilary; T1632: Ric. Thomas/Kea; T1637: Humphrey Trigeon/Sancreed, Wm Trugens/Kenwyn; Marshall, op. cit. 526, 531, 555; *W. Engl.* i, 135–6, 141 sqq., 295, 298; ii, 8, 45–7, 54; Norden, op. cit. 20; *Surv's. Dial.* 224 (2nd occ.); Fitzherbert, *Husbandrie*, f. 6; Folkingham, op. cit. 25; T. Westcote, *View Devon in 1630* 1845, p. 55; R. Carew, *Svy Corn.* 1769, f. 19v.; Lennard, art. cit. 30–1, 35–6; *Rep. & Trans. Devon Assoc.* l, 270–1.

[1] Ibid. xli, 215 sqq., esp. 226–7; B.M., Egerton 3134, ff. 174 sqq., 199;Marshall, op. cit. ii, 47, 81, 118.

[2] Ibid. i, 79, 135–6, 186, 191–4, 295; ii, 53, 102–3, 117; *S. Dept*, 517, 523–4, 531, 542, 577; W. Borlase, *Nat. Hist. Corn.* 1758, p. 87; Carew, op. cit. f. 20; Lennard, art. cit. 37, 42; Apperson, op. cit. 164; H. Hulme, 'Prob. Inv. goods & chattels Sir Jn Eliot', *Camd. Misc. xvi*, Camd. 3rd ser. 1936 lii; Worthy, op. cit. 22–3, 180, 273; Camden, op. cit. i, 30, 49; T. Risdon, *Chorographical Descron or Svy Co. Devon* 1,723 p. 4; A. L. Rowse, *Engl. Eliz.* 1950, p. 103; *Rep. & Trans. Devon Assoc.* xli, 226–7; invs.:—Corn. R.O., Cons. Ct A/d Corn.; Wilts. R.O., Dioc. Reg. Sarum.; Soms. R.O., Cons Ct Bath. & Well., Cons. Ct A/d Taunton; D.D./W.O., Fineton recpt bk 1599; B.M., Harl. 71, f. 57 (68); Add. 21608, f. 277; P.R.O., Exch. A.O., Parl. Svys Corn. 9, f. 16; 25, f. 3; ff. 2–3; Devon 6A, f. 19; Cash, op. cit. 1 sqq., 15 sqq., 27–8, 31 sqq., 140 sqq., 168–9; Norden, loc. cit.

and cider-mills, though it was not much produced for the market, except in South Hams.[1] Whether in permanently cultivated arable, of which half was in tillage and half mown and grazed in rotation, or in temporary moorland tillage plots, the land was commonly laid down under oats, for wheat could only be grown as a first crop. Since beat-burning destroyed whatever grass had originally been growing, worth-while leys could be formed only by sowing hay-seed, when they could endure from five to ten years in the best and deepest soils, less in others, before being invaded by ferns and thistles. Furzy and heathy moorlands, which were broken up only once every twenty or thirty years, were not seeded down, but left to recover their former state of rough grazing.[2]

While they were awaiting their turn to be broken up, the vast expanse of rough grazing on Dartmoor, Exmoor, Bodmin and other moors were used as summer pastures. Sheep wintered in lowland enclosures were, by a species of transhumance, summered in the moorland plateaux and valleys. Exmoor and Dartmoor, e.g. were heavily stocked in summer by large flocks driven from far and wide. Although great parts of both moors were overgrown with heath, there were some patches of good greensward, as by Badgeworthy Water, and, despite mists and fogs, both made summer pastures able to fat both sheep and cattle for the butcher. It was therefore the practice to preserve bottom grass-lands for winter pasture and to drive many of the sheep and cattle to the moors, where their human companions resided in the same stone cabins that fiction has placed at the disposal of pixies and of Sherlock Holmes. The outskirts of the large moors were commons for the stock of the 'venville' or bordering manors, while their heartlands were agisted with the flocks of more distant townships.[3] None of the farmers had great flocks and most of them acted as their own head shepherds. They bred, reared and stocked sheep mainly for the wool and mutton.[4] Horses were not much used for carting, but as pack-animals, for which they were con-

[1] Ibid. 214; Defoe, Tour i, 222; Marshall, W. Engl. i, 27–8, 300; ii, 119; Worthy, op. cit. 22–3, 26–7; invs.:—Devon R.O., Cons. Ct Exon. no 43; Corn. R.O., Cons. Ct A/d Corn. P1618: Mk Payne/Stratton, Mary Pearse/Calstock; B.M., Add. 21605, ff. 36 sqq.; Harl. 71, f. 58 (69); 5827, f. 8; P.R.O., Exch. A.O., Parl. Svys Corn. 5, f. 1.

[2] Ibid. 25, f. 3; Marshall, op. cit. i, 135–6, 138; ii, 45–7, 53, 59–60; S. Dept, 523–4, 544, 554, 572–3.

[3] Ibid. 531, 604; W. Engl. i, 268; ii, 23–7, 55, 71; Rowse, op. cit. 104; Markham, op. cit. pt v, 32; P.R.O., Chanc. Proc. ser. i Jas I, R. 8/36; Exch. L.R., M.B. 207, f. 35 (33)v.; A.O., M.B. 358, f. 68 (3); Parl. Svys Corn. 46, f. 3; Devon 6A, f. 45; Soms. 18, ff. 4–5, 7–8; B.M., Harl. 5827, f. 8v.

[4] Ibid. f. 10; Carew, op. cit. f. 23; Apperson, op. cit. 167–8; Childrey, op. cit. 13; Mascall, op. cit. 217; Marshall, op. cit. i, 259–60, 269, 302; ii, 7, 44–7, 55–6, 118, 121, 146, 151; S. Cos. i, 378; S. Dept. 526, 547–8; all invs. ut sup.; Worthy, op. cit. 14–15, 22–3, 26–7, 33, 35–6, 87, 182–3, 193, 204, 220, 272–3; Borlase, op. cit. 286.

stitutionally fitted, being bred from the best of the small, sturdy, moorland ponies. All farm carriage was by pack-horse, except that oxen were sometimes yoked to harvest or dung-sledges ('gurry-buts'). Muck, sand and even marl were usually carried to the land on horse-back, in strong, coarse panniers with drop-bottoms, known provincially as 'dung-pots'. Cattle formed the chief stock and plough-teams were made up of two or four oxen or six steers, or some such combination, led by one or two horses. Oxen were shod, but were often hard put to gaining a footing in hilly lands. These teams usually made two journeys a day, morning and afternoon, each of about four hours.[1] The cattle were of the middle-horn class. Generally, they had no claim to be a dairy breed and were valued chiefly for draught and for feeding, though all the farms had domestic dairies. The distinctive feature of dairy practice was that cream had to be raised from indifferent milk by the gentle application of culinary heat; and the resultant clotted cream was highly regarded for itself. Only a little hard skimmed-milk cheese was made, and occasionally goats' milk cheese, and, except in the Vale of Exeter, not much butter. Although some cattle and sheep were fatted for local markets, the great object of farming was the breeding and rearing of beef cattle. These were brought up by their dams in the best grasslands, reared in rough grazings and moorland pastures, worked until four or five years of age, and then sold to graziers in plain and vale countries further east.[2] The system of cultivation well suited this breeding and rearing, for the temporary leys, although not good fatting grounds, were excellent for cows and calves, and the 'new springuyng grass' they enjoyed gave rise to good beef stores.[3]

WALES

Largely mountainous and inarable. Wales formed a distinct farming country that occupied most of the principality and extended beyond it, there being little coincidence between administrative, linguistic and agricultural boundaries. Here, then, Wales signifies the region where

[1] Ibid. 88, 288; Worthy, op. cit. & invs.—as prev. no.; Fiennes, op. cit. 264–5, 267; Lennard, art. cit. 33; Norden, *Corn.* 20; Carew, op. cit. f. 19v.; Childrey, op. cit. 12; Marshall, op. cit. 525, 580; *W. Engl.* i, 30–1, 113, 116, 119, 121–3, 155, 238–9, 293–4; ii, 58, 116, 142, 186.

[2] Ibid. i, 239 sqq., 249–50, 302, 324; ii, 117, 119–20; *S. Dept*, 526, 581–2; Borlase, op. cit. 59, 286–7; Childrey, op. cit. 13; Norden, loc. cit.; Apperson, op. cit. 175; Hulme, art. cit.; *Rep. & Trans. Devon Assoc.* xx, 84 sqq.; Soms. R.O., D.D./T.H., inv. Abraham Pollard 1677 Chard; Worthy, Cash & invs. ut sup., esp. Cons. Ct Exon. no 49, & Dioc. Reg. Sarum. Jn Clare 1586 Netherbury; Andr. Burrow als Barby & Jn Loming 1680, Ric. Horswell als Cole 1686/Uffculme.

[3] B.M., Harl. 5827, f. 8v.

the characteristically Welsh system of husbandry prevailed. A further and internal distinction may be made between the lowlands or Englishry and the uplands or Welshry, for the former had mostly deep soils and the latter thin ones, in which corn could scarcely establish roots, so the depth of soils was more significant than their variety, which ranged from valley gravels to sands, woodland clays, loams, black peat-earths and fen-moulds. Excessive rain, too, heightened the obstacles to cereal cultivation in the Welshry, while the somewhat drier summers and longer autumns enjoyed by the lowlands of Anglesey, Cardiganshire, Pembroke- shire and Gower made them more apt for corn and grass.

Much of the Englishry, especially in the south-west, was formerly permanent tillage, with regular tilths deeply ploughed by strong teams, and called 'errable or corne grownde', meaning 'the best sorte of corne grownde and such as will endure to be plowed for corne everye yeere'. Here the chief crops were oats, winter wheat, rye, barley, peas and beans. Wheat and rye, whose seed was sown under furrow, were pre- ceded by a summer fallow, which was either folded with sheep or mucked with manure from the farmyards and from the cotes where the sheep wintered. Pulse was grown on the stubbles after corn. Barley, which was grown more near the coast than elsewhere, gave yields of between ten and fourteenfold about 1600 on land composted with seaweed or dressed with sea-sand, marl or lime.[1]

In the Welshry, the narrow valley bottoms were meadows, the lower and gentler slopes arable, the higher slopes and table-lands rough grazing and the heights and eminences barren wilderness. Although the slopes were barely eligible for corn, the farmers were ever assiduous in aration and took the plough wherever possible, so that while the area of tillage was small, that of arable was great.[2] As a later sixteenth-century surveyor puts it, 'they doe often convert their pasture into errable and

[1] C. Hassall, *Gen. View Ag. Co. Pembroke* 1794, p. 19; id. *Carm.* 1794, pp. 13, 15; T. Lloyd, id. *Cards.* 1794, pp. 10, 29; Davies, *S. W.* i, 122; *N. W.* 143; B. E. Howells, 'Eliz. Squirearchy in Pembs.', *Pembs. Historian* no i, 37–9; 'Pembs. Farming c. 1580– 1620', *N. L. W. Jnl.* ix, 246, 248; F. V. Emery, 'W. Glam. Farming c. 1580–1620', ibid. 397, 399–400; E. L. Barnswell, 'N. on Perrot Fam.', *Archaeologia Cambrensis* 1866 xii, 357; E. Rowley-Morris, 'Hist. Par. Kerry', *Coll. Hist. & Archaeol. Montgom.* xxvii, 117; P.R.O., Exch. L.R., M.B. 206, ff. 6 sqq., 53 sqq., 75 sqq., 118 sqq., 216 sqq., 227 sqq.; 260, ff. 14 sqq., 23; N. L. W. Episc. Cons. Ct Hereford invs. 1691–2 Mar.: Wm Gunter/Cusop; 1726 May: Hy Andrews/Byton; G. Owen, *Taylors Cussion* 1906 pt i, ff. 3, 35; pt ii, f. 115; *Descron Penbrokeshire* H. S. C. Rec. Ser. 1892– 1936, pt i, 59–60, 63, 74–5.

[2] Ibid. 61–2; J. Bradney, *Hist. Mon.* 1904–34 iii pt ii, 230; Lloyd, op. cit. 8, 21; Davies, *S. W.* i, 308; J. Clark, *Gen. View Ag. Co. Radnor* 1794, p. 13; W. Rees, *Svy D.L. Ldps in W. 1609–13* 1953, pp. 239–40, 248, 261; Slack, op. cit. 65, 67–8, 70, 73, 87, 94; B.M., Add. 27605, ff. 7, 116–17, 143v., 147–8, 158–61; P.R.O., Exch. L.R. M.B. 185, f. 143 (43)v.; 205, ff. 1 sqq.; 239 ff. 1 sqq.; 258, ff. 3 sqq.; 260, ff. 14–17, 55, 84 sqq., 216 sqq.

their errable into pasture, for that it will not contynue good longe in tilledge.' Another surveyor explains that

'by . . . errable or pasture . . . is ment, for the most parte, wylde grownde called in Welsh *tir mynyth* or *tir mane*, such as yeldeth corne but once in xx or xxiiij yeeres . . . and at all tymes ells lyeth grown with small furse or heath and serveth for pasture for sheepe or yong cattell; and . . . by . . . pasture (whereof yow shall fynde very little) is ment such as serveth for pasture at all tymes and to none other use.'

The poorest arable, indeed, would 'beare corne but once in xxx yeeres'.[1] At least a year before sowing was intended, a selected corn-plot might have installed upon it a running fold of hurdles for the reception of all the cattle, horses and sheep that could be mustered, in order to crop short the herbage, consolidate the soil and impregnate the sod. Every night from mid-March to mid-November, or as long as the weather was clement, the stock were driven to this pinfold. In this way the equivalent of twenty beasts or 200 sheep would fold-muck two acres in six months. In November or December the plot was ploughed and in March sown to oats. Another crop of oats might follow and the succession, indeed, was often prolonged until harvest failed to return the seed. If the crop failed to ripen, it was cut green for hay. Otherwise it fed both humans and horses and provided the cattle with straw for the winter. In extraordinarily favourable situations some barley was grown, or even, on newly folded land, a little rye or summer wheat ('holywheat'), which ripened only precariously.[2] Winter corn could be grown only after paring and burning, which was a recognized alternative to folding. In the commoner practice, that of 'clean beatland', all the sward was dug up or skimmed off with a broad-winged share in early summer and then left to lie root upwards to dry out. In autumn the turves were burned in heaps and crops sown in the scattered ashes 'to an incredible production of oats', rye, peas or vetches, or even of winter wheat. Finally there would be a farewell crop of black or naked oats, or perhaps of vetches and hayseed; but the land would not bear corn again for a score of years or more. Another method was called 'pied beatland', where only half the turf was dug up with a 'bettax' (adze) and alternate furrows were left untouched. When the turves had been burned, the whole field was ploughed, mixing in the ashes, ready for a succession of oats that might

---

[1] Ibid. ff. 16v., 23; B.M., Add. 27605, f. 117v.
[2] Coles, op. cit. cap. cxliv; Leland, op. cit. iii, 17; Davies, *N. W.*, 151; Lloyd, op. cit. 23; Clark, loc. cit.; *Gen. View Ag. Co Brecknock* 1794, pp. 34, 36; G. Kay, *id. N. W.* 1794, Carn. 11, 17; A. Llwyd, *Hist. I. Mona* 1833, p. 6; Marshall, *Sheep*, 14; Owen, op. cit. pt i, 59–62; T. M. Owen, 'Some Lleyn Invs. 17th & 18th cents.', *Trans. Carn. Hist. Soc.* xxi, 71 sqq.; Rowlands, op. cit. 189.

last as long as five or six years. Shifting cultivations in Wales and in the West Country thus resembled each other in both name and nature. Tillage abandoned, the land was simply thrown open to gain a sward as best it could. If the plot had been 'clean beatland', little or no herbage would be forthcoming for at least a year or two; if fold-land, and ploughed moderately, it was apter to grass over. Yet what grass did come would soon be invaded by fern, heath and furze.[1] Having degenerated into rough grazing, the land could not be ploughed up again until rested a long time, when its turn came to be folded or beat-burned. Cultivation was thus merely temporary, and since the soils were so fleet, all ploughing was necessarily shallow, and the normal team of two shod oxen led by two ponies hardly more than scratched the surface.[2]

Even amongst the heights many a valley or combe (*cwm*) grew good grass in summer, and thither cattle were driven when the bottom grass-lands were shut up for hay. In this transhumance some members of each family normally accompanied the herds. A detachment, including some women-folk to tend the in-milk cows and make butter or cheese, spent the summer in specially constructed cabins in this *hafod* or *hafod-tref*, as the encampment was called.[3]

Formerly almost every township had a *maes* or common field, but usually this was only temporary, a mere tillage plot in shifting cultivation distributed ridge by ridge amongst the commoners as in other mountainous countries; and large tracts of permanent common-field land were found only in Gower and in Pembrokeshire's 'Little England beyond Wales'. In these permanent common fields the field-course was exactly the same as in the town fields of the Lancashire Plain. In winter the land was always fallowed in preparation for spring crops. Had any-one sown winter corn, it would only have been eaten off by the common herds. Thus when the enclosure of these common fields commenced about 1560, more wheat was grown than before.[4]

[1] Ibid. 187–9; D. G. Owen, *Eliz. W.* 1962, pp. 24, 80; Camden, op. cit. ii, 813; Folkingham, op. cit. 27–8; Fuller, op. cit. iii, 530; Norden, *Surv's. Dial* 208–9; B.M., Add. 27605, f. 31v.; P.R.O., Exch. L.R., M.B. 260, f. 23; G. Owen, op. cit. pt i, 63.

[2] Ibid. 62; Davies, op. cit. 318; *S. W.* i, 289; Fox, *Glam.* 39; *Mon.* 16; Hassall, *Pembs.* 19; Clark, op. cit. 36; Kay, op. cit. Anglesey 18; Rowlands, op. cit. 94.

[3] Rees, *S. W. & March*, 217–18; H. J. Randall, *Bridgend* 1955, p. 34; R. A. Roberts, 'Trends in semi-nat. hill pastures fr. 18th cent.', *4th Internat. Grassland Cong. Rep.* 1937, pp. 150–1.

[4] P.R.O., Exch. A.O., Parl. Svys Pembs. 2, f. 2; L.R., M.B. 205, ff. 25, 28, 30, 135; 206, ff. 39, 53 sqq.; 238, f. 37; 239, ff. 125–8; 260, ff. 66, 222; B.M., Add. 27605, ff. 5 sqq., 22–3, 26v.–7, 32–3, 36, 44 sqq., 164v. sqq.; Marshall, *W. Dept*, 166; Kay, op. cit. Carn. 21; Lloyd, op. cit. 29; Hassall, op. cit. 20–1, *Carm.* 21; Fox, *Glam.* 41; Davies, op. cit. i, 220–3; Clark, op. cit. 24; Slack, op. cit. 77, 94, 115–16; E. J. Jones, 'Enclo. Movemt in Anglesey (1788–1866)', *Anglesey Ant. Soc. & Fd Club Trans.* 925, pp. 25 sqq.; E. M. Jones, *Exch. Proc. (Eq.) concerning W.: Hy VIII–Eliz.* 1939,

Both tillage and the application of extraneous fertilizer were undertaken mainly with the object of bettering grasslands, for breeding and rearing sheep and cattle were the farmers' main business. Large numbers of goats allowed many cows to be spared from domestic dairies, and ewes, too, were milked. The farmers had ponies and a few horses, and often large flocks of sheep, but their chief stock, in point of value, was of breeding and rearing cattle. Some larger farms had 200 breeding cows, 150 rearers and 700 sheep couples. Cows were suffered to suckle and bring up their calves in good pastures, while the rearing beasts were turned into rough grazings in the summer months and perhaps employed in folding tillage plots. Meanwhile, the meadows were left for hay and the cows taken to the *hafod*. Sheep, too, roamed the rough grazing in spring and summer. Then, in autumn, many or most of the steers, bullocks, hogs, and wethers would be sold off, leaving the remainder of the stock to winter in or near the farmsteads, where from early December onward they were housed or cotted.[1] As the biggest were often retained for draught, it was the far more numerous lesser bullocks and runts— 'the Spanish fleet' of Wales—that provided the greatest single item in farm income when they were sold off for fatting in inferior pastures in the Midland Plain, Wealden Vales and Cheese, Butter and Saltings countries.[2]

---

pp. 297–8, 301–2; Howells, art. cit. 315–16, 327–9; M. Davies, 'Open Fds Laugharne', *Geog.* 1955 xl, 170 sqq.; 'Rhosili Open Fd & rel. S. W. Fd Patts.', *Ag. H.R.* iv, 80 sqq.; G. Owen, op. cit. pt i, 61; *Taylors Cussion* pt ii, f. 115.

[1] Ibid. pt. i f. 8; *Penbs.* pt i, 61–2; Holinshed and Harrison, op. cit. 221; E. Powell, 'Pryce (Newton Hall) Corr. &c.', *Coll. Hist. & Archaeol. Montgom.* xxxi, 72–4; A. H. Dodd, *Ind. Rev. in N. W.* 1933, pp. 2, 4; D. R. Phillips, *Hist. V. Neath* 1925, pp. 210–11; invs.:—N. L. W. Episc. Cons. Ct Hereford; Glouc. Lib. Cons. Ct; B'ham Lib. 324074; P.R.O., Exch. L.R., M.B. 260, ff. 23, 71v.; E. A. L. 'Goods & Chattels Cards. Esq. in 1663', *Cards. Ant. Soc. Trans.* xi, 28–9; Roberts, art. cit. 150; Emery, art. cit. 19–21, 23, 27–8, opp. 32; E. D. Jones, 'Inv. Pembs. Squire's Chattels 1629', *N. L. W. Jnl* viii, 222–4; E. M. Jones, op. cit. 122, 125, 189; Rees, *D.L. Ldps,* 239–40; T. M. Owen, loc. cit.; G. D. Owen, op. cit. 24; Howells, art. cit. 240 sqq., 249–50; 'Eliz. Squirearchy', 37–9; Barnswell, art. cit. 348, 353 sqq.; W. S. K. Thomas, 'Swansea Inv.—Jn Moris', *Gower* x, 58–61; Slack, op. cit. 69; Kay, op. cit. Merioneth 12; Davies, op. cit. i, 161, 308; ii, 227, 251; Lloyd, op. cit. 23; Hassall, loc. cit.; *Carm.* 12; Fox, *Mon.* 10, 32; M. I. Williams, art. cit. 174 sqq.; Defoe, op. cit. ii, 54–5, 59; Merrick, op. cit. 11; Fuller, op. cit. iii, 484.

[2] Ibid. 508; Dors. R.O., A/d Ct Dors. inv. 1693: 11; Ess. R.O., D./D.P. F224, m. 5; F234; B.M., Add. 34162, f. 4 (5); P.R.O., St. Ch. Jas 54/10; Exch. K.R., Sp. Commn 5021; L.R., M.B. 206, f. 3; Llwyd, op. cit. 7; Davies, *N.W.* 310–11; Boys, op. cit. 147; Hassall, op. cit. 35; Dodd, op. cit. 7–8; *Stuart W.* 20; C. Skeel, art. cit.; 'W. under H. VII', in *Tudor Studies* ed. R. W. Seton-Watson 1924, p. 14; K. Williams-Jones, 'Drover's A/c', *Jnl Merioneth Hist. & Rec. Soc.* ii, 311; M. I. Williams, loc. cit.; W. O. Williams, 'Anglesey Gentry as Bus. Men in Tudor & Stuart Times', *Anglesey Ant. Soc. & Fd Club Trans.* 1948, pp. 105, 109; T. B. Lennard, 'Exts. fr. Household A/c Bk Herstmonceux Cas. 1643–9', *Suss. Archaeol. Colls.* xlviii, 109.

THE NORTH-EASTERN LOWLANDS

In and between Weardale and the Wooler district lay a country of coastal plains, hills, hillocks and vales, with mainly pale, deep, cool, retentive clays and clay loams, standing partly on limestone but mostly on red boulder clay, becoming progressively weaker and cooler inland, but giving way in the Wooler district to absorbent sandy and gravelly loams. Although no wetter than the Vale of York, and little harder in winter, the Lowlands were less favoured in their summers and had a more backward climature. No corn could be cut before August and little before September.

In earlier times there were common fields, with their ley lands and grassy balks, common meadows, pastures and marshes.[1] A three-field course generally prevailed, successive seasons being sown to winter and to spring corn and then bare-fallowed for a year. The winter crops were wheat, rye, maslin, and bigg, the northern winter barley; and the spring ones oats, except by the coast, where peas and beans were also grown.[2] What is remarkable is that the typical common field was merely a shifting, temporary cultivation and that outside a few of the deepest soils anything of a more permanent character was hardly known.[3] The first crop in a new plot was usually oats, followed by first a bare fallow and then winter corn, this succession being continued for a dozen or score years until the land was exhausted, whereupon it was abandoned to grass, heather and rubbish. No grass-seeding was attempted.[4] Nor was the land dunged. Cultivation itself was suspended. Having been plough-ed out of heart, the land was left to recover as best it could. Whereas the Midland common fields gave tenfold increases of harvest over seed, these temporary fields gave only threefold, except perhaps fivefold of

[1] E. Bateson, op. cit. i, 152–3, 234–5, 287, 355; ii, 45, 128–9, 156–7, 300, 307, 367, 412–13, 451, 478; v. 161–4, 202, 204–5, 208, 258, 332, 369–70, 376–7, 416–17, 421–2, 424, 493; vi, 92–3, 95, 101; vii, 252, 260, 312–13; viii, 264, 345; ix, 4–5, 119, 194, 324–7; xii, 173; xiii, 230–1; xiv, 213, 244, 247–9; Marshall, *N. Dept*, 141; E. Hughes, *N. Country Life in 18th cent. N.E. 1700–50*, 1952, p. 134; Exch. L.R., M.B. 192, mm. 5 (1) d. sqq., 16 (12) d. sqq., 29 (26) d. sqq., 38 (34), 40 (36) d.–43 (39), 47 (43) d. sqq., 64 (61)–65 (62), 68 (65) d., 70 (67) d.–71 (68).

[2] Ibid. mm. 5 (1) d., 19 (15), 21 (17) d., 22 (18) d.–23 (19); Lisle, op. cit. 152; Hughes, op. cit. 135–6; *Wills Invs.* (Surtees S.) pt i, 335 sqq., 365–6; pt ii, 159–60, 304–5, 326 sqq.; pt iv, 140–1, 243–5, 206; Bateson, op. cit. ii, 300, 307, 464; v, 256–8, 331, 374, 392, 395, 416–17, 424, 465; vii, 312–13; ix, 5.

[3] Ibid. i, 234–5, 274, 287; ii, 369, 381–2, 418, 478; v, 201–3, 376–7, 416–7, 421–2, 424, 488; ix, 119, 324; xiv, 211–12; Nef, op. cit. i, opp. 307; *Wills & Invs.* pt i, 335 sqq.; Purvis, *Causes in Tithe*, 100; Hughes, op. cit. 137; P.R.O., Exch. L.R., M.B. 192, m. 32 (29).

[4] Bateson, op. cit. ix, 193, 197; Marshall, op. cit. 49; *Yks.* ii, 278, 315; *Wills & Invs.* pt i, 335 sqq.

oats as a first crop in a new plot.[1] When cultivation was discontinued,
the land was merely rough grazing, 'no more than a barren heath', sur-
charged by intercommoning townships, and further impoverished by
needy peasants digging turves and pulling heather for their own fuel,
and despite by-laws to the contrary, for sale, even where coal-seams
lay near the surface and when there were coal-pits in the self-same
common.[2] That the land could bear only temporary cultivation was due
to its poverty when brought under the plough. Poor swards meant light
stocking, so the land to be ploughed was unenriched, and there was a
chronic shortage of farmyard manure. Along the coast, and where it
was least needed, seaweed was often used, but only in the Wooler district was the land safe for folding sheep, and elsewhere common grazings consisted almost entirely of ox-pastures, which left as the sole source
of fertilizer the cattle bred and reared for draught and dairying and 'for
servynge of there fallow'. In consequence, as a survey of Shilbottle says
in 1567, 'the arable land ys a waisted, leane lande, for that they are not
able to donge yt as the same wold be. Yt ys a baire clay grounde and
will take much soile or donge before yt be brought to any good perfeccon
of fertylytye.'[3] There was little possibility of improvement through
heavier stocking, for the common pastures were so heathy and moory
they were well suited only to goats, which, indeed, were often kept in
some numbers for domestic dairies, especially in the Wooler district,
where some men had herds of up to thirty. One surveyor did suggest
farmers elsewhere be encouraged to keep more goats, as the only way to
break out of this vicious circle of poverty;[4] but even this could have been
no more than a palliative.

THE NORTH COUNTRY

The North Country consisted of gritstone table-lands, mountainous
crags and slopes, and narrow valleys. The plateaux were wide, bleak,
rarely cultivable heaths and moors on pale, cold weak soils of sand and
vegetable mould. Where insufficiently sloped for drainage or overlain

[1] Ibid. pt iii, 158–9; pt iv, 140–1; Bateson, op. cit. v, 331, 374, 392, 395, 413.

[2] Ibid. 208, 368, 372, 424–5; vii, 308; xiv, 211, 248.

[3] Ibid. i, 287, 342–3; ii, 44, 128–9, 156–7, 300, 368, 412–13, 421, 424–5; v, 201, 208, 290, 331, 376–7, 392, 395, 413, 416–17; vii, 312–13, 394–5; ix, 119; xiii, 228, 243–4; Bailey & Culley, *Northumb.* 4; Blome, op. cit. 179; P.R.O., Exch. L.R., M.B. 192, mm. 18 (14), 21–1 (16–17), 64–5 (61–2); *Wills & Invs.* pt i, 133–4, 169–71, 192–4, 244–6, 335 sqq., 365–6, 377–9, 399–400, 437–8; pt ii, 81–3, 147–9, 159–60, 214, 299–300, 304 sqq.; pt iii, 54–5, 145–6; pt iv, 140–2, 157–8, 240–1, 274–5, 306.

[4] Ibid. pt i, 181–4, 335; pt ii, 49 sqq., 219–21; pt iii, 145–6, 158–9; pt iv, 173; Bateson, op. cit. v, 425.

by clay, the base was retentive, giving to rise wet, black, peaty soil. Generally, at heights of 1,200 feet or more, where rainfall was between 56 and 62 inches a year, there were many large, deep bogs; while from 750 to 1,200 feet, where it was only some 42 inches, moors and heaths were more extensive and bogs fewer and smaller. Heather moors were thus commonest on well-drained uplands of moderate elevation. The mountains had none but the most stunted and windswept of trees and the highest grew nothing but islands of heather amidst great stretches of dark brown peat-bog. Fertile land was almost confined to the narrow valleys and dales that penetrated far into, or even through, the mountains; and here most of the villages and hamlets were sited. Wensleydale and Swaledale were better than most, but the richest valley district was in the Hexham basin, with its expanse of excellent calcareous loam lying on mountain limestone. Similar loams were found also between the River Lowther and the Lake district, and above all in Craven. This region was neither valley, nor vale, nor plain, nor plateau. Stretching between Settle, Keighley and Clitheroe, it was an uneven upland, in which only some of the high swells had cool, clay soils, while the rest had calcareous loams. In the extreme north were the conical Cheviot Hills, with their many rounded slopes, covered from base to summit, some exposed rock excepted, with vegetation or peat. The lower slopes were fertile and bore natural greensward; the summits were crowned with thick layers of peat; and in between lay tracts of heath. In the extreme west were the rocky, slatestone mountains of the Lake District. Here the proportion of inarable land was very high. The crags themselves were quite barren, but the fell slopes consisted of moorlands, where inferior herbage grew amongst the slaty shivers and pulverized slate. In the North Country generally, it could be said, the winter lasted nine months and the rest of the year was cold. The springs were backward, and especially so north of Stainmore Forest. The rainfall was everywhere high and in the Lake District rose to 100 inches and more a year. Since the country was so mountainous, the land's inclination was crucial. Where the sun's rays could hardly make themselves felt, as in parts of the Tyndales, there was much fog and mist, and even if the soil were warm and fertile, little corn could be grown, though, in compensation, the herbage was fresh and winter-hardy. Where the reflection of these rays was multiplied, corn could be ripened the more easily.

In some of the wider and sunnier valleys there may have been a few small permanent common fields, but shifting ones in the moors were typical.[1] As a whole, the country was ill adapted to permanent cultiva-

[1] Ibid. iii, 102; iv, 317, 328, 357, 381, 403; x, 133–6, 270, 273, 276, 366–7, 387–8; xii, 142, 157–9, 166, 184, 191, 239, 318–19; Lancs. R.O., D.D. X. 160/3; P.R.O., Exch. L.R., M.B. 193, mm. 104 (36) sqq., 112 (44); 195, mm. 1 sqq., 38–41, 64, 67d.–8, 72–4, 75d. sqq., 90 sqq.; Raistrick, op. cit. 17, 20, 42–3, 54–5, 68; J. P.

F

tion, still less to permanent tillage. Most tillage was merely temporary, either in up-and-down land in permanent enclosures in the valleys, or in temporary ones made from the moors for the shifting cultivation of wild land. The lowest valley closes were meadows and permanent grass, but the higher ones were tilled from time to time, with the twin objects of bettering the sward and snatching a little corn. Although these stone-walled arable enclosures were added to in the early modern period, their extent was never great.[1] The only wide expanse of arable was in the moors and here tillage was necessarily limited in both size and duration. In cultivating the 'moors', by which was meant all common pastures whatsoever, it was usual for proprietors and tenants to meet together and determine what land was to be brought into tillage and how divided between them, always in proportion to the extent of their holdings and of their common rights in the moors. The plot selected had then to be cleared. Heather, ling and moss were extirpated and the stones that came to light removed for walling and other construction. The land was then ploughed to remove any sod that might be. Weeds, sods and rubbish were next heaped and burned, in winter preferably, lest the fires spread. Then the ashes were scattered and mixed in the soil by a second ploughing, and a seed-bed prepared for rye or bigg by a third. A short succession of oat crops on single earths might follow, after which the plot was abandoned to reclothe itself with herbage as best it could. In the event of the plot being limed and manured, however, red or white clover and some sweet grass might flourish for a time until the natural vegetation came into its own again. Shifting cultivations like this were made in moors in all parts, from Rawdon Moor to the slopes of the Cheviots, and traces of them long remained upon the ground.[2] The chief crops were thus, in descending order, oats, bigg, and rye; and in warmer and deeper soils in sunnier locations some wheat, peas and spring barley were grown. Oats constituted the principal food grain of the lower orders, in the form of clap-bread, bannocks and porridge.

Rylands, *Lancs. Inqs. retd into Chanc. D.L., Stuart Per.* 3 vols. Rec. Soc. Lancs. & Ches. iii, xvi–vii 1880–8 ii, 287; C. M. L. Bouch & G. P. Jones, *Short Econ. & Soc. Hist. Lake Cos. 1500–1830* 1961, p. 77; M. Hartley & J. Ingilby, *Yks. Vil.* 1953, pp. 7, 238; 241–2.

[1] Ibid. 243; Leonard, art. cit. 110; Ess. R.O., D./D.L. E54; P.R.O., Exch. L.R., M.B. 192, mm. 27d.–9 (23d.–6); 195, mm. 64–6, 75, 77 sqq., 110d.; A.O., Parl. Svys Wmld I, ff. 3–4; *Wills & Invs.* pt ii, 335–6; Brown, *Yks. Deeds*, 32–3; T. S. Willan & E. W. Crossley, *3 17th-cent. Yks. Svys* Yks. Archaeol. Soc. Rec. Ser. 1941 civ, 146–7; Willan, art. cit. 255–6; A. Pringle, *Gen. View Ag. Co. Wmld* 1805, p. 310; Tuke, op. cit. 32; Bateson, op. cit. iii, 101; Raistrick, op. cit. 78.

[2] Ibid. 57, 62; T. Robinson, *Nat. Hist. Wmld & Cumb.* 1709, p. 20; Marshall, *N. Dept*, 8; *Archaeologia Aeliana* 1894 xvi, 138–9; Bateson, op. cit. vi, 383; x, 270; xii, 157.

Oats, bigg, and sometimes even wheat, were made into indifferent malt. Winter feed and fodder were provided by preserved pastures of winter-hardy grass, by the small hay crops, by straw, and especially by oats in the straw.[1] Farmyard manure was spread on the 'infield' of home and lower closes. Turf and peat were dug for fuel, and perhaps for compost-ing, and the ashes of moorland swards likewise provided fertilizer. From the middle of the seventeenth century onwards, perhaps before, marling and liming were sometimes undertaken.[2]

Except when tilled, the moors were common rough grazings, the lower parts of which were stinted for horses and cattle under the management of the township and its herdsmen. To save the labour of herding and attendance, these hams were sometimes mounded off with dry stone walls as common closes.[3] In summer, when the valley closes were mostly put up for hay, the better parts of the moorlands were used as cattle pastures. As soon as the spring corn was sown, many of the cattle were driven to these elevated grazings by a party composed of persons drawn from all the town's households. Most of these people remained on the high moors 'scattering and summering' with the beasts, living in more or less permanent cabins and milking cows for cheese. Thousands of acres of moorland were given over to this summering and temporary hamlets, called variously 'shiels', 'shields', 'stallings', 'stel-lings', 'summerskills', 'summerlodges', 'erghs', 'arks', 'satters' and 'setts', are commemorated in place-names throughout the country. These stellings also made convenient places for temporary tillage plots, on which the cattle could be penned at night, known as 'rivings', 'ridings', 'riddings', 'stubbings' or 'burnt moors'. Thus, in May, a Haughton gentleman had cattle at 'the stelling', and, in August, a Cheeseburn Grange gentleman had not only beasts 'at the stelling' but also two old geese, winter corn (including bigg), hay, oats, and a plough with gears. These stellings were likewise eligible situations for new townships, hamlets or farmsteads, and some actually developed into permanent settlements.[4]

[1] Ibid. vii, 183; Hudleston, op. cit. 34–5, 39, 89; S. H. Scott, *Wmld Vil.* 1904, pp. 78–81; Hartley & Ingilby, op. cit. 28, 78–9, 105; Gras, *Eng. Corn Mkt,* 403–4; Raine, op. cit. 52–3, 145, 181–4, 225–6, 249 sqq.; *Wills & Invs.* pt i, 242, 367–8, 393–4, 397–9, 410–12; pt ii, 29–30, 75–7, 121–2, 161, 246–8, 325–6, 335–6; pt iv, 196–7; invs.:—Lancs. R.O., Cons. Ct Cestr.; Richmond A/d: Furness, Kendal & Copeland deaneries; Cumb. R.O., Cons. Ct Carliol.; Leeds Lib. R.D./A.P. 1; Fiennes, op. cit. 192–3; *Wills & Admins. Knaresborough* ii, 204–5, 207–8, 229–30.

[2] Ibid. ii, 204–5, 229–30; Robinson, loc. cit.; Stat. 7 Jas c. 17; Lancs. R.O., Rich-mond A/d, Furness deanery invs.: Jas Preston 1630 Cartmel, Ellen Peppery 1632 Cark; Darby, *Hist. Geog. Engl.* 374; Raine, op. cit. 169, 225–6, 249 sqq.; Fiennes, op. cit. 192; *Wills & Invs.* pt ii, 121–2; Willan & Crossley, op. cit. 1 sqq.

[3] Ibid. 77–8; Raistrick, op. cit. 20, 45–6; Bateson, op. cit. xii, 239; Brown, op. cit. 45–6; P.R.O., Exch. L.R., M.B. 193, m. 112 (44); 195, mm. 1 sqq., 38–41, 43 sqq., 58–60, 61d.–4, 66d.–70, 90 sqq.; Harley & Ingilby, op. cit. 7, 246.

[4] Ibid. 68, 250; Hudleston, op. cit. 145; Raistrick, op. cit. 93; Bateson, op. cit.

Homebred sheep of various breeds roamed the moors unshepherded throughout the year, save for yeaning time. All were agile and hardy, giving poor fleeces but sweet mutton, and the wethers and other surplus increases were sold for fattening in the English lowlands, as far afield as the Saltings Country. Especially were the Cheviots sold to the Wooler district of the North-eastern Lowlands, the Herdwicks to the North-western Lowlands and the Lancashire Plain, and the Lanks to the Lancashire Plain.[1] On the eastern side of the mountain range, shorthorn cattle predominated, and on the western, longhorn. Some cows were reserved for domestic dairies, kept in cow-houses in winter and then perhaps taken summering; but most were applied to breeding and suffered to bring up their own calves. Breeding cows were depastured in the more distant valley and hillside enclosures, where byres were provided for them and their calves. In summer the breeders stayed mostly in the open; in winter they more often took refuge in their byres, whither hay was brought them. The cows calved in spring and raised their young in summer; but no feed or fodder could be spared to rear more than were needed for domestic dairies, farm work and further breeding, so all surplus calves were sold off in autumn to the North-eastern Lowlands and the Lancashire Plain, where they could be reared. The chief store-producing districts were those where the cattle grew biggest and best, i.e. in the better dales and the Hexham basin, whence came most of the short-horns, and the Craven district, where the majority of long-horns originated. In Craven there was a little tillage for oats and barley, and Lank sheep were stocked on the higher swells, but the rest of the land was reserved for breeding cows. Thanks to the rich, wholesome pastures, which were much given to perennial red clover (cow grass), and their natural upbringing, Craven calves developed excellent constitutions. They were sold to the Lancashire Plain for rearing and thence to the Cheshire Cheese Country, the Midland Plain and elsewhere for dairying and grazing.[2]

By no means all North Country farmers grew corn, and even if they did, their livestock interests were greater, usually overwhelmingly so.

x, 269, 387–8; *Wills. & Invs.* pt i, 236–8, 410–11; D. L. W. Tough, *Last Yrs Frontier* 1928, p 51.

[1] Lancs. R.O., D.D. Pt 1, A/c bk starting 1616, 1620 entry; Robinson, op. cit. 2; Defoe, *Pl. Eng. Comm.* 283; Marshall, op. cit. 97–8, 198, 202–3, 323–4, 328, 406, 489–91; *Sheep*, 1–2, 5–6, 9–10, 47; Bailey & Culley, *Cumb.* 268; W. F. Rea, 'Rental & A/cs. Sir Ric. Shireburn 1571–7', *Trans. Hist. Soc. Lancs. & Ches.* cx, 50.

[2] Ibid. 50–1; Marshall, *Midl. Cos.* i, 317; *N. Dept.* 91; Savine, op. cit. 194–5; Raistrick, op. cit. 82; Harland, op. cit. 9; Long, art. cit. 113; Northants. R.O., F.(M.) Misc. 918; Lancs. R.O., D.D. To. K/35; D.D. Pt. 1, A/c bk starting 1616, cattle a/c 1617; Cons. Ct Cestr. inv. Jn Bayley 1594 Downeham; Hartley & Ingliby op. cit. 246; & sup. 146.

Riding and pack-horses were kept, for roads were few and there were no wheeled vehicles other than tiny carts. In some of the wider valleys horses were employed also in draught and in the Lake District small ones formed the majority of what plough-teams there were. Most sheep-flocks were small enough to be managed by the farmers themselves. It was only in the Cheviot Hills and the Lake District that great specialist sheep-masters existed. In the former, the ewe, lamb, hog, and gimmer flocks of a farm each had its own shepherd; in the latter, there were similar flocks with 4,000 or more sheep; and in both sheep-farming was supreme. An important one throughout the country, wool was here the largest single item of farming income, which, in the Lake District, was derived, as a rule, only indirectly, for the landowners and sheep-masters were accustomed to letting out their flocks with their fell farms, each of which might have some 5,000 acres; and the tenants themselves were little more than shepherds working on commission. Oxen were employed in ploughing and in all the more fertile localities domestic dairies were maintained, and sheep and feasts fattened for local consumption. Yet in other less favoured parts it was impracticable to keep cows for the dairy, and here goats were stocked instead. It was not out of the way for a farmer to have one or two score goats, sometimes to the virtual exclusion of sheep. The chief objects of farming were cattle-breeding and the breeding and rearing of sheep for wool and for sale as stores. In the Cheviot and Lake districts sheep were of the first importance, elsewhere cattle. Most occupiers, it is true, had only modest stocks even of breeding cattle; but the more substantial of them had two or three score or even as many as 200 head.[1]

THE PEAK-FOREST COUNTRY

What is here called the Peak-Forest Country consisted of High Peak, Trawden, Rossendale and Sherwood forests, and associated districts.

[1] Marshall, op. cit. 92, 95–8, 100, 199, 239; Hartley & Ingilby, op. cit. 28, 78–9, 242–3, 250; Fiennes, op. cit. 192, 194; Bouch & Jones, op. cit. 105; Scott, op. cit. 78–80; Hudleston, op. cit. 50, 54–5, 79–80, 91, 117, 145, 147, 181–2, 195; Bateson, op. cit. iv, 260–1; v, 474; vii, 183; x, 266, 269; Rea, loc. cit.; 'E. R. & Purveyance Contt', Trans. E. R. Archaeol. Soc. i, 80–1; Woodworth, op. cit. 78; Childrey, op. cit. 158; Earwaker, op. cit. xxviii, 151–2; Raine, op. cit. 10–11, 14–15, 52–3, 145, 169–71, 181–4, 225–6, 249 sqq., 284–6; Wills & Invs. pt i, 128, 146–7, 236–8, 242, 312–13, 367–8, 393–4, 397–9, 410–12; pt ii, 29–30, 34–5, 75–7, 121–2, 125–6, 161, 246–8, 325–6, 335–6; pt iv, 196–7, 235–6, 273; Wills & Invs. Knaresborough i, 4–5, 29 -30; ii, 204–5, 207–8, 210, 214, 229–30, 233–4; Dickson, op. cit. 114; Lancs. R.O., D.D. Pt. 1, A/c bk starting 1616, 1620 entry; invs.:—Cons. Ct Cestr.; Richmond A/d: Furness, Kendal & Copeland deaneries; Cumb. R.O., Cons. Ct Carliol.; Leeds Lib. R.D./A.P.1.

The mass of mountain limestone forming both the High Peak and the Low gave rise to a vast extent of rough grazing; and they were surrounded by successive belts of shale, of millstone grit, and of other sandstones. The prevailing soils were black, cold, peat-earths, with great tracts of moor covered with heather, cotton grass, and bilberry shrubs; thin, infertile grits or sands; and deeper sandy soils able to support oak and birch woods, ling, broom, bracken, Yorkshire fog and hair-grasses. There were also patches of gravelly and sandy loams, and of clay and clay loam or 'mainland'. In the south and south-east of the country, where the largest amount of cultivable soil was found, human settlement was possible only where springs occurred, and these were few and far between. As for climate, it grew steadily worse with each rise in elevation, and consorted ill with the soils, so that the pervious sands, which needed most rain, received the least, while the High Peak suffered harsh winters, short, cool summers, and 60 inches of precipitation.

Small permanent common fields were widely found, and new intakes from the wild were often held in common by two or three occupiers under neighbourhood arrangements;[1] but most of the farms consisted of much rough grazing and a few cultivated enclosures, the lowest-lying of which were meadows and the others up-and-down land.[2] Such an arable close was usually called a 'pasture', so that it was possible for a man to have 'entered the pasture . . . and trod down the corn growing there'.[3] Not surprisingly, the jury of a court of survey cannot 'conveniently soe distinguish between the arable, meadow and pasture as is required, by reason that the most part . . . is used for all the said purposes of plowing, mowinge and pasturage as occasion and necessite doth urge the occupyers'.[4] The land was ploughed up for one or two crops of

[1] P.R.O., Exch. A.O., Parl. Svys Derbs. 19, ff. 7, 14–16; Notts. 10A, ff. 1–2; 17, ff. 1 sqq.; 22, ff. 1, 5, 9; L.R., M.B. 201, ff. 274 sqq.; 230, ff. 66–7; K.R., M.B., 38, f. 10v.; R.&S. G.S. 14/83, ff. 3 sqq.; B.M., Add. 6702, f. 100v.; R. 18064; Lowe, op. cit. 21; Marshall, *Midl. Dept*, 15, 123; Chippindall, op. cit. 47–9; 'St. Ch. Hy VIII & Ed. VI', *Colls. Hist. Staffs.* 1912, p. 144; Brown, op. cit. 150–1; id. iii, 25; Farrer, op. cit. i, 347; ii, 203, 359; G. H. Tupling, *Econ. Hist. Rossendale* Chetham S. 1927 lxxxvi, 50, 100–3; Fishwick, *Rochdale*, 106, 119, 126, 210, 215, 245–6.

[2] Ibid. 12, 28, 36 sqq., 42, 47, 74, 178–9, 183, 186–7, 196 sqq., 220, 222, 228, 230, 232, 236–8, 241; Lowe, op. cit. 45; Marshall, op. cit. 65, 131; Tupling, op. cit. 64; J. W. Clay, op. cit. ii, 111–12; B.M., Add. 6702, f. 100v.; 36906, f. 203; 36912, ff. 1 sqq.; Deene ho. Brudenell Maps & Pls. 31–43; Lancs. R.O., D.D. K. 1462/1–7; Charlesworth, op. cit. 111 sqq., 135 sqq., 163 sqq.; P.R.O., Chanc. Proc. ser. i Jas I, S. 22/71; D.L., R.&S. 5/12, ff. 3v.–4; Exch. A.O., Parl. Svys Derbs. 19, ff. 6–9, 12–13; Notts. 14A, f. 1; M.B. 369, ff. 91 (34) sqq.; L.R., M.B. 230, ff. 54 sqq.; K.R., M.B. 38, ff. 1 sqq.

[3] Ibid. Deps. by Commn 40–1 Eliz. Mich. 34, ex parte quer. & def.; 'St. Ch. H. VIII & Ed. VI' ut sup. 144, 146.

[4] Fishwick, op. cit. x.

oats, barley or peas, with occasionally a little wheat or rye, and then laid down to grass.[1] By far the greater part of the farmland was open moor or heath, both known by the generic name of 'moor'. Their poor, heathy swards were common pastures for unshepherded flocks. In summer, when horses and cattle also went on the moors, the sheep preferred the higher lands; in the depth of winter they descended to enclosures, where they were permitted free ingress and egress.[2] Despite many mountainous and inarable tracts, parts of most moors and heaths, even Sherwood, were subjected to shifting cultivation, in consequence of which wide areas were eventually thrown into ridge and furrow.[3] Heathy swards were often prepared for tillage by being stocked up with mattocks and then winter-fallowed. Next summer slaked lime might be applied at rates between four loads and six quarters to an acre, spread with shovels, and ploughed in about mid-September, for rye, which gave a twelvefold increase. After a fallow in the following winter, barley was sown in April and gave a tenfold increase. Next year, after a single ploughing in March, white peas were sown. Were the land still in some heart, a crop of common oats might then be taken. After the peas or common oats, a farewell crop of black oats or 'skegs' was sown, tillage abandoned, the dead hedges removed, and the plot thrown open to common of pasture. Several other methods were employed. Lime was often applied to the heath three or four years before it was broken up, producing a superior sward and so a more fertile tillage plot. Sometimes the heath itself was ploughed under and seeds harrowed into the inverted sods for two successive years, so giving two crops for a single ploughing and rotting and killing the heath into the bargain. Any further crops then needed but a single ploughing each. Another alternative was to dig up the sod or pare it off with a breast-plough, dry it out, burn it, blend the ash with lime, and plough the mixture under in autumn in preparation for barley, which might be followed by oats, rye and oats again, all on single ploughings. In Sherwood a usual succession was (1) oats or peas, (2) barley, (3) rye, (4) oats, (5) skegs. The 'mainland' patches were often brought into cultivation by marling, in preparation for maslin and subsequent spring crops. Hot, sandy soils could

[1] Pitt, *Staffs* (1794) 86; T. Brown, *Gen. View Ag. Co. Derby* 1794, p. 27; B.M., Add. 6668, ff. 54 sqq.

[2] C. Whone, *Ct R. Manor Haworth* Bradford Hist. & Ant. Soc. 1946 iii, 1 sqq.; Dickson, op. cit. 572; Stewart-Brown, *Lancs. & Ches. St. Ch.* 45; Farrer, op. cit. i, 289, 380; ii, 44, 203; iii, 270, 299, 403; Tupling, op. cit. 109–12; P.R.O. Exch. K.R., Deps. by Commn 40–1 Eliz. Mich. 34, ex parte quer.; A.O., M.B. 369, ff. 91 (34) sqq.; Parl. Svys Derbs. 25, f. 2.

[3] Marshall, op. cit. 17, 124; 'St. Sh. Hy VIII & Ed. VI', ut sup. 184, 186; Lowe, op. cit. 21; Pitt, loc. cit.; Plot, *Staffs.* 109, 343; *Eng. Reps.* cxxiii C.P. i, 36; J. D. Chambers, *V. Trent 1670–1800*, 5; W. B. Crump & G. Ghorbal, *Hist. Huddersfield Woollen Ind.* 1935, p. 43.

likewise be improved by marling for seven or eight crops, once the
broom and gorse had been stocked up. Moorish peat-earths could be
brought into cultivation temporarily, but even with a dressing of marl
at 400 loads to an acre, they could only bear albeit long successions of
oats and perhaps a little barley. Were the peat-earths not marled, oats
could be grown on a single ploughing of the turf and then twice more
after similar cultivations of the stubble. Thus, though the land was
poor, fertilizers abounded. Several varieties of marl were available.
Limestone could readily be quarried and the expansion of coal-mining
made it increasingly cheap to burn.[1] Ash itself was an excellent manure.
Great piles of turf were ignited, usually in winter, and their fires stoked
continually for three weeks. Earth was sometimes laid on the ashes to
prevent them blowing away, or the whole heap might be made in
alternate layers of turf, stubble and earth, so that it needed only one
firing and covered its own ashes. Ash was mixed in the composts, or
used alone, when it would improve wet lands for two years and dry
ones for seven, and kill moss in the meadows.[2]

The chief tillage crops were, in descending order, oats and skegs,
feed barley, rye, peas, wheat and beans. Oats served all purposes and
long remained the staff of life, but no tillage crop was grown for any but
local markets. Domestic dairies were maintained and teams of two or
three horses did the ploughing. Sheep fed the moors and heaths in large
numbers, but were mustered from innumerable small flocks and from
very few great ones. Most farms were run by family labour and farmers
acted as their own shepherds. Nevertheless sheep made important contributions to farm incomes, for, in the absence of cereal sales of any size,
the proceeds of wether and wool weighed heavily in farmers' budgets.
No less profitable was the sale of in-calvers and cows with calves at their
feet. Even these commodities, however, loomed larger in the mass than
in the economy of any particular farm. Agriculture was so frequently
combined with some other occupation, often industrial, and so many

[1] Ibid.; Lowe, op. cit. 6, 21–2, 148; Pitt, loc. cit.; Brown, loc. cit.; Marshall, op.
cit. 149, 167, 173; Fishwick, op. cit. viii–x, 162, 215, 235; Farrer, op. cit. ii, 306;
iii, 87, 382; Kynder, art. cit. 184; Folkingham, op. cit. 28; Lisle, op. cit. 157; Fitzherbert, *Surveyinge*, ff. 46v., 47v.; I. R. in Fitzherbert, *Husbandry* ed. Skeat, 133; J.
D. Chambers, *Notts. in 18th cent.* 1932, opp. 154, 156; P.R.O., Exch. K.R., Deps. by
Commn 40–1 Eliz. Mich. 34, ex parte quer. & def.; L. R., M.B. 201, ff. 290, 293v.,
303, 314, 328, 332–3; A.O., Parl. Svys Derbs. 28, f. 8; Notts. 10A, ff. 1–2; 11, ff. 1,
3, 8, 10; 14A, f. 2; 17, ff. 1 sqq.; 22, ff. 5, 8; Lichfield Jt R.O., Cons. Ct invs.: Robt
Blythe 1591 Woodsetts Dale, Roger Thornell als Skinner 1615 Bamford; W. M.
Bowman, *Engl. in Ashton-under-Lyne* 1960, p. 404; Plot, op. cit. 109, 115, 119,
343–4.
[2] Ibid. 115, 334, 355; Bowman, op. cit. 556–7; Tupling, op. cit. 117; Stewart-
Brown, op. cit. 43–5; Farrer, op. cit. i, 241; Stat. 7 Jas c. 17; P.R.O., Exch. A.O.,
Parl. Svys Derbs. 28, f. 8; 'St. Ch. Hy VIII & Ed. VI', 1910, pp. 72–3; Preston,
op. cit. 7, 61–3, 99–100.

farms were part-time businesses only, that mere subsistence rivalled stock-breeding as the great object of husbandry.[1]

THE BLACKMOORS

The northernmost part of the limestone range, in which the Cotswolds were the greatest eminences, emerged to form the Blackmoors. Here, however, the limestone was extremely thin and the moors stood also on a variety of other rocks, including a hard, compact sandstone, called 'moor grit', and some impervious clayey shales. In the north-west the country ended abruptly in a precipice; in the south it dipped gently into the Vale of Pickering; and in between lay high moors and bleak, barren heaths intersected by narrow valleys. Black peat-earth, i.e. a mixture of sand and vegetable mould, was the prevailing soil, and there were also patches of yellow 'grout', which was an infertile mixture of clay, sand and gravel, and, in the Esk Valley, of clay and clay loam. The coastal soils were generally deeper and more productive. Here and there tracts of deep peat and peat-bogs were found, but by far the greater part of the surface was moorland, of which two main types were distinguished. The soil of the low moors was shallow, and these were called 'thin moors'. On the high moors, the peat-earth was usually thicker, and might be as much as 4 feet deep. These 'fat moors' supported heath, ling, bilberry, bog moss, purple moor-grass (flying bent), rush, and cotton-grass, the thin moors chiefly heath, sheep's fescue, bent and hair-grasses, which made good grazing for sheep.

In the dales and coastal lowlands, the lowest closes were usually permanent grass and the others up-and-down land.[2] Wheat could be grown only in the most favoured parts and oats and rye were the chief crops. Some bigg was sown, but spring barley would not ripen. In the moors, especially the thin ones, there was some shifting cultivation of temporary tillage plots by agreement of the commoners. The sod was pared and burned in heaps and rye sown in the mixed soil and ash. A short succession of oat crops on single ploughings might follow. Yet even such cultivation was severely limited and the tillage area formed only a

[1] Ibid. 7, 13, 21–2, 33–4, 39–42, 48–9, 55–7, 61 sqq., 99–100, 107 sqq., 131–4, 140–2, 147–50; Marshall, op. cit. 170; Pitt, op. cit. 86, 140–1; Ashley, op. cit. 177–8; Holt, op. cit. (1795) 56; Markham, op. cit. pt i, 88–9; Woodworth, op. cit. 77–8, 80; 'E. R. & Purveyance Contt' ut sup. 80–1; B.M., Add. 6668, ff. 54 sqq.; Cartwright Hall, Heaton 1B, 2B, 4B, 5B, 6B, 7B, 8B, 9B; Kennedy, op. cit. 16–18, 22, 53–4, 84–5, 94, 100, 106, 108, 110–12, 118–19, 122, 125–6; Blome, op. cit. 74; invs.:— York, Dean & Chap.; Lichfield Jt R.O., Cons. Ct & Pecs.; Lancs. R.O., Cons. Ct Cestr.

[2] P.R.O., Exch. A.O., M.B., 422, ff. 84 sqq.; Parl. Svys Yks. 50, ff. 1 sqq.; Willan, art. cit. 280.

small portion of the whole.[1] Seaweed and sludge were used near the coast, and ash was often added to composts; but other extraneous fertilizers were hardly known. The chief method of moorland improvement was to fire the heather as it grew. This encouraged new growth, which was more leafy and nutritious for sheep.[2]

The land was applied mainly to breeding and rearing. Sheep were the chief, and on the high moors the sole, stock; yet, on the average, it took ten acres to keep one of them. The sheep were of a distinct, hardy, white or speckled, moorland breed, with coarse, hairy fleeces, but giving sweet mutton. Except for yeaning time, they spent all the year on the open moors.[3] Many farms had domestic dairies, but more attention was paid to breeding and rearing shorthorn cattle. Milkers and breeders were kept in the valleys, while rearing beasts were depastured on the thin moors. Ploughing, when undertaken at all, was frequently performed by a small team of horses. A few horses were bred and some farmers kept poultry, though by no means all grew enough grain for chicken feed. Store sheep and cattle and wool were the main commodities produced; but few farmers operated on any large scale or had as many as 500 sheep.[4]

THE HIGH WEALD

The High Weald was a tract of wild, heathy, woody upland with weak, shallow soils. In the east, a range of barren, sandy hills and an old sea-cliff marked the country's limits. Here and elsewhere the soil was mostly a light, black sand, much given to heather. In addition there were a few silver sands, sandy loams, gravels and gravel loams, and, in some valleys, pale, weak, retentive, 'woodland' clay or 'marl cope' soils, besides a little clay loam and middle loam or 'hazel mould', which had been improved from clay in association with grass growth. Rainfall was relatively heavy, varying with elevation between 30 and 35 inches. Summers were cooler than in the surrounding vales and the springs later. However, since most of the soils were warm, the climature was far from being the country's least favourable feature.

Although some new enclosures were still being made in the early modern period, there remained great stretches of sandy soil given over to cony warrens, woodland and rough grazing. Common fields there were none and the cultivated area consisted of some wet meadow and

[1] Helmsley & Area Gp Yks. Archaeol. Soc. op. cit. 195, 197; York, invs. Pec. Ct Dean York; Crossley, art. cit. 49 sqq.; Marshall, *Yks.* ii, 226.

[2] Ibid. 315; *N. Dept*, 477.

[3] Ibid. 490; *Yks.* ii, 281.

[4] Ibid.; York, invs. Pec. Ct Dean York; Crossley, loc. cit.; Raine, op. cit. 223.

more temporary tillage.[1] Neither marling, nor liming, nor chalking, nor ley farming could make most of the country more than briefly fertile. Even after marling, the soils were generally too weak to bear peas or barley, and wheat could be grown only immediately after such a dressing. The chief corn was oats, and then largely 'pillotes' or naked oats. A first crop of oats or 'pillotes' might be followed by a second and similar one, under which the land was laid down again to thin, weak, spindly rye-grass and superior crowfoot.[2] Hardly had these poor swards formed than they were invaded by such numbers of ferns and brakes that the farmers grew accustomed to regard these almost as crops and to mow them in summer as a kind of hay to be thrown to sheep and cattle. Brakes were also brought in to litter cattle yards in winter and had rotted down by the time these were mucked out.[3]

The High Weald was a nursery for 'Sussex' cattle. The calves were reared at the teat, running with their dams, a practice as favourable to breeding as it was ruinous to the dairy. Breeding cows and their calves were accorded the luxury of permanent grass or temporary leys, while rearing beasts were relegated to rough grazings. At the end of the summer, calves surplus to the requirements of the breeding herds (and of draught teams) were sold off, for there was no fodder to winter them.[4] About three sheep were kept to every head of cattle, partly to provide opportunities for mixed grazing. They were of an aboriginal breed, degenerated by feeding poor pastures, somewhat resembling Dartmoor sheep.[5]

THE NORTH-WESTERN LOWLANDS

The North-western Lowlands included the Kendal, Carlisle and Appleby districts and the adjoining coastal plain. Foremost amongst its soils were calcareous loams on mountain limestone, red, sandy loams on red sandstone, and reddish sands on red freestone. These latter were light, loose and hungry, demanding frequent fallowing and heavy

---

[1] Markham, *Weald*, 3; Marshall, *S. Cos.* ii, 102; B.M., Add. R. 31162, 31357; Harl. 2192, ff. 2 sqq.; 6721, ff. 4, 248v.; S. P. Vivian, *Manor Etchingham c. Salehurst* Suss. Rec. Soc. liii, 1, 27, 200 sqq.; E. Straker, *Buckhurst Terrier 1597–8* id. xxxix, pp. i sqq., 19–21, 26 sqq., 44–7, 53–4, 56–9, 72–3; D'Elboux, op. cit. 1–2, 128–9, 132 sqq., 156 sqq.; Daniel-Tyssen, art. cit. xxiii, 243–4, 246–7, 251–2, 255; xxiv, 193.

[2] Kent R.O., Cons. & A/d Cantuar. invs.; Melling, op. cit. 20; W. Turner, op. cit. 73; Marshall, op. cit. ii, 149–51.

[3] Ibid. 150; Norden, *Surv's. Dial.* 227–8 (2nd occ.); Boys, op. cit. 20.

[4] Invs. ut sup.; B.M., Harl. 6721, f. 248v.; Melling, loc. cit.; Marshall, op. cit. ii, 134, 145–6, 149; Cornwall, op. cit. 84.

[5] Ibid.; art. cit. 68; Melling, loc. cit.; Marshall, op. cit. ii, 146–7; invs. ut sup.

applications of farmyard manure. Their natural vegetation was fern, heath, and inferior grass, except in the valley bottoms, which made fair meadowland. The calcareous and sandy loams were fertile and productive, and, if deep enough, would bear several kinds of corn, grass rich enough to fatten some stock, and even fruit-trees. The summers were generally cool and winters somewhat mild. Although higher in the Kendal district than near Carlisle and Appleby, precipitation was rarely excessive, and since most of the soils were warm, the climature for crops was generally no worse than in the Lancashire Plain.

Small common fields existed in many places, but with few exceptions were merely shifting cultivations or 'rivings'.[1] Holme Cultram copyholders, for instance, were accustomed to plough up the greater part of Colt Park for three years at a time and then to leave it unsown as a stinted common for six years. There were also other lands called 'acredales' or 'rivings', comprising some 344 acres. These were divided into four 'rivings', each in turn sown for three years and then thrown open as common pasture for nine.[2] The closes near the farmsteads were mostly up-and-down arable. The sandy soils, if pared and burned, could be made to bear corn, and, if limed and mucked, fairly good grass; and the other ones needed less elaborate treatment. When a ley became overrun with moss, between four and ten years old, the turf was ploughed up and sown to oats. A second crop of oats would follow, or perhaps one of bigg. The third and last crop was usually oats once again. In certain favoured locations, the more substantial husbandmen sometimes tried their luck with small crops of peas and beans or of spring rye or wheat, which they sowed in March. With the last crop, the field was laid to grass, naturally, as a rule, for the land was grass-proud and hay could be cut in the first year of a spontaneous ley. Only after paring and burning was it usually necessary or advantageous to seed down with hay-seeds. The first purpose of ploughing was to restore good grass to leys that deteriorated quickly, and the second, to grow corn for the household and oats in the straw for the cattle.[3] Lime was useful on some

[1] Man. Lib. Lancs. Deeds L. 6, 7, 15, 445–6; Gray, op. cit. 227 sqq.; T. H. B. Graham, 'O. Map Hayton Manor', *Trans. Cumb. & Wmld Ant. & Archaeol. Soc.* vii, 42–3; G. Elliott, 'Enclo. Aspatria', ibid. lx, 99–100, 107; P.R.O., R.&S. G.S. roll 986; Exch. A.O., Parl. Svys Cumb. 8, f. 12; Lancs. 18, ff. 3 sqq.; K.R., M.B. 37, ff. 4 sqq.; L.R., M.B. 220, ff. 18 sqq., 27 (1) sqq.; 213, m. 52; 212, ff. 377–9.
[2] Ibid. f. 316; A.O., Parl. Svys Cumb. 6, ff. 16, 24.
[3] Ibid. 8, f. 12; Lancs. 7, f. 3; 18, f. 27; L.R., M.B. 220, ff. 2–3, 7, 18–20, 29–31 (3–5), 38 (12), 51 (25); R.&S. G.S. roll 986; Northants. R.O., Mont. Lancs. 3/6, 7; Lisle, op. cit. 152; Coles, op. cit. cap. lxxi; W. Turner, *Names Herbes* E. D. S. 1881, p. 42; Holinshed & Harrison, op. cit. 169; Robinson, op. cit. 53; Raine, op. cit. 215 sqq.; Earwaker, op. cit. xxviii, 223–5; invs.:—Lancs. R.O., Richmond A/d: Furness, Kendal, Copeland & Lonsdale deaneries; Cumb. R.O., Cons. Ct Carliol.; Leeds Lib. R.D./A.P. 1; Marshall, *W. Dept*, 28–9; *N. Dept*, 77, 183, 191, 232–3, 235–6.

of the soils and seaweed and sludge were available near the coast. In default of spring barley, malt was made of oats and bigg, and oatmeal was the basis of diets.[1]

Although a few oxen were yoked, a small all-purpose horse served generally for carting, ploughing, and riding. Theaves of the black-face and Herdwick breeds were wintered for North Country farmers and wethers fattened on summer grass. Most farms had longhorn dairy herds to meet domestic and local demands for liquid milk, cheese, and butter. A few beasts were fatted on summer grass and the country bred and reared its own cattle. Some pigs and poultry were also stocked.[2] Farm produce, including wool, sold locally, but hardly outside the country, and it was not imported much. Commodity production was feeble and the object of husbandry was simply to supply one's own household. Some landowners, it is true, had large farms, but here again, they were intended to meet the needs of housekeeping and hospitality.[3] Under these circumstances, little innovation was to be expected. 'Improvement' signified only extending the area of cultivation. Some small marshes were converted to arable or permanent grass, but no great movement for land reclamation developed. Salt-marshes were defended by seawalls, but it is doubtful if the sea lost more than it regained.[4]

THE VALE OF LONDON

The numerous heaths of the Vale of London stood on poor, sandy soils. Sandy loams were found in many parts and generally between the Thames and the Uxbridge road and between the Lea and Enfield Chase; silty loams along these two river valleys; pale, woodland clays in and about Epping Forest; and, for the rest, mainly clays, clay loams and heavy clays. As a rule, the lighter soils stood on flint and gravel and the heavier on blue clay. Apart from some isolated hills, like the conical ones at Harrow and Greenford, the floor of the vale was more or less level. The climate favoured agriculture, but cold bases made much of the climature backward.

In the south-east, common fields survived only as remnants amidst a patchwork of intermixed enclosures. Elsewhere, especially towards the

[1] Ibid. 169, 190; P.R.O., Exch. A.O., Parl. Svys Lancs. 13, f. 3.

[2] Earwaker, loc. cit.; Raine, op. cit. 10–11, 21–3, 27–9, 107, 188–9, 215 sqq.; P.R.O., R.&S. G.S. roll 986; Exch. A.O., Parl. Svys Cumb. 4, f. 3; 6, ff. 44–6; invs. ut sup.; Marshall, op. cit. 184–5, 197–8, 203, 237–8.

[3] Ibid. 181–2.

[4] Raine, op. cit. 21–3, 215 sqq.; *V.C.H. Lancs.* ii, 289; Rylands, *Lancs. Inqs.* pt i, 6; pt ii, 415; P.R.O., Exch. L.R., M.B. 220, f. 11; K.R., M.B. 47, ff. 60 sqq.; A.O., Parl. Svys Cumb. 6, ff. 18 sqq.; Lancs. 14, ff. 3, 12; 18, f. 32; 30, f. 3.

west, common fields of permanent tillage and grass, with ley lands, grassy balks, and Lammas grounds, ordinarily persisted throughout the early modern period, as did a multitude of common meadows along the rivers and on aits in the Thames.[1] Most of the fields had two- and three-field courses;[2] but in free-working common fields with ready access to London manure, every year's ground, in which bare fallows and uniform courses gave way to continuous cropping, was frequently met with.[3] Most townships had common herds and flocks. Either heath-croppers, largely homebred, or Chalk Country sheep, mostly imported wethers, were close-folded on the tillage at night in large flocks, at rates of between one and three to an acre of fallow, according to the amount of sheep-walk available, the size of the breed, and the area of the acre.[4] Extensive sheep-walks were provided by numerous heaths and commons like Blackheath, Richmond Hill, and Hounslow Heath, where some 6,000 heath-croppers were constantly feeding in 1790.[5] These heaths naturally produced needle-furze (small whin), ferns, heather, ling, broom, goose-grass, hair-grasses and such, though the sheep helped to encourage good swards.[6] Although parts of Hounslow Heath were

[1] E.g. W. M. & F. Marcham, *Ct R. Bp Ldn's Manor Hornsey 1603–1701* 1929, p. 62; Marshall, *Mins.* i, 13. *Experimts & Obs. concerng Ag. & Weather* 1779, frontis. & intro.; *S. Dept*, 101–2, 117, 355–6; P. Foot, *Gen. View Ag. Co. Mx* 1794, frontis.; James & Malcolm, *Bucks.* 27–8; *Sy*, 45–8; Kalm, op. cit. opp. 91; Aubrey, *Sy* ii, 3; K. N. Ross, *Hist. Malden* 1947, pp. 75–6; L.C.C. *Ct Mins. Sy & Kent Sewer Commn 1569–79* 1909, p. 297; Wimbledon Com. Cmtee, *Exts. from Ct R. Manor Wimbledon* 1866, pp. 51, 123; V. B. Redstone, 'Diary Sir Th. Davies,' *Sy Archaeol. Colls.* xxxvii, pt i, 2–3; ibid. v, 87; xli, 47–9; Hull, op. cit. 12–13, 28, 35–6; N. G. Brett-James, 'Some Extents & Svys Hendon', *Trans. Ldn & Mx Archaeol. Soc.* 1935–7 vii, 36 sqq., 248 sqq., 546 sqq.; S. J. Madge, 'Rural Mx under Comm.', ibid. 1921–2 iv, 302, 409–11, 427, 453.

[2] Ibid. 414–15; B.M., Add. 21558, f. 15v.; Bucks. Mus. 445/29 Ct R. Taplow; Mx R.O., acc. 446/E.M. 37 svy Iver; acc. 16/8; Tusser, op. cit. 113; Marcham, op. cit. 62; Foot, op. cit. 20; J. Middleton, *View Ag. Mx* 1798, p. 151; James & Malcolm, op. cit. 38, 45.

[3] Ibid. 45–8; *Bucks.* 27–8; P.R.O., Exch. L.R., M.B. 226, ff. 24 sqq.

[4] Marshall, op. cit. 110, 132, 145, 391; Kalm, op. cit. 140; *Wimbledon*, 93, 103, 111, 117, 147; P.R.O., Exch. L.R., M.B. 197, f. 115; 199, ff. 98 sqq.; D.L., M.B. 127, f. 19; Chanc. Proc. ser. i Jas I, C. 16/66, compl.; B.M., Add. 21206, ff. 10, 41; 21558, f. 15; Harl. 779, ff. 3 sqq.; Herts. R.O., B. 36; B. 48, p. 4; B. 119; Northants. R.O., Mont. Bucks. 2/1, 2; box P, pt i, X. 890, Ct R. Chalvey; Sy R.O., 2/1/6; acc. 137, f. 12; Bucks. Mus. 43/51 Wraysbury; 445/29 Taplow; Mx R.O., acc. 248/1a; acc. 180/2, f. 76; acc. 249/69; acc. 262/16, f. 76; acc. 446/M102, 104–5 Ct R. Harmondsworth; *Sy Archaeol. Colls.* v, 139.

[5] Ibid. 94–6, 136–7; Marshall, op. cit. 110, 145; *Sheep*, 30; Aubrey, op. cit. i, 15; Redstone, loc. cit.; Mx R.O., acc. 180/2, f. 62; P.R.O., Chanc. Proc. ser. i Jas I, B. 35/3, compl.; Exch. L.R., M.B. 197, f. 115; A.O., Parl. Svys Sy 25, ff. 2–3; 31, f. 6; 38, ff. 13–14; 45, f. 5; Marcham, op. cit. 50, 80, 154.

[6] Ibid. 154; Gerarde, op. cit. 1139–40, 1199; Blith, op. cit. 86–7; Kalm, op. cit. 36; Ray, op. cit. ii, 1303–4, 1307; Sy R.O., 2/1/6; Mx R.O., acc. 248/1a; acc. 446/M105 ut sup.

enclosed in 1545 and East Bedfont Heath was divided and allotted at much the same time,[1] much open heathland remained, despite which some farmers and townships were unable to keep all the sheep they required, so their needs were met by petty sheep-masters from the Blackheath Country, who brought their own heath-croppers to fold lands in the vale.[2] As the vale was a highly residential district, thousands of acres had been enclosed into numerous parks, and further empark-ment was undertaken from time to time.[3] Not all this land was lost to husbandry, for many parks were cultivated by their owners or disparked and let to farmers. Hampton Court was disparked in 1548–9 and let out again to the former tenants. A hundred years later a good deal of it was still arable.[4] As is well known, George III had hobby farms in Windsor Park. Other and lesser parks were likewise cultivated. In 1607, e.g. part of Woking Little Park was in tillage and Henley Park contained a close of 'plowed land'.[5] Although there was nothing approaching a general enclosure movement, an already large acreage of closes was being aug-mented in early modern times.[6] Nor should any be regarded as purely common-field districts, for their demesne farms were often made up of enclosed fields.[7] All told, it is doubtful if more than half the farmland of the vale was in common field even in the early sixteenth century. Along the banks of the Lea and the upper Thames lay some marshes and many wet meadows, which had been walled against unwanted floods and drained by open ditches. Here much hay was cut, many cows and horses depastured, and some sheep fattened. Banks and sluices were kept in repair by customary works and contractors, the expenses being met by special drainage rates, and the supervision often supplied by elected marsh-wardens.[8] In the Thames estuary, extensive drained salt-marshes, such as the marshes at Deptford, Charlton, and Battersea, and the levels of West and East Ham, Ripple, Barking, Dagenham, and

[1] P.R.O., R.&S. G.S. 3/11; Stat. 37 Hy VIII c. 2.

[2] Blith, loc. cit.; Laurence, op. cit. 68.

[3] *Sy Archaeol. Colls.* v, 147 sqq.; B.M., Harl. 3749, ff. 14–16; P.R.O., Exch. L.R., M.B. 216, ff. 21 sqq.; A.O., Parl. Svys Berks. 36, f. 1; 38, f. 2; Herts. 27, ff. 10; Kent 18, ff. 2, 6, 8; Madge, art. cit. 431, 444–6.

[4] Ibid. 446; *V.C.H., Mx* ii, 88.

[5] B.M., Harl. 3749, ff. 14–16.

[6] Madge, art. cit. 429; *V.C.H. Mx* ii, 91–2; P.R.O., Req. 393/128, compl. & deps.; Chanc. Proc. ser. i Jas I, C. 16/66, compl.; Exch. A.O., Parl. Svys Mx 16, f. 8.

[7] Corbett, art. cit. 75; Mx R.O., acc. 446/E.M. 44/4.

[8] Ibid. 44/8; M102, 105 ut sup.; acc. 16/8; P.R.O., D.L., M.B. 125–6; 127, ff. 33 sqq.; Exch. L.R., M.B. 199, ff. 98 sqq.; 220, f. 116 (7); A.O., Parl. Svys Berks. 12, f. 1; 14, ff. 3, 5; 28, f. 2–5; Herts. 24, f. 12; 30, f. 9; B.M., Add. 21558, f. 15; Herts. R.O., B. 58, pp. 112–13; Bucks. Mus. 155/21 Taplow; Northants. R.O., Mont. Bucks. 2/2; *Sy Archaeol. Colls.* xii, 39; Madge, art. cit. 413–15, 423; Dugdale, op. cit. 65; L. E. Harris, op. cit. 37–8; Stevenson, *Sy,* 59–60; Marshall, *Mins.* i, 2; *S. Dept.* 101–2, 138, 356.

the Isle of Dogs, were all protected against high tides by great embankments with sluices.[1] These drained marshes were ploughed up for such crops as wheat and madder,[2] alternating with grass. Cow-keepers' cattle and road horses were accommodated, but most of the grass was mown once or twice a season and then preserved to be grazed in winter by muttons and beeves bought by the London grazing butchers from the Midland Plain and elsewhere. This stock was sold fat to cutting butchers in the course of the winter months, when grass meat was otherwise unobtainable, and reached consumers under the name of marsh beef or mutton.[3] Most enclosures were treated as up-and-down land and grouped or divided into shifts for arable cultivation. Here as elsewhere, 'pasture' meant a close that was sometimes in grass.[4] In these closes and cultivated parks there was no uniformity of courses or rotations and it is the utmost generalization to say that hemp and oats were common crops on the inverted turf; barley usually preceded wheat, until the latter was no longer needed as a nurse crop for grass; peas, horse-beans and tares were also grown; and no art was used in laying down to grass beyond cleaning cultivations, heavy manuring, and sowing hay-seeds.[5] Plough-teams were mostly of horses. The chief consumption crops were beans, peas and rye, each grown as extensively as barley, of which only a portion was for feed. The lesser consumption crops, in descending order, were oats, tares and buckwheat. Most of the tillage needed bare summer fallows from time to time, and wheat often a whole year's cleaning. Barley was grown only about half as much as wheat. The strong loams,

[1] Ibid. 140; Cardigan, art. cit. 114; Hants. R.O., 15 M50/391, 397; Ess. R.O., D./S.H. 7, pp. 1, 23, 47, 79; P.R.O., Exch. T.R., Bk 148, pp. 37-9; A.O., M.B, 425, ff. 1 sqq., 41 sqq.; Parl. Svys Kent 56, f. 10; L.C.C. op. cit. 187, 297; Dugdale. op. cit. 59, sqq., 65, 69 sqq., 81-2.

[2] Norden, *Surv's. Dial.* 235; Fuller, op. cit. ii, 113-14; P.R.O., S.P.D. Chas vol. 174 no 22; Ess. R.O., D./D.P. F234.

[3] Ibid.; Cardigan, loc. cit.; Defoe, *Tour* i, 9; ii, 130; Kalm, op. cit. 83-4; Westerfield, op. cit. 199; P.R.O., Exch. T.R., Bk 148, pp. 37-9; A.O., M.B. 425, ff. 1-2, 45 & 2nd foliation 61 (54); Parl. Svys Ess. 17, ff. 2, 19.

[4] Ibid. Berks. 18, ff. 1-3, 9; Bucks. 12, ff. 6, 10-11; Herts. 24, f. 7; Kent 56, ff. 2-3, 7; Sy 23, ff. 3 sqq., 12; 24, ff. 3 sqq., 32, ff. 2-4; 44, ff. 2 sqq.; 56, ff. 2, 5; 58, ff. 2-3; 60, ff. 2-4; 67, ff. 2 sqq.; M.B., 425, 2nd foliation 46, 49; L.R., M.B. 196, ff. 18v., 20, 85, 206v.; 197, ff. 195, 200-1; 198, ff. 30v.-4, 35v.-6, 88v.-91; 210, ff. 194 sqq., 204; 218, ff. 121, 123, 131, 140-1, 148-9; 220, ff. 117, 132, 140, 147, 158, 161, 164, 169 (8, 23, 31, 38, 49, 52, 55, 60); Foot, op. cit. frontis.; Madge, art. cit. 409-11, 423, 446, 451-2, 454-5; Marcham, op. cit. 12, 44, 68, 71; Northants. R.O., F-H 119; Ess. R.O., D./D.P. E25, f. 72v.; E26, ff. 4-5; B.M., Add. 34683, f. 3; Harl. 3749, ff. 14-16; Guildford Mun. Rm, 97/6/13, ff. 3, 16; Marshall, *Mins.* i, 24; V.C.H. Mx ii, 88; Emerson, op. cit. 258-9.

[5] Ibid.; Middleton, op. cit. 234; Tusser, op. cit. 113; Blith, op. cit. 254; P.R.O., Req. 392/93, ans. & deps.; Northants. R.O., F-H 617; Mx R.O., acc. 446/E.M. 37-8, 44/4; B.M., Add. 37682, ff. 173-4; Marshall, op. cit. i, 118, 180; S. Dept. 135, 382.

especially those of the Vale of Harrow, were amongst the best wheat land in England, and Heston wheat was a byword. For this reason, and as malt was more economically imported, wheat was the main market crop in the vale.[1]

Despite all local peculiarities, the vale was fashioned into a distinct farming country by the presence of the great and growing city. Most Londoners lacked farms, accommodation closes, orchards, gardens, or even hen-coops; yet all needed food and preferred it fresh. Under this powerful influence, the whole vale was drawn into the supply of food and fodder to the city and received in return an abundance of the city's natural produce of refuse and muck.

Since Londoners had no kitchen gardens, market gardens proliferated, in the latter sixteenth century, wherever free-working soils lay within reach of economic supplies of city manure. In 1651 old men could still remember the first gardeners setting up in and about Fulham; yet by 1610 the town was already famous for its carrots and parsnips. By 1597 Hackney was noted for the small turnips women from the village brought to sell on Cheapside. About Chertsey and Weybridge the gardeners converted heathland to carrot cultivation. Closes in Mitcham and common fields in Chelsea, Fulham and Kensington were alike transformed into gardens. The vale's gardeners produced turnips, cabbages, carrots, parsnips, cauliflowers, rathe-ripe peas and other vegetables for the table; carrots, cabbages and turnips for the city cow-keepers; and tobacco for apothecaries and pipe-smokers. Turnips, carrots and cabbages grown nearest to London, or to the Thames and its barges, were usually consigned direct to Covent Garden or Cheapside, while those from more distant parts were bought up by the great cow-keepers.[2] Similarly, numerous orchards, nurseries, cherry-gardens and hopgardens sprang up in the vale.[3]

[1] Ibid. 39, 135; *Mins.* i, 27, 81, 320; *Sy Archaeol. Colls.* xxxi, 14; James & Malcolm, *Sy*, 48; Middleton, op. cit. 166, 180, 186, 193, 198; *V.C.H. Mx* ii, 87, 206–7; Norden, *Mx & Harts.* 11–12; Childrey, op. cit. 88; Fuller, op. cit. ii, 310; Gerarde, op. cit. 82; Eland, *Shardeloes*, 59; B.M., Add. 37682, ff. 173–4; Harl. 570, ff. 11v.–2; R. T19; P.R.O., Exch. A.O., Parl. Svys Sy 38, f. 2; Mx R.O., acc. 446/E.M. 37, W. Drayton; Northants. R.O., F-H 617; Wmld 5. vii, inv. Th. Fyssher 1586 Crayford; invs.:—Hants. R.O., Cons. & A/d cts; Herts. R.O., A/d St. Albans; Melling, op. cit. 25–6; Folkingham, op. cit. 42.

[2] Ibid.; R. Child in Weston, op. cit. (1651) 11; Fuller, op. cit. iii, 200–1; A. Speed, *Adam out of Eden* 1659, pp. 18–20; Gerarde, op. cit. 178; Norden, *Surv's Dial.* 212; C. M. MacInnes, *Early Eng. Tobacco Trade* 1926, pp. 79, 81–2; Baxter, art. cit. 186; Madge, art. cit. 452; Stevenson, op. cit. 279–80; James & Malcolm, op. cit. 38; Marshall, *S. Dept*, 136–7, 394; F. J. Fisher, 'Developmt Ldn Food Mkt', in E. M. Carus-Wilson, *Essays in Econ. Hist.* 1954, pp. 141–3; Sy R.O., 2/5/4; P.R.O., Req. 392/93, compl., ans. & deps.; Exch. A.O., Parl. Svys Sy 32, f. 5; 38, f. 7; & v. Ben Jonson, *Alchemist* act v sc. iii.

[3] Fisher, art. cit. 141, 143; P.R.O., D.L., M.B. 127, f. 65; Exch. L.R., M.B.

Since Londoners had no domestic dairies and fresh milk could not be transported any great distance, cow-keeping developed. Unless they had the chance of buying milk from dairies in some of the parks, city-dwellers obtained their supplies from cows stall-fed on grain, hay, turnips, cabbages and carrots. Cow-keepers in places like Moorfields multiplied as the city grew, until by 1794 there were reckoned to be over 8,000 of them. Dairy-farmers necessarily maintained a certain standard of cleanliness, for unless the utensils were daily scalded in boiling water, butter and cheese would sour before they were made; but cow-keepers sold only liquid milk. Their cows, too, were confined throughout the year in dark, close sheds and stalls that promoted pulmonary consumption, and fed on stale, rank, and often foul food, so that they could not maintain their health above two years. Perhaps the best way of providing for children and invalids was to buy the milk of the asses that were driven from door to door, for this could not be tubercular; but the general consumer was in large measure protected by the cow-keepers' cupidity, for the best and most profitable cow-keeping practice was to buy in shorthorns at their third or fourth calving, when their yield was at its peak, milk them for one season, and then withdraw them, throw some fat on them as quickly as possible by forcing them on brewers' grains, bean shells and cabbage leaves, and sell them off as cow-beef, so that conversion rates were maximized and tuberculosis risks incidentally minimized.[1]

Since the vale could not hope to furnish all the cheese and butter consumed in the city, and these could more economically be bought elsewhere, most farmers had only domestic dairies. However, butter kept less well than cheese, so that the freshest product could always command a premium, and in and near Epping and Hainault forests, from grass in summer and from hay and grain in winter, much cream and butter was made for sale in the city.[2]

Since beef and mutton could be brought to London on the hoof from some distance, the farmers of the vale produced little of either. There was a good deal of grazing, but mostly by or for grazing butchers, who bought fat stock from other countries, either on the farms themselves or at the markets at Smithfield, Brentwood, Epping, Bishop's Stortford, Uxbridge and elsewhere, and kept it fat on preserved pastures and

---

198, f. 30v.; 220, f. 117 (8); A.O., Parl. Svys Sy 24, f. 2; 38, f. 3; 56, f. 2; Mx R.O., acc. 16/4.

[1] Marshall, op. cit. 108, 110, 136–7, 394; *Mins.* i, 48; Kalm, op. cit. 160–1; Lisle, op. cit. 276–7; Gras, op. cit. 361; Speed, op. cit. 23; J. C. Drummond & A. Wilbraham, *Englishman's Food* 1939, pp. 230–1; B.M., Add. 37682, ff. 173–4.

[2] Ibid.; Harl. 570, f. 15; R. T19; Norden, *Ess.* 9; Marshall, *S. Dept*, 148; Steele, op. cit. i, 40, 49.

aftermaths until it was taken off their hands by the cutting butchers.[1]

As veal and lamb could not be brought in on the hoof, they had to be produced in the vale itself, largely to the exclusion of the commercial dairy, for each longhorn cow acted as a nurse to several lean calves, which had been bred on the farm or brought from Midland and other dairy-farmers. From the more distant parts of the vale, fat calves were transported in the same way as the lean, by cart or by water, and nearer to London they went to the butchers on horseback.[2] Similarly, more house-lamb was suckled in the vale than in any other country. Ewes of the house-lamb ('Dorset') breed were bought in and allowed to raise their own lambs, which were most often twins. If a ewe lost her lambs, she was forced to suckle others, often by being yoked. The ewes were highly fed on grain, chaff, hay, rye, and root crops bought from the gardeners.[3] Another speciality was cramming table birds on barley bought but later rejected by the maltsters.[4] Hogs were also fatted at breweries, distilleries and starch factories on brewers' grains and other by-products.[5]

The number of riding, wagon and coach horses in the city was prodigious. By 1636 there were no less than 6,000 private or public-hire coaches. Horses demanded accommodation closes, especially out of term and season, and these were supplied by marsh and upland pastures. The demand for hay was enormous. To provender the stables and cow-sheds of London, the meadows of the Thames valley were mown for hay to be sold off the farm. Here, and at Marylebone, St Pancras and Islington, there were many specialized hay farms where nothing was done but mow hay and manure the meadows with stable dung brought back by the hay wagons and barges, except that their aftermaths served to accommodate horses or feed butchers' fat stock in the winter. From all about the vale, vast stores of hay were brought to the Haymarket and elsewhere for the use of the city.[6]

Extraneous manures supplemented the sheep-fold and farmyard

---

[1] B.M., Harl. 570, f. 15; R. T19; Melling, loc. cit.; Defoe, op. cit. i, 9; ii, 130; Kalm, op. cit. 84, 167; Westerfield, op. cit. 199; Emerson, op. cit. 89–90, 330–1; Ess. R.O., D./D.P. F224, mm. 5, 11d.; Fisher, art. cit. 144.

[2] Ibid.; Marshall, op. cit. 93–4, 108, 142, 363, 407, 411; *Mins.* i, 49; Kalm, op. cit. 167, 372–3; Laurence, op. cit. 130–1; Mortimer, op. cit. 169; Pitt, *Northants.* 197, 270–1; Houghton, op. cit. (1681) ii, 163; A. Wilkinson, 'Obs. on Mx Ag.' *Ann. Ag.* xxii, 55; Bodl. Hearne's diaries 158, p. 60; Northants. R.O., Wmld 5. vii, inv. Fyssher ut sup.; Mx R.O., acc. 446/E.M. 37; Woodworth, op. cit. 77–8, 82.

[3] Ibid.; B.M., Harl. R. T19; Melling, loc. cit.; Fisher, loc. cit.; James & Malcolm, op. cit. 29; Speed, op. cit. 29; Houghton, op. cit. ii, 164; Laurence, op. cit. 146; Ellis, *Sheep*, 53–4, 247 sqq.; Marshall, op. cit. i, 52–3, *S. Dept.*, 145, 363, 411.

[4] Ibid. 135; 'Nat. Hist. Dorking', *Gent's Mag.* xxxiii, 220.

[5] James & Malcolm, op. cit. 34–6; Marshall, op. cit. 144.

[6] Ibid. 40; *Mins.* i, 36 sqq., 44; Atwell, op. cit. 102; Brentnall, 'Longford MS.', 19; Parkes, op. cit. 66, 109.

manure. Marling was practised and snail-cod and moor-earth were dug from the beds of the Thames and the Colne and from nearby ponds flooded for this express purpose. By the application of these fertilizers even sandy soil could be made to bear tillage for a dozen years.[1] The chief resource of the farmers and gardeners was, however, stable and cow-shed manure, slaughter-house refuse, and street sweepings, which contained much coal-dust. These were all collected and taken to the farms by barge, wagon and horseback. Stable manure was mostly barged to market gardens and hay farms near the Thames and applied more especially to the sandy loams. Street-soil was generally used on the clay loams.[2]

[1] P.R.O., Chanc. Proc. ser. i Jas I, C. 16/66, compl.; Mx R.O., acc. 446/M 105 Ct R. Harmondsworth 11 June 1652; Norden, *Surv's Dial.* 223, 226 (2nd occs.); Blith, op. cit. 143.

[2] Ibid. 87; Norden, op. cit. 226–7; Childrey, op. cit. 88; Child, loc. cit. 45; Brentnall, loc. cit.; James & Malcolm, op. cit. 45, 59; Baxter, loc. cit.; Fisher, art. cit. 143; P.R.O., Req. 392/93, ans. & deps. ex parte def.; Marshall, op. cit. i, 31, 36–7; *S. Dept*, 40, 388–9.

CHAPTER III

UP-AND-DOWN HUSBANDRY

THE backbone of the agricultural revolution was the conversion of permanent tillage and permanent grassland or of temporary and shifting cultivations, to permanently cultivated arable alternating between temporary tillage and temporary grass leys.

The new husbandry that revolutionized farming and replaced the system of permanency is nowadays called 'ley farming', convertible, alternate or 'field-grass' husbandry. Here it will be known by its historical and descriptive name of 'up-and-down' husbandry, and the land subjected to it as 'up-and-down land', as it is still called. In up-and-down husbandry everything hinged on the arable fields, known as 'pastures', being laid down to grass for a few years and then ploughed up and tilled for a time, all the farmland, saving some pieces of wet meadow and permanent grass, being subjected to the same treatment.[1] In the form we find this system taking in the Midland Plain, where it had the greatest scope,

'the outlines of management consist in keeping the land in grass and corn alternately, under a singular system of practice; and in applying the grass to the breeding of heifers for the dairy, to dairying, and to the grazing of barren and aged cows, with a mixture of ewes and lambs, for the butcher; all together, a beautifully simple system of management; and, being prosecuted on large farms, and by wealthy and spirited farmers, becomes a singularly interesting subject of study'.

Why up-and-down land is difficult to find in early modern records and has usually been mistaken for permanent grass is because the new

---

[1] Marshall, *Midl. Cos.* i, 81, 184 (quot.), 268; *N. Dept*, 373; *Midl. Dept*, 11, 59, 66, 131, 168–9, 199–200, 220, 291; Crutchley, op. cit. 10, 12; Fitzherbert, *Husbandrie*, f. 5v.; *Surveying*, f. 53; Blith, op. cit. 2, 71–4; Moore, *Crying Sin*, 12; Lee, op. cit. 23; Morton, op. cit. 44–5; Plot, *Staffs.* 341–3; Laurence, op. cit. 45; Lisle, op. cit. 61, 86, 151–2; Donaldson, op. cit. 27; Fiennes, op. cit. 220; 'Incola', 'Nat. Hist. Sutton Coldfield', *Gent's. Mag.* xxxii, 403.

husbandry necessitated a fresh terminology, which was only devised and accepted after some delay, so there was considerable confusion, recently worse confounded by the misuse of agricultural terms of art. The main medieval categories of land states were arable, pasture and meadow. Modern ones are much different. Tillage and temporary leys are arable; permanent grass includes pasture, meadow and grassland mown and fed in rotation; and, lastly, there is rough grazing. In early times, arable and tillage were synonymous terms, for nearly all arable was permanent tillage. Meadow meant wet, riverside meadows. Pasture was intended to mean permanent pasture. The more didactic surveyors explained the inadequacy of the old terms and tried to devise new ones. 'There are two sorts of meddowes, low and moist, and upland and dry', says Norden.[1]

'The upland meddowes have but the name of meddowes; for indeede they are but the best pasture grounds laid for hay. And to distinguish betweene that kinde of meddowe and pasture ground, or between pasture and arable is frivolous; for that kind of meddow is most properly pasture and all pasture grounds may be tilled. For when we say arable, it is as much as if wee said, it is subject to the plough, or land that may be plowed. . . . I confesse a surveyor may note the quality of everye kinde as he findeth it in the time of his perambulation and view. But, peradventure, the nexte yeare, he that comes to distinguish them, may enter them cleane contrary to the former. And therefore it is not amisse, in all such entries, to adde the word "now", as to say, "now tilled" or "now pasture".'

Norden himself did not usually enter the state of the land at all in his surveys, which was the simplest solution, but both he and others sometimes followed his tentative suggestion of merely entering the present state. Most surveyors persisted with conventional and almost meaningless terms like 'close of pasture', 'close or pasture', 'close of meadow', and so on. The best, however, stated the alternative land uses, in medieval terminology. Grassland fed and mown in rotation could thus be described as 'meadow or pasture' and enclosed up-and-down land as a 'close of arable or pasture', 'clausum pasture sive arrabile', and similar variants.[2]

Turning again to the great Midland Plain, we soon see that, for the most part, the manorial surveys retained conventional terminology, recording 'closes of pasture' and 'closes of meadow'. This usage, never-

[1] Norden, *Surv's Dial.* 201–3.

[2] My *Svys Manors Philips E. Pembroke & Montgom. 1631–2* Wilts. Archaeol. & Nat. Hist. Soc. Recs. Br. 1953 ix, 1, 5, 28, 33, 35, 116, 124; B.M., Add. 6027; P.R.O., R.&S. G.S. 2/46, ff. 125, 134; Exch. T.R., Bk 157.

theless, was colloquial. In the vernacular, 'a pasture' was simply an enclosed field, of either permanent grass or up-and-down land. A survey of Water Stratford records a 'peece or parcell of arrable land . . . commonly called or knowne by the name of the Pasture Feild'.[1] There is explicit reference to 'the *pastures*, by which are meant the inclosures, in contradistinction to the commons'.[2] This is why the surveys so frequently speak of 'a close or pasture': the words were synonymous, as were also 'close of pasture', 'ground' and 'piece'. The 'pasture' could equally well be permanent grass or arable, including temporary leys. Paradoxically, the word 'pasture' was commonly employed to mean an arable field. Rights of common were claimed in 'pastures' when the corn was harvested.[3] Witnesses were examined as to whether any 'pastures' were ploughed,[4] and allegations made that the defendants 'entered the pasture . . . and trod down the corn growing there and broke the hedges inclosing the same'.[5] Casual references were made to corn and woad growing in 'pastures' and Blith spoke of 'plowing on pasture and resting another'.[6] In fine, a 'pasture' simply meant a close. Yet even if used in the modern sense, 'pasture' would have to be taken to include temporary as well as permanent grass. For all these reasons, statements of land use in formal surveys, and there were hundreds of them, cannot be used in evidence of land utilization; and it is necessary to reject everything written on the false assumption that they could be.

Some Midland surveys recorded alternative states, as by saying 'arable or pasture' for up-and-down land. At Creslow in 1607 there were 15 acres of warren, 10 of permanent grass, and 766 of up-and-down land.[7] Bearing in mind that descriptions of parcels are only as accurate and up to date as the conveyances and terriers shown in courts of survey,[8] it may be concluded that up-and-down husbandry was practised in most Rowington farms in 1606. One copyhold farm had 8 acres wet meadow, 3 acres permanent grass and 7 closes of up-and-down land, of which one was 7 acres, now divided in two, two others 6 apiece, one 4 and three 3 acres each. The demesne farm, much larger, was also composed mostly of up-and-down land, and likewise a farm at Kington. Up-and-down husbandry was general practice at Knowle in 1605.[9] In a

[1] Ibid. A.O., Parl. Svys Bucks. 19, f. 7.

[2] Marshall, *Sheep*, 18.

[3] P.R.O., St. Ch. Hy VIII 19/11.

[4] P.R.O., Exch. Deps. by Commn 14 Chas Mich. 25, mm. 1, 4v.

[5] 'St. Ch. Hy VIII & Ed. VI', *Colls. Hist. Staffs.* 1912, p. 144.

[6] Ibid. 23–4; 'Chanc. Proc. temp. Eliz.', id. 1926, pp. 132–3; Blith, op. cit. 79; Shak. Bpl. W.de B. 1024a, 1080; Northants. R.O., F-H 1140; Leics. R.O., A/d invs.:— 1627: 140; 1672: 96; 1707: 126; 1709: 73.

[7] P.R.O., Exch. L.R., M.B. 210, ff. 40, 42.

[8] Kerridge, op. cit. ix–xi.

[9] P.R.O., Exch. L.R., M.B. 228, ff. 65 (1) sqq., 149 (1) sqq.

similar way it is recorded at Brampton, Ampthill, Chicksands, Hadden-
ham, Hardwick, Bedwardine, Tibberton, Chilesmore, Gretton and
elsewhere.[1]

Other surveys adhere to formal terminology, but nevertheless add
explanatory notes. Thus the surveyors of Hampton-in-Arden in 1649
record,

'One close of pasture ground called the Hill Feild, now devided into
foure severall parts, whereof some part thereof is att present plowed, and
the rest of it unplowed, it being a usuall course with the inhabitants to
plow their ground which they doe call pasture for twoe or three yeares
together, and then to lett it lye for pasture fifteene or twenty yeares and
then plowe it againe, and this they doe with a greate part of their pasture
ground. And therefore wee thought good to give it as pasture ground,
it being soe called by them, for the ground that is this yeare pasture is
sometimes the next yeare plowed and the ground that is this yeare
plowed is the next sometimes layd for pasture, it being counted with them
att an equall estimate when eyther plowed or not plowed.'

The very next parcel is 'one close of pasture ground commonly called
. . . Ley Hill, now devided into twoe severall parts, whereof the one
parte is plowed and the other not plowed, as aforesaid'. There is also
'one close of pasture ground called the Castle Hills, being now devided
into seaven parts, whereof some parte thereof is att present plowed, it
being a usuall course thereabouts soe to doe, as is before exprest'.
Finally, we find 'all that parcell of pasture ground called the Old
Parke there being some small part thereof plowed as aforesaid'. Hampton-in-Arden was then in the last stages of enclosure;[2] and a survey in
1634 shows large common fields, but already some 'closes of pasture',
of which one was 'a close of pasture called Lea Hill now devided into
twoe and some parte of one of them plowed'.[3] The commonwealth surveyors who had been engaged at Hampton-in-Arden held court also at
Rudfin in Kenilworth. After abstracting some closes and pastures, they
record

'one close of ground being now plowed called . . . Slies Close, it being a
usuall course with the inhabitants thereabouts . . . to plow their pasture
grounde for twoe or three yeares together and then to lett it lye for tenne

[1] Northants. R.O., F-H 570, 27 Feb. 1728; Cave & Wilson, op. cit. 64, 66, 155;
B.M., Harl. 4781, f. 2; 6288, ff. 28 v., 77; P.R.O., Ct R. G.S. 207/25, 17 Apr. 14
Chas, 9 Apr. 16 Chas; Exch. L.R., M.B. 196, ff. 49 sqq.; 198, ff. 20 sqq., 53; 204,
mm. 2–4; A.O., Parl. Svys Hunts. 3, f. 10.
[2] Ibid. War. 12, ff. 6, 19, 21, 35.
[3] Ibid. M.B. 419, f. 53.

or twelve yeares and so to plow it againe; and this they constantlie doe with the greatest parte of their pasture ground, it being counted with them att an equall estimate when it lieth for pasture or plowed'.

The next parcel is 'one close of ground being at present plowed as aforesaid', and subsequent 'closes of pasture' can be taken as up-and-down land, for amongst them are 'one close of ground being nowe plowed', 'one other close of ground being now plowed comonlie called . . . the Pease Close', a parcel of rough ground now divided into four, 'some parte thereof being plowed, it being counted with them att equall estimate when it is plowed or lyeth for pasture', Rudfin Park, containing 160 acres, 'some small parte thereof being att present ploughed', and a 'close of meadow', now divided into four, 'some parte thereof being at present ploughed'. The whole lordship was enclosed up-and-down land in the occupation of two farmers. Some indication of how long up-and-down husbandry had been practised here may be gained from two groups of parcels. There was an impaled ground called the Paddock, now divided into several closes, namely, a 'close of pasture' called Stocking Ground, one other close of ground being now plowed', another 'close of pasture', a parcel of rough ground, 'some parte thereof being plowed', and three 'closes of meadow', whose names suggest wet meadow. The whole paddock had 'not bene made use of otherwise then now it is for the space of fortie yeares or thereabouts'. Duck Park, too, had been disparked, divided into two 'closes of pasture', one of which was now subdivided into fields for the field-course, and 'one close of meadow', 'some parte thereof being at present plowed'.[1] Up-and-down husbandry had thus been introduced at Rudfin no later than about 1600. The survey of Kenilworth manor is formal, merely listing so-called 'pastures';[2] but that of Hog Park resembles the one for Rudfin. Some parcels are conventionally described, but there is also 'one close of pasture ground . . . some parte thereof being att present plowed', 'one other parcell of ground . . . now devided into twoe closes, parte thereof being att present plowed', 'one close of pasture ground . . . called Plowed Close', and 'one parcell of ground . . . now devided into twoe parts, one parte being at present plowed called . . . the Corn Feild'. Hog Park was clearly disparked up-and-down land.[3] In Kenilworth Old Park, similarly, we find 'a close of pasture grounde . . . being att present plowed, it being usuall there to plow their ground a yeare or two . . . and then to lett it lye againe for pasture'. Three other 'pastures' were each 'now devided into three severall parts, parte thereof being att present plowed'. In short, Old Park for about fifty years had been dis-

---

[1] Ibid. Parl. Svys War. 32, ff. 1, 2, 5, 6, 8, 9, 12–14, 17, 19–21, 26, 29.
[2] Ibid. War. 15.
[3] Ibid. 21, ff. 1 sqq.

parked up-and-down land.[1] Similar parcels were to be found elsewhere in Kenilworth manor: numerous 'pastures' and 'grounds', some of which were under the plough at the time of survey and some of which were in temporary grass, 'one close of ground being at present plowed', 'a parcell of Lamas ground being att present plowed', and another similar ground also 'att present plowed'. All these had been withdrawn from the common field, but there was also 'one close of ground being at present plowed and formerly belonging to a certaine springe called Edibourne Spring'.[2] Further, one notes a 'parcell of ley land, parte thereof being at present plowed, now devided into 4 severall parts', one Lammas close being ploughed temporarily, and two others formerly part of the Hale ground, one of which was then under the plough and divided into two parts, and the other 'sometimes plowed'. There followed two other parcels of ground, of which one was 'devided into five severall parts, some . . . at present plowed' and the other 'usuallie plowed, now devided into six severall closes',[3] and then 304 acres of 'impalled ground . . . called the Castle Hills Park . . . some parte thereof being lately plowed'.[4] A similar survey of part of Lillington shows up-and-down husbandry there also.[5] In Cookesey and Huddington the number of closes at present being ploughed puts the general practice of up-and-down husbandry beyond doubt.[6] In Shuttington the occupiers of Hale Close had long been accustomed to plough it up for corn from time to time.[7] In 1625, East Lilling was all enclosed up-and-down land 'altred at the pleasure of the tenante'.[8]

As already seen in passing, surveys explicit about up-and-down husbandry also record the division of closes into parts for rotating temporary tillages. When the plough was taken round the farm, fieldcourse shifts were composed not always of single closes, but might be of two or more small closes or part of a large one. In Hog Park, for instance, lay a ground 'now devided into twoe parts, one parte being at present plowed'. Similar ploughing divisions, made by movable railings or 'fence fleaks', or by permanent mounds, are found elsewhere in Kenilworth, Hampton-in-Arden, Creslow, Cookesey, Huddington and Shuttington.[9] That these

[1] Ibid. 20, esp. ff. 4, 8, 10.
[2] Ibid. War. 16; 15, ff. 18–19.
[3] Ibid., War. 17.
[4] Ibid. 22, ff. 1 sqq.
[5] Ibid. 24, ff. 3–4.
[6] Ibid. Worcs. 4, 6.
[7] Ibid. M.B. 380, f. 18.
[8] B.M., Harl. 6288, f. 27.
[9] P.R.O., Exch. A.O., M.B. 380, f. 13; 419, f. 53; Parl. Svys War. 12, ff. 5, 6, 19–21, 30, 32; 16, ff. 5, 7, 9; 17, ff. 2, 3, 5, 6, 12; 20, ff. 4, 5, 8–10; 21, ff. 3, 6; 22, f. 4; 32, ff. 7, 12–13, 17–18, 21; Worcs. 4, ff. 3, 4, 6, 11–12, 15, 22–5, 27; 6, ff. 3, 4, 8, 10–11, 16, 22; L.R., M.B. 210, f. 40.

parts or shifts were for the purpose of up-and-down husbandry is shown
also by a Market Bosworth particular which says, 'The oulde parke is a
severall pasture of the demesnes which hathe byn divided in three
partes, but it is nowe all on pasture, the moundes of partition lyinge
unmayntayned; yt is but course pasture'.[1] In Neville Holt in 1638 a
quickset hedge across Sheep Close divided off sixteen acres intended to
be ploughed up.[2] When people at Great Alne declare 'the lande at the
Woodhowse ys devyded into fyve partes notwithstandinge' its enclosure,
they intend to support their contention that the equivalent of 'iij
yarde lande ys styll in tyllage'. The incumbent of Great Packington
describes 'a lesowe called the Broome Feild . . . which . . . I divided into
two with a good quickset to till one part and graze the other'.[3] Hence
such partitions provide circumstantial evidence of up-and-down
husbandry in the farm they formed part of. In this way up-and-down
land is disclosed even by otherwise formal surveys and particulars.
Many closes in Winwick were divided into parts, several being 'arable';
one was 'meadow and arable land', another 'pasture and plowed land',
yet another 'pasture ground and arrable called the further part of the
park, now divided into two parts'.[4] Breedon-on-the-Hill Park was
divided into six or seven parts, some of which were 'arable', some
'pasture', and some 'meadow'.[5] At Dunham in 1651 a close of 'meadow'
and a 'pasture' were each now divided into two, while lease covenants
stipulated extra rent for every acre 'plowed and sowed'.[6] In 1650 an
otherwise purely formal survey of Launton records a close of arable and
ley ground now divided into two closes.[7] A particular of Ingarsby about
1660 says, 'the lord and owner . . . hath lately bine att a great charge in
makeing devisions in many of the said grounds, which are ditcht and
quicksett and are very advantageous to the tenants'.[8] At Kenilworth and
Rudfin, where up-and-down husbandry was practised in the early seventeenth century, divided closes provide circumstantial evidence of it as
far back as 1581.[9] Many other records of divided closes testify to widespread up-and-down husbandry after 1560.[10] More rarely, the 'pastures'

[1] Leics. R.O., D.E. 40/22/2.

[2] Ibid. D.E. 53/93.

[3] War. R.O., D.R.O. 72 (a) terrier 1612; Shak. Bpl. Gt Alne 'A declaration of all
the inclos. made'.

[4] Northants. R.O., R.H. 45, ff. 2 sqq.

[5] P.R.O., Exch., A.O., Parl. Svys Leics. 6, f. 2.

[6] B.M., Add. Ch. 53392, mm. 11–13, 15–18.

[7] Oxon. R.O., J. vii. 2, f. 4.

[8] Leicester Mus. 35/29/340.

[9] P.R.O., Exch. L.R., M.B. 185, ff. 32, 36, 50v.

[10] Ibid. ff. 15 (14), 100v., 134 (135)v., 156 (50); 222, f. 21; 228, ff. 73 (9), 104
(39), 155 (7), 165 (17); A.O., M.B. 369, f. 35 (7); Parl. Svys Hunts. 3, f. 3; Northants. 15, f. 3; 20, f. 18; Ruts. 13, f. 1; War. 10, f. 5; Wds, Feodaries' Svys Northants.
bdl. 30 pt ii no 702; R.&S. G.S. 26/66, f. 10; Salt Lib. D. 1765/27, svy; Staffs. R.O.,

were not too large for the shifts of up-and-down husbandry, but too small, so that two or more closes needed to be thrown together and the hedges razed. This process provides additional circumstantial evidence of up-and-down land.[1]

Particulars, although often formal and no more accurate than those issued by estate agents today, frequently yield evidence of up-and-down husbandry. A mid-seventeenth-century particular of Wychbold describes some closes as 'pasture' and some as 'arable', meaning grass and tillage respectively. There is a close with four acres 'arable' and the rest 'meadow', and several 'closes of pasture', including one 'nowe in tillage', another 'in tillage nowe', one 'lately in tyllage', one 'in areable grownds, but nowe in pasture', two more 'now in pasture, that formerly was in tillage', and another now divided into three several closes.[2] A less formal particular, of Rotherby in 1678, mentions a close that was first in grass, then ploughed for seven years, then laid down again for the past year.[3] Another of Kirby about 1650, specifies 'the meadow ground now wheate', a great pasture to be divided, grounds to be ploughed, and 'grounds that have bine plowed'. A seventeenth-century particular of Duddington glebe and tithes remarks, 'there are some enclosures plough'd up. But as much feild land is layd down'.[4] An Aldborough valuation says several closes were apt to run to whins and suggests 'four or five crops might be worth the soil and lay down again in some heart'.[5] In these and similar ways, particulars and analogous documents provide evidence of up-and-down husbandry between 1597 and 1734.[6]

Still further evidence is found in law and equity pleadings, especially

---

D. 260, 16 (b) ct of svy, ff. 1 sqq.; Northants. R.O., F-H 119, Skinnand; 272, ff. 8, 24–6; 298, p. 6; Deene No. Brudenell A.S.R. 562, p. 7; O.x. 14; B.M., Add. 34683, f. 4v.; W. K. Boyd, 'Chanc. Proc. temp. Eliz. 1560–70', *Colls. Hist. Staffs.* 1906, p. 199; L. Stone, *Crisis Aristocracy 1558–1641* 1965, p. 324; E. M. Hartshorne, *Memls Holdenby* 1868, app. pp. xxi–ii; Barratt, op. cit. i, 6–7, 40–2, 102–3; Cave & Wilson, op. cit. 60, 129, 160.

[1] Ibid. 60; P.R.O., Exch. L.R., M.B. 185, ff. 67, 69, 74, 90, 92, 95, 115 (3, 5, 10, 26, 28, 31, 51).
[2] B'ham Lib. 478550.
[3] Leicester Mus. 35/29/427.
[4] Northants. R.O., F-H 1145, 3712A.
[5] Lawson-Tancred, op. cit. 43, 45.
[6] Northants. R.O., F-H 4177; Mont. Northants. 13/12; War. 4/46; Clayton 61, 70, 128; Wmld 7. xv: letter stwd/1d & enclo. rental; Maps 571, 1493; Staffs. R.O., D. 150, 300/2, 301a; Leicester Mus. 35/29/27–8, 32, 35, 39, 95, 376, 397; Berks. R.O., D./E.Bp E15; Shak. Bpl. Leigh: Stoneleigh svy demesnes 1623; W.de B. 1080; B'ham Lib. 382959, f. 9v.; Oxon. R.O., J. vii. 6, esp. ff. 1–2, 3v.; B.M., Add. 36981, f. 12; Barratt, art. cit. 147–9; H. Gill & E. L. Guilford, *Rector's Bk Clayworth* 1910, pp. 46–8, 110; Deene ho. Brudenell I. iii. 7; & v. Maps 22, 34–6.

in tithe suits. Both complainant and defendant agree that 153 acres in Bretford Pasture in Brandon has for twenty years been 'used at their wills and pleasure either to plough or lay to pasture . . . as to them hath alwayes seemed best, and have, as they have allwayes thought yt fittest, used and imployed part thereof in tillage and part in pasture, sometime in one place thereof and sometime in another'.[1] It is similarly deposed, of land in Desford, that 'some part of the said closes have beene sometimes used as pasture grounds and some part thereof as arrable'. At Quinton the Grange Close was divided into nine separate closes, and the answer to the interrogatory, 'how many acres of ground have bin plowed and sowed with corne yearely in the said closes one yeare with another', is that four or five acres have been ploughed and sown to corn 'one yeare with another for the said tenne yeares'. Up-and-down husbandry is likewise shown to have been general in the Grafton, Hellidon and Charwelton districts.[2] Between 1560 and 1660 especially, many other similar instances occur in the pleadings.[3]

Anti-depopulation legislation and proceedings likewise testify to the prevalence of up-and-down husbandry after the early sixteenth century. The enlightened Act of 5 and 6 Edward VI caput 5 has a proviso exempting anyone who:

'hath or shall turne or convert to tyllage and errable grownde as much pasture ground or leise within the same . . . village . . . where anny suche lande so hath byn or hereafter shalbe converted from tyllage to pasture, and doo suffer the same lande so turned from pasture to be errable, withowte turninge the same to pasture againe, so longe as the landes turned to pasture as aforesaid shalbe used in pasture'.

After being laid aside for a long time, the same exemption for up-and-down husbandry is restored in the statute of 39 Elizabeth caput 2, by which it is

---

[1] P.R.O., Chanc. Proc. ser. i Jas I, Y. 1/25.

[2] P.R.O., Exch. K.R., Deps. by Commn 15 Chas East. 6, esp. m. 74; 15–16 Chas Hil. 8; 1656 Mich. 17.

[3] 'Chanc. Proc. temp. Eliz.', *Colls. Hist. Staffs.* 1926, pp. 13–14, 132–3; 'St. Ch. Hy VIII & Ed. VI', id. 1912, pp. 23–4; P.R.O., Chanc. Deps. Jas, F. 13/16 arts. 2–6, 8; Req. 129/45; Exch. K.R., Sp. Commns 5554, 6507; Deps. by Commn 38–9 Eliz. Mich. 8, esp. art. 5; 42–3 Eliz. Mich. 2, esp. art. 13; 8 Jas East. 4; 12 Jas Hil. 11, ex. parte quer.; 21 Jas Mich. 13, mm. 3, 5–6; 16 Jas Hil. 18; 3 Chas East. 1; 4 Chas Mich. 24; 9 Chas Mich. 47, esp. art. 2; East. 10; Trin. 4; 10 Chas Mich. 48, arts. 3, 4, 17, 20–1; Trin. 12, arts. 7, 10–11, 13–15, 18; 11 Chas Trin. 9, mm. 1–3; 12 Chas East. 24, mm. 2–4, 6, 7d.; 13 Chas Mich. 59; arts. 4, 7; 14 Chas Mich. 25, mm. 1, 4 (5)d.; 15 Chas East. 19, mm. 1d., 2, arts. 19, 20, 25; 1657 East. 9; 1659 East. 42, esp. art. 2; 19 Chas II Trin. 2; 35 Chas II East. 3; supp. bdl. 902 no 42; St. Ch. Jas 40/22, m. 110.

'provided allsoe, that if anie such occupier or possessor of grounde . . .
hath broke upp or laide forthe, or shall breake upp, converte or lay
forth into tillage anie grounde not liable to this present lawe . . . and
lyinge within the same . . . towne . . . or within two myles of the same
lande formerly tilled, that for such quantitie onlie and for so longe time
as he hath soe done or contynued, or shall so doe or continue, he shall
not incurre anie penalty . . . but that it shall be lawfull for anie suche
occupyer or possessor, at his liberty and pleasure, and accordinge to his
best commodity and husbandry, to change and alter from tyme to tyme
such grownde put or to be put in tillage, so that every such occupier doe
kepe the somme or totall of the quantitie or proporcon of his growndes
. . . in tillage'.

A defendant, accused of conversion to 'pasture' in Waterperry,
answers that his predecessor 'did put parte thereof to pasture and parte
to tyllage',[1] while he himself

'hath put parte of the sayd land to tyllage and parte converted to pasture
untyll nowe of late, that ys to saye, aboute v or vj yeres last past, the sayd
defendant hath suffred such parte and parcell of the sayd land as afore
that tyme was occupied with tyllage to be converted to pasture from
tyllage, bycause the sayd land so occupied yn tyllage become so barreyn
that hyt wold no longer bayre any corne or grayen; and durying whiche
tyme he converted other parcelles of the sayd cc acres to tyllage, and so
hath occupied the sayd cc acres of land parte yn tyllage and parte yn
pasture'.

In answer to a charge of depopulation at Great Alne, it is declared that[2]

'wher thre ploughes are supposyd to be decayed within the sayd lord-
shipe, one at the farm and ij at the Woodehowse, the fermer kepithe at
this present xij oxen and tyllythe as moche as for his comoditie and
benefitt he thynkithe meate; and the lande at the Woodhowse ys
devyded into fyve partes notwithstandinge: iij yarde land ys styll in
tyllage whiche ys as moche as ever was tyllyd, so that neither howse nor
ploughe ys decayed'.

Some defendants of depopulation suits in 1607—and those who as yet
are not known to have been found guilty—pleaded the up-and-down
proviso of the 1597 act. Men from Houghton, Colworth, Farnborough
and North Stoke[3] all claimed to have ploughed up grassland to replace

---

[1] Ibid. Hy VIII 22/352; 24/221; vol. 6, f. 176.
[2] Shak. Bpl. Gt Alne 'A declaration of all the inclos. made'.
[3] V.C.H. Hunts. ii, 89–90; P.R.O., St. Ch. Jas 10/4, m. 3; 15/12, m. 10; 16/13, m.
3; 18/12, m. 8.

tillage laid down. William Belcher answered that all the common fields of Nortoft had been enclosed by agreement about 1590 and the allotments largely made in greensward. He had, nevertheless, kept a good deal of his in tillage and recently ploughed up twenty acres of grassland. Thomas Throgmorton admitted laying down 200 acres at Weston Underwood, but said he had ploughed up forty acres of old grassland and half the land was laid down 'for a short space onlye to the intent and purpose that yt may gayne and gather to ytselfe hart and strengthe, beinge before that tyme verye feeble, barren and out of hart'. This he did 'intend and fullie purpose to putt to tillage agayne nowe the next season fitt for that purpose, havinge beene laid for pasture only foure yeeres or thereabouts'. John Ingram, it was said, had seven acres in Oving 'many yeares togither plowed and sowen with corn in soe muche as the saide lande by reason of the longe and often tilladge thereof became unfytt to be longer tilled'. He had therefore allowed it 'to lye freshe and untilled . . . for the space of two yeares or thereabout'. He then conveyed the property to one Richard Saunders, who for the next year 'did likewise suffer the said seaven acres to lye freshe and untilled and did with his beastes feede upon . . . the pasture therof and hath sithence, when he thought the said land fitt to be againe tilled, plowed the same and sowen the same with corne'.[1] Whether these persons were found guilty or not, they considered a plea of up-and-down husbandry plausible precisely because the practice was common. Indeed, some of the presentments themselves concede that the land laid to pasture was now being ploughed up.[2] That up-and-down husbandry was already general is shown by the answer of Sir Thomas Humfrey of Swepstone. He pleads, 'he hath converted from pasture to tillage . . . as much pasture ground as hee hath there converted from tillage to pasture, which he hath done for the better husbandinge of the said ground according to the course of husbandry of the said countrie'.[3]

Common-field lease covenants usually forbade ploughing up old greensward.[4] For enclosed farms, however, it was usual to forbid ploughing up 'pastures' under a penalty of £5 a year per acre. These penalties were not intended to prevent ploughing up: on the contrary, landlords were solicitous to persuade their tenants to do just this.[5] The purpose of covenants was to ensure the landlord an increased rent and prevent over-ploughing. They do not prove a particular field in any one year was up-and-down land, but show the contingency landlords

[1] Ibid. m. 17; 10/23, mm. 3, 5.
[2] L. A. Parker, 'Depop. Returns for Leics. in 1607', *Trans. Leics. Archaeol. Soc.* xxiii, 259.
[3] P.R.O., St. Ch. Jas 16/13, m. 2.
[4] E.g. P.R.O., Exch. A.O., Parl. Svys Berks. 35, f. 5.
[5] Marshall, *Midl. Cos.* i, 23; Northants. R.O., F.(M.) Corr. 221/101.

provided against and argue that up-and-down husbandry was general. Sir William Cope paid £800 for the assignment of the lease of a manor farm on the understanding he could plough up various parts of the 2,000 acres of 'pastures' and marsh on payment of £1 ploughing rent an acre, and this consent was confirmed by a fictitious action. Covenants were intended to regulate, not to prevent, the plough-up of 'pastures'.[1] A mother chides her son for losing £3,000 or £4,000 in six years, as she says, by failing to plough 'pastures' as directed by his late father and allowed by the lease covenants.[2] The Tubney farmer is accused not of ploughing up 'pastures', but of ploughing more than his lease allowed, with the intention of exhausting all the farm before the expiry of his term.[3] Many such covenants are found in surviving seventeenth-century leases,[4] but only a fraction of those originally made, for most indentures did not recite, but merely alluded to the covenants, which were usually recorded separately in special articles of agreement. The indenture itself was obtained for various considerations of which one was a payment and another a promise to abide by covenants and cropping agreements.[5] Articles of agreement setting out such covenants have survived less frequently than indentures, but one may be taken as typical. In 1669 the incoming tenant of Dishley Grange Farm agrees, under covenant, that 'the Nether Jacksone Close and Pingle and Dunkirke Close, with the Cow Close, shalbe plowed within 12 yeares after the date of the lease if the said John Shillcock pleaseth. Also the Dishley Feild shalbe holden and enjoyed whether plowed or not as he pleases as it was formerly in George Thorps tyme'.[6]

Where a probate inventory expressly states crops were growing in closes or 'pastures', where both cropping and stocking are consistent with up-and-down husbandry, where this husbandry is already known to have been usual local practice—where all these circumstances coincide, it is a reasonable inference that this particular farm was up-and-down land. Such circumstantial evidence is readily forthcoming after 1590, notwithstanding that it was only fortuitously the appraisers even

---

[1] P.R.O., Chanc. Proc. ser. i Jas I, C. 22/82; & v. P. A. J. Pettit, 'Econ. Northants. R. Forests 1558–1714', ts. thesis D.Phil. Oxon. 1959, pp. 386–8; F. P. Verney, *Mems. Verney Fam. during Civ. War* 1892–4 i, 77.

[2] Beds. R.O., O. 190/145.

[3] P.R.O., Chanc. Proc. ser. i Jas I, M. 13/57.

[4] Gooder, op. cit. 29–30; Ruston & Witney, op. cit. 176; Leeds Lib. T.N./C.O./2; N.R. R.O., Z.C.V. 54, 24 Oct. 1705; Northants. R.O., S.(G.) 297; F.(M.) Misc. 191–2, 200, 202; Misc. Vol. 194; 437, p. 20; Leics. R.O., D.E. 10 Herrick's A/c Bk 1620–36, ff. 225–6; D.E. 53/64, 93, 350; Leicester Mus. 35/29/27; Beds. R.O., L. 4/314; A.D. 1043; B.M., Add. Ch. 53392, mm. 7, 11, 13–14, 16, 18; B'ham Lib. 501864.

[5] Ibid. Winnington 45, 52; Worcs. R.O., B.A. 68 Woodmanton le covenant memo. 1612.

[6] Leicester Mus. 35/29/272.

mentioned the closes or 'pastures'.[1] Also some inventories not referring to closes, nevertheless record crops growing in farms or fields known to have been enclosed. Sir William Whitmore's crops were almost certainly grown in Apley and Hord parks.[2] The 'pastures' corned in Beaumont Leys were closes.[3] Potters Marston fields were enclosed before they were cropped in 1695.[4] The crops at Lee Grange and Staunton Lodge were presumably growing in enclosures.[5] The oats and barley the Hon. Henry Howard had at Winwick in 1663 were almost certainly grown in his closes, which the 1652 survey showed as up-and-down land.[6] Apethorpe demesnes were already enclosed in 1542 and the crops the Earl of Westmorland grew there in 1629 were likely in 'pastures',[7] as were the Countess of Leicester's at Kenilworth in 1634[8] and Sir Humphrey Ferrers' at Tamworth Castle in 1608.[9] The same may be said for William Peyto's at Chesterton in 1609, for this farm was certainly in up-and-down husbandry soon afterwards, while the township had long since been enclosed.[10] Similar assumptions may be made about crops at Elford Hall, Naneby, Primethorpe, Peckleton, Burton Lazars, Muston and elsewhere.[11]

Furthermore, agricultural writers bear witness to up-and-down husbandry. Marshall rightly considered it had been practised in some places since time immemorial. It was well known in the north-west of the Midland Plain, and so to Fitzherbert, by 1535. In 1650 the great

[1] Emmison, op. cit. 123–4; Raine, op. cit. 98 sqq., 200 sqq.; Lawson-Tancred, op. cit. 175 sqq.; B'ham Lib. 277414 281291–2, 350279, 351983, 422770; Northants. R.O., F-H 1140; I.(L.) 769; Shak. Bpl. Leigh: inv. Hy Chambers 1735 Langley; W.deB. 1651; B.M., Add. 36582, ff. 81v., 127; Leeds Lib. T.N./M7/1; invs.:— Worcs. R.O., Cons. Ct 1546: 110; Lichfield Jt R.O., Cons. Ct H1592: Martin Holbache/Fillongley; Leics. R.O., A/d 1612: 215; 1614: 175; 1627: 78, 140; 1632: 45, 56; 1636: 132; 1637: 90, 92, 105, 176; 1638: 209; 1639: 61, 101, 133; 1642: 7; 1660 small: 28, 107, 125; gt: 235; 1661 A/d: 244; 1663 Commy: 52; 1667: 72; 1668 A/d: 13, 136; 1669: 78; 1691: 81; 1693 V.G.: 11, 88; 1695: 94; 1696: 118; 1697: 29; 1702: 38; 1704: 41; 1705: 105; 1706: 28; 1707: 113, 126; 1708: 35; 1709: 28, 47, 100; 1710: 14 & Wm Moore/Aston Flamville; 18th-cent.: Geo. Brewster 1728 Gt Dalby, Th. Tilecoat 1741 Nelson.

[2] *Trans. Salop. Archaeol. & Nat. Hist. Soc.* 1914 iv, 305 sqq. N.B. 'in the field' not necessarily in com. fd, v. Leics. R.O., A/d inv. 1633: 6.

[3] Ibid. 1671: 205; 1707: 130; 1708: 79.

[4] Ibid. 1695: 34; Leicester Mus. 8D. 39/25/1/4.

[5] Leics. R.O., A/d invs. 1636: 111; 1710: 20.

[6] B.M., Add. R. 13588; Northants. R.O., R.H. 45, svy ff. 2–4.

[7] Ibid. Wmld 4. xx. 3; 6. v. 1, 2.

[8] J. O. Halliwell, *Anc. Invs.* 1854, pp. 40, 42; sup. 185–6.

[9] B'ham Lib. 437935.

[10] Shak. Bpl. W.deB. 1024a; W. Smith, *Hist. Co. Warwick* 1830, p. 91; inf. 212.

[11] *Yks. Archaeol. Jnl* xi, 279 sqq.; *Wills & Invs. Knaresborough* i, 129 sqq.; B'ham Lib. Elford Hall 294; Leics. R.O., A/d invs.:—1614: 175; 1626: 141; 1637: 176; 1666: 56; 1673: 96; 1708: 67; 1709: 28.

G

expert in up-and-down husbandry was Walter Blith, who hailed from the east of the plain. It was the same practice in the central and eastern parts that Edward Lisle remarked upon.[1] Later, William Marshall became the authority on the system.

In the early sixteenth century, up-and-down husbandry was confined to the north-west and to a few farms elsewhere. It expanded and spread rapidly after 1560 and fastest between about 1590 and 1660, by which time it had conquered production and ousted the system of permanency from half the farmland. In this expansion, up-and-down husbandry progressed at the expense of permanent tillage, mostly in common fields, and of permanent grass, partly in common fields, partly in en-closures. Much permanent grass was converted to up-and-down land between 1590 and 1660. At this time, as has been seen, many parks were disparked and both these and the larger 'pastures' divided up into arable fields. The great wave of tithe disputes that broke at the close of the sixteenth century was caused precisely by this conversion of permanent grassland.[2] Probate inventories still continue to show some pure graziers; but they give an exaggerated impression of the extent of permanent grass. Such inventories are deceptively difficult to understand, because they list everything and explain nothing. Inventories reveal graziers who undertook no ploughing, but this does not necessarily mean their 'pastures' were all permanent grass. Closes could be, and frequently were, leased singly to farmers for a term of years, during which they might be tilled;[3] and they could equally well be let out for ploughing to halves or thirds (share-tenancy and share-cropping).[4] This gave graziers the advantage of temporary leys without any cares of cultivation. It was this period that saw the rise of itinerant woadmen and flaxmen. Woad, especially, was rarely grown otherwise than as the first crop in newly broken 'pastures', and from 1590 to 1660 the plain became famous for this crop. Woad and flax were often cultivated in 'pastures' by neither owner nor occupier, nor even by a local farmer on a short letting or share-cropping agreement, but by itinerant woadmen and flaxmen under special agreements whereby they might take a single industrial crop and a few subsequent corn crops and then relinquish the land and pass on somewhere else.[5] In these ways the conversion of permanent grass to up-and-down land is partially concealed, to such an extent, indeed, that it is difficult to find a clear example of a grazing farm. For instance,

[1] Fitzherbert, op. cit. ff. 52–3; Blith, op. cit. 97 sqq.; Lisle, op. cit. 94, 151–2; Marshall, *Yks.* i, 297.

[2] Sup. 189.

[3] E.g. Verney, op. cit. i, 129; Finch, op. cit. 48, 114, 130, 147.

[4] E.g. Leicester Mus. 7D. 51/1; B'ham Lib. 394772; Worcs. R.O., Cons. Ct inv. 1563: 83.

[5] Blith, op. cit. 99, 226; Morton, op. cit. 17; Hurry, op. cit. 69; A. Young, *Farmer's Tour through E. Engl.* 1771 i, 57–8, 60.

the 500 acres of Moorbarns pastures had 'only a shepparde house upon the whole premisses', but were none the less ploughed.[1]

The conversion of common fields to up-and-down land was perhaps even more extensive. On their enclosure, where, say, half the land was previously permanent grass and half permanent tillage, the usual procedure was to lay most of the tillage to grass, leave the wet meadow and perhaps also the home closes as before, and plough up as much old greensward as would result in between one-half and four-fifths of the farm being up-and-down land. Much the same resulted, too, in the ploughing up of old enclosed greensward. Thus about a quarter of the farm was tillage. The proportions of both up-and-down arable and of the tillage in it varied according to soils, markets, and individual circumstances, but less variation occurred in the arable than in the tillage area, which might occasionally form no more than one-tenth of the farm.[2] Fitzherbert suggests each man take his share of 'leys' in the common field to form one close, of common pasture for a second, and of meadow for a third. One close should likewise be made from each of the three tillage fields.[3]

'Yf any of this three closes that he hathe for his corne be worne or ware bare, then he maye breake and plowe up his close that he had for his leyse, or the close that he had for his commen pasture, or bothe, and sowe them with corne, and lette the other lye for a tyme, and so shall he have alwaye reyst grounde the which wyll beare moche corne with lytell dongue.'

Enclosure of common field indeed, usually resulted, on conversion to up-and-down farms, in a diminution of tillage. Even if the land were no longer down than up, tillage could hardly cover half the farm, since there had to be some wet meadow and permanent grass. The conversion of permanent-grass farms to up-and-down land, however, necessarily augmented both arable and tillage. When up-and-down husbandry, therefore, replaced the system of permanency, the arable was extended while the tillage remained much the same.

Land long under the plough, more particularly permanent common tillage, was prone to grass and could easily be laid down, but took between

[1] Leicester Mus. 35/29/378; P.R.O., Exch. K.R., Deps. by Commn 12 Chas East. 24, m. 7d.; E. F. Gray, 'Temples of Stowe & their Debts . . . 1603–53', *Huntington Lib. Q.* ii, 412–13.

[2] Marshall, *Midl. Dept*, 220, 291; *Midl. Cos.* i, 187–8, 234, 263; Tuke, op. cit. 32; Ingleby, op. cit. 17; T. Birch, *Coll. State Papers Jn Thurloe Esq.* 1742 iv, 686; Mills, art. cit. 86; P.R.O., Exch. K.R., Deps. by Commn 16 Jas Hil. 18; 9 Chas Trin. 4; 10 Chas Trin. 12, arts. 10–11; Sp. Commn 6507; Chanc. Deps. F. 13/16; St. Ch. Jas 16/4, m. 3; 16/13, m. 2; Northants. R.O., Mont. War. 4/46.

[3] Loc. cit.

seven and twelve or more years to produce good turf, and in the meantime up-and-down husbandry could not be pursued.[1] Old permanent
grass was equally difficult to convert to tillage, by reason of its rankness
and infestation with wireworm and leatherjacket. Paring and burning,
rolling, harrowing, hand-picking, close-folding sheep, driving stock to
and fro, or putting in ducks, or any combination of these methods, might
destroy leatherjackets. Wireworms, which were extremely destructive of
roots, especially those of wheat, and usually most virulent in the second
year after breaking up old grassland, were more obdurate enemies,
though not invincible. Dressings of quicklime or salt might prove help-
ful, and so might the heavy roller; but the simplest thing was to starve
the worms out by an eighteen-month bare fallow or by sowing crops
they could not eat. Hemp and flax sometimes succeeded in this, but the
only infallible remedy was woad, which was sown as the pioneer crop
and left in the ground for two, three or four years, during which the
worms were exterminated at no cost to the farmer.[2] Further risk lay in
the rankness of newly ploughed grassland, which might be so rich that
even specially selected strong-stalked wheat or barley would grow to
such a height it would easily lodge. This was reason enough to make the
first crop woad. After two years of woad, the land had abated its strength
enough for barley. Other suitable crops were flax, hemp, rape, madder
and liquorice. How difficult it was to deal with over-rankness, even in
up-and-down land is illustrated by the account of it a Midland farmer
gave to Lisle. He had chosen great wheat for a rich new-broken
'pasture'. This first crop was followed by beans, but the land was still too
rank for barley or oats, and he was thinking of sowing a mixture of
great and red-straw wheat, so the former might support the latter.[3]
Thus the creation of up-and-down land took several years, during
which some old permanent grass might as yet lie unploughed and some
old permanent tillage unturfed. The whole farm needed reorganizing.
If the conversion were being made from permanent grass only, one
farm might have to be split into two; if from common field, several farms
might be amalgamated into a unit commensurate with the capital
employed; if from old enclosure, some 'pastures' might need to be
thrown together and many divided; if from open land, the new closes
might at first be large and then made smaller as opportunity presented
itself. New ponds might also be needed. Conversion, in short, was not an

[1] Marshall, op. cit. ii, 39–40; *Yks.* ii, 87.

[2] Marshall, *S. Cos.* i, 93–5; Morton, op. cit. 480; Markham, *Weald*, 11, 17; *Eng.
Husbandman*, 50–1; R. Lennard, art. cit. 44; Farey, op. cit. ii, 123; Pitt, *Leics.* 75;
Murray, op. cit. 58; Shak. Bpl. W.deB. 1652B, Heath to Laxton 8 July 1661; 1711,
woad a/c 9 June, barley a/c 1 & 20 May; Collier, art. cit. 49; Laurence, op. cit. 67;
Lisle, op. cit. 61, 120; Blith, op. cit. 132–3.

[3] Ibid. 97, 107, 226; Morton, op. cit. 399; Marshall, *Midl. Cos.* i, 244; Lisle, op. cit.
151–2.

enterprise to be lightly embarked upon. That it was undertaken at all
was due only to the immense superiority of up-and-down farming.

The leys were always long, varying in duration, in early modern
times, between six and a score years, but mostly between seven and
twelve, according to local circumstances and market conditions.
Periods of tillage were likewise various. On the least ameliorated soils
they might be as short as two years, and on the most as long as five, but
the best managers on middling soils favoured three or four. If marled,
the tillage might continue eight or nine years; and if woaded, for seven,
though six was long enough for the best results from both tillage and ley.
Without either marling or woading six or seven years in tillage were
usually too much; and those who ploughed for nine, ten, or even twelve,
earned well-merited censure. Yet no hard and fast rules were applied.
Farmers tended to till one shift until another destined to take its place
was ready to plough up; and to graze one ley until the turf had formed
on one elsewhere. Leys were thus somewhat longer than in later times,
but tillages about the same.[1]

The leys were usually broken up, from February to April, by a single
ploughing lengthways of the ridges for oats (or sometimes barley, peas
or beans, woad, flax or hemp), the turf simply being torn up and inverted. After a crop of oats (or some alternative), the stubble field was
winter-fallowed ('pin-fallowed') for barley (or occasionally oats), by
ploughing lengthways of the ridges in November or thereabouts, across
them in February or March and then lengthways again, after which it
was left in clods ready for sowing. Barley might be repeated, or be
followed by pulse, usually peas; but, more generally, a single barley
crop was succeeded by one of wheat. For this the stubble was ploughed
two or three times, first lengthways, then across, and then lengthways
again, but always gathered at last either into a bout, laying two plits
(furrow slices) back to back, or, in heavier soils, into elevated ridges
with water-furrows, for surface drainage. This last crop was mucked, for
the sake less of the wheat than of the grass the land was now laid to.
In shorter tillages, wheat was usually omitted altogether, and in lighter
soils, replaced by rye or maslin or, in the north, by bigg. Sometimes

---

[1] P.R.O., Exch. K.R., Deps. by Commn 38–9 Eliz. Mich. 8, art. 5; 8 Jas East. 4;
4 Chas Mich. 24; 9 Chas Trin. 4; 10 Chas Trin. 12, arts. 14–15; 11 Chas Trin. 9;
12 Chas East. 24, m. 7d.; 14 Chas Mich. 25; 15–16 Chas Hil. 8; 1657 East. 9; supp.
bdl. 902 no 42; A.O., Parl. Svys War. 12, f. 6; 20, f. 4; 32, f. 6; Berks. R.O., D./E.Bp
E15; Leicester Mus. 35/29/95, 272, 427; Northants. R.O., Clayton 70, 100a; F.(M.)
Misc. Vol. 194; Corr. 176/10, 220/42–3, 222/39, 44; Mont. Northants. 13/12; Wmld
7. xv, Apethorpe tithe agrt 1700; F-H 3712A; Ruston & Witney, op. cit. 102;
Lennard, loc. cit.; Fitzherbert, op. cit. ff. 44, 53; J. Moore, op. cit. 12; Blith, op. cit.
97–9, 103, 106, 111–12, 132, 138; Plot, op. cit. 341; Worlidge, op. cit. 33; T. Nourse,
Campania Foelix 1700, p. 54; Laurence, op. cit. 45; Marshall, *Yks.* i, 296; *Midl. Cos.* i,
187.

winter corn preceded barley, but the former was best left to the end to be a nurse for the grass. There were thus about six ploughings in a dozen years and a crop of corn or grass every year.[1]

The two chief corn crops were barley and oats, while wheat covered rather more, and peas somewhat less, than half the barley acreage. Rye and maslin were grown, and some dredge, bigg, and beans. Thus more oats were grown in up-and-down than in common-field land, more wheat, less barley and much less pulse. Beans and peas for horses were largely replaced by crushed oats, feed barley and 'cut meat' (i.e. oats in the straw cut up small), and 'cut meat' and hay were employed for a little stall feeding.[2]

Farmers with enclosed up-and-down farms had livestock similar to that of the old graziers and managed it in much the same way, save only in the following points. The graziers in permanent-grass farms did not keep large dairy herds or allow milkers on their best fatting pastures, for they would have taken too much out of the soil, making up-and-down husbandry inevitable; but the new-style farmers were under no such disability. Dairying was general on up-and-down land throughout the plain, but tended to concentrate towards the west and in the extreme north. Cheese was the chief product, except in the south, far north and north-east, where butter took its place, and in the north-west, where both were important. And with dairying went pigmeat, especially bacon production. The herds might contain up to fifty cows, which

[1] Ibid. i, 23, 145, 187–8, 195, 209, 234–5, 239–41, 243–4; ii, 29–30; *N. Dept*, 396; *Midl. Dept*, 66, 220; Norden, op. cit. 222 (both occs.); Fitzherbert, op. cit. ff. 44, 46v.–7; *Husbandrie*, f. 5v.; Mortimer, op. cit. 43; Bailey, op. cit. 127; Laurence, op. cit. 59, 67; Blith, op. cit. 99, 101, 104, 214, 226, 254–5; Worlidge, op. cit. 33, 41; Plot, loc. cit.; *Oxon.* 241; Morton, op. cit. 480, 482; Lisle, op. cit. 61, 86, 94–5, 324; Pitt, op. cit. 29, 95, 109; *Staffs.* 76, 78, 83; *Northants.* 73, 78–80, 95, 107; Gill & Guildford, op. cit. 46–8, 99, 106, 110–11, 116, 121, 124, 127, 133; M. Campbell, *Eng. Yeo.* 1942, p. 180; Wedge, *War.* 13–14; P.R.O., St. Ch. Jas 40/22, m. 110; Exch. K.R., Deps. by Commn 38–9 Eliz. Mich. 8; 42–3 Eliz. Mich. 2, art. 13; 8 Jas East. 4; 4 Chas Mich. 24; 9 Chas Mich. 47, art. 2; 11 Chas Trin. 9, mm. 2d.–3; 12 Chas East. 24, mm. 2, 3d.; 14 Chas Mich. 25; 15 Chas East. 19, mm. 1d.–2, arts. 19, 20, 25; 1657 East. 9; 1659 East. 42; 13 Chas II Mich. 44; Chanc. Proc. ser. i Jas I, C. 22/82; Shak. Bpl. W.deB. 1080, 1711; Berks. R.O., D./E.Bp E15; Leics. R.O., A/d invs. 1708: 55; 18th-cent.: Wm Coltman 1754 Wigston Magna; Brewster & Tilecoat—ut sup.; Northants. R.O., F-H 3711A, 3712A.

[2] Ibid. 1140; Halliwell, loc. cit.; Hall, op. cit. 153; Lawson-Tancred, op. cit. 175 sqq.; *Yks. Archaeol. Jnl* xi, 279 sqq.; Raine, op. cit. 19–21, 98 sqq., 132 sqq., 200 sqq., 243 sqq.; *Wills & Invs.* (Surtees S.) pt ii, 96–8, 237 sqq.; *Wills & Invs. Knaresborough* i, 129 sqq.; Wilts. R.O., acc. 88, A. 1/17a; Dioc. Reg. Sarum. inv. Nic. Johnson 1619 Grove; Lancs. R.O., D.D.F. 1072; B'ham Lib. 277414, 351983, 422770; Shak. Bpl. W.deB. 1651; Leics. R.O., A/d invs. 1602: 126, 1627: 78, 140; 1632: 56; 1637: 90, 92, 105; 1638: 238, 309; 1639: 133; 1661 A/d: 244; 1691: 81; 1695: 94; 1696: 118; 1702: 38; 1704: 41; 1708: 35; 1710: Jn Lewin/Syston; 18th-cent.: Geo. Fisher 1726 Barrow-on-Soar; Leeds Lib. T.N./M7/1; Marshall, *Midl. Cos,* i, 135–6, 244–5, 362.

calved down in February. In this way the periods of highest lactation and fastest grass growth coincided. In May, production was commenced of factor's cheese, which was mainly thin until the later eighteenth century, when Stilton was introduced. Farmers bought in steers, bullocks, heifers and in-calvers; but bred more calves than did the graziers and reared both cow and bull calves; and were, consequently, less dependent on imported stores. The farmers also had more working horses and oxen, for they needed powerful plough-teams of about five horses or of four or six oxen. Horses were more usual, but ox-teams were by no means out of favour, especially in earlier times.[1]

Before about 1660 land was usually laid down by leaving the natural grasses to form a sward of themselves. The first essential in laying down, although it is Irish to say so, was not to have ploughed the field out of heart. The form in which land was laid down was also important. In both respects, some farmers merited censure. Blith expatiates on this:[2]

'As I cry up plowing as a soveraigne meanes of a great advancement, so I also as much decry over-plowing, or the plowing of lands as most doe; some plow as long as it will beare any corne, and others as long as it will beare good corne; and others they plow on any fashion, lay their lands as though they were over-running them, both to corne and graze, and when they lay it downe, some lay downe warme dry land very high, ridge and furrow, and small land too, very prejudiciall to their land and

---

[1] Ibid. i, 268–9, 349, 352–5, 361–2, 367, 440–1; ii, 220, 222–4; *Midl. Dept*, 208–9, 231; *E. Dept*, 61; *Yks*. ii, 271–2; *N. Dept*, 378–9, 403, 406, 485, 488; Granger, op. cit. 42; Pitt, op. cit. 36–7, 130, 137–8, 194–5, 197; T. Burton, *Hist. & Ant. Hemingborough* 1888, p. 362; Lowe, op. cit. 28–9; Hall, loc. cit.; Lawson-Tancred, loc. cit.; Plot, *Staffs*. 108; Freeman, art. cit. 102–3; Farnham, op. cit. 200; Emmison, op. cit. 50, 54–5, 69–70, 77–8, 81–2, 114–15; Kennedy, op. cit. 85 sqq.; Raine, op. cit. 19–21, 98 sqq.; 107–9, 132 sqq., 200 sqq., 243 sqq.; Kirk, art. cit. 251–2; *Yks. Archaeol. Jnl* xi, 279 sqq.; Crossley, art. cit. 94 sqq.; *Wills & Invs*. pt i, 109–10, 161–4, 271–2; pt ii, 77–9, 96–8, 237 sqq.; pt iii, 41–4; pt iv, 203; *Wills & Invs. Knaresborough* i, 129 sqq.; Purvis, art. cit. 449–52; Brown, *Yks. Deeds* iii, 47–9; Blome, op. cit. 201; *Trans. Salop. Archaeol. & Nat. Hist. Soc*. 1914 iv, 305 sqq.; Halliwell, op. cit. 40–2; J. West, *Vil. Recs*. 1962, pp. 97–8, 104–5, 112, 114; M.A. Rice, *Abbots Bromley* 1939, p. 214; Verney, op. cit. i, 128, N. E. McClure, *Letters Jn Chamberlain* 1939 ii, 252; Kent R.O., U. 269/A413, A423–4; Lincs. R.O., Andrews 1; H. 97/22/1, 2; Salt Lib. D. 1734/4/1/6–11; Lancs. R.O., D.D.F. 1072; B.M., Add. 36582, ff. 39–40, 81v., 86, 107–8, 127; R. 13588, 32859–60; B'ham Lib. 277414, 281271, 281291–2, 350203, 351983, 437935, 468177, 477329; Bournville Vil. Trust. 14; Elford Hall 294; Shak. Bpl. W.deB. 898, 1024a, 1651, 1654 'Laings forth in the yeare 1636'; Stratford: Wills & Invs. 22; Leigh: inv. Hy Chambers 1735 Langley; Herts. R.O., 8442; Beds. R.O., F.N. 1094, 1097; A.B.P./W. 1607/98; T.W. 3, p. 79; Leics. R.O., D.E. 53/78; Northants. R.O., F-H 574, 1140, 2431–2; I.(L.) 195a, 508, 769, 1491; F.(M.) Misc. 897, 903; Wmld 5. vi, inv. L. le Despenser 1626; 6. v. 1, 2; Crutchley, loc. cit.; Leeds Lib. T.N./M7/1; & invs. listed App. B.

[2] Op. cit. 103–4.

themselves too, and are justly reproveable; others lay down strong cold
land flat unopen'd, some part plowed, some unplowed, full of balkes,
holes and hils; as if they would secure or ingrosse all the coldnesse and
venom of all the water and hunger that is either naturally upon it, or
that falls upon it, or passeth by it; they matter not after what manner
they leave it, nor after what graine. I therefore prescribe onely three or
four yeares to plow unto this sort of land, and to raise it every yeare not
less, because the rush, filth and earth will not be rotted, nor well com-
pounded, nor the nature of the land changed with fewer tilths, nor the
lands brought to a good height, roundnesse and drinesse in lesser time,
for if it be cold land, all that can possibly be done will not lay it high
and dry enough, nor the mould wrought to her perfect tendernesse and
true mixture, whereby it may yeeld more fruitfulnesse; but if the land
be very rich of nature, and not well wrought, nor the rush perfectly
destroyed, nor the lands brought up to a convenient height and roundnesse, then one yeare more may doe well, which yeare shall yeeld the
best crop out of all question, but will draw a little more from the
strength of the land then any of the other yeares did; and if the land be
in strength, it may very little prejudice it'.

The great point of restricting tillage was so that grass would come
again when wanted. The secret was to preserve the grass 'turf' in the soil
throughout. It was for this that the turf was simply inverted for the first
crop of oats, which thus grew in the very roots of the grass. It was for
this that cultivations were restricted to the minimum and summer fallow
stirrings eschewed. The new ley of natural grass was raised on the ruins
of the old, for radical particles of the ploughed-up grasses were still
there when the land came to be laid down again. The pin-fallow checked
the development of these particles and corn kept them under. When the
last corn crop had been taken, the natural grasses no longer had to con-
tend for supremacy with anything but casual intruders, which were
handicapped by late arrival, so that in the first year the natural grasses
recovered, and in the second they resumed the appearance, and much of
the quality of old grasslands.[1]

The choice of the nurse crop was also of some importance. Clay
loams and soils slow to grass over were best laid down

'upon wheat, meslen or rye stuble, which will exceedingly thicken and
improve the soarding . . . because it hath one halfe yeare more to soard
in then after the lenton tylth and so is somewhat soarded before oates,
barley or pease are sowen; . . . because winter corne groweth thin, long
and a stronger straw, and gives more liberty to the grasse to grow and

[1] Marshall, *Midl. Cos.* i, 145; ii, 29, 40–3, 46; *S. Cos.* ii, 325; Lisle, op. cit. 264;
Pitt, *Leics.* 114.

spread and thicken, and the soard will also be very rich and fruitfull'.

A fine wheat tilth, too, left the ground even and smooth for grazing. Cold retentive soils had, in laying down, to 'be left high and round, the colder in nature the higher and rounder . . . and each furrow be scoured up as cleanly as you can possibly'. Lastly, what would ensure a good sward even on land least disposed to grass was to muck it during the ploughings for the last straw crop. Blith advises further,[1]

'if possibly you could run over a good part of this land with dung after you have plowed it before you sow your last crop, or so much as you could, it would bestow a double advantage of the cost bestowed towards the soarding of it. And if, after you have reaped your last crop, you could then run it over againe with any quantity of muck or compost, it might so nourish your land, and that for many yeares after, possibly it might be as neare as goode againe upon the soarding as it was before; for you would wonder how much good one load of manure doth upon the land so tender wrought and mixed, beyond what two or three load will doe on old soard or old pasture'.

Then, as the ley was forming, judicious management was important. The best course was to put cattle on the grass as soon as it could bear them, but not a moment before. After midsummer the weeds and broken grass were to be swept down with a scythe. Sheep were not to be put in until the third year.[2] As the old ley had been largely composed of perennial rye-grass, perennial red clover and wild white clover, the new one was much the same. At the worst, more creeping bent grass might have invaded the field; and this was hardy, withstood early treading well, and made good aftermath and 'bottom' (late-flourishing) grass. Moreover, all species of grass made good grazing when young, and creeping bent compared well with others in point of nutrition and palatability. Good leys were thus made simply by creating the best possible conditions for natural swarding.

If too many corn crops had been taken, however, and the succession interrupted by a still, or even worse, by a stirred summer fallow, natural swarding would be slow and inferior, and in these circumstances resort might be had to hay-seed composed of indigenous clovers and grasses. If so, the rye-grass might become well established in the first year but the ley would not be of much service until the second or third.[3] The

---

[1] Op. cit. 59–60, 104–5, 107; & Lisle, op. cit. 61; Plot. op. cit. 341.

[2] Blith, op. cit. 111–12; Norden, op. cit. 208; Marshall, *N. Dept*, 483; *Yks.* ii, 86–7.

[3] Ibid. 86; Worlidge, op. cit. 34; Tuke, op. cit. 48; P.R.O., Exch. K.R., Deps. by Commn 15–16 Chas Hil. 8.

eighty-two acres in New Close at Burton Lazars ploughed for five successive years about 1650 were worth less for grazing three years after
laying down than before ploughing up, although improved year by
year. Home Close at Rotherby was mismanaged to the extent of being
ploughed for seven years. When first laid down it was not worth half its
pre-ploughing rent and, in an effort to remedy this, 200 loads of farmyard manure had been laid on its 18½ acres of new sward.[1]

Properly managed the new ley would begin to wear the face of old
grassland after one or two years. If laid down under spring corn, land
usually took two years from the time of sowing to form good grazing, and
two years might be needed even under wheat in the coldest soils; but
most clays, if ploughed moderately and laid down carefully under
winter corn, would keep as many cattle on first-year grass as in the year
before plough-up.[2] Just before being broken up the old ley had probably
passed its best, and new leys did not usually reach their peak until the
third year. For this reason leases of single closes commonly prescribed
that tillage should be laid down three years before expiry.[3]

Midland up-and-down husbandry was thus ley farming in a grass-
arable rotation. The leys were long, three-quarters of the farm was
grass and the main object was animal produce. What this plan of
management achieved was farming without the waste of a drop of urine
or a blade of grass. It married the livestock to the soil and extracted the
greatest possible cereal and animal produce from the farm, whilst continuously improving its fertility.[4]

The temporary leys of up-and-down husbandry were generally better
than permanent grass. 'Woodland' clay soils could not be left in grass
above a dozen or fifteen years without becoming overrun with moss and
yielding only scanty feed from coarse, slow-growing herbage. If only to
kill this moss, the Kenilworth farmers ploughed up their 'pastures' every
twelve or fifteen years.[5] Fitzherbert tells the farmer to look to his 'pasture' and

'yf it ware mossye in wynter, then wold it be plowed agayne and sowen
with dyvers cornes, as the grounde requyreth. And at the fyrste plowynge
it wolde be plowed a square forowe, as depe as it is brode and layd
flatte and sowen with otes, that the mosse maye rotte, and than to lye
falowe one yere, and than to be sowen with wheat, rye or barley, as the
husbande thynketh mooste convenyente. And yf it shulde lye falowe the

[1] Leicester Mus. 35/29/95, 427; & Northants. R.O., F-H 4177.

[2] Blith, op. cit. 59–60, 97, 103–4, 110–11; Norden, loc. cit.

[3] Lisle, op. cit. 264; Pitt, op. cit. 114; Northants. R.O. F.(M.) Misc. Vol. 194;
Corr. 176/10, 220/42–3.

[4] G. Stapledon, *Way of the Land* 1943, pp. 185–6.

[5] P.R.O., Exch. A.O., Parl. Svys War. 20 f. 4; 32, f. 6; Blith, op. cit. 80, 97–8;
Fitzherbert, op. cit. f. 5v.; Norden, op. cit. 208, 221.

fyrste yere, the mosse wyll not rotte, and at wynter it wyll be wette and drowne all the wheate and rye that it toucheth. And yf a man have plentye of suche pasture that wyll be mossye, every thre yere let hym breake up a newe pese of grounde and plowe it and sowe it, as I have sayd before, and he shall have plentye of corn.'

The plough was the sovereign remedy for weedy, mossy, gorsy, broomy, ferny, heathy, rushy, hilly, or waterlogged grounds; and the only possible cure for cold soils infested with rushes, moss and other rubbish. Here the plough was used as 'a medicine, not as a calling'.[1] Norden says these cold and watery grounds yielded only long-stalked, sour and unprofitable grass, rushes and rank moss. Drainage would have cured this, 'but commonly these grounds are of clay, and clay will never give way or evacuation to the water, because the ground is hard and stiffe'. The only thing was to plough up and dress the tillage with hot chalk, lime, coal dust or ashes, chimney soot and fine, dry sand, and then return it to grass. Blith regarded it as 'a husbandman old principle' that 'woodland lands' be 'tilled every ten yeares, yea, some every eight', because

'all the woodlands are apt to runne to mosse, and fearne, gosse and broome, and to be so extremely overrunne therewith that it bears nothing else; and if they be not tilled, according to that ancient principle all husbandmen retaine, every ten or fifteene yeares, they will runne into these extremes so far as that they will be of little use; so all the lands of a better nature subject to these extremes, no better way can possibly be than moderate tillage'.

Sad, moist, cold clay soils were improved more than others by alternating tillage with grass. Even very cold clays gave better grass after a period under the plough. Sandy and gravelly soils and loams could bear neither tillage nor grass for long; but on all these a first-year ley could be as good as the grass the year it was ploughed up; and a wheat-stubble sward could be better eighteen months after the corn was sown than the old ley had been. The best clay loams and loams carried excellent permanent grass applied almost exclusively to fatting, which took little out of the soil. Yet even the best of these fatting pastures could be improved by ploughing, and they were, indeed, broken up, and all too often over-ploughed, for the sake of the abundant corn they yielded.[2]

Farmers and agricultural workers knew up-and-down land was best

[1] Ibid. 221 (2nd occ.); War. R.O., D.R.O. 72(a) Gt Packington terrier 1612; Fitzherbert, *Surveyinge*, ff. 44 sqq.; Blith, op. cit. 80, 97, 109–10, 124.

[2] Ibid. 80, 96–7, 106, 110–11, 132; Norden, op. cit. 203; Atwell, op. cit. 100; Folkingham, op. cit. 22; H. Platte, *Jewell Ho. Art & Nat.* 1594 bk ii, 21.

for both corn and grass. Mill Field at Grafton was 'good ordinary ground', but the consensus of opinion was, it was best in up-and-down husbandry. Richard Cleaver, the Charwelton shepherd, judged, 'by experience of other grounds in other places in like manner used', that if Mill Field were tilled moderately, three or four years after it had been laid down again, it would be improved in all ways and keep more and healthier sheep. Richard Flaxney, an experienced gentleman farmer from Charwelton, thought the ground would be bettered by ploughing, which would remove ant-hills, avoid lameness in the sheep, and leave the soil 'better mingled'. Robert Cleaver, of Hellidon, said in his experience grassland ploughed up for woad and corn for seven years gave better pasture than before and kept more cattle.[1] A Higham Ferrers farmer asked permission to plough up a 'pasture' because it was too 'high' for either mowing or grazing, whereas after three years of tillage, it could be laid down in handsome order.[2] The improvement by ploughing showed itself in landowners' rentals as well as in farmers' profits. Moorbarns 'pastures' let at £350 a year before ploughing, £600 during the five years of tillage, and between £400 and £500 after laying down.[3] In fine, it was generally accepted that all grasslands whatsoever needed to be ploughed up at least every twenty years if they were to give of their best.[4]

Ploughing grasslands reduced the incidence of disease, especially in sheep. Common-field lands, when wet, put sheep in danger of rot, but cold-soil 'pasture' was no safer, and waterlogged permanent grass fatal. Heavy soils waterlogged easily and the consequent appearance of moss and rushes was not merely a sign the leys were outrun, but also a warning the sheep were in mortal danger. Every four or five years some kind of sheep rot broke out. In wet years, when the great rots occurred, it was the permanent grasslands inflicted the greatest number of casualties.[5] Liver-rot touched sheep mostly at the onset of autumn rains. They throve mightily for about ten weeks, but then decayed, fell away, and died in late winter or early spring. Foot-rot could be overcome by cutting away and tarring infected parts, by washing the sheep from time to time and by changing their ground, putting them if possible into dry tillage or heathland. It was not only the sheep had to be cured, however, but also the field. Richard Cleaver testifies that

[1] P.R.O., Exch. K.R., Deps. by Commn 15–16 Chas Hil. 8.
[2] Northants. R.O., Clayton 100a–b.
[3] P.R.O., Exch. K.R., Deps. by Commn 12 Chas East. 24, m. 7d.
[4] Nourse, op. cit. 54; Worlidge, op. cit. 33; Blith, op. cit. 80, 97–8, 131.
[5] Ibid. 75, 97–8, 112; Ellis, *Chiltern & V.* 18; *Sheep*, 316–17; Pitt, op. cit. 210; *Staffs.* 62; Vancouver, *Cams.* 109, 112, 123; Marshall, *Sheep*, 18; *Midl. Cos.* i, 376; Leics. R.O., A/d inv. 1632:160; Northants, R.O., Mont. Northants. 13/12; J. Bentham, *Xn Conflict* 1635, p. 320; Lisle, op. cit. 338; P.R.O., Exch. K.R., Deps. by Commn 15–16 Chas Hil. 8.

'many others . . . who had grounds subiect to lameness of sheepe . . . have caused their grounds to be ploughed up for the cure thereof and it is reputed that the ordinary cure for lame sheep is by ploughing, for . . . sheep taken out of the grounds subiect to the disease . . . have been putt and folded in the common feildes upon arrable and thereby have been cured . . . and there is no such certaine cure for lameness of sheep and purginge of the ground but by ploughinge'.

Ploughing cleared the ground of moss and of the mole and ant-hills, which caused water to stand in pools. Richard Flaxney said 'most iudicious grasiers' agreed the trouble was in the ground. He himself had removed a flock of mostly lame sheep into the stubble of a newly ploughed 'pasture', with the result they recovered over winter. He thought the only way to rid ground of the 'infection' was to plough it up; and this was the general opinion. Up-and-down husbandry was thus a great asset to the health of livestock; but, on the debit side, on grass newly laid down, both sheep and calves were liable to wood-evil ('moor-evil' or 'blacklegs'), with its locking of the joints, drawing up of the limbs, and dysentery or chronic constipation. Mrs Glover, who had a flock infected in Mill Field at Grafton, tried to cure them with herbs, but as many ewes died 'as would fill a muck cart'. It was generally agreed the infection spread from the ground itself and could only be stamped out by ploughing up the ley again. Two men who rented 'a pasture' in Greens Norton lost £100 when their sheep contracted wood-evil. The next taker was persuaded to plough up and purge the ground, and he apparently overcame the trouble.[1] Wood-evil affected mostly lambs and calves and so rarely ravaged herds or flocks, for young leys were mostly depastured only by feeding cattle, and the danger was further reduced by laying down under winter corn on a smooth and well-prepared tilth.[2]

Up-and-down husbandry gave better grass blade for blade. Young grasses of all species are highly nutritive and palatable, for they grow quicker than old swards and throw up a greater proportion of blade, where the goodness principally resides. Temporary leys, then, gave more nutrients an acre than permanent grass and so produced more milk and meat. Fitzherbert knew temporary leys gave better grass than permanent ones; shepherds, that they could keep more sheep; farmers, that young grass fattened beeves and muttons better, and gave more milk and richer cheese.[3] Blith summed up contemporary opinion in these words.[4]

[1] Ibid.; Lisle, op. cit. 337–8; Fitzherbert, *Husbandrie*, f. 23v.; Morton, op. cit. 10; Mascall, op. cit. 232; Ellis, op. cit. 319–20; Smyth, *Hund. Berk.* 31; Blith, op. cit. 112.

[2] Ibid.

[3] Ibid. 102; Fitzherbert, *Surveyinge*, f. 44v.; Marshall, op. cit. i, 353.

[4] Op. cit. 111–12.

'Doe but you looke into and upon much of your new layd-down-land to graze, which being continually grazed doth put more proofe into all sorts of goods, breed better, feed faster, milketh fruitfuller than old pasture that is richer, for tenne, fifteene or twenty yeares together. I have bought the purest mutton out of land the third, the fourth or fifth yeare after ploughing, being about eighteene or twenty shillings per acre, than any land in those parts of neare thirty shillings an acre hath afforded; and in reason it must needs be so, because what grasse comes fresh, is pure, without mixture and sweet, being young and tender, and having no corrupt weeds or filth to annoy it, and fruitfull, having heat and strength left in the land to feed it; and for continuance fear it not, if grazed, for the very grazing will inrich it every yeare and improve it untill it grow so old againe and overrunne with mosse, ant-hils, rushes or other corruptions, that it requires ploughing.'

Not for nothing did Blith say temporary leys would 'breed better' or farmers declare 'all breed is put in at the mouth'.[1] It was largely due to temporary leys that the improved Midland livestock came into being. Unlike the sheep, cattle here did not evolve a distinct breed. Farmers on up-and-down land largely bought their cattle, including cows and calves, from the Lancashire Plain; but despite excellent pastures, this large race degenerated and by the third descent were no better than homebreds, partly because of inferior bulls and partly because the stock-breeders in the Lancashire Plain let the calves suckle as long as they would, whereas in the Midlands the whole milk went for cheese or butter and the calves were weaned as soon as possible on skim and whey.[2] Distinct breeds of sheep existed in common fields and in 'pastures'. Field or fallow sheep were usually of a horned downland or a polled heath (forest) breed from barren sheep-walks like Cannock Chase and Charnwood Forest. Both were short-woolled.[3] The pasture sheep were polled and long-woolled, had up to twice the value of fallow sheep, twice the weight both of fleece and of flesh, and a propensity to fatten well at three years. The distinction between fallow and pasture sheep was of ancient origin, but as 'pastures' multiplied, so did the pasture breed.[4]

[1] Pitt, op. cit. 46.

[2] Lisle, op. cit. 275.

[3] Leics. R.O., A/d invs.:—1632: 160; 1639: 133; 1642: 34; 1647: 43; 1661 Commy: 111; 1662 V.G.: 21; 1663 Bp's Visitation: 5; 1667: 118; 1668 A/d: 143; 1669: 1, 151; 1700 unstamped: Ric. Overton/Burbage; 1708: 43, 55, 77, 95; 1709: 11, 34, 61; 1710: 49; Boyd, art. cit. 93–4; Morton, op. cit. 10, 16; Pomeroy, op. cit. 10; Marshall, S. Dept, 500; Sheep, 37; Midl. Dept, 50–1, 181, 300, 394, 594; Midl. Cos. i, 376–7; R. H. Tawney & E. Power, Tudor Econ. Docs. 1924 iii, 101–2.

[4] Ibid.; E. Power, Wool Trade in Med. Engl. 1941, p. 21; H.M.C., MSS. D. Buccleuch & Queensberry at Mont. Ho. iii, Mont. Papers 2nd ser. 1926 vi, 40–1; Discourse Com. Weal Realm Engl. ed. E. Lamond 1929, xliii. Pace P. J. Bowden, Wool Trade in Tudor & Stuart Engl. 1962, p. 31. Inf. 313–14.

Up-and-down husbandry made not only richer grass, but also better corn. Fitzherbert said it gave 'plentye of corne with lytell donging'; and Blith agreed that 'sometime plowing on pasture, and resting another' made 'fresh land and restey' that would 'beare more corne without manure, than it did before with it'.[1] Manure was applied in up-and-down husbandry not for the corn but for the grass. The fertility provided by ploughing in a sod impregnated with droppings and urine was made accessible to tillage crops by the excellent soil structure formed by the roots of the previous ley. The first constitution of this crumbly structure after converting permanent tillage to up-and-down land might require a ley lasting a score of years; but once made, either by temporary or permanent grass, the structure could be maintained by shorter leys. Except when done fortuitously by sheer graziers, the creation of this crumbly structure was thus part and parcel of the initial conversion to up-and-down land. Heavier stocking on temporary leys produced greatly increased quantities of manure, which was partly reserved for ploughing in with the last corn crop. Temporary leys permitted what permanent grass forbade—efficient application of fertilizers. Merely laid on the surface of permanent grass, farmyard manure was largely wasted in the air, but in up-and-down husbandry could be properly worked in with the soil. The temporary tillage period is 'when one load of manure will goe as far as two or three' and one load does more for a temporary ley than 'two or three load will doe on old soard or old pasture'.[2] From about 1580, liming was practised more and more widely. Permanent grass could not be limed efficiently and the expense was beyond most common-field occupiers, but in up-and-down land the farmers took advantage of temporary tillage to apply lime (or chalk), marl, sand, all sorts of dung, hedge-bank and ditch mould, rags, malt dust, salt, ashes and all manner of farm and extraneous manures and dressings.[3] They knew from experience that this 'maketh good pasture grounds followe'.[4] The heaviest and almost the only dunging was reserved for the last straw crop and the grass it nursed, but corn was the residual beneficiary.

That one acre well manured would yield as much as three half-starved passed as currency among farmers,[5] and with the swards of

[1] E. Maxey, *New Instruction* 1601; Blith, op. cit. 72, 79–80.

[2] Ibid. 105, 124; Norden, op. cit. 203.

[3] Ibid.; Blith, op. cit. 132–3; Marshall, op. cit. i, 23–4; W. Burton, op. cit. 2; Platte, loc. cit.; Lisle, op. cit. 3, 15, 27, 30–1, 61; Morton, op. cit. 480–1; Plot, op. cit. 341; Verney, op. cit. i, 130; Pitt, *Leics.* 137; Incola, art. cit. 403; R. Hardy, *Ct. R. Par. Tatenhill* 1908, p. 222; Bodl. Hearne's diaries 159, f. [255]; B.M., Harl. 7180; Shak. Bpl. Ct R. Solihull 15 Oct. 1653; W.deB. 1652 B, Heath to Laxton 8 July 1661; Salt Lib. D. 1734/4/1/6; Leics. R.O., A/d invs.:—1638: 105; 1669: 109; 1709. 44; 18th-cent.: Geo. Fisher 1726 Barrow-on-Soar.

[4] Lennard, art. cit. 44.

[5] Blith, op. cit. 80.

temporary leys as their matrix, tillage crops could not but be abundant.[1] Anything in the nature of statistics of crop yields in this period is hard to come by, because farm accounts and cropping books are rare and because there was no uniformity in either square or dry measures. Blith says that in up-and-down husbandry 'one acre beareth the fruit of three, the two acres are preserved to graze', i.e. when common field is converted to up-and-down land and the tillage is reduced to one-third of what it was, as much corn will be raised as before.[2] In the hypothetical comparison of equal areas of permanent and temporary tillage, in the courses usual on each, respectively, fallow, tilth and breach, and oats, barley and wheat, the latter, *ceteris paribus*, produced half as much corn again as the former. But everything else was not equal. In common fields a tenfold increase of harvest over seed was considered good.[3] In temporary tillage Edward Peyto obtained over a nineteenfold increase of barley at Chesterton in 1638;[4] elsewhere twentyfold increases were reported; and it was the praises of twentyfold increases in ploughed 'pastures' that Robert Herrick sung.[5] It is reasonable to suppose that crops in 'pastures' yielded twice as heavily as those in common fields. This would make the total product in an acre of temporary tillage thrice that of an acre of common field, as Blith stated. But in up-and-down husbandry the tillage area was reduced, so the total corn product acre for acre of farmland was, again as Blith said, about the same. In other words, tillage diminished, but tillage crops did not.

Account must also be taken of the great crops of grass in up-and-down husbandry, for although the acreage of tillage was reduced, that of arable was increased and, as Blith said, two of the three acres were reserved to grass. Whereas about half the common-field land was permanent tillage and half permanent grass, three-quarters of an up-and-down farm was arable and one-quarter permanent grass. The acreage of temporary grass was thus about the same as that of permanent tillage in an equal extent of common-field land, namely, one-half. It is instructive to strike a rough comparison of their respective products. For the first four or five years of its life an acre of temporary ley produces more starch equivalent and two or three times as much protein than one of tillage can.[6] The temporary grass of an up-and-down farm would, then, have been twice as productive as common-field tillage. Thus, when permanent tillage and permanent grass were converted to up-and-down land, the total product can hardly have failed to have

[1] Marshall, op. cit. i, 244; Bentham, loc. cit.

[2] Op. cit. 80–1.

[3] Plot, op. cit. 340.

[4] Shak. Bpl. W.de B. 1711, barley a/c 1638.

[5] Plot, op. cit. 205; Herrick, *Noble Numbers*, 'A thanksgiving to God for his ho.' Caveat: latter ref. not specifically Midl.

[6] G. Stapledon & W. Davies, *Ley Farming* 1948, pp. 40–1.

doubled. There was no more corn, but more milk and meat. Moreover, the costs of corn production bushel for bushel were much less than on common-field tillage. On up-and-down land five ploughings in ten years gave a crop of corn or grass every year. The three-field course in common fields demanded five ploughings in three years.[1] So, in ten years, on equal areas of farmland and for the same amount of corn, it required three times as much ploughing in common fields as in up-and-down land. Prime corn production costs were, therefore, three times as high in common fields as in up-and-down farms. But total costs per unit were even higher, for the grass nutrients of up-and-down farms have also to be taken into account. The common-field farms had three times as much ploughing on two-thirds of the extent of arable, as compared with up-and-down farms. Farm for farm, production costs were twice as high. But the total produce of a common-field farm was only half that in a comparable up-and-down one. Therefore total unit costs were four times as high in common fields as in up-and-down land, always supposing production to have been in the same scale in each. But it was not. In common fields, family farms had an average of seven acres of tillage crops per horse, and working farms ten;[2] but up-and-down farms had eleven.[3] Horse-acre and man-acre ratios were much the same.[4] Costs on up-and-down farms, by economies of scale alone, were much lower than in common-field ones. Hence, all considered, up-and-down husbandry had total unit costs less than one-quarter of those in common fields.

As a result of up-and-down husbandry, the output of industrial crops, of flax, hemp, skins, hides, wool, and especially of woad, was greatly expanded. Not only the introduction, also the continuance, of convertible husbandry, occasioned woad cultivation.[5] Middling 'pastures' were considered best for mere corning, but the richest were often first woaded and then corned, partly because woad, like flax, needed a rich ley for its matrix, and partly because, as explained above, the richest 'pastures' were too rank for corn when first ploughed.[6] Such land was usually woaded for two, three or four years and then corned, in the best

[1] Marshall, op. cit. ii, 43, 226–7; sup. 92–3.
[2] Sup. 97 n.1.
[3] Sup. 199 n.1.
[4] T. Davis, op. cit. 111; Venn, op. cit. 146; H. Levy, *Large & Small Holdings* 1911, p. 158.
[5] Shak. Bpl. W. de B. 1080, 1711; Berks. R.O., D./E.Bp E15; Lichfield Jt R.O., Cons. Ct inv. B1598: Robt Beachcroft/Derby; P.R.O., Exch. K.R., Deps. by Commn 9 Chas Mich. 47, art. 2; East. 10; 12 Chas East. 24, mm. 2–3; 'Descron Beds.', *Gent's. Mag.* xxxiv, 57; H.M.C., *Middleton MSS.* 459, 497 sqq.; *Eng. Reps.* cxxiii, C.P. i, 806; Fiennes, op. cit. 31; Blith, op. cit. 107, 226; Hurry, op. cit. 69; Barratt, op. cit. i, 67–8.
[6] Ibid., Pitt, *Staffs.* 83; Hurry, op. cit. 11; Blith, op. cit. 97, 107, 226.

management, for about the same period. The field was then laid to grass and after a dozen years could be woaded again. Woad plants were not, however, purely industrial, for at the end of each season, the crop gathered, they could be folded to sheep, who ate them readily, especially if sweetened by one or two frosts.[1] For two or three years five or six cuts of woad might be taken annually, the first cut, especially of virgin woad, excelling later ones.[2] Thus from 39 acres woaded at Norton in 1619 and after, the virgin cut gave 5 tons, the second 5 also, and the third only 3, worth £190, £90 and £25 respectively. In the second year all the cuts together were worth only £180 and in the third year only £100.[3] While returns diminished, however, so did costs. The first year was necessarily expensive. Cabins and houses had to be built for the woadmen, and the mill and other works installed. All the ploughing, too, fell in the first year, and woad was usually sown on three earths. Then, if the sward were old, the couch grass had to be pronged out. Often 'grubs', similar to turnip flies, had to be picked off the plants. Every year the crop was hoed, cut (i.e. picked with a twisting motion), carried, ground and boaled. For seed, the woad had to be mown, cocked and threshed in the last year.[4] The hey-day of woading was from 1590 until 1660, coinciding with the peak period in the conversion of permanent grass to up-and-down land.[5] One peculiarity of woading was, it was only economic on a scale large enough to utilize fully the installations and the services of the woadmen, without whose supervision few farmers ventured to grow the crop.[6] Thus at Pattishall 35 acres were woaded at a time, at Norton 39, at Chesterton 126 and at Charney 146½.[7] Another peculiar feature of woad cultivation lay in the itinerant woadmen. They sometimes worked under contract to an owner-occupier;[8] but tenant farmers had little chance of profiting from woading, for landlords would prefer to deal directly with the woadman; and mere graziers, though their 'pastures' were often ripest for woading, had little ability or inclination to supervise, even perfunctorily, such laborious operations. Therefore the usual way was to entrust the business to a woadman, who hired the

[1] Ibid. 99, 226; Pitt, *Northants.* 107; P.R.O., Exch. K.R., Deps. by Commn 12 Chas East. 24, m. 7d.; Kent R.O., U. 269/A415, A423; Mavor, op. cit. 230; Hurry, op. cit. 11, 15–18, 65–6.

[2] Ibid. 14–15, 17–18; Blith, op. cit. 226 (recte 229) & bet. 232–3; Worlidge, op. cit. 41.

[3] P.R.O., Exch. K.R., Deps. by Commn, supp. bdl. 902 no 42.

[4] Ibid. 9 Chas East. 10; 12 Chas East. 24, m. 2d.; Chanc. Proc. ser. i Jas I, C. 22/82; Kent R.O., U. 269/A415, A423; Shak. Bpl. W. de B. 1711; Blith, op. cit. 228; Hurry, op. cit. 23–5.

[5] Ibid. 62; Blith, op. cit. 226.

[6] Ibid. 226–8; Pitt, op. cit. 107.

[7] P.R.O., Exch. K.R., Deps. by Commn 9 Chas Mich. 47; supp. bdl. 902 no 42; Berks. R.O., D./E.Bp E15; Shak. Bpl. W.de B. 1080.

[8] Ibid. 1024a, 1080, 1707–11; 1706 summary of a/c 1622, pp. 4–5.

'pasture' for a few years. A farmer might take the land again afterwards and profit from the woad barley, but a tenant grazier hardly could, and the subsequent corn crops might be grown either by the woadman himself or by a farmer. This was easily organized, for 'pastures' were mostly let out singly for short terms to various tenants and the landlord had only to keep in hand those he wanted woaded and hire them out for a few years or have them cultivated by some special arrangement.[1]

Wool was another important industrial crop, a profitable by-product of mutton production and a not inconsiderable item in farmers' and graziers' incomes. Fully grown pasture wethers gave over four pounds of wool to a fleece;[2] but the average pasture sheep rather less. Contrary to common belief, however, wool was not the grazier's, far less the up-and-down farmer's chief aim, even in respect only of sheep. Beef and mutton were the principal objects of the one, and meat, dairy produce, and corn of the other. Wool, hides, fells, tallow, and horn were merely by-products.[3] Graziers and farmers adjusted the proportions of sheep and cattle according not to variations in market prices of by-products, but to the state of the weather, the natural mortality of their sheep and the age and condition of their 'pastures'. Mixed feeding kept these in trim, because sheep, cattle and horses all graze differently and have distinct preferences for particular grasses, but sheep would harm first- and second-year leys. These and similar considerations resulted in rates of stocking of one beast and two sheep on two acres of temporary ley and half as many on permanent grass.[4] Up-and-down husbandry swelled supplies of industrial by-products, because temporary leys gave four times as much nutriment as permanent grass. Substituted for mere grazing, up-and-down husbandry doubled, and replacing common fields, quadrupled rates of stocking. Each pasture sheep, however, produced twice as much wool as each fallow one, and, since the proportions of sheep and cattle remained about the same in the one as in the other, the change-over from common fields to up-and-down land increased

[1] Pitt, op. cit. 107–8; Young, *Farmers' Tour* i, 57–8; *Gen. View Ag. Co Lincoln* 1799, p. 197; P.R.O., Exch. K.R., Deps. by Commn 9 Chas East. 10; Chanc. Proc. ser. i Jas I, C. 22/82.

[2] Inf. 313.

[3] Invs. ut sup. 112 n.1, 199 n.1, esp. Leics. R.O., A/d 1636: 164; 1642: 34; 1671: 205; Lincs. R.O., Cons Ct 1632–3: 204; Wilts, R.O., acc. 88, A. 1/17a; Boughton ho. Sir Ed. Montagu's A/cs, bk ii, ff. 22–5; 30, 34–5; bk iii, ff. 45 sqq., 66, 77 sqq.; Shak. Bpl. W.de B. 898, 1024a; B'ham Lib. Bournville Vil. Trust 14; Salt Lib. D. 1734/4/1/6–11, esp. 8, ff. 10, 22, & 9, f. 39; Kent R.O., U. 269/A421, A423–4; Northants. R.O., F-H 3712A; I.(L.) 1491; P.R.O., Req. 45/100; Bankes, op. cit. 23; Winchester, op. cit. 176; Finch, op. cit. 41–3, 45–6, 171–2; Huntington Lib. S.T. 48, pace Gay, art. cit. 421, who exag. Temple's own wool rects in 1601–5 by adding in those fr. one Wotton's in 1601.

[4] Marshall, op. cit. i, 367, 409; Fitzherbert, *Husbandrie*, f. 30; Mascall, op. cit. 69–70.

wool production eightfold. What resulted was less carding wool for the woollen industry from fallow sheep and vastly more combing wool from pasture sheep to boost the manufacture of hosiery, knitwear, worsted, serges, tammies, shalloons, bays and other new draperies and stuffs.[1]

The new up-and-down farms were cornucopias of beef, veal, mutton, lamb, cheese, butter, pork, bacon, eggs, barley, wheat, wool, hides, skins, woad, horses, and poultry. Edward Heath's small farm in Cottesmore had 120 sheep, 40 hog sheep, a dairy herd worth £26, 43 swine, 13 horses, 39 acres of barley, 22 of oats and peas, 3½ of wheat, and stacks of oats, barley, hay and peas.[2] In 1609, Peyto had on Chesterton farm 3,049 sheep, worth nearly £2,000, 16 draught oxen, 3 fat bullocks, 22 milking cows, 3 geldings, 9 mares, 3 suckling colts and 3 older ones, 1 filly, 3 sucking calves, not to speak of pigs, poultry and swans, and he had yet to buy in his store cattle for feeding. In his stores were butter, cheese, bacon, tallow and wool, in his granaries £70 worth of barley, wheat and maslin, in his malt house £50 worth of malt, and in his ricks £64 worth of hay. Winter corn in the ground was already worth £30 and barley and oats had yet to be sown. In his yards stood 2 carts, 2 tumbrels, 2 pairs of harrows, 3 iron-bound wains and 7 ploughs. Just before 1624 he had woaded at least 126 acres and in 1638 he was woading again on much the same scale, for his first year's expenses ran into three figures. At the same time he was harvesting 181 q. 3 b. of barley from 9 q. 3 b. of seed, giving him a return of nineteen for one.[3]

By 1650, up-and-down husbandry had built up scores of years of experience, had established a complete system, and had developed into the most productive and important, even if not yet, as it easily was 100 years later, the most extensively practised general plan of management in the Midland Plain.

First among the countries not altogether unlike the Midland Plain, and where a similar and simultaneous revolutionary introduction of up-and-down husbandry took place, is the Fen Country, whose southerly and easterly uplands evidenced Midland affinities in the great and growing number of enclosures, especially on demesne land, where corn and grass were alternated in an up-and-down system.[4] In the high lands between the wolds and the sea and in Holderness, the closes were mostly divided and grouped into shifts for up-and-down husbandry. The first crop was usually barley on a single ploughing of the turf, and the

[1] Morton, op. cit. 16; Plot, op. cit. 258; H.M.C., *MSS. in Var. Colls.* iii 1904, p. 96; Northants. R.O., I.(L.) 1491.

[2] Shak. Bpl. W.de B. 1651.

[3] Ibid. 1024a, 1080, 1711.

[4] *V.C.H. Hunts.* ii, 90; Herts. R.O., G'bury xi. 11, f. 60; P.R.O., S.P.D. Mary vol. 9 no 67; Northants. R.O., Wmld 7/16B; Mont. Hunts. 26/27; 26/28 Ct R. Bk 18 Apr. 2 & 3 P. & M.; F.(M.) Misc. 211; Corr. 178/24; Somerville, op. cit. i, 308; Darby, *Draining Fens*, 16.

second might be barley or wheat. Both clay loams and warps could be tilled a score of years with little or no manure save when laying down, and with a whole-year bare fallow only one year in seven to ensure good wheat and bean crops.[1] In the Isle of Axholme, the demesnes had largely been enclosed of old and enclosure now made greater inroads into the common fields. After about 1560 most of these closes came to be treated as up-and-down land. In Epworth demesne closes, which have stiff clay soil,[2]

'In one entire close the tennant useth to mowe parte, feede parte, and plough other parte, as is most advantagious for him; nor doth he constantly use any one parte of the close for meadow, pasture or tillage, but that parte which nowe is pasture, may the nexte yeare be plowed upp for tillage, and that parte which nowe is arrable, the nexte yeare laid downe for pasture, as he shall thinke moste convenient for him.'

Hemp was widely grown as a first crop on the turf, and so were flax, woad and mustard. Then oats, rye or barley might be grown for one or two years, followed perhaps by wheat. Amongst the other crops were beans, lentils, peas, maslin, and bigg.[3]

Up-and-down husbandry wrought a similar change in the Vale of Evesham, only to a lesser extent, for although it was only in the suburbs of Gloucester and Tewkesbury that a few 'all-green' farms continued, this country was one where the common fields were mostly late to disappear.[4] In enclosing and converting to up-and-down land, some old permanent grass had to be broken up, often by ploughing sward and ant-hills in the spring, cross-ploughing in summer, harrowing in autumn, and then sowing to wheat, whose seed was buried deep. A succession of

[1] B.M., Egerton 3003, ff. 91–3, 104–7; Lincs. R.O., HEN. 3/3; P.R.O., Exch. A.O., Parl. Svys Yks. 27, f. 5; 34, ff. 2–3; 35, ff. 9, 11.

[2] Ibid. Lincs. 16, ff. 11–12, 14–17; M.B. 390, f. 37v. (quot.); Jackson, art. cit. 89; Tomlinson, op. cit. 66; Vancouver, op. cit. 155 sqq., 185, 217; Marshall, *E. Dept,* 253.

[3] Ibid. 6, 49, 209, 229–31, 234, 253, 255–6, 282, 288–9; Defoe, *Tour* ii, 100; Darby, op. cit. 87, 164–5; Pitt, op. cit. 105; Folkingham, op. cit. 14, 22; Blith, op. cit. 58, 251–2; Gerarde, op. cit. 213; Vancouver, op. cit. 158 sqq., 188; Morton, op. cit. 8; Dugdale, op. cit. 144–5; Thirsk, art. cit. 21; *Fenland Farming,* 37; *Lincs. Historian* 1951 no 7, pp. 263–4; Hurry, op. cit. 69; Foster, op. cit, ii, 69, 86, 110, 155; iii, 98–9; W. Gooch, *Gen. View Ag. Co. Camb.* 1813, pp. 160, 167–9; B.M., Add. 37521, ff. 5v.–6, 16v., 42, 43v., 48v., 52; 41168, ff. 1 sqq.; Northants. R.O., F-H 119, Dowdyke; invs.:—Lincs. & Nfk R.O.s, Cons. cts; York, Snaith Pec.; P.R.O., Exch. L.R., M.B. 285, f. 12; A.O., Parl. Svys. Lincs. 11, f. 3; 43, f. 4; K.R., Deps. by Commn 40–1 Eliz. Mich. 19.

[4] Ibid. 1653 East. 2; A.O., M.B. 379, ff. 27–9, 42 sqq.; Worcs. R.O., B.A. 494 partic. Morton Underhill 1648; Glos. R.O., D. 184/M24, pp. 199, 203; D. 326/E1, ff. 1, 7v., 14v. sqq.; Cave & Wilson, op. cit. 35; Pomeroy, op. cit. 13; Phillimore & Fry, op. cit. i, 7–8, 130; Marshall, *Glos.* i, 18, 21, 48, 62.

as many as six wheat crops, each on a single ploughing, might then follow.[1] Alternatively, woad or flax might be used as a pioneer crop.[2] Land was generally laid to grass under oats. At Welcombe in 1617 many ridges were 'sowed with otes and were layd downe to sword'.[3] Hay-seeds were frequently used in laying down from permanent tillage. These did include some rye-grass and clovers; but, whatever was sown, the vale's natural perennial rye-grass and wild white clover soon asserted themselves and produced good swards.[4] Grasslands were generally managed as excellently as the tillage. They were mostly mown and fed in rotation and the time of shutting up for hay was carefully adjusted to the nature of the soil. Cold and backward fields were seldom fed in the spring, while warm and forward ones were depastured until the beginning of May.[5]

Then there was one common-field country, the Vale of Pickering, where the change-over to up-and-down husbandry, when it came in the years from 1560 onward, although involving a smaller area, was swifter and more thorough-going and revolutionary than even in the Midland Plain. The central woodlands, pastures and meadows were enclosed, the folding flocks put down, and sheep-walk and tillage sundered. Isolated farmsteads and hamlets multiplied in the inner vale and the moors and wolds escheated to the Blackmoors and the Northwold Country.[6] The vale was thus enclosed in the 200 years after 1560, by local or partial agreements, or, especially in the north-west, by piece-meal exchanges, and so into numerous small closes only somewhat less intermingled and dispersed than the common-field parcels they re-replaced.[7] Under the new plan of management, both grass and tillage were more temporary than permanent. Upon enclosure, it was usual to lay the old permanent tillage to grass, temporarily, and to convert the former permanent grass to up-and-down arable, by tilling portions of it in turn. The same treatment was thenceforward accorded to both former common fields and grasslands.[8] As the small dairy farmers who came to occupy most of the vale had only a perfunctory interest in cereals,

[1] Ibid. 67–8.

[2] Cf. ibid. 67.

[3] Shak. Bpl. Stratford: Misc. Docs. vol. xiii no 45.

[4] Pomeroy, op. cit. 10; Marshall, op. cit. i, 158–61, 164, 166–7.

[5] Ibid. 197–8.

[6] Marshall, *Yks.* i, 17, 256, 292; ii, 218.

[7] Ibid. i, 52, 98; Jeffery, *Thornton-le-Dale*, 78–9; Leonard, art. cit. 110; Helmsley & Area Gp Yks. Archaeol. Soc. op. cit. 207; Turton, op. cit. i, 217, 220–1, 259; B.M., Harl. 6288, f. 62; 7180; P.R.O., Exch. A.O., Parl. Svys Yks. 39, f. 1 sqq.; L.R., M.B. 186, ff. 71 sqq., 92v., 94; 229, ff. 264, 278–80; 230, ff. 72 sqq.; D.L., M.B. 124, f. 33.

[8] Ibid.; Exch. L.R., M.B. 186, ff. 92v., 94; 229, ff. 278–80; 230, ff. 72 sqq.; A.O., Parl. Svys Yks. 39, ff. 1 sqq.; B.M., Harl, 6288, f. 62; Marshall, op. cit. i, 292, 297.

the tillage area was restricted. There was nothing approaching a regular crop rotation, but wheat was usually preceded by a bare fallow, and flax was sometimes the first crop of a succession. A ley's duration was decided primarily by the condition of its sward, and a field once ploughed up was kept in tillage until another 'pasture' was in need of being broken up. Leys were formed of perennial grasses and clovers, usually by a mere cessation of tillage, and often negligently, so the best part of a score of years might expire before a full crop of grass ensued, so long did it take natural grasses to drive out the weeds. If the soil were exhausted, hay-seeds were sometimes sown, but, again, in the slovenly manner characteristic of small dairymen, the seeds being either taken from the loft at random, foul with weeds as they were, or obtained from soft meadow grass, cultivated separately and threshed, but less suitable than perennial rye-grass. The objects of farming were butter, cows, oxen, saddle-horses, fat bullocks and sheep, bacon and oats. Other crops, including wheat, were for home consumption only. Cattle and sheep were likewise sold on mainly local markets. Oats, ordinary butter and bacon went to North Country industrial centres. Saddle-horses were bred and reared for London and abroad. Best bacon and prime butter, made from spring and summer grass milk, likewise sold for consumption in, and redistribution from, the metropolis. In short, the grass was applied chiefly to cows, for butter, and its by-products.[1]

A transformation not unlike that in the Vale of Pickering, but on a smaller scale, was witnessed in the Cheese Country. Here, the original settlement had usually been in hamlets and lone farmsteads, and the tendency was for each farmstead to stand in the midst of its fields, those nearer the house being mostly pastures and the more distant ones meadows. But much of the country was forest, and in 1540 Pewsham (Chippenham), Blackmore (Melksham), Selwood (Gillingham), and Braydon forests were all well wooded. In 1608 they still contained tens of thousands of both timber trees and dotards and hundreds of acres of coppice; but by 1650 most of the woods had been cleared, and the remainder thenceforth covered only about one-twelfth of the land.[2]

[1] Ibid. i, 256, 293–6, 409; ii, 69, 83 sqq., 195, 218; Defoe, op. cit. ii, 199; York, invs. Ampleforth Pec. & Pec. Ct Dean; P.R.O., Exch. L.R., M.B. 229, ff. 278–80.

[2] Ibid. 191, f. 163; K.R., Sp. Commn 4577; Deps. by Commn 41–2 Eliz. Mich. 4; A.O., M.B. 420, ff. 7 sqq.; Parl. Svys Wilts. 45; S.P.D. Jas vol. 71 no 107; D.L., M.B. 108, ff. 84v.–5; 115, f. 83; Ct R. 127/1912; Wilts. R.O., acc. 212B, B.F. 14a; Marshall, Glos. ii, 142; Leland, op. cit. i, 133; vi. 97, 106; E. of Kerry, 'K.'s Bowood Pk', Wilts. Mag. xli, 409; J. E. Jackson, 'Chippenham N.' ibid. xii, 286–7; 'On Hist. Chippenham', ibid. iii, 35; 'Selwood Forest', ibid. xxiii, 282 sqq.; F. H. Manley, 'Parl. Svys Crown Lands in Braden Forest (1651)', ibid. xlvi, 176 sqq.; R. C. Hoare, op. cit. Hund. Warminster, 84; Darby, Hist. Geog. Engl. 398–9; Straton, op. cit. i, 187–8; B.M., Lans. vol. 34, no 38, f. 102; Aubrey, Wilts. Topog. Colls. 67; Nat. Hist. Wilts. 21.

Cattle and sheep were at once the agents and beneficiaries of this clearance, for by feeding in the woods they prevented the establishment of seedlings and prepared the ground for swarding. Man also lent a hand by felling and grubbing. When Chippenham and Melksham were disforested, many trees and bushes had to be removed before fields could be laid out, and much clearance was needed in Selwood.[1] The country had also had small but numerous and widespread common fields, even within the forests; but the enclosure of fields, pastures and meadows was so rapid after 1540 that it was almost complete by 1670.[2] Energetic improvement accompanied this enclosure of common lands. After grubbing up the underwood and enclosing with pales, ditches and quicksets, a common pasture, formerly overgrown with brambles and briars, was said to have improved its rental value over twelvefold. Narrow, elevated ridges and open ditches often laid the close dry enough; but sometimes turf, stone or wood underdrains were needed. Thistles had to be mown down, moles killed, old watering pools cleansed and new ones made.[3] The spread of up-and-down husbandry, while it entailed some loss of tillage in former common fields, increased the arable acreage where once had been commons, woodlands, parks, and forests, so the total proportion of tillage stayed much as before, and the rest lay mostly in grass.[4]

Up-and-down husbandry progressed in the Wealden Vales mainly by making inroads into the woodlands. In the early sixteenth century many

[1] Ibid.; Jackson, 'Selwood', 282 sqq.; P.R.O., D.L. Ct R. 127/1912; Exch. K.R., Sp. Commn 4577.

[2] Ibid. 4697; L.R., M.B. 187, ff. 170 sqq.; A.O., Parl. Svys Berks. 13, ff. 1 sqq.; Soms. 27, f. 4; S.P.D. Jas vol. 71 no 107, ff. 10, 21, 23, 40, 42, 44, 53–4 (321, 332, 334, 351, 353, 355, 364–5); Wds, Feodaries' Svys Wilts. unsorted bdl. Jn Bryant 1620 S. Marston; Chanc. Proc. ser. i Jas I, F.11/62; St. Ch. Jas 63/10; Req. 56/18; D.L., Exams. & Deps. 89/29; R.&S. 9/26, ff. 2 sqq.; Wilts. R.O., acc. 88, Charlton Este Papers box B, Svy Bk Charlton, Brinkworth, Hankerton & Brokenborough, ff. 60 sqq.; Moores box 1, Charlton enclo. agrt 1631; Bristol Univ. Lib. Trowbridge Dauntsey Ct Bk. ff. 29, 49, 51, 62; acc. 31, Ct Bk Hannington vol. A; Berk. R.O., D./E.Pb E42, E66A; M3, pp. 65–6, 179; Aubrey, *Wilts. Topog. Colls.* 309; C. B. Fry, op. cit. 8, 27, 30–1; W. Morris, op. cit. 507, 509 sqq.; Tawney, op. cit. 420–1; *Wilts.Mag.* xxviii, 254; G. M. Young, 'Some Wilts. Cs in St. Ch.', ibid. l, 447; Atkyns, op. cit. 548; T. Davis, op. cit. 117–18; Mavor, op. cit. 147; *Cals. Proc. Chance. in reign Q. Eliz.* ii, 302; Marshall, *Glos.* ii, 146, 151.

[3] P.R.O., St. Ch. Jas 63/10; Wds, Feodaries' Svys Wilts. 250; Young, loc. cit.; Goldney, op. cit. 201–2; Phillimore & Fry, op. cit. i, 101–2; Norden, op. cit. 197; Marshall, *W. Engl.* ii, 208; *Glos.* ii, 148.

[4] Ibid. 142, 151; Straton, loc. cit.; W. L. Bowles. *Par. Hist. Bremhill* 1828, p. 270; B.M., Add. 34566, f. 11 sqq.; R. 37571; Bristol Univ. Lib. Trowbridge Dauntsey Ct Bk; Wilts. R.O., acc. 212B, B.F. 14a; acc. 84, Clayton 2; Ct Bk Latton c. Eisey & Down Ampney, ff. 36 sqq.; acc. 34, Hobhouse Papers A, 25/5; P.R.O., S.P.D. Jas vol. 71 no 107; D.L., M.B. 108, ff. 57 sqq.; 115, ff. 69 sqq.; R.&S. 9/26, ff. 2 sqq.; 9/30; Exch. A.O., Parl. Svys Wilts. 36, 45, 47; L.R., M.B. 191, f. 132; K.R., Sp. Commn 2395.

farms here consisted largely of woody and bushy grounds and small, ragged cattle pastures.[1] Then, between 1540 and 1650, owing to simultaneous demands for agricultural land, for constructional timber, and for wood for the nearby iron, glass and dye-works, the woodlands were speedily cleared. More timber was cut at this time than in any period of like duration before or since.[2] Clearance was rapid, maintenance difficult. Unless ploughed, the land would revert to wood, and unless enriched would bear little of corn or grass.[3] Indeed, it was marling alone made the soils here into good up-and-down land, so that the measure of one is the measure of both.[4]

In the Oxford Heights Country up-and-down husbandry took the place of common fields, meadows and pastures, with their permanent tillage and permanent grass. Enclosure was swift. About 1560 one-quarter, and by 1650 more than half the land was enclosed.[5] Agreements to this end were concluded at Hatford in 1577, at Bremhill in 1579, at Keevil and Bulkington in 1603 and 1613, shortly afterwards at Rowde and Bromham, and in 1686 and 1710 at Sevenhampton.[6] Most of the land suited convertible, sheep-and-corn husbandry conducted in enclosures. Even the clayey vale soils were converted to up-and-down husbandry in the early seventeenth century, resulting in excellent wheat crops.[7]

In the Cotswold Country, too, wet meadows aside, many of the enclosures were, from 1560 at least, cultivated in a convertible system, not only on the hills, but also in the valleys, where woad was sometimes a first crop on old grassland.[8] At Haseldon in 1617 was 'one close called

[1] Leland, op. cit. ii, 30; Markham, *Weald*, 1–4; Norden, op. cit. 219, 222 (1st occs.).

[2] Ibid. 219–22 (1st occs.); Gulley, op. cit. 48; Bodl. Hearne's diaries 158, f. 43.

[3] Norden, op. cit. 219, 222 (1st occs.); Markham, op. cit. 2.

[4] Inf. 246.

[5] C. B. Fry, op. cit. 28–9; P.R.O., Exch. L.R., M.B. 191, ff. 145 sqq., 158v. sqq.; R.&S. G.S. roll 709; S.P.D. Eliz. Add. vol. 12 no 22, ff. 44 sqq.; Bodington, art. cit. xli, 122–3; B.M., Harl. 3961, ff. 64 sqq.; Wilts. R.O., acc. 40 Sevenhampton Ct Bk 1541–1624.

[6] P.R.O., Chanc. Proc. ser. i Jas I, E. 1/51; B.M., Add. 37270, ff. 105v., 114; Bowood ho. Svy Bremhill 1629; Wilts. R.O., acc. 122 Svys Bromham, Bremhill, Rowden & Stanley: Bromham Ct Bn 25 Sept. 16 Jas; Keevil & Bulkington Ct Bk 44 Eliz.—2 Chas: 3 Mar. 45 Eliz., 14 Mar. 1 Jas, 16 Apr. 11 Jas; Aubrey, loc. cit; Mavor, op. cit. 148; M. W. Farr, *A/cs. & Svys Wilts. Lands Adam de Stratton* Wilts. Archaeol. & Nat. Hist. Soc. Recs. Br. 1959 xiv, pp. xxxi–ii.

[7] '1614 Customs Xn Malford', 174; Bodl. Aubrey 2, f. 87.

[8] Phillimore & Fry, op. cit. i, 51–2; ii, 2; iii, 53; P.R.O., D.L., Sp. Commn 663; Exch. A.O., Parl. Svys Soms. 42, ff. 4–6; L.R., M.B. 191, f. 1v.; 202, ff. 169 sqq.; 224, f. 76; 225, ff. 43, 152; T.R., Bk 157, p. 85 (f. 45); Ct R. G.S. 208/35, mm. 3, 5; R.&S. G.S. 2/46, f. 134; St. Ch. Jas 18/12, m. 9; B.M., Add. 34683, f. 4; R. 18517, 32972; Harl. 4606, f. 1 (3) sqq., 12 (25) sqq.; Glouc. Lib. 28917, svys Alderley & Tresham 1674; Glos. R.O., D. 184/M24, pp. 165 sqq.; Wilts. R.O., Stourhead:

Thistlye Leaze, sometymes layde for arrable', another 'used comonlie for arrable' and a third 'close arrable or pasture', of 40, 79 and 55 acres respectively. Some of the other fields had evidently been ploughed as long as possible and were now about to be laid down.[1] When Robert Bridges took a lease of the manor farm of Rowell and Godstone in 1620, he decided, on the advice of local husbandmen, to plough up most of the old grassland enclosures.[2] Temporary tillages were made to bear about three crops of oats, barley and wheat, but fewer were perhaps taken when the grass was broken by raftering or sod-burning.[3]

Up-and-down husbandry expanded in the Chalk Country also. From about 1560 until 1720 the plough was, as we have seen, making more or less continual inroads into the downs. In 1614 Bulbridge Farm included seventy-two acres of 'newe broke arrable ground belonging to the sheep-sleight'. At Dinton and Teffont, what was in 1567 sheep-down in severalty, had by 1631 become 'arrable land in one field inclosed, severall only to the farme'.[4] Occasionally such new ploughings were retained as permanent tillage, but once ploughed, most downs could only be employed in a convertible system.[5] At Winterbourne Bassett in 1567 the West Field contained a forty-acre close 'noviter inclusus qui aliquando seminatur et aliquando jacet ad pasturam'.[6] Even in the valleys, water-meadows apart, only a small and probably decreasing extent of grass was permanent.[7] Woad was increasingly cultivated in the half-century after 1585, largely as a first crop on the many newly ploughed rich old grasslands.[8] The farmer of Collingbourne Ducis evoked an outcry from the tenantry by ploughing a common pasture for woad. When Richard Kennell ploughed up meadow and pasture at Norrington for a succession of woad and grain, various people testified the land would be much improved in value if laid down again to grass before too long. This, as

---

Ct. Bk Ld Stourton's Manors 1644–92, E. Chelborough 1674, Purse Caundle 29 July 2 Jas II; Soms. R.O., D.D./P.O., svys Compton Dando 1656; D.D./S./W.H., Svy Bk Chew Sutton, Knowle & Stone 1615; Bristol R.O., 4490, f. 13v.

[1] P.R.O., Exch. T.R., Bk 157, pp. 55–6 (f. 29); B.M., Add. 6027, ff. 31–3 (30–2).

[2] P.R.O., Chanc. Proc. ser. i Jas I, B. 35/23, m. 71.

[3] Marshall, *Midl. Dept*, 472; Shak. Bpl. Leigh: Ct R. Longborough 24 Apr. 1712; B.M., Add. R. 18517.

[4] Straton, op. cit. i, 228; Wilton ho. Svys Manors 1631 i, Dinton & Teffont, f. 2 (3); ii, Bulbridge &c. f. 2 (3).

[5] Ibid. i, Fugglestone, f. 11 (12) marginalia; Naish, op. cit. 142, 154–5; Pugh, op. cit. 71; Vancouver, *Hants*. 264–5; Wilts. R.O., acc. 283, Lib. sup. Amisburie, f. 25v.; Svy Amesbury 1635, ff. 43–4, 55–7, 59; A/d Wilts. inv. Jn Benger 1635 Pewsey.

[6] Straton, op. cit. i, 265–7.

[7] Vancouver, loc. cit.; Naish, op. cit. 87; inf. next 2 nn.

[8] Blith, op. cit. 99, 225–6; Hurry, op. cit. 62, 69; B.M., Lans. vol. 49 no 54 (24), f. 124 (111); no 57 (27), f. 130 (117); no 60, f. 143 (131).

Robert Toppe, a gentleman farmer of Bridmore, said, was 'by reason of the great plentie of corne which the same groundes have borne'.[1]

The systems of convertible husbandry instituted in drained fens and marshes are described below. They had much in common with the up-and-down farming we have seen, and they expanded their scope no less rapidly.[2] In the Saltings Country, to name but one of those concerned, an unprecedented amount of marshland was tilled between 1590 and 1650.[3] In the Northdown Country, too, more fresh marsh was periodically ploughed up for crops, whose great yields may be gauged by the high corning rents paid over and above the usual pasture ones. We find, for instance, a farmer near Margate offering £1 fine an acre for the right to plough up marshland.[4]

That the extent of up-and-down land in the Lancashire Plain and the Cheshire Cheese Country was growing, as more and more land was won from heaths and mosses, is indicated by a greatly increased use of marl, until saturation point was reached and marling had to be dropped in favour of liming.[5] Similarly, in many other countries, the spread of woad cultivation[6] may be taken as a sign that permanent grass was being converted to up-and-down land. Woading enjoyed its golden age around the close of the sixteenth century,[7] simply because this marked the height of the up-and-down revolution.

Probably the most spectacular of all advances made by up-and-down husbandry were those in the North-eastern Lowlands, for here ley farming was not replacing permanent tillage and permanent grass, for there had not previously been much permanent cultivation at all, but mainly temporary and shifting cultivations of the wild. Indeed, it is often extremely difficult to distinguish between agreements for the allotment of temporarily cultivated plots, those for dividing up townships,[8] and those for permanent enclosure and the extinction of common rights, all of which were sanctioned by manorial ordinances, by multipartite indentures, or by decrees in the palatinate courts. What is clear is that most common-field lands were enclosed into permanent severalty between about 1562 and 1673, and nine-tenths of them by 1720, chiefly by agreement, sometimes by unilateral action. True, some common

---

[1] Wilts. R.O., Savernake: Ct Bk Collingbourne Ducis 25 Apr. 1593; P.R.O., St. Ch. Jas 7/6, 156/4; H.M.C., MSS. in Var. Colls. iii, 139-40.

[2] Inf. 226, 235-6.

[3] Gramolt, op. cit. 213, 314 sqq.; Burrell, op. cit. 146; J. Kirby, Sfk Traveller 1764, p. 2; Ess. R.O., D./D.K. F2/10.

[4] P.R.O., Chanc. Proc. ser. i Jas I, B.1/68.

[5] Inf. 246-8.

[6] Sup. 209-10, 214, 218.

[7] Hurry, op. cit. 62.

[8] E. Bateson, op. cit. i, 351, 355; ii, 128-9, 367 sqq., 416, 418-19, 458, 478; v, 202, 332, 372, 424, 488, 497; vii, 305, 307, 315; ix, 325-6; xiv, 211-3.

pasture and tillage lingered on into the later eighteenth century, but usually only in townships already mostly enclosed and where the demesne lands had long since been in severalty, as often they were even in the early sixteenth century.[1]

Upon enclosure, the tillage was put down to graze and the grazing partly broken up for tillage, in such a way as to reduce the acreage of rough grazing and temporary cultivation and increase that of permanent cultivation, arable and, usually, tillage.[2] After enclosure, crop rotations were little changed, the prevailing succession of (1) oats (or pulse near the coast), (2) summer fallow, (3) wheat, rye or bigg, being continued for between two and four summer fallows and the field then laid to grass for at least seven years.[3] The staples of diet thus remained unchanged: bread was made of wheat, rye or bigg, porridge and cake of oats, and malt of oats, bigg or 'blandlings', a miscellany of oats and barley.[4] Itself of only minor technical significance, enclosure was thus inextricably bound up with an agricultural revolution, and whereas common-field farms had been in the hands of peasants concerned only with subsistence, enclosed ones were conducted in high style by farmers who had both the capital and the spirit for good husbandry. Excepting a few specialist dairy-grazing farms near the burgeoning industrial centres, these new men treated their fields as up-and-down land. They grew a good deal of grain, but their chief object was breeding and rearing sheep and shorthorn cattle. Nearly all the enclosed farms bred and reared 'mugs', as the local pasture sheep were called. Most farmers also fattened some mugs on summer grass, but the greater part of the sheep reared inland were sold in autumn to the coastal plain, whose rich grass eminently suited mutton production. Some farms also imported North Country sheep to feed on summer grass. All told, at the height of the season, a single farm might stock up to 3,000 sheep. Indeed, in the Wooler district, where Cheviot sheep predominated, farmers relied

---

[1] Ibid. i, 153, 234–5, 256–7, 268, 274–5, 351, 353–4; ii, 45, 129, 159, 378, 386–7, 424–5, 458, 478, 482, 485; v, 202–3, 212, 258–9, 424, 430, 498; vi, 101–2; vii, 315, 370; viii, 241, 264, 345; ix, 4, 25, 124–5, 325–6; xii, 172–3; xiii, 147; P.R.O., Exch. L.R., M.B. 192, mm. 9 (5)d., 11 (7)d., 20–1 (16–17), 27 (23), 36 (32)d. sqq., 50 (47)d. sqq., 58 (55)d. sqq., 68d.–9 (65d.–6); Hughes, op. cit. *N.E. 1700–50*, pp. 131, 133–4; Leonard, art. cit. 111–13; Marshall, *N. Dept.*, 141; Bailey, op. cit. 86; Laurence, op. cit. 46; *V.C.H. Durh.* ii, 238–9.

[2] Ibid.; Leonard, art. cit. 117; Bland, Brown & Tawney, op. cit. 525–6.

[3] Hughes, op. cit. 135–6, 138; Marshall, op. cit. 49, 74, 78; Bailey, op. cit. 127; P.R.O., Exch. L.R., M.B. 192, mm. 36 (32)d. sqq., 50 (47)d. sqq., 68d.–9 (65d.–6); *Wills & Invs.* (Surtees S.) pt i, 181–4, 317–20, 347 sqq., 364–5, 434–7; pt ii, 49 sqq., 129 sqq., 138–40, 183–6, 188 sqq., 207–9, 243–6, 256–8, 266–8, 302–4, 315–18; pt iii, 158–9; pt iv, 29–31, 103–5, 148–9, 143–5; Bateson, op. cit. i, 158–9, 354; v, 228, 303–4, 403–4, 465; vi, 171–2; viii, 241.

[4] Ibid. ii, 421; v, 309, 413; Marshall, op. cit. 29, 77; Hughes, op. cit. 141; *Wills & Invs.* pt i, 181–4, 420–3; pt ii, 152 sqq., 188 sqq.

more on their flocks than on their herds. However, most farms, and
virtually all the large ones, reared both their own calves and many
others bought in from the North Country. Fifty or sixty calves might be
reared on whole milk in a single season by a farmer who devoted hardly
more than a dozen cows to the dairy; and it was not uncommon for a
single farm to have up to 300 head of cattle, including eighty cows, and
to sell eighty steers or bullocks a year. Some oxen, too, were retained for
the plough, even in the eighteenth century, though they were being
increasingly replaced by horses. Coastal farms also engaged in fattening
both their own stores and others purchased inland, selling them as grass
beef, at about three-and-a-half years, to the big towns and to shipping.[1]
Most of the cattle reared, however, were sold as stores to the Midland
Plain, or to the Wealden Vales, Romney Marsh, the Sandlings Country
and elsewhere.[2] A good system of ley farming in enclosed farms permitted much heavier stocking, leaving more manure for the tillage,
which, after giving increased yields, especially of wheat and bigg, could
be laid down in good heart. Farmers could afford to be lavish with their
farmyard manure and still employ extraneous fertilizers like marl, sea-
coal ashes, soot, sea-sand, seaweed, and lime.[3]

In view of the growth of old-established systems of up-and-down
husbandry and the revolutionary innovation of the ones just recounted,
it is not surprising that what so impresses an acute Swedish observer in
1748 is that the 'English custom, for the most part, is, by turns, to lay
down ploughed fields to meadows, and meadows to ploughed fields'.[4]
The up-and-down revolution was complete.

[1] Ibid. pt i, 151–4, 181–4, 222–4, 235–6, 243–4, 266–8, 280–3, 317–20, 335 sqq.,
347 sqq., 377, 417 sqq., 434–7; pt ii, 43 sqq., 49 sqq., 56 sqq., 62–4, 129 sqq., 135–7,
147 sqq., 152 sqq., 183–6, 207–9, 219–21, 225 sqq., 231–2, 243–6, 256–8, 264 sqq.,
286–8, 302–4, 315–18; pt iii, 44–5, 105–6, 158–9; pt iv, 29–31, 103–5, 148–9, 158–
60, 173, 200, 237, 243–5, 260–1, 314–15; Hughes, op. cit. 138, 141; Marshall, op.
cit. 54–5, 91–2, 95–7, 99, 101–2; *Sheep*, 47; Bailey, op. cit. 230 sqq., 246; Bateson,
op. cit. i, 158–9; v, 303–4, 309, 403–4; vi, 171–2; vii, 348–9, 397, 443; ix, 202.

[2] Lodge, op. cit. 3, 5, 7, 32; B.M., Harl. 127, ff. 17 (28), 22 (37)v.; Kent R.O.,
A/d Cantuar. invs. 1665: Jn Pell/Pluckley, Robt Platt/Buckland; sup. 79, 111, 133,
136.

[3] Marshall, *N. Dept*, 70, 150; Laurence, op. cit 78–81, 86; Hughes, op. cit. 135.

[4] Kalm, op. cit. 216. Pace Ashton, *Ind. Rev.* 28.

CHAPTER IV

FEN DRAINAGE

SECOND only in significance to the supersession of permanent tillage and grass by up-and-down land, was the powerful outburst, between 1560 and 1720, particularly before 1660, in the drainage of fens, i.e. those low, flooded grounds known variously also as marshes, moors or mosses, some being salt, some fresh, some formed of peat, others of silt, and a few of both.

Along a great part of the estuaries and coasts facing the English Channel and North Sea, in the South Sea-coast, Northdown, Saltings, Sandlings and Fen countries, in Romney Marsh and the Vale of London, tides of redoubled force were, directly and indirectly, the chief agents not only of coastal erosion, but also of the continual formation of saltings. The self-same tides provided power for numerous mills, of which the one in Woodbridge is amongst the few survivors. In constructing a tide-mill, part of the estuary waters had to be drawn off and penned up, causing silt to collect until eventually the mill-ponds and carriages themselves might be transformed into marshland.[1] And the great tides, by their ebb and flow, and by throwing up shingle banks, behind which silt and sand accumulated, laid the very foundations of the saltings. When these deposits had risen to somewhere near the mean tide level, they supported aquatic vegetation. Then glasswort, samphire and the like established themselves and consolidated the banks. Later, cotton-grass, common salt-marsh grass, and other herbage invaded. Grazing then improved the coarse sward and the sea's recession made it gradually fresher. At this stage the salting was eligible for defence by walling with clay, chalk rubble, blown sand, and wood, faced on the seaward side with a 'needlework' of bramble and thorn faggots on a timber frame, and, later, perhaps, when this had grassed over, with brick or ragstone. Outside this sea-wall a new salting might now start to form, in which event the old wall became a grassy embankment acting as a second line of defence to a fresh marsh. Through what had

[1] Marshall, *S. Cos.* ii, 228–9.

formerly been a spacious foreshore, numerous creeks emptied into the
sea along square troughs, where sluice-doors, or 'tankard-lids', opened
and shut under the pressure of fresh and salt waters.[1]

In the Saltings Country, some two-thirds of the present-day fens
were walled and drained before 1560, and by far the greatest part of the
residue between then and 1715, in what was an exceptional burst of
activity,[2] both here and in the Sandlings Country, especially, perhaps,
at Walton, Trimley and Felixstowe.[3] In the South Sea-coast Country,
between 1628 and 1636 an attempt was made to enclose further salt-
marshes at Hilsea.[4] Drainage likewise increased the area of fresh marsh
available in the Northdown Country.[5] Some salt-marshes in the Norfolk
Heathlands, like those at Holkham were already drained and enclosed
by 1560, but many excellent opportunities still presented themselves
over the next 100 years. In 1637, the tenants and demesne farmer of
Burnham agreed to have their common salt-marshes walled and drained
by contractors. In the same year the salt-marsh embankments at Salt-
house were renewed by Dutch undertakers; and further sea-walls
were under construction here in 1649. About 1640 Blakeney and Cley

[1] Ibid. i, 360, 367–8, 370–1; *E. Dept*, 156–7, 284; Mortimer, op. cit. 21–2; Darby,
Draining Fens, 13, 24–5, 44; Blith, op. cit. 47–8; Gerarde, op. cit. 17, 19–20; Thirsk,
Fenland Farming, 14–17; Dugdale, op. cit. 275 sqq.; Brown, *Yks. Deeds*, 36–7; Steers,
op. cit. 410, 437, 517 sqq.; Saunders, op. cit. 104, 107, 117; Somerville, op. cit. i,
308; Spratt, op. cit. 221, 224; Northants. R.O., F-H 119, Dowdike; 1136; F.(M.)
Misc. 918–19; B.M., Add. 24782, f. 77 (116)v.; Cott. Augustus I/i/24; Egerton 2994,
f. 51; 2999, f. 96v.; Harl. 702, f. 14; Lans. vol. 654, f. 11 (14); PRO, Maps & Pls.
MPC/11; D.L., M.B. 112, ff. 33–4; 119, ff. 85v., 90, 170v., 113, 167, 201, 235, 259v.,
375v.–6, 381; Exch. L.R., M.B., 229, ff. 295 sqq.; 230, ff. 18, 33, 87, 182, 187, 208v.,
210v., 219–22; 256, ff. 3 sqq., 44–6, 283; 286, f. 82; A.O., M.B. 390, ff. 38–41; Parl.
Svys Kent 26, f. 6; Lincs. 13A, ff. 1–4; 18, f. 7; 20, ff. 33, 43; 27, f. 4; 35, ff. 1 sqq.;
Yks. 34, ff. 7–8; 35, ff. 3, 5, 12–13; Lincs. R.O., Massingberd 26; Ess. R.O., D./D.K.
E1, p. 18; D./S.D. 1, ff. 34, 38; D./S.H. 7, pp. 97–8, 107; M.T. Derville, *Level & Liberty
Romney Marsh* 1936, pp. 25–7; Gramolt, op. cit. 189, 217 sqq., 230–1, 234, 243–4,
246–7.

[2] Ibid. 38, 44, 62, 66, 72, 75, 91, 100, 115, 118, 122, 138, 140, 142; L. E. Harris,
op. cit. 37–9; Steers, op. cit. 396; Chalklin, op. cit. 13–14, 184–5; R. H. Goodsall,
Whitstable, Seasalter & Swalecliffe 1938, p. 29; B.M., Harl. 590, f. 1; 6697, f. 8; Cott.
Augustus I/i/51; Hull, op. cit. 63–4; P.R.O., Chanc. Proc. ser. i Jas I, C. 3/69;
Exch. A.O., Parl. Svys Kent 42, ff. 6–8; Ess. R.O., D./D.K. E1, p. 18; D./D.Th
M17; D./S.D.1, esp. ff. 38, 39v., 73v.–4; D./S.H. 7, pp. 75, 101; J. H. Evans, 'Up-
church Marshes in Time 1st Eliz.', *Arch. Cant.* lxxvi, 163; 'Rochester Bridge Lands in
Grain', ibid. lxviii, 185 (& opp.), 191.

[3] Dugdale, op. cit. 298; Burrell, op. cit. 121–3, 125–7, 134; *Shotley Par. Recs.* Sfk
Green Bks 1912 xvi, 267, 276, 278; B.M., Add. 21042, f. 6 (7); 21054, ff. 65–6;
23955, f. 22; 32134, f. 30 (23); R. 26341, Aldeburgh 16 Eliz.; E. Sfk R.O., 50/1/74(1),
p. 36; (12), f. 1; 50/22/3(1); S. 1/10/9. 12, f. 23; V. 5/18/10(1), pp. 5–6, 19.

[4] S. A. Moore, op. cit. 258–9, 290–1; *A.P.C.* Jan.–Aug. 1627, pp. 203–4.

[5] P.R.O., Exch. L.R., M.B. 197, ff. 72v., 74v., 101v.–2; 198, ff. 8–10, 23, 38–9;
218, ff. 189 sqq., 203–4, 255, 305; 219, ff. 65 sqq., 328, 338; A.O., Parl. Svys Kent 26,
ff. 6, 12; B.M., Stowe 858, ff. 1, 6, 10, 12, 17, 22, 27, 42, 62, 66.

marshes were walled and drained.[1] The Fen Country, too, saw many saltings newly inned, notably on the southern shores of the Wash, about Croft and Wainfleet, and on the northern spit of the Humber.[2]

Along the west coast, especially in the Lancashire Plain and the Cheshire Cheese Country, the saltings came to be protected from the sea by walls whose foundation was of sand blown on the westerly winds. Many of these coastal dunes were also brought into cultivation. Experience showed that self-sown 'star-grass', i.e. probably, sea wheat-grass, followed by lyme and marram grasses, served to consolidate the shifting sands. Some time before 1600 farmers in the Lancashire Plain started to plant star-grass on their dunes and in due course this practice was made obligatory by lease covenants. When sufficiently stable and productive, the improved 'hawes' were used as sheep pastures, so that flocks fed in coastal marshes were now afforded an excellent change of soil and diet and in return still further enriched and consolidated the ground, enabling good rye crops to be taken.[3] Romney Marsh, whose sewers were entrusted to a corporation, was walled and drained in early times and was the best defended marshland. Walland Marsh and Pevensey, Pett and Mountney levels had been similarly recovered, and although inundations occurred from time to time, the damage was always repaired.[4] In the early modern period, however, reclamation took a new lease of life. By 1562 Guldeford Level had been recovered, and a parish church erected, while New Romney had ceased to be a seaport. Denge Beach and Dungeness continued to grow appreciably, and salt-ings to be enclosed, but almost all the reclamation had been accom-plished by 1644, when farmers had at their command nearly 100,000 acres of rich, drained marshland.[5]

Although the extent of new reclamation was smaller, and the net gain less discernible, in the Vale of London, constant battles were

[1] Riches, op. cit. 95; Gray, op. cit. 326–7; Tawney, op. cit. 245; Blith, op. cit. 208; H.M.C., MSS. D. Rutland 1905 iv, 263; P.R.O., St. Ch. P.&M. 3/42, compl.; Steers, op. cit. 352–3.

[2] Ibid. 417; Darby, op. cit. 44; Thirsk, op. cit. 16–17; Dugdale, op. cit. 165–7; Moore, op. cit. 253, 281–2, 284, 292, 414, 424; J. Chamberlayne, 'A/c Sunk I. in R. Humber', Phil. Trans. R.S. Ldn abr. C. Hutton, G. Shaw & R. Pearson 1809 vi, 423; P.R.O., D.L., M.B. 119, ff. 170, 204–5; Exch. K.R., Memoranda, Recorda, Trin. 8 Jas I, rot. 187; L.R., M.B. 285, f. 224; A.O., Parl. Svys Lincs. 27, ff. 2, 37.

[3] F. A. Bailey, Hist. Southport 1955, pp. 11–12, 24; E. Salisbury, Downs & Dunes 1952, pp. 211, 213, 293.

[4] Lambard, op. cit. 158; PRO, Maps & Pls. MPC/11; D.L., M.B. 112, ff. 33–4; B.M., Cott. Augustus I/i/24; Mundy, op. cit. 35–6; W. Holloway, Hist. Romney Marsh 1849, pp. 132–3, 136; Dugdale, op. cit. 16 sqq., 83 sqq.

[5] Ibid. 16–17; Cornwall, op. cit. 204; Holloway, op. cit. 141, 147, 169, 181; Steers, op. cit. 314, 320, 327–8, 331; Chalklin, op. cit. 14; C. J. Gilbert, 'Evolution Romney Marsh', Arch. Cant. xlv, 263.

fought against the waters here. Wapping Marsh was recovered about 1543. After Woolwich, Plumstead and Erith marshes had been drowned about 1530, and tides had breached East Greenwich walls in 1545, the commissioners of sewers, under an Act of Parliament, entrusted recovery to Sir Edward Boulton, who failed to complete his contract, whereupon another was placed with Ferdinando Poins and Company. Experts from Romney Marsh were consulted and in 1586 a wall was built of heavy earth, chalk and sludge, all well beaten down with beetles. In 1606-7 followed an Act for the recovery of Lessness and Fants marshes. William Burrell secured this contract. Further reclamation in Erith and Plumstead marshes was undertaken in 1629 by Joas Croppenburgh the younger, with whom was associated another Dutchman by name of Cornelius Vermuyden. They eventually recovered nearly 500 acres. About 1594, 1620, and again in the early eighteenth century, breaches had to be stopped in the walls protecting Havering, Dagenham, Barking and Ripple levels.[1]

Away from the coast, hindered rather than helped by Nature, the drainers' work was still more difficult and demanded even heavier investments of capital. Yet it is a striking fact that here the outburst of draining activity was more powerful than elsewhere.

Along the banks of the streams in the Sandlings Country, some fens still awaited improvement until early modern times. In 1601, for instance, John Norden noticed between Rendlesham and Butley, on the brook running through the latter, a fen ground lately enclosed and drained to form good pasture.[2] Of the marshes inland from Romney, Wittersham and the Upper and Rother levels were finally reclaimed only after much delay. In 1629 Wittersham Level had 1,000 acres of high marsh and 1,500 of low, which were respectively winter and summer-grounds. The owners of the 5,000 acres in Upper Level had previously drained them by a sewer following a circuitous route through Appledore; but finally found only a direct cut to the sea would remove all the waters; and any new cut straight enough to be effective had to pass through Wittersham Level. The new works, mutually agreed in 1629, involved turning the navigable Rother into a new channel 50 feet wide. In attempting this, the Upper Level waters unfortunately irrupted and drowned Wittersham Level and it was not until 1644 that the works were finally completed.[3]

---

[1] Dugdale, op. cit 63-5, 81-2; Defoe, op. cit, i, 9; Harris, op. cit. 37; Holinshed & Harrison, op. cit. 1540-3; Stats. 35 H. VIII c. 9; 37 H. VIII c. 11; 23 Eliz. c 13; 27 Eliz. c. 27; 4 Jas c. 8; Priv. Acts 5 Eliz. no 36; 8 Eliz. no 222; 14 Eliz. no 15; P.R.O., St. Ch. H. VIII 18/2, compl. & ans.; Chanc. Proc. ser. i Jas I, S. 9/55, compl.

[2] E. Sfk R.O., 50/1/74 (12), pp. 20-3; V. 5/22/1, ff. 11v.-12, 21v.-2.

[3] Holloway, op. cit. 150, 163 sqq.; Dugdale, op. cit. 16-17; Moore, op. cit. 222.

H

Even more extensive improvements were made from the mosses of the Lancashire Plain and the Cheshire Cheese Country. In their unenclosed state these were summer pastures for cattle and sheep and great sources of fuel to the neighbouring farmers, who had common of both pasture and turbary, and possessed spades, carts and houses for the peat and turf they burned in their hearths and lime-kilns or composted at the bottom of their dung-hills.[1] Mosses were drained with banks, walls, sluices and floodgates, and with characteristic sod-drains. These were broader top than bottom, where they had a gully roofed with turves, the like of which also filled the whole trench. First opened about 1 foot deep and 18 inches wide, the trenches were left to drain off a while, and then deepened by stages to some 4 feet. At the bottom, the gullies were about 5 inches wide and 18 inches deep, with 6-inch shoulders on either side to bear the covering turves, which had been selected from those dug at the first opening and laid sward downwards in the meantime. Sod-drains of this kind were laid at regular 6-yard intervals and every 100 yards connected to main drainage ditches. After drainage, one of two courses was adopted. Sometimes the land was ploughed and harrowed, marled at the rate of 3,000 or 4,000 marl-cart loads an acre, and left to weather in sun and frost until oats were harrowed in. Alternatively, the sward was pared off with a push-plough and burned, the ashes scattered, ploughed in on a shallow furrow and compressed with the heavy roller, and the land then mucked, at the rate of 1,000 tumbrel loads an acre, for a crop of oats. After paring and burning, moss-land would not bear tillage above three years, but whatever the previous treatment, the usual course was formerly three successive crops of oats, the last of which nursed a ley. Yet courses were far from uniform and a good deal of barley and some wheat and rye were grown. Drained mosses were highly fertile and much firmer, but shrinkage and burning made them liable to subside about 2 feet, and a special moss-plough fitted with a broad-winged share was drawn by horses wearing pattens to prevent them sinking to their houghs.[2]

[1] Leland, op. cit. iv, 2; Sutton, art. cit. v; Farrer, op. cit. i, 87; Shaw, *Kirkham*, 712, 731–2; Rylands, op. cit. iii, 3, 7–8, 13, 23–4, 204; Piccope, op. cit. xxxiii, 105 sqq.; li, 52–5; liv, 58 sqq.; Earwaker, op. cit. iii, 60 sqq., 151–3; xxviii, 149–50; Raine, op. cit. 90–3; Stewart-Brown, *St. Ch.* i, 11, 24–5, 67–8; Fishwick, *Du. Ct* xxxii, 3–4; xxxv, 184–6; xl, 11, 13–14, 16–17; Twemlow, op. cit. 252–3; Defoe, op. cit. ii, 260; Candidus, loc. cit.; Benevolus, art. cit. 563; Marshall, *W. Dept*, 111; Harland, op. cit. 52, 104; Deene ho, Brudenell H. vii. 6; Man. Lib. Ches. Deeds C. 135; Lancs. do L. 250; Smith & Webb, op. cit. 17; Lancs. R.O., D.D. Pt 22, Ct Bk Billington 1–8 Eliz. p. 10; Cons. Ct Cestr. invs.: Geoff. Barnes 1634 & Robt Adamson 1677 Broughton, Th. Hey 1680 Gt Sankey, Ralph Gregson 1699 Penwortham.

[2] Dickson, op. cit. 458–9, 466–7, 469–70, 507; Holt, op. cit. (1794) 58; (1795) 104–5, 100, 111, 113; C. Leigh, op. cit. bk i, 65; Fiennes, op. cit. 184–5; Walker, op. cit. 42; Bailey, op. cit. 23–4; Plot, *Staffs.* 345; Houghton, op. cit. i, 57; ii, 95.

Although no recent departure, reclamation took on greater impetus after 1560. Piecemeal, twenty or thirty acres at a time, hundreds and thousands of acres were recovered, at Kirkham alone some 400 merely between 1657 and 1677. By 1700, Pilling, Marton, Meols, and Tarleton mosses had been reclaimed, as well as Bootle Marsh and Marton and Martin meres.[1] How the original drainage was often completed before 1700 and then followed at a later stage by repairs and renovations, is well illustrated in the history of Martin Mere. In or slightly after 1692 Thomas Fleetwood of Bank Hall leased the mere and drained it by a new straight cut through the embanked salt-marsh near Birkdale, converting a fishing lake to arable winter-ground. But during the great inundations of 1715 and 1720, the sea flooded in. In 1781, Thomas Eccleston, lord of Scarisbrick, renovated the works and by 1786 barley and oats were again being grown in the mere bed. Then once more the land deteriorated to summer-ground, until in 1809 the drainage was restored again and cultivation resumed.[2]

In none of the countries heretofore mentioned, not even the Lancashire Plain, did inland and peat fens generally dominate the farming scene, as they did in the Fen Country, whose essential character was moulded by its immense tracts of water-formed land. It was these rich, free-working soils that saw the mightiest and most revolutionary changes there.[3] The crucial significance of drainage is shown by the fact that its allotment of recovered land might be worth more than all the rest of the farm put together, and this after a third of the fen had been given to the undertaker.[4]

The Fen Country had seen great drainage works in previous ages, but fresh developments were on a strictly minor scale until the last third of the sixteenth century, when the tempo noticeably quickened.[5] In 1568 Maud Foster drain was cut through West Fen and a new outfall sluice erected. In 1577-81 new works initiated in Caldecote Fen entailed Sir Edward Montagu cutting a ditch from Whittlesey Mere westwards to a point between Caldecote and Stilton. In 1577 the draining of fens to the south of Gedney Hill was commissioned. About 1588 a new sewer was cut in Wawne. In 1590 the Earl of Bedford brought over three

---

[1] Fishwick, op. cit. xxxii, 3–4; V.C.H. Lancs. ii, 288, 290; Shaw, op. cit. 278; Steers, op. cit. 106; H. T. Crofton, 'Broughton Topog. & Manor Ct', in Chetham Misc. ii Chetham S. 1909 lxiii, 22; Man. Lib. Lancs. Deeds L. 250; L'pool R.O., Fam. & Persl Recs. K. 434, Svy Bk Sir Th. Aston 1636, ff. 41–4; Lancs. R.O., D.D.F. 101, 112, 1939, 1978, 1984; D.D.K. 1451/1, m. 3; 1452/1, mm. 26, 28; 1454/3, m. 1; 1455/1, mm. 16, 25; 1456/2, m. 1; 1467/1–6.

[2] Fiennes, loc. cit.; Leigh, op. cit. bk i, 17; Bell, op. cit. 67; Bailey, op. cit. 10–12, 24.

[3] Marshall, E. Dept, 228–31; Sinclair, op. cit. 13; Dugdale, op. cit. 174–5.

[4] B.M., Add. 36906, f. 157.

[5] Dugdale, op. cit. 204, 241–3.

Netherlanders to inspect Thorney Fen with a view to drainage. In 1591 Milton common fens were enclosed. About this time some fens near Ely were drained. Other works were undertaken at Conington, Elm, Soham, and elsewhere. Shortly after 1596, Upwell Fen was drained by new works financed by three businessmen whose allotment was appropriately named Londoner's Fen. In 1599 Clow's Cross was commenced with the object of improving the passage into Shire Drain.[1]

By 1604 the state of drainage was as follows. The Marshland and Holland siltlands had mostly been drained long since, and a great deal of peat fen, if not dry in winter, was at least summer-ground. To the west, Catt Water bore the floods of Peterborough Fen to Old South Eau and passed them into Shire Drain, which went through the sea-wall near Tydd St Mary. Between Old South Eau and the sea were various sewers, like Sutton Drain, that ran parallel through the sea-wall to the saltings. These drains were connected in turn by cross-drains, of which the chief is now called South Holland Main Drain. Two loads, located where North and South Drove Drains now are, emptied the waters of Deeping Fen into the Welland near Spalding. From Catt Water through Thorney one drain ran into the Wryde and thence, by way of Wisbech Drain, to Wisbech Cut, while two others ran from west to east to join Gold Dike, which crossed the Wryde on its way to the sea. A whole series of sewers ran from near Peakirk through Peterborough Fen, then south of Crowland Fen into the Great Shepeau, and through Whaplode Fen to the salt-marshes of the Wash. South of Morton's Leam a network of delfs and loads led to the old bed of the Nene and connected transversely also with the Leam itself, encompassing Whittlesey and Whittlesey Turf fens. East of the old Nene, where Sixteen Foot Drain now is, West Water and the Leam ran north-eastwards to Wisbech, both being connected to Old Croft River, whence further loads ran off to the Ouse. Sewers radiated in all directions from the Isle of Ely: west to Morton's Leam, south and south-west to West Water and the Ouse, east to the Ouse, and north to the cross-drains. Thus a network of loads covered the main body of peat fens. Many fens along the Witham were similarly drained, but Wildmore, East and West fens were in worse state, and Crowland 'fields' and a third of Hatfield Chase were fit only for fishing and fowling. The presence of Whittlesey, Ugg, Ramsey, Benwick, Stretham and Soham meres pointed to great drainage achievements in the surrounding fens, for they were

[1] Northants, R.O., Mont. Hunts. 26/28, 25 Sept. 19 Eliz., 25 Feb. 1581; B.M., Add. 33466, f. 160; P.R.O., Chanc. Proc. ser. i Jas I, W.11/61, compl. & ans.; Exch. K.R., Sp. Commn 3047; Camden, op. cit. i, 550; Harris, op. cit. 19–20; Darby, op. cit. 11–12, 14, 15, 19–21, 32, 34–5, 43; Spufford, op. cit. 109–10; J. A. Sheppard, 'Draining Marshlands E. Yks.', ts. thesis Ph. D. Ldn Univ. 1956, p. 115; T. Badeslade, *Hist. Anc. & Pres. State Navig. Pt K's. Lynn* 1725, pp. 68–9.

necessary reservoirs preserving them from drowning under floods from the uplands.[1]

Yet artificial rivers were lacking to carry the waters away to the sea, for the sinking of the peat fens, silting up of the outfalls, failure to improve them, neglect of old rivers and increasingly sluggish flow to the sea all brought the whole drainage system into a parlous state.[2] Growing stagnation compelled recourse to pumping mills, whose function was to maintain locally the continuous flow of water that new cuts alone could produce throughout the levels. In 1588 Holbeech mill was pumping up more water than the outfall could handle. In 1592 Coldham fens were being drained only by means of an engine. In 1618 Tydd St Giles sewers were lower than the outfall, so that 'an artificiall water engine or myll' was needed 'to cast forth' the water. In 1619 the ready remedy for Somersham Fore Fen was to install 'an engine . . . to withdraw the water if occation be'. Pumps were ever more essential accessories and it was in the knowledge of this that William Folkingham of Helpringham wrote:

'Surrounded grounds may be won by sewing them with competent draines, tonnels, goats, sluces, and such like, if the water-fall be sufficient; otherwise some enginarie aide must bee assistant, to mount the water by screwes, pullies, poizes, by causing vaccuums, or reinforcing of spirits into narrow straights and cylinders.'

Parochialism might declare the difficulties to arise solely from neglect of existing local works; but the root of the trouble was that these very works had outgrown the main rivers and outfalls.[3]

This they none the less went on doing. Starting in 1599 or just after, Capt. Thomas Lovell eventually made good summer and winter-ground of Deeping, Spalding, Pinchbeck South, Thurlby, Bourne South and Crowland (Goggisland) fens. He spent the £12,000 rates voted for the project, only to see his banks destroyed by rioters. A private Act of Parliament in 1602–3 then allowed him three years to make good his works, else the commoners to re-enter. The Earl of Exeter now bought Lovell's allotment of one-third of the drained land, but employed him as chief engineer. In 1615 the earl said he had spent £17,000 in five years on this drainage scheme, which involved making great banks to con-

---

[1] Ibid.; Sheppard, op. cit. 118–19, 124–6, 287–8, 300; Tomlinson, op. cit. 83–4; Harris, op. cit. 64–5; B.M., Cott. Augustus I/i/79; Add. 33453, f. 87; Darby, op. cit. 33, 44, 67.

[2] Ibid. 16, 18–19, 21, 36–7, 95–6, 267; Sheppard, op. cit. 113, 119; Harris, op. cit. 129; B.M., Add. 33466, ff. 6, 139, 156, 160.

[3] Ibid. ff. 6, 137–9, 143–4, 183; Folkingham, op. cit. 20; Darby, op. cit. 16, 19; Brace, op. cit. 21.

tain the Welland and the Glen. In 1617 he dug the first spit in the Welland's bed at Stamford to inaugurate the deepening that was to make it navigable for boats, hoys and keels, as well as to enable it to carry away the increased flow of water from the drained fens.[1] About 1606–9 Popham's Eau was cut between the Old Nene and the Ouse and some 6,000 acres of fen were drained at Waldersea and Coldham. Around 1612 a new cut, later discontinued, was commenced between Ely and Littleport.[2] In 1618, when Wisbech River had recently been widened from 40 feet to 60 feet, the commissioners ordered the cutting of a new sewer at Little Thetford, the repair of Stanground, Farcet and Whittlesey banks, and the erection of a new dike to stop a backwater from drowning King's Delf.[3] In this period a great deal of draining was effected. John Norden said much drowned ground had been made firm by Capt. Lovell, William Englebert ('an excellent ingenor') and others. Rowland Vaughan knew Lovell as a masterly drainer.[4]

One single document, hitherto neglected, is fatal to the argument that peat-fen drainage was merely nebulous and indeterminate until Vermuyden came on the scene. The survey made of the fens in 1619 clearly shows that although only about a third of the fenland around Peterborough was dry, and only half that south of Holland and Marshland, very little remained drowned east or south of the Ouse, south-east of Ely or about Somersham. Deeping Fen was perhaps deteriorating. The survey originally declared it mostly well drained by the Earl of Exeter's undertaking, but a later hand denied this was any longer so. Even the drained fens, however, were mostly only summer-ground, or wet meadow overflowed in winter. At Cottenham, e.g. some fens, say the surveyors,

'uppon extraordinarye flourde are sometimes overflowed and uppon the fall of the river doe forthwith draine againe, as the upland meadowes doe; but unlesse the sayed flourde happen to overflow them in the summer season (which is very seldome), we doe finde that the sayd groundes receave more benefit then hurte thereby and are thereby much bettered and enriched; for those growndes which lye lowest and are oftenest and longest overflowne in the winter season are the most fertile growndes and yeald the beste yearlye value . . . unlesse it be some dry yeare when they are not overflowne, for then the white fodder is decayed and the

[1] Stat. 16 & 17 Chas II c. 11; P.R.O., St. Ch. Jas 111/25, m. 1; Exch. A.O., Parl. Svys Lincs. 14, f. 25; B.M., Harl. 702, f. 1; Add. 33466, ff. 25, 148; W. R. Scott, *Jt Stk Coys* 1910–11 ii, 353; Dugdale, op. cit. 194–5, 205–7, 218–19; Darby, op. cit. 45–6.

[2] Ibid. 31–2, 36, 43; Harris, op. cit. 27; Stat. 4 Jas c. 13.

[3] B.M., Add. 33466, ff. 11–12, 69; Ch. 33101.

[4] Norden, *Survs. Dial.* 195; R. Vaughan, *His Booke* ed. E. B. Wood 1897, p. 142; M. F. Bond, *MSS. H. L. xi add. 1514–1714*, 1962, pp. 33–5.

growndes turne muche to a kinde of small hammer-sedge which the cattell like not so well.'

Recently banked and drained anew, the commons here now grew a smaller variety of grass, giving far less to mow or feed in all but the wettest years. Some of Mildenhall Fen had been under water the previous February but this was due to extraordinarily heavy falls of snow and rain; and neither here nor at Brandon was ever as much lost in winter by overflowing as was gained from a single acre in summer. Landbeach High Fen was a hedged and ditched common cow-pasture, only a small part of which was ever drowned in winter. The state of Somersham was similar.[1] South-east of Holland and Marshland the peat fens were mostly of the nature of wet meadow.[2]

Nevertheless, notwithstanding all that had been accomplished, fen drainage as a whole was in a critical position, for nothing had as yet been done to make new straight cuts to the sea and clear the outfalls. Humphrey Bradley, one of the men commissioned to survey the fens in 1588, had reported that 'the most expedient and only way to redeem the lands from the waters is to draw off the waters by directing them along the shortest tracks to the greatest outfalls'. In 1593 he submitted to Burghley a comprehensive fen-drainage plan on precisely these lines. In 1605 the commissioners of sewers concluded that 'the making of a new river from Earith Bridge through Sutton, Byall and Westmore fens to Welney River and thence through certain fens of Norfolk into the Ouse about Mayd Lode would be most necessary, and that without so doing the fens could never be drained'. Next year Bradley's plans were momentarily revived, and in 1618 the commissioners restated their previous conclusion, pointing to the imperative need to improve the Ouse, Nene and Welland outfalls.[3]

In 1626–7 Vermuyden's syndicate carried out works in Hatfield Chase intended to lay the grounds dry enough for tillage. Just how much land was drained is, however, uncertain. The level contained in all 73,515 acres, of which part, as at Warton, had previously been enclosed and drained, and the rest was either summer pastures, mow-fens or peat-hags, 'at such tymes as the waters ar low, for most of the commons is often drowned or overflowed with waters', or else fisheries and navigable waters, as at Thorne and Fishlake. Vermuyden doubtless made much new summer-ground, but hardly succeeded in draining the whole

[1] B.M., Add. 33466, ff. 139–40, 143–5, 148, 160–1, 163–5, 172–3, 179–80, 182 sqq., 192, 195, 198, 200. Cf. Harris, op. cit. 15–18.

[2] Ibid. 75; P.R.O., Chanc. Proc. ser. i Jas I, B. 1/37, mm. 1, 4, 7; S.P.D. Chas. vol. 152 no 84; Exch. L.R., M.B. 201, ff. 174 sqq.; A.O., M.B. 419, ff. 58–9; Spratt, op. cit. 209; Darby, op. cit. 25, opp. 50, 51.

[3] Ibid. 18–19, 267; Harris, op. cit. 23, 26–8, 129; B.M., Add. 33466, f. 48.

level. Besides leaving washes to receive sudden downfalls, he unwisely abandoned the old Don and gambled on one new river replacing three former ones, with the result that while he made some flooded land dry, he also flooded some dry land, especially around Fishlake, Sykehouse and Snaith, a situation not remedied until Dutch River was cut shortly after 1633.[1] Vermuyden also took charge in the Great Level, which he undertook to make all good summer-ground. Upon the old drainage network he superimposed a new set of straight cuts to the outfalls, such as had long been advocated. The main new cut was the Old Bedford River, 70 feet wide and 21 miles long. Yet even in 1637, when the contract had been declared fulfilled, complaints were voiced against allegedly ineffective drainage, especially in the Over, Cottenham, Willingham and Ely districts. Once again, it is difficult to see how successful the drainage was, the more so since Vermuyden had hardly finished his contract to make good summer-ground before he undertook to convert this in turn to winter-ground and set works on foot for this purpose. By 1642 he had made a fresh bank south of Morton's Leam, a new cut 60 feet wide and 2 miles long on the Nene to improve the outfall below Wisbech, a sluice at Stanground to turn the Nene into the Leam, and another at Shire Drain outfall, all these being modifications of his previous system. At this juncture popular disturbances halted work and the most Vermuyden could claim was fleeting success.[2]

Meanwhile, in the course of this unprecedented draining boom, other contractors had also been busy. Between 1630 and 1642 were drained Brandesburton and Watton carrs, 500 acres of Soham's fens and over 1,000 of Tydd St Mary's. Sir Anthony Thomas and others drained West and East fens. The Earl of Lindsey undertook the drainage of over 70,000 acres of the Witham fens in Lindsey Level. Further work was done in the fens between Bourne and North and South Kyme by cutting Bourne Eau and South Forty Foot Drain, which was made navigable for twenty-four miles. Seven hundred acres of Somersham manor's fens were enclosed and improved and the marshes between West Fen and Bolingbroke reclaimed. Peterborough Little (Flag) Fen was also recovered. Works were undertaken in Pinchbeck North and Spalding South fens, this latter containing some 16,000 acres, and in Holland Fen, where about a third of the 21,500 acres had previously

[1] G. Stovin, 'Bf A/c Drainage Levells Hatfield Chase & pts adj.', *Yks. Archaeol. Jnl* xxxvii, 386, 390; 'Nat. Reading & Commnrs Sewers Level Hatfield Chase', ibid. xviii, 184; Collier, art. cit. 36–7, 52; Tomlinson, op. cit. 65–6, 82–5, 94–5; Rylands Lib. Eng. 216, ff. 17, 38, 43, 47, 56, 58, 63–4; P.R.O., R.&S. G.S. 13/87; Exch. L.R., M.B. 193, mm. 130 (63) sqq., 145 (78)d. sqq.; 230, ff. 300 sqq.; 256, ff. 52 sqq., 107–8, 194; A.O., M.B. 390, ff. 36–7; Parl. Svys Lincs. 16; Dugdale, op. cit. 140, 144; Harris, op. cit. 41, 43–6, 49–50, 52–3.

[2] Ibid. 61, 63 sqq., 71–2, 75, 85; B.M., Egerton Ch. 1451; P.R.O., S.P.D. Chas vol. 491, no 94; Dugdale, op. cit. 207; Darby, op. cit. 39–42, 44, 58–61.

been overflowed. The drainage of 19,000 acres in Ancholme Level was completed. Finally, in 1641, Ayliffe and Thomas directed further works in Deeping Fen, which made it all good summer-ground and likely to be good winter-ground too.[1]

Thus by 1642 immense levels had been completed, but by no means does it follow that all the land in them was previously drowned. The round and ample acreages of the contracts included portions of land already well drained. In Holland Fen only about 7,000 acres were formerly completely flooded, though 21,500 were written into the contract. Moreover, of the directors and contractors, only Lovell, Thomas and Vermuyden had undertaken to make winter-ground. Furthermore, not all the land hitherto drowned was now laid dry, for meres, sikes and washes still had to be left. In Deeping Fen the meres and sikes covered about 200 acres. Some of Vermuyden's washes were several miles long and one mile wide. Washes could be used as wet meadow, but both they and the meres, sikes and carriages were targets for the complaints of those who had seen their dry land flooded.[2] Even apart from this, it is doubtful if all the draining was successful. Vermuyden's works in Hatfield Chase were so defective he was obliged to cut a new channel from Turnbridge to Goole at his syndicate's expense. In the Great Level he made many of his banks not of clay and gravel as the dike-reeves did, but of sedge hassocks and light, porous peat earth, which would shrink, and 'both burne and swim'. Nor were new works necessarily proof against floods. Perhaps the disastrous thaw of 1613 was too much for Exeter's works in Deeping Fen, for under the pretext that the Welland was threatening to flood and engulf whole townships the 'slodgers' turned out at dead of night to make a slacker through the wall and so re-inundate the fens.[3] Finally the various new works had not long been completed, or were still in progress, when rioters tampered with them and put many of the fens under water once again.[4]

[1] Ibid. 44, 46, 48; Leonard, art. cit. 109; Marshall, op. cit. 94; *Jnl H. L.* iv, 220; *V.C.H. Lincs.* ii, 332-3; P.R.O., Exch. L.R., M.B. 230, ff. 33, 35 sqq.; 286, f. 196; A.O., Parl. Svys Hunts. 7, f. 34; Yks. 27; Dugdale, op. cit. 151-2, 208.

[2] Ibid. 207-8; Blith, op. cit. 54; Darby, op. cit. 50-1, 67; Thirsk, art. cit. 26; Harris, op. cit. 45, 130; D. G. C. Allan, 'Agrarian Discontent under early Stuarts', ts. thesis M.Sc. Ldn Univ. 1950, p. 129; B.M., Add. 33466, f. 25; Northants. R.O., Wmld 7. xvi.

[3] Dugdale, op. cit. 206-7; P.R.O., St. Ch. Jas 111/25, mm. 1-3; A. Burrell, *Excs. agst Sir Cornelius Virmudens Discourse* 1642, pp. 2, 4, 11, 13; *Briefe Relation Discovering Plainely . . . the gt Levell of Fenns* 1642, pref.; Harris, op. cit. 52-3, 86.

[4] Ibid. 50-1; Allan, op. cit. 113-15, 118 sqq., 126 sqq., 141; Sheppard, op. cit. 114; *V.C.H. Lincs.* ii, 333; *Jnl H. L.* ix, 118; S. R. Gardiner, *Reps. Cs in Cts St. Ch. & High Commn* Camd. S. 1886 xxxix, 59-60; P.R.O., Exch. A.O., Parl. Svys Hunts. 7, ff. 19, 35; Lincs. 14, f. 25; Dugdale, op. cit. 145-6, 152-3, 208; Darby, op. cit. 55-6, 61-3.

About 1649 fen drainage was taken up anew. By 1652–3 Vermuyden had made the Bedford Level winter-ground. There were other works too,[1] but no general reclamation of Lindsey Level or of East, West, Wildmore and Holland fens, which remained largely summer-ground. From 1653 onwards none but minor works were anywhere undertaken and even these aimed merely at conservation. Persistent shrinking of the peat and silting up at the outfalls combined with some negligence in repairs to turn conservation into deterioration. The Great Level was seriously flooded in 1653, 1673 and 1694, Deeping Fen about 1660–3, Hatfield Chase in 1687. Once more, riddance could only be had by recourse to pumps and windmills. The wheel had turned full circle. Drainage reverted to local occupiers and landowners. New mills were installed and maintained by them, not by the Bedford Level Corporation. Such circumstances suited management by commissions of sewers, but these were not restored, and instead the corporation was reorganized on a local basis. Then, between 1720 and 1735, during the lowest depths of depression, fen drainage was allowed to go to rack and ruin.[2] Only in the latter part of the century was serious consideration given to the recovery of drowned fens; but by then the necessary capital and labour were employed in canals elsewhere, and no far-reaching plans could be entertained. No cure being possible, the utmost aspiration was to improve the palliatives. But James Watt was diverted by the stronger demand for steam-mills and it was not until 1819–20 that the steam-engine was brought in to power the pumps.[3]

In fine, drainage activity culminated in its greatest intensity between 1590 and 1653. Thenceforth activity declined. At no time was either none or all of the fens dry, but the greatest coincidence of maximum draining activity with maximum winter and summer-ground was about 1637.

True, the land might be drained not wisely but too well, so depriving it of essential sediments and solutions or laying it too dry for good grassland. Some soils were 'very dust' and had 'ther lieffe and succor from the waters overflowinge'. When Cottenham common fen was re-drained, the commoners were driven to seek pastures elsewhere and 'to set barne dores overwharte the river to stancke the water to help water

---

[1] Ibid. 67–8, 70 sqq., 81–2; Harris, op. cit. 89–90, 92–3; Lennard, art. cit. 45; Morton, op. cit. 8; Sheppard, op. cit. 116.

[2] Ibid. 135, 139, 142–4; Stats. 14 Chas II c. 17; 16 & 17 Chas II c. 11; 22 Chas II c. 14; Darby, op. cit. 80–1, 94 sqq., 118 sqq., 134 sqq., 144 sqq.; *Hist. Geog. Engl.* 458–9; Fuller, op. cit. i, 221; Defoe, op. cit. ii, 100; Tomlinson, op. cit. 102, 284–7; Dugdale, op. cit. 152–3; Cams. R.O., L. 1/20, f. 12; Northants. R.O., Misc. Led. 145, p. 541; F.(M.) Misc. 1006; Marshall, op. cit. 94.

[3] Ibid. 21–2, 231, 237–40; Vancouver, *Cams.* 191; Pitt, *Northants.* 168; Webb, op. cit. i, 184; Darby, op. cit. 464; *Draining Fens*, 129 sqq., 136, 141–3, 145–8, 150–2, 179 sqq.

into theire ditches for theire cattell'.[1] It was to meet such situations that warping was developed. Where basically poor or sandy soils were bereft of essential alluvial dressings, little ingenuity was required to pierce small slackers through the embankments to allow in as much silt as was needed. Such warping was especially important about the Ouse and Trent estuaries, in Holderness and the Isle of Axholme. Although only brought to public notice by William Marshall, this practice was probably not much posterior to the drainage that necessitated it.[2] With this remedy at hand, it is impossible to see anything but advantage in the draining of the peat fens.

Despite the summer-grounds being mostly for grazing or mowing, some parts of them had long been occasionally cultivated. Several years might pass without the farmer growing any corn at all in the fens, because they had never dried out enough; but when a dry season came along, the fen-mould might be ploughed up for spring crops.[3] Some fens had long been, and more became, good winter-ground, which was mostly arable in a distinct system of convertible husbandry.[4] Fen-moulds were moory, deep and spongy, but needed only an intermixture of clay marl at the outset to be excellent in cultivation. Moistness made their climature backward, seed-time being ten days behind that in the Northwold Country, yet sun smiled on the crops.[5] So rich in humus was the land, that its swards had to be pared and burned, lest the crops be too rank. With the sod, albeit ploughed as shallow as could be, was burnt some of the mould itself, especially when the fires 'pitted in' and smouldered underground, perhaps as deep as 2 feet; and the heaps themselves were interlayed with peat fuel dug for the purpose. Burning thus destroyed superfluous humus, dried out the land and guarded against soil pests; but it also lowered the field and eventually impaired drainage.[6] The main cereal crop was oats, which served for bread, drink,

[1] B.M., Add. 33466, ff. 184, 187, 200; P.R.O., Chanc. Proc. ser. i Jas I, B. 1/37, mm. 4, 7; Morton, loc. cit.; Marshall, op. cit. 17–18, 229, 238–40; Darby, op. cit. 51; Thirsk, art. cit. 26.

[2] Ibid.; Adkin, op. cit. 133–4; Marshall, op. cit. 4, 103–4, 111, 113; N. Dept, 388–91; Harris, op. cit. 47, 49; Rider-Haggard, op. cit. ii, 181–2; W. Tatham, Nat. Irrigation 1801, pp. 110 sqq.

[3] Marshall, E. Dept, 233; Thirsk, op. cit. 37; Darby, op. cit. 155, 174–5; Tomlinson, op. cit. 84; Blith, op. cit. 47, 59, 61.

[4] B.M., Egerton 2994, f. 51; Northants. R.O., F-H 119, Dowdike; F.(M.) Misc. 207, 216, 453–4, 459, 1033; Corr. 178/24; Misc. Vols. 76, 187; P.R.O., D.L., M.B. 119, ff. 205, 224, 228–9, 230v.–2; Exch. L.R., M.B. 211, ff. 57, 59–60, 73, 81–6, 89–90; 285, ff. 15, 28, 43–4, 67–8; A.O., M.B. 395, ff. 2, 4–5, 9–11, 19, 22 sqq.; Parl. Svys. Lincs. 26, f. 6; 43, f. 4.

[5] Morton, op. cit. 8, 36–7, 45; Marshall, op. cit. 17; A. Bloom, Fm in Fen 1944, pp. 85, 110; Rider-Haggard, op. cit. ii, 31.

[6] Ibid. 13; Bloom, op. cit. 62, 96–8, 132; Morton, op. cit. 37, 482; Darby, op. cit. 84; Blith, op. cit. 61; Vancouver, op. cit. 156, 158 sqq., 185–8; Marshall, op. cit. 23, 39, 49–50, 57, 209, 255–6, 289.

potage and provender if need be. Sometimes the land was sown to oats until exhausted and covered with twitch, to which fen-moulds were all too prone. Oat stubbles were generally burnt off, for they had no other use, and this and various cleansing operations obviated the necessity for whole-year bare fallows.[1] The best fen-mould was hardly ever kept in tillage above eight years and the inferior three or four, upon which it was laid down and the resultant 'layer' was left as long as it remained good.[2]

The predominant and characteristic first crop on fen-mould was rape or cole-seed.[3] This old-standing English crop was being grown in the Fen Country in the early sixteenth century. In 1551, Turner related, 'The long rooted rape groweth very plenteously a little from Linne, where as much oyle is made of the sede of it.' Of this colza oil Langham says in 1578, 'there is great plentie of it made in Marshland, neere to Linne.' In 1597 Gerarde writes of 'our common rape, which beareth the seed whereof is made rape oile and feedeth singing birdes'. When Folkingham lays it down in 1610 that 'Rapes require a broken-up lay and a rich layer', it is his own Fen Country he has in mind.[4] By 1603, if no earlier, Boston was regularly exporting the seed.[5] In 1599 William Aleff of Terrington left ten combs of rape-seed valued at £7 10s, in 1605 Richard Cook of Sutton 57 acres of cole-seed worth £60, Roger Greene of Whaplode 3¼ acres worth £3, and Thomas Cooke of Pinchbeck some newly sown rapes at 30s. Cole-seed was a usual field crop in Gedney and district in and before 1608. In 1610–11 John Dethe, a Gosberton gentleman, had 'vj accers of wheat, rye and rapes' valued at £10. After draining, a great part of Haxey Carr in the Isle of Axholme was sown with rape. By 1629, at the latest, cole-seed was being cultivated in Dowdyke.[6] In 1632 some 4,000 acres sown to cole-seed in Sutton

[1] Ibid. 51, 228 sqq., 287; Invs.:—Nfk R.O., Cons. & A/d cts; York, Snaith Pec.; Lincs. R.O., Cons. Ct.; Northants. R.O., Cons. Ct Petriburg. Hunts. Invs.; Cams. Bds & Invs.; F-H 119, Dowdike; F.(M.) Misc. 902, 904, 917, 919; Misc. Vol. 55; E. Sfk R.O., 50/13/10.2; Cams. R.O., L. 93/139; Morton, op. cit. 9, 484; A. Harris, op. cit. 35; Vancouver, op. cit. 137, 158; Coles, op. cit. cap. cxliv; Darby, op. cit. 164; Gooch, op. cit. 105–6.

[2] Ibid. 104; Blith, op. cit. 59–60, 62; E. Sfk R.O., 50/13/10.2; Northants. R.O., F.(M.) Misc. 453–4; Misc. Vols. 76, 194; Marshall, op. cit. 228, 253, 255, 288.

[3] Ibid. 49, 51, 209, 228 sqq., 236, 253, 255–6, 282, 287, 289–90; *Midl. Dept*, 599, 639; *Yks.* ii, 30; Vancouver, op. cit. 145, 154, 158 sqq., 185–7; Gooch, op. cit. 104; Barley, 'E. Yks. Manorial Bye-Laws', 44; Darby, op. cit. 84–5, 164–5; Morton, op. cit. 8; Northants. R.O., F.(M.) Misc. Vol. 76.

[4] Gerarde, op. cit. (1597) 179; (1633) 233; Folkingham, op. cit. 36; Turner, *Herbal* pt ii, f. 113; W. Langham, *Gdn of Health* 1579, p. 521; W. Salmon, *Eng. Herbal* 1710, p. 929; Stat. 2 & 3 P. & M. c. 2; Winchester, op. cit. 184.

[5] Brace, op. cit. 17; R. W. K. Hinton, *Pt Bks Boston 1601–40* Lincs. Rec. Soc. Pubns 1956 l, 23, 25, 59, 85, 129, 131, 215, 217, 247 sqq., 281 sqq., 315–17, 319, 321.

[6] Dugdale, op. cit. 145; Northants. R.O., F-H 119; invs.:—Lincs. R.O., Cons. Ct

brought a profit of the order of £10,000. In 1633 Robert Tysdale of Tydd St Mary had cole-seed on the ground worth £7 and John Donne of Frampton had a small patch of the crop valued at half a crown. Andrew Burrell, a Wisbech gentleman, testified that between 1632–3 and 1640 he made about £300 a year on his farm in Wisbech and Elm from rape cultivation alone, while a tenant of his at Waldersea had a crop worth £500.[1] In 1652 Anthony Williamson of Kenwick had over 15 acres of cole-seed growing.[2] By now tens of thousands of acres were under the crop throughout the length and breadth of the country.[3] In short, as more fen-mould was made winterground, so the crop spread.

The cole-seed, or giant rape, was brushed in at intervals from about May onwards, July being the peak month and the best for germination. Thus from August and September onwards a succession of crops was available for folding off to fatting sheep in autumn and winter. When intended to stand through the winter for seed, the crop was not sown until August. Cole-seed produced about fifteen tons of green food an acre and no less than twenty hundredweights of starch equivalent, appreciably more than did common turnips. After being fed in the winter season, spring frosts might kill the crop, and then oats were sown in its stead; but in mild springs the cole-seed continued to flourish. In summer it was reaped, spread on sail-cloth for about a fortnight to dry and then threshed with ordinary flails. After winnowing, the seed was sold for farmers, or to oil-mills for crushing. The colza oil expressed gave illumination or lubrication or went to make soap. The stubble was useless for anything but burning where it stood. Selling seed off the farm tended to deplete soil resources, but these could easily be restored by purchasing rape-cake made from the crushed seeds and feeding it to cattle, so that the ground received back much of what it had given up. Cole-seed was primarily a crop on the turf, but in the best fen-moulds it could be repeated in the succession, being then sown after two fallow stirrings heavily dunged, often succeeding wheat and preceding a farewell crop of oats.[4]

––––––––––

1604–5: 139B, 150, 276; 1610–11: 209; Nfk R.O., Cons. Ct 1598–9: 144; P.R.O., Exch. K.R., Deps. by Commn 6 Jas Hil. 30, Hy White's dep. to art. 4.

[1] Ibid. 6 Chas Trin. 2; L. E. Harris, op. cit. 87–8; Burrell, *Excs.*, 13; Lincs. R.O., Cons. Ct invs. 1632–3: 75, 217.
[2] Northants. R.O., F.(M.) Misc. 918.
[3] Ibid. Cons. Ct Petribur. Hunts. Invs., Cams. Bds & Invs.; invs.:—Lincs. R.O., Cons. Ct; Nfk R.O., Cons. & A/d cts.; Lennard, art. cit. 36; Blith, op. cit. 58–9, 61, bet. 248–9; Worlidge, op. cit. 41–2; *Jnl H. L.* iv, 337; J. Moore, *Hist. or Narrative Gt Level* 1685, p. 62; J. L. *Discourse concerning gt benefit Drayning* 1641, pp. 3–4, 13; Verney, op. cit. iii, 207; L. E. Harris, op. cit. 113–14; A. Harris, op. cit. 35, 42; Darby, op. cit. 62, 77, 84–5, 87, 281.
[4] Ibid. 167; Brace, op. cit. 17, 21; Marshall, *Midl. Dept*, 639; *E. Dept*, 49, 209,

Contrary to some prejudiced and tendentious predictions, the new drainage works did not deprive farmers of forage and fodder. Temporary grass ensured ample hay and grazing, and cole-seed fresh winter feed more than compensating for any loss of coarse fen-fodder. Sheep were now fattened also in winter, when they fetched better prices, and cole-seed mutton nicely filled the gap between grass and turnip meat.[1] Moreover, the native 'Lincolnshire' sheep were now stocked in far greater numbers.[2] Despite forebodings, grass was now plentiful enough to allow greater summer beef production, so that the native shorthorns had to be reinforced by larger draughts than before of North Country and Scottish stores. The cheese and butter dairy, too, flourished, and therefore veal and pig-meat production likewise. Now as before, brood mares of the massive fen strain of the shire breed supplied draught in teams of two or three, and gave biennial foals into the bargain. Going unshod on soft fen-moulds caused the colts' hooves to splay out in a way ideally suited to heavy horses and made the Fen Country their perfect nursery; but whereas the peat fens had formerly been unable to bear the weight of ponies of over thirteen hands, they could now stand shire horses of seventeen hands or more, so the breeding of them became much more widespread.[3]

287, 289–90; Vancouver, op. cit. 154 sqq., 185–7; Gooch, loc. cit.; Morton, op. cit. 484, 491; Blith, loc. cit.; Ellis, *Sheep*, 212; Blagrave, op. cit. 232–4; invs. as prev. n.; Northants. R.O., F.(M.) Misc. 918.

[1] Ibid. 477, 902, 904, 907, 916–20; Misc. Vols. 52, 55; invs., esp. Cons. Ct Petri-burg. Hunts. Invs. E. 1609–94, Robt Edmunds 1638 Yaxley; Cams. Bds & Invs. 1662: Mary Clements/Waterbeach; 1669, Jn Parrish/id.; Peterboro' Invs. 1693: Th. Spicer/Gunthorpe; Peterboro' Wills &c. 1724 (a): Wm Marriot/Dogsthorpe; Nfk R.O., invs. ut sup., esp. Cons. Ct 1598–9: 114A, 144; 1611: 13, 93, 150–1; 1631: 39, 206; 1638: 203; Woodworth, op. cit. 78–80; *Lincs. Historian* no 7, pp. 261 sqq.; Foster, op. cit. ii, 85–6; Thirsk, op. cit. 30–1; Morton, op. cit. 8.

[2] Ibid.; Vancouver, op. cit. 205; Ellis, op. cit. 44, 322; Marshall, *E. Dept*, 63; J. L. op. cit. 8; Strickland, op. cit. 231; Defoe, op. cit. ii, 89, 94, 96.

[3] Ibid. 94–5; Markham, *Wealth* pt i, 89; Stat. 8. Eliz. c. 8; Camden, op. cit. i, 549; Woodworth, loc. cit.; Cunningham, art. cit. 261–4, 276; Fuller, loc. cit.; Morton, loc. cit.; Spratt, op. cit. 210; Thirsk, op. cit. 27–30; Darby, op. cit. 89, 94; Mascall, op. cit. 69; Foster, op. cit. ii, 65–6, 85–6; iii, 98–9, 227–8; Purvis, art. cit. 450–1; Best, op. cit. 105, 112–13; Steele, op. cit. i, 203; Marshall, op. cit. 57; *Midl. Dept*, 636–7; Spufford, op. cit. 27–8; Raine, op. cit. 12; *Lincs. Historian* no 7, pp. 264–5; E. Sfk R.O., 50/13/10.2; Cams. R.O., L. 93/139; B.M., Add. 37521, f. 59v.; Bodl. Hearne's diaries 158, f. 131; Northants. R.O., F.(M.) Misc. 792–3, 902, 904, 907, 916–22; Misc. Vol. 55; invs.:—York, Snaith Pec. esp. Wm Bateman 1664 & Jn Scholes 1690 Balne; Lincs. R.O., Cons. Ct. esp. 1604–5: 139B, 150, 276; 1610–2: 209; 1632–3: 75, 167, 217; Nfk R.O., A/d & Cons cts, esp. Cons. Misc. 1637–68: A/1; 1593: 10, 44; 1598–9: 92, 114A, 143A, 144, 154; 1611: 13, 16, 85, 93, 150–1; 1631: 39, 45, 206, 210; 1632: 75; 1633: 362; 1634: 12, 101; A/d 1674–5: 30; Northants. R.O., Cons. Ct Petriburg. Northants. Bds & Invs. 1684, esp. Jn Catlin/Maxey;

Hunts. Invs. E. 1609–94, esp. Edmunds ut sup.; K. 1613–87, esp. Jn Knight 1676
Ramsey; Cams. Bds & Invs. 1662, esp. Clements ut sup.; 1669 esp. Parrish ut sup.;
Peterboro' Invs. 1693, esp. Robt Hickling/Glinton, Laurence Stoxe/Northborough,
Robt Willemot/Peterboro', Spicer ut sup; Peterboro' Wills &c. 1724(a) Jn Eaton/id.,
Robt Tyers/Maxey, Marriott, ut sup.

CHAPTER V

FERTILIZERS

AGRICULTURAL improvement spelled outlay and investment, not least in manures, which were to be had in abundance by farmers with capital and spirit. The most widely used were farmyard manure and the sheep-fold. Hugh Latimer made a generalization valid for many countries and almost all common fields when he said, 'A ploughland must have sheep; yea, they must have sheep to dung their ground for bearing of corn; for if they have no sheep to help fat the ground, they shall have but bare corn and thin.'[1] Some innovations and improvements enhanced the fold's value, and most of them augmented the muck heaps, which in some countries were swelled by composts from sheep-cotes. The best manures were, for general purposes, dung from sheep and corned horses; for dry grassland, from pigeons and poultry; and for dry soils, from pigs. In warm soils, well-rotted composts of short dung were preferred, and in cold, long dung that opened the land and decomposed in it.[2] For composting, vegetable matter was readily available. Old thatch, offal straw, rushes, bracken, thistles, fallen leaves and other things were soaked in ponds, or used as litter, or laid upon the ways to be trampled in the mire that was predestined for the compost heaps.[3] Near the coast, seaweed (ore) was much used, especially in Wales and the West Country, where it assisted in the difficult business of growing good barley. Sometimes ploughed in green, and more usually rotted down in composts, ore was effective for one year.[4] Green manures were in no

[1] *Sermons* Everyman, 215.
[2] Blith, op. cit. 132, 145, 147–8; Lisle, op. cit. 14–15, 324; Morton, op. cit. 481; Worlidge, op. cit. 66–7; Plot, *Oxon.* 241, 244; Berks R.O., D./E.Ah E5/1, 2; Folkingham, op. cit. 24, 29; Atwell, op. cit. 107.
[3] Ibid.; Marshall, *Nfk* i, 15; *S. Dept*, 32; Lisle, op. cit. 18, 24; Norden, *Surv's Dial.* 228 (2nd occ.); Blith, op. cit. 151; Morton, loc. cit.; Mavor, op. cit. 363; Verney, op. cit. i, 130; Fussell, op. cit. xix; C. Leigh, op. cit. bk i, 55; Glouc. Lib. 16526/102; 18253, f. 1v.; Soms. R.O., D.D./W.O., Ct Bk Trevelyan Manors, p. 22; Folkingham, op. cit. 23, 30; B.M., Harl. 5827, f. 7v.
[4] Ibid.; Blith, op. cit. 141–2; Norden, op. cit. 223 (2nd occ.); Worlidge, op. cit.

wise neglected. Buckwheat, lupines, and tares, ploughed under when in flower, did much to improve poor, sandy lands.[1] All kinds of waste and refuse were pressed into service, often at considerable expense in transportation. Nothing was overlooked, neither sticklebacks, offal pilchards, sea-sand, sludge, peat, turves, pond mud, soot, nor wheat chaff and rape-cake, nor old clothing and footwear.[2] Urine was applied to meadows, but otherwise human waste was usually eschewed and buried deep and well out of the way. Not until the later eighteenth century were covetous eyes cast upon London night-soil, and even then, fortunately, most of it was disposed of other than to farmers.[3] Of all the extraneous fertilizers, lime, chalk and marl enjoyed the widest use. The numerous varieties of this last may be classified into chalk, clay, and stone or slate marls. The first were especially applicable to heavy soils, the second to light, and the third, not soapy and slippery like the others, to thin peat-earths on upland moors. According to the natures of marl and soil, improvements of long but varying duration resulted.[4]

Seed-steeps also partook of the nature of fertilizers. Gathering cold land into high ridges guarded against blights by keeping both seeds and corn dry, but rusts, smuts and bunt admitted no cure. That these could be transmitted to wheat and barley crops through the seed was proved experimentally in the years 1633–9 by a Shrewton farmer named Robert Wansborough.[5] These mildews could, however, be prevented by assiduous pickling. Sown wheat might be dressed with a mixture of

---

65; Borlase, op. cit. 86–7; Westcote, op. cit. 55; Owen, *Penbs.* pt i, 75; Boys, op. cit. 139, 141; H. Rowlands, *Idea Agriculturae* 1764, pp. 190–1; Emery, art. cit. 400; Vancouver, *Hants.* 347; Marshall, op. cit. 270, 432, 540–1; *N. Dept*, 70, 190, 477, 519; Folkingham, op. cit. 30.

[1] Ibid. 30, 35; Plot, *Staffs.* 346; Gerarde, op. cit. (1597) 82; Clarke, op. cit. 23; Lisle, op. cit. 174.

[2] Ibid. 14–17, 24; Platte, op. cit. bk ii, 49, 59; Atwell, loc. cit.; Morton, loc. cit.; Plot, *Oxon.* 244–5; Fuller, op. cit. i, 301, 394; Boys, op. cit. 138–9, 141; Laurence, op. cit. 78–9; Borlase, op. cit. 87; Blith, op. cit. 132, 142–4, 147, 150; Walker, op. cit. 39; C. Leigh, loc. cit.; Folkingham, op. cit. 23–4, 30; Norden, op. cit. 226 (2nd occ.); Lennard, art. cit. 36; Leicester Mus. 4D.51/1, p. 161; Kent R.O., U. 214/E7/44; Marshall, op. cit. 190, 477; *Yks.* ii, 255; *Nfk* i, 15, 27–9, 33; *W. Dept*, 135, 142–4; *E. Dept*, 373; *S. Cos* i, 400; ii, 55; *S. Dept*, 10, 14, 432, 525.

[3] Ibid. 32, 131–2, 177, 388–9; *Mins.* i, 31; Jacks, op. cit. 198; Morton, op. cit. 480; Plot, *Staffs.* 346; Worlidge, op. cit. 69; Vancouver, op. cit. 461; B'ham Lib. 505455; Bodl. Hearne's diaries 159, p. 226; Blith, op. cit. 142, 150.

[4] Ibid. 132, 135; Fitzherbert, *Surveyinge*, f. 47v.; Folkingham, op. cit. 23–4, 31–3; Plot, op. cit. 119–20, 341–2; Morton, op. cit. 61–2; Lisle, op. cit. 26–7; Laurence, op. cit. 85; Smyth, *Hund. Berk.* 40–1; Fuller, op. cit. i, 394; Norden, op. cit. 223 (2nd occ.); Owen, op. cit. pt i, 71–4; Godfrey, op. cit. 92; Marshall, *Nfk* i, 16; B.M., Add. 6027, f. 17 (16); 28529, f. 132 (143) v.; Harl. 5827, f. 8; Shak. Bpl. Throckmorton: Ct R. Sambourn 12 Oct. 1640.

[5] Bristol Univ. Lib. Shrewton 37; my 'N.-bk Wilts. Farmer', *Wilts. Mag.* liv, 416 sqq.

lime and ashes, but it was far better to pickle the seed in brine, lime or red lead. Wheat seed generally, barley sometimes, was steeped in a solution of salt and lime strong enough to float a new-laid egg. When the whole had been well stirred, the scum was skimmed off. The remaining seeds were then strained, spread on the floor and dried in lime. Thus the good ones were disinfected and the light discarded. Steeping was undertaken with the object also of quickening the seed, for which was added a liquid manure composed of chalk, soot, ashes, salt and urine or dung, preferably pigeon's. Francis Bacon demonstrated that human urine was the best quickening agent and this was perhaps occasionally used. Steeps thus often had dual purposes and even those intended for pickling served also somewhat to quicken the seed.[1]

Poverty led many cottagers and small farmers to burn not only fern and turf, which could as well have been added to composts, but also straw and cow clots. Aubrey says, 'Where fuell is very scarce, the poore people doe strow strawe in the barton, on which the cowes doe dung; and then they clap it against the stone walls to drie for fuell, which they call ollit.' These composts were not rich, since mostly from milking cows, and their ashes usually returned to the land;[2] but township governments did what they could to reduce the wastage. None but cottiers were to gather such fuel from the commons and even they were ordered to have a supply of firewood in their yard before the onset of winter.[3] When enclosure increased supplies of kindling wood and mining advances had their effect in cheap coal,[4] the land could receive more manure. Every advance in industry, indeed, swelled supplies of extraneous fertilizers. Without the rise of the coal industry, farmers could not have used lime so liberally. Augers developed for prospecting mines proved invaluable in marl-digging.[5] Sea-coal ash, dust and soot were highly esteemed. So was urry, a clayey substance dug from near the

[1] Ibid. 420; Blith, op. cit. 127; Lennard, art. cit. 37–8; Morton, op. cit. 401–2, 478–9; Worlidge, op. cit. 56–7, 191; Lisle, op. cit. 87; Platte, op. cit. bk ii, 35–6; Markham, *Wealth* pt v, 6; Plot, op. cit. 350; *Oxon.* 40; Boys, op. cit. 82; Pitt, *Staffs.* 92; Westcote, op. cit. 57; F. Bacon, *Opera Omnia* 1730 iii, 86–7; B.M., Sloane 3815, f. 157v. (p. 352); Basset Down ho. N. Maskelyne's A/c Bk, ff. 279–80; Bodl. Aubrey 2, f. 84.

[2] Ibid. ff. 88v.–9; Plot, op. cit. 241; Morton, op. cit. 481; W. Burton, op. cit. 2; Norden, op. cit. 222 (1st occ.); A. Moore, op. cit. 27; Fuller, op. cit. ii, 223; *Jnl H.C.* xxx, 741–2; E. Laurence, *Duty Stwd to his Ld* 1727, p. 29.

[3] B.M., Sir Th. Phillipps' Tracts: Topog. & Geneal. iii: 'Wanborough Ct R.' pt i, 10, 31; pt ii, 52, 54, 57, 60; Add. R. 49701, 19 Apr. 13 Eliz.; Bucks. Mus. P. 24/2 Ct R. Pitstone 20 Apr. 13 Chas; Northants. R.O., Higham Ferrers presentmts 5 & 6 Eliz.; Irchester Ct R. 19 Eliz.; I.(L.) 128, Ct R. Lamport 25 Oct. 11 Eliz. Scaldwell ords.; Deene ho. Brudenell O. xxiv, 1 Ct Bk Wardley Oct. 18 Eliz.; Shak. Bpl. Throckmorton: Ct R. Weston Underwood 28 Oct. 1736.

[4] Nef, op. cit. esp. i, 196; & v. A. Standish, *Coms. Compl.* 1611, p. 8.

[5] Smyth, op. cit. 41–2; Platte, op. cit. bk ii, 27; Fitzherbert, loc. cit.; Rowlands, op. cit. xxv–vii; Bodl. Hearne's diaries 158, p. 24.

coal-face and spread on grasslands.[1] The growth of soap-boiling gave rise to greater amounts of the soap-ash the boilers had drawn their lyes from, and this, when sifted on to swards 'like a hoare frost', promoted the growth of wild white and perennial red clover. Applied at the rate of 150 sacks an acre, it would remedy rushiness in meadows. From about 1590 soap-ashes came into increasing use in the West Country; and not long after a certain Mr Broughton introduced into the Vales of Hereford the practice of buying them from the Bristol soap-boilers.[2] The expansion of the iron industry augmented supplies of the pulverized slag that served the same purposes.[3] Salt and waste brine from salt pits, pans and flashes made valuable fertilizers.[4] Amongst the other industrial by-products employed by farmers were tanner's muck (rotten bark), stone chippings, and saw and malt-dust.[5]

Farmers increasingly bought in refuse from big towns and cities. From Ware, Hertford and Hitchin, where barley was malted for London, farm carts and wagons brought back malt-dust. The barges and wagons that took corn, malt and provisions from the Chalk and Chiltern countries and the Norfolk Heathlands for London and other centres returned laden with stable manure, street refuse, soot, ashes, rags, furriers' clippings, horn shavings, sheeps' trotters, leather shreds, bones, and all manner of refuse. Bones might be calcined, and rags and waste leather cut up, and then all were ploughed in or sown with the corn.[6] The farmers of the Lancashire Plain bought in ashes and stable-dung by the cart-load. Manure from the Yarmouth stables, which were littered with sand, was especially valuable for the clay loams of the East Norfolk broadlands.[7]

Whilst it cannot be said that many important new fertilizers were

[1] Norden, op. cit. 203, 226 (2nd occ.); Worlidge, op. cit. 24; Blith, op. cit. 150; Westcote, op. cit. 56; Lisle, op. cit. 24; J. Laurence, op. cit. 78–80; Folkingham, op. cit. 23; Boys, op. cit. 138; Marshall, *Nfk* i, 15, 31; Weston, op. cit. 45; Lennard, art. cit. 36.

[2] Ibid. 35; Leigh, loc. cit.; Fuller, op. cit. i, 394; Worlidge, loc. cit.; Westcote, loc. cit.; Folkingham, loc. cit.; Beale, op. cit. 53–4; Hitt, op. cit. 149; B.M., Harl. 5827, f. 8; Bodl. Aubrey 2, ff. 85, 153; Hearne's diaries 159, p. 229; Nfk R.O., Cons. Ct inv. 1742–63: 175; W. Sfk R.O., Episc. Commy Ct Bury St Edm's. inv. 1670: 182; J. Mitchell, J. 'On Prep. & Uses var. Kinds Potash', *Phil. Trans.* ix, 575; Norden, op. cit. 227 (2nd occ.).

[3] Ibid.; Straker, *Wealden Iron*, xii, 27, 222–3, 323, 358, 457–8; Glouc. Lib. Cons. Ct invs. 1668: 14; 1690: 74; Folkingham, op. cit. 23–4.

[4] Ibid. 24; Blith, op. cit. 132, 150; Westcote, loc. cit.; Pomeroy, op. cit. 34; Marshall, *S. Dept*, 525; *W. Dept*, 144; Platte, op. cit. bk ii, 14–15, 42–3.

[5] Ibid. 49; Morton, loc. cit; Atwell, loc. cit.; Folkingham, op. cit. 27; Laurence, op. cit. 79; Lisle, op. cit. 14–17; Plot, op. cit. 241, 244–5; Marshall, *Nfk* i, 15.

[6] Ibid.; *S. Dept*, 10, 14; Walker, loc. cit.; Mavor, loc. cit.; Folkingham, loc. cit.; Plot, op. cit. 244–5; Atwell, op. cit. 106; Laurence, op. cit. 78; Kalm, op. cit. 144; Lisle, op. cit. 17; Norden, op. cit. 226–7 (2nd occ.); *Cal. S.P.D. Ven.* xv, 249; Bodl. Hearne's diaries 158, p. 38.

[7] Cf. Marshall, *Nfk* i, 32.

introduced in the 200 years after 1560, the evidence suggests more manure was applied. Especially is this clear in respect of sea-sand, marl, and lime. Sea-sand was in wide use along the coasts and nowhere more markedly than in the West Country, which had a relatively long littoral and so a great supply, as well as a special demand, since after peat-burning, if anything more than one good first crop and a short and indifferent succession were desired, heavy applications of fertilizer were essential. This was why West Country farmers gained renown for ingenuity and diligence in dressing and manuring. Calcareous sea-sand, or rather broken and pulverized shell, mixed with sand, slime, ooze and mud, dug from the foreshore, was increasingly used on both coastal and inland farms, though more sparingly on the latter, on account of the cost of transport by barge and pack-horse. So much was sea-sand employed, that its digging, transport and sale became a recognized occupation. From the early seventeenth century, tenants habitually covenanted to lay 300 sacks of sea-sand on every acre converted to tillage for four crops, or 240 for two. Sea-sand was applied in one of two ways: either, in 'clean-sanding', by itself; or, more usually, combined with well-rotted farmyard manure, pond-mud, ditch-mould, headland earth, rotten pilchards, the scrapings of yards and lanes previously littered with straw or fern, and such like, in a single compost. This made good corn on a small straw—the barley ear might be as long as the stalk—and was even better for the subsequent ley of clover and sweet grass.[1] In Wales, similarly, sea-sand was carried to farms often four or five miles inland.[2]

Sand, of any kind, wrought the greatest benefit when mixed with tough clay, and clay, when laid on tender sand. Such intermixture, as practised in the Vale of Berkeley, East Norfolk, and elsewhere,[3] was closely akin to marling, where chalk marls were spread on clay, and clay marls on sandy soils. And marling appears also to have increased, in the sixteenth century, for instance, in the Chalk, Southdown, Northdown, Butter, Sandlings, and Peak-Forest countries, in the Breckland, Romney Marsh, East Norfolk, and the Midland Plain.[4] Not that marl

---

[1] B.M., Harl. 5827, f. 7v.; Add. 21608, ff. 130–1, 192, 276v.–7; P.R.O., Exch. L.R., M.B. 207, ff. 40 (38), 56 (54); Stat. 7 Jas I c. 18; Soms. R.O., D.D./W.O., Ct Bk Trevelyan manors, p. 22; Seaton A/c Bk 1616, disbursemts; Corn. R.O., Cons. Ct A/d Corn. inv. P1639: Jn Picken/St Cleer; Lennard, art. cit. 33–5; Westcote, loc. cit.; Folkingham, op. cit. 25, 27, 30; Borlase, op. cit. 82–3; Carew, op. cit. ff. 19v., 27; Childrey, op. cit. 11; Norden, *Corn.* 20; *Surv's. Dial.* 224 (2nd occ.); Blith, op. cit. 141; Rowe, op. cit. 218–20; Fuller, loc. cit.; Marshall, *W. Engl.* i, 79–80, 154–5, 297; ii, 14, 58; *S. Dept*, 516, 524–6, 541; D. Cox, 'Improvemt Corn. by Sea-sand', *Phil. Trans.* ii, 206–7.
[2] Rowlands, op. cit. 98–9, 115–17, 135 sqq.; Owen, op. cit. pt i, 74–5.
[3] Ibid. 75; Norden, op. cit. 203; Smyth, op. cit. 41; Marshall, *Nfk* i, 15–16.
[4] Ibid.; *S. Cos.* ii, 235, 238; *S. Dept*, 158–9; Plot, *Staffs.* 341, 343–4; Worlidge, loc.

was dug more now, perhaps, than in remote times, but it lasted in the soil only permanently, not perpetually, and it would seem that even land heavily marled, say, in the high Middle Ages, was often ready for a further course of treatment by 1560 or before. Applied at the conventional rate of 300 loads to an acre, marl was now quadrupling the rental value of many fields in the Oxford Heights Country;[1] and chalk marl was heavily applied in the Norfolk Heathlands.[2] Moreover, there were some countries where other improvements made in the period after 1560 entailed the use of marl for the first time. Clay marls were often imperative when ploughing up peat marshes in the Fen Country, the Lancashire Plain and elsewhere.[3] In yet other countries, the area of permanent cultivation, or of up-and-down husbandry, could best be increased by means of marling. From about 1560 marls were more and more employed in Wales. Clay marl was spread on leys and fallows in the summer and left to weather down in winter. Marl, laid on a fallow or ley, made possible spring barley as the first crop of a long succession, or continuous oat cropping for a dozen or score years. Applied to the hillsides, clay marl destroyed fern, furze, heath and broom, and gave rise to a fine sward replete with white or red clover. Stone marl was quarried from the mountains and worked a slow improvement in fertility as it scaled off.[4] Marl was widely distributed and much used in the High Weald in the seventeenth century. The clays, clay loams and white or silver sands responded to the methods described below for the Wealden Vales; but the black sands demanded somewhat different treatment. After dressing with marl, they were ploughed deeply and sown to wheat, then fallowed for twelve months and stirred in summer, in preparation for another wheat crop.[5]

---

cit.; Fuller, loc. cit.; Smyth, op. cit. 41–2; Laurence, op. cit. 85–6; Lisle, op. cit. 26; Gerard, op. cit. 93; Lennard, art. cit. 32; Brentnall, 'Longford MS.', 16; Godfrey, op. cit. 92; Young, *Suss.* 42; Postgate, op. cit. 106; Melling, op. cit. 20, 55; *Wills & Invs. Knaresborough* ii, 204–5; P.R.O., Exch. L.R., M.B. 207, f. 79 (76) v.; St. Ch. Jas 155/27; Sp. Coll. Shaftesbury Papers 32/7; B.M., Harl. 5827, f. 8; Add. 28529, f. 143 (132) v.; Soms. R.O., D.D./W.O. Ct R. Seaton 10 Oct. 1632; Farway svy 1609; Herts. R.O., G'bury x.B.3a, 4 Oct. 38 Eliz.; Kent R.O., U. 214/E7/44; Norden, op. cit. 223, 225–6 (2nd occs.).

[1] Ibid. 222 (1st occ.); Bodl. Aubrey 2, f. 86.
[2] R. A. C. Parker, 'Coke Nfk & Agrarian Rev.', *Ec.H.R.* 1955 viii, 165; J. H. Plumb, 'Sir Robt Walpole & Nfk Husbandry', ibid. 1952 v, 87; Riches, op. cit. 32, 77 sqq.; Marshall, *E. Dept.* 354; *Nfk* i, 16; H.M.C., *Rep. on MSS. D. Portland* 1901 vi, 159.
[3] Sup. 226, 235.
[4] Owen, op. cit. pt i, 71–4; Rowlands, op. cit. xxi–iii.
[5] Daniel-Tyssen, xxiii, 249, 253, 256, 263, 267, 270; xxiv, 194; Norden, op. cit. 223 (2nd occ.); Heresbach, op. cit. f. 19v.; Straker, op. cit. 101, 108, 223, 263, 387, 393; Cornwall, op. cit. 210; Melling, op. cit. 20; Markham, *Weald*, 17.

Finally, marling became of paramount importance in certain countries. In the Wealden Vales, about 1585, it was taken up as the grand basis of improvement. Four kinds of marl lay at hand in veins in the hillocks: grey, blue, yellow and red; and all were good, earthy, fatty and slippery as soap. Hazel moulds might be ploughed deeply (any sub-soil turned up would soon weather down), and marl then laid on, at the rate of 500 cart-loads an acre, to lie throughout the winter and summer, until the land was ploughed for wheat. Alternatively, oats might be sown before marling, to kill the grass, the land stirred in summer, the marl applied and left for a year, and wheat sown. In a wet summer, peas went better before the wheat, to keep down the weeds. Otherwise a bare fallow was the best matrix for the heavy first wheat crop on marled hazel moulds. Wheat having been taken twice, the land would be laid down to grass for five or six years, when the fine sward, replete with clover, would start to become broomy and mossy, and was ploughed up again for two more wheat crops, under the second of which the field was once more laid down. Hazel moulds were thus made into good up-and-down land. Clay soils could likewise be improved. Dressed with 200 or 300 loads of marl an acre and fifty of farmyard manure, the clays were made to give good oats, wheat and grass. If the old sward were, as all too often, coarse and weedy, the marl was best laid straight on, without any ploughing, in order to rot away the herbage. Next spring the land could be tilled for oats, then summer-fallowed and sown to wheat. Marled land had to be ploughed in narrow, shallow furrow-slices, for the goodness worked downwards. High, narrow ridges with deep water-furrows were needed to keep the wheat dry, but in sloping fields the ridges had to be 7 or 8 feet broad, lest the marl wash away. Cross-guttering was advantageous only if the gutter-ends were stopped to prevent the richness escaping. Directly after marling, the land was always stiff, and the best remedy was to stock heavily and dress with ditch and headland moulds. The more clayey the soil, the less marl was needed and the more farmyard manure, but with the correct combination of fertilizers all the vale lands could be improved to bear good crops. If, however, marled land were over-ploughed or cropped for six or seven years continuously, all the goodness of both marl and soil was taken away, leaving a desert of barren clods.[1]

In the Lancashire Plain and the Cheshire Cheese Country, in and about the period 1560–90 most farmers marled in the ordinary course of business and to such purpose that they often doubled the value of their land. Although slate, stone, and shale ('steel') marls were all employed, pre-eminence belonged to the clay marl on which so many of the soils

[1] Ibid. 4, 8–11, 13 sqq.; Boys, op. cit. 19–20; Heresbach, loc. cit.; Marshall, *S. Cos.* i, 348; ii, 142; Lodge, op. cit. 81, 151, 157–8; Gulley, op. cit. 143 sqq.; Chalklin, art. cit. 36–7; Norden, loc. cit.

stood. It looked like dun clay, was esteemed in direct proportion to its calcareosity, gave body and retentiveness to light soils, and made heavy ones workable and permeable. Marl was usually applied in summer, about forty loads to an acre, left to disintegrate in sun and frost, and given a shallow ploughing in spring. The field could then be cropped for several years and still make good grass at the end. Sandy and gravelly soils, otherwise only able to bear three years of rye, buckwheat and oats, were made as rich as any by marl and muck. Though sometimes laid on winter fallows, marl was most efficacious on turf. If left unploughed, the grass grew through the marl and any feed lost the first year was more than made up in the next. More usually, marl was laid on grass intended to be ploughed the next season. New ploughings from marled grass were tilled for six or seven years and then laid down again after a succession of this sort: (1) fallow wheat, (2) barley after winter fallow, (3) brush peas, (4) brush wheat, (5) brush barley, (6) brush oats. Sometimes two or three further crops, of beans and vetches, were taken, but brought light soil dangerously near exhaustion. Heavier soil, when marled, could give eight or nine crops and still make good grass, if only well manured with dung and lime. The richest soils could be tilled even longer, but only after a year of bare fallowing and summer stirring, which was seldom thought worth while, for farmers wanted grass more than corn. Tilled in moderation, marled land gave leys abounding in perennial rye-grass and wild white clover, and this was the main purpose in marling.[1]

The longer the application of marls was persisted in, the further afield or deeper down had they to be sought, by the early seventeenth century at five or more fathoms.[2] The necessarily increased costs roughly coincided with peculiarly diminishing returns, for repeated marling eventually defeated its own end, when the land was glutted and extra marl only lowered fertility, and what was needed instead was lime or manure.

[1] Ibid.; Folkingham, op. cit. 32; Houghton, *Coll.* (1681) i, 55–7, 121–2, 125; Bankes, op. cit. 8, 12–15, 19, 21, 23, 25, 30, 34; Shaw, *Kirkham*, 278; *R. Forest*, 455; Raine, op. cit. 90–3; Leigh, loc. cit.; Laurence, op. cit. 45; Holt, op. cit. (1795) 64; Marshall, *N. Dept*, 286–7; *W. Dept*, 24–5, 135–6, 138–40; Fitzherbert, op. cit. f. 45v.; I.R. in Fitzherbert, *Husbandry* ed. Skeat, 134; Leland, op. cit. iv, 2; Stewart-Brown, *Lancs. & Ches. St. Ch.* 94–5; W. L. Sachse, *Diary Roger Lowe* 1938, p. 61; A. W. Boyd, *Country Par.* 1951, p. 11; Smith & Webb, op. cit. 18; Benevolus, art. cit. 563; Candidus, loc. cit.; Markham, *Eng. Husbandman*, 41; Lancs. R.O., D.D.Bl. 54/8; D.D. F. 158; D.D.K. 1453/1–2, 1463/1–2, 1464/1, 1470/1, 1471/1–2; D.D. Pt. 39, svy Dunkenhalgh 1657–72; Cons. Ct Cestr. invs. Geoff. Barnes 1634 Broughton, Wm Barton 1690 Tarlscough; Ches. R.O., Nedeham & Killmorey: Ct Bk Badington Bromall 22 July 11 Jas, 15 July 4 Chas; valn id. c. 1650; Chetham Lib. Mun. Rm, Sir Wm Meredith, svy his lands at Bowden & Altrincham 1726; Man. Lib. Ches. Deeds C. 135; L'pool R.O., Norris Papers 656; Fam. & Persl. Recs. K. 434, Svy Bk Sir Th. Aston 1636, ff. 3 sqq.

[2] Smyth, op. cit. 41–2.

This saturation point was widely reached in the Lancashire Plain and the Cheshire Cheese Country towards the end of the sixteenth century, and thenceforward lime was increasingly fetched from Wales, the Peak-Forest Country, the Craven and Clitheroe quarries and elsewhere. In the west, limestone, and near the coast, beach, were burned in farm kilns.[1] By 1607 marl had given way to lime in the Sandlings Country.[2] In the Wealden Vales, marl-sated land was ploughed up, or even pared and burned, and lime or chalk applied. Lime was often burned in kilns in the fields and ploughed into the fallows for wheat; but chalk was preferred and could easily be carted to most farms from the neighbouring downlands. By about 1630 the vales had largely been cleared, the basic marling completed, and the second phase of chalking and liming entered.[3] Similar stages of first marling and then recourse to lime, chalk, sludge, sand and manure are found in other countries also, and in some backward areas, e.g. Anglesey, this second phase was not started until shortly after 1650.[4]

Lime, it hardly need be said, was far from being merely the natural successor to marl; it sweetened acid soil and released hitherto untrapped fertility, and it is not surprising it became the farmer's standby almost everywhere, especially as coal fuel now reduced the cost of producing many of its forms. In country after country, after 1560, and still more after 1590, liming, or chalking, though not in itself an entirely new practice, grew so greatly in extent, frequency and volume, that it became effectually revolutionary.[5] At a rate of about sixty loads an acre, lime

[1] Marshall, op. cit. 135, 139; *N. Dept*, 292, Benevolus, loc. cit.; Candidus, loc. cit.; Lisle, op. cit. 31; Folkingham, loc. cit. 23–4, 27–8; Houghton, op. cit. ii, 96; Leigh, loc. cit.; Plot, op. cit. 341–3; Harland, op. cit. 49–50, 150, 172, 199, 230; Norden, op. cit. 224 (2nd occ.).

[2] Ibid. 225 (2nd occ.); E. Burrell, op. cit. 66.

[3] Chalklin, loc. cit.; Markham, *Weald*, 5; Norden op. cit. 224 (2nd occ.); *A.P.C.* 1621–3, p. 338; Leconfield, *Sutton & Duncton*, 80; Marshall, *S. Cos.* i, 348–9; ii, 143; *S. Dept*, 479–80; Boys, op. cit. 19, 20, 77, 142; Aubrey, *Sy*, iv, 175; Gulley, op. cit. 149–51; J. Cornwall, 'Ag. Improvemt 1560–1640', *Suss. Archaeol. Colls.* xcviii, 123; Kenyon, art. cit. 115–16, 119–22; Lodge, op. cit. 81, 157, 176, 180, 187; W. Suss. R.O., Cons. Ct Bp Cicestr. for A/d Cicestr. invs., esp. Jn Brooker 1669 Chiltington; 1670: Mathew Ireland/Wisborough Green, Jn Capeline/Ashington.

[4] Rowlands, op. cit. xxv–vii, 167–9.

[5] Leconfield, op. cit. 61; Lennard, loc. cit.; Nef, op. cit. i, 187; Standish, loc. cit.; W. Hooper, *Reigate* 1945, p. 199; Fiennes, op. cit. 192; Worlidge, loc. cit.; Kynder, art. cit. 184; Fuller, loc. cit.; Westcote, loc. cit.; Fitzherbert, *Surveyinge*, f. 47v.; Folkingham, op. cit. 28; Boys, op. cit. 139; Plot, op. cit. 341–2, 344; Robinson, op. cit. 20; Aubrey, op. cit. Evelyn's pref.; 'Nat. Hist. Dorking', 221; A. R. Bax, 'N. & Exts. fr. A/c Bk Ric. Bax', *Antiquary* 1882 vi, 164; Melling, op. cit. 35, 37–8; Ess. R.O., D./D.L. E61, a/c 1586; invs.:—W. Suss. R.O., Cons. Ct Bp Cicestr. for A/d Cicestr. Jn Penfould 1663 Petworth, Ed. Streater 1670 Pulborough; W. Sfk R.O., Episc. Commy Ct Bury St Edm's. 1667: 38; Marshall, op. cit. 160; *N. Dept*, 150, 477, 519; *S. Cos.* ii, 238; *Nfk* i, 15, 30; *Yks.* ii, 255.

was increasingly applied in the Butter and Cheese countries at these times, and in the Midland Plain.[1] As a result of the transformation wrought in the Vale of Pickering, lime now took the place of the sheep-fold as the sheet-anchor of husbandry. Almost every substantial farmer on the horse-shoe belt had his own kiln; and the smaller farmers and those in the central vale bought supplies from 'sale-kilns'.[2] In the North-eastern Lowlands, liming became a major innovation. Coal and lime were near at hand and mining inventions cheapened both, thus at once ending the impoverishment, and promoting the improvement of grass-lands.[3] In southern Wales and the Butter Country, liming on a large scale started about 1565. Merrick writes in 1578, 'Now of late yeares, since the knowledge or use of lyminge was found, there groweth more plentye of grayne.' Rough grazings and woodlands were converted to arable, and sweet grass ousted furze, ferns, heath and scrub. Here, too, lime-burning was facilitated by the frequent proximity of coal and limestone veins. The stone was hewn to the size of a man's fist, burnt in coal-fired kilns, and mixed in composts or ploughed in by itself. In 1652 white shell marl, i.e. shell lime, was found in Anglesey.[4] At much the same time as in southern Wales, liming made its impact on the West Country. If pools of water formed in meadows, the farmers would soak them up by 'puddening' with a mixture of dung and lime, first piling the compost in the place affected and then spreading it over the rest of the field. Lime, too, had special application to clayey and sandy soils and to fields glutted with sea-sand. Burnt from shelly beach or marble with furze and coal, lime was put on three-crop land at the rate of fifty double Winchester bushels an acre. Marble was also used crude. Norden notes,[5]

'certaine maine rockes of a most hard black flint which the countrey

[1] Ibid. 273; N. Dept, 384–5; Midl. Cos. i, 23–4; S. Dept, 248, 270; W. Engl. ii, 145; Childrey, op. cit. 157; Lennard, art. cit. 44; Houghton, Coll. no 7, June 15, 1682, p. 95; Morton, op. cit. 481; Burton, op. cit. 2; Platte, op. cit. bk ii, 21; Merrick, op. cit. 11; Lisle, op. cit. 3, 27, 30–1; Blith, op. cit. 132; Plot, op. cit. 341; Norden, op. cit. 203; Hardy, op. cit. 222; Salt Lib. D. 1734/4/1/6; Leics. R.O., A/d invs. 1636: 105; 1709: 44; 18th-cent.: Geo. Fisher 1726 Barrow-on-Soar; Bodl. Aubrey 2, f. 85; Hearne's diaries 159, p. [255]; B.M., Harl. 7180; Shak. Bpl. W.deB. 1652B, Heath to Laxton 8 July 1661.

[2] Blome, op. cit. 248; Marshall, Yks. i, 333.

[3] Laurence, op. cit. 80–1; Marshall, N. Dept, 70, 150; Hughes, N. Country Life: N.E. 1700–50, 135, 138.

[4] Emery, art. cit. 399; Merrick, op. cit. 11, 120; Rowlands, op. cit. xxv–vii, 167–9; Owen, op. cit. pt i, 64–6, 68, 70–1; T. Churchyard, Worthines of Wales 1776, pp. 51–2.

[5] Lennard, art. cit. 33; Westcote, loc. cit.; Borlase, op. cit. 85; Childrey, op. cit. 5; Marshall, S. Dept, 517; W. Engl. i, 79, 156–7; ii, 8, 58; Fuller op. cit. i, 301; Soms. R.O., D.D./W.O., svy Nettlecombe &c. 1619, f. 36; Bodl. Aubrey 2, f. 153; B.M., Harl. 5827, ff. 7v.–8; Norden, op. cit. 226 (2nd occ.).

husbandmen beate out with extreme toyle and with intollerable diffi-
cultie beate it as small as a mans fist and cast it on their land, which
doth yeerely cast a kinde of scale, which fats the earth so as it needes no
other helpe in a douzen yeares'.

Temporary tillage plots in the Sandlings were dressed with lime burnt
from shingle,[1] and from about 1718 with the newly discovered red crag,
composed of fossilized molluscs in their earthy beds, which was in the
nature of instant lime.[2] Hardly known before 1595, liming was undertaken in the Chalk Country in the next century,[3] as it also was in the
Chiltern Country. For the flinty clay loams, however, chalk was better
than lime. The great extent of such soils here, and the smaller one in the
Chalk Country, were rendered dark and fertile by assiduous chalking.[4]
In the Salting Country, marshlands were usually dressed with chalk
rubble before being ploughed from grass, and the upland clays were
chalked every score years, so being transformed into rich, mellow, clay
loams. Chalk was brought by sea and road from the North Downs and
ploughed in with the turf at the rate of six wagon loads an acre.[5] The
farmers of the Vales of Hereford, too, now made much greater use of
lime, at first chiefly on heavy soils, and then, from about 1647, more
particularly on the ryelands, where it produced mighty crops of rye,
enabled wheat to be grown, improved the pastures, and worsened,
perceptibly, the quality of Ryeland wool.[6] Patently, they were highly
conspicuous threads that Blith drew together in forming his conclusion
that whole countries formerly barren were now improved for corn-
growing by the application of lime.[7]

Thus extraneous fertilizers contributed much to the agricultural
revolution, and raised the rental value of farm land, according to their
potency and endurance succinctly expressed in the adage, 'A man doth
sande for himself, lyme for his sonne, and marle for his grandechild.'[8]

[1] Ibid. 225 (2nd occ.).

[2] Gent's. Mag. xxxiv, 233; Rider-Haggard, op. cit. ii, 426–7; Burrell, op. cit. 17,
70–3; Kirby, op. cit. 77; R. Pickering, 'On Manuring Land w. Fossil Shells', Phil.
Trans. ix, 82.

[3] Aubrey, Nat. Hist. Wilts. 105; Bodl. Aubrey 2, ff. 85, 153; Lisle, op. cit. 30, 32.

[4] Ibid. 26–7; Norden, op. cit. 225 (2nd occ.); Walker, op. cit. 31; Blith, op. cit.
144, 151; Atwell, op. cit. 107; Plot, Oxon. 243; Kalm, op. cit. 152; Herts. R.O.,
G'bury x.B. 3a, 4 Oct. 38 Eliz.; Hants. R.O., 5 M. 50/2531; T. Davis, op. cit. 56;
Marshall, S. Dept, 15–16, 306.

[5] Ibid. 158–60, 176–7; Lisle, op. cit. 26, 86; Defoe, op. cit. i, 99–100; Emmison,
art. cit. 7; & v. Burrell, op. cit. 10.

[6] Bodl. Aubrey 2, ff. 149, 152–3; B'ham Lib. Winnington 45; Laurence, op. cit.
67; Mortimer, op. cit. 58; Lennard, art. cit. 33; Beale, op. cit. 53; W. H. Howse,
'Harley Misc.', Trans. Woolhope Nats.' Fd Club xxxv, 302, 305.

[7] Op. cit. 132–3.

[8] Owen, op. cit. pt i, 75.

CHAPTER VI

FLOATING THE WATERMEADOWS

GRASS hay came formerly from two main sources, from dry or upland meadows, and from bottom, wet or water meadows. As Norden says:

'There are two sorts of meddowes, low and moist, and upland and dry meddowes; of these kinds the low is commonly the best, because they are aptest to receive these falling and swelling waters, which for the most part brings fatnesse with it; and besides it moisteneth the ground and makes the grass to grow cheerefully. . . . The upland meddowes have but the name of meddowes; for indeede they are but the best pasture grounds laid for hay.'

These wet and dry meadows, however, had different qualities, for as Harrison observes:

'Our medowes are either bottomes . . . or else land meade . . . The first of them are yearelie and often overflowen . . . The others are seldom or never overflowen and that is the cause wherefore their grasse is shorter than that of the bottomes, and yet it is farre more fine, wholesome and batable, sith the haie of our low medowes is not onlie full of sandie cinder, which breedeth sundrie diseases in our cattell, but also more rowtie, foggie and full of flags, and therefore is not so profitable for stover and forrage as the higher meads be.'

Nevertheless, bottoms gave about three times as much hay an acre as dry meadows. Therefore, every incentive existed to extend the area of wet meadow, by baying up and forcing the stream into trenches to irrigate the grass; and if need be a Persian wheel could induce the necessary flow. According to Fitzherbert:

'Another maner of mendying of medowes is, yf there by any runnynge water or lande flodde, that may be set or brought to ronne over the

medowes, from the tyme that they are mowen unto the begynninge of
Maye, and they wyll be moche the better, and it shall kyll, drowne and
dryve away the moldye-warpes and fyll up the lowe places with landes
and make the ground evyn and good to mowe. All maner of waters be
good, so that they stande not styl upon the grounde; but specyally that
water that cometh out of a towne from every mannes myddyng or
dunghyll is best and wyll make the medowes most rankest. And fro the
begynnynge of Maye tyll the medowes be mowen and the hay gotten in,
the waters wolde be let by and ronne another way for dyvers con-
sideracyons.'

Norden says:

'I perswade men to make meanes, where it may be done, to induce out
of streets, lands, wayes and ditches all the water that by some extra-
ordinarie raine passeth through them into their grounds, by making
some little dam or barre to draw them into their grounds; for the matter
which this water bringeth with it is commonly so rich and fat as it
yeeldeth a marvailous refection to all the grounds high or low into which
it may be brought.'

Winter flooding did only good and even remedied bogs, but if the water
stayed on the ground too long the grass would be killed, so 'there must
be some meanes used for evacuation' and the drains had to be scoured
to maintain a current of water. Folkingham agrees that 'land-flouds,
fatte rivers and gulfs of water participating of a slimie and muddy substance induced and brought into the meddowes and pastures in the
spring by draines, dams, inversions from towne ditches, sewers, wayes,
streetes, tilthes, do very much comfort and revive them'.[1] Thus the
surveyors expose the whole art of watering meadows and grasslands
in the sixteenth and seventeenth centuries and show how widespread the
practice was.[2]

[1] Norden, op. cit. 199 sqq., 205–6; Folkingham, op. cit. 24, 33; Worlidge, op. cit.
17–18; Fitzherbert, *Surveyinge*, f. 43v.; W. Harrison, *Descron Engl.* ed. F. J. Furnivall
1877, supp. 132–3; B.M., Sloane 3815, f. 97 (p. 218).

[2] Lisle, op. cit. 262; Aubrey, *Wilts. Topog. Colls.* 55; Marshall, *W. Dept*, 403;
H. U. M. Lyte, *Hist. Dunster* 1909, pp. 315, 317, 435; C. O. Moreton, *Waddesdon &
Over Winchendon* 1929, p. 132; Harland, op. cit. 199, 230; Phillimore & Fry, op. cit.
ii, 135; Baigent, op. cit. 225, 254; Fussell, op. cit. 37; 'Humberstone's Svy', *Tks.
Archaeol. Jnl* xvii, 151; 'Chanc. Proc. temp. Eliz.', *Colls. Hist. Staffs.* 1926, pp. 67–8;
B.M., Lans. vol. 59 no 36, f. 78; Northants. R.O., F.(M.) Misc. Vol. 433, Stamford;
Mont. Northants. 7/66/4 Ct files Weekley 20 May 6 Eliz., 27 Oct. 7 Eliz.; Aynho Ct
R. 20 Oct. 1 Jas II; Deene ho. Brudenell E. vi. 22; Leics. R.O., D.E. 53/434; D.E. 10,
Ct of svy Beaumanor 1656; Herts. R.O., G'bury ii. D. 2; Beds. R.O., A.D. 1060,
partic. Mr Dudley's lands Turvey May 1660; P.R.O., R.&S. G.S. 20/16, f. 1; D.L.,
Ct R. 80/1101, 7 Oct. 6 Eliz.; Exch. L.R., M.B. 221, ff. 270, 274, 276; 222, f. 293.

Watering was seen at its best in the West Country and the Vale of Taunton Deane. The vale's bottom meadows were renowned for their excellence and stood in little need of artifice, but the sides of the hills that ringed it were highly eligible. West Country meads were generally good—Crediton Lord Meadow was one of the best in England—and gave a first bite as early as February; but were naturally severely restricted in extent, and in all but the narrowest valleys were usually watered by art. The gentler hillsides might also be irrigated. Artificial rills and leats, formed by taking channels off dammed streams, were led along the contours, to supply mill-ponds, watering pools and farmsteads, and then to convey to the highest point of the grassland the waters, perhaps now deliberately enriched with farmyard manure, that were caused to spill over their banks down the slopes. Such leat-grounds or 'waterleats' were watered from the hatch intermittingly throughout the winter, depastured by sheep couples or other stock, and later put up for hay. Although less valuable than valley meadows, leat-grounds were immensely superior to dry pasture, as may be seen from the numerous enclosed 'waterleates' or 'waterlands' at Wellington.[1] Similar watering was practised in the Vales of Hereford, for in a survey of Eyton a marginal entry concerning a common pasture reads: 'Memorandum that this oxepasture of Somergilles may be overflowen in the winter in time of grete floods by letteng in the flodd in iij or iiij places above the bridge and owt of the pasture next above, soe the renes may be filled and the pasture yerely amended, as it was in Januarie anno 1582'.[2] This kind of watering was undertaken too by Robert Loder at Harwell in the Chalk Country,[3] and in Pallavicino's manor of Babraham in the Chiltern Country.[4]

Thence it was no great step to the new development of 'floating upwards', or drowning, which was effected by making a dam and floodgates across the river where it flowed out of the mead. By this means the water could be penned up and forced back over the meadow. The famous Orcheston meadow was described as:

[1] Ibid. 202, ff. 274, 283, 285; 255, f. 207; A.O., Parl. Svys Devon 6a, ff. 19, 29; Marshall, *W. Engl.* i, 30, 204, 206–8, 299–300, 305; ii, 269, 308 sqq.; *S. Dept*, 535; *S. Cos.* ii, 332; Lyte, op. cit. 315, 317, 435; Lennard, art. cit. 45; Billingsley, op. cit. (1798) 264–5; Norden, op. cit. 199–201, 205; R. Fraser, *Gen. View Ag. Co. Corn.* 1794, p. 44; *id. Devon* 1794, p. 37; C. Vancouver, *id.* 1808, p. 314; Westcote, op. cit. 56; Soms. R.O., D.D./C.N., Ct Bk Jn Francis 1573–87, pp. 230–1, 268; D.D./N.N.F., Ct R. W. Bagborough 31 Sept. 10 Eliz.; D.D./W.O., svy Farway 1609; svy Farway, Seaton, Sherford & Whitewell 1682; svy Nettlecombe, Rowden & Woodadvent 1619, ff. 2–3, 6, 9, 10, 36v.; Exeter Lib. M.B. 8d. Ld Dynham's Svy Bk 1566, f. 35; Devon R.O., Arlington Parsonage terrier 1679; B.M., Add. 21608, f. 192; Harl. 5827, f. 8.
[2] Ibid. 7369, f. 22v.
[3] Fussell, op. cit. 14, 16, 89, 194; T. Davis, op. cit. 30.
[4] O.S., Normal Nat. Grid Ref. 552250; W. Smith, *Obs. on Water-meadows* 1806, pp. 116–17; Gooch, op. cit. 258–9; Marshall, *Midl. Dept*, 633–4; *Midl. Cos.* ii, 57–9.

'one continuous pool of stagnant water. Not on the scientific principle of circulation; but on the more simple and natural one of flooding; agreeable to the obsolete practice of floating upwards: a practice which, it is highly probably, it was once prevalent in this part of the island. The term "drowning", which is now inaptly applied to the modern practice, strongly corroborates this suggestion'.

'Floating upwards' tended to produce an elephantine strain of rough-stalked meadow grass, so sweet that pigs ate it with relish and so strong it had be to cut with a pea-hook.[1] Here in the Chalk Country, 'floating upwards' was perhaps practised in favourable situations from about 1560, when Amesbury Priory Farm included flood hatches, where was no water-mill, but a field suggestively named 'Water Meade'. The Avon is here so serpentine that not much art would have been needed either to flood the meadows or to draw off the water.[2] At Statfold, in the Midland Plain, some meadows were 'floated upwards', and possibly in the extreme south-east of the Cotswold Country;[3] but the system well suited only fairly level alluvial river valleys.

A parallel, and infinitely more important development was floating properly so-called, as introduced in the Vales of Hereford. Rowland Vaughan of New Court and White House, the inventor and innovator, described his works in a book dictated in old age in 1604 and published in 1610. His chance references to a court of Ward's suit that 'bredd more white haires in my head in one yeare than all my wetshod water-workes in sixteene' and to cleaning out his 'trench-royal' in 1601 show his innovation could not have been started later than 1589.[4] Vaughan floated meadows near Peterchurch, Vowchurch, New Court and White House. His 'trench-royal' or master-carriage began at a weir on Trenant Brook and ran through Poston Court, Turnastone Court and Chanstone Court farms, floating hundreds of acres along two miles of the Golden Valley. By 1610 'hee that doth drowne is a good husband' was proverbial in the vales.[5] The 'communi prati vocati le Flott' at Kimbolton, recorded in 1608, was apparently a floated meadow.[6] By 1657 the system was normal amongst gentlemen farmers and cultivating

[1] Ibid. 57–8; *S. Cos.* ii, 342–3 (quot.); Davis, op. cit. 30–1; Norden, op. cit. 199, 205–6; Worlidge, op. cit. 29; Aubrey, *Nat. Hist. Wilts.* 51; J. E. Jackson, 'V. Warminster', *Wilts. Mag.* xvii, 301–2; Folkingham, op. cit. 27.

[2] Ibid.; Wilts R.O., acc. 283, Lib. sup. Amisburie, f. 18; Smith, op. cit. 20.

[3] Pitt, *Northants.* 192–3; *Leics.* 38, 202; Lowe, op. cit. 102; Farey, op. cit. ii, 468 sqq., 477–80; Wedge, *War.* 16; Marshall, *Midl. Cos.* i, 287–8; ii, 57–60, 94, 107; inf. 257.

[4] R. Vaughan, *Most approved & long experienced Water-workes* 1610; *His Booke*, xiii sqq., xviii, 126.

[5] Ibid. xiii, 141, 144.

[6] P.R.O., Exch. L.R., M.B. 217, f. 317.

landowners. Floated meadows had been constructed the length of the Golden Valley, in thousands of acres bordering the river Arrow, beside the Teme near Tenbury, and along the Lugg for some twenty-five miles before it joined the Wye. This river's flow was too great, but floating spread to smaller streams in all the vales.[1]

The floating was of the catchwork type, which suited hillsides, not alluvial valleys, and carried the waters by a feeder, topping, or braving trench to the highest level of the whole work. A weir or sluice was placed at, or slightly above, the level of the banks to be floated, and hence the water was carried along the contour of the hill, down whose slope it was then passed, by way of a descending array of gutters. A headlong flow downwards was prevented by 'stanks' or dams in the gutters, along which the water was forced until it spilled over the gutters' lips through a series of small outlets and was thus evenly distributed over the whole hillside. Between one gutter and the next, the water passed over the grass as a moving sheet or film about 1 inch deep, depositing sediment amongst the grass roots, stalks, tillers and blades. When the water had passed through the catchwork and was now running clear, it was returned to the stream by an 'everlasting trench' or bottom drain. In summer, clear water was briefly passed over the meadow solely to encourage grass for hay. Sandy ground could absorb much more water, but a cold soil needed to be floated only once in May and then again two or three days before mowing. Winter floating was only intermittent. True, some streams, like the Arrow, had their sources amidst calcareous or siliceous hills, but strong solutions were not generally to be expected. Consequently, the floater's main reliance was on the muddiness of the waters after heavy rains and on floods from streams that washed along with them the rich moulds of ditches and fields. The floodgates were opened only when a flush of sediment-bearing water occurred, and this was played over the meadows at controlled points, which were varied from day to day, until the water ran clear and was allowed to resume its natural course. In the summer, the meadow gave one or two hay crops, but in spring was depastured by sheep, and even more by cattle. At the beginning of March, it was left a few days to dry off and kept as dry

'as a child under the hands of a dainty nurce: that the continuance of cold water in the body of your ground in the spring breed neither rush, boult nor spiery grasse; but grasse much more profitable, thick, long, and fine, voyde of all mosse, hard-heads, cowslips or any weede whatsoever'.

[1] Hereford Lib. Local: dr. 16 no 480, p. 3; Gaut, op. cit. 123–4; Fox, *Mon.* 16; Hassall, *Mon.* 76; A. Yarranton, *Improvemt Improved* 1663, pref.; Beale, op. cit. 37–8; T. S. Willan, *R. Navig. in Engl. 1600–1750* 1936, p. 45; Marshall, *W. Dept*, 288.

The meadow could then be grazed until put up for hay.[1]

Not only old meadow and pasture was floated in this way. Arable was converted to rich meadow, raising its annual value six, eight or tenfold. A barren sandy rabbit-warren could be made into the best meadow. Old meads newly floated trebled their value. Vaughan reckoned his demesne land grew seven or eightfold in value after an expenditure of £2,000, and that after four years of floating his capital outlay had been returned between four and sixfold. Beale reported the improvement by floating to be eightfold, in terms of rents paid, and described the innovation as the metamorphosis of wildernesses.[2] Increased production, profits and rents resulted from an invention that gave not only almost unlimited hay, but also an early bite in March, when fodder was scarce and other grass unready.

It now needed only to graft the techniques perfected in catchwork floating to those evolved in 'floating upwards', to create the ridge-and-furrow system of floating for use in alluvial valleys. Vaughan had recommended his invention to the Earl of Pembroke, and it is possibly more than coincidence that led to ridge-and-furrow floating being early recorded on the Herbert estates in the Chalk Country.

Certainly this new system of floating flowing meadows, as they were called, was designed expressly for the Chalk Country, just as the catchwork one was for the Vales of Hereford, and each was the chief improvement in its own country. Before the innovation of flowing meadows the problem of providing winter fodder remained a difficult one in the Chalk Country, and sheep stocks, and hence the arable acreage and yields, were consequently restricted. Spring grass came fully a month later than in the neighbouring plain and vale countries, and the meadowland could not give enough hay to over-winter as many sheep as the arable could utilize. Wether lambs had to be sold off in autumn, ewe lambs often, and horses and cattle partly, wintered in the Cheese, Butter and other nearby countries, and hay imported thence.[3]

The home sources of hay were wet meadows beside the rivers, streams and bournes; and upland ones. These latter were the richest pieces of downland, mown in alternate years and therefore more accurately described as 'meadow or pasture'.[4] Around 1600, the increasing need to

[1] Ibid.; Beale, op. cit. 52–3; Claridge, op. cit. 36; T. Wright, *Frmn & Managemt Floated Meadows* 1808, opp. 188 sqq.; Vaughan, op. cit. 74, 95 sqq., 106–7, 114–17, 127, 135, 137.

[2] Ibid. xiii, 122; Beale, op. cit. 38; Gaut, op. cit. 123.

[3] Lisle, op. cit. 306, 338; Davis, op. cit. 17; Bennett, art. cit. 35–8; Wilton ho. Ct Bk Var. Pars. 1633–4, f. 6; Wilts. R.O., Dioc. Reg. Sarum, invs. Jn Palmer 1637 Calne, Wm Coward 1596 & Eliz. Goddard 1564 Sedgehill; P.R.O., St. Ch. Eliz. A.11/8; A.34/10; Bristol Univ. Lib. Shrewton 37, f. 2v.; Straton, op. cit. ii, 440–1.

[4] Ibid. i, 34; Norden, op. cit. 199–203; Harrison, loc. cit.; 'Soc.'s MSS.: Chiseldon

distinguish upland from bottom meadows led to special designations such as 'drie grounde', 'dry meadow', 'dry close', 'drye hurst' and 'drye pasture grounde'.[1] But the greatest innovations were made in the bottom meadows, most of which had been flooded naturally in the winter months, and the rest artificially watered or 'floated upwards'.[2] By this last system the land was flooded, with this disadvantage, that were the water retained too long, the grass was spoilt, and even when the floodgates were opened to let the stream by, some standing water might still be left, unless drains were made to convey it away. This, it may be surmised, helped prepare the way for floated flowing meadows.[3]

From the seventeenth to the nineteenth century, the floated watermeadow, the crowning glory of agricultural technique, was an integral part of Chalk Country farming. The overwhelming majority of wet meadows, both in common and in severalty, were floated, almost all the rivers being both calcareous and small enough for the purpose. Some catchwork meadows were floated along the chalk escarpment; but the immense majority were of the ridge-and-furrow variety.[4]

The floated flowing water-meadow[5] was a 'hot-bed for grass'. April—the month of 'interregnum' between hay and grass—was the crucial period of the farmer's year. His hay was spent and the grass not ready for feeding. The livestock he was able to carry through the year depended, therefore, on the amount of feed and fodder in April. Moreover, lambing was impossible until spring grass was available to the couples, and rams had consequently to be put to the ewes at a time that would ensure they did not yean before their keep was ready. The two great functions of the floated water-meadow were to produce an abundance of grass in April and provide hay to last right through until then.

A single large hatch was constructed to dam the river where it

& Draycot', *Wilts.Mag.* xxxi, 175–6; Wilts. R.O., Savernake: Svy Chisbury 44 Eliz. f. 2; Svy Collingbourne Kingston 1595, f. 50; P.R.O., D.L. M.B. 108, f. 55v.; Bodl. Aubrey 2, f. 115; Wilton ho. Svys Manors 1631 i, Foffonnt f. 9(11).

[1] Ibid. ii, Netherhampton; Svy Flambston 1631; P.R.O., Wds, Feodaries' Svys Wilts. unsorted bdl. Baskervile confession 19 Jas; cert. improved val. Wm Noyse 1618; B.M., Add. 28529, ff. 143 (132), 164 (155)v.; Bodington, art. cit. xl, 263, 267, 270; Kitchin, op. cit. 179, 181.

[2] Sup. 253–4.

[3] Norden, op. cit. 205–6; Davis, op. cit. 30–1; Marshall, *S. Cos.* ii, 342–3.

[4] Ibid. 331; *S. Dept,* 49, 77, 243, 246, 292–3, 344–5, 467; Davis, op. cit. frontis.; Pearce, op. cit. 51; Mavor, op. cit. 371; Young, *Suss.* 43–5; Vancouver, *Hants.* 265, 268 sqq.; Claridge, op. cit. 34–6; Driver, op. cit. 19.

[5] Foll. descron based on Blith, op. cit. 16 sqq.; Claridge, loc. cit.; Marshall, *W. Dept,* 441–2; *S. Cos.* ii, 331 sqq.; Smith, op. cit. 70 sqq.; G. Boswell, *Treatise on Watering Meadows* 1801, pp. 34 sqq.; J. Browne, *Treatise on Irrigation* 1817; Wright, op. cit.; *A/c Advantages & Method Watering Meadows* 1789, v–vii; Vancouver, loc. cit.; Davis, op. cit. 30 sqq.

entered the mead and to master its water. When allowed through the hatch, the water passed along a main carrier or stem across the meadow, and then down a series of minor carriers branching out along the crowns of ridges that intersected the 'pitch of work' at regular intervals. Between each pair of ridges and the carriers that lay upon them like canals upon an embankment, was a drain or drawing furrow, which took off and conducted the water into a main drain at the lower end of the meadow and parallel to the stem. This main collected the outflow of all the furrows and then rejoined the river below the pitch of work. In the main carrier, sluices obstructed the flow sufficiently to direct it into the branch carriers, where smaller sluices or stops slowed it down, if necessary, to ensure the water trickled over the carrier's lips to pass as a moving sheet over the grass. Thus the whole was covered with a 'regular disposition of the water-carriages and water-drains, which, in a well laid-out meadow, bring on and carry off water as systematically as the arteries and veins do the blood in the human body'.[1]

The layout of a pitch depended on the lie of the land and on whether the meadows were common or in severalty. Different designs were devised for all circumstances; but whatever the one adopted, great capital expenditure was inevitable. The whole pitch had to be levelled and prepared under an expert 'floater' or 'waterman', the land twice gathered into high ridge and sunken furrow, an immense length of works dug, all the carriers and furrow drains walled with boards, hatches and sluices built of iron and timber, and, finally, either grass sown, or the original turf removed, replaced and rammed.[2] Estimates of cost necessarily varied with time and place, but flowing meadows were considerably more expensive than catchwork ones, and no seventeenth century estimate fell much below 5s an acre.[3] In 1632 the Wylye farmers who supplied all materials and unskilled labour, paid the floater 14s an acre merely for his fee and assistants' wages.[4] Maintenance costs were not extremely heavy, however, for the works had only to be scoured and repaired annually. The return on this investment was great, sometimes immense. Estimates of improved rental values arising from floating varied according to circumstances, but the range lay between three and sixtyfold increases.[5]

The effect of precipitation upon the height of the water-table in the Chalk Country was to cause a marked increase in the flow of rivers and bournes in late autumn and early spring. Turbulent floods bore down

[1] Ibid. 31.

[2] Blith, op. cit. 29–30.

[3] Ibid. 41; Vaughan, op. cit. xiii; Wright, *Floated Meadows*, 89; Boswell, op. cit. 118; Davis, op. cit. 34; Marshall, op. cit. ii, 335–6.

[4] Wilton ho. box 25 Ct R. Var. Manors 1632, Wylye 10 Sept. 1632, m. 4.

[5] Blith, loc. cit.; Wright, *Watering Meadows*, 1; Bodl. Aubrey 2, f. 86; Hants. R.O., 5 M 50/2558.

with them much chalky sediment, and the higher the degree of sus-
pension or solution in the water, particularly if calcareous, the greater
its value for floating. Even if, as often, apparently clear, the water was
charged with a chalky solution of the highest nutritive value. This was
by no means the only advantage, for the flowing water provided a
blanket for the grass, protecting it from frosts.[1] In all senses, the floated
water-meadow was a hot-bed for grass. When floated, the meadow was
covered by an evenly distributed and continuous sheet of running water
to a depth of about 1 inch. Thus, in addition to the warmth provided,
all the sediment was deposited amongst the stalks, blades, roots, and
tillers.

When the autumn rains had swelled the river, the floater passed it
over the meadow. The water was then 'thick and good', being the first
washing of the banks since spring. This sheet was kept flowing the greater
part of the winter time and as long as ground frosts remained sharp.
But were the water left flowing too long without intermission, harm
resulted; so floating was occasionally interrupted to allow the grass a
breath of air. The danger signal feared by floaters was scum appearing
on the water's surface, for this meant the grass was suffocating. Normally, the forced growth of grass, now 5 or 6 inches high, was ready to
be fed by sheep about the middle of March, long before a first bite was
elsewhere to be had. Then the main hatch was closed and the meadow
left to dry off for a day or two to ensure it was safe for sheep. By the end
of April the sheep would have eaten the meadow off close. The flow of
water would then be resumed for a few days and the meadow put up for
hay, which by June would be ready for mowing, since the grass tended
to be long and stalky and had to be cut young when juicy and leafy.
Excellent hay resulted. A floated mead could be relied upon in all
years to crop about four times as heavily as other meadowland. If still
more hay were needed, a repetition of the same process would produce
a second or even a third crop; the farmer with floated meadows need
never fear a shortage of winter fodder. However, a crop or two sufficed
and most floated meadows were given over to dairy cattle in late summer and early autumn. To reap the fullest advantage from floating it
was necessary to keep a substantial dairy, because the meadows were
unsafe for sheep in early autumn. In September the floated meadows
were made to carry the greatest possible stock of cattle, that the grass
might be eaten off cleanly. Afterwards, in or about the middle of
October, the carriers and drains were righted up, scoured out and repaired where damaged by hooves. The meadows were then ready for
the admission of the highly prized November flood-waters.

Floating provided an early bite for lambs and ewes, whose yeaning
was timed to coincide with the opening of the meadows, of which they

[1] Brentnall, art. cit. 8.

then had exclusive use. The feed of the couples was thus vastly improved and the breeding of early lambs made possible. Grass was hurdled out in portions day by day, creep-hurdles permitting the lambs to feed forward. Since water-meadow grass was often over-moist, some hay was usually provided for the ewes. While the couples were in the water-meadow by day, they were folded on the barley by night. One day's feeding on an acre of floated meadow sufficed the 500 couples needed for an acre of arable. The couples were not allowed on with empty bellies or while dew was still on the grass, so they started the day with a snack else-where and then went on the water-meadows from ten or eleven in the morning until four or five in the afternoon. None but those who have seen this kind of husbandry can appreciate justly the value of the fold of ewes and lambs, coming immediately from a floated water-meadow, with their bellies full of young, quick grass, and how much it could increase the quantity and quality of a crop of barley. The value of such a fold was reckoned equal to a quarter of barley on every ridge. Most of the good barley-lands had the support of floated water-meadows and the two were often in juxtaposition. When in the floated meadows, therefore, the sheep were hardly suffered to drop dung or urine. All the manure was for the arable and as soon as they were full and seen disposed to lie down, the sheep were straightway hurried to the tillage.[1]

Not merely old meadows could be improved by floating, but all types of land within the reach of a main carrier. Marshes were highly eligible and made as good water-meadow as any. Arable, too, was often floated and converted to meadow. Although many indigenous meadow grasses were recommended for seeding down water-meadows and the original turf was often used, the initial variety was not of much consequence, for floating itself induced the most suitable grass to the exclusion of all others. Provided the land were well drained, the nature of the soil was similarly a matter of indifference, for floating continued over a number of years deposited on the meadow fresh soil of the greatest fertility, and this was deepened and improved year by year. This rich soil's luscious grass was not without effect upon the livestock. The milk and early grass feed enjoyed by young stock largely determine their constitutions, and since the floating of water-meadows improved both these, it was accounted one of its greatest benefits that it played a crucial part in increasing the size of the Chalk Country horn sheep. Without the floated water-meadow, the country could never have supported so many sheep of so great a size.[2]

Davis disclaimed any knowledge of the date of its first innovation,

---

[1] Davis, op. cit. 35, 38 sqq.; 60–1; Smith, op. cit. 70; Marshall, S. Dept, 246; Vancouver, op. cit. 275.

[2] Ibid.; Marshall, S. Cos. ii, 412; Davis, op. cit. 23.

but suggested floating had been generally introduced between 1650 and 1750. Worlidge, who published in 1669 and resided in the Chalk Country, described floating as 'one of the most universal and advantagious improvements in England within these few years', and said he had seen the same river used for floating several miles together. He could hardly have expressed himself in such terms unless the floating of flowing water-meadows was already widespread. Aubrey says, more particularly:

'The improvement of watering meadowes began at Wylye about 1635, about which time, I remember, we began to use them at Chalke. Watering of meadowes about Marlborough and so to Hungerford was (I remember) about 1646; and Mr John Bayly of Bishop's Down (near Salisbury) about the same time made his great improvements by watering there by St Thomas Bridge; much about the same time St Nicholas Meade at Salisbury (14 acres) was let for 15 *li.* per annum: now 'tis improved to sixty pounds per annum.'

Clearly Aubrey intends 'watering' to mean floating, as in common parlance once the floating of water-meadows had generally superseded 'floating upwards' and mere irrigation. He also says,

'The watred meadows all along from Marlborough to Hungerford, Ramsbury, and Littlecot, at the later end of April, are yellow with butter flowers. When you come to Twyford the floated meadowes there are all white with little flowers . . . The graziers told me that the yellow meadowes are by much the better, and those white flowers are produc't by a cold hungry water.'

According to Aubrey, then, the floating of water-meadows was first undertaken at Wylye and Chalke about 1635, and near Salisbury and in the Kennet valley about 1646. He was accurate in dating Bishop's denshiring at Martin and the records again corroborate his remarks.[1]

Manorial surveys reflect some activity in the improvement of meadows about 1600. In Netherhampton a copy of court roll taken out in 1627 mentioned a parcel of meadow called 'wett mead'. A copyhold tenement leased in 1592 included an enclosure of 'wett ground' called 'Water Close'. Other copies, of which the earliest was dated 1609, spoke of 'water closes'. By 1632, moreover, the common marsh had been divided among the tenantry and enclosed, as though for some special improvement. Similarly, a Broadchalke copy taken out in 1605 described an enclosure 'called the Wett Mead'; and one of the parcels of Chilmark

[1] Ibid. 30; Worlidge, op. cit. 16–17; Aubrey, loc. cit.; Bodl. Aubrey 2, f. 86.

demesne farm, when leased in 1619, was ten acres of meadow called 'Wett Meade'.[1]

Quarter sessions records suggest floating was being introduced in the second quarter of the seventeenth century. In 1639 the Shalbourne constable presented Richard Clifford, gentleman, for 'raysing up a new hatch in his meadow whereby the water is bayed back', barring the way to church. The same year Richard Constable, a Broad Hinton gentleman, was presented for turning an ancient watercourse to the annoyance of his neighbours. In 1641 the floodgate lately set up in Tidpit common meadow by Henry White, gentleman, and maintained and used by the occupiers of Toyd Farm, was presented as a common hurt, because, it was alleged, the overflowing water gave the sheep 'coathe' or rot. These incidental allusions should be seen in the light of the fact that both Constable and White had certainly floated their meadows at the latest by 1661.[2] Almost certainly, then, the nuisances complained of arose from works entailed in introducing floating, and such damages were always difficult to avoid.[3]

At Dinton and Teffont the meadowland was mostly enclosed by 1631 and measured out by statute acre, suggesting enclosure by agreement. William Baberstoke, who had three copyhold tenements, held, amongst other parcels, 'one close of meadowe called water mead containing three acres'. This description dates from 1616, when the copy was granted. A grant in 1624 of a one-acre 'arrable close converted into meadowe' almost irresistibly suggests floating. This inference is strengthened by the knowledge that the demesne meadows here were floated by about 1650 at the latest, for shortly afterwards the following marginal note was inserted beside the entry of Simon Newe's cottage and two acres of enclosed meadow:[4]

'Memorandum: not to grant any new estate in the premisses unlesse they submitte to the flotting of the demesnes lands gratis, except the charge of flotting the meadow belonging to the premisses, which is improved by the drowning (above the damage) 20s per annum. For the consent of this tenant to drowne and flott the farm meadowes, the farmer was constreined also to give 10 sheeplease in his flockes'.

Aubrey is likely right about the date of introduction of floating in the

---

[1] Wilton ho. Svys Manors 1631 ii, Netherhampton, ff. 2(3), 10(11)–12(13), & pass.; Broad Chalke, f. 9(13); Svys Manors 1632–3, Chilmark & Rudge, f. 3.

[2] B. H. Cunnington, *Recs. Co. Wilts.* 1932, pp. 129, 139–40; Wilts. R.O., Savernake; Mildenhall partic. c. 1650; acc. 212B, B.H. 8; acc. 84, Clayton 6.

[3] Berks. R.O., D./E.Mt M3, m. 7; Wilton ho. box 25, Ct R. Var. Manors 1632, Wylye 10 Sept. 1632, m. 4; Svys Manors 1631 i, Dinton & Teffont, f. 8 (9).

[4] Ibid. ff. 8 (9), 13 (14), 19 (21) & pass.

Chalke demesne meadows, for he himself was the farmer there;[1] and, as has been seen, the survey suggests meadowland improvements were being made thereabouts from 1605 onwards. Striking confirmation of Aubrey's account of the first floating at Wylye is found in the records. The 1631 survey makes no mention of floating, but one entry in the court roll in 1632 is an order for the general floating of all meadows and marshes in the township. An agreement was made between two freeholders, the undertenants of the other freeholders, the customary tenants and other inhabitants of the one party, and John Knight of Stockton of the second, whereby the latter, apparently a professional floater of some experience, undertook to float, manage, and maintain for an initial period, pitches of work in the Marsh, Nettlemead and the Moors. The first party agreed to make and maintain all the timber works, hatches and bays with labour supplied by themselves, to allow Knight and his workmen to dig trenches, conduits and works for the bays wherever he decided, to defray from a common purse all damages arising, and to pay Knight 14s for every acre floated and 2s an acre annually for maintenance. Although some of them were enclosed, common management was, not unusually, instituted for all the meadows, for floating entailed close co-operation in utilizing the water. This agreement shows floating was well understood in the district, that specialist engineers had already been called into existence, and that farmers, tenants, and manorial lord (the Earl of Pembroke and Montgomery) were all aware of the innovation's advantages. This means in turn that the farmers and estate officers had almost certainly seen floating successfully practised elsewhere in the vicinity. That the floating at Wylye was carried out according to intention is shown by an order for righting up in September 1633;[2] and a similar order at Stanton Bernard in 1634 suggests floating was being practised there too.[3]

From about 1629, indeed, evidence of floating in numerous places becomes precise and plentiful. In Puddletown court baron on October 15th that year, with the lord, Henry Hastings, himself present, after 'a great debate beinge theare had and questions moved by some of the tenants about wateringe and improvinge theire groundes', it was ordered with the full consent and agreement of the court that Mr Richard Russell should be allowed to water and improve Broadmoor and make watercourses as 'begann, and in parte wrought by the said Mr Russell in the last springe and in part before', and to make his trench, bays, dams and sluices as had then been proposed, in agreement and co-operation with his neighbour Mr Woolfries. On November 10, 1636, in the hundred

[1] Ibid. Broad Chalke, f. 3 (7) addendum; sup. 261.
[2] Wilton ho. Svys Manors 1631 ii, Wylye; box 25, Ct R. Var Manors 1632, Wylye 10 Sept. 1632, m. 4; Ct Bk Var. Pars. 1633–4, f. 2.
[3] Ibid. f. 41.

court, a further agreement provided for more and similar floating to be undertaken by Russell and others in Broadmoor. When John Aylinge concluded an agreement for the lease of Tyle House Farm in West Harting in 1632, one of the articles bound the lessee 'to improve his rent, att the judgment of two indifferent men, as the land shall be improved by wateringe att the lessors charge'. A neighbouring farmer already had amongst his meadowlands 'one roode flowed' and some other 'land flowed'.[1] Between 1634 and 1639 Mr Ayliffe floated Imber farm meadows. Circumstantial evidence of at least watering or 'floating upwards' at Netherhampton from about 1592 has been shown above; and direct evidence proves meadows were floated there some time before 1651, when the manor court ordered righting up to be performed by Michaelmas. Another ordinance in the same court imposes pains and penalties on 'whosoever shall refuse or neglect to pay his ratable proporcion for the drowning and watering the meadow groundes . . . or shall at any time hereafter refuse to be ordered and ruled by the drowner or floter for the tyme being in all things relating to that worke'. The agreement made in 1635 for floating the common meadow in Winfrith Newburgh had been implemented by 1658 at the latest. In the nearby townships of Moreton and Bovington, the demesne meadows were floated before 1649.[2] In 1654 it was ordered and agreed at Colthrop that the demesne farmer might water Aldershot grounds if he compensated any damages inflicted on other tenants. An estate agent's particular of Mildenhall, drawn up just after 1650, confirms Aubrey's relation of the floated meadows in that district. In Upper Farm ten acres of 'meadow watred' were valued at £25 a year; Lower Farm had fifteen acres of 'watred meadow' and sixteen of dry; and in the Manor Farm Mr Richard Constable (probably the self-same man who was in quarter sessions for turning a water-course), held a copyhold farm of £90 annual value that included eleven acres of dry and eleven 'of watred meadow'.[3] In Damerham, near to where Henry White's floodgate was complained of as a nuisance, a 1661 particular refers to 'Battingtons, a meadowe taken out of farmes, improved by water'.[4]

[1] B.M., Add. 28529, ff. 89 (74), 157 (145) v., 204 (194); Dors. R.O., D. 39/H2, ff. 60, 189.

[2] Ibid. D. 29/E65 arts. agrt 27 Mar. 1683, 7 Oct. 1649, map. c. 1700; D. 10/E103, MSS. endorsed 'This note subscribed by the tenants of Winfryth 1635' & 'Agreement for Watering Winfrith Medow'; & v. 'Orders 1665', Agrt 4 Sept. 1678 & all others in 1st batch E103 save that endorsed 'Rate for sheepe made 1598 Winfryth'; Devizes Mus. Papers rel. to prosecution Th. Chambers/Imber; Wilton ho. Papers rel. to Var. Manors: copies of svys &c.:—Netherhampton Ct R. 27 Mar. 1651; Ct R. 1666–89, Netherhampton 31 Dec. 1666; sup. 261.

[3] Berks. R.O., D./E.Mt M3, m. 7; Wilts. R.O., Savernake: Mildenhall partic. c. 1650.

[4] Ibid. acc. 84, Clayton 6.

About the same date a Downton Newcourt particular values a piece 'of medowe, drowned by art, 70 acres, att 30s the acre'.[1] In 1663 the overflowing of water penned up for use on Burghfield Sheffield meadows was adjudged no nuisance by the court baron.[2] In 1664–9 floated watermeadows were as well established in the south-west of the Chalk Country as in the south-east.[3] Before 1678 further meadows had been floated at Winfrith.[4] In 1681 a lease of White's Farm in Boxford contained a covenant that the water-meadows be properly maintained and their produce retained on the farm. By this date, and probably before, several meadows were floated here, including White Mead and Miller's Plot. By 1711 at the latest, Boxford Common meadows were being floated. The impediments to floating presented by the established rights of millers, had already been partially overcome in this village. By his lease terms the miller was obliged to let the water flow by, for the exclusive use of floaters, from the beginning of December until that of August, on Thursdays from midnight until 4 p.m. and from 11 a.m. every Saturday until 8 a.m. on Mondays. Thus a compromise was reached between mill and farm.[5] In 1694 some 400 acres of floated flowing meadows were constructed at Britford Lower Farm, apparently to supplement older works made about 1670.[6] About 1705–9 the Dairy Meads in Englefield were newly floated.[7] Between 1696 and 1709 the existing floated meadows at Houghton were considerably extended.[8] When How Benham was enclosed, the agreement of 1713 allocated to its various parties their responsibilities in maintaining old floated meadows, and arranged for a new hatch on the Kennet for floating the common marsh. This was to be divided and allotted, but the floating was to be a common work financed by a rate levied on the occupiers. Floating was similarly introduced in the Dry Grounds; and in 1734 further pitches of work were under consideration. By a similar agreement, in what was the standard pattern for the common floating of meadows in severalty, it was ordered in Burcombe and Ugford manor court in 1716, that Mathew Pitt esquire might set up a pair of hatches for floating three of his own meadows and several others belonging to four different tenants, who were to allow him to make works wherever convenient in their own grounds as well as in his. All the meadows were then to be

[1] Ibid. 8.

[2] Berks. R.O., D./E.Sw M20, art. 13.

[3] Lennard, art. cit. 45; Naish, op. cit. 97–8; Hants. R.O., 5M50/2531, 2557–8, 2561; & v. 5M53/748.

[4] Dors. R.O., D.10/E103, Agrt 4 Sept. 1678.

[5] Berks. R.O., D./E.Ah E5/1/3 & T7.

[6] G. Gynn, '1000 Gal. Herd on Water-meadows', *Farmer & Stockbreeder* 1954 lxviii, 70; ex inf. Maj. F. H. T. Jervoise, T.D., D.L., J.P.

[7] Berks. R.O., D./E.By E68.

[8] Hants. R.O., 5M50/2536–8.

floated by arrangement between the five contracting parties. They were to choose and pay a head floater, who was to direct operations and set out stems for them all.[1] In 1728–40 the easterly part of the country, already well furnished with floated meadows, was still finding room for extensions and additions.[2]

In fine, the gestation of ridge-and-furrow floating occupied the period 1600–28, while by 1680 floating was an old-established part of the general plan of management. Then, the statement that 'The meadow-land is water'd by the foot like Canaan and with the turne of a hand'[3] is no less platitudinous than curious. Everything points to the years between 1629 and 1665 as the period when floated meadow construction was at its height. This was when an innovatory technique was generally introduced to revolutionize production itself. The movement continued to run its course in the latter part of the seventeenth century and the early part of the eighteenth, but the accomplishments of this period consisted in the extension and improvement of an established productive process, in the completion of a floated meadow network whose essential pattern had already been determined.

Floating belonged peculiarly to the Vales of Hereford and the Chalk Country, but was practised elsewhere to a limited extent, for instance by Sir Richard Weston.[4] Some ridge-and-furrow meadows were floated in the Chiltern Country. They were to be found towards St Albans, Hatfield and Hertford in the mid-seventeenth century, when their first crop might be worth £5 an acre or five times that of unimproved meadows, and in other parts of the extreme south-east and on the Duke of Bedford's Woburn estates in the eighteenth.[5] Flowing meadows were made, too, in the Poor Soils Country between Fordingbridge and Ringwood.[6] On the south-eastern margins of the Cotswold Country a few meadows were 'floated upwards' or in pale imitation of the Chalk Country style;[7] and in the West Country a small number of leat-grounds were made to resemble catchwork meadows by the addition of gutters, stops and other works.[8] Instances of genuine floating were not altogether rare

[1] Berks. R.O., D./E.Ah E2 & E4/1–4; Wilton ho. Ct R. Manors 1689–1754, box ii, Ct Bk Burcombe & Ugford, pp. 40–1.

[2] Naish, op. cit. 89, 95–8; Willan, op. cit. 28–9.

[3] Brentnall, art. cit. 8, 18–9, 47.

[4] D. McDonald, *Ag. Writers* 1908, p. 67; Speed, op. cit. 35; Hants. R.O., 5M53/748.

[5] Batchelor, op. cit. 484 sqq.; Atwell, op. cit. 87; Walker, op. cit. 23–4; A. Young, *Gen. View Ag. Herts.* 1804, pp. 178–81; & v. Herts. R.O., 19271 Nortonbury 7 Sept. 1609; G'bury ii. D. 2, copy of ct r. 7 Dec. 5 Chas.

[6] Driver, op. cit. 292–3.

[7] Marshall, *W. Dept*, 403, 440–2; Atkyns, op. cit. 21; G. Turner, op. cit. 26–7; Aubrey, *Wilts. Topog. Colls.* 55; Bodl. Aubrey 2, f. 65.

[8] Vancouver, *Devon*, 314–15; R. Smith, 'Some A/c Frmn Hillside Catchmeadows in Exmoor', *Jnl R. Ag. Soc. Engl.* xii.

in the Midland Plain. In the hilly district bordering the west, notably at Dunclent, catchwork floating had been introduced by about 1650 and hundreds of acres of hillsides and barren, sandy coney-warrens transformed into verdant meadows. By 1682 catchwork meadows at Drayton Park were bearing forty loads of hay on thirty-five acres.[1] In the later eighteenth century the acreage of catchwork meadows was still being expanded in the Birmingham and Tamworth district. Further east, too, by this time, floating of one kind or another was being undertaken by many favourably-situated farmers, notably by Paget of Ibstock, Moor of Appleby and Wilkes of Meesham. The most famous exponent here of the ridge-and-furrow method was Robert Bakewell. After spending some time studying Chalk Country practice, he set out a pitch of work at Dishley, diverting a small brook along the farthest boundary of his farm and turning it down a narrow valley into the meadows. The main carrier not only floated about 200 acres, but, since it ended in the ponds near the farmhouse, served to convey turnips from the fields to the sheds, the roots simply being thrown in to be borne along by the current.[2] Thus, while it is true that only two countries ever adopted floating generally, the combined effect of all these scattered floated meadows was far from negligible, and a few of them, as we shall see, made indispensable contributions to livestock improvement.

[1] Plot, *Staffs.* 356–7; Gooder, op. cit. 30; Gaut, op. cit. 123–4; Worcs. R.O., B.A. 494, Dunclent partic. c. 1660.

[2] Marshall, *Midl. Cos.* i, 284–6; *Sheep*, 33–4; Pitt. *Leics.* 32–4, 202 sqq.; & v. sup. 254 n.3.

CHAPTER VII

NEW CROPS

OF the many new crops introduced, tobacco is perhaps the best known. The culture of English tobacco was already well established in the Vale of Evesham by 1619, and continued to flourish, especially in the sandy loams of the middle vale, in despite of the government, until about 1700. In 1627 tobacco was also being grown in similar soils in or near Wootton Bassett, in the Oxford Heights Country.[1] Another new crop was weld (dyer's weed). This was introduced in the Northdown Country, especially in the valley of the Great Stour, about 1610, and not long after in the Norfolk Heathlands, notably in Narford, and in the Chiltern Country. Weld was usually sown under oats or barley, and sometimes, later, together with clover. In its first year, the weld was fed by sheep, and in the second was cropped, for the sake of its yellow dyestuff.[2]

Otherwise the new crops were all intended exclusively for forage and fodder, and largely for winter stockfeed. They fall into two main classes: coles and roots, and clover and grasses.

The first root crop of any significance was the carrot, and this in the Sandlings Country. From 1597 onwards most herbals follow Gerarde in saying 'carrots are sowen in the fieldes' as well as in gardens. It would not be surprising if it were to this country that Gerarde alluded, for it was the sole one in which the field cultivation of carrots might then have been generally undertaken. Norden found it already established there. The hot, sandy soil, he says, is good for carrots, 'a beneficial fruit, as at

[1] (Nicotiana rustica=hyoscyamus luteus—yellow henbane—Eng. tobacco). Gerarde, op. cit. (1597) 284–6; Coles, op. cit. cap. cvii; J. Parkinson, op. cit. 711; Ray, op. cit. i, 715; A. Rive, 'Consumption Tobacco since 1600', *Econ. Hist.* i, 60; Willcox, op. cit. 158–61; MacInnes, op. cit. 76–8, 84, 86–9, 91–2, 103–4, 108, 111 sqq., 117 sqq., 126, 129, 184; *A.P.C.* Jan.–Aug. 1627, pp. 409–10; Fuller, op. cit. i, 546.

[2] Ibid. ii, 113–14; *V.C.H. Ess.* ii, 366; Blith, op. cit. 223–2 (recte 222–3), 224; Worlidge, op. cit. 139; Mortimer, op. cit. 127; Blagrave, op. cit. 234–5, 237; Marshall, *S. Dept,* 393–4; *S. Cos.* ii, 414; *Nfk* ii, 26–7; P.R.O., Chanc. Proc. ser. i Jas I, B.14/17.

Orford, Ipswich and many sea townes in Suffolke: as also inland townes, Berrie, Framingham, and others in some measure, in the same shire, Norwich and many places in Norfolke, Colchester in Essex', and else-where.[1] As he refers to Framingham as being in Suffolk, he must in-tend Framlingham, which lay in the Sandlings Country. Norden clearly regarded this country as the centre of carrot cultivation, both the Great Sandling, which achieved the highest fame for this piece of husbandry,[2] and the lesser ones towards Orford and near Colchester; and soon after 1590 they all took to exporting carrots. Probate in-ventories show carrot husbandry in the Great Sandling, at Nacton in 1633, possibly, and at Sudbourne in 1638, certainly.[3] Its innovation thus belongs to the turn of the sixteenth and seventeenth centuries. The country was peculiarly favourable to carrots. In its deep, sandy soils they could apple out well and throw roots down to the subsoil below the plough-pan. The fields were winter-fallowed and seeds harrowed in about the end of March. During growth, the carrots were hoed two or three times to a depth of about 7 inches. They were then left to stand in the field, all winter if necessary, and pulled when required for provendering horses.[4] About 1670–90 a second great carrot-growing region sprang up in the Vale of Taunton Deane, where cultivation and utilization like those in the Sandlings Country became general in all but the extreme south.[5] Elsewhere carrots never became a crop of the first magnitude, but were somewhat cultivated in the Breckland, about Bury St Edmunds, by 1618, and perhaps in East Norfolk also.[6] By the early eighteenth century farmers had taken up the crop in the few suitably sandy soils in the Chalk Country and the Midland Plain.[7]

It hardly need be said, all the roots and coles, and especially carrots, turnips, and cabbages, were widely grown in kitchen and market-gardens, for the table, in eating varieties, and likewise by farmers as market-garden crops, long before they were taken up, in fodder varie-ties, by farmers in their fields, for the purpose of stockfeed. This may not be realized so readily in the instance of table turnips, as they are less eaten than formerly. Farmers in parts of Wales commonly grew table turnips in market-garden fashion in the sixteenth century. In parts of

[1] Gerarde, op. cit. 872; (1633) 1027; Coles, op. cit. cap. ccli; Parkinson, op. cit. 901–2; Norden, *Survy's. Dial.* 212–3; Salmon, op. cit. 158.

[2] Young, *Sfk*, 42; Rochefoucauld, op. cit. 180–1.

[3] Hull, op. cit. 84 & app. 6; E. Burrell, op. cit. 56; Nfk R.O., Cons. Ct invs. 1633: 287; 1638: 40.

[4] R. Blome, *Gent's. Recreation* 1686 pt ii, 220; Marshall, *E. Dept*, 446, 450.

[5] Soms. R.O., Cons. Ct A/d Taunton invs.:—Wm Batt 1672, Nic. Stodgell 1676 N. Petherton, Pet. Curnelius 1691 Hinton St Geo., Abraham Allen 1730 Alcombe.

[6] Norden, op. cit. 212; Cash, op. cit. 157.

[7] Pitt, *Leics.* 34; Morton, op. cit. 484; Lisle, op. cit. 233; Soms. R.O., Cons. Ct A/d Taunton inv. Meredith Joanes 1693 Merriott.

the Chalk Country, too, such root cultivation was being practised, e.g. at Burbage in 1574. By 1598 parsnips, at least, and by 1636–40, onions, carrots and probably turnips, were being grown here in closes where they alternated with corn and grass. Burbage's brown, sandy loams were excellent for root crops and hand-hoeing, and Aubrey remarked on its fine peas and turnips, which were 'not tough and stringy like other turnips, but cutt like marmalad'. In other words, they were grown for the table, and were, in fact, sold widely for this purpose, principally to Bath. Root crops had not entered farming practice and were grown only in market-garden style.[1] Table turnips also made a good crop to cultivate under hops in hop-gardens, and cottagers were wont to grow them in their hemp-gardens after the hemp was pulled.[2]

In the middle of the seventeenth century, however, there suddenly took place in High Suffolk an agricultural revolution, by the introduction of turnip husbandry, i.e. the field cultivation of fodder turnips in stockfeed varieties.

Some slight hint of later developments was given in the field cultivation of carrots about Framlingham in the early seventeenth century,[3] and by the sowing of carrots and parsnips in Bradwell fields in 1620.[4] Turnips, however, were as yet grown only in hop, hemp, kitchen and market-gardens, and it was still in market-garden fashion that Abraham Baly had, in September 1646, 'rootes, turnupps and cabbadges now growinge uppon the ground' at Oakley.[5] From then till 1661 no probate inventories for High Suffolk are available, but in May of that year Richard Hill, a gentleman farmer of Toft Monks, had 'three great turnip bullocks' and '3 turnipe howes'. In September 1662 a Chedgrave farmer had 'one peece of turnupps' worth £12. That October, Deborah Godfrye, a Weybread widow and farmer of substance, had £2 worth of 'turnups on the ground'. Next month Miles Sinklen, a St Olaves' yeoman, had some 'turnup cowes and 2 bulles' valued at £10 and 'on haystacke by the turnup shed', while 'all the turnups' on his farm were worth £10.[6] The same month, Richard Vynor, a Met-

---

[1] Aubrey, *Nat. Hist. Wilts.* 36; *Wilts. Topog. Colls.* 381; *Essay towards Descron N. Div. Wilts.* 1838, p. 71; Bodl. Aubrey 2, f. 88; Worlidge, op. cit. 42; T. Wentworth, *Off. & Duty Exors* 1641, pp. 61–2; Owen, *Penbs.* pt ii, 366; Taylors *Cussion* pt ii, f. 115; Wilts. R.O., Savernake: Svy Burbages 1574, f. 21; Ct R. Burbage Esturmey 11 Oct. 1598; invs.: Pec Ct Dean Sarum. reg. 12 no 41; Preb. Ct Husborne & Burbage 1/3, 11; 2/19; Gerarde, op. cit. (1597) 872.

[2] Ibid. 178; Marshall, *S. Cos.* i, 140; *E. Dept.* 442–3; Parkinson, *Ruts.* 49; Leics. R.O., D.E. 53/350.

[3] Norden, op. cit. 212.

[4] P.R.O., Chanc. Proc. ser. i Jas I, U. 2/35, compl.

[5] Marshall, loc. cit.; Gerarde, loc. cit.; Nfk R.O., Cons. Ct invs. 1646: 71; 1664: 12; Misc. 1637–68: A./91; 1718–21 stamped: 157.

[6] Ibid. 1662: 68, 27, 29, 97.

tingham gentleman, left 'foure acres of turneps' valued at £4.[1] About 1664 turnip cultivation had reached as far as Wattisfield, where it was introduced by William Swatman, who had just removed from Wrentham, where he had become experienced in the art.[2] In 1665 John Sharpe of East Dereham had 'six acres of turneps upon the ground'. In the summer of 1666, Thomas Wille of Wortham left some young turnips, and that winter John Reade, a yeoman of Barnham Broom, had 'aleven acers of turnips', appraised at £11.[3]

To evaluate this evidence the following should be borne in mind. First, no inventories are available for the period 1647–60. Secondly, the only accessible ones for High Suffolk immediately thereafter are a few accompanying wills proved at Norwich. Of these only about one in ten is of the goods and chattels of a farmer, for the country was one of large farms, and most of the inventories concern farm-labourers, cottagers, weavers, shipwrights, fishermen and others. Of the inventories of High Suffolk farmers, only a handful were made during the turnip season, and the references to turnip hoes and turnip bullocks at Toft Monks are purely fortuitous, for one year's turnips were all consumed and the next year's not sown. High Suffolk farmers' inventories made in the turnip seasons of the early 1660s are very few, but what is significant is that they mostly allude to the cultivation of turnips, and not least in the years 1661 and 1662. Of no less moment are the references to turnip cows, turnip bullocks, turnip hoes and a turnip shed, all integral parts of High Suffolk turnip husbandry, for these show that turnip culture had already passed the experimental stage. It would not have been possible for appraisers to have used these terms of art unless and until they had become part of farming terminology and the things themselves recognized parts of an established husbandry. The valuation of eleven acres of turnips in 1666 makes it possible to estimate the value of an acre of them at about £1 and so shows that the crops being grown in 1661 and 1662 ranged between two and ten acres a farm and were thus comparable with root acreages on farms in this district today. It may be concluded that turnip husbandry was already established when these inventories were made. Furthermore, the three great turnip bullocks at Toft Monks in 1661, must have been turniped on a crop sown in the late summer or autumn of 1660 and hoed with the special implements listed. Hence turnip husbandry was already established in 1660. The next previous reference to turnip culture was in 1646, and then, and before then, only in market-garden fashion.[4] Hence it is certain that

---

[1] Ibid. 1669: 53.

[2] Cullum, op. cit. 251.

[3] Invs.:—W. Sfk R.O., Episc. Commy Ct Bury St Edm's. 1666: 133; Nfk R.O., Cons. Ct 1665: 26; 1666: 55 (pr. 1 Feb.).

[4] Ibid. Cons. & A/d cts invs.

turnip husbandry was both introduced and established in High
Suffolk between 1646 and 1660.

Small areas of land in this country were tithed for turnips between
1650 and 1660 and it has been concluded that their cultivation was in
the experimental stage, simply because these areas were small. However, the small acreages argue not that turnip culture was experimental,
but that High Suffolk turnip husbandry was already established in its
final form, in which turnips were mainly fed to milch kine and only
partly to fatting beasts; for when turnips were fed to cows for milk,
tithe was taken not in the roots, but in dairy produce; and turnips
themselves were only tithed when grown expressly for feeding beef or
mutton. Hence the small tithes argue an established husbandry.[1]

Before 1646 writers mentioned turnips growing in fields only in
market-garden fashion. By 1652 Blith knew they were grown in summer
for winter feed and had heard of turnip husbandry.[2] The first allusion
to High Suffolk turnip husbandry is contained in a little book on new
farming methods published in 1659, namely, Adolphus Speed's *Adam
out of Eden*. Speed makes no particular mention of a specific locality,
but his description cannot have applied to any farming country but High
Suffolk at a time when no turnip husbandry was elsewhere practised.
Milking cows, says he, are sometimes kept in the yard and fed on nothing
but turnips. A gentleman of his acquaintance sows a large field with
turnips every year, builds a shed for feeding cattle in the midst of it and
fats some turnip cattle for the market.[3] Such an authentic description
could hardly have been written unless the practice itself had been
established about three years before publication. Hence it is certain that
the turnip husbandry of High Suffolk was introduced and established as
ordinary practice between 1646 and 1656. By 1695 High Suffolk was
already famous for its vast improvement by employing great acreages in
turnips,[4] and Defoe was well informed when he said of High Suffolk:
'this part of England is also remarkable for being the first where the
feeding and fattening of cattle . . . with turnips was first practised'.[5]

From commonwealth times up to the present day, the specific features
of High Suffolk turnip husbandry have been these. Land that would
otherwise have been bare or buckwheat-fallowed, was ploughed as soon
as the corn was in, i.e. before August, and the turnips sown on a single,
well-mucked earth. Each tillage succession was usually fallowed once

---

[1] Spratt, op. cit. 203, 205; P.R.O., Exch. K.R., Deps. by Commn 1650 Mich. 17;
E. Sfk R.O., S. 1/2/6.7; Doughty, op. cit. 146; R. Green, *Hist., Topog. & Ant. Framlingham & Saxted* 1834, pp. 243–4, 254, 261; R. Loder, *Hist. Framlingham* 1798, pp.
442, 445–6.
[2] Gerarde, loc. cit.; (1633) 232; Coles, op. cit. cap. lxxxviii; Blith, op. cit. 261.
[3] Pp. 23, 28.
[4] Worlidge, op. cit. 42; Camden, op. cit. i, 438.
[5] *Tour* i, 58.

for a whole year, and this season was now sown largely to turnips. During growth the turnips were hand-hoed at intervals. In autumn the first were ready to be fed and some were drawn and stored in the turnip shed for immediate use, while the remainder were left in the ground to be lifted as required. From the shed, turnips were carried, together with hay or straw, to the milking cows in yards or houses, so that milk production continued uninterruptedly throughout the winter months, the last of the turnips not being pulled until the field was prepared for barley about March. Some might be left for seed even after this date. In addition, some bullocks were fattened on turnips in winter.[1]

Turnip husbandry then spread, in the years 1666–71, or thereabouts, as Marshall discovered, from High Suffolk to East Norfolk, where it was already well established when first recorded in 1674–5 growing in fields of up to fifteen acres on farms in Herringby, Kerdiston with Reepham, Hellesdon, Hoveton St John, and elsewhere. What was transferred to East Norfolk was, however, the minor variety of turnip husbandry as practised in High Suffolk; namely, the feeding of bullocks for winter beef.[2]

Turnip cultivation made its next advance in the Norfolk Heathlands. The earliest known reference to turnips as a field crop here dates from 1673, when the elder Walpole was growing considerable quantities on his farm at Houghton. When these proved successful, he encouraged his tenants in their cultivation.[3] In September 1677 Edward Chamberlayne esquire, of East Winch, left turnips valued at £5; and the inventory's wording suggests his crop was nothing unusual.[4] These early crops were evidently of hard turnips to be pulled for cattle. In 1681 turnips, presumably white ones, for feeding off by sheep, were being grown at Shropham, and in 1684 at Norton.[5] Well before 1700, turnip

---

[1] Ibid. 58–9; Speed, loc. cit.; Spratt, op. cit. 205; J. Laurence, op. cit. 110; Camden, loc. cit. (added 1695); Blome, op. cit. pt ii, 221; Marshall, op. cit. 458; S. Switzer, *Diss. on True Cythisus of Ancs.* 1731, p. 79; invs.:—E. Sfk R.O., A/d: 1684–5: 14–15, 93, 101, 126, 129, 131, 159–61, 166, 172: W. Sfk R.O., Episc. Commy Ct St Edm's. 1696: 65, 67; 1699: 55; 1701: 23, 27, 49; 1702: 5; Nfk R.O., Cons. Ct, Misc. 1628–68: 32; 1662: 27, 29, 68, 97; 1664: 66; 1665: 26; 1666: 55; 1668: 66; 1669: 53; 1673: 44, 70; 1674: 86; 1675: 56; 1677: 3, 150; 1683–5: 33, 105; 1685: 14–15, 101, 116, 118, 126, 129, 146, 163, 166, 172; 1688–9: 18, 59c (formerly 49), 59i (formerly 56), 65, 191; 1690–1: 12B, 105; 1704–5: 11, 79, 89, 91, 127, 130, 136, 158; 1705–13: 4, 8, 16, 33, 77, 99, 143, 153; 1718–21 stamped: 54, 56, 91, 129, 138, 156–7, 187, 196, 198, 252; 1740: 24; A/d Ct 1692: 157; 1702: 34, 66, 95, 114, 127, 133.

[2] Ibid. 1674–5: 148, 187, 191 (cat. erron. 19); 1682: 20, 104, 247, 290; 1692: 113, 117, 138, 145, 207; Cons. Ct 1675: 25; 1690–1: 84; 1718–21 stamped: 11, 86, 186, 189, 260; unstamped: 16; 'Person of Honour', *St Foine Improved* 1674, p. 2; Allison, op. cit. 64; Marshall, *Yks.* ii, 257; *Glos.* i, 233; E. Dept, 369, 382; inf. 298.

[3] J. H. Plumb, *Sir Robt Walpole* 1956, p. 85; Person of Honour, loc. cit.

[4] Nfk R.O., Cons. ct inv. 1677: 85.

[5] Ibid. 1683–5: 107; Riches, op. cit. 85.

husbandry for cattle and sheep was established practice on Townshend's home farm at East Raynham,[1] on Sir Robert Walpole's at Houghton, and on most tenant farms.[2] By 1712 turnip seeds were being exported from the Heathlands to other parts of England, and by 1718 what had been an innovation was now ordinary. The general introduction of turnip husbandry here thus belongs, as Marshall discovered, to the period 1670–80.[3]

To this, however, the exception must always be made of a narrow strip of poor, sandy soils in the extreme north, where much heathland and 'breck' cultivation remained even in the nineteenth century. Marshall rightly thought the introduction of turnip husbandry had been delayed here until about the second quarter of the eighteenth century.[4] The earliest known reference to the field cultivation of turnips in this part of the Heathlands is to two turnip carts at Thornage in 1720, and the second concerns the hoeing of seventeen acres of turnips at Holkham in September 1723.[5] Moreover, it was not until the third quarter of the century that improvement by turnips could be said to be complete in the extreme east of this locality, between Cromer Ridge and the north coast.[6] It remains now only to explain that quaint myth whose principal authors were Arthur Young and Nathaniel Kent. William Marshall had already explained the established turnip husbandry of East Norfolk. 'This would seem', he says, 'to have given umbrage to the splendid meteors which then blazed, or were beginning to blaze, amid the dark regions of rabbit-warrens and wild sheep-walks in the more northern parts of the county'.[7] Young proceeded, by means of repeated attacks on Marshall, to publicize a tardy variation on an old theme as a first innovation.[8] Kent was also to blame in that he spread the 'Turnip' Townshend story, in which Townshend was supposed to have learnt the new invention of turnip cultivation in Hanover, when attending George I, to have brought back some of this rare seed, and to have introduced turnip husbandry into England. This story has two main defects: first, that turnips were not then cultivated in Hanover; and, second, that they had long since been introduced into English farming, not least on the Townshend estates themselves.[9]

Meanwhile, turnip husbandry had spread to many other regions, and

[1] Ibid. 32, 85; H.M.C., *Portland MSS.* vi, 159.

[2] Plumb, art. cit. 86–7.

[3] Nfk R.O., Cons. Ct invs. 1718–21 stamped: 69, 158, 214, 244, 270; Morton, op. cit. 483; Lisle, op. cit. 239; Marshall, op. cit. 369.

[4] Ibid. 368, 370; Slater, op. cit. 79.

[5] Riches, op. cit. 85; R. Parker, art. cit. 160.

[6] Ibid. pass.; Sinclair, op. cit. I,

[7] Marshall, op. cit. 368.

[8] Riches, op. cit. 39–40.

[9] Stevenson, *Sy*, 242–3. Townsend–Townshend.

earliest, probably, to the Sandlings Country. The turnips first recorded at Theberton in 1674 were evidently of a hard variety, suited only to pulling; but those found in old-established crops in the early eighteenth century were mostly white varieties introduced about 1684 for feeding off to sheep.[1] After having been first introduced, probably in a hard variety, perhaps about 1653, turnips became part of everyday practice in the Chiltern Country sometime in the period 1673–1700.[2] They well suited the sandy, gravelly and chalky loams here; could be grown on the flinty clay loams, if necessary, it was discovered, on ridges elevated for the purpose; and were excluded only from some shallow chalk soils and the chalky clays, where their roots were obstructed shortly below the surface and refused to apple. Here, probably for the first time, white turnips were grown especially for sheep to feed off on the ground. Chiltern turnip husbandry for sheep became second to none[3] and prepared the way for the spread of the new husbandry in heavier soils and, above all, for sheep in the chalk downlands. In the Northdown Country, despite Sir Richard Weston's earlier experimental clover-flax-turnip rotation, we find the farmers taking up turnip husbandry for sheep and making it part of their usual plan of management only in the period 1675–80.[4] At much the same time turnips were introduced in the Oxford Heights Country,[5] and in the Breckland, where in 1682 Thomas Longe, a Croxton Park yeoman, left ten acres of them.[6] Simultaneously, the innovation was made in the Chalk Country. By 1675 turnips were in field cultivation in the belt of deep sandy soils from Calne to Crewkerne, and in the Vale of Pewsey; and wherever else in the country suitable turnip land was available, they had become normal field crops for sheep some years before 1699. The fields were limed in preparation and the

[1] Doughty, op. cit. 146; Defoe, op. cit. i, 58; Ess. R.O., D./D.K. F2/10; E. Burrell, op. cit. 58–9; E. Sfk R.O., A/d invs. 1685: 93; 1702: 16, 81, 97, 98? (sic); 1704–5: 18, 26, 111, 117, 143; 1705–13: 3, 16, 34–5, 45, 51, 65–6.

[2] Cullum, op. cit. 250–1; Marshall, *S. Dept*, 28, 37; Young, *Herts.* 102; Ellis, *Sheep*, 214–15; *Chiltern & V.* 353; Herts R.O., 22101; invs.:—A/d St Albans: Th. Hills 1685 St Paul's Walden, Robt Morgan 1693 Watford; A/d Hunts. Hitchin Div. sep. invs. Jn Field 1690 Bps Hatfield; Geo. Crawley 1703 Harpenden; Sam. Bassill 1708 Watton at Stow; Geo. Beech 1730 Flamsted; W. Sfk R.O., Episic. Commy Ct Bury St Edm's. 1700: 18, 50; J. Houghton, *Coll. for Improvemt Husbandry & Trade* ed. R. Bradley 1727–8 i, 213; iv, 142.

[3] Ibid.; Kalm, op. cit. 151, 230; Ellis, op. cit. 16, 284, 353; Spufford, op. cit. 30; Marshall, *Midl. Dept*, 628.

[4] R. Weston, *Discourse Husbandry used in Brabant & Fland.* 1652; Stevenson, op. cit. 243; Boys, op. cit. 92; Marshall, *S. Dept*, 394, 411; Kent R.O., U. 234/A. 10, Aylesford A/cs. starting 1679, 14 June 1680; A/d Cantuar. invs. 1680: Jn Heyward/Sandwich, Ric. Gallant/St Dunstans, Steven Neale/Faversham.

[5] Devizes Mus. Wm Gaby His Booke, rev. a/c 1 Aug. 1680.

[6] Allison, op. cit. 63; Clarke, op. cit. 23–4; Postgate, art. cit. 95; Spufford, loc. cit.; invs.:—Nfk R.O., A/d Ct 1682: 165; W. Sfk R.O., Episc. Commy Ct Bury St Edm's. 1701: 39; 1702: 17, 27; 1703: 12.

turnips hand-hoed. In the stiffer 'clays', the seeds were simply brushed in with a bush harrow, so they grew on top of the soil rather than in it.[1]

The innovation was now taken up at all hands: there was no longer any single axis of advance, or even a limited number of thrusts, but a fanning-out in all directions. Turnips were introduced in the fen-moulds of the Fen,[2] Cheshire Cheese[3] and Saltings countries.[4] 1680 saw them growing in the Vale of Evesham.[5] By the opening of the next century, they were old-established in certain widely scattered localities in the Midland Plain.[6] However, experience showed turnips did not suit most farms here, and nothing like a tenth of Midland arable was sown to them at one time.[7] Their cultivation was confined to pockets of sandy loams, calcareous gravels and gravel loams, and to the rich loams of the flood plains of the Soar, the Nene, the Avon and other large rivers. In such places, as at Wanlip, the grass-arable rotations of up-and-down husbandry were sometimes abandoned in favour of an arable-grass rotation in which root crops were regularly cultivated.[8] By 1720 turnip husbandry had been popularized in the Cotswold Country by Richard Bishop,[9] and had established itself in the tillage 'breaks' in Sherwood,[10] in the Northwold Country,[11] and in the North-eastern Lowlands[12]—

[1] Invs.:—Soms. R.O., Cons. Ct A/d Taunton, Jn Bryne 1674 Crewkerne; Wilts. R.O., Dioc. Reg. Sarum. Stephen Smith 1675 Calne; Lisle, op. cit. 233, 237–8, 329, 335; Tull, op. cit. 324; Ernle, op. cit. (1961) 135; H. C. Brentnall, 'Doc. fr. Gt Cheverell', Wilts.Mag. liii, 437.

[2] Northants. R.O., F.(M.) Misc. Vol. 76; Blagrave, op. cit. 233; Blith, op. cit. bet. 248–9; Marshall, E. Dept, 229-30, 253; Darby, Draining Fens, 164.

[3] Plot, Staffs. 345, where Salt Lib. copy has transcript Sir Simon Degge's nn. on turnip cultivation (Degge d. 1708); Houghton, Coll. (1681) i, 57; ii, 95.

[4] Burley, op. cit. 59; Melling, op. cit. 29–31; Marshall, op. cit. 477; Young, Ess. ii, 90; Ess. R.O., D./D.K. F2/10.

[5] Houghton, op. cit. i, 56.

[6] Yarranton, op. cit. 35; Blith, op. cit. p. befe 249; Lisle, op. cit. 233–5; Morton, op. cit. 481; Ellis, Sheep, 210; Murray, op. cit. 107; Franklin, op. cit. 90.

[7] Marshall, Midl. Cos. i, 253, 255; Leicester Mus. 3D.41/40/71–2. Pace J. Thirsk in V.C.H. Leics. ii, 243–4.

[8] Leicester Mus. 3D./42/40/71–2, 75, 85; Leics. R.O., D.E. 10 Ct Bk '1815 to 1829'; Crane & Walton A/c 166, 16 June–21 July, 23 Nov.–19 Dec. 1829; A/d invs. 19th-cent.: Ric. Hayward 1812 Newton Burgoland, Jn Rawson 1813 Kirby Muxloe; Northants. R.O., Wmld Misc. Vol. 42, p. 11; Misc. Led. 146, p. 13; Daventry 549b, 27 Oct. 1740; Prob. Recs. Petriburg. A/d Ct Northampton inv. Northants Wills & Admins. Jan.–Mar. 1725: Hy Perrin/Towcester; Shak. Bpl. Trevelyan: Ct R. Snitterfield & Bearley 1 Dec. 1742; Leigh: Stoneleigh Ct R. 29 Oct. 1764; Murray, loc. cit.; Lisle, loc. cit; Parkinson, Ruts. 49; Pitt, Leics. 34; Northants. 64–5, 76, 78; Morton, op. cit. 483; Young, Oxon. 122; Mavor, op. cit. 166; Marshall, op. cit. i, 253; Midl. Dept, 609–10.

[9] Atkyns, op. cit. 21–2.

[10] Marshall, op. cit. 167; Lowe, op. cit. 22; Chambers, V. Trent, 38.

[11] Eland, Shardeloes, 61; Leatham, op. cit. 41; Marshall, Yks. ii, 252-3, 257.

[12] Marshall, N. Dept, 49, 70; Hughes, N. Country Life: N.E. 1700–50, 142.

in a word, wherever a reasonable opening, however restricted in scope, could be found for it. By about this time, too, small turnip crops were being taken even in the Woodland,[1] and in the West Country.[2] By 1756 turnips had finally penetrated the obscurity of the North-western Lowlands.[3]

In soils too heavy or too shallow for turnips, dwarf rape provided a good alternative, and as such made its appearance in the Midland Plain at the latest in 1686,[4] and became hardly less important than English and Swedish turnips, here, in the Vale of Pickering, and in the Chalk Country.[5] Cabbages, too, could well be grown instead of turnips, especially in heavy soils. They were first introduced as a field crop by Sir Anthony Ashley at Wimborne St Giles, in the Poor Soils Country, about 1660–70.[6] In the eighteenth century, they supplied extra winter feed in some stiff Midland soils, and partly replaced turnips.[7] Finally, in the latter part of that century, in High Suffolk, when the fly became too much of a pest, drumhead (cattle) cabbages were sometimes substituted for turnips. They were more difficult to grow and needed the field earlier, but were less affected by drought. So turnips and cabbages together came to supply winter feed.[8] For similar reasons, at the same time, Swedish turnips were often substituted for common ones, despite their inferior leafage.[9]

Finally, graduating from the kitchen garden, the potato became the characteristic moss-land crop and the show-piece of cultivation in the Lancashire Plain, whence all England learned the practice. It was about 1650 that the field cultivation of potatoes was started in the 'hawes' and silty marshes of Formby and North Meols; but not until shortly before 1690 that it became both general and usual.[10] Sometimes

[1] Steer, op. cit. 268, 270.

[2] Borlase, op. cit. 89; Cash, loc. cit.

[3] Hughes, op. cit. ii: *Cumb. & Wmld*, 226.

[4] Deene ho. Brudenell Map 8; York, invs.:—Dean & Chap. B.2: Jn Barton 1693 Riccall; Selby Pec. Wm Knowles 1729–30 Hambleton; Morton, op. cit. 484; Gill & Guilford, op. cit. 74; 82, 105–6, 120, 123; Pitt, *Northants.* 98.

[5] Ibid. 79–80; *Staffs.* 85–6; *Leics.* 34, 36, 39–42; Marshall, *Yks.* ii, 29–30; sup. 26.

[6] Bodl. Aubrey 2, f. 88.

[7] Pitt, op. cit. 34–6, 42; *Northants.* 99; Marshall, *Midl. Cos.* i, 259–61.

[8] Marshall, *E. Dept*, 454, 458; Young, *Sfk*, 21, 41; '5 Days Tour to Woodbridge &c.', *Ann. Ag.* ii, 139; Rochefoucauld, op. cit. 191–2.

[9] Leicester Mus. 3D. 42/40/75; Leics. R.O., A/d inv. 19th-cent.: Ric. Hayward 1812 Newton Burgoland; Marshall, *S. Dept*, 395; Pitt, op. cit. 98; *Leics.* 29–30, 34, 39, 43.

[10] F. Bailey, op. cit. 24; R. N. Salaman, *Hist. & Soc. Infl. Potato* 1949, pp. 451–2; Steers, op. cit. 103; J. Forster, *Engl's. Happiness Incr.* 1664, pp. 2–3; Lancs. R.O., invs.:—Cons. Ct Cestr. 1690: Wm Barton/Tarlscough, Jn Johnson/Gt Crosby, Wm Holland/Bickerstaffe, Jn Ball/Becconsall; 1691: Wm Mercer/Linacre, Jn Nodder/ Lathom, Th. Aughten/N. Meols; 1699; Ralph Gregson/Penwortham; 1700: Hy Blackhurst/the Holmes, Ric. Ball/the Banks; Richmond A/d, Amounderness Deanery B. 1686–96: Isabel Bennet/Pilling.

grown in the fallows for wheat and commonly as the first crop on moss-land turf, the tubers, though often gracing humble tables, were primarily succulent fodder for cattle.[1] By this time, the Cheshire Cheese Country had followed suit,[2] but not even in the West and Fen countries, or Wales, did the potato elsewhere assume the role played in the Lancashire Plain.[3]

Although sainfoin was not the first 'artificial grass' to be experimented with, it was the earliest to be received into the general practice of husbandry. It was no accident either that this innovation, albeit by a narrow margin of time, was commenced in the Cotswold Country, which stood in the greatest want of it. The same inevitable exhaustion that made the tillage need regularly to be laid to grass, rendered this very step difficult, and especially so in the stonebrash. Selected sainfoin provided a complete and perfect answer. Aubrey says, 'The improvement by clover-grass/cinqufoile (which now spreds much in the stonebrash lands) was first used at North Wraxall by Nicholas Hall (who came from Dundry in Somersetshire) about the yeare 1650. It turned to great profit to him, which hath made his neighbours to imitate him.' Indeed, sainfoin spread so rapidly that it was an ordinary crop by 1675.[4] Sainfoin made it possible and profitable to make most sheep sleights and hill-pastures convertible, with the result that the proportion of arable in the country as a whole rose from half to nine-tenths.[5]

In this innovation, the English sainfoin stole a march on French, for much of the research and development had been done by Sir Richard Weston of Sutton, who was experimenting with what was probably Giant or French Sainfoin as early as 1645. At this time Common or English Sainfoin was neither selectedly cultivated nor grown for seed. But in the event it was English Sainfoin as introduced in the Cotswold Country, that most farmers adopted, for, although giving but one cut a year instead of two, it lasted five years or more, as compared with two, and suited the majority who wanted long leys. In the Northdown

---

[1] Bailey, loc. cit.; Aikin, op. cit. 18–19; D. Hudson & K. W. Lockhart, *R.S.A. 1754–1954* 1954, p. 64; Holt. op. cit. (1795) 21, 57, 59.

[2] Ibid. 57; Boyde, op. cit. 7; Man. Lib. Lancs. Deeds L. 36a; Lancs. R.O., Cons. Ct Cestr. inv. Th. Hey 1680 Gt Sankey; Salaman, op. cit. 433.

[3] Ibid. 409, 433; Forster, loc. cit.; Borlase, loc.cit.; Darby, loc. cit.; Marshall, *E. Dept*, 231.

[4] Blith, op. cit. 186–7; Mortimer, op. cit. 31; Worlidge, op. cit. 24, 27–8; Plot, *Oxon.* 153–4, 242; Morton, op. cit. 482–3; Atkyns, op. cit. 21–2; Jeffery, *Gt Rollright*, 27; R. L. Rickard, *Prog. N. Wdn Woodward for Wilts. Estes New Coll. Oxf. 1659–75* Wilts. Archaeol. & Nat. Hist. Soc. Rec. Br. 1957 xiii, 29, 56; Gaut, op. cit. 97; M. A. Havinden, 'Ag. Prog. in Open-fd Oxon'. *Ag. H.R.* ix, 76; 'Rural Econ. Oxon.' 185, 194; *Trans. Bristol & Glos. Archaeol. Soc.* l, 249; R. Davis, op. cit. 13; Bodl. Aubrey 2, f. 85; Hearne's diaries 158, pp. 73, 83; Worcs. R.O., Cons. Ct inv. 1690: 287; Marshall, *Glos.* ii, 63.

[5] Ibid. 11; G. Turner, op. cit. 10–11.

Country, from 1651 sainfoin of some sort was being grown successfully at Cobham Park and in other infertile chalky ground where nothing else would flourish; and by 1675 the English variety was firmly established in Northdown general practice, on exhausted fields on a chalky subsoil within reach of its tap-root, as a hay ley to be broken up for corn when invaded and smothered by natural grasses.[1] From its base in the Cotswold Country, sainfoin spread like wildfire to the Oxford Heights,[2] Chalk, and Chiltern countries. In the Chalk Country, it rapidly entered general practice shortly after 1650,[3] but was far less sown than in its country of origin, since it hardly was worth while cultivating anywhere except on the thinnest and most-exhausted of soils. Here its great use was the restoration of burnbaked redland soils, any of which could be put back into heart by folding and sainfoin.[4] In the early 1650s sainfoin was introduced into the Chiltern Country and entered into general cultivation over at most the next twenty years.[5] Sir John Turner is said to have learned sainfoin husbandry in the Cotswold Country and to have transferred it to the Norfolk Heathlands, where it had certainly become common by 1674.[6] By about this time, too, sainfoin had been taken up in the Northwold Country[7] and the Breckland.[8] All the main opportunities had thus been quickly seized, but smaller ones were still sought, sometimes in vain. The Midland Plain was hardly a promising field for sainfoin, yet experimental crops were being grown from 1651 onwards, and those who did not realize it was only apt to calcareous soils or know the calcareousness of their land, were still toying with it as late as 1724. In the small areas appropriate, however, it was already an established crop in the late seventeenth century. The wonder is not that sainfoin was never generally introduced here, but that it found its way

[1] Weston, op. cit. (1652); (1651) 2; Blith, op. cit. 186; Fuller, op. cit. ii, 113; Aubrey, Sy iii, 326; D. C. Coleman, 'Econ. Kent under later Stuarts', ts. thesis Ph.D. Ldn Univ. 1951, p. 63; Melling, op. cit. 24, 26–7; Chalklin, op. cit. 87; Speed, op. cit. 37, 42; Kent R.O. A/d Ct inv. Augustine Spaine 1678 Elham; U. 214/E7/9; U. 234/A.10, Aylesford A/cs starting 1679, 1 Aug. 1680; Marshall, S. Dept, 397, 399–400.

[2] Farr, op. cit. xxxii; Bodl. Hearne's diaries 158, p. 22.

[3] Ibid. 159, p. 226; Wilts. R.O., acc. 84, Clayton 9; Marshall, S. Dept, 56; Worlidge, op. cit.28; Naish, op. cit. 47–8; Brentnall, 'Longford MS.', 16; Lisle, op. cit. 55, 112.

[4] Ibid. 30, 55; Marshall, S. Cos. ii, 324, 329; Mavor, op. cit. 289; Bodl. Aubrey 2, f. 83; Hearne's diaries 159, pp. 226, 229.

[5] Worlidge, op. cit. 27–8; Blith, op. cit. 185–7; Ellis, Chiltern & V. 16, 273; Kalm, op. cit. 151; Plot, op. cit. 250; Mortimer, op. cit. 31; Young, Ess. i, 239; James & Malcolm, Bucks. 19; Marshall, Midl. Dept, 489; E. Dept, 454–5; Hine, Hitchin i, 59; Herts. R.O., 8479–81, 8483–7, 8579; A/d Hunts. Hitchin Div. inv. Jn Deard 1672 Hitchin.

[6] Person of Honour, op. cit. 4, 6; Atkyns, op. cit. 22.

[7] Barley, op. cit. 81; Thirsk, Eng. Peasant, 171.

[8] Spufford, loc. cit.

so unerringly to the few suitable fields.[1] Lastly, about 1750, sainfoin was introduced into as unlikely a place as the West Country.[2]

As we have seen,[3] it was not clover cultivation that was new in the mid-seventeenth century, for white and red clovers ('claver-grass' 'honeysuckle grass') were being added to hayseeds to form leys by 1607 at the latest,[4] but the selection of the seeds of a particular variety of clover for sowing either separately or as a measured proportion in a prepared mixture of clover and 'seeds' for temporary leys. The adoption of this latter practice is difficult to follow, since it passed almost entirely unrecorded, for it involved only minute changes in farming methods and the produce concerned—grass and hay—escaped the particular notice of appraisers in probate inventories, the latter because it was indistinguishable from other mixed hay crops, the former because it passed with the land and was not, therefore, included amongst the goods and chattels inventoried.[5] Fortunately, the difficulty is more apparent than real, for, in practice, clover seed was selected and clover grown for seed with both pure clovers and mixtures in view. What we need to know is when farmers, with a view to supplementing or supplanting crops of tares and ready-mixed hayseed either with clover alone or with proportioned mixtures of clover and of rye and other grasses, started to buy these in a purportedly pure and unmixed state. But we must not forget that red clovers are mostly for short hay leys and white for long grazing ones.

Experiments with clover as a selected crop started in the first half of the seventeenth century. Shortly before 1645, Weston promoted the sale of Flemish clover seeds, which he was himself growing under barley and oats on thirty and forty acres at a time. He also cultivated trefoil (nonsuch or 'hopclover'), which although not a true clover, served as one, and was especially suited to chalky soils and to sheep.[6] It may thus well have been due in large measure to his efforts that trefoil was, about 1655 probably, introduced in nearby Worplesden, where it was used in producing butter for the London market.[7] Similar research, development, and cultivation for seed was undertaken by others also, including,

---

[1] Morton, op. cit. 56–7; Worlidge, op. cit. 27; Blith, op. cit. 185–6; Pitt, *Staffs.* 25; *Northants.* 102; Crutchley, op. cit. 11; Berks. R.O., D./E.Bp E15; B.M., Lans. 1056, f. 153; Oxon. R.O., Wi.x.34, 1st pagination, 1; Northants. R.O., Map 1382; F.(M.) Corr. 176/16, 222/39.

[2] Borlase, loc. cit.

[3] Sup. 29–32.

[4] Norden, op. cit. 207–8; Folkingham, op. cit. 25, 87; L. Carrier, *Begs. Ag. in Am.* 1923, pp. 239–40.

[5] B.M., Lans. vol. 615, f. 55; R. Burn, *Eccl. Law* 1767, iv, 212–13.

[6] Weston, op. cit. (1652); (1651) 51; Speed, op. cit. 33, 35, 37; Blith, op. cit. 178; Yarranton, op. cit. 3–4; McDonald, op. cit. 67.

[7] Aubrey, *Sy* iii, 326–7.

perhaps, Andrew Yarranton in the vales of Hereford, and a Chiltern farmer by the name of Howe, to whom Cromwell is said to have given a reward for his pains and achievements.[1]

However, the first evidence we have of the successful innovation of clover refers to the Wealden Vales. Here the newly selected wild and Dutch white, perennial red, and broad clovers, and perennial rye-grass 'seeds', had been introduced as early as 1649, and had become ordinary husbandry by 1661 probably, by 1669 certainly. Clover, sown by itself, now served also as an alternative to peas and beans. Nonsuch and Dutch clover were sown occasionally, the latter perhaps as a part-contributor to the first year of long leys.[2] Much the same innovations were made in the Midland Plain at this time. Wild white and perennial red clovers were natives of the Midland grasslands, but clover of any sort was rarely selected for temporary leys before 1660. Nevertheless, trial crops had been grown as early as 1652 and were continued in the next few years.[3] By 1662 clover seeds were on sale in Kidderminster, Bromsgrove, Birmingham, Dudley, Wolverhampton, Walsall, Sutton Coldfield and other western towns, and were being sown on farms in Maddingley and Harston in the extreme east.[4] By 1675 clover cultivation had become general. However, Midland farmers had little use for clover by itself. What they needed was a mixture of clover and 'seeds' for the rapid formation of long leys. Perennial rye-grass was best for this: it was an indigenous and chief constituent of both permanent and temporary leys; but although probably collected for use in earlier times, and certainly bought in mixed hay-seed, it was not generally selected for seed and sale before 1650, and appears not to have been cultivated regularly until about 1670.[5] By 1675 mixtures of clover and perennial rye-grass were commonly employed in laying down, and by the early eighteenth century were considered ordinary.[6] Sometimes trefoil, melilot or yellow

[1] Marshall, *S. Dept*, 28, 39; Yarranton, op. cit. 1, 3; Blith, op. cit. 177–9, 181–2.

[2] B.M., Add. 34164, f. 86; Lodge, op. cit. 237, 242, 253, 432–3; Kenyon, art. cit. 111, 119–20, 151; Boys, op. cit. 20, 77–8; Mortimer, op. cit. 27–8; T. B. Lennard, art. cit. 109; invs.:—Kent R.O., A/d Ct Cantuar. 1679: Jn London/Staplehurst; 1680: Jacob Dive/Headcorn, Ric. More/Marden; W. Suss. R.O., Cons. Ct Bp Cicestr. for A/d Cicestr. Alex. Bennett 1668 Thakam, Jn Barnard 1671 Chiltington; 1672: Nic. Randole/Lurgashall, Wr. Payne/Northchapel, Laurence Tillet er/ Billingshurst; Jn Stone er 1675 Nuthurst; Geo. Weller 1690 Warnham.

[3] Blith, op. cit. 177–9, 181–2; Worlidge, op. cit. 24–6, 28.

[4] Yarranton, op. cit. 46; Atwell, op. cit. 101; Spufford, loc. cit.

[5] Morton, op. cit. 482; Plot, *Oxon.* 154; A. M. Mimardière, 'War. Gentry 1660–1730', ts. thesis M.A. B'ham Univ. 1963, pp. 143–4.

[6] Ibid. 128, 143–4; J. M. Martin, 'Soc. & Econ. Trends in Rural W. Midls. 1785–1825', ts. thesis M. Comm. B'ham Univ. 1960, pp. 79–80; Bodl. Hearne's diaries 158, p. 14; invs.:—Shak. Bpl. Stratford: Wills & Invs. 22; Leigh: Hy Chambers 1735 Langley; Leics. R.O., A/d 1691: 81; Lichfield Jt R.O., Pec. cts Humphrey Arkoll

suckling clover were preferred, but the usual mixture was of two parts of perennial rye-grass to one of wild white or red clover. The resulting ley was mown for one or two years, and then horses, rams, and cattle were turned in belly-deep.[1] Although it is only in 1662 that we hear of clover seeds grown in the Vales of Hereford being marketed throughout western England, this marks not the beginning but the end of their introduction in the vales, for selected wild white and red clover had arrived on the scene shortly after 1650. Yet clover and 'seeds' cannot be said to have become commonplace among all classes of farmers up and down the length and breadth of the vales until just before 1690.[2]

Aubrey possibly intended to say clover was introduced in the Cotswold Country in 1650; but clover and 'seeds' were not generally adopted here before the period 1700–15, when they were vigorously promoted by Richard Bishop the seedsman.[3] Since West Country leys on beatland had perforce to be sown down, great reliance had long been placed on hay-seeds and collected grasses, so clover and 'seeds' found a ready opening. By 1664 clover was on sale in Exeter and other towns, and was sometimes grown by itself in South Hams. More usually, however, it was sown in a mixture with the local 'ever' or 'evergreen' strain of perennial rye-grass. This method was probably started about 1664 and certainly long before 1736, when it was being stipulated in lease covenants, which normally were content to follow precedents and lagged far behind current practice. White clover, trefoil or melilot trefoil were sometimes substituted, but otherwise it was usual to sow amongst the sprouting oats a mixture of twelve gallons of 'evergreen' to ten pounds of broad clover.[4]

1695 Penkridge; Worcs. R.O., Cons. Ct, Ric. Elly 1718 Ombersley; Deene ho. Brudenell Map 8; Houghton, op. cit. (1681) i, 56; Franklin, op. cit. 90; Lisle, op. cit. 247; 'Descron Graysbrooke in Yks.', Gent's. Mag. xxxiii, 532; Morton, op. cit. 482–3.

[1] Ibid. 483; Mimardière, op. cit. 144; Plot, loc. cit.; Crutchley, op. cit. 11, 14; Worlidge, op. cit. 29; Pitt, Staffs. 24; Leics. 35; Northants. 101; Marshall, Midl. Cos i, 23–4, 234, 263, 266–7, 353; Beds. R.O., L. 4/333; invs.:—Shak. Bpl. Leigh: Chambers as prev. n.; Leics. R.O., A/d 19th-cent.:—Jn Willmat 1810 Shepshed, Ric. Hayward 1812 Newton Burgoland.

[2] Bodl. Aubrey 2, f. 152; Hereford Lib. Local: Deed 3682; B'ham Lib. Winnington 217; Fox, Mon. 14; Marshall, W. Dept, 279; Beale, op. cit. 53; H. Holland, Gen. View Ag. Ches. 1808, p. 179; Howse, art. cit. 301–2; C. Radcliffe-Cooke, 'Jn Noble's Household & Fm A/cs. 1696–1719', Trans. Woolhope Nats.' Fd Club xxxvi, 201; Yarranton, op. cit. 46; Houghton, loc. cit.; invs.:—N. L. W. Episc. Cons. Ct Hereford 1691 Sept.: Jn Powell/the Wolhead; 1691–2 Mar.: Mich. Mann/Ross; 1695: Ed. Hoskins/Kings Caple; Cons. Ct Dean Hereford 1723: Herbert Haines/ Haywood; Glouc. Lib. Cons. Ct 1690: 74, 161; 1703: 112, 114; 1704: 85.

[3] Ibid. 1703: 171; 1715: 173, 198; 1718: 134; 1722: 105A; Morton, op. cit. 482–3; Atkyns, op. cit. 21–2; Plot, op. cit. 153–4; Havinden, 'Rural Econ. Oxon.', 194; sup. 278.

[4] Marshall, S. Dept, 406, 542; Midl. Dept, 601; W. Engl. i, 78–80, 136, 202–3,

Much the most remarkable instance of the adoption of clover, and, incidentally, the one most destructive of conventional notions as to how the innovation was made, relates to the Vale of Taunton Deane, where the crop was suddenly taken up in the early 1660s. In 1664 Robert Huish of Corfe had been growing clover hay. In 1667 one Stephens of Lydeard St Lawrence had 'haye and clover' worth £5. In 1669 William Barrett of West Bagborough left £2 worth of clover. In 1671 Richard Larcombe of Wembdon had clover seed worth 30s in his house. In short, clover was universally adopted and widely grown for seed. Trefoil was also cultivated.[1]

In East Norfolk clover came in at much the same time as in the Vale of Taunton Deane. It was now substituted for a large part of the summer grain, and, with grass 'seeds', for the natural grasses of summerleys. In September 1665, Richard Lacey, yeoman, of Sloley, had 'eight hurryes of clovergrass' worth £7, compared with only 'foure hurryes of hey' (meaning meadow-hay), worth £3. In 1666, Gilbert Wyatt, a Ludham beer-brewer and farmer, had £4 worth of 'clover seed sowne'. In 1668, Thomas Smyth of Belaugh left 'in the pease howse pease in the straw and some clover haye' worth £4, and 'in the barne called Cannells barne one small cullett of clover and gray pease in the straw', which, together with some barley, were valued at £10. In 1669, Thomas Moone of Hoveton St John had '2 load of clover and 2 load of hay' worth £3.[2] Farm inventories all over East Norfolk in 1671 no less than in 1681–2 and 1690–2, show that clover, and occasionally trefoil, crops were already old-established, and worth, when new sown, about half a crown, when ready to harvest, about £1 an acre in the first year and somewhat less in the second. Thus Marshall's opinion that clover was of old introduction here receives ample confirmation.[3]

High Suffolk did not fail to keep pace. Clover was being grown for hay at Edwardstone in 1664, at Bildeston in 1665, at Thurlton in 1668, and at Boxford in 1669. By 1675 the inventories generally find it necessary to distinguish meadow from clover hay, so the new crop must already

295, 325; Fraser, *Corn.* 33; R. Lennard, art. cit. 34, 36; Rowe, op. cit. 222; Borlase, op. cit. 88–9; Cash, op. cit. 148; Soms. R.O., Cons. Ct A/d Taunton inv. Geo. Hill 1671 Winsford.

[1] Ibid. Robt Huish 1664 Corfe,—Stephens (wid. Maria) 1667 Lydeard St Laurence; Wm Barrett 1669 W. Bagborough; Ric. Larcombe 1671 Wembdon; Jn Bennett 1688 Milverton; & v. 1689: Jos. Welshawe/Crowcombe, Wm Roosen/Spaxton; 1690: Wm Jeffrey/Michael Creech, Jn Cunditt/Kilve, Jn Good/Bridgwater; 1691: Francis Bryant/Staplegrove, Jn Gooding/Halse; Marshall, op. cit. ii, 170; Billingsley, op. cit. (1794) 158–60.

[2] Marshall, *Nfk* i, 252; Nfk R.O., Cons. Ct invs. 1665: 87; 1666: 3, 66; 1668: 49; 1669: 92.

[3] Ibid. 1671: 12; 1675: 25, 32; 1682: 6, 29; A/d Ct 1682: 3, 20, 41, 69. 104, 140, 210, 299; 1692: 63, 77, 107, 117, 138, 169, 175, 204, 207; Marshall, op. cit. i, 302.

have been taken up widely. In 1684, to take some further instances, it was grown at Rushmere and Whitton-cum-Thurleston, in 1686 at Stoke by Nayland, in 1687 at Layham and at Assington. Clover was now commonplace, and this the inventories[1] conclusively prove, all the more if we bear in mind it was not often sown by itself here, being merely an occasional crop like tares, and as such was seldom recorded.[2] With ample green fodder, there was little call to expand hay production. Convertible husbandry continued as before and what was needed was still the long ley of a grass-arable rotation. For similar reasons nonsuch (trefoil) was rarely grown. Perennial red clover (cow grass), however, was widely employed in 'seeds' mixtures with annual meadow grass, called 'Suffolk grass' because uniquely cultivated there. Despite its short life, Suffolk grass had the advantage, in a dry climate, of constantly reseeding itself and of impregnating the rich loams with its seed. The grass sward thus stayed young and firm for a long time, and consequently contained vast amounts of nourishing new blades. Cow grass and Suffolk grass were the natural produce of High Suffolk long leys and provided rich feeding for cows.[3]

We must next consider a number of countries where the nature of the evidence prevents us fully tracing the course of the introduction of clover, but permits us to see by what time it had been innovated. Amongst these by a strange chance, are the Northdown and Chiltern countries, which had probably witnessed some of the earliest research and development in this field. Yet, in the former, it was not until about 1670 that clover (including trefoil) passed into general use. Before then it is not noticed in inventories, but afterwards is listed as frequently as the nature of the crop permits. By 1675 the famous Kentish wild white clover was also being grown for seed, exported from Rochester to London and distributed thence to the rest of England. By this time, clover, 'seeds' and sainfoin between them had reduced hay to one-third its previous price.[4] Yet even these could not form the sole diet of sheep or

---

[1] Marshall, *E. Dept*, 455; invs.:—Nfk R.O., Cons. Ct 1671: 43 (inv. 4 Jan. 1668 O.S.); 1675: 39; 1690–1: 105; A/d Ct 1692: 157; W. Sfk R.O., Episc. Commy Ct Bury St Edm's. 1664: 22; 1666: 105; 1670: 182; 1685–6: fnd loose, Jn Partridge/ Stoke by Nayland; 1688: 10, 15; 1692: 106; 1696: 65, 84; 1700: 8; E. Sfk R.O., acc. 519, Wm Green 1715 Battisford; A/d 1684–5: 27, 31, 37; 1702: 3.

[2] Ibid. 1702: 31, 66, 89; 1704–5: 91, 111; 1705–13: 6, 106, 133; Nfk R.O., Cons. Ct 1718–21 stamped: 88, 191 & Robt Selfe 1718 Gissing.

[3] Ibid. 191; E. Sfk R.O., A/d 1705–13: 6; Marshall, loc. cit.; *Nfk* i, 301–2; N. Kent, *Hints to Gent. of Landed Prop.* 1775, pp. 30–1.

[4] Yarranton, op. cit. 3, 11; Aubrey, *Sy* iii, 326, 363; Lisle, op. cit. 109; D. Coleman, op. cit. 63, 65; Melling, op. cit. 26–7; B.M., Add. 34164, f. 86; Kent R.O., A/d Ct Cantuar. invs.:—1671: Mary Allen/Doddington; 1678: Josh. Pix/Frinsted, Jn Allen/ Borden, Wm Charleston/Boughton, Jn Aphly/Faversham; 1679: Jn Bennet/Staple, Stephen Luck/Thornham, Ric. Marrian/Bobbing, Hugh Maynard/Leeds; 1680: Jn Tharpe/Rainham, Robt Seth/Bobbing, Jn Spillet/Boughton Malherbe, Roger

horses, and the new crops only partly replaced and supplemented the much-grown podware. Some summer fields were prolonged into a second year under clover; and as natural grasses were replaced in leys, these became quicker yielding. In the Chiltern Country, the early history of the great clovers,[1] of trefoil,[2] and of selected perennial rye-grass[3] is almost a complete blank. We only know they had all been generally introduced by 1675. Trefoil, melilot-trefoil, white clover and rye-grass provided excellent sheep feed in the richer Chiltern soils.[4] Broad red clover, trefoil, and perennial rye-grass were all introduced in the Norfolk Heathlands by 1674 and had become part of normal farm practice, at the partial expense of tares, in most of the country by 1682,[5] and even in the Holkham District by, at the latest, 1692, when William Man of that town had '23 akers of clover'.[6] In this third quarter of the century the new crops were apparently taken up in the Oxford Heights Country[7] and no more years elapsed before we find them being generally grown in the Chalk Country.[8] Here the usual mixtures were rye-grass

Pottles/Linsted, Th. Sandridge/Newington, Ed. Brewer/Faversham, Wm Clagett/ E. Sutton, Alex. Godwin/Chartham, Mich. Denne/Littlebourne; Stevenson *Sy*, 303, 309; Marshall, *S. Dept*, 396–7.

[1] Ibid. 28, 39; Cullum, op. cit. 249–50; Young, *Herts*. 55; Worlidge, op. cit. 24–7; B.M., Add. 36233, ff. 218–19; R. 32971, m. 6; Herts. R.O., 8154, 2nd foliation 14; 8579; Plot, *Oxon*. 153.

[2] Ibid. 153–4, 240, 250; Worlidge, op. cit. 28–9; Blith, op. cit. 185, 187; Aspley Hth Sch. op. cit. 19 sqq.; Herts. R.O., 22101 A/d St Albans inv. Th. Hills 1685 St Paul's Walden.

[3] Cullum, loc. cit.; Plot, op. cit. 154, 240, 250; Ess. R.O., D./D.Kw E2.

[4] Ibid.; Plot, op. cit. 154, 240; Ellis, *Chiltern & V.* 16, 264, 268, 284, 286; Kalm, op. cit. 151–2; W. Sfk R.O., Episc. Commy Ct Bury St Edm's. inv. 1692: 58; Herts. R.O., A/d Hunts. Hitchin Div. Wills & Invs. Jn Bradley 1690 Bps Hatfield; & v. 3 prev. nn.

[5] Nfk R.O., invs. Cons. Ct 1718–21 stamped: 222, 259; A/d Ct 1682: 5, 89, 135; 1692: 58; sup. 279 n.6.

[6] Nfk R.O., A/d Ct inv. 1692: 156.

[7] Farr, op. cit. xxxii; Wilts. R.O., Cons. Ct Sarum. inv. M. 1676–1720: Th. Manfield/Tytherton Lucas.

[8] Laurence, op. cit. 68; Lisle, op. cit. 109–10; Naish, op. cit. 50–1; Brentnall, 'Longford MS.', 16; Wilton ho. Ct Bk W. Overton starting 1724, 1725; invs.:— Dors. R.O., A/d Ct Dors 1689: 59 (31); 1693: 2; 1695: 19 (117); 1701: 28 (47); 1711: 18 (161); 1712: 1 (70); 1714: 31 (60); 1718: 59 (11); 1725: 8 (85); Wilts. R.O., Dioc. Reg. Sarum. Jn Humby 1682 Downton, Th. Pavy 1717 Plaitford, Ed. Parker 1719 Gt Wishford, Wm Chipp 1733 Alton Pancras; Cons. Ct Sarum. A1584– 1700: 77; Hants R.O., A/d Ct, 1675: Robt Budd(s) Ropley, Ric. Soper/N. Oakley; 1691: Jn Grundy/Ewshott; Cons. Ct, 1676: Th. Smith/Priory ho.; 1688: Ric. God-win/Hambledon; 1690: Margery Heberden/Steep, Jn Ransome/Hungerford, Nic. Morris/Fordingbridge; W. Suss. R.O., Cons. Ct Bp Cicestr. for A/d Cicestr. Th. Scarvill 1687 Funtington, Jn Locke 1688 Rogate, Robt Penfold 1690 Bepton, Ric. Alyling 1691 Chithurst; Berks R.O., D./E.Ah E5/1, 2.

and broad red clover below the hill and rye-grass and 'hop-clover' above the hill, both being sown under barley or oats. Perennial rye-grass was the 'seed' employed everywhere: it was best and cheapest. Sometimes broad red clover and trefoil ('hop-clover') were sown alone amongst the green wheat in March, for a single year's hay ley or perhaps a second year's grazing as well. Rye-grass and mixtures were usually sown on well-mucked soils, and broad red clover was occasionally grown with sainfoin or even with beans. Thus sainfoin and mixtures of rye-grass and 'hop-clover' were used for temporary leys on the downs: mixtures of rye-grass and red clovers for those in lower situations; and pure clover crops as an alternative to tares and horsemeat, though clover never entirely replaced these, since it could not be grown so frequently. Perennial rye-grass survived better below than above the hill, but everywhere the natural grasses eventually ousted the artificial, so the chief advantage of rye-grass mixtures was that they provided leys rapidly, and this was why natural grass seeding became something of a rarity.[1] By 1679 at the latest, red clover had been generally introduced in the Saltings Country too, partly as an alternative to beans, mainly mixed with perennial rye-grass.[2] The older way of laying to grass was superseded by clover and 'seeds' especially selected, in this last quarter of the century, in the Fen, Southdown and South Sea-coast countries, and in favoured parts of the Blackheath Country and the Breckland.[3]

In some other countries, although one might suppose clover and 'seeds' were introduced early, we have as yet not much evidence of this. In 1662 clover seed was on sale in Worcester, but was not much sown, apparently, in the Vale of Evesham, before about 1690.[4] Clover husbandry started in the Petworth District about 1673 and had been

[1] Ibid. E.5/1, 2; Wilts. R.O., Enclo. Awards Fovant & Broad Chalke 1792; invs.:—Dioc. Reg. Sarum. Pavy & Parker as prev. n.; Hants. R.O., A/d Ct, 1675: Budd(s) as prev. n.; 1720: Jn Hobbes, er/Breamore, Wm Whicher/Buriton; Brentnall, art. cit. 16–18; Mavor, op. cit. 284, 287; T. Davis, op. cit. 18, 43, 47–8; Naish, op. cit. 87; S. Switzer, Compendious Method 1729, p. 25; Lisle, op. cit. 25, 27, 46, 49, 52, 109, 111, 113, 161, 241, 266.

[2] Ibid. 86; Marshall, S. Dept, 158; Chalklin, op. cit. 97; Melling, op. cit. 29–31; Vancouver, Ess. 148–9; Ess. R.O., D./D.K. F2/10; D./D.P. E25, f. 70; Kent R.O., A/d Ct Cantuar. invs. 1679: Ric. Marrian/Bobbing; 1680: Robt Seth/id., Jn Tharpe/Rainham.

[3] Collier, art. cit. 50; Barley, 'E. Yks. Manorial Bye-Laws', 51; Morton, op. cit. 484; Northants. R.O. F.(M.) Corr. 178/24; invs.:—Hants. R.O., A/d Ct 1690: Jn Bursey/Milton; 1691: Jn Chitty/Heathley; Cons. Ct 1690: Th. Hicks/Efford, Barnaby Gantlett/Bockington; 1692: Jas Parkes/Iver; 1720: Jn Stears/Hayling Southwood; W. Sfk R.O., Episc. Commy Ct Bury St. Edm's. 1688: 116; W. Suss. R.O., Cons. Ct Bp Cicestr. for A/d Cicestr. Mich. Raynor 1670 Appledram; Wm Lelam 1674 Almodington; Jas Dalley er 1690 Selsey; 1693: Jn Gibberish/Barnham, Wm Squier/Hunston; Th. Holliday 1678 Sompting; Wm Osborne 1693 Fernhurst.

[4] Pomeroy, op. cit. 13; Yarranton, op. cit. 46; Glouc. Lib. Cons. Ct inv. 1721: 166; & inf. 292–3.

generally accepted by 1689. Perennial red clover was being grown in 1694.[1] In the Woodland, clover was grown a little in the later seventeenth century, to replace tares; but these themselves had never been important, and hardly any scope existed for pure clover crops,[2] with the result we are left largely in the dark. In the Vale of Berkeley[3] and the Cheshire Cheese Country,[4] broad clover seeds were introduced in the mid-seventeenth century, but were unsuited on any scale. All we know of clover in the Sandlings Country is that it was an old-established crop in the early eighteenth century.[5]

Finally, some countries appear to have introduced clover and 'seeds' only tardily. This is true of the Poor Soils and Northwold countries,[6] of Wales, where they were only partially taken up even in 1700,[7] and of the North-eastern Lowlands, where the selective seeding of broad clover, trefoil, and perennial rye-grass may not have become general practice until shortly before 1720.[8] Lastly, in the Vale of Pickering, and in the backward North-western Lowlands, selected clover only made its appearance about 1750.[9]

In considering this evidence of clover and 'seeds' cultivation, its inevitably fragmentary and incomplete nature must be remembered. Whilst it is hardly possible to chronicle the innovation with all the precision and certitude we would, certain salient facts emerge clearly. Experimental crops of Dutch clover for short leys were being grown from 1645 onwards, but most supplies of this little-grown variety have always come from Holland and central Europe. The introduction of selected clover as a farm crop, other than in permanent leys, started in 1650 or just after. About 1661 commenced a great clover and 'seeds' boom that spread to all suitable countries but the northernmost, first to the plains and vales, and then to the downlands, and reached its peak around 1670. Although all the best opportunities for this innovation had been

[1] Leaconfield, *Sutton & Duncton*, 55–6; W. Suss. R.O., Cons. Ct Bp Cicestr. for A/d Cicestr. invs. Hy Courtney. 1673 Petworth; 1689: Ric. Nayno/Easebourne, Jn Humphery/Tillington; 1692: Jn Morison/Midhurst, Jn Talmey/Fittleworth; Eliz. Browing 1693 Grafham.

[2] Steer, op. cit. 269, 271; Burley, op. cit. 60; W. Sfk R.O., Episc. Commy Ct Bury St. Edm's. invs. 1670: 127; 1699: 36.

[3] Marshall, *Glos.* ii, 94; Lennard, art. cit. 36.

[4] Chetham Lib. Mun. Rm, Sir Wm Meredith, svy his lands at Bowden & Altrincham 1726; invs.:—Lichfield Jt R.O., Gnossall Pec. Jn Edwards 1695–6 Mill Meece; Lancs. R.O., Cons. Ct. Cestr. Jon. Travis 1690 Cuardley; Houghton, op. cit. i, 56; Wedge, Ches. 28–9; Yarranton, op. cit. 46; Marshall, *W. Dept*, 6, 28.

[5] Ess. R.O., D./D.K. F.2/10; E. Sfk R.O., A/d invs 1704–5: 128; 1705–13: 106.

[6] Leatham, op. cit. 41; Marshall, *Yks.* ii, 252–3; Dors. R.O., A/d Ct Dors. inv. 1712: 20 (18).

[7] Emery, art. cit. 30; Fox, *Mon.* 14; Hassall, *Carm.* 12; *Pembs.* 11.

[8] Marshall, *N. Dept*, 49, 88–9; Hughes, op. cit. *N.E. 1700–50*, 137–8, 143.

[9] Ibid. ii: *Cumb. & Wmld*, 226; inf. 342.

taken by 1675, modest advances occurred until about 1720, most markedly in the Northwold Country and the North-eastern Lowlands. Now all objectives were attained and tasks fulfilled. This chronological outline is dramatically confirmed by contemporary writers. It was in about 1661, with the Wealden Vales foremost in mind, that Sir Roger Twysden wrote, 'Now there is a newe device of cloverseed that spoyles all meadowland'.[1] Around 1673–96 John Aubrey remarks that in the Northdown Country, 'clover-grass has reduced the price of meadow-hay from three pounds to twenty shillings per load'.[2] In 1676–7 Petty related how clover had helped to depress food prices.[3] In the Chalk Country, about 1680, the cheapness of hay was attributed to 'the greate quantytys of clover and other grass sowed'.[4] By 1700 or earlier Timothy Nourse was inveighing against clover and other 'foreign weeds' for having spoilt the price of grass grounds. 'To be in clover' was already a common saying.[5]

We cannot leave this account of new crops without mentioning two being grown in the later seventeenth and early eighteenth centuries: spurrey, occasionally, for the winter feed of sheep, in some sandy soils, as at Thorpe Malsor and Cransley, in the Midland Plain;[6] and lucerne, which, outside the Northdown Country, was not much cultivated, except experimentally, or on hobby farms, or as a special suburban crop, chiefly for the green soiling of horses, i.e. it was cut and fed to them green.[7] Nor should we overlook one instance of the use of an old crop for a fresh purpose, in what, although an old piece of husbandry else-where, was a new one in the Breckland. Rye usually preceded barley in the successions, but from about 1580 it became increasingly the practice not to let the rye stand, but to feed it off to sheep and then plough it in as the matrix for barley. Alternatively, rye was sown in place of the oat or summer corn shift or instead of leaving the land in 'summerley' and fed off and ploughed in for a succeeding crop.[8]

We have tried to show how the new crops came to be generally introduced in various parts of the kingdom, but will be the first to admit that complete adoption came somewhat later, and, indeed, that

[1] B.M., Add. 34164, f. 86.
[2] *Sy* iii, 363.
[3] *Econ. Writings* ed. Hull 1899 i, 288, 303.
[4] Berks. R.O., D./E.Ah E.5/1, 2.
[5] Op. cit. 86–7, 92.
[6] Morton, op. cit. 56–7; Worlidge, op. cit. 24.
[7] Ibid. 28; Crutchley, op. cit. 11; Pitt, *Northants.* 103; *Staffs.* 25; Morton, op. cit. 483; Blith, op. cit. 187; Plot. *Oxon.* 154; Boys, op. cit. 96; Melling, op. cit. 36, 38–40, 45, 48; Marshall, *S. Cos.* i, 69, 153; ii, 12, 33; Leics. R.O., Crane & Walton A/c 166, 9 May 1829.
[8] P.R.O., Chanc. Proc. ser. i Jas I, L. 15/7; W. 11/60; Req. 65/52; Nfk R.O., Cons. & A/d cts invs. esp. Cons. Misc. 1637–68: A./41.

universal adoption never has been. By general introduction we mean that those farmers and owner-occupiers who cultivated between them most of the farmland of a particular country had accepted the practice as an ordinary, everyday piece of husbandry. But this does not mean that all, or even the overwhelming majority of cultivators had followed suit. On the contrary, no doubt most of the smaller farmers lagged behind. What we mean by complete adoption is when the majority of small farmers likewise took up the new practices. When this had occurred, the innovations were as complete as any innovations ever can be. We now need to discover then, when the new crops became adopted completely, and this we can do by studying the history of common fields, where most of the occupiers were petty family and part-time farmers.

The same new crops that modified up-and-down husbandry changed or even revolutionized many of the dwindling number of Midland common fields. In 1662 clover was being grown in Maddingley breach field instead of pulse.[1] Somewhat later common fields were being laid down with rye-grass and clover mixtures for biennial and even triennial leys, which replaced parts of the pulse and corn of the breach field and of the succeeding bare fallow or hitching. In this and similar ways, many common fields changed from a system of permanency to arable-grass rotations not unlike those in some enclosed turnip soils. This entailed division or alteration of the shifts and reorganization of the field-course. It was in this way that ley farming was first introduced into the common fields; at this time that the hitherto rigid field-courses often underwent change; and at this time that common-field husbandry became more flexible and productive.[2] Contemporaneously, coles were introduced in suitably soiled common fields. From 1688 at the latest rape was being grown in Clayworth common fields and it was occasionally cultivated in the eighteenth century in those of Childerley and Kettering.[3] The usual root crop in common fields was turnips, which generally preceded barley.[4] By 1723 turnips had become a regular crop in Snitterfield and Bearley fields; by 1735 at the latest in Yarwell; by 1739 in Brigstock; and by 1740 in Hellidon.[5] By the latter half of the

[1] Atwell, op. cit. 101.

[2] B.M., Add. 36584, f. 118; Oxon. R.O., Wi.x.34, 1st pagination 1, 17; 2nd 98; Shak. Bpl. Trevelyan: Ct R. Snitterfield & Bearley 10 Oct. 1694, 14 Oct. 1698, 13 Oct. 1703, 26 Oct. 1715, 10 Oct. 1716, 29 Oct. 1723, 6 Oct. 1729; Northants. R.O., Ecton 1191, ords. 24–5; Daventry 549b, ords. 5–6; Misc. Led. 146, p. 13; Crutchley, op. cit. 8–9; Young, *Oxon.* 122, 124; Pitt, *Northants.* 76–8; Parkinson, *Ruts.* 49; Batchelor, op. cit. 339; Thirsk, *Eng. Peasant,* 185; Marshall, *Midl. Cos.* ii, 226; Vancouver, *Cams.* 100–2, 109, 121.

[3] Ibid. 122; Gill & Guilford, op. cit. 81–2, 105–6, 120, 123; Pitt. op. cit. 77.

[4] Ibid. 76–8; Parkinson, loc. cit.; Marshall, loc. cit.

[5] Shak. Bpl. Trevelyan: Ct R. Snitterfield & Bearley 29 Oct. 1723, 1 Dec. 1742; Northants. R.O., Wmld Misc. Vol. 42, p. 11; Daventry 549b; Misc. Led. 146, p. 13.

K

eighteenth century, rape, common turnips and swedes were old-established crops in suitable common fields.[1] Common-field farmers were not
averse from this improvement, but sometimes experimented with turnip
crops only to find their soil too heavy. Indeed, in most soils the farmers
later laid turnips aside, except perhaps in a year when fodder was
exceptionally scarce. For instance, 'the Shuttington farmers, by general
consent, turneped their fallow field. The consequence was, they constantly lost their barley crop; and for this reason . . . the practice was
discontinued'.[2] Even when grown, then, turnips did not necessarily
become a regular crop; nor were they included in the rotations in most
common fields. Nevertheless, clover and 'seeds', rape, turnips and swedes
between them necessitated many new field-courses, much rearrangement of shifts and greater flexibility of management, as well as newly
devised, rigorously enforced, and often complicated by-laws. At Marsh
Baldon in 1724 one of the three fields was divided into two to accommodate clover and 'seeds', thus making a four-field course.[3] From 1694
at the latest, Snitterfield and Bearley common fields were thrown into
quarters and seeded down and ploughed up in a rotation based on four
shifts. At Geddington a four-field course of (1) turnips (later swedes),
(2) barley, (3) clover, (4) wheat was adopted.[4] At Hellidon and elsewhere the whole-year and eighteen months' fallows of the old three-
field course were utilized for clover crops without any other change.[5]
At Rothwell a three-field course was maintained, but half the 'red-land'
fallow was fenced off temporarily with coppice underwood and sown
to turnips, while the other half was bare-fallowed for wheat. Turnip and
bare fallows were alternated, so the succession became (1) turnips, (2)
barley, (3) promiscuous breach crops, (4) bare fallow, (5) wheat, (6)
breach crops as before. At Kettering the three-field course was preserved by a succession of (1) bare fallow, (2) wheat, (3) beans, (4) rape,
(5) barley, (6) clover. The three-field course at North Luffenham also
continued in a new guise, each field being divided into three shifts for
(1) bare fallow, (2) tilth wheat and barley, (3) breach field for peas and
beans, (4) turnip fallow, (5) barley, (6) oats, or brush barley, (7) clover,
mown once, (8) wheat, (9) breach field as before.[6] Sometimes these new

[1] Pitt, op. cit. 64, 75–8; Young, op. cit. 122; Parkinson, loc. cit.; Tate, op. cit.
261–2; Crutchley, loc. cit.; Marshall, *Midl. Dept*, 609–10; *N. Dept*, 344; Ruston &
Witney, op. cit. 181.

[2] Marshall, *Midl. Cos.* ii, 215–16, 226.

[3] Oxon. R.O., Wi.x.34, 2nd pagination 98.

[4] Shak. Bpl. Trevelyan: Ct R. Snitterfield & Bearley 10 Oct. 1694, 14 Oct. 1698,
13 Oct. 1703, 26 Oct. 1715, 10 Oct. 1716, 29 Oct. 1723, 6 Oct. 1729, 1 Dec. 1742;
Pitt, op. cit. 64, 76.

[5] Ibid. 76–8; *Leics.* 95; Crutchley, op. cit. 9; Wedge, *War.* 15; Vancouver, op. cit.
12, 101–2; Northants. R.O., Daventry 549b.

[6] Pitt, *Northants.* 64, 76–7, 301–2, 306; Parkinson, loc. cit.

crops were grown under compulsory, sometimes under permissive, by-laws. At Brigstock, e.g. an order in 1739 permitted the fencing of lands sown with clover and 'seeds', provided sheep goings were proportionately reduced.[1] In 1740 a similar order at Hellidon permitted turnip cultivation on 'sharp' land in the hitching field when the vetches were finished.[2] In these ways, the common-field farmers were tardily able to participate in improvement; and in turnip soils common fields often made a fair imitation of the arable-grass rotations practised in some enclosures. Nevertheless, up-and-down land still yielded half as much again as common fields.[3]

   In the Cotswold Country likewise, common-field husbandry embraced these new crops. Sainfoin and 'seeds' were being cultivated in Great Tew common fields from 1691 at the latest, and by-laws kept sheep off the former in its first year.[4] At Aynho a by-law in 1702, on condition he throws the aftermath open to the commoners and abates three sheep from his common stint in the first year, permits that 'Mr Cartwright shall sowe what sandfoyle or other grass seed he pleases on the further side of London way beyond brooke, provided he mound it apart for the first yeare after it is sowed'. In 1700 Taston, in 1708 Spelsbury, and 1715 Fulwell common-field farmers were sowing sainfoin, by no means all for the first time.[5] In 1712 the lord of Longborough agreed the tenants might plough up Greenhill and the Downs, hitherto reserved for sheep-pasture, for a period of four years, each tenant breaking up two acres, provided he laid it down with two bushels of grass 'seeds' an acre.[6] At Great Rollright in 1732 three furlongs were ordered to be sown down with 'seeds' under barley. Those who had already sown sainfoin were allowed to mound it off for all the first year. In 1733 sainfoin was to be sown elsewhere.[7] In 1748 clover hitchings were introduced at Whichford and became as regular as the pea and vetch ones. Clover was chiefly reserved for feeding off to the horses in common, but part could be cut for hay. In 1750 all the ploughed hillground called Whichford Hill was ordered to be sown to clover by the yardland at the jury's direction.[8] Clover, sown under barley, was regularly cultivated at Brailes by 1752. By 1758 at the latest a clover hitching had been introduced at Adlestrop.[9] In 1762 a hundred weight of clover, bought by the constable

[1] Northants. R.O., Misc. Led. 146, p. 13.

[2] Ibid. Daventry 549b, arts. 5–7.

[3] Marshall, *Midl. Dept*, 172; Pitt, op. cit. 61, 81–2, 95; Laurence, op. cit. 45.

[4] Webb, op. cit. i, 81, 83.

[5] Northants. R.O., Aynho Ct R. 12 Oct. 1 Anne; Havinden, art. cit. 76–8.

[6] Shak. Bpl. Leigh: Ct R. Longborough 5 May 1691, 24 Apr. 1712.

[7] Jeffery, *Gt Rollright*, 27.

[8] B.M., Add. 36585, ff. 255, 262, 268v.–9, 277, 284v., 285v., 299–300, 313–14.

[9] B'ham Lib. 168125, 16 Oct. 1752; Shak. Bpl. Leigh: Adlestrop Ct R. 20 Mar. 1758, 14 Apr. 1760, 26 Apr. 1762.

out of the common purse, was sown under barley in Steeple Aston fields and one entire furlong laid to sainfoin. Next year as much clover was sown in a new hitching.[1] From the fourth decade of the century or before, turnip cultivation entered the common fields. In the spring of 1743 each Adlestrop man was ordered to sow turnips for hurdling off to his own sheep; and some had grown them the previous year.[2] In 1747 Great Rollright jury agreed, perhaps not for the first time, 'to sow turnips at the further side of West Field so farr as the neighbours think fitt'; and in another part turnips were to be sown for hurdling off to sheep.[3] At Whichford in 1754 the old clover hitching was ordered to be sown with turnips to be fed off to sheep, pulled for them or sold off as desired.[4] In 1756 the common-field farmers of Great Tew were allowed 'to lay as many sheep upon the turnips as they will'. The general upshot of these innovations in the common fields was that the field-courses became similar to those in enclosed farms, narrowing the gap that had widened between the two after 1650.[5] Hence the enclosures that shortly ensued made little difference to farming practices, except that some old greensward balks were now converted to arable, usually after being sod-burned for turnips.[6]

Similarly, in the Vale of Evesham, by 1699 Alveston and Tiddington heath had been broken up for corn and thrown into four quarters like the rest of the common fields. In 1704 there is an order 'that the first break of the heath shall be laid down this next crop and sown with grass-seed'. The commoners are also 'to break up another part of the heath this yeare ensuinge', evidently in a mature arable-grass rotation. In 1713 it was the turn of the 'black ground' to be sown with oats and grass-seed, while the first heath quarter was now ploughed up for six crops. Meanwhile, the wheat stubble on the heath was to be ploughed for a last crop of oats as a nurse for grass-seeds bought out of the common purse. At the same time the upper Great Rye Field was to be broken up and the lower laid down. In 1719 the black ground seeded down in 1713 was to be broken up after one further year, and the wheat stubble summer-fallowed, sown to barley and oats in the spring and then laid down with clover and 'seeds' at the discretion of the field overseers. In 1720 the next two Rye Field quarters and the Milking Place in the cow-pasture were to be ploughed up for three crops and eight years respectively, before all were seeded down. The year 1724 saw similar orders for ploughing up and laying down. By 1728 turnip cultivation had been established under common regulations, for some land was now to be

---

[1] C. C. Brookes, *Hist. Steeple Aston & Middle Aston* 1929, pp. 130–3.

[2] Shak. Bpl. Leigh: Adlestrop Ct R. 21 Mar. 1742–3; Atkyns, op. cit. 22.

[3] Jeffery, op. cit. 27–8.

[4] B.M., Add. 36585, f. 299.

[5] Webb, op. cit. i, 81 sqq.

[6] Brookes, op. cit. 133; Jeffery, op. cit. 29; Marshall, *Glos.* ii, 38.

ploughed to turnips and some already in turnips sown to barley and clover, for mowing in the first year and feeding to sheep in the second, before being broken up for wheat. This shift was then to continue in tillage for six crops, including a last one of clover. Similar orders were made in subsequent years, e.g. in 1730, when Alveston Townsend was to be turnip fallow next summer, the turnips being divided into breaks by the overseers and fed to the common flock. In 1732 Sand Field was to be marled when broken up for turnip fallow. In 1751, 1759 and 1761 similar practices continued. At Shottery in 1711 the common fields had much the same arable-grass rotation.[1]

A similar pattern of development can be seen in the Chalk Country. The tenants in many townships, convinced at length of the advantage of rye-grass and clover, came to an agreement to sow them in all or part of their spring field, previous to a wheat crop, instead of suffering the ground to be bare-fallowed. In some instances they altered their fields for this purpose, by making a fourth where there were originally but three; in others the three fields still remained and the grass stood for one year only. Elsewhere clover sometimes replaced tares in the hitching field.[2] In 1677 the tenantry of Wylye agreed to restrict peas to one-third of the West End fallow fields each year, showing that the hitching was large, but not until 1723 was clover certainly sown in it. By 1716 clover was being grown in Chalke common fields. In 1706 the Ibthorpe and in 1723 the Burcombe tenants agreed to sow the summer field to grass under barley. In the same year the Netherhampton tenantry restricted 'horsemeat' to one-quarter of the wheat field and agreed to sow the rest to grass. By 1725 clover and 'seeds' were old-established crops in the common fields of West Overton and Chalke. In 1749 the tenants of Netherhampton specified broad clover, 'hop-clover' (trefoil) and rye-grass as the crops to be sown under barley. In 1752 it was first presented as the custom of Burcombe that the sowing of turnips, fallowing and raftering, presumably after clover and 'seeds', were not to commence before July 5. The new common fields laid out at Fovant, Broad Chalke and Stoke Farthing were to be sown with broad clover, 'hop-clover' and rye-grass under barley or other lent grain.[3] Thus, even if tardily,

---

[1] Shak. Bpl. Ct R. Alveston & Tiddington 11 Oct. 1699, 20 Oct. 1704, 17 Oct. 1712, 30 Oct. 1713, 25 Oct. 1719, 21 Oct. 1720, 30 Oct. 1724, 4 Oct. 1728, 13 Oct. 1730, 4 Nov. 1731, 20 Oct. 1732, 10 Oct. 1740, 23 Oct. 1751, 26 Oct. 1759, 21 Oct. 1761; Ct R. Shottery 16 Apr. 1711.

[2] T. Davis, op. cit. 43–4; Slater, op. cit. 20.

[3] Naish, op. cit. 44; Wilton ho. Ct R. 1666–89, Wylye 25 Sept. 1677; Ct R. Manors 1689–1754, box ii, Burcombe & Ugford, p. 57; Chalke, pp. 134, 136, 148, 157, 164; box iii, Netherhampton & Washerne, p. 69; box iv, Wylye, p. 86; Ct Bks starting 1724: Burcombe 1724, 1752–82; W. Overton 1725, 1728, 1732, 1736; Chalke 1728, 1729, 1731, 1735; Ct Bks starting 1742–3: Netherhampton 1749, 1750; Ct Bk Netherhampton starting 1752, init.

common fields participated in these improvements, all eminently suited to permanent tillage or arable-grass rotations. The usual tenantry three-field course now became (1) wheat, (2) barley, (3) clover and 'seeds', part mown, part fed. The best four-field course was (1) wheat, (2) barley, (3) clover and 'seeds' fed or mown, (4) clover and 'seeds' fed until summer fallowing for wheat; and the worst, (1) wheat, (2) barley, (3) oats, (4) clover and 'seeds', part fed, part mown. Sometimes there was a six-field course of (1) wheat, (2) barley, (3) oats, (4) clover and 'seeds' mown or fed, (5) oats or barley, (6) summer fallow for wheat; and occasionally a five-field, like (1) wheat, (2) barley, (3) rye-grass, fed off in spring to sheep for (4) turnips, fed off in turn to sheep for (5) barley.[1] These courses might be changed, but were strictly enforced.

In the Oxford Heights Country, again, the innovations later spread to the surviving common fields. Cumnor fields were thrown into four quarters or seasons to accommodate the new crops.[2] In 1748 the common-field farmers of Watchfield agreed to divide their land into four 'partitions' or quarters for a four-field course of (1) wheat, (2) barley, (3) beans, clover, peas, tares or oats, (4) fallow. Clover was grown in only part of the third season, being sown under one acre of barley in a yardland, i.e. on about a tenth of the partition. Exhausted parts of the field were laid down with sainfoin, and others with perennial rye-grass and 'hop-clover' for sheep-pastures.[3] Lastly, in the Chiltern Country, by 1685, sainfoin was being grown in Hitchin common fields by arrangement between the different occupiers.[4]

In short, all the important new crops started to come about 1650. By around 1673 they had made their major impact. By 1720 they had spread everywhere and percolated far down, but it was only between then and about 1760 that the innovations were virtually completed on the most backward farms. Incidentally, we may add that the cultivation of turnips, clover and grass seed was generally introduced into the lowlands of Scotland in the third quarter of the eighteenth century, and this may be taken as the last lap of the course run by the new crops in Britain.[5]

[1] Davis, op. cit. 44 sqq.; Pearce, op. cit. 29; Slater, loc. cit.; Brentnall, 'Longford MS.', 16–18; Wilts. R.O., Enclo. Awards, Fovant & Broad Chalke 1792; Berks. R.O., D./E.By E70.

[2] Mavor, op. cit. 147, 166–8.

[3] Berks. R.O., D./E.El, E2; D./E.Pb E52/1, 2; E53.

[4] Hine, *Hitchin* i, 59.

[5] J. E. Handley, *Scot. Farming in 18th cent.* 1953, pp. 145 sqq., 155 sqq., 203–4, 213.

CHAPTER VIII

NEW SYSTEMS

IT was in the natural course of events that the new crops gave rise to new systems of husbandry.

High Suffolk remained self-sufficient in corn and grain. Winter corn, barley and summer corn continued much as before, but tares gave some ground to clover and wheat and beans were grown more. One pair of punches abreast became the usual plough-team. Small numbers of sheep were fed as formerly and beeves, newly including Scots ones also, were now fattened also in winter. The farms had as many poultry and hogs as before. Hemp remained a speciality about Diss, Eye and Beccles. Barley usually succeeded turnip (or cabbage) fallows and wheat a crop of clover or pulse. One succession commonly employed was (1) turnips (or cabbages), (2) barley, (3) beans or clover, (4) wheat. Bare summer fallows were not altogether abandoned, however, least of all in preparation for wheat, and smothering crops of mustard were taken occasionally. Butter now became of paramount importance. Butter made from the milk of cows fed on turnips, cabbages, hay and straw was scarcely if anything inferior to that from grass milk and better than hay butter. As turnip or cabbage cream cheese was not as good as that from grass, and 'bang' stored so well that it commanded a good price as a provision for long voyages, there was little point in producing winter cheese, whereas High Suffolk had a virtual monopoly of winter butter and commanded the market. Therefore the dairies concentrated more and more on butter and summer cream cheese. About 40,000 dun cows were applied to butter and cheese production, each cow in milk yielding about six gallons a day or eight at the height of the grass season.[1] High Suffolk winter dairy produce was unique. Turnip and

---

[1] Invs.:—E. Sfk R.O., A/d 1684–5: 14–15, 37, 93, 101, 126, 129, 159, 161, 166, 172; 1702: 34, 66, 95; W. Sfk R.O., Episc. Commy Ct Bury St. Edm's. 1685–6 fnd loose Jn Partridge/Stoke by Nayland; 1688: 10, 15; 1692: 106; 1696: 65, 84; 1699: 55, 67; 1700: 8, 1701: 23, 27, 49; 1702: 5; Nfk R.O., Cons. Ct. 1662: 27, 29, 68, 97; 1666: 55; 1677: 3, 150; 1668: 45, 80; 1675: 39; 1685: 33; Misc. 1628–68: 32; Blome,

cabbage butter ensured essential fresh supplies throughout the year. In addition, High Suffolk helped to fill the gap in winter beef supplies and supplied the model for the speciality of turnip beef in East Norfolk.

Here turnips and clover with rye-grass became integral parts of a new six-field course.[1] Since the soils were so uniform and the new general plan of management hinged on the production of fat stock from arable crops, East Norfolk became unique for the uniformity of its field-courses. Since East Norfolk alone of all improved countries developed a regular field-course, this achieved fame as the Norfolk system.[2] As field-courses are often confused in the lay mind with crop rotations, this system, in turn, was misnamed the 'Norfolk rotation'. Finally, due to the system being erroneously supposed to have been based on a four-field course and to a dim awareness of some confusion between field-course and crop rotation, the systematic field-course became publicized as the 'Norfolk four-course rotation'.

East Norfolk farms mostly comprised a score of small enclosed fields, True, some 'pightles' were tiny and bettered by being thrown together, but the fields generally remained small and numerous from the need to distribute evenly over the whole farm, turnip crops that were not fed off but pulled, and then not stored in sheds and given to cattle in houses, but thrown to them in the fields. These were grouped into six shifts, each shift containing three or four closes. Each year one or two fields in each shift were under a 'shift crop', i.e. were cropped according to the following regular succession: (1) wheat, (2) barley, (3) turnips, hoed as a fallow crop, (4) barley, undersown with clover and perennial rye-grass, (5) rye-grass and clover hay, (6) rye-grass and clover ley, fed off until midsummer, or until the bullocks went to market, and then broken up for summer fallows, usually by raftering. The summerley was stirred three or four times, being ploughed and harrowed alternately throughout the rest of the summer in a thorough-going way, with the object of extirpating weeds and ameliorating the soil in preparation for wheat. This bare, much-stirred, summer fallow was 'the very corner stone, the firm foundation of Norfolk husbandry', and summerley wheat was worth twice as much as clover wheat. While the 'shift field' of each shift was under a shift crop in this regular succession, the other closes in the same shift might be, and often were, outside the shift

---

Brit. 207; Rochefoucauld, op. cit. 75, 193; Defoe, op. cit. i, 59–60; Young, *Sfk.* 21, 23–4, 41–2; Mortimer, op. cit. 147; Childrey, op. cit. 101; Norden, *Survy's. Dial.* 213; Coles, op. cit. cap. ccxlii; Griggs, op. cit. 18; Vancouver, *Ess.* 64–6; Marshall, *Midl. Dept,* 477–8; *Nfk* i, 133, 362–3; *E. Dept,* 385, 429–30, 436, 442–4, 454–5, 457, 460–1, 467.

[1] Ibid. 382; *Nfk* i, 132.
[2] Ibid.; *E. Dept,* 136–7.

succession and not under the shift crop. Instead they might be sown with oats, tares, peas or buckwheat or be given a whole year's fallow, or even eighteen months' bare fallow, with summer stirrings, which was considered enough to restore heart to the most exhausted land. No field, however, missed the turnip fallow or the summer fallow of the succession, except when fallowed for a year or more.[1] Thus the six shifts of the course succeeded each other not in particular fields, but only in particular shifts, and not necessarily in all the fields of each shift. No field was subjected to the shift crops of the succession in two six-year periods one after the other, but in one of these was rested from the shift crops for a time, peas, oats or buckwheat being grown instead of barley or tares, peas or buckwheat instead of rye-grass and clover ley, or a bare substituted for a turnip fallow in order to restore the land to heart and prepare a clean tilth. It was not every fifth and sixth year that the same field bore clover, but only more occasionally, so the land could not become clover-sick.[2] Another reason for the intricacy of the six-shift course, apart from the danger of clover-sickness and the occasional necessity for whole year's bare fallows, was that it was necessary to have a flexible system that permitted readjustment in the event of crop failure. If the turnips failed, the farmer might sow wheat, and if the clover and 'seeds' did not take well, peas might be substituted. Yet when a field was not a shift field under a shift crop, it was never cultivated in such a way as to prevent it being brought back into the shift the next year. The six-shift system combined the maximum flexibility of cropping with the minimum regularity consonant with the desirable policy of keeping the land in course.[3] A remarkable feature of the six-field course was that each field was fallowed every third summer, winter fallowed every sixth year after wheat, and given a twelve or eighteen months' bare fallow as occasion required. So far from the new husbandry expelling bare fallows from the farm, these formed an essential part of the system and farmers covenanted to fallow all the tillage every third year.[4]

Most of East Norfolk used the six-field course, but it did not suit the broadland clay loams, where the danger was not one of exhausting the soil, but of insufficiently tempering its strength to prevent the crops being too rank and so in peril of lodging at the first storm. Moreover, the fen-grounds made temporary grazing leys unnecessary. A common succession here was (1) wheat, (2) barley, (3) clover for hay, (4) wheat, (5) oats.[5] The general result of six-field courses and broadland successions was that barley was the grain most grown. Barley and wheat were

---

[1] Ibid. 331, 342–5, 347, 379, 382, 392; *Nfk* i, 131–3, 142; Nfk R.O., invs., esp Cons. Ct. 1671: 12; A/d Ct 1674–5: 148, 165.

[2] Marshall, *Midl. Dept*, 478; *E. Dept*, 136–7.

[3] Ibid. 137, 320–1.   [4] Marshall, *Nfk* i, 75.   [5] Ibid. ii, 191–2.

the market, and clover and rye-grass, turnips, oats, peas, tares, buck-wheat and natural grasses the consumption crops. In addition, some weld, hemp and hops were grown and a little cole-seed.[1]

The grand basis of husbandry was the turnip crop for beef. In all but the worst weather, the turnips were pulled and thrown to bullocks in the stubbles, leys and fallows. The soil suited pulling and the fields were small enough to enable the turnips to be thrown almost anywhere on the farm, so carting was reduced to the minimum.[2] The great object of farming was bullocks that were first fatted on turnips in winter and then finished on rye-grass and clover for sale between mid-May and mid-June, during which period East Norfolk beef reigned supreme in the markets, precisely filling the gap between the stall-fed beef of High Suffolk and elsewhere and the grass beef of the Midland Plain and similar countries.[3] Homebred beasts were joined, no later than 1660, by imported Scots cattle.[4] Perennial rye-grass, that most valuable of species, was also the best for finishing off turniped bullocks. As it nursed clover in the first year and in the second was first fed off close and then broken up as soon as the bullocks left the field, it never ran up too high.[5] Apart from fen-grounds in the broadlands and wet meadows, which were in a state of nature, watering by art being quite unknown, there was little natural grassland. Long leys were seldom employed, and then of Suffolk and cow grass usually.[6] Domestic dairies were kept, but most herds were now converted from milking to breeding and rearing, for the supply of feeding bullocks.[7] Fatting oxen were never worked for exercise and draught was supplied solely by punches. Two sufficed for a plough-team, but a string of five was used to draw wagons. In winter the punches were provendered mainly on barley straw, with some clover or tare hay, but, when working, hay oats or barley, both with the chaff, and in summer, clover, tares or aftermaths.[8] Very few sheep were stocked, even in summer. Most farmers had none. Over-wintered flocks and sheep-folds were rarities found only in landowners' parks, about the few remaining heathlets, and on a small number of the capital farms. Where available, the sheep-fold was highly valued for barley and considered the surest preventive of turnip fly,[9] but the universal fertilizer

[1] Ibid. i, 125–6, 133, 375–6; E. Dept, 349; Nfk R.O., Cons. & A/d cts. invs.

[2] Ibid.; Marshall, loc. cit; Nfk i, 256, 284, 287–8.

[3] Ibid. 35, 125; E. Dept, 332; invs. ut sup.

[4] Marshall, Nfk i, 323–4; Nfk R.O., invs. Cons. Ct Misc. 1628–68: 3; 1668: 27; A/d ct 1674–5: 148, 170.

[5] Marshall, op. cit. i, 303–4; ii, 12; E. Dept, 391–2.

[6] Nfk R.O., Cons. Ct inv. 1690–1: 29; Marshall, Nfk i, 301–2, 310, 312, 317, 319–20.

[7] Ibid. 127; Nfk R.O., Cons. & A/d cts invs.

[8] Ibid.; Marshall, op. cit. i, 42, 44, 46, 48–9, 126.

[9] Ibid. i, 35, 127, 362–3; ii, 1, 14–15, 26–7, 30, 35; invs. ut sup., esp. A/d Ct 1674–5: 91.

was the rich 'teathe' of fatting bullocks, which was ploughed in at the very first opportunity, and wheat was not usually top-folded with sheep when too rank; instead cattle were pressed into service.[1] Although the dairy was, in a manner, put down, some hogs and many turkeys were fattened as before.[2]

Sheep-and-corn husbandry remained the outline of management in the Chiltern Country. More and better sheep-feed meant more and better cereals and a new line in mutton. Wether tegs were bought in at two or three years of age, folded on fallows for two years and then fatted; while breeding ewes were likewise folded except when yeaning. In late autumn and winter, sheep fed on turnips sown in the fallows in successions in early summer. They then passed to rye, winter vetches, and clover and 'seeds' leys. Before they went on turnips, their tails were docked, so rank was the feed; and this had the advantage of making them look plumper. Turnips were carefully hurdled off and the sheep had no more than they could eat up clean the same day. The essential point in sheep management was, they were always divided into two flocks, of stores and feeders respectively, and the latter always preceded the former over the same grounds. Early in the morning, one after the other, the two flocks were folded on turnips. In this first passage they were not given time to eat the turnips clean up, but were passed continually to new feed, and then brought back again to finish off the turnip offals. This done, they were yet again put on to turnips, fresh ones this time, that they might return full to the nocturnal fold. After March the sheep had a change from turnips. On being let out of the fold in the early morning, they were left in the fallow field, to eat down weeds and browse in the hedge-greens until two or three in the afternoon. Then they moved to rye for a time, and afterwards to temporary pastures of rye-grass, white clover, trefoil and similar mixtures. Here they stayed until nightfall, when they returned to the fold, now set up in a fresh part of the tillage. Rye was replaced, at the turn of April and May, by winter vetches, and these, in late summer, by tares and other pulses. Since sainfoin now provisioned the horses, the sheep had the tares and summer pulses to themselves. Then, in late summer and early autumn, there were always stubbles to be grazed. In heavy soils sheep could not be folded in wet weather and the shepherd let them out to shelter in the hedge and coppice-rows. This apart, the fold was unremitting and there were usually 300 or more folding nights a year. Both store and fatting flocks were folded for corn, save the fat wethers, which were finished off on turnips and then sold in late winter or early spring, when grass mutton was scarcest, cole-seed mutton expended and turnip mutton at a premium. Although it entailed a sacrifice of quality

[1] Marshall, op. cit. i, 15, 33–4; ii, 199.
[2] Ibid. i, 372, 375–6; invs. ut sup., esp. Cons. ct 1666: 3.

in the wool, which came to rank amongst the worst in England, the addition of a fatting flock, and the improved diet of both stores and feeders, greatly increased both the quantity and quality of the sheep-fold, especially for barley.[1]

Barley remained the chief market crop. The fields, even if common, were generally thrown into three or four shifts, one of which was usually fallowed each year. Most of the fallow was sown with turnips in preparation for barley. This, in turn, was undersown with clover and 'seeds' for one or two years as a matrix for wheat, or for rye, which was fed off in spring in preparation for wheat. Sometimes a turnip, instead of a rye fallow preceded wheat; and sometimes wheat was followed by oats undersown with 'seeds'. From time to time, too, barren soil was laid to sainfoin for seven years or so, the hay mown and the aftermath grazed by horses and cattle.[2] The general plan of management was vastly improved in the third quarter of the seventeenth century, but not changed in basis. The objects were wheat, winter mutton and, first and foremost, barley, especially malting barley.

In the Petworth District, the area of cultivated herbage was greatly reduced and instead of leys of natural grasses in a grass-arable rotation, there were only clover leys of one year's duration, i.e. an arable-grass rotation, which is the modification of permanent tillage to include short leys, involving the partial substitution of clover for tares. The difference between such arable-grass rotations and permanent tillage is more verbal than real, and, it may be said, whereas the great clovers are commonly supposed to have been the essential prerequisite of convertible husbandry, their function in this district was to displace convertible husbandry with natural grass leys in favour of an arable-grass rotation or quasi-permanent tillage. The arable acreage remained much as before, but the tillage was considerably extended. The reason given by farmers for their preference for a one-year clover ley was that longer leys would encourage the sod-worm, to the destruction of the wheat. Wireworms, and leather-jackets, would certainly have been a danger, but were not an insuperable obstacle to long leys, and the crucial factor in deciding farmers in favour of one-year leys must have been that tillage crops were more useful to them than

[1] Herts. R.O., 22101; invs.:—A/d St. Albans: Wm Weedon 1683 Bushey, Th. Hills 1685 St Paul's Walden, Robt Morgan 1693 Watford; A/d Hunts. Hitchin Div. sep. invs. Geo. Crawley 1703 Harpenden, Sam. Bassill 1708 Watton at Stow. Geo. Beech 1730 Flamsted; Wills & Invs. Jn Burley 1690 Bps Hatfield; W. Sfk R.O., Episc. Commy Ct Bury St Edm's. 1692: 58; Plot, Oxon. 240, 244, 250; Marshall, S. Dept, 15; Midl. Dept, 603; Kalm, op. cit. 230; Ellis, Sheep, 43, 51–2, 209 sqq., 219–21, 224–6, 228, 243; Lisle, op. cit. 425.

[2] Ibid. 86; Kalm, loc. cit.; Ellis, op. cit. 217; James & Malcolm, Bucks. 21–2; Walker, op. cit. 30; Marshall, op. cit. 561; R. Davis, op. cit. 12; Childrey, op. cit. 85; Stone, Beds. 18.

temporary pastures and that clover was sown as an alternative to tares.[1]

In the Sandlings Country, some of the new successions employed were (1) turnips, (2) barley, (3) carrots; (1) carrots, (2) barley with rye-grass and clover for hay, (3) the same fed off, (4) peas, (5) rye; and (1) turnips, (2) barley, (3) rye or peas, (4) carrots.[2] The introduction of turnips permitted the production of some winter mutton and butter. Otherwise sheep-and-corn farming was continued with little change, but it now went with horse-and-carrot husbandry and the breeding and rearing of punches for sale to other parts of East Anglia.

The fold-course system of the Norfolk Heathlands impeded any improvement in the field-course and the introduction of profitable fallow crops. In some localities where the fold-course persisted, it still prevented turnip cultivation even in the eighteenth century.[3] Its abolition thus became imperative to the farmers, but was not easily accomplished. The tenants might, as at Kenninghall, buy out the liberty of the fold-course;[4] but this was expensive. Dismembering and selling off a manor destroyed the liberty, but was rarely practicable.[5] The only solution satisfactory to small farmers and acceptable to landlords and proprietors of fold-courses was a general enclosure of the township and the extinction of both common rights and fold-course liberties. This was the course adopted. Some heaths and rough grazings remained open in the early eighteenth century, but by this time most common fields had been enclosed by agreements that extended also to the extinction of fold-courses.[6] The introduction of turnips and other fallow crops defeated the fold-course and reconciled landowners to its demise by offering profitable alternatives to all concerned.

Clover and 'seeds', and turnips, constituted two components of the new husbandry. A third was enclosure by agreement and the defeat of fold-courses. The fourth was the increased use of old fertilizers. The sheepfold was of great antiquity, the application of chalk marl far from a novelty. The fifth component was embanking and draining salt-marshes and converting them from fatting grounds for sheep to arable in a convertible system.[7]

The changes introduced built on the old system rather than made a

[1] Marshall, *S. Cos.* ii, 170, 188; W. Suss. R.O., Cons. Ct Bp Cicestr. for A/d Cicestr. invs., esp. Hy Courtney 1673 Midhurst; 1689: Ric. Nayno/Easebourne, Jn Humphrey/Tillington; Jn Talmey 1692 Fittleworth, Eliz. Browing 1693 Grafham.

[2] Marshall, *E. Dept,* 445–6; Rochefoucauld, op. cit. 182; E. Sfk R.O., A/d invs.

[3] Marshall, *Midl. Dept,* 638; Gooch, op. cit. 145.

[4] Spratt, op. cit. 254.

[5] P.R.O., Req. 102/45, compl.

[6] Corbett, art. cit. 83–4; Allison, op. cit. 60, 65–6, 70–3; Riches, op. cit. 47 sqq.; Marshall, *Nfk* i, 1, 116; ii, 365.

[7] Sup. 223–4, 245.

clean sweep. The land had been disposed in arable and heath. Now most of the heathlands were made arable in permanent cultivation, and the old arable-grass rotations vastly improved. Field-courses and crop rotations had formerly been varied from place to place, but had been ossified to meet the requirements of the fold-course. Now regular field-courses and crop rotations were done away with. Apart from the meadow, a few permanent grasslands, and the drained marshes, which were in a convertible system, the whole of the farmland was given over to series of varied arable-grass rotations. Some of the many successions employed were (1) turnips, (2) barley, (3) clover for hay, (4) wheat; (1) turnips, (2) barley, (3) clover and 'seeds' hay, (4) clover and 'seeds' fed off, (5) wheat; (1) turnips, (2) barley, (3) clover and 'seeds' for hay, (4) the same, fed off, (5) peas, (6) wheat; (1) wheat, (2) barley, (3) turnips, (4) barley, (5) clover and 'seeds' hay, (6) clover and 'seeds' fed off; (1) turnips, (2) oats, (3) clover for hay, (4) wheat; (1) whole-year bare fallow summer stirred, (2) wheat, (3) turnips, (4) clover and 'seeds' hay, (5) clover and 'seeds' fed off, (6) wheat. Countless other variations were made on the same and similar themes, but were all mixed and interchanged, so that the same succession was rarely used twice running. The first of the successions exemplified, the mythical 'Norfolk four-course rotation', was regarded as unprofitable for the tenant and bad for the landlord, because insufficient fodder and too much market corn was produced, but could be employed where plenty of drained salt-marsh was available. Fixed courses and rotations were mostly impracticable, but this particular succession could never be repeated until it became a rotation, because the land became clover-sick and the eel-worm multiplied, so that clover would not take. The most that can be said is that turnips, clover and 'seeds', wheat and barley became the chief crops, that rye and peas, and some vetches, continued to be grown, that cole-seed was cultivated in the marshes, that turnips were normally fed off for barley, and that wheat was usually grown on a matrix of clover and 'seeds'.[1]

Great flocks of sheep continued to be bred and reared, but were now folded on 'seeds' leys and turnips, causing a great increase in the production less of marsh than of turnip mutton that was sold off between March and Easter.[2] Dairies continued much as before, except that turnips were added to the diet, leading to an increased volume of winter milk; but feeding overshadowed milking and although more calves

---

[1] Nfk R.O., Cons. & A/d cts invs., esp. Cons. 1718–21: 69, 158, 214, 222, 244, 259, 270; A/d 1692: 156; Sinclair, op. cit. 5, 10; Plumb, art. cit. 87–9; Slater, op. cit. 331; R. Parker, op. cit. 160–2; L. W. Moffit, *Engl. on Eve Ind. Rev.* 1925, p. 279; Marshall, *Midl. Dept,* 478; *E. Dept,* 136–7, 373; Riches, op. cit. 82–3.

[2] Ibid. 101–4; Ellis, op. cit. 212; invs. ut sup., esp. Cons. 1677: 85; Plumb, art. cit. 87–8.

were now reared, many North Country and Scots runts were bought in early autumn to be fatted on turnips and sold off in March or April. Nevertheless, beef was always less important than mutton.[1] Clover and 'seeds', in reality mainly trefoil and perennial rye-grass, were for hay in the first season, but their aftermath and second year's growth were grazed by the sheep before they passed to turnips. Sainfoin remained no more than an occasional crop on exhausted land. Horses continued the chief source of tractive power.[2] Thus, in the new sheep-and-corn husbandry, the chief objects became wheat, barley and turnip mutton; and the chief consumption crops turnips and clover and 'seeds'.

The outline of farm management in the Northdown Country, too, remained sheep-and-corn husbandry. Barley and wheat were the chief market crops, but fruit and hops, wheat and clover seeds, and mutton were also important. To the old consumption crops of natural grasses and podware, selected grasses, broad clover, trefoil, sainfoin and turnips were now added, together with some lucerne and rape. Farming was thus greatly improved, while remaining basically the same.[3] Wheat was usually preceded by clover or podware, but on flinty clay loams, when grown for seed, or where quality was the first consideration, by a summer, whole-year or eighteen months' bare fallow, it being held that, to produce its best, the 'land must have a holiday'. The great benefit of clean fallowing was precisely appreciated, as in the inventory of Thomas Carter of East Sutton in 1680. His 4½ acres of fallow wheat were valued at £10 odd and his 8¼ acres of gratton wheat at £11. Even when preceded by tares or other podware, wheat was usually given an autumn, and barley a winter bare fallow. Barley sometimes followed a turnip or rye fallow, the crop being fed off by sheep in winter or spring respectively. Occasionally too, rye was fed off for a succeeding turnip fallow. Barley remained the chief and best crop, especially in the Isle of Thanet, being grown about one-third as much again as either wheat or forage. On sandy loams, rye and turnip fallows were more numerous, and in the stiffer lands west of the Isle of Thanet and in the Maidstone and Canterbury districts, wheat and bean crops.[4] Wheat, rye-grass and clover were

[1] Ibid. 86–8; invs. ut sup., esp. Cons. 1679: 89; 1688–9: 61; A/d 1674–5: 92; Riches, op. cit. 97.

[2] Ibid. 107; Sinclair, op. cit. 8; invs. ut sup., esp. Cons. 1677: 85.

[3] Marshall, *S. Cos.* i, 68–9; ii, 11, 26–7, 403, 406, 409, 411; Boys, op. cit. 61–2, 64 sqq., 73–5, 95–6; Lisle, op. cit. 109; Lambert, op. cit. ii, 65; *Arch. Cant.* lxi, 60 sqq., 69–72; 'Nat. Hist. Dorking', *Gent's. Mag.* xxxiii, 221; B.M., Add. R. 16280; Herts. R.O., 22042; Kent & Hants. R.O.s, Cons. & A/d cts invs.: H.M.C., *Portland MSS.* vi, 77; R. Arnold, *Yeo. of Kent* 1949, pp. 33–5; Chalklin, op. cit. 86–7; Melling, op. cit. 36.

[4] Ibid. 24–7, 35 sqq., 69–71, 73–5; Childrey, op. cit. 69; Marshall, *S. Dept.* 382, 391–3, 432–3, 440; *S. Cos.* i, 69–70, 80–1, 95, 117, 137–8; ii, 11–14, 36–7, 406; Boys, op. cit. 14, 18, 61, 64 sqq., 72–3, 75; R. Lennard, art. cit. 35; invs. ut sup., esp.

extensively cultivated for seed, which was distributed through London.[1]
To mention one of the minor innovations, burnbaking was introduced
between 1635 and 1675 for breaking up poor land, and as the usual way
of preparing downs for turnips and sainfoin leys for wheat.[2] The only
new departures with horses and cows concerned their feed. Sainfoin was
widely used for foddering horses, especially in the Isle of Thanet and
near Maidstone. In these places, too, and particularly in the Isle of
Thanet, where it was sown broadcast on the open downs, lucerne became a common crop, which it did in no other farming country. This
gave excellent hay for horses, and sainfoin and lucerne aftermaths were
usually reserved for the tethering of horses and cows.[3] Flying flocks of
wethers bought in for fatting and resold at two or three years of age,
made up most of the sheep stock. Every morning, at six o'clock in
summer and at first light in winter, the shepherd moved his hurdles and
set up the fold afresh in readiness for penning. Then the flock was
driven to the more distant or inferior keep, to down-pastures if any.
At midday it was brought back to the fold for two or three hours, while
the shepherd had his dinner, and a nap in summer. In the afternoon
the sheep were gradually led towards the best feed on the farm, that they
might be replete when returned to the fold in the evening. Tares and
other podware remained the chief staple of sheep diet, except in the Isle
of Thanet, where red clover and trefoil were more important. These
were grown for sheep, to some extent, everywhere; so too, in many
places, were common or, later, Swedish, turnips, or rape; and weld was
fed by them in its first year of growth. In winter, the flocks now had
clover as well as meadow and tare hay. Thus the sheep had a great range
and variety of feeds. During the day they moved from one to another,
gradually working their way to the richest.[4]

As a result of the last wave of innovations in the Chalk Country, the
usual successions in severalty became: on the 'whiteland', (1) wheat,
(2) barley or oats, with clover and 'seeds', (3) part mown, part raftered
for wheat, i.e. substantially the old three-field course; or (1) wheat, (2)

A/d Cantuar. 1660: Eliz. Pelham/Sittingbourne, Jn Sole/Chislet; 1678: Wm Whiting/
Chislet; 1680: Jn Spillet/Boughton Malherbe, Th. Sandridge/Newington, Jn Allen/
Lenham, Th. Carter/E. Sutton.

[1] E.g. Kent R.O., A/d Ct Cantuar. invs. 1680: Mich. Denne/Littlebourne, Wm
Clagett/E. Sutton.
[2] Boys, op. cit. 65; Aubrey, Sy i, Evelyn's pref.; Marshall, op. cit. ii, 32.
[3] Ibid. i, 56–7, 69, 320, 322; ii, 10–12, 31–4, 404, 411; Kent & Hants. R.O.s,
Cons. & A/d cts invs.; Arch. Cant. loc. cit.; Melling, op. cit. 24–7, 36, 38–40, 45, 48;
Ess. R.O., D./D.L. E61, a/c 1586; B.M., Add. R. 16280; Herts. R.O., 22042; Lennard, art. cit. 31; Weston, op. cit. (1651) 8: Boys, op. cit. 96.
[4] Ibid. 110, 139, 155; Marshall, op. cit. ii, 11, 36–7, 411, 413; S. Dept, 391 sqq.,
409–11; Stevenson, Sy, 481; Aubrey, op. cit. ii, 306–7; J. Parkinson, op. cit. 603.

half clover and 'seeds', half barley and oats, (3) half ley and half beans, peas and vetches, this being regarded as the best three-field course; or (1) wheat, (2) barley or oats undersown with clover, (3) clover, mown or fed, and followed by a winter fallow, (4) summer fallow on foul land and beans, peas and vetches on the remainder; in flinty loams, (1) wheat, (2) barley, (3) clover, mown, (4) summer field fallowed for wheat, but part hitched for tares; in sandy loams, (1) wheat, on one earth, (2) turnips, fed off, (3) barley, (4) clover, mown or fed; or (1) wheat, (2) barley, (3) clover, (4) turnips, fed off; or (1) wheat, (2) turnips, (3) barley, (4) clover, followed by a late summer fallow; in the sandy soils of the Vale of Pewsey, (1) wheat, (2) half beans and pulse, or tares, or turnips, half barley or oats, (3) part clover and 'seeds', part bare fallow; and in the deeper 'redland' soils, (1) wheat, (2) barley, (3) turnips, (4) oats, (5) clover and 'seeds' for two years. It should not be thought, however, that there was much uniformity in these successions, for they were frequently changed or modified to suit individual circumstances, and variations were legion. In general, all that can be said is that wheat mostly continued to precede barley, and sainfoin restored burnbaked lands.[1]

New systems appeared similarly in the Cotswold Country with the introduction of sainfoin, turnips, clover and 'seeds', and when Bishop showed Cotswold farmers 'how to become an opulent people'.[2] Some land could still bear corn only once before laying down, but all these new crops led to the development of fresh two-tier multi-field courses, of which one may be instanced, namely, (1) turnips, (2) barley, (3) clover and 'seeds' for hay, (4) the same, grazed, (5) wheat, (6) oats or peas. This or a similar succession was repeated several times, and the exhausted soil then sown down with sainfoin under oats or barley after turnips, or under wheat. The first year the sainfoin ley was little or no use, but in the next gave a cut of hay excellent for horses and an aftermath to be fed also by sheep and cows. Some farmers threw soot on the sainfoin aftermath to prevent the sheep eating it off too short. When seven or eight years old, the sainfoin ley was pared and burned for wheat or turnips. It was notable that in this country, exceptionally, sainfoin was cultivated so extensively, it was not the especial preserve of horses, but was shared by all the farm stock. Winter feed for sheep was provided chiefly, however, by turnips hurdled off to them. Vetches were still grown for sheep, and peas sometimes but now clover and 'seeds'

---

[1] Lisle, op. cit. 46, 49, 55, 60, 246; T. Davis, op. cit. 53–5; Pearce, op. cit. 28; Marshall, S. Cos. ii, 325–6; Bodl. Hearne's diaries 159, p. 226; invs.:—Hants. R.O., A/d & Cons. cts; Wilts. R.O., Dioc. Reg. Sarum, A/d Wilts., A/d Sarum., Preb. Ct Husborne & Burbage, Pec. Ct Dean Sarum., Cons. Ct Sarum.; Dors. R.O., Cons. & A/d cts; W. Suss. R.O., Cons. Ct Bp Cicestr. for A/d Cicestr.

[2] Atkyns, op. cit. 21.

often gave both grazing and fodder. The chief crops were, for the market, barley, wheat, mutton and wool and, for consumption, oats, peas, turnips, vetches, sainfoin, trefoil, broad clover, melilot, rye-grass, and natural grasses.[1] New crops and management ameliorated the soils to such an extent that wheaten bread now replaced barley even on farm servants' and labourers' tables.[2] The new husbandry, adopted first in severalty and later in common fields, needed fewer plough-works than the old and yet left the extent of tillage, no less, and of arable greater, than before. In the old husbandry, the twin objects were corn and sheep; but now, in the new, mutton, especially from turnips, was preferred. While the acreage in arable grew, and under wheat vastly, sheep numbers doubled.[3]

Similar but less drastic changes were made in the Oxford Heights Country. Turnips were fed to sheep, clover partly replaced tares, and sainfoin, to break up which burnbaking was introduced in 1674, improved exhausted soil and provided hay for the horses.[4] The Breckland was too poor in its soils and climature to take full advantage of the new fodder crops, and it was thanks chiefly to rye that farmers were enabled to feed and sell more muttons; and this husbandry was both cause and consequence of the defeat of the fold-course. Mutton, however, never became as important as in the Norfolk Heathlands. The paramount object of farming remained cereals, now chiefly barley, the crops of which were improved by the preceding rye fallows.[5] Thus the Breckland and the Norfolk Heathlands became two clearly distinguished farming countries, which formerly they were not.

The Southdown Country likewise recast its husbandry to accommodate the new crops. In the eighteenth century, some rape was grown to provide the sheep with a supper while on their way from the downs to the fields. In early summer, before they passed to the wheat stubbles, the sheep were often folded in preparation for turnips that were hurdled off to them in the winter months. Clover had been introduced; but winter and spring vetches continued to hold their own as hay and fodder crops. The best source of extra spring feed was in rye, or maslins of rye, black oats, winter vetches and rape, or any two of them. Rye was

[1] Ibid. 22; G. Turner, op. cit. 10–11, 13–14, 21, 27; Marshall, *W. Dept*, 413; *Midl. Dept*, 472, 488; *Glos.* ii, 10, 36–7; Havinden, 'Rural Econ. Oxon.', 194; invs.:— Wilts. R.O., Cons. Ct Sarum., Dioc. Reg. Sarum., A/d Wilts.; Soms. R.O., Cons. Ct Bath. & Well.; Northants. R.O., A/d Ct Northampton; Lichfield Jt R.O., Cons. Ct; Worcs. R.O., Cons. Ct; Glouc. Lib. Cons. Ct.; Bodl. Cons. & A/d cts Oxon.

[2] Bodl. Aubrey 2, ff. 83–4.

[3] Marshall, op. cit. ii, 10–11, 27, 36, 79; *W. Dept.* 409; Morton, op. cit. 483; Atkyns, op. cit. 21; J. Dyer, 'The Fleece' (1770) bk ii, 108; invs. ut sup.

[4] Bodl. Aubrey 2, ff. 83, 85; Wilts. R.O., Cons. Ct Sarum. invs.

[5] Invs.:—Nfk R.O., Cons. & A/d cts; W. Sfk R.O., Episc. Commy Ct Bury St Edm's.; sup. 288.

much sown for hurdling off, especially to the couples.[1] The cultivation of these crops constituted the chief improvement made in the plan of management, which remained basically unchanged.[2]

In the Northwold Country, as the new crops spread on the upper wolds, to the destruction of cony-warrens, they were often accompanied by the extinction of common rights,[3] and preceded by the systematic stubbing up of the whins, which had previously been cut only for fuel and dead hedging.[4] In these thin soils it was not unusual to burnbake for turnips, which were folded to sheep in preparation for two successive crops of oats, and perhaps a further one of barley, with clover and 'seeds' sown under whichever came last. One succession in the deeper vale soils was (1) turnip fallow, folded off, (2) barley, undersown with (3) clover and 'seeds', (4) wheat. Sainfoin provided the horses with hay, leaving more of the other fodders for the sheep, and gave some aftermath for horses and cows.[5] Already before the introduction of the new crops the practice had arisen of buying in Scots cattle. These found even the poor wold pastures so much better than their native moors that they soon put on flesh. This tended to slacken the demand for marsh and lowland grass lettings, a call then further lessened by new crops. 'Since the practice of improveing lands with turnops is set up,' as a contemporary says, 'they take that way of so improveing their own lands and feeding the sheep themselves, or can now sell 'em (tho' leane) into those countreys where they practice turnop improvement.'[6] Hence the introduction of turnips led to the partial discarding of lowland annexes and out-farms and slightly diminished the size of the country. Farmers hardly fatted more sheep than before, though they now concentrated on winter mutton and lamb, and the chief benefit of the new crops was seen in the enrichment of the sheep-fold and the extension and intensification of cereal cultivation.[7] Wethers never displaced the flock from its key position, and the general plan of management continued to be the breeding of folding flocks for the production of cereals. Barley, particularly malting samples, and wheat, remained the principal objects of farming.

As a result of clover cultivation, the general plan of management in

[1] W. Suss. R.O., Cons. Ct Bp Cicestr. for A/d Cicestr. invs.; Young, *Suss.* 39, 67; Marshall, *S. Dept*, 485, 487–8, 504–5; *S. Cos.* ii, 279, 333.

[2] Ibid. 383–4.

[3] Marshall, *Yks.* ii, 245–6; Barley, op. cit. 81.

[4] Crossley, 'Test. Docs.', 95, 102.

[5] Marshall, op. cit. ii, 245, 252–3, 257; Stone, *Lincs.* 39; Leatham, op. cit. 48; invs.:—Lincs. R.O., Cons. Ct; York, Prerogative Ct Abp, Mkt Weighton & N. Newbald Prebs. Cf. Tenn. 'N. Farmer O.S.' x.

[6] Lincs. R.O., Monson: Newton Papers 7/13/232; invs. ut sup.; Eland, *Shardeloes*, 60–1.

[7] Ibid. 61; Barley, loc. cit.; Lincs. R.O., M.M. VI/5/2, 9, 30, 32; invs. ut sup.

Midland up-and-down husbandry was modified. Sown alone or in a mixture, clover made possible annual, biennial or triennial leys, which could be employed in arable-grass rotations. Most farmers continued to prefer long leys, but annual or short ones were often adopted in turnip soils and combined with turnip and cabbage fallows in arable-grass rotations that differed radically from the grass-arable ones on most of the up-and-down land. Either way, animal products remained a chief object, but in arable-grass rotations temporary leys of natural grasses were abandoned, so no reason was left to eschew turnip fallows or summer stirrings. In these localities, root and clover crops entailed abandoning long leys in a grass-arable rotation for short leys in an arable-grass one, and up-and-down husbandry in favour of ley farming of another kind.[1] Up-and-down husbandry lost some ground; but as it gained in turn from permanent tillage and grass, its predominance was not threatened; and as the districts of turnip soils and arable-grass rotations were small and scattered, no new farming country can be said to have been created. Whereas formerly two systems of husbandry had competed, namely, up-and-down husbandry and permanency, now three systems existed cheek by jowl.

At the same time the old grass-arable rotation was improved, for 'artificial' clover and 'seeds' speeded laying to grass. Formerly, only good managers got a useful ley in the first year. Now, a hay crop was virtually certain.[2] This advantage, however, was partially offset, for after a year or so the clover began to fail and give way to the now aggressive natural grasses, especially perennial rye-grass. While the two joined battle, the produce of each was restricted, until the latter's victory resulted in the final creation, three or four years after laying down, of an excellent long grazing ley in which natural grasses, clovers and herbs predominated. As farmers say,

'second years "seeds" are the worst grass: because the clover is then gone off and the natural grasses, having been checked by the pinfallow and kept under by the barley and the clover, have not yet recovered themselves: but the third year, having nothing to struggle with, they *rise again*; resuming the appearance and, in a considerable degree, the profitableness of old grass lands'.[3]

Since the leys were now established so quickly, advantage no longer

---

[1] Morton, op. cit. 483; Pitt, *Leics.* 34–5; Stapledon, op. cit. 185; Leicester Mus. 3D. 42/40/72, 85; Leics. R.O., Crane & Walton A/c 166; Marshall, *Midl. Cos.* i, 234, 263, 266–7.

[2] Ibid.; sup. 202.

[3] Plot, op. cit. 154; Morton, loc. cit.; Lisle, op. cit. 247, 259, 264; Pitt, *Northants.* 114; Marshall, op. cit. ii, 42.

attached to laying down under wheat, and since the leys were now productive sooner, it was pointless to retain them after their peak, now between the fourth and seventh years. Hence the most usual succession in the early eighteenth century had become turf oats, brush wheat, pin-fallow and barley with 'seeds' for a sexennial or septennial ley—five ploughings in ten years and a crop every year.[1] The improvement made in up-and-down husbandry in the second half of the seventeenth century was thus considerable. To Young's ill-considered remark that 'forty years ago, the knowledge of a true system was to be found only in the practice of Norfolk and Suffolk, and that solely on turnip soils', William Marshall was clearly correct to add that the improved practice of the Midland Plain was of 'much older date'.[2]

Much the same changes were made in the Vale of Evesham. Until the new fodder crops were introduced, the closes were mostly of up-and-down land, on which woad and flax were often first crops on the turf. Later many enclosed farms passed to an arable-grass rotation, and in others up-and-down husbandry was improved as it was in the Midland Plain[3] and other plain and vale countries.

Carrots and clover were both introduced early in the Vale of Taunton Deane, and liming soon became important. Wheat, the most-prized crop, was usually the first in successions. Specimen eighteenth-century rotations were, in the sandy loams, (1) wheat, (2) peas, (3) barley, (4) winter vetches, fed twice in spring and then ploughed once for carrots, or occasionally for turnips; and, in the clay loams, (1) wheat, (2) beans, (3) barley, (4–5) clover; but clover was eschewed when impairment of the wheat was intolerable. Only in the stiffest soils was wheat preceded by bare fallows, which were fertilized with lime, farmyard manure and headland earth, it being the practice to spread this mould on the tillage. Bare summer fallows were rare and the usual cleaning cultivations were summer carrot, turnip or cabbage fallows or bare winter ones.[4]

In the mosslands of the Lancashire Plain and the Cheshire Cheese Country, the farmers adopted, as a first crop, occasionally, turnips, and,

---

[1] Ibid. i, 187–8, 234, 244; ii, 41, 43; Yarranton, op. cit. 8–9.

[2] Marshall, *Midl. Dept*, 477.

[3] Marshall, *Glos.* i, 66; Pomeroy, op. cit. 13; Glouc. Lib. Cons. Ct invs.; sup. 308.

[4] Marshall, *W. Engl.* ii, 170; Billingsley, op. cit. (1794) 158–60; (1798) 269–70, 279–81; Soms. R.O., Cons. cts Bath. & Well. & A/d Taunton invs., esp. A/d Taunton: Ed. Sherwood 1713 Dunster; Wm Gatcomb 1715 N. Petherton; Robt Gadd 1716 Trull; Wm Strawberidge 1720 Cannington; 1721: Pet. Chappell/Milverton, Hugh Paine/Minehead, Jn Dodridge/N. Petherton, David Rawl/Porlock, Ed. Cole/ Stogursey; Reynoll Taylor 1723 W. Monkton, Lawrence Edney 1725 Cannington; 1729; Wm Brewer/Stogursey, Hy Cornish/Kingston, Alex. Harding/Luccombe; 1731: Wm Burnoll/Stogursey, Lavinia Durk/Bicknoller; Ric. Turner 1734 Goathurst; Jn Bond 1736 Heathfield, Jn Nichols 1745 Middle Alcombe, Hy Paris 1749 Chedzoy.

most often, potatoes. The latter, especially, were a usual fallow crop in preparation for wheat, and one course pursued was (1) potatoes, (2) wheat, (3) barley, undersown with rye-grass and clover.[1] The Saltings Country had as its chief consumption crops, beans, oats, grass, barley, cole-seed, mustard, turnips, and clover; and as market ones, wheat and barley, much more the former than the latter; besides, of course, canary and rape-seed.[2] In the Fen Country wheat came to be sown often on a clover ley. Perennial rye-grass and white or red clover were usual, and plantain and trefoil occasional constituents in the mixtures, and the resultant leys were generally left down for half a dozen years.[3]

By about 1720 the West Country had developed a system of ley farming incorporating lime, potash, clover and 'seeds', and comparable in its maturity to the husbandries of the Midland 'pastures' and of East Norfolk.[4] And the basis of this system was already firmly established by 1657–8, when Oliver Cromwell gave his opinion that West Country husbandry was the best in England.[5] Lastly, the Vales of Hereford underwent further modernization and never looked like lagging behind the Northdown Country in cultivating clover and 'seeds' for sheep or in producing clover seed for sale.[6]

[1] Holt, op. cit. (1795) 57; Boyd, op. cit. 7; Dickson, op. cit. 467; Man. Lib. Lancs. Deeds L. 36a; Lancs. & Ches. R.O.s, Cons. Ct Cestr. invs., esp. Th. Hey 1680 Gt Sankey, Wm Barton 1690 Tarlscough.

[2] Kent R.O., A/d & Cons. cts. Cantuar. invs., esp. Cons. 1678: Wm Whiting/ Chislet; 1679: Ric. Marrian/Bobbing; 1680: Jn Tharpe/Rainham, Robt Seth/ Bobbing; Ess. R.O., D./D.K. F.2/10; Melling, op. cit. 29–31.

[3] Vancouver, Cams. 146, 154, 158 sqq., 162–3, 185–7; Gooch, op. cit. 104; Parkinson, Ruts. 60–1; Marshall, E. Dept, 4, 6, 51, 209, 289; Morton, op. cit. 484; Northants. R.O., F.(M.) Corr. 178/24.

[4] Marshall, Midl. Dept, 477.

[5] Bodl. Aubrey 2, f. 83.

[6] Ibid. fo. 152; Howse, art. cit. 301–2; Pomeroy, op. cit. 13; Fox. Mon. 14; Marshall, W. Dept, 279; Hereford Lib. Local: Deed 3682; B'ham Lib. Winnington 217; invs.:— N.L.W. Episc. Cons. Ct Hereford & Cons. Ct Dean Hereford esp. Episc. 1691 Sept.: Jn Powell/the Wolhead; 1691–2 Mar.: Mich. Mann/Ross; 1695 Ed. Hoskins/Kings Caple; Dean 1723: Herbert Haines/Haywood; Glouc. Lib. Con. Ct esp. 1703: 112, 114; 1704: 85; 1717: 15A & B; 1719: 61; 1721: 126; 1722: 53; 1730: 81.

CHAPTER IX

NEW STOCK

BY now the reader will have rightly concluded that the innovations of the agricultural revolution were designed first and foremost to increase the volume and range of fodder and forage crops turned out by English farmers; and this being so, it was in the natural order of things that farm livestock should undergo changes, and improvements be effected upon the original breeds of sheep, cattle and horses.

Eight main breeds of arable sheep were formerly stocked, and seven of them were primarily folding sheep. Of these the most widely diffused, in the Chiltern and Northdown countries, the Vale of London, the Isle of Wight, the Midland Plain, and elsewhere, as well as in its native haunts, was the Chalk Country breed, sometimes called 'Western', 'Wiltshire', or 'Hampshire'. This was a big, hardy animal. It had a large head, big eyes, roman nose, long arched face, wide nostrils, horns (in both sexes) falling back behind the ears, a wide, deep chest, straight back and long, sturdy legs. Both face and legs were white. With a long but light frame, the sheep was naturally active and agile, a good walker and climber. It could pass with ease up and down the hills, often abrupt, that separated the nightly fold from the daily pasture. A greedy feeder, it was slow to fatten, but sometimes attained great weight and its mutton was good. It bore a fleece of about two pounds of good carding wool, but the underparts, from sympathy with the warm, dry soils, grew only a short silvery hair. For long bred on open downs, this sheep was a strong, healthy, intelligent animal, well suited to its habitat and function. It was held in the highest esteem for its folding quality, for its propensity to leave its droppings on the arable at night, and for its ability as a walking dung-cart, robbing the downs for the sake of the tillage, but maintaining the down pastures by feeding them closely.[1]

[1] Davis, op. cit. 23; Marshall, S. Dept, 58, 347; S. Cos. i, 327; ii, 345–6, 412; Sheep, 26; Lisle, op. cit. 427; Vancouver, Hants. 266; Ellis, Sheep, 41–2; Luccock, op. cit. 85–6, 272–3; Youatt, Sheep, 244–5; Bodl. Aubrey 2, f. 122; Notestein & al. op. cit. vii, 499.

The Southdown Country had its own aboriginal Old Southdown breed, polled, black-faced and with a tuft of white wool on their foreheads. About the same size as the unimproved 'Wiltshire' sheep, they were similarly active and hardy animals, sharp-backed, high in the shoulders and strong in the leg, well able to gather a living from the scanty down herbage, with only a little hay in winter, to travel miles between fields and downs, and to endure the fold throughout the year. Their mutton was lean and sweet and they bore a fleece of about two pounds of fine clothing wool.[1] In the Norfolk Heathlands, the Breckland, the Sandlings Country, and thereabouts, flourished the East Anglian breed, often called 'Norfolk'. They had black or mottled skins, and long bodies, legs and horns which were long and spiral in rams and straight in ewes and wethers. This was an active and hardy breed, designed for picking up a living off heaths and folding the tillage. It produced sweet mutton and short, fine fleeces of between one and two and a half pounds of carding wool.[2] The Oxford Heights Country had its 'Berkshire' Nott breed, good folding sheep and, as their name implies, polled and so well suited to enclosures.[3] The Old Northwold sheep were another polled, short-wool breed, active, hardy and bred for the fold, yielding fleeces of about two pounds and a half of excellent clothing wool.[4] Old Cotswolds were small-faced, white-skinned and polled, with long, spare, big-boned frames, long necks, square bulks and broad buttocks. They were active and intelligent folding sheep. Thanks to the sparseness of feed, the exercise and exposure entailed by folding, and the protection of the cote in winter, they bore three-pound fleeces of fine, silky clothing wool, in quality second only to that of the Ryeland breed. They also gave excellent mutton.[5] Ryelands were smallboned, well-shaped, dark-skinned, polled sheep, giving excellent mutton, and fleeces, which, though often weighing only one pound and seldom as much as two, even in the best wethers, yielded a peerless, fine, silky, carding wool. Cotting spared the sheep many ailments and improved their fleeces, but abruptly checked bodily growth and made

[1] Ibid.; Cornall, op. cit. 151–2; 'Farming in Suss.', 49; White, op. cit. 173; Young, *Suss.* 48; Vancouver, op. cit. 366; Defoe, op. cit. ii, 49; Marshall, op. cit. 32; *S. Dept,* 499–500; *S. Cos.* ii, 370–1; Youatt, *Compl. Grazier,* 222.

[2] Ibid. 212–3; Marshall, *Nfk* i, 364–5; *E. Dept,* 465; Riches, op. cit. 101–2; Reyce, op. cit. 38; Young, *Sfk,* 33–4; B.M., Harl. 127, f. 22 (37); K. J. Allison, 'Flock Management in 16th & 17th cents.', *EcH.R.* 1958 xi, 104–6. Cf. Bowden, op. cit. 35.

[3] Marshall, *S. Dept,* 94; Mavor, op. cit. 380–2; W. Fream, *Els. Ag.* 1918, p. 521.

[4] Best, op. cit. 24; Marshall, *N. Dept,* 520–1; *Yks.* ii, 259; A. Harris, op. cit. 32; H.M.C., *14th Rep.* App. pt iv, 1894, p. 573; Strickland, op. cit. 231; Lincs. R.O., HEN 3/2.

[5] Wilts. Clothier, op. cit. 53; Defoe, op. cit. ii, 32; Folkingham, op. cit. 8; Smyth, *Hund. Berk.* 4; G. Turner, op. cit. 9; E. Leigh, op. cit. 77; Dyer, 'Fleece' bk ii, 108; Oxon. R.O., Dashwood VIII/34 valn Harrison's fm; Kent R.O., U.269/A.421; Marshall, *W. Dept,* 416; *Glos.* ii, 79.

them delicate, though they had the ability to gain a living on the poorest pasture.[1]

Bred and reared in the Butter Country and sold far afield, especially to the South Sea-coast Country, the Petworth District, and the Vale of London, the 'Dorset horn' or 'house-lamb' breed had white skin, straight horns projecting forwards and a heavy fleece of short, middling to fine, close-textured, mainly carding wool. This animal's two distinctions were hardiness and fecundity. It could thrive on almost any land and endure folding on the tillage, which was its first purpose. The ewes took the ram in spring, so yeaning in autumn, had propensity for twinning, and made excellent nurses. The breed was thus admirably adapted to the production of suckled house-lamb in autumn and winter.[2]

Of the five main closely allied breeds of pasture sheep, the two from the Midland Plain are perhaps best known to historians. 'Warwick' or 'old Leicester' sheep, which flourished in all the plain, but least in the vales of York and Stockton, were heavy polled animals, with big bones, large loose frames, long, thick legs and slaw feet. They had up to twice the value of fallow sheep, twice the weight both of fleece and of flesh and a propensity to fatten well at three years. Their fleeces, weighing between four and seven pounds in wethers, were of mainly combing wool, suitable for hosiery and worsteds. While fallow or heath sheep fattened well in 'pastures', pasture sheep starved in common fields or heaths, so unlike were their natures. The distinction between the two was of ancient origin, but as enclosures multiplied, so did the pasture breed.[3] Fallow sheep were best for folding, for carding wool and for sweet mutton, pasture sheep for the rapid production of great quantities of mutton and for combing wool. When as yet stores, they were sometimes folded on fallows at night, and their dressings were worth a third again as much

[1] Ibid. 233–6; *Sheep*, 20, 23–4; Markham, *Wealth* pt i, 107–8; Mortimer, op. cit. 177; Worlidge, op. cit. 150; Pomeroy, op. cit. 10–11; Beale, op. cit. 51, 54–5; H.M.C., *Salisbury MSS.* pt xiii, 54–5; Fuller, op. cit. ii, 68.

[2] Ibid. i, 451; Ellis, op. cit. 43; Plot, *Oxon.* 188; Coker, op. cit. 5; Lisle, op. cit. 338; Melling, op. cit. 36; Bodl. Aubrey 2, f. 116; Hearne's diaries 158, pp. 37, 39, 103; Marshall, *W. Engl.* ii, 151; *S. Dept,* 252–3.

[3] Ibid. 94; *Midl. Cos.* i, 376, 378–80; *Sheep,* 19–20, 37; *Midl. Dept,* 50–1, 300, 603; Lowe, op. cit. 126–7, 129; Pitt, *Northants.* 203, 207–8, 210; Crutchley, op. cit. 14–15; Ellis, op. cit. 43–4; Defoe, op. cit. ii, 89; Mortimer, loc. cit.; Fuller, op. cit. i, 193; iii, 267; Youatt, op. cit. 215–6; W. Burton, op. cit. 2; Morton, op. cit. 16; Markham, op. cit. pt i, 108; Lisle, op. cit. 309; Dyer, 'Fleece', bk ii, 109; Notestein & al. loc. cit.; Boyd, art. cit. 93–4; H.M.C., loc. cit.; *Buccleuch & Queensberry MSS. at Mont. ho. vol. iii, Mont. Papers 2nd ser.* vi, 40–1; *Discourse Com. Weal this Realm Engl.* ed. E. Lamond, Camb. 1929, p. xliii; Power, op. cit. 21; Maxey, op. cit.; Tawney & Power, op. cit. iii, 101–2; Herts. R.O., 8442; Huntington Lib. ST. 48; Salt Lib. D. 1734/4/1/6; Northants. R.O., I.(L.) 1491; Cons. Ct Petriburg inv. Hunts. K. 1613–87: Jn Keble 1636 Caldecote; Leics. R.O., A/d invs. 1639: 36; 1642: 34; 1661 Commy: 111; 1664: 3; 1695: 94; 1700 unstamped: Ric. Overton/Burbage; 1707: 11; 1709: 11; 1710:20. Pace Bowden, op. cit. 31.

as those of field sheep; but their wool was too long and their legs too short to permit regular folding in permanent tillage, and they could neither manage on sparse feed nor endure to be close-folded, and would make every endeavour to escape from the hurdles.[1] In the vales of York and Stockton lived a race of large, long-bodied, polled, loose-limbed, long-wooled pasture sheep, similar to those of the rest of the plain with which they were often crossed or exchanged. This Teeswater strain was perhaps the best and almost the biggest sheep in England, frequently produced twins, and bore a heavy fleece of combing wool.[2] The 'Mugs' of the North-eastern Lowlands, with their muff of wool over eyes and faces, were a similar, long-wooled pasture sheep that rose to pre-eminence with the great enclosures there.[3] The Fen Country rejoiced in its famous 'Lincolnshire' breed, a strain of pasture sheep even larger than those of the Midland Plain with which it was frequently interbred. Despite largely bare legs and belly, it gave a twelve-pound fleece of mediocre combing wool. This sheep was inured to wet ground and sur-vived where most upland ones would have rotted, but rot and wood-evil might still decimate flocks. For the sake of their size and propensity to fatten slowly to great weights, Midland farmers bought fen tups to im-prove their own pasture sheep and some idea of their stature may be gained from the danger in yeaning into which they put Midland ewes.[4] Lastly, the Romney Marsh or 'Kent' breed, which were found also in Pevensey Level and temporarily in part of the Northdown Country, were the largest pasture sheep, with long legs, deep paunches, thick necks and heavy fleeces of very long, semi-lustrous combing wool, well suited to all but the finest worsteds. These sheep were excellent feeders, having a marked propensity to fatten young. Thanks to their habitat, they were exceptionally hardy to climatic extremes and able to thrive on the coldest pasture. In feeding, shearing and constitution, they al-ways excelled any other breed, not excepting the Dishley strain of Midland pasture sheep.[5]

The other group was of hill sheep, as found in the North Country, where they roamed the moors unshepherded throughout the year. Over

[1] Maxey, op. cit.; Marshall, *Midl. Dept*, 298, 535, 594, 603.

[2] Defoe, *Pl. Engl. Comm.* 283; Markham, loc. cit.; Youatt, op. cit. 219; Granger, op. cit. 35; B.M., Add. 25079, f. 55; Marshall, *S. Cos.* i, 380; *N. Dept*, 489, 491; *Sheep*, 44–5.

[3] Ibid. 47; *N. Dept*, 99, 101–2; Youatt, loc. cit.; Hughes, *N. Country Life: ii Cumb. & Wmld.*, 10.

[4] Morton, op. cit. 8; J. L. op. cit. 8; Defoe, *Tour* ii, 89, 96; Dyer, loc. cit.; Strickland, loc. cit.; Vancouver, *Cams.* 205; Ellis, op. cit. 44; H.M.C., *Salisbury MSS.* pt xiii, 54–5; Lisle, op. cit. 309; G. Culley, *Obs. on Livestock* 1786, pp. 75–6; Markham, loc. cit.; Mortimer, loc. cit.; Marshall, *E. Dept.* 63; *Sheep*, 19, 39–42; Youatt, op. cit. 218.

[5] Ibid. 220; Lodge, op. cit. 21; Defoe, op. cit. i, 125; Boys, op. cit. 150; Fuller, op. cit. ii, 112; Chalklin, op. cit. 113; B.M., Add. 34258, f. 6; Marshall, *S. Cos.* i, 378–80.

most of the country flourished a distinct black-face moorland breed, with black or grey skins, large spiral horns, and fleeces of three pounds or more of coarse, wavy, loose-textured, shaggy, hairy wool, some of which suited hosiery, but was mostly too coarse for carding and too short for combing, and therefore used to make carpets. Though slow to fatten, these lively, agile little animals were noted for excellent mutton, and were hardy enough to spend all their lives, lambing time apart, on the bleak moors. They could exist on a diet more of heather and furze than of grass and even in the severest winters only about one in ten died of exposure or starvation. In the Cheviot Hills, the native breed of polled, white-skinned sheep gave good mutton and a three-pound fleece twice as valuable as that of the black-faces, but still far from fine and best employed in tweeds. These Cheviot sheep, though they lived all the year on the hillsides, were somewhat less hardy than the black-faces, as they could obtain natural shelter from the bleakest winds and fed on superior grasses. The Herdwick sheep of the Lake District were extremely hardy, with white or speckled skins and curved horns in the rams. They bore short, strong, open, two-pound fleeces, inclined to be hairy, especially about the neck, and used in Kendal cloth. Finally, in the Craven District, lived the Lank or Lonk breed of large, nimble, prolific sheep with short, close fleeces of soft wool, and mutton second to none. The rams had large horns that projected well out and were turned once or twice according to age, while the ewes had more slender and straighter ones.[1] In Wales, the sheep were mostly small, white, wild, hardy 'mountaineers', giving small quantities of lean, sweet meat, and one-pound fleeces of coarse, short, hairy, close-textured wool, suitable for cottons and flannels. The rams were horned. In Anglesey and other lowland parts there were larger and better strains of the same breed. About Kerry Hill, Clun Forest and Wenlock Edge obtained the much superior polled 'March' or 'forest' sheep, which gave good wool for carding and were sold to be fattened in the Midland Plain and Cheshire Cheese Country; whereas the 'mountaineers' were too wild to be confined in ordinary pastures and sold only to Romney Marsh and the Saltings Country, where sewers kept them within bounds.[2] The breed generally stocked in the Peak-Forest Country was the Gritstone, so named after its place of origin. These hardy, white, polled sheep were famed for their lean mutton and excellent hosiery wool. Sherwood had a similar if smaller old, grey forest sheep, with fine fleeces of up to two

[1] Bailey & Culley, *Cumb.* 268; Youatt, op. cit. 211; Marshall, *N. Dept.* 97–8, 198, 202–3, 323–4, 328, 406, 489–91; *Sheep*, 1–2, 5–6, 9–10, 47.
[2] Ibid. 14–15; Davies, *S.W.* ii, 243; *N.W.* 323–5; Fox, *Mon.* 15; Fiennes, op. cit. 181; Owen, *Taylors Cussion* pt i, f. 2v.; Ellis, op. cit. 50; Markham, loc. cit.; Dyer, 'Fleece', bk ii, 108; H.M.C., loc. cit.; Barnswell, art. cit. 357; Kent. R.O., A/d ct inv. 1665: Robt Tilby/Tenterden; Ess. R.O., D./D.P. F.224, m. 5; Boyd, art. cit. 93.

pounds.[1] Of the West Country breeds, the polled Dartmoor and horned Exmoor were small, hardy animals, noted for sweet mutton and short, hairy fleeces, while the South Hams Nott was larger, with long, curly wool, suitable for kerseys, hosiery, worsted, and grograms.[2]

In one respect, however, the foregoing account is over-simplified, for no breed gave all combing or all carding wool and, as now, the wools produced by the different breeds of sheep had to be sorted into the different parts of the fleece or fell and then distributed according to their varied uses. Of a long-staple fleece, head-wool and bay-wool were for heavy blankets, carpets, baize, and yarn stockings; long wool for worsteds; middle wool and best tail-wool for duffields, blankets, hats and rugs; and worst tail-wool for collars, wrappings and tilt-cloths. Of a short-staple fleece, the neck, breast and bottom belly-wool was for the warp and weft of woollen cloth; back and rib-wool for the abb thread of drugget; flank and buttock-wool for long worsted thread, for druggets and for the weft of serges and other new draperies; and tail-wool for lists for cloth and for rugs and blankets. This explains how it was that some Chalk Country and Southdown wool was used in the new draperies of nearby industrial centres, why the wool of the East Anglian arable sheep was employed largely for the worsted industries of East Norfolk, and why new-drapery converters resold some of their pasture wool to the carding-wool clothiers.[3]

Cattle fell into the longhorn, middlehorn, shorthorn, and polled classes. Of these the longhorns, which stemmed from the western North Country and the Lancashire Plain and occupied west central England, were the most numerous. Both sexes of this brindled, finched-back breed had the tips of their slightly incurved horns a yard apart. The cows excelled in cheese-making, for their milk produced much curd. The bullocks could be fattened rapidly to a great weight of first-class beef or made good draught animals, for they were large, big-boned and strong.[4] The three main middlehorn breeds had much in common, being all large, reddish beef cattle, well suited to the yoke, but of small repute in the dairy. Second to none for beef, and able to fatten well on mediocre pastures, the massive Herefords were sold as two-year stores

---

[1] Plot, *Staffs.* 109; Lowe, op. cit. 124, 129; Marshall, *Midl. Dept*, 50–1, 180–1.

[2] Youatt, op. cit. 211–2; Borlase, op. cit. 286; Carew, op. cit. f. 23; Childrey, op. cit. 13; Marshall, *W. Engl.* i, 259–60, 302; ii, 7, 44–7, 55 sqq., 121, 151; *S. Cos.* i, 378; *S. Dept*, 526, 547–8; B.M., Harl. 5827, f. 10.

[3] Plot, *Oxon*, 278; Dyer, 'Fleece', bk ii, 94–5; Atkyns, op. cit. 23; Bowden, op. cit. 42, 63; *A.P.C.* 1616–17, pp. 178, 180; Stat. 1 Ed. VI c. 6; Lisle, op. cit. 427; Winchester, op. cit. 178; B.M. Add. 34258, ff. 5v.–6; Wilts. R.O., Dioc. Reg. Sarum. inv. Augustine Pearson 1610 Stapleford; Leics. R.O., A/d invs.:—1614: 2; 1697: 9.

[4] Blome, *Brit.* 132; Fuller, op. cit. ii, 189–90; Childrey, op. cit. 166; C. Leigh, op. cit. bk ii, 5; Marshall, *Midl. Cos.* i, 317.

over much of midland, southern and eastern England.[1] The Wealden breed of 'Sussex' or 'Kent' cattle was similar.[2] 'Devon' cattle were less• uniform. To the west and north of the West Country they were smaller and darker, in and about the moorlands coarser and stunted, and in South Hams and other favoured locations larger and better at the pail.[3] East Norfolk had its own small, red, horned, hardy, thrifty breed, with short legs, light bones, and a propensity to fatten early and produce superior flesh. They were like miniature Herefords and probably contained some Hereford blood.[4] The Vale of Evesham gave rise to a middlehorn dairy breed, the old 'Gloucesters'. These were mostly dark red or brown, with black muzzles and legs, and finched backs: i.e. white rump, tail and spinal markings.[5] In Wales the native cattle were black middlehorns. Although they sometimes attained considerable stature and could give prime, if slow-maturing beef, individual sizes depended largely on the feed available and varied from great oxen down to the lowest runts.[6] On the easterly slopes of the North Country, shorthorn cattle were bred for rearing in the North-eastern Lowlands. But these dual-purpose beasts had not as yet as much currency as longhorns.[7] Lastly, High Suffolk had the Suffolk duns. They were large, with well-knit, long bodies, broad foreheads, deep sides and great milk-bags, the only hornless breed then known, and famed for their high prices and excellent milking qualities. The sole and sufficient explanation of their virtues is, 'the husbandman saith good pasture makes the best cattle'.[8]

Ponies abounded on Dartmoor and Exmoor, in Wales and elsewhere, but the lightest horse used in farming was the Cleveland Bay, which was bred and reared mainly in the vales of York and Stockton. The Cleveland was a horse of general utility, much used in leading bullock-teams, harrowing, carting, riding and drawing coaches.[9] The largest and commonest draught horse was the Shire or Old English Black horse. The chief single source of Shires was the Fen Country. Some breeding was undertaken elsewhere, but heavy horses were mostly bred

[1] Campling, op. cit. 72; Marshall, *Glos.* ii, 226–7, 230.

[2] Marshall, *S. Cos.* ii, 134.

[3] Youatt, op. cit. 5–6; Norden, *Corn.* 20; Childrey, op. cit. 13; Borlase, op. cit. 286–7; Marshall, *S. Dept*, 526; *W. Engl.* i, 239 sqq., 302; ii, 117.

[4] Marshall, *Nfk* i, 323–4; & v. Campling, loc. cit.

[5] Markham, op. cit. pt i, 89; Bodl. Hearne's diaries 158, p. 180 (170); Marshall, *Glos.* i, 211–31, 215, 218–19.

[6] R. Wallace, *Fm Live Stock of G.B.* 1907, pp. 140–3.

[7] Marshall, *N. Dept*, 91; Tuke, op. cit. 61; Granger, op. cit. 34–5; Markham, loc. cit.; Defoe, op. cit. ii, 95.

[8] E. Sfk R.O., A/d inv. 1582–3: 251; Reyce, op. cit. 39–40.

[9] Long, art. cit. 107; Granger, op. cit. 42; Culley, op. cit. 15; Marshall, op. cit. 378–9; *Yks.* ii, 272, 274; Fuller, op. cit. iii, 394–5; Defoe, op. cit. ii, 219, 221.

in waterlands and reared in the plains.[1] East Anglia was alone in possessing a specialist farm horse or punch, a short-legged, thickset, compact animal. East Norfolk originally had its own brown-muzzled punches, noted for hard work and hard keep, and the Sandlings Country was the home of the Suffolk Punch.[2]

Before attempting to assess what improvements were made upon livestock, it is well to expunge from our minds the notion that little heed was aforetimes paid to its quality. In fact, in the sixteenth century and after, in common-field townships, common flocks and herds had not a little care bestowed on them. Horses with mange or fashions, distempered cattle and rotten sheep were forbidden the commons. Animals dying of infectious diseases had to be buried well out of the way.[3] If the duty did not fall on the parson or other freeholder,[4] the township itself often supplied common bulls and boars.[5] Each common flock had its complement of good public rams, to the exclusion of ridgels, and perhaps of all rams of less than a specified monetary value.[6] The picture Henry Best draws of sheep-husbandry in the Northwold Country shows us how careful farmers were for their stock. As no

[1] Marshall, *S. Dept*, 92; *Glos.* i, 207; *S. Ços.* i, 320; *Midl. Cos.* i, 306, 311; Stat 32 Hy VIII c. 13.

[2] Reyce, op. cit. 42–4; Marshall, *Nfk* i, 42.

[3] Colman, op. cit. 127–8; Smyth, op. cit. 20; Crossley, 'Test. Docs.', 87, 101; Jeffery, *Gt Rollright*, 26; J. F. Ede, *Hist. Wednesbury* 1962, p. 112; J. H. Glover, *Kingsthorpiana* 1883, p. 32; *Oxon. Archaeol. Soc. Rep.* 1911 (1912) 136; Clay, *Yks. Deeds* v, 98; Farrer, op. cit. i, 380; Marcham, op. cit. 154; Darbyshire & Lumb, op. cit. 65; Farnham, op. cit. 6; Wimbledon Com. Cmttee, op. cit. 49; C. Jackson, art. cit. 90; B.M., Add. 23150, ff. 15, 21–3; 33454, f. 18; 36585, f. 164; 36875, f. 25; 36908, ff. 8, 40; R. 37391; P.R.O., D.L., Ct R. 82/1133, mm. 28–9; 84/1155; Ct R. G.S. 195/79, m. 7d.; 82, m. 1; Berks. R.O., D./E.C. M114/1; Bucks. Mus. P. 24/1 Pitstone; 155/21 ct files Taplow; Herts. R.O., 677; B. 119; Beds. R.O., H.A. 5/1, f. 22v.; O.R. 804, 816; S.19, 20; Northants. R.O., Higham Ferrers Du. Ct; Mont. Northants. 7/66/5, 6, 9, 10; 7/72; 17/160; 18/160; Misc. Led. 145, pp. 21–2, 98–9, 184; I.(L.) 128; Wmld 5.v.1; F-H 516, 834; Old Par. Recs. fd offrs' bk 1738–9; Grafton 3422; Salt Lib. D. 1750 Ct R. Madeley Holme; Leics. R.O., D.E. 10 Barrow Ct R. & files; D.E. 40/37/7, 40/46/3; Shak. Bpl. Henley-in-Arden Ct R.; Whitchurch ct files; W.de B. 703b, 1194; Leigh: Stoneleigh Ct Bk, p. 43; Cams. R.O., L. 1/10; L. 88/4; Deene ho. Brudenell O. xxiv. 1; Bucks. R.O., acq. 35/39 by-laws & regs. Padbury fds 1779; Stat. 32 Hy VIII c. 13; M. Bateson, op. cit. ix, 119.

[4] Ibid. x, 273; P.R.O., Req. 129/45; B.M., Add. R. 28264; *Eng. Reps.* lxxii K.B. i, 626; Northants. R.O., Higham Ferrers Burg. R. fd ords. 1696–1725.

[5] Ibid. Mont. Northants. 7/66/5; 16/98; Barley, op. cit. 98–9; M. Hartley & J. Ingilby, *Yks. Vil.* 1953, p. 243; W. G. Fletcher, *Hist. Loughborough* 1887, pp. 45, 47; War. R.O., D. 19/44; Shak. Bpl. Alveston & Tiddington Ct R.; N.R. R.O., Z.A.X. 2, p. 445; P.R.O., D.L., Ct R. 81/1119, m. 14d.; 106/1529, m. 1d.; 1535, m. 1; Ct R. G.S. 195/82, m. 1; B.M., Add. 36585, f. 162; Deene ho. Brudenell O. xxiv, 1; B'ham Lib. 168124.

[6] Ibid. 167919, 168163; Northants. R.O., Misc. Led. 129; 145, p. 99; Mont. Northants. 7/72; Hunts. 26/28; Leics. R.O., D.E. 10, Barrow Ct R. & files; D.E. 40/22/1, f. 22; D.E. 40/40; Ches. R.O., Vernon (Warren) Ct R. 11.

NEW STOCK   319

marsh or vale grassland was available on the smaller farms, ewes were not usually tupped until the latter part of October, so lambing at the end of March. Otherwise the full-mouthed ewes were kept together with the rams throughout the year, so that all the lambs should not fall together and small numbers of them could continually be sold fat. Often all the ewes were kept with the tups throughout the year, but then good sheep-masters clouted the gimmer shearlings to avoid inferior lambs. In Henry Best's experience, too, 'the most judicious sheepe-men endeavour by all meanes possible to provide goode tuppes for their ewes'. One tup would serve forty or fifty, but it was surer to allow four to every hundred. They were often encouraged by being put on the oat and barley stubbles. During lambing, bottom grass was the best feed for ewes, but they could be given peas and oats in the straw morning and evening and then driven straightway to water. Sometimes oats were threshed and fed to them in troughs; and sometimes they were put on newly ploughed land to eat the grass and weeds, because they were held to be good for the milk. Lambs were usually gelded when about a fortnight old, and could be put to grass after four or five weeks, but were normally allowed to suck as long as they liked, for the farmers' prime concern was breeding and rearing sound, healthy sheep.[1] Nor did Best exaggerate the care taken in providing good sires. In 1602 Sir Robert Spencer of Wormleighton, which lay in a district noted for its superior strain, received an order for pasture ewes and tups from a sheep-master seeking to improve his flocks in the northernmost part of the Midland Plain. Around 1650 selected Midland pasture rams were selling at £10 apiece. Moreover, Midland graziers and farmers improved their breed by importing marsh tups from the Fen and Saltings countries and longhorn cattle from the Lancashire Plain. In 1605 Sir Robert Drury of Hawstead, in the Woodland, had a herd of fifty Hereford bulls and steers in one of the few bull farms we have record of. Little as we know as yet of such activities, it is clear that breeding was a point of husbandry much attended to.[2]

We do not know exactly how much sixteenth-century farm horses differed from present-day ones in respect of strength and stature; but the statutes of 27 Henry VIII caput 6 and 33 Henry VIII caput 5 show the minimum size for a hackney stallion was fourteen hands, just as it is now; and the statute of 32 Henry VIII caput 13 lays down a minimum of fifteen hands for all stallions commoned in those parts where shires and punches were bred and reared. As their average heights are now seventeen and sixteen respectively, there appears to

[1] Best, op. cit. 1 sqq., 12, 20, 27-8, 75-6.
[2] Campling, loc. cit.; B.M., Add. 25079, f. 55; Winchester, op. cit. 173; Lisle, op. cit. 275, 309; Fuller, op. cit. i, 193; Marshall, *Midl. Cos.* i, 317.

have been little improvement in the meantime, and that mainly to the finer points of breed. The greatest change was probably in the Suffolk Punch, and especially in and about the Great Sandlings. The greater part of the carrot crop went to provender farm horses, replacing hay and oat-straw, which were thus released for sheep and cattle. The punches' usual diet became eighty bushels of carrots a week to a stable of six, with as much chaff (two parts of straw to one of hay) as they wanted, but little pure hay, rarely oats, and corn of any sort only when it was intended to put them to extraordinary exertions. On summer evenings, however, they were allowed into paddocks or aftermaths. On this fare they worked strongly from six in the morning to six at night, with an intermission of two hours and a half at midday; and under this management the Suffolk Punch ousted others and became the best breed of specifically farm horses. Their peculiar characteristics were strength and compactness, arched, thick-set necks, chestnut colour, featherless fetlocks, iron constitution and courageous, never-say-die attitude to the heaviest work.[1]

Nor did the various breeds of cattle change much. The floating of water-meadows doubtless led to some improvement in the Herefords,[2] and new crops in the West Country cattle, but in the Midland Plain, where most longhorns and shorthorns were employed, as dual-purpose milking and beef breeds, the general plan of management prevented the generality of farmers from effecting any radical improvement in the breeds themselves.[3] Indeed, these were only spared degeneration by the importation of stores from the North Country and the Lancashire Plain, where some attention was paid to breeding and rearing. Nevertheless, specialist breeders arose in the Midland Plain and it was to these that the advances eventually made were due. Since the stock had to be constantly maintained by importations, it followed it could be ameliorated by care in selecting the beasts imported. In this way was developed the superior strain of Teeswater or so-called 'Durham' shorthorns, whose first famous sire was 'Studley Bull', which was calved in 1737. One of the earlier breeders of longhorns to concentrate on this kind of selection was Captain Tate, who flourished at the turn of the seventeenth and eighteenth centuries.[4] By this means Webster of Canley, near Coventry, had, about 1750, built up a superior longhorn herd and become the leading breeder in the plain. It was from the Canley herd that Princip of Croxall, Bakewell of Dishley and, later, Fowler of Rollright, drew their stock for the development of a specialized beef breed. Bakewell's

---

[1] Marshall, *E. Dept*, 446; Reyce, op. cit. 43–4; Rochefoucauld, op. cit. 75–6, 180–1; Young, *Sfk*, 42; *Tours in E. & W.* 76 sqq., 96–7; *Gent's.Mag.* xxxiv, 71.

[2] Cf. Wallace, op. cit. 114.

[3] Sup. 198–9.

[4] Lisle, op. cit. 275; Culley, op. cit. 24–5.

first famous bull, 'Twopenny', came from a heifer bought from Canley. These new beef cattle were, perhaps, open to criticisms similar to those levelled at the Dishley sheep, but the chief objection to them was, they were unwanted and vanished almost as quickly as they had appeared. This was because nearly all Midland farmers continued to need only dual-purpose cattle.[1] Had such a beef breed been demanded, Bakewell and the others would almost certainly have been more successful had they worked not with the traditional imports, but with the middle-horn breeds, for these were already primarily beef cattle of the finest quality. As it was, tampering with the longhorn breed brought it into disrepute and the way was prepared for its replacement by the new shorthorns.[2]

Far greater were the changes wrought in sheep breeds in the course of the agricultural revolution. Fed on sainfoin, rye-grass, turnips and clovers instead of on the short grass of the old sleights, and crossed with Midland pasture sheep, the Cotswold breed was transformed. The sheep remained polled, but their legs shortened and their carcasses became larger and fleshier. Meanwhile, the wool was altered from fine clothing quality to a progressively coarser long-staple variety pre-eminently suitable for worsteds, though the huge fleeces contained some short wool used for coarse cloth. Whereas the sheep had previously been folded in summer and cotted in winter, they were now, almost all, spared the wearying discomfort of the trip to and from the close fold, to which their short legs and long wool rendered them unsuitable, and denied the unhealthy comfort of winter cotting, which had improved their wool but stunted their growth. Formerly sheep were bred for the fold and the cote, with fine flesh and wool secondary considerations, but now they were primarily intended to produce mutton. By the middle of the eighteenth century, the new breed, the product of richer feed, different management, and selective and cross-breeding, was already so well and so long established that no one could accurately recall the old.[3] As a result especially of floating, the Chalk Country sheep gradually became larger in stature, longer in the leg and higher and heavier in the fore-quarters, a bigger animal altogether. Another advantage of this innovation was, it permitted some lambs to be sold fat instead of lean,[4] which was as well, for forcing the sheep to a great size made them less attractive as stores to farmers in the Chiltern, Northdown and other countries without floated meadows, where they were in-

[1] Marshall, *Midl. Cos.* i, 315, 318 sqq., 325, 331, 341, 345.

[2] Marshall, *S. Dept*, 494–5.

[3] Atkyns, op. cit. 23; Pomeroy, op. cit. 10; Marshall, *Glos.* ii, 79–80; *W. Dept*, 416–17.

[4] T. Davis, op. cit. 30; Vancouver, *Hants.* 275; Marshall, *S. Cos.* ii, 348–9, 370, 412; *S. Dept.* 408–9.

L

creasingly supplanted by Southdowns. Lastly, superior feed, especially clover, coarsened Chalk Country wool.[1] Lime improved the pastures and fodder enjoyed by Ryeland sheep enough to worsen perceptibly the quality of their wool also.[2] Improved feed, too, caused the Norfolk or East Anglian sheep, or most of them, to grow in weight and stature and produce more twins and triplets. Their mutton was not as sweet and lean as formerly, but they put on more flesh and fatted freely at two years, and yet retained sufficient of their folding qualities to be employed in arable flocks and bear with remarkable fortitude the drift to Lynn, Norwich and Smithfield.[3] Partly by feeding on the new crops, partly by being crossed with fen sheep themselves improved by drainage, the Northwolds gave birth to a new breed yielding more meat and a clip of up to six pounds of long wool. Wethers of this New Northwold breed were weaned on sainfoin, fed on clover and 'seeds' and finished off for the butcher on turnips; and this management, adapted for the rams and ewes, was largely instrumental in making the new breed.[4]

By the same token, some down and heath countries retained their old sheep in their pristine form. In the Brecklands, e.g. the old type of Norfolks continued to flourish under the name of 'heath sheep'. Not altogether dissimilarly, Southdown sheep failed to increase in stature as Chalk Country ones did.[5]

Selective breeding had long been employed in improving Midland pasture sheep. Larger animals of the same type were kept in the Fen and Saltings countries, whence rams were imported into the Midland Plain. The fen sheep were so much bigger that all but the largest of the Midland pasture ewes were endangered in yeaning. This importation of fen sheep effected a continuous improvement, all the more as drainage made for less hairy fleeces. In the middle of the sixteenth century a sheep-master of Glapthorne declares, 'I would fain mend my breed', and buys in sheep from the Saltings Country. Other farmers about the same time bought from the Fen Country. In the early eighteenth century, breeders like Major Hartopp and Captain Tate were purchasing fen rams that had been forced to a great size on cole-seed.[6] Then, from pasture sheep bought from Stone of Goadby, near Melton Mowbray, Joseph Allom of Clifton first developed, by a combination of superior feed and selective inbreeding, the New Leicester pasture sheep

[1] Ibid.; *S. Cos.* i, 327; Wilts. Clothier, op. cit. 52; Lisle, op. cit. 404, 424; & v. ibid. 425; Ellis, op. cit. 43; Melling, op. cit. 26.

[2] Bodl. Aubrey 2, f. 153.

[3] Marshall, *Nfk* i, 363–5.

[4] Marshall, *N. Dept*, 520–1; *Yks.* ii, 260; Eland, *Shardeloes*, 61; Lincs. R.O., M.M. VI/5/2, 9, 30, 32.

[5] Marshall, *S. Cos.* ii, 370; *Nfk* i, 363–4.

[6] Winchester, op. cit. 173; Lisle, op. cit. 309.

further developed by Robert Bakewell in the first dozen years after he took over the management of Dishley Grange Farm in 1755. He was not the originator of the system of breeding in-and-in, which had long been used by race-horse breeders; but was the first to realize its potentialities for fashioning sheep eminently suited to cross-breeding and the production of great supplies of mediocre grass mutton.

These improvements in the Midland pasture sheep depended on innovations made in other farming countries, but no less, on those effected in the plain itself in the second half of the seventeenth century. The ram breeders set up as specialists in the districts of turnip soils and arable-grass rotations, more particularly in the rich alluvial valley of the Soar, at such places as Clifton, Dishley, Ibstock, Quorndon and Hoby. It was to improve their stock that the ram breeders became such great growers of cabbages, swedes, turnips, rape and other coles. Their work depended largely on these crops and on short leys of clover and 'seeds'. Bakewell either developed or propagated a new strain of cabbage especially suited to sheep fatting.[1] The floating of water-meadows also played an important part in livestock improvements. It was in those valleys with turnip soils and arable-grass rotations that floating was notably developed, with the object of raising abundant hay. Bakewell, the most famous of the breeders, had 200 acres of flowing meadows on which hay could be cut four times a season.[2] Furthermore, it was thanks to the rich leys of up-and-down husbandry that the pasture sheep had already become such a worthy object of improvement.

The propensity selected by Bakewell for exaggeration and inbreeding was that of forming flesh quickly. No attention was paid to wool, suitability to the fold, or any other attribute but these. The method was a combination of feeding and breeding. First, the ram lambs were forced to a great size on rye-grass and clover leys and then fattened to the limit on cabbages, swedes, turnips, other coles, corn and hay. The fattest and fastest fatting of these rams were then selected for breeding. Secondly, these selected rams were put to ewes reared from couples that had been fed in spring on rape. Thirdly, these rams and ewes were bred in-and-in, i.e. the sire was put to his own offspring and her own offspring to the dam.[3] The Dishley strain of the New Leicester breed of pasture sheep was thus not the work of any one man or even of any one farming country, and it was certainly not due merely to breeding in-and-in. First, the 'pastures' themselves maintained a distinct breed of pasture sheep. These were improved both by the temporary leys of up-and-down husbandry and by cross-breeding with the larger pasture sheep

---

[1] Pitt, *Leics.* 34–6; Marshall, *Midl. Cos.* i, 260–1, 380–1.

[2] Ibid. 284 sqq.; *Sheep*, 33–4; Pitt, op. cit. 32; sup. 267.

[3] Marshall, *Midl. Cos.* i, 296 sqq., 381–2, 397, 402, 419; Pitt, op. cit. 34–6; H. C. Pawson, *Robt Bakewell* 1957, pp. 59–60.

from the Fen and Saltings countries. The cultivation of short clover and 'seeds' leys enabled the ram lambs to be forced. Cole crops, arable-grass rotations and floated meadows, borrowed from the Chalk Country and the Vales of Hereford, enabled them to be fattened rapidly. The rams originally imported from the Fen and Saltings countries were raised there partly on rape and this practice, translated into the idiom of the plain, and applied to the couples, was an essential part of improvement. Sheep fatted on cole-seed had long commanded a premium[1] and the method adopted by the ram breeders was an old one. Selective breeding had been practised for hundreds of years. Nor was inbreeding an eighteenth-century innovation. The new pasture sheep were only perfected by Bakewell. Their creation was the work of Joseph Allom, Major Hartopp, Captain Tate, Mr Stone and successive generations of improvers.

The new sheep were pre-eminently suited to rapid feeding and fatting. To compare them with the old fallow sheep would be unrealistically to telescope historical development; and it would be incorrect to regard the new pasture sheep as better than the old. The old pasture sheep was too good to lose and was not completely replaced by the new. The new sheep were an improvement on the old only in the sense that they were based on the old breed. In much the same way, the passenger may be said to be an improvement on the goods train. The new pasture sheep was an altered breed demanding not only praise but assessment. Bred entirely for fatting, it had about one-quarter less wool than the old pasture sheep, and this of inferior quality. In compensation, the new sheep fattened well at two years on coles and at two and a half on pastures, instead of the three years previously required. The new pasture sheep were bred for the butcher and not for the hosier or worsted-weaver, while the old had reconciled the interests of both. As long as the demand for pasture wool was maintained, therefore, many farmers continued to prefer the old breeds. Bakewell deliberately disregarded wool altogether and agreed with the staplers that his Dishley sheep necessarily gave poor fleeces. Moreover, while the old pasture sheep could be folded as stores, the new could only waddle about and their constitutions were too delicate to permit folding.[2] Furthermore, the new sheep sacrificed the quality of mutton to quantity. They fattened younger than the old breeds and had less bone, yet about the same dead weight. With the new breed, therefore, the farmer could produce much more mutton to the acre. Fatted on grass at two years and a half, the lean mutton of the new sheep was not inferior to that of the old. When put

[1] Northants. R.O., F.(M.) Corr. 222/54.

[2] Marshall, op. cit. i, 380, 402–4, 409–11, 449–50; *Midl. Dept*, 278–9; *Sheep*, 36–7; 'On new Leics. sheep', in A. Hunter, *Georgical Essays* 1803, pp. 388 sqq.; *S. Dept*, 500; Crutchley, op. cit. 15; Pitt, op. cit. 74; Boys, op. cit. 150.

on roots at two years, however, the new pasture sheep had a propensity not merely to fatten quickly but to run to sheer fat. Like all turnip mutton, it tended to be watery and would not answer its weight when killed.[1] The new sheep were thus greatly to the advantage of the sheep-master, but conferred rather smaller benefits on the butcher and consumer. Its introduction was accompanied by 'the folly of over-fatting livestock'. Even William Marshall, who had done so much to bring Bakewell's achievements to the notice of the public, considered as 'highly creditable' the comment that

'there has, for some years, been a prevailing rage, a ridiculous kind of competition among graziers, to produce the largest cattle, and the fattest meat . . . Sheep have been likewise commended, not for the sweetness and tenderness of their flesh, but for their weight per quarter; though the tallow chandler is chiefly benefited by the excess to which fatting has been carried'.

Not all of the extra weight of meat carried by the new sheep was lean, and in so much as it was fat, none but the coarsest palates were advantaged.[2] Great quantities of mediocre mutton were indeed produced for the mass urban and industrial market, but fattiness perhaps tended to repel the discriminate. The chief advantage of the new race was thus in extending the range of sheep breeds, each of which had a distinct purpose and peculiar attributes, and in providing a stock from which, by judicious cross-breeding, improvements could be made on the old pasture sheep of various countries and on mountain sheep such as the Cheviots.[3]

[1] Lisle, op. cit. 335; Pitt, *Northants.* 207–8.
[2] Ibid.; Marshall, op. cit. 92.
[3] Marshall, *Midl. Dept,* 603; *Midl. Cos* i, 412.

CHAPTER X

THE FRUITS OF ENTERPRISE

EARLY modern English farmers were bursting with industry and enterprise. It is impossible not to be struck by the desire for good husbandry
and improvement. The well-breeched, go-ahead farmer travails to
acquire riches.

'He improveth his land to a double value by good husbandry. Some
grounds that wept with water or frowned with thorns, by draining the
one and clearing the other, he makes both to laugh and sing with corn.
By marl and limestones burnt he bettereth his ground and his industry
worketh miracles by turning stones into bread.'[1]

Yet few would risk their livelihood and throw over their plan of
management, with all its elaboration of checks and balances, for the
sake of what might prove a catchpenny device. The attitude of mind
that resisted the blandishments of eighteenth-century publicists and
refused to replace horses by oxen, was captured by Folkingham when
he said, 'Wee are too wise, holding it ridiculous to innovate, nay to
imitate, anything not approved by continual practise, howsoever we
have authenticke records from antiquities to animate us thereunto.'
Innovation proceeded at a familiar tempo. First, a few enterprising
individuals developed new systems of production, which when successfully proved, the generality of capitalist farmers hastened to adopt.
Witness the rapidity with which floating spread. It is remarkable at
what speed practical and suitable innovations were made. Selected
clover cultivation, once perfected, was soon taken up. Turnip husbandry
was generally introduced in High Suffolk in the space of ten years.[2]
    Foreign influence contributed something to the agricultural revolu-
tion. Some early supplies of clover, sainfoin and lucerne seeds came from
the Low Countries and France, potatoes and tobacco from the Americas.

[1] T. Fuller, *Holy State & Profane State* 1841, p. 107.
[2] Folkingham, op. cit. 26.

But it would be wrong to exaggerate this influence. Long before their seeds were selected for leys, English grasslands included wild white and perennial and broad red clovers, trefoil (yellow clover, 'hop clover', medick, nonsuch), birdsfoot trefoil, common sainfoin, burnet and melilot.[1] A little Dutch white clover was grown, but was so short-lived as to be of value only in grazing leys of short duration or as a minor constituent of the clovers sown in long-ley mixtures; and so had but small application. It need hardly be added, however that 'Dutch' is the name of a variety of white clover, not a designation of its invariable place of growth. Like French leave and Dutch courage, it was easily naturalized in England. Some Dutch white clover was and is grown in England, but it is true, most of the Dutch white seed employed here was and is imported, partly from or through Holland. However, at the time when the term was coined, Dutch did not mean specifically Hollander or pertaining to the United Provinces, but merely Germanic. In short, we grew a little Dutch white clover, partly from our own seed, but mostly from seed imported from the Spanish Netherlands, Holland, and central Europe. A wide variety of superior English-grown clover seeds was available in ample quantities, but as far as Dutch white was concerned, it was well to import a good deal of Continental seed.[2] Similarly, it was common or English sainfoin that was mostly grown, not the French variety. Virtually every agriculturally valuable grass, not excepting meadow catstail (timothy), was indigenous.[3] Nearly all the cole and root crops were likewise native to England: at least two varieties each of common turnip, rape or cole-seed, and carrot. Some Dutch cole-seed was imported, mostly by way of exchange of seed, for the Dutch bought ours in return. That cole-seed was first brought to England by Vermuyden and the Dutch, as has been unsupportedly alleged, is incorrect.[4] Almost the only new introduction from abroad was the Swedish turnip, which arrived only in the later eighteenth century. Some Flemish horses and a few Friesian cows were imported. Many

[1] Ibid. 25, 87; Salisbury, op. cit. 42; Yarranton, op. cit. 7; Blith, op. cit. 177–8; Gerarde, op. cit. (1597) 840, 887–9, 1017–8, 1021–2, 1024, 1034; (1633) 1185–6; Coles, op. cit. cap. cxxxii, ccxcviii; Norden, Surv's. Dial. 208; Beale, op. cit. 53; Ray, op. cit. i, 345, 617, 878 (recte 876)–7, 943–4, 949–52, 967–8; Worlidge, op. cit. 29.

[2] Ibid. 24; Blith, op. cit. 177–8, 181; Lisle, op. cit. 241; Mortimer, op. cit. 28; Speed, op. cit. 33, 37; Yarranton, op. cit. 1, 3–4, 6–7, 45–6; Weston, op. cit. (1652); Gerarde, op. cit. (1633) 1185; (1597) 1018.

[3] Ibid. 1 sqq.

[4] Ibid. 177 sqq., 872; Coles, op. cit. cap. lxxxviii, ccli; Mortimer, op. cit. 121–3; Laurence, op. cit. 130; Lisle, op. cit. 234; Ray, op. cit. i, 800–1; Turner, Names Herbes, 55, 67; Salmon, op. cit. 158, 1203; J. Parkinson, op. cit. 862–4, 901–2; Blith, op. cit. p. foll. 248. For cole-seed, sup. 236–7. Cf. B. H. Slicher van Bath, 'Rise Intensive Husbandry in Low Countries', in J. S. Bromley & E. H. Kossmann (eds.) Brit. & Nthlds 1960, p. 139. Pace Thirsk, Eng. Peasant, 30, 127–8.

Dutch drainers were employed over here, but this was due less to their engineering than their financial ability. English engineers had more experience and expertness in fen drainage. The Dutch were admittedly skilled in banking silt levels, but such impoldering was not draining and contributed little or nothing to drainage technique. Even where the Dutch had the greatest expertise, in the reclamation of saltings, they played only a minor part.[1] Floating was an English invention and the up-and-down husbandries of the plain countries were uninfluenced by Continental ideas. England seems to have borrowed precious little.

As both industrial[2] and agricultural changes were proceeding simultaneously, interaction between the two is hardly to be wondered at. Drainage improved inland navigations. Woad-growing literally supplied a foundation for the dyeing industry. Advances in farming changed the available quantities of the various grades of wool and remoulded the textile industries. The extension of cultivation, the expansion of the cheese and butter dairy, with their demand for wood fuel, and the growing use of lime, all encouraged, directly or indirectly, the expansion of the coal industry. The rise of dairy farming also stimulated the extractive and metallurgical industries, for every dairy needed an extensive range of utensils. Rising agricultural incomes provided a deepening home market for English industry. Conversely, the early industrial revolution gave farmers cheap fuel for domestic heating, lime-burning and other uses, and extraneous manures; and improved techniques lowered relative industrial prices and so swelled real agricultural incomes.[3]

We make no bones about asserting that the agricultural revolution dominated the period between 1560 and 1767 and that all its main achievements fell before 1720, most of them before 1673, and many of them much earlier still. In order to prove this we have had no need whatsoever to refer to either net yields or gross volumes of production. Nevertheless, it would be gratifying if we could find the various revolutionary innovations mirrored in these, and this we shall now attempt.

To measure livestock improvement is extremely difficult. In 1618 in the Chalk, and about 1720 in the Cotswold Country, cows going on the commons gave a gallon of milk a day. About the same time, the Shuttleworth domestic dairy, presumably of longhorns, to judge by the cheese and butter made from their milk, yielded each about one gallon and a third a day. By the same token, Fen Country cows, about 1656,

---

[1] Gramolt, op. cit. 141; C., H. *Discourse concerng Drayninge Fennes & Surrounded Grounds* 1629; L. E. Harris, 'Sir Cornelius Vermuyden & Gt Level of Fens. New Judgt', *Proc. Camb. Ant. S.* xlv, 18, 20, 22; sup. 223–5.

[2] Nef, op. cit.; *Conquest Material World* 1964, pp. 121 sqq.

[3] Ibid. 121 sqq., 240 sqq. For woad, v. P. L. Hughes & J. F. Larkin, *Tudor R. Proclamations* i, 1964, p. 454.

gave around one and a half. These are averages over a year, of course, and daily figures varied with the season. They suggest gross annual yields of about 300 or 400 gallons. Suffolk duns gave even more. Little significance attaches to these figures, however, except to show the yields were much like modern ones and varied according to diet.[1] No particular advantage derives from high milk yields, except to farmers forbidden to water their milk after it has left the cow, for the more the milk the lower the proportion of butter-fat and of solids-not-fat. Crude yields have risen much, but, on the same diet, it is doubtful if modern cows can make significantly more butter or cheese than seventeenth-century ones did.

It is similarly difficult to judge improvements in fat stock. The weight of livestock sold at Smithfield in the eighteenth century did not increase much, and even if it had done, little significance would attach, for the fashionable size for joints changes, and graziers have to suit consumers by fattening stock of a particular size and age. The largest oxen, for instance, victualled the East Indiamen, for their thick beef long retained its juiciness. In any event, it is impossible to increase the weight of lean flesh and not that of bone, for the size of muscles is related to that of the bones they move. The only significant measure of progress would be conversion rates, and these are unknown.[2]

Nor is it easier to measure agricultural progress by reference to the yields of corn per acre. Historically, the absence of any uniformity in measures of volume and of superficial area precludes the possibility of any but the most vague and meaningless estimates. Any valid statistics moreover, would have to apply to exactly the same plots of land and be capable of bearing septennial averages. No such are, in fact, available and all that can be said, for what it is worth, is that medieval wheat yields are usually estimated at about a quarter an acre, and late sixteenth-century ones at two quarters.[3] This estimate of two quarters agrees with what Robert Loder garnered. Many yields were higher. In 1634, 533 quarters of woad barley were grown on 146½ acres at Charney, in the Midland Plain.[4] As the size of neither bushel nor acre

---

[1] Harland, op. cit. 216; Fussell, op. cit. 156; Verney, op. cit. iii, 209; Oxon. R.O., Dashwood VIII/34 valn Harrison's fm; Marshall, *E. Dept*, 461.

[2] Culley, op. cit. 32; G. E. Fussell, 'Size Eng. Cattle in 18th cent.', *Ag. Hist.* iii, 160 sqq.; B.M., Harl. 7017, nos. 26, 29 (27).

[3] Ernle, op. cit. (1927) 10; Harrison, op. cit. suppl. 133; Venn, op. cit. 95; N.S.B. Gras, *Hist. Ag. in Eur. & Am.* 31; A. P. Usher, 'Soil Fertility & Exhaustion & their Hist. Significance', *Q. Jnl. Econ.* xxvii, 394; W. Beveridge, 'Statistical Crime of 17th cent.', *Jnl Econ. & Bus. Hist.* i, 525–6; 'Yield & Price Corn in Middle Ages', *Econ. Jnl* i, 155 sqq.; 'Wheat Measures in Winchester Manors', *Econ. Hist.* ii, 19 sqq.; M. K. Bennett, 'Brit. Wheat Yield per ac. for 7 cents.', ibid. iii, 13 sqq.

[4] Fussell, op. cit. 23, 28–9, 42, 47–8, 57, 74–5, 92–3, 109–11, 124–6, 139–40, 142, 160, 162, 175, 177; Berks. R.O., D./E.Bp E.15.

is known, not much can be argued from this, but it would seem that yields per acre in the seventeenth century compare not unfavourably with modern English ones, the average of which has only increased as it has in more recent times through the abandonment of poorer lands.

One measure of early modern agricultural progress is the comparison of seed-harvest ratios within the self-same countries and field-courses, for estimates of yields in terms of the increase of seed obviate difficulties arising from diversities in soils and measures. Walter of Henley's ideal was a fivefold increase of wheat. In and about the thirteenth century, sixfold increases were obtained in the Tamar Valley in the West Country, and between two and two-and-a-half fold in the Cotswold Country. Wheat and barley increases in Harwell were about four and fivefold respectively. Other medieval yields were of the same order.[1] In Tudor and Stuart times, the average increases in shifting cultivation in the North-eastern Lowlands were about threefold. Permanent common fields could now give tenfold increases. In the late sixteenth century, the tillage of the Englishry in Wales often gave between ten and four-teenfold increases of barley. In the early seventeenth century wheat yields in the Cotswold Country were between four and fivefold. In the middle of this century, average wheat yields in the West Country were between ten and fourteenfold, much the same as at the end of the eighteenth. In the later seventeenth century, tenfold increases were reckoned good in common fields in the Midland Plain. Between 1612 and 1620, when harvests were middling, Robert Loder, a conservative-minded farmer of little experience, in a two-field course in Chalk Country common fields, on the self-same Harwell demesne farm, obtained wheat increases ranging between five-and-a-half and twenty-fold and averaging twelvefold; and barley increases ranging between five and elevenfold and averaging eightfold.[2] Clearly, between the thirteenth and mid-seventeenth centuries, without any change in the general plans of management, increases from lean land and ordinary common fields about doubled, and this striking progress was mostly achieved after 1500. But this is less than half the story, for no account has yet been taken of the improvements wrought by the conversion of permanent tillage and permanent grass to up-and-down land; and everything known about permanent tillage and ley farming today suggests that the substitution of the latter for the former about doubles

[1] Gras, *Corn Mkt*, 261–4, 267–8; ex inf. Mr J. Titow; Finberg, op. cit. 114–5; Rees, *S.W. & March*, 189; J. Saltmarsh, 'Coll. Home Fm in 15th cent.', *Econ. Hist.* iii, 165–6; B. H. Slicher van Bath, 'Yield Ratios, 810–1820', being *A.A.G. Bijdragen* 10, pp. 30 sqq., 112 sqq.

[2] Ibid. 47; Fussell, loc. cit.; Owen, *Penbs.* pt i, 60; *Taylors Cussion* pt ii, f. 115; Marshall, *W. Engl.* i, 189; R. Lennard, art. cit. 39–40; Plot, *Staffs.* 240; *Wills & Invs.* (Surtees S.) pt iii, 158–9; pt iv, 140–1; E. Bateson, op. cit. v, 331, 392, 395, 413; Maxey, op. cit.

yields. The increases from up-and-down land in the Midland Plain were indeed about twice those of common fields in the same country. Seventeenth-century writers estimate the increases in up-and-down husbandry at twentyfold. Barley yields at the end of the eighteenth century were between twenty and twenty-fivefold and they were hardly less a century and a half earlier.[1] Twentyfold seems about the average. This means that where up-and-down husbandry was introduced, increases were redoubled. Inferior practices in the seventeenth century gave increases twice as great as the medieval standard of excellence, and the best, increases four times as great as the best medieval ones. At the end of the eighteenth century, yields were hardly more than in the early seventeenth. That is the measure of the advance that had been made by then.

But it would be artificial to consider corn and not grass yields, for grass became as important a crop as corn, and its yield also indicates the state and numbers of livestock depending on it. The conversion of permanent tillage and permanent grass led to about a fourfold increase in the production of grass nutrients, an advance that laid the foundation for a great expansion of animal husbandry. Floating catchwork and ridge-and-furrow meadows multiplied the production of meadow grass and hay about fivefold, permitted heavier stocking and earlier lambing, and in turn increased corn yields. In the Chalk Country, for instance, floating raised barley yields by about a quarter an acre. Roots, coles, clover and 'seeds', and sainfoin allowed stock to be carried and fattened in winter as in summer. Marshland drainage prepared the way for the growing of more corn, without sensibly diminishing grazing. The upshot of these improvements was the production of more and larger Hereford cattle and Chalk Country sheep, more Ryeland, Devon Nott and pasture sheep, more Shire horses, more and improved Suffolk Punches, more grass lamb, mutton and beef, more fresh winter meat, more superior dairy cattle, and more dairy produce, both in spring and summer and in winter, all per acre of farmland.[2] Combining the increases both of corn and grass nutrients and of other forage and fodder, the improvement of yields, between the later Middle Ages and the end of the seventeenth century, must have been enormous. Corn and grass yields rose about fourfold, and the yields of the fallows increased out of recognition. All told, it is difficult to resist the conclusion that yields rose up to tenfold, and fivefold on the average.

What this increase in yields meant in terms of gross product can best be seen in relation to population changes and exportable surpluses. It

[1] Ibid.; Marshall, *Midl. Cos.* i, 187, 192; Norden, loc. cit.; Plot, *Oxon.* 151–2; R. Herrick, *Noble Nos.* 'Thanksgiving to God, for his Ho.'; sup. 208.

[2] Carew, op. cit. f. 23; Borlase, op. cit. 286; Childrey, op. cit. 13; B.M., Harl. 5827, f. 10; sup. 320–4.

is generally accepted that the kingdom's population reached about 3 million in the period 1250–1350, but that medieval agriculture was unable to maintain so many people more than temporarily and precariously, so thereafter the population declined and stagnated until the latter part of the fifteenth century. By about 1540 the population had recovered to some 3 million; and by 1700 it had risen to about 6 million. At some time between 1540 and 1700, then, the population had doubled, and the Jacobeans were well aware of this rapid increase.[1] All this time England was more or less self-sufficient in foodstuffs, but in the sixteenth century London and other corn-deficient areas had to rely on foreign grain in times of bad harvest, whereas from the middle of the seventeenth century onwards England developed a considerable and more or less constant net export trade in corn. Net corn exports amounted to about 300,000 quarters a year in 1675–7, 350,000 in 1697–1731 and 675,000 in 1732–66. Net wheat exports alone averaged about 112,000 q. a year in 1697–1726 and 324,000 in 1727–56. Roughly speaking, then, English cereal exports were sufficient to feed 150,000 persons in 1675–7, 175,000 in 1697–1731 and 340,000 in 1732–66. Assuming that English diet remained much the same, foodstuff production must at least have doubled between 1540 and 1700. That the volume of meat and dairy produce increased greatly is already known, and exports of both probably grew, as did those of beer, ale, perry and cider.[2]

However, the indications are that common diets improved during the agricultural revolution, and not least amongst the lowest ranks of society. The staples of farm-workers' diet were bread, beer, beef and cheese. The lower classes, it is true, did not always eat wheaten bread, but the rye bread, oat cakes, barley bannocks and maslin flours sometimes substituted were not vastly inferior. Rye has almost as much protein as wheat, oats only a quarter and barley only a third less, while all have much the same carbohydrate equivalent, except oats, which, however, have more fat. Oats formed the staple corn only in Wales, the North and Peak-Forest countries, the North-western Lowlands, and such like places; but here agricultural wage-workers were hardly to be found.[3] Moreover, farm improvement led to the wider consumption of wheat, so that by the middle of the seventeenth century, the poorer sort

[1] Stat. 1 Jas c. 5.

[2] Gras, op. cit. 77, 101 sqq., 113–14, 192, 245, 437; D. G. Barnes, *Hist. Eng. Corn Laws 1660–1846* 1930, p. 299; E. Leigh, op. cit. 184; Gerarde, op. cit. 61; Standish, op. cit. 43; Steele, op. cit. i, 203, 219–20; Hughes & Larkin, op. cit. 500; *A.P.C.* ix, 280–1; Stats. 1 & 2 P. & M. c. 5; 3 Jas c. 11; 14 Chas II c. 26; 22 & 23 Chas II c. 13; 25 Chas II c. 1 sect. 31; C. H. Firth & R. S. Rait, *Acts & Ordinances Interregnum* 1911 ii, 1044–5; S. G. E. Lythe, *Econ. Scot. in its Eur. Setting* 1960, p. 224; Chalklin, op. cit. 175; Bland, Brown & Tawney, op. cit. 415; H.M.C., *MSS. Marquis Salisbury at Hatfield Ho.* pt ii 1888, p. 147.

[3] Marshall, *W. Engl.* i, 27; Spratt, op. cit. 158–9; sup. 156, 162–3, 168–9, 171, 173.

were largely eating wheat instead of rye or barley.[1] The servants of gentlemen farmers fared less well than their masters. In the Northwold Country, the Bests ate bread of rye, peas and barley and pastry of wheatmeal; while their servants had pastry of rye, peas and barley and puddings of barleymeal, except during harvest, when wheatmeal was substituted, or when tail wheat was used. Servants to working farmers, however, though perhaps sitting at separate tables, usually dined in the same room with their masters and off the same food.[2]

Wherever wheat was a main crop it formed the usual bread of both masters and servants and was consumed in ample quantities. Each man ate about a peck of wheat a week; seven-tenths of a peck of barley malt was consumed in beer; and each had also a good deal of bacon and of meat, much of which was salted in earlier times, about a quarter of a pound of cheese, some butter, milk and fish and a little fruit, spice, salt, hops and oatmeal. This was the regimen in Loder's household.[3] Every day two pounds of bread and four pints of beer were amply supplemented by high-protein foods, fruit and vegetables. Farm-workers, no less than other folk, enjoyed fresh or preserved peas, beans, carrots, cabbages, turnips and the like.[4] The quantities of meat consumed are difficult to estimate, but throughout the period both men and maid-servants expected as of right roast meat for supper at least twice a week.[5] In Lent fish took the place of meat and a little fish was eaten at other times also. Butcher's meat and bacon could also be supplemented by hares, rabbits, larks, bustards and other game. Eggs were readily available, and numerous varieties of fruit and nuts, many of which could be kept for or through the winter.

Two pounds of wheaten bread contained about 114 gm. second-class protein, 14 gm. fat, 355 mg. calcium, 1·8 gm. phosphorus, 27 mg. iron, 1·8 mg. carotene, 2,130 international units of vitamin A, 960 of vitamin B_1, 0·18 mg. riboflavin (vitamin B_2), and 3,000 calories. Four pints of beer provided over 700 calories and some of the vitamin B complex. The cheese eaten gave about 20 gm. first-class protein, 30 gm. fat, 1 gm. calcium, 0·6 gm. phosphorus, 2 mg. iron, 400 calories and 2,000 units of vitamin A. 4 oz. lean meat a day would have given 25 gm. first-class protein and 3 mg. iron. Fat meat, butter and milk would have provided 100 gm. fat, and some vitamins A and D, calcium, phosphorus and calories. At the least the diet contained 159 gm. protein, of which only 45 were first class and 114 second class, the latter having only

[1] Bodl. Aubrey 2, ff. 83–4; J. O. Halliwell, *Autobiography of Sir Simonds D'Ewes* 1845 i, 180.

[2] Best, op. cit. 104; Fussell, op. cit. 45.

[3] Ibid. 22–3, 28, 30, 44, 67–8, 86–7, 106–7, 136, 152, 162, 173.

[4] Holinshed & Harrison, op. cit. 208.

[5] Tusser, op. cit. 136; Verney, op. cit. ii, 225; Drummond & Wilbraham, op. cit. 124.

60 per cent of the biological value of the former, so that the whole amounts to some 120 gm. first-class protein equivalent. The rest of the diet consisted of about 144 gm. fat, 2 gm. calcium, $2\frac{1}{2}$ gm. phosphorus, 32 gm. iron (no more could have been absorbed), 1·8 mg. carotene, 5,000 units of vitamin A, 1,000 of vitamin B, 100 of vitamin C and adequate amounts of vitamins D and E. All told the diet provided upwards of 4,000 calories a day. The farm servant's food contained enough fat, calories, and vitamins of all sorts, and ample calcium, iron, phosphorus and protein.[1]

This diet was somewhat better than that thought to have been enjoyed by the average fifteenth-century husbandman.[2] As compared with a modern 'poverty' diet, such as that of the unemployed during a depression, the food of the early modern farm servant contained twice as much protein, somewhat more fat, more calories, seven times as much calcium, nearly four times as much iron, ten times as much vitamin A, four or five times as much of the vitamin B complex, perhaps six times as much vitamin C, considerably more vitamin D and adequate amounts of vitamin E, which was almost entirely lacking from the 'poverty' diet. As compared with modern 'middle-class' diet, that of sixteenth and seventeenth century farm servants contained at least as much fat, more calories, three times as much calcium, twice as much phosphorus, as much of vitamins A, C and D, more vitamin E and twice as much of the vitamin B complex, and more than twice as much iron.[3]

Although it can hardly be shown, we have every reason to suppose that outdwelling servants and day-labourers generally fed as well as indwelling servants. The former were recruited from amongst the latter and it is hardly likely that the worker's food was appreciably worse, on the average, after than before marriage. Outdwelling servants and labourers had their own cows, pigs, poultry, kitchen gardens and even field plots sometimes; and in addition to these resources they continued on occasion to receive a greater or smaller part of their diet from the farmers.[4] It may be guessed, therefore, that most regular farm workers enjoyed much the same food.

From this it would follow that the gross output of consumers' goods on English farms must have doubled and may well have trebled during the agricultural revolution.

To all appearances the first half of the eighteenth century was a period of depression and stagnation, broken by short outbursts of restricted progress in the spread of what were by now almost completed innovations.

[1] Ibid. 83, 90–3, 100–4, 138, 155–6, 301–2, 352, 450, 495, 502, 514, 561–2. Wheat had somewhat less protein in wet summers, but bread then fortified with beans.
[2] Ibid. 561.
[3] Ibid. 565.
[4] Fussell, op. cit. 76, 80, 86, 106, 117.

No new round of innovations started, and there was retrogression in some places, e.g. the Fen Country. Industrial expansion, too, which had previously been rapid, now slowed down. The population did grow, but only by about one-sixth. Between 1534 and 1696 the London population rose from about 60,000 to about 530,000. It increased rapidly also in the second half of the eighteenth century, but only slightly from 1696 to 1750.[1] Then, in the third quarter of the century followed a period of recovery and of further livestock improvements.

About 1774, England entered a period of secondary industrial revolution and of a second and comparable great prosperity, and the population began to rise rapidly once again; but no second agricultural revolution materialized to match up to that of the previous period, no revolutionizing of technique, no radical reshaping of any of the agricultural industries, no great increase in yields and not much in the gross product. Between 1750 and 1850 the population doubled, but the number of souls fed with home-grown food did not. From 1757 onwards, and even more from 1767, corn imports became both larger and more regular. In 1773 it became necessary to restrict corn exports in the interests of the home population and the export bounty now fell into desuetude. Exports were negligible after 1789 and were prohibited in almost all years. Instead of on corn exports, in 1795–6 and 1800–1 bounties were placed on imports.[2] This change is shown even more clearly by the wheat trade. In the period 1757–86, exports shrank to an average of some 16,000 quarters a year; and by 1787–1816, the balance had changed altogether and there was a net average annual import of about 400,000 quarters. Between 1750 and 1801, it follows, British farmers only increased their gross output sufficiently to feed an extra 2 million persons, even assuming that standards of diet were maintained. In fact, at this time, considerable economies had to be effected both in food and in the industrial use of corn. Tea started to be substituted for beer, and starch-making was restricted. The diet of the poorer sort declined and there was probably a fall in consumption of food per head.[3] The gross output of English farms cannot have risen more than by about one-third between 1750 and 1801 and perhaps by no more than a quarter.[4] After the end of the eighteenth century largely, and before that partly, the increase of population was fed by imports. This tendency continued in no uncertain fashion. By 1817–27 net imports

[1] Gras, op. cit. 75; Nef, *Brit. Coal Ind.* i, 20, 123–4; *War & Human Prog.* 1950, pp. 291–2; sup. 234.

[2] Gras, op. cit. 114; A. Smith, *Wealth of Nations* 1904 ii, 10; Barnes, op. cit. 299–300.

[3] Ibid. 72, 75, 77, 82, 85; C. R. Fay, *Corn Laws & Soc. Engl.* 1932, p. 37; E. J. Hobsbawm, 'Brit. Std Living 1790–1850', *EcH.R.* 1957 x, 49–50.

[4] Agreeable with Mr Fussell (cited Ashton, *Ind. Rev.* 146) & P. Deane & W. A. Cole, *Brit. Econ. Growth 1688–1959* 1962, p. 65.

had reached over 500,000 quarters a year, and by 1828–40, over 1,500,000. By 1850 about one-quarter of all the flour consumed was imported from overseas.[1] But these figures serve only to mask the actual stagnation in gross output. True, home agriculture did continue to supply most of the food consumed, but this was thanks less to advances in agricultural technique than to the concentration of agriculture on supplying the domestic food market at the expense of exports and of the production of drink corn and industrial and forage and fodder crops. It is a statistical crime to compare populations and argue from them as Dr Mingay does, without so much as breathing a hint that England about 1870 was a net importer and about 1700 a net exporter of farm produce; or that she became a great importer of dairy produce, pig-meat, rough grains, bone dust, nitrates, guano, potash and phosphates; or that imported tea, coffee, cocoa and sugar had largely been substituted for home-grown malt and hops; imported cotton, wool, hemp, flax and jute for home-produced fibres; imported oils and seeds for butter and cole-seed; Virginian tobacco for that of the Vale of Evesham; overseas hides and skins for English ones; foreign dyestuffs for English-grown woad, weld and madder; and steam-engines consuming coal for horses consuming grass, hay and corn.[2]

In the absence of anything in the nature of gross farm output statistics we can hardly do more than guess, but it does appear that the great spurt in production between 1540 and 1700 was quite unmatched in the years from 1750 to 1880, and this is inconsistent with the view that an agricultural revolution occurred then, but consistent with the revolution we have described.

It is, of course, no part of our argument to deny that improvements and innovations were made either before 1560 or after 1767. On the contrary, many notable changes readily spring to mind. In the Fen Country, for instance, Morton's Leam, dug in 1478–90, was significant not only on account of its size. It was the first large straight cut and the first English canal primarily intended for navigation.[3] The introduction of hop-growing was important in several ways, not least that it enabled economies to be made in malting barley and facilitated the preservation of malt liquor. The varieties originally introduced from the Low Countries suited spongy and fenny grounds and were cultivated in High Suffolk and the Woodland chiefly, in the bottoms of the Vales of Hereford to a limited extent, and in the north-east of the Wealden Vales eventually. Later special upland varieties were developed and took hold in the Northdown Country, especially in the Maidstone District

[1] Barnes, op. cit. 300.

[2] Chambers & Mingay, op. cit. 207–8; G. E. Mingay, 'Ag. Rev. in Eng. Hist.', Ag. Hist. xxxvii, pp. 123 sqq.; Ashton, loc. cit.

[3] L. E. Harris, op. cit. 18; Darby, Hist. Geog. Engl. 367, 449.

and, about 1600, in the Vale of Farnham; in the Chalk Country, especially near the brewing towns of Salisbury and Wilton; in the Oxford Heights Country, mostly near Bromham; and in the higher lands of the Vales of Hereford. These places had free-working soils just shallow enough to allow the roots to draw nourishment from their chalk or limestone subsoils and light enough to facilitate hoeing. The hop-merchant going his rounds of the farmhouses became a familiar figure in many countries, but the few specialist hop-gardeners worked on a small scale only and farmers always treated hops as a subsidiary crop. In the Vales of Hereford, which had become second only to the Northdown Country in this business, in 1650, £30 or £40 a year was a good profit from a hop garden.[1] After 1767, a few minor crops were newly introduced, such as mangolds, Italian rye-grass and crimson clover ('trifolium'). Significant changes, including some for the better, were also made in farm livestock breeds. From 1784 shorthorn improvements were continued by the brothers Charles and Robert Colling, who farmed near Darlington. They made the breed still more compact and weighty, without any sacrifice of milking quality and so did much to promote it as a replacement for the longhorn. When the Dishley sheep craze was at its height, so much reverse crossing took place that the Fen Country strain of pasture sheep was largely lost, and Bakewell's stock even found its way into the Norfolk Heathlands, though it never took a foothold except in some pleasure parks, as it was wholly unsuited to arable flocks.

[1] R. Scot, *Perfite Platforme of a Hoppe Garden* 1576; Coles, op. cit. cap. ccxx; Gerarde, op. cit. 4; Norden, op. cit. 212; Marshall, *S. Cos.* i, 22, 67, 140, 346, 397, 399, 400; ii, 47–8, 55; Fuller, op. cit. i, 493; *W. Dept*, 277; Reyce, op. cit. 31–2; Tusser, op. cit. 55–6; Lodge, op. cit. 43, 179; Steer, op. cit. 52–3, 99, 134, 148, 179; Kitchin, op. cit. 179; Cunnington, op. cit. 116; *Wilts. N. & Q.* viii, 383; Aubrey, *Sy* iii, 346–7; *Arch. Cant.* lxi, 60 sqq., 69–72; Melling, op. cit. 24, 35, 37–8, 43, 49; Chalklin, op. cit. 92–5; Wilton ho. Svys Manors 1631 ii, Wilton ff. 1 (3)–3 (4), 5 (7); Svys Manors 1632–3, Bishopstone f. 2; Devizes Mus. Svy Bps Cannings Rect. & Manor Cannings Canonicorum 1661, ff. 81–2; Commonplace Bk Sir Hy & Sir Ed. Baynton 1614–79, rev. p. 1e; P.R.O., Exch. L.R., M.B. 219, f. 409; A.O., Parl. Svys Ess. 12, f. 5; Sfk 15, f. 5; Chanc. Proc. ser. i Jas I, A. 8/36; D. 9/74, compl. & ans.; Herts. R.O., G'bury xi. 11, f. 122; Ess. R.O., D./D.P. M186, p. 30; D./D.Pr. 426; D./D.Qs. 58/6; T./B. 65/1; Worcs. R.O., B.A. 68 Woodmanton valn 1611; B.A. 494 Lickhill partic. 1656; Hereford Lib. Local: Deed 3540; Gaut, op. cit. 92; Beale, op. cit. 47–8; Tawney & Power, op. cit. i, 313–14; B'ham Lib. Winnington 52; B.M., Add. 27605, f. 100v.; 29890; 34162, f. 19v.; R. 17751; invs.:—Wilts. R.O., A/d Sarum. Wm Sharpe 1637 Fugglestone; Dioc. Reg. Sarum. Mich. Hibberd 1610 S. Burcombe; N.L.W. Episc. Cons. Ct Hereford, 1664 May: Joyce Barrett/Collington; Cons. Ct Dean Hereford, 1727: Jn Tully/Holmer; Kent R.O., A/d Ct Cantuar. 1660: Denise Honey/ Bethersden; 1665: Wyatt Chowne/Boughton Monchelsea; 1678: Wm Charleton/ Boughton; 1680: Th. Carter/E. Sutton; Beeleigh Abb. Th. Wilson 1627 Bocking; Nfk R.O., Cons. Ct 1633: 315; 1664: 66; E. Sfk R.O., A/d 1583–4: 318; S. 1/7/5.10; R. C. Temple (ed.) *Travs. Pet. Mundy in Eur. & Asia: 1608–67: iv, Travs. in Eur. 1639–47* Hakluyt Soc. ser. II 1925 lv, 40.

In the last two decades of the eighteenth century, John Ellman of Glynde improved the old Southdowns and developed a new strain by breeding in-and-in. His work was taken up and completed by Jonas Webb of Babraham, in the Chiltern Country. The result was a new breed bearing a fleece of about three pounds, much better for fatting on 'seeds' leys and roots, but less adapted for feeding the downs and folding the tillage. It soon established itself in the Chiltern and Northdown countries and in the Norfolk Heathlands. The New Southdowns tolerated folding and gave more meat than the improved Norfolks and Chalk Country sheep they replaced, but the chief reasons why the newcomers found favour were, they were polled, and so better suited to enclosures, and the over-extension of tillage in its own home had brought about the downfall of the Chalk Country breed. The New Southdowns were important not only in themselves, but also because they were crossed with the Chalk Country Horns to produce the Hampshire Downs, and with the East Anglian sheep to produce the Suffolks, while the Hampshire Downs in turn were crossed with the New Cotswolds to make the Oxford Downs.[1]

At this juncture the reader may well wonder why more agricultural advances were not made in the last quarter of the eighteenth century and the first half of the nineteenth. The answer is no major innovation was possible, and little room remained for further improvement, for the simple reason that all the opportunities for such had previously been exhausted: the wheel had turned full circle and was never to turn more.[2]

If we ask, for instance, why more floating was not undertaken, why the practice did not spread ever more widely, the answer is, it was neither possible nor advantageous. In the Southdown Country, due to the narrowness of the downs, virtually all the streams arose not in the chalk but in the vale, so they were not highly calcareous or suitable for floating. Furthermore, the valley bottoms were retentive of water, and so unsafe for sheep in all but the driest seasons. Few floated meadows were constructed and none successfully. The meadows were thus good only for hay and for aftermath, which was usually fed by cattle. Early spring feed had to be sought by other means, none of which was so effectual as floating.[3] The Northdown Country, by the same token, was even less suitable, and only a few catchwork meadows were floated. The innovation for similar reasons, was equally impossible in the Northwold and Oxford Height countries and most of the Chiltern Country.[4] In the Vale of London, the Thames, and in the Poor Soils

[1] Wallace, op. cit. 57, 60–1, 64; Marshall, *Sheep*, 41; *E. Dept*, 353; *S. Dept*, 41, 499; sup. 322, 325.

[2] Marshall, op. cit. 28.

[3] Ibid. *S. Cos*. 369–70, 382.

[4] Ibid. *S. Dept*, 354, 360, 366, 376; sup. 266.

Country, for the most part, the Avon, which were almost the only rivers, were too big and wide to allow the construction of pitches of work.[1] For similar topographical reasons, hardly any floating was ever undertaken in the Cotswold Country, while in the Breckland, the Heathlands of Norfolk and the Blackheath Country, the very streams were mostly lacking. In these places, watering never entered generally into farm practice, far less floating. In High Suffolk the meadowlands were neglected also, but here because it was easiest and best to remedy their deficiencies by growing more tillage crops.[2] Indeed, in the Chiltern Country, the Norfolk Heathlands, East Norfolk and High Suffolk, turnips supplied the want of hay better than any kind of floating ever could have done. Nor could floating have often been worth while in the Cheshire Cheese,[3] Butter and Cheese countries, or the Vale of Pickering, where dairy-grazing was the principal business, for in these hay was to be had cheaply and in abundance. Finally, in northerly hill-farming regions, like most of the Peak-Forest Country, Wales and the Blackmoors, even the watering of meadows was rarely attempted, so it is hardly surprising that any kind of floating was almost unknown. Here the shortages of hay were caused by a lack not of grass, but of sun and warmth to make it grow, ripen and dry. There was no point in growing two crops of hay a year when it was the utmost endeavour to secure one before the autumn rains set in.[4]

If the cultivation of turnips made little progress after 1750, this was not, as has been assumed by some,[5] because it was only just starting, but because it had already gone almost as far as it possibly could; and if it was not general throughout the farms of the kingdom by 1750, then this was solely because it would have been bad husbandry to have made it so, either because it was impossible, or because it was unnecessary, or disadvantageous, and therefore uneconomic. In the Midland Plain, turnip fallows were rarely attempted and only on a few exceptional soils and on specialist breeding farms did they become the rule.[6] Where grown, they commonly preceded barley and occasionally wheat, which suffered accordingly. Turnips sown in June or July, after stirring and

[1] Marshall, op. cit. 124, 360; sup. 255, 266.

[2] Ibid. *E. Dept*, 457.

[3] Dickson, op. cit. 510; Holland, op. cit. 247–8; J. Plymley, *Gen. View Ag. Salop.* 1803, pp. 238–9.

[4] Ibid. 238; Marshall, *Yks.* ii, 293; T. Brown, op. cit. 26; Farey, op. cit. ii, 469 sqq., 477 sqq.; R. Brown, *Gen. View Ag. W.R. Yks.* 1799, p. 148; Hassall, *Carm.* 12; *Pembs.* 10–11; Lloyd, op. cit. 8–9; Kay, op. cit. Denbigh 12; Merioneth 11; Montgom. 14, 20; Carn. 15; Anglesey 19; Fox, *Glam.* 23; J. Clark, op. cit. 15–17, 35; Davies, *N.W.* 305–7. 309; *S.W.* ii, 195 sqq.; Youatt, *Compl. Grazier*, 20; Defoe, *Tour* ii, 54.

[5] J. Thirsk, in *V.C.H. Leics.* ii, 243–4.

[6] Pitt, *Leics.* 116–17; *Staffs.* (1794) 77–8; *Northants.* 79–80; Crutchley, op. cit. 10–11; Marshall, *Midl. Dept,* 66; *Midl. Cos.* i, 145, 187–8, 253; ii, 195.

liming, were hurdled off to sheep in late autumn or thrown on pastures to help in finishing fat beasts.[1] Outside these localities, however, and in general, Midland farmers steadfastly resisted all blandishments and, after experimenting with turnips on the heavier soils, deliberately and correctly excluded them from their courses, which lacked a summer fallow to accommodate them. Turnips would, indeed, have gone a long way to defeat the very system of up-and-down husbandry, because a turnip fallow with its hoeings would have delayed the formation of the next temporary ley by as much as a year. Turnips could be gained only at the expense of grass,[2] and, top and bottom, would have given only about half the feed value and twice as much water. The exchange would only have been worth while had fresh winter feed been at a premium. Yet it was spring and summer grass the farmer needed most, for he specialized in grass meat. Even had turnip soils predominated, turnip fallows could not have advantaged the farmer much. What he needed was an abundant supply of grass. Turnip soils, in any event, were rare; and in all retentive ones turnips were singularly ineligible. They could not be folded off to sheep without rotting the flocks and poaching the land, nor be pulled and thrown to beasts without leaving the field full of waterlogged holes.[3] Similar conditions obtained in the Cheshire Cheese Country. Outside the mosslands and the market-gardens that had made 'Manchester' turnips an established trade name by 1611, root crops could hardly obtain general acceptance, and were superfluous to cheese production.[4] A few turnips were raised in the Lancashire Plain in the eighteenth century,[5] but the crop could not be cultivated widely. Turnip soils were likewise few and far between in the Butter and Cheese countries, the vales of Berkeley and Pickering and the Wealden Vales, and turnips were of little or no use.[6] It was the same in the Woodland. From 1728 at the latest small turnip crops were occasionally taken, but a turnip fallow before wheat would normally have gained a penny and lost a pound.[7] In the Chalk Country, the turnip crop was intended primarily for the winter feed of sheep and it was reckoned that thirty acres of turnips, tops and roots, would fatten 400 wethers. Turnip was, however, inferior to grass mutton: 'perfect water would run out between the skin and the flesh'. Hence it was only in the sandy loams and especially the Vale of Pewsey that the new introduction had much

[1] Ibid. i, 234–5, 240–1; ii, 220 sqq.; Morton, op. cit. 483; Leics. R. O., Crane & Walton A/c 166, 16 June–21 July, 23 Nov.–19 Dec. 1829.
[2] Crutchley, op. cit. 8–9; Marshall, op. cit. i, 187–8; ii, 38, 43, 215–16, 226.
[3] Ibid. i, 254–5; Pitt, op. cit. 98; Wedge, War. 13–14.
[4] Lancs. R.O., Cons. Ct Cestr. inv. Geoff. Barnes 1634 Broughton; Harland, op. cit. 34, 197; Holland, op. cit. 164; Marshall, W. Dept, 7; Crofton, 'Broughton', 32.
[5] Holt, op. cit. (1795) 64.
[6] Chalklin, art. cit. 37, 40; Boys, op. cit. 20; Marshall, S. Cos. ii, 139; S. Dept, 268.
[7] Steer, op. cit. 268, 270.

effect on farm management. Here bare fallows were restricted, tending to the destruction of the summer sheep-flock, in place of which farmers wintered sheep from the neighbouring uplands, where turnips were not generally grown, partly because they could hardly apple in the thinner soils, and partly because they were unnecessary, by reason of the abundance of meadow-hay now available.[1] In the Northwold Country they were more needed, but even less possible.[2] Turnips may have been of early introduction in the Vales of Hereford, but floating rendered them unnecessary. A few turnips were grown in the Blackheaths, but the soil was mostly too shallow for root crops of any description; and the same goes for the Poor Soils Country.[3] Finally, in hill-farming countries like the West and Peak-Forest, and Wales, neither climate, nor soil, nor plan of management was suited to turnip husbandry on any scale. These countries were not backward in cultivating turnips—indeed, farmers in parts of Wales grew table turnips in market-garden fashion very early on—they were simply unfit for turnip husbandry. In any event, turnips are good for fatting stock and feeding milch kine, but not for raising sound young beasts and sheep.[4]

Why sainfoin cultivation did not continue to gain ground is likewise readily explicable: there was no ground to gain. If sainfoin did not spread further in the Southdown Country, despite its being an otherwise ideal habitat, it was because the higher downs were rarely ploughed.[5] Elsewhere it failed to appear, as in Wales and the West Country, because chalky subsoils were absent.[6]

The relatively negligible spread of clover and 'seeds' after 1750 is to be explained along similar lines. First, some countries possessed few soils rich enough to bear clover. Amongst these may be cited the Breckland, the Blackheath, Wales, and the Peak-Forest. Where clover was possible, it was introduced early enough—in parts of Wales, e.g. by 1700—but the possibilities were limited.[7] Secondly, in some countries, clover, especially broad clover, could well be grown, but would have been positively disadvantageous. In the Cheese Country, the natural grasslands were composed mainly of perennial rye-grass, dogstail and

[1] T. Davis, op. cit. 19. 55–6; Lisle, op. cit. 335.

[2] Eland, *Shardeloes*, 61; Leatham, op. cit. 41, 45–6; Marshall, *Yks.* ii, 252–3, 257; *W. Dept*, 283; Yarranton, op. cit. 35; Pomeroy, op. cit. 13.

[3] White, op. cit. 6, 21; Vancouver, *Hants.* 81–4; Claridge, op. cit. 19.

[4] Marshall, *S. Dept*, 525, 542; *W. Engl.* i, 80; *Midl. Dept*, 167; Borlase, op. cit. 89; Lowe, op. cit. 22; Pitt, *Staffs.* (1794) 86; Chambers, *V. Trent*, 38; Owen, *Penbs.* pt ii, 366; *Taylors Cussion* pt ii, f. 115; Bodl. Aubrey 2, f. 88; Lloyd, op. cit. 24; Hassall, *Pembs.* 17.

[5] Young, *Suss.* 41; Marshall, *S. Cos.* ii, 280, 381.

[6] Borlase, loc. cit.

[7] Blith, op. cit. 182; Switzer, *Compendious Method*, 33–5; Emery, art. cit. x, 30; Fox, *Mon.* 14; Hassall, op. cit. 11; *Carm.* 12; W. Suss. R.O., Cons. Ct Bp Cicestr. for A/d Cicestr. inv. Wm Osborne 1693 Fernhurst.

wild white clover. Broad red clover was introduced, but never much favoured, partly on account of the superabundance of grass, which permitted hay to be exported to the Cotswold and Chalk countries by the wain-load, and partly because broad clover would not make the kind of milk needed,[1] for the farmers' great concern was to increase the 'sowre herbage' that made this 'sour, woodsere country . . . so proper for good cheese', or to maintain the rich fatting grounds like the Idovers at Dauntsey.[2] In the Cheshire Cheese Country, in the Vale of Berkeley, and in a large part of the Vale of Evesham, circumstances were almost exactly as in the Cheese Country; and in the Butter Country[3] and the Vale of Pickering, not much different. In this latter country, selected ryegrass and clover seeds were introduced about 1750, but only in the teeth of opposition, and were not much accepted. Even at the end of the century, annual and biennial leys were almost unknown. Clover was little grown and still excited some prejudiced antipathy, which was not, however, entirely unjustified, for in a grassland country like this, there was little advantage in clover.[4]

Adverting now to marl, we have already seen how beyond a certain point, further marling became too costly and did more harm than good, and this is why it was discontinued.

As for ley farming, the reason it made only slight headway after 1750 was, it already had substantially replaced both shifting cultivation and permanent tillage and permanent grass. Some farms still existed where these improvements had yet to be made and some in which they would always remain impracticable, but by and large the change had been accomplished. Convertible husbandry, in the form either of arable-grass rotations with single crops or short leys of clover and 'seeds', and with long sainfoin (or lucerne) leys, or of grass-arable rotations with up-and-down husbandry and long grazing leys of selected and natural grasses, had become standard English practice. If the transition to convertible husbandry appears slow in the second half of the eighteenth century, this is merely because it was already virtually complete.

Then, to turn to a somewhat different case, good reasons were sometimes present for postponing improvement until a late date. In 1620–1 King James contemplated enclosing some 12,000 acres of the sedgemoors in the Western Waterlands, and Vermuyden undertook to drain

---

[1] Marshall, *Glos.* ii, 144, 150–1; Lisle, op. cit. 304; Basset Down ho. N. Maskelyne's A/c Bk ff. 8, 29–30, 36–7, 191; Wilts. R.O., Cons. Ct Sarum. invs. Ric. Clarke 1637 Brinkworth, Th. Mills 1647 Purton, Th. Sheppard 1631 Benacre; T. Davis, op. cit. 119; P.R.O., D.L., R.&S. 9/26, ff. 6, 8; Aubrey, *Nat. Hist. Wilts.* 37; *Wilts. Topog. Colls.* 216.

[2] Ibid. 266; Bodl. Aubrey 2, f. 101.

[3] G. Turner, op. cit. 35; Marshall, op. cit. i, 65, 154–5, 210; ii, 94; R. Lennard, art. cit. 36; Smyth, *Hund. Berk.* 4, 31, 249–50.

[4] Marshall, *Yks.* ii, 83 sqq.

4,000 in King's Moor but his contract remained unfulfilled; in 1638 large tracts near there were still 'hurtfully surrounded'; and in 1655 these plans were finally abandoned.[1] It is noteworthy that all attempts to drain King's Sedgemoor met with stubborn local opposition, in 1621, 1655 and about 1680; and it was only in the teeth of great hostility that large tracts of the Brue Marshes and Sedgemoor were laid dry at the end of the eighteenth century.[2]

This retarding of drainage arose because the Western Waterlands conformed to the general pattern of the western vales and plains in being devoted to dairying. Consequently drainage to winter-ground was not the great advantage it might have otherwise been.

Real reasons exist, moreover, to explain why certain farming countries remained almost untouched by the agricultural revolution. The Vale of London, for instance, was virtually excluded from participation. The growth of London formed the farming country, but also reduced its extent. More and more agricultural land was taken over for housing, stabling, cow-sheds, market gardens, orchards and such, not to speak of industrial premises. Furthermore, agriculture was forced into a suburban pattern and already began to exhibit modern characteristics. Butcher-grazing, cow-keeping, market-gardening, house-suckling, pig farming, poultry cramming, hay farming—all these trades and monocultures were portents of impending dissolution. The influence of the city made the vale remarkably backward in respect of innovations or improvements. New field crops were introduced extremely tardily. Despite some monoculture of 'artificial' grass 'seeds', clover and 'seeds' mixtures were little used. Hay-seeds were so plentiful and cheap, they held the field even in the late eighteenth century. Root crops were virtually confined to market-gardens. There was little watering and no floating, nor even the improvement of heathlands by burnbaking. Drainage was almost the only practice not to lag behind, and even in this the vale was far from being in the vanguard. It was for such reasons that Walter Blith was moved to cry out against the 'ill husbandry discovered along the river Thames, both wayes much barren land near London . . . Halfe of it is scarce used, though so much needed. . . . Many hundred, if not thousand acres . . . are neglected.' And William Marshall knew from experience that the farmers of the vale were just as homely as anywhere and 'far less enlightened and intelligent than those in many parts'.[3] Some other countries played only small roles in the agricultural revo-

[1] L. E. Harris, op. cit. 117–20; *Jnl H.L.* iv, 227; P.R.O., Exch. L.R., M.B. 202, ff. 255–8; Dugdale, op. cit. 101–2.

[2] Ibid. 111–12; Harris, op. cit. 121; Camden, op. cit. i, 75; Soms. R.O., D.D./ S.A.S. Aller custumal 1653; D.D./X./M.K.G. svys Netherham 1662, 1699; D.D./ S./W.H. svy Milton juxta Wells 11 July 19 Jas; D.D./X./H.O. Ct Bk Tintenhull 10 Apr. 1662, 30 Mar. 1668, 21 Oct. 1714; Marshall, *S. Dept*, 586, 594–5.

[3] Blith, op. cit. 86–7; Marshall, *Mins.* i, 25.

lution for the simple reason they were, and are, naturally almost un-improvable. In this class, we may mention the North and Peak-Forest countries, Wales, the Blackmoors, and, perhaps what was the clearest example, the High Weald. Here, in 1657–8 the parliamentary sur-veyors recommended various rough grazings be converted to tillage and grassland by dint of marling and liming; but the greater part of the country they thought fit merely for woodlands, cony-warrens, sheep-walks and rough grazings. The only object farming could set itself, they reported, was the breeding of young cattle.[1] Finally, certain countries escaped the full effects of the agricultural revolution for the good reason that they had already been improved almost as much as they possibly could be. Not much further change could be made in the Cheese Country. It was by nature deep and enclosed and once the woodlands were cleared and common rights extinguished it had essentially attained its modern form. The simple and effective husbandry of the Woodland admitted little improvement.

Not the least of the fruits of agricultural innovation was the general and great prosperity reflected in rising prices, profits, wages and rents after the mid-1560s. England then enjoyed a prosperity similar in all essentials to the one it has passed through in the last score years. Rents and prices rose to a peak in the 1610s, but the nation then had its first glimpse of the horrors of plenty, of that avalanche of goods that follows great innovations and crashes through the old price structure. Rents, which had risen threefold, suddenly broke. By 1620 corn prices were less than two-thirds of the thirty-one-year mean. From 1617 to 1620 they had almost halved. Prices of dairy produce, meat, cattle and wool had also declined sharply.[2] No very dear year had occurred since 1613, and the consequence was, in 1621 some capital farmers had as much as five years' corn in store. In February 1620, Chamberlain writes, 'We are here in a straunge case to complaine of plentie, but so yt is that corne beareth so lowe a price that tenants and farmers are very backward to paye theyre rents; and in many places plead disabilitie.'[3] By November, he is bewailing,[4]

'Plentie hath made us poore, so far foorth, that tenants generally can-not pay theyre rents, and many make suit to geve up their leases. The reason we cannot yet reach unto, but that there is a generall want of monie; but whence that shold proceed, let them looke to yt whom yt

[1] Daniell-Tyssen, art. cit. xxiii, 243–4, 246–8, 251–3, 255–6, 260, 263, 267, 270; xxiv, 193–4; & v. Marshall, S. Cos. ii, 132–3.
[2] My 'Movemt Rent 1540–1640', EcH.R. 1953 vi; McClure, op. cit. ii, 289; Notestein & al. op. cit. ii, 29, 178–9, 357, 379; iii, 213–14, 281, 345; iv, 19, 357; v. 147; vii, 214.
[3] Ibid. ii, 179.
[4] McClure, op. cit. ii, 327–8.

most concernes; corne and cattle were never at so low a rate since I can remember; wheat at two shillings a bushel, barley at seven shillings a quarter, *et sic de cæteris*; and yet they can get no riddance at that price, so that land falls everywhere; and yf you have monie, you may buy goode land at thirteen or fowreteene yeares purchase.'

By February 1621 the crisis had become deeper and his complaints of low prices even shriller:[1]

'England was never generally so poore since I was borne as yt is at this present, insomuch that all complaine they cannot receve their rents; yet is there plentie of all thinges but monie: which is so scant, that countrie people offer corne, or cattle, or whatesover they have els in lieu of rent, but bring no monie, and corne is at so easie rates as I never knew yt, wheat 20 and 22*d*. a bushell, barley at nine-pence, and yet no quantitie wil be taken at that price . . . but the strangenes of yt is how this great defect shold come and be perceved but within these two or three yeares at most.'

This was when English people largely lost the habit of eating rye. 'All farmers generally murmured at this plenty and cheapness; and the poorer sort that would have been glad but a few years before of the coarse rye-bread, did now usually traverse the markets to find out the finer wheats.'[2] By contemporary standards the affluent society had arrived, and the fear of want was removed. Objections to the free export of corn could now be put aside, for the danger of dearth had vanished. As John Smyth of Nibley reported to the Commons, 'Our husbandry, by marlinge, chawkinge, seasand, lymynge, more earth, oadynge old pastures, plowing up warrens, parks and wood grownds, with gods ordynary blessinge, freeth us from that feare.'[3]

But the fruit of the agricultural revolution was not yet fully formed and did not ripen until 1670, when rents and prices suddenly collapsed. For forty years rents languished at about three-quarters of their previous level,[4] despite the bounty laid on corn exports in 1673.[5] Contem-

---

[1] Ibid. 342; *A.P.C.* 1620–1, pp. 342, 344.

[2] Halliwell, *D'Ewes*, i, 180.

[3] Notestein & al. op. cit. v, 384.

[4] Index here & hrnar based on Wilton ho. Stoke Verdon, Flambston, Foffont, & Broad Chalke Svys 1705; Svys Manors & Fms, pp. 405 sqq.; Svy Manor Alvediston 1706 & 1758; Svys Stanton Barnard 1705 & 1792–1805; & supported by B. D. Henning, *Parl. Diary Sir Ed. Dering 1670–3* 1940, p. 100; Thirsk, op. cit. 194; Leicester Mus. 35/29/370; Worcs. R.O., B.A., 494 partic. Stoulton c. Wadborow 1653, reviewed 1687; Northants. R.O., Clayton 100a; F-H 298, p. 15; Mont. Northants. 13/12, partic. Brigstock 1694; F.(M.) Misc. Vol. 55, distraint inv. Francis Smith

poraries were well aware it was the general adoption of improvements that had depressed rents. They saw 'a strange paradox, that plenty should make the kingdome poor'.[1] Part of the fall was sometimes attributed to imports of Scots and Irish cattle and of Spanish wool, and to declining woollen exports,[2] but even these were the roundabout result of agricultural innovations, whose direct effects were even more powerful. Turnip and cole-seed husbandry led to a fall in marshland grazing rents in the Fen Country and elsewhere.[3] Clover cultivation depressed the rents of wet meadows. As Sir Roger Twysden said around 1661, 'Now there is a newe device of cloverseed that spoyles all meadowland, so as wee are forced to abate 5 or 6s. the acre of good land in Romney Marsh'.[4] A Chalk Country man complains 'that by reason of the cheapnesse of hey . . . occasioned by the great quantytys of clover and other grasse sowed, hee cannot lett the meadows at the rate he could have done by 30 l. per annum.'[5] 'Artificial' grasses brought down meadow hay prices from £3 to £1 a load and reduced grassland rents by about one-sixth.[6] In 1676–7 Petty notes

'that England . . . doth so abound in victuals, as it maketh laws against the importation of cattle, flesh, and fish from abroad, and that the draining of fens, improving of forests, inclosing of commons, sowing of saint-foyne and clovergrass be grumbled against by landlords, as the way to depress the price of victuals. [To him] it is manifest that by reason of the dreyning of fens, watering of dry grounds, improving of forrests and commons, making of heathy and barren grounds to bear saint-foyne and clovergrass, meliorating and multiplying several sorts

---

1744; 194; Corr. 176/10, 16, 26; 179/41; 220/42–3; 222/13, 39, 44–5; Misc. 900, 902, 904, 917; Wmld 7. xv, letters fr. stwd to E. 15 June 1734, 19 Dec. 1732; Berks. R.O., D./E.Ah E5/3; Shak. Bpl. Leigh: distraint inv. Hy Chambers 1735 Langley; Bowden, op. cit. 211, 215; Martin, op. cit. 149 sqq.; H. F. Howard, *A/c Fin. Coll. St Jn* 1935, pp. 67, 309; E. Hopkins, 'Releasing Ellesmere Estes 1637–42', *Ag. H.R.* x, 26; G. E. Mingay, 'Este Managemt in 18th-cent. Kent', ibid. iv, 109–10; 'Ag. Depression 1730–50', *EcH.R.* 1956 viii, 323 sqq.; S. J. Madge, *Domesday Cr. Lands* 1938, p. 276; G. S. L. Tucker, *Prog. & Profit in Brit. Econ. Thought 1650–1850* 1960, pp. 11–12; S.H.A.H. (ed.) *Diary Jn Hervey 1st E. Bristol* 1894, p. 70; *Letter-Bks Jn Hervey 1st E. Bristol* 1894 i, 228–9; ii, 123, 167–8, 187; iii, 233–4, 238, 243, 401; T. Culpeper, *Tract agst High Rate Interest* 1668 pref.
[5] Stat. 25 Chas II c. 1 sect. 31.

[1] Person of Honour, op. cit. 4.
[2] Bodl. Aubrey 2, f. 123; Anon. *Treatise of Wool & Manufacture of it* 1685, pp. 6–7, 9, 16–17; Bowden, op. cit. 211, 215; Nourse, op. cit. 91; Eland, op. cit. 60.
[3] Ibid. 60–1; Howard, op. cit. 67.
[4] B.M., Add. 34164, f. 86.
[5] Berks, R.O., D./E.Ah E.5/1, 2, memo.
[6] Aubrey, *Sy* iii, 363; Person of Honour, loc. cit.

of fruits and garden-stuffe, making some rivers navigable, &c.—I say it is manifest, that the land in its present condition is able to bear more provision and commodities than it was forty years ago.'

Nourse inveighed against 'clover, saint-foin, rye-grass, and other foreign weeds' for having spoilt the price of meadows and feeding grounds.[1]

In the second decade of the eighteenth century, there was a sudden and sharp but short-lived rise in the rents contracted on new leases. For a time rents were higher than ever before; but this was merely an interruption in a period of depressed rents that lasted approximately from 1670 to 1750. Newly contracted rents could easily be adjusted, but the rents of old leases could not be reduced fast enough to prevent many farmers failing. The selling up of farm stock in distraint of rent was even more common in the period 1720–50 than it had been in the decade 1670–9. Shortly before 1750 both rents and corn prices were the lowest they had been since 1580. During the brief boom of the second decade of the century improvement received some stimulus, but otherwise the first half of the eighteenth century was a period of depression and stagnation, with little bettering and some deterioration of technique. Not until 1750–9 did final recovery commence. In this third quarter of the century corn prices rose strongly and rents on new takings trebled, even without making allowance for the fact that landlords now passed back to their farmers the burden of taxes shouldered during the depression.[2] Thereafter, as is well known, British economic development, including agriculture, was dominated by an industrial revolution. The agricultural revolution was no more.

*   *   *

In 1523, when Fitzherbert extolled the virtues of up-and-down husbandry, innovation was in its infancy and the agricultural revolution cannot be said to have commenced until about 1560–3. From then until 1580 there was an upsurge of activity in up-and-down husbandry, fen drainage, 'floating upwards', marling, swarding, and cole-seed cultivation. The period 1585–1612/13 witnessed an upsurge both longer and stronger, with the innovation of catchwork floating, carrot cultivation, extensive woading and liming, larger-scale fen drainage and floating

---

[1] Nourse, op. cit. 86–8; Petty, op. cit. i, 287–8, 303.

[2] For taxes, v. Wilton ho. svys ut sup.; B.M., Add. 21608, f. 130; Howard, op. cit. 66, 308–9; Martin, op. cit. 95; Northants. R.O., F.(M.) Misc. 77; Corr. 222/53; Shak. Bpl. W.deB. 1080; Leicester Mus. 35/39/272; Mingay, 'Ag. Depression', 331–3; & v. V. M. Lavrovsky, 'Expropriation Eng. Peasanty in 18th cent.', *EcH.R.* 1956 ix, 277–8.

upwards, more marling and cole-seed cultivation and rye-growing for sheep, the introduction of soap-ash, and the more rapid advance of up-and-down husbandry. Between 1621 and 1656, further advances were made in all the above improvements, save marling, and, in addition, the following innovations were made: ridge-and-furrow floating, burn-baking downlands, and sainfoin, clover, turnip and rye-grass cultivation. Blith, who flourished at this time, was able to scan in one sweep the great innovations of floating, draining, up-and-down husbandry, clover, sainfoin, and turnips.[1] By the end of the revolutionary period, about 1690, when potatoes had just been introduced, writers vied with each other in extolling floated meadows, disforesting, up-and-down husbandry, marling, liming, burnbaking, carrots, turnips, sainfoin, rye-grass, trefoil and clover as epoch-making achievements;[2] and the fall in rents was authoritatively ascribed to the general introduction of sainfoin, floated water-meadows, root crops, clover and rye-grass 'seeds', fen drainage and similar improvements.[3] Contemporaries were thus quite clear that they lived in the age of the agricultural revolution. Medieval England had accepted as an ineluctable fate the vicious circle of poverty imposed by the cessation of grass growth in the winter months. In early modern England private enterprise found half a dozen ways to break this circle and with characteristic vigour adopted them all in an agricultural revolution of unparalleled achievement.

[1] Op. cit. 2–3 & pass.

[2] Brentnall, 'Longford MS.', 16–18; Blome, *Gent's. Rec.* pt ii, 208 sqq., 220–1; Switzer, op. cit. 25, 30.

[3] Petty, op. cit. i, 288, 303; Nourse, op. cit. 87–8, 92; Aubrey, *Sy* iii, 363; Bodl. Aubrey 2, f. 123; Person of Honour, op. cit. 4–6; B.M., Add. 34164, f. 86; Berks. R.O., D./E.Ah E.5/1, 2, memo.

APPENDIX A

Additional References to Midland Common-field Farms

Invs.: Northants. RO, Cons. Ct Petriburg. Hunts. Invs. E1609–94: Jn
Egbarrow/Orton Longueville; K1613–87: Abraham Kinge/Toseland;
Northants. Bds & Invs. 1683: Th. Goodfellow/Luddington; Peterboro'
Invs. 1693:13, Th. Worlidg/Oundle, Robt Pratt/Gt Weldon, Wm Salsbury/
Helpstone, Jas Cunnington/Warmington, Hy Joyce/Winwick, Jn Lee &
Robt Naylor/Lowick; Peterboro' Wills 1724(a): Wm Green/Helpstone;
A/d Ct Northampton, Northants. Invs. 1661: Jn Forsberie/Hardingstone,
Simon Colli(n)s/Wellingborough, Jn Hawford/Clapton, Anthony Sayer/
Denford, Mary Austine/Chipping Warden; 1664: Th. Smith/Rushden;
1660–99: 2, 13, 33, 45, 50; Northants. Admins. 1661: Th. Lyne/Long Buckby,
Mich. Bugby/Oxendon; 1697:7, 11, 13, Ed. Elward/Blisworth; Northants.
Wills & Admins. 1725 Jan.–Mar.: Jn Dale/Doddington Magna; May–
Sept.: Francis Landon/Naseby, Vincent Barker/Earls Barton, Jn Ashe/
Sulgrave; Lichfield Jt RO, Pecs.: Jn Adderley, 1661–2, Chillington; Nic.
Adye, 1698, Chorley; Francis Allen, 1664, Fradley; Jn Alport, 1662, Gt
Wyrley; Jn Anneley, 1665, Fradley; Wm Atkins, 1691–2, Bishton; Wm
Averill, 1697, Cannock; Eleanor Clarke, 1667, L. Saredon; Wr Collier,
1663, Gt Wyrley; Th. Eaton, 1722, Egginton; Wm Eginton, 1728, Hilton;
Mark Evans, 1727, Armitage; Th. Gelforde, 1689–90, Lichfield; Th.
Gnosall, 1691, Rack End; Ric. Gratley, 1690, Huntington; Ric. Greene,
1667, L. Wyrley; Anne Greenwood, 1694, Longdon; Th. Griniley, 1663,
Whittington; Th. Marshall, 1661, Longdon; Wm Marshall, 1662, K's.
Bromley; Ric. Mason, 1660, Harbourne; Robt Massey, 1667, Colwich;
Jn Moore, 1668–9, Hammerwich; Th. Mountfort, 1663, Water Eaton;
Cons. Ct: A1560: Robt Alcock/Draycott, Chris. Adnit/Stretton, Jn Assheborn/Keresley; A1563: Ralph Allen/Benty Lee, Robt Alldryche/Melbourne;
A1564: Th. Addams/Ockbrook, Jn Atkyns/Thurlaston; B1541: Jn Baytman/
Clifton, Jn Barber/Long Ash; B1544: Th. Baytman/Clifton, Nic. Byrch/
Withybrook, Ric. Bateman/Pailton, Robt Browne/Nuneaton, Th. Bruman/
Tunstall, Roger Beech/Checkley, Ric. Bykerd/Solihull; B1545: Ralph
Bedull/Keele, Wm Blakeman/Bradley; B1547: Wm Bryan/Wolvey, Hy
Borton/Long Lawford, Jn Brereley/Fillongley, Ric. Broke/Longdon; Ba
1563: Jn Bache/Solihull; Bo 1563: Ed. Browne/Whitnash, Jn Bouross/
Wilnecote; Ba1566: Th. Benche/Lillington, Jn Benson/Broadwell, Jn
Bagnall/Stoke-on-Trent, Ralph Bold/L. Saredon; B1568: Thomasine Birche/
L. Bloxwich; B1569: Chris. Breamer/O. Whitacre; B1591: Jn Belcher/
Bretby, Th. Baker/Willington, Robt Barghe/Dalbury, Th. Bartram/Foston;
B1598: Jn Bearne/Burnaston, Chris. Bentley/Rodsley, Hy Bayard/Newton
Solney, Th. Baker/Napton-on-the-Hill; C1565: Wm Crosse/Spondon,
Oliver Cowper/Ockbrook; C1616: Robt Copson/Burton Hastings, Th.
Crocksall/Shustoke; E1694: Jn Eglestone/Chaddesden; F1591; Roland Fletcher/Shenstone; G1633: Edm. Godfrey/Barton-under-Needwood, Robt

Gregg/Lindon, Ed. Greene/Wheaton Aston, Hy Gretton/Gt Gate, Jn German/Woodhouses; G1635: Ric. Good/Flecknoe, Ed. Gee/Wolvey; G1637: Hy Good/Stockton, Wm Gumbley/Hillmorton; G1638: Th. Godridge/Stanton; H1592: Agnes Hollier/Bentley; H1593; Jn Hawley/Stockton, Wm Hand/Newbold Paunton, Ric. Heywood/Grandborough, Jn Hodgkyns/ Coventry, Jn Harrison/Chilvers Coton; H1617: Hy Hawkins/Church Lawford, Gavyn Hobleys/Coventry, Th. Hollin/Exhall; H1619: Ric. Hewit/ Wappenbury, Th. Aston/Water Orton; I-K1616: Jn Johnson/Aldridge; M1547: Ric. Mockslow/Coleshill; M1549; Jn Mansfylld/Darley; M1563: Jn Myllner/O. Whitacre, Ric. Maycoke/Harbury; M1566: Ric. Marlowe/ Erdington; M1567: Harry Mason/Withybrook; M1569: Jn Myllward als Howell/Hill, Hy Mylward/Aston, Jn Millward/Handsworth; M1597: Th. Mitchel/Repton, Robt Man/Farnborough, Humphrey Mogsley/ Ockbrook, Joan Meryman/Kirk Langley; M1633: Pet. Mytchell/Spondon; P1545: Jn Pegge/Burnaston, Th. Pall/Gt Harborough, Wm Pall/Southam; P1567: Wm Prophette/Farnborough; P1631: Wm Pershall/Sutton Coldfield; P1633: Geo. Patchett/Hurley; P1634: Margery Prensopp/King's Newton; Q-R1545: Jn Robinson/Druffield; 1549: Robt Russell/Uttoxeter; S1610: Ed. Swanne/Hartley Green; S1611: Jn Stokes/Essington; S1618: Edm. Shepperd/Lullington; S1634: Wm Steele/Nether Shuckburgh, Wm Sowthar/Weston; T-V1567: Humphrey Unett/Tittensor; T-V1614: Wm Twycrosse/King's Newton; W1593: Th. West/Shotteswell, Humphrey Whiteheade/Seckington, Th. Watson/Willoughby, Robt Watsonn/Ruytonupon-Dunsmoor, Robt Webb/Long Lawford; W1595: Jn Wilcoxe/Enfield; W1597: Ric. Whitworth/Weston Underwood, Wm Whorwood/Moxull, Roger Wright/Gresley; W1599: Th. Walker/Solihull, Ric. Webb/Newbold Paunton, Jn Weste/Thurlaston; W1613: Ed. Walle/Sheldon, Margery Weste/Shotteswell, Th. Welch/Southam, Ric. Westley/Marton, Chris. Woulf/Bramcote: W1615: Nic. Webb/L. Harborough, Th. Walker/Draycott, Th. Walton als Callowe/Aston; 1723: Wm Proctor/Loughton: Worcs. RO. Cons. Ct Wigorn.: 1545: 82, 84, 139, 146, 148, 162, 249, 289, 291, 298, 361, 382; 1546: 27, 111, 196; 1563: 15–17, 49, 53, 77–8, 81, 84, 86–7; 1566: 74, 115; 1568: 53, 55–7, 78; 1592: 25, 35, 100, 145c; 1596:8, 17c, 23a, 24, 26a, 40–1, 49, 73, 84; 1598: 5, 7, 10, 15, 60; 1612: 19, 50: 1615: 30, 89, 93b–c, 103–4a, 116, 150d, 230; 1617: 1, 97, 144c, 147; 1618: 79, 97a, 109, 112, 130, 143–4, 164d; 1632: 61, 180; 1633: 32, 37, 46, 166, 172; 1635: 227; 1637: 25, 33, 91, 119, 126, 154; 1638: 130, 135–6: Leics. RO, A/d: Ric. Shipton 1535, Wm. Colinson 1544, Th. Keckwick, 1558, Robt Tympson, 1561, Th. Taylor, 1570, all of Leicester; early sixteenth-century.: 8, 34–5, 37, 65, 82, 84, 92, 105, 126, 143, 154–5; mid-sixteenth-cent.: 14, 22, 51, 59, 71, 93, 96, 100, 102–4; 1599: 18, 40, 53; 1602:7, 20, 55, 75, 83, 86, 96, 143, 181; 1603: 67, 105; 1608: 51, 63, 105, 112, 189; 1612: 170; 1614: 2, 122, 177, 189(28); 1616: 6, 20–1, 28, 54, 84, 97; 1618: 26, 202; 1621: 42, 132; 1625: 120: 1626: 8, 85, 151, 191; 1627: 16, 56, 69, 107; 1628: 2, 7, 28, 57, 108, 221; 1631: 42, 108, 125; 1632: 27, 132, 280; 1633: 10, 93, 170, 180; 1636: 49, 62, 74, 78, 132, 194, 196, 204, 226, 240; 1637: 92–3, 105, 125, 159, 170; 1638: 36, 144, 203, 293, 301; 1639: 15, 22, 44, 46, 100, 114, 123, 125, 127, 129–31, 137, 139, 141; 1641: 54, 70; 1643: 19; 1645:41, 91; 1647; 29, 85; 1649: 21,

32, 63; 1660 small: 72; gt: 56, 165, 314, 318; 1661 Commy: 43, & Anthony
Fowler/Hothorpe: 1662, Commy: 30; VG: 21, 85; 1663, Commy: 23, 116;
Bp's Visitation: 19; 1664: 46, 48, 117; 1665: 34, 54, 75, 90, 127; 1667: 1,
147; 1668, A/d, 91, 150; 1669: 35, 45, 105, 109, 207; 1693 VG: 110, 125;
1695: 17; 1700 unstamped: Ric. Overton/Burbage; 1703: 21; 1704: 22,
48; 1705: 13, 88, 92; 1708: 77, 87, 123; 1709: 11, 29, 42, 45–6, 52, 65, 68,
71, 74, 80–1, 85, 88, 111, 113, 118; 1710: 11, 27–8, 57, 85, 91, 102, & Hy
Cantrell/Blackforby, Th. Tomson/Shepshed, Francis Clarke/Gt Easton,
Robt Lount/Kibworth Harcourt, Jos. Thompson/Stoney Stanton, Mary
Howett/Dunton Bassett, Th. Crane/Gt Dalby, Wm Carter/Leire, Robt
Kirkeman/Hemington, Lewis Russell/Gt Bowden, Jn Butler/Whetstone,
Jon. George/Waltham-on-the-Wolds, Stephen White/Bagworth; eighteenth-
cent.: Christine Bent/Cranoe, Wm Blankly/Sproxton, Anthony Collins/
Foxton, Wm Mayes/Barrow-on-Soar, Ric. Lowe/Sapcote, Rebecca Hall/
Arnesby, Chas Harrison/Markfield, Th. Hutchinson/Netherseal, Jn Hunt/
Croft, Geo. Baker/Barton-in-the-Beans, Sam. Whitworth/Overseal, Hy
Fancoate/Stanton-under-Bardon, Ric. Barraws/Nelson, Geo. Marshall/
Orton-on-the-Hill, Jn Seagrave/Friskby-on-the-Wreake, Th. Glover/ Cas.
Donington, Th. Porser/Bruntingthorpe, Th. Parker/L. Appleby, Robt
Scampton/Birstall, Jn Bruard/Thornton, Geo. Holmes/Bagworth; Rothley &
Evington Commy Cts: 1, 7, 9–12, 21, 23, 27, 45, 47; Ric. Bayliffe 1614,
Ric. Beeby, 1616, Jn Johnson, 1591, Wm Johnson, 1613, Robt Palmer,
1589; Leeds Lib. MSS.RD/AP, 1: Janet Bell, 1562 & Geo. Allenson, 1564,
Cundall; Jn Dayle, 1563, Wm Dodgesson, 1564–5 & Ric. Sworde, 1634,
Rainton; Alice Aldburgh, 1565, Knaresborough; Hy Maxwell, 1591,
Thornbrough; Brian Abbay, 1564, Joan Abbey, 1591–2, Eliz. Atkinson,
1595 & Jn Abbay, 1596, Kirk Hammerton; Jn Davison, 1592, Farnham;
Th. Fetham, 1592, Ric. Murthwat, 1595, Jn Allen, 1612, Pet. Ostler &
Martin Carter, 1615–6, Aldborough; Chris. Dixson, 1592, Kirklington; Ric.
Abbay, 1590, Jas Gaytell, 1595, Chris. Picke, 1611, Gt Ouseburn; Th.
Mawer, 1611–12, Anne Mawer, 1614, Wm Cooke, 1635, Hutton Conyers;
Anne Mason, 1614, Long Cowton; Jn Topham, 1631, Norton-le-Clay; Jn
Clarke, 1632, Newton-le-Willows; Wm Walker, 1633, Goldsborough; Ric.
Clapham, 1634, L. Crakehall; Jn Dobinson, 1635 & Ric. Harrison, 1637,
Brompton-upon-Swale; Robt North, 1616 & Jn Adamson, 1637, E. Cowton;
Ed. Kay, 1638–9, Holme; Edm. Best, 1562, Middleton Quernhow; Wm
Blackburne, 1562, Francis Atkinson, 1592–3, Marton-le-Moor; Th. Buk,
1562, Robt Barnight, 1565, Dishforth; Robt Butt, 1562–3, Mylby; Wm
Ayecryke, 1563, Ellerton-on-Swale; Jn Beckwith, 1566, Haythrop; Wm
Cooke, 1569, Brearton; Wm Dearlowe, 1569, Jas Goodridge, 1612–13
Scotton; Jn Marshall, 1590, Jn Pybus, 1613–14, Kirkby Fleetham; Ric.
Monckton, 1591, Marton; Janet Clerke, 1591–2, Burton; Jn Allane, 1596,
Gt Crakehall; Ralph Mytchell, 1597, Exelby; Jn Akers, 1597, Staveley;
Geo. Marshall, 1597, Asenby; Jn Atkinson, 1611, Malmerby; Chris. Benson,
1616, Gt Langton; Jn Praunce, 1617, Wm Precious, 1619, Jn Earle, 1635,
Minskip; Ed. Dawson, 1617, Whixley; Eliz. Dicconson, 1618–19, Copgrove;
Percival Cooke, 1631, Easby; Th. Flint, 1631, Ripley; Dennis Casse, 1636,
O. Dunsforth; Cuthbert Collin, 1637, Gt Smeaton; Ed. Atkinson, 1637,

Gatenby; Jn Screwton & Wm Thompson, 1639, Aldburgh; York, Pec. Ct Dean: Wm Tindall, 1661, Spittle, Matt. Kilburne 1661, Beilby, Wm Cobb, 1664, Fangfoss; Dean & Chap.: B2, Jn Barton, 1693, Riccall; D1; Th. Daines, 1630; G1: Ric. Gilbie, 10 Eliz., Eliz. Gibson 1633—all of Askham; T1: Jn Thompson, 1660–1, U. Poppleton; Robt Touke, 1659–60, Robt Tuke, 1690, Riccall; Ed. Thompson, 1669, L. Ouseburn; T2: Francis Thompson, 1699, Acomb; Var.: Robt Scadlocke, 1660–1, Acomb, Chris. Saunders, 1662, Riccall; Ampleforth Preb.: Wm Harrison, 1699, Heslington; Bp Wilton Pec.: Th. Charlton, 1694–5, Ed. Cooke, 1695–6, Youlthorpe; Robt Blanshard, 1723, Th. Stephenson, 1727–8, Bolton; Temple Newsam Manorial Ct: 25, 38, 104, 116, 128; Snaith Pec.: Alex. Salmon, 1661–2, Jn Lawe, 1691, Pollington: Wm Ashton & Robt Heaton, 1691–2, Gt Heck; Wm Heppnestall & Geo. Makinge, 1664, Wm Nutt & Mary Rawden, 1725, Hensall; Wm Awcocke, 1664, Carlton, Robt Patricke, 1664, Airmyn; Selby Pec.: Wm Saunders, 1659–60, Robt Hall, 1660, Barley; Wm Clarkson & Jn Bromley, 1728, Brayton; Wm & Alice Halley (Haleye), 1662, Dorothy (1694) & Robt Sugden, 1695, Selby; Hy Scowcroft, 1663, Thorpe Willoughby, Margery Sharp, 1729, Lund; Th. Brayshaw, 1662, Francis Browne, 1664–5, Th. Sharpe, 1666–7, Eliz. Higgins, 1694, Hambleton; Ann Brooke, 1667–8, Kath. Ball, 1669, Gateforth; Hy Beedforth, 1691, Jn Beame, 1719–20, Burn.

APPENDIX B

Additional References to Midland Up-and-down Farms

Invs.: Leics. RO, A/d: mid-sixteenth cent.: 18, 18a; 1598: Ralph Freeman/
Newark Grange; 1599: 98; 1602: 99, 126, 205, 1612: 103, 215; 1614: 33, 99,
175; 1618: 56; 1621: 173; 1625: 101; 1626: 141; 1627: 78, 111, 130, 140,
197; 1628: 28, 79, 82, 89, 129, 158, 174, 241; 1631: 90, 122; 1632: 45, 56,
124, 148, 160; 1633: 31, 43, 74, 96, 155; 1636: 23, 105, 111, 132, 164; 1638:
158, 195, 238, 309; 1639: 23, 36, 59, 61, 64, 101, 133; 1641: Robt Bonner/
Lindridge; 1642: 7, 34; 1643: 31; 1644: 28; 1647: 43, 81, 90; 1660 small:
28, 170, 125; gt: 220–1, 235; 1661, Commy: 111; A/d: 242, 244; 1662 VG:
61; 1663, Commy: 45, 52; 1664: 119; 1665: 56, 60; 1666: 56; 1667: 8, 72,
138; 1668 A/d: 13, 32, 49; 1671: 205; 1673: 1, 96; 1691: 81; 1693 VG: 11,
66; 1695: 34, 94; 1702: 38; 1704: 41, 64; 1705: 105; 1706: 28; 1707: 11, 117,
126, 130; 1708: 35, 44, 55, 78–9, 95, 101; 1709: 28, 44, 47, 100; 1710: 14,
21 & Josh. Wallin/Temple Hall; eighteenth-cent.: Th. Tilecoat, 1740–1,
Nelson; Worcs. RO, Cons. Ct Wigorn. 1546: 110; 1568: 76; 1618: 132a;
1637: 80; 1638: 162; Lichfield Jt RO, Pecs.: Hy Agarde, 1661, Brereton, Jn
Cresswell, 1662, Barnhurst, Jn Alcocke, 1620–1, Fauld, Wm Griniley, 1666,
Fisherwick, Jn Eardley, 1724, Eccleshall, Humphrey Arkoll, 1695, Penk-
ridge, Wm Averne, 1694, Rugeley; Cons. Ct: 1541: Wm Bowyer/Knyper-
sley; A1560: Anthony Abell/Ticknall, Wm Adams/Wolvey, Jas Austen/
Normcott Grange; Br1566: Randoll Bradshaw/Chesterton; H1592: Martin
Holbache/Fillingley; T–V1569: Jn Tailor/Burton Extra; W1597: Robt
Whithall/Stanton; 1694: Sam. Brown/Walter-upon-Trent; Northants. RO,
Cons. Ct Petriburg. Hunts. Invs. K1613–87: Jn Keble/Caldecote; Cams.
Bds & Invs. 1662: Th. Edwards/Long Stanton; Peterboro' Invs. 1693:
Wm Deacon/Belsize; Peterboro' Wills & c. 1724(a): Jn Austin/Titchmarsh;
A/d Ct Northampton, Northants. Admins. 1661: Ric. Canwarden/L.
Harrowden; Northants. Invs. 1660–99: 8; Northants. Wills & Admins
1725, Jan.–Mar.: Hy Perrin/Towcester; Leeds Lib. RD/AP/1: Geo. Bar-
rows, 1562, Knaresborough, Robt Constable, 1566, Langthorne, Jn Garth,
1595, E. Layton, Francis Askwith, 1631, Mowton, Robt Stannel, 1634,
Ellingthorpe, Hy Earle, 1637, Rockcliffe, Th. Smithson, 1638, Melsonby,
Wm Nicholson, 1638, Akebar, Th. Squire, 1639, Anderby Steeple, Chris.
Nicholson, 1640, Bedale; York, Dean & Chap. 1488–1691: Isabel Parkin-
son/Beaumont Hill; Bp Wilton Pec. Wm Blanchard, 1721, Bolton; Selby
Pec. Jn Harland, 1666, Newand, Wm Knowles, 1729–30, Hambleton.

M

GLOSSARY

abroad: open to common of pasture.

accommodation close: one to accommodate non-farm livestock.

agist: to set or accept livestock for depasturing upon payment.

aldercarr: marshy ground replete with alders.

all-green: of a farm without tillage.

alternate husbandry: convertible husbandry, q.v.

arable-grass rotation: one in which the leys are short and the emphasis is on tillage.

arden: woodland, wood-pasture.

artificial grass: sown and grown by art and not by nature.

bare fallow: naked one, without crops.

bastard ley: one incompletely formed.

bay: low dam in carriage of floated meadow.

beat, beet: to remove turf with an adze; turf so removed.

beatburning: i.q. burnbaking, sodburning, denshiring, paring and burning q.v.

blackland: thin, black soil on slopes of downs; clay loam in plains.

blackleg: i.q. wood-evil, q.v.

blandlings, blendings: dredge, mixture, usually of spring corn.

boozy: of cheese—made from hay.

bottom grass: late-flourishing variety in a mixed sward.

bout: two furrow slices laid back to back.

brassica: coles, i.e. cabbages, turnips, cole-seed, coleworts, etc.

breach: opening of dead hedges round common field after harvest; ploughing up the stubble.

break: breck, q.v.

breast-plough: push-plough.

breck: division of land for shifting, temporary cultivation.

brookland: wet meadow.

brote: stubble.

brush: stubble; to mow down overgrown grass stems.

bullimong: dredge, q.v.

burnbake, burnbeat: i.q. denshire, q.v.

butt: ridge.

butty: fellow; of field—common, mean.

cade: decayed sheep.

carcass butcher: wholesaler, slaughtering wholesaler.

carr: marsh.

cast: of ridges—to couple them.

catch crop: minor one snatched between two main crops.

catchwork: system of floating on hill-sides.

champion: open land, as opposed to woodland or wood-pasture.

chilver hog: theaf, q.v.

chisely: flinty, gravelly.

chough: self-actuating sluice.

cinq(ue)foil: often for sainfoin.

cledge: flinty clay or clay loam, formed from clay-with-flints.

climature: effective climatic environment of plant life.

close-fold: to fold densely.

clove: of wool—7 lb.

clover-sickness: disease of clover associated with minute eel-worms in stem, found especially in red (broad) clover.

comb: balk, unploughed green furrow.

cone wheat: *triticum turgidum*.

consumption crops: those destined for consumption on the farm.

convertible husbandry: where the land alternates between grass and tillage.

coom: i.q. maam, q.v.

coomb: 4 b.

couple: ewe and lamb.

cow grass: perennial red clover.

crag: shell-marl.

creachy: calcareous and gravelly.

creep-hurdle: permitting egress and ingress to lambs only.

crone: old ewe.

cutmeat: provender, generally oats in straw, cut in short lengths.

cutting butcher: retailer.

cwm: Welsh spelling of combe.

denshire, devonshire: to pare and burn vegetable cover, sowing seed in scattered ashes.

dill: for till, q.v.

dredge: miscellany of barley and oats.

drowner: floater, q.v.

dung-pot: tumbrel; coarse pannier with drop bottom.

ear: to plough.

earth: a ploughing; soil having been ploughed.

eaver, ever, evergreen: strain of perennial rye-grass.

etch: ploughing of the stubble.

every year's land: cropped every year without any fallow.

feeder: fatting beast.

field-course: course of cultivation, as distinct from rotation of crops.

fielden: champion and largely in common fields.

field-grass husbandry: i.q. convertible husbandry, q.v.

flash: flooded or flushed pit, quarry or hollow.

flat: furlong.

fleak: hurdle.

float: to pass thin sheet of water over a meadow; to lay out meadow for this passage.

floater: professional expert in floating.

flowing meadow: floated by ridge-and-furrow system.

flying flock: one bought in only for resale in near future.

fold-course: special rights pertaining to folding flock of sheep.

foxbench, foxglove soil: cold, wet, retentive clay soil, such as favours foxgloves.

fremmy: apt to grass over.

frouse: mixture of horse beans and grey peas.

full-mouthed: with full set of teeth.

gate: pasture right.

gather up: of ridge—to form from the flat.

gimmer: young ewe.

goat: sewer.

going: i.q. gate, q.v.

grass: all herbs valuable for mowing or grazing.

grass-arable rotation: one in which the leys are long and the emphasis is pastoral.

gratton: common of pasture in common fields.

grazing butcher: wholesaler who carries stock on grass.

green furrow: balk.

green wall: old sea-wall grassed over.

grip, gripe: surface cross-drain.

growan: black sand or gravel.

gurry-but: dung-sledge.

hafod, hafod-tref: Welsh for shiel, q.v.

ham: narrow riparian ground.

hawe: coastal sand-dune.

hazel mould: soil of improved structure created from clay by cultivating grass.

headley: headland in grass.

heath-cropper: heath sheep.

hen-land: hazel mould, q.v.

hey: hedge; hedged field.

heyward: hedge-warden, field officer for bounds strays, etc.

highland: upland, as opposed to low marsh.

hitching, hitchland, hookland: part of fallow under crop.

honeysuckle-grass: clover.

hop-clover: variety of clover; or misnomer or provincialism for trefoil.

horse-meat: mixture of tares, peas or lentils, with oats for them to climb by, all cut together for horse fodder.

house-lamb: housed for suckling.

hurlock: stony chalk rock.

hurst: field enclosed by coppice-rows.

improvement: amelioration in at once the fertility and the produce of the land; in north—intake from waste, common or forest.

ing: wet meadow.

in: to get in harvest; to take in land.

kealy: calcareous and gravelly.

kebb: rotting sheep, cade.

knee-sick: weak in stalk, sagging at joint.

laine: season or division for field-course; ley, q.v.

lamb hog: hog.

land: imperfect provincial synonym for ridge, q.v.

layer: ley, q.v.

lea: grazing; right of common pasture.

leat: artificial rill.

ley: land laid to grass.

ley farming: form of convertible husbandry.

lid: coarse, rank fen hay.

linch, linchard, linchet: balk, greensward mere.

load: corn 5 lb., straw 36 trusses of 36 lb., old hay 36 trusses of 56 lb., new hay *id.* of 60 lb., timber unhewn 40 cu. ft, squared 50 cu. ft.

load, lode: drain.

lodge: of corn—be beaten down by rain or wind.

long: of dung—with straw unrotted.

loon: ridge.

lynchet: i.q. linchet, q.v.

maam, malm, mawm, mawme: chalky clay loam.

maes: Welsh for field, especially town field.

mainland: clay soil or clay loam.

marlcope: pale woodland clay soil.

moor, more: tract composed largely of peat-earth or fen-mould.

moor-earth, more earth: river-bed ooze.

moor-evil: wood-evil, q.v.

mound: field bound of any kind, but especially an earthen bank.

mug: type of pasture sheep.

needle-work: facing of bramble and thorn faggots on earthwork.

nott: of stock—hornless; of cereal—beardless.

olland: old land, ley land.

ollett, ollit; compost of cow-dung and straw, especially when used as fuel.

ore: seaweed for manure.

over-winter: to keep over winter.

oxgang: fiscal unit of assessment for rating farms.

pack: of wool—240 lb.

park: in West Country—any enclosure.

pasture: in Midlands—a close.

pightle: small, narrow close.

pilez, pillas, pilles, pillotes: naked oats.

pinder: field officer, heyward, q.v.

pinfallow: winter fallow.

pitch of work: meadow floated from a single main hatch.

plain: land never gathered into ridge and furrow.

plit: furrow slice.

plough: in west—often the team, not the implement.

plough-pan: hard bed formed beneath tilth by plough-share.

rafter: to plough alternate furrows, inverting those ploughed on those unploughed.

ray-grass: i.q., rye-grass.

rayne, rein, run: furrow.

redland: red soil; red soil on tops of downs; deep, red sandy loam; deep, red clay loam.

rew: i.q. row.

rhine: drainage sewer.

ridge: ploughed land between two open or water furrows.

ridge by ridge: temporary, shifting, common-field tillage.

ridgel: immature ram.

rift, riving: new ploughing.

rive: to make a rift.

rivet wheat: cone wheat, q.v.

roweless: roofless, as of a tenement without a messuage.

run-rig: ridge by ridge, q.v.

rushland: heavy, well-textured clay loam on retentive base, apt to turn to rushes.

ryeland: sandy soil, suited to rye.

ryne: i.q. rhine, q.v.

sack: of wool—two weys=354 lb.

salting: undefended salt-marsh, saline mud-bank.

scalding fallow: one stirred in high summer.

seeds: agriculturally, includes all that sown with the botanical seeds; grass seeds; young seeded grass.

several: free of common rights.

severalty: state of being several; several land.

sharp: of land—light and acid.

shiel, shield, shieling: temporary pastoral encampment in glen, dale or combe.

shippen, shippon: cow-house; sheep-pen.

short: of dung—well-rotted, with straw broken up.

shub: river-bed ooze, moor-earth, q.v.

sike: drain to remove overflow.

six-teeth: of sheep from shearing at 2 years to shearing at 3 years, when teeth are so many.

skegs: black oats.

skirt, skirwinkle: to pare off alternate furrows of sward.

skirt soils: highly organic silty clay loams.

sleech: i.q. sludge.

sleight: open pasture.

slodger, sludger: inhabitant of interior of undrained fens.

soap-ash: by-product of soap-boiling.

sodburn: to pare and burn the sod, to denshire, q.v.

sodworm: i.q. wireworm.

soil: season or shift in field-course.

spearwort: sheep-rot; *ranunculus flammula, ranunculus lingua*.

staffherd, staffhold: to depasture flock in charge of shepherd with staff.

stank, stanch, staunch: dam.

star-grass: probably sea wheat-grass, perhaps also lyme and marram grasses, possibly too for sea couch, sand couch and their hybrid.

starry: of soil—shallow and barren.

stelling: shiel, q.v.

stitch: ridge, q.v.

stitchmeal: ridge by ridge, q.v.

streak-fallow: rafter (q.v.) for a fallow.

stripe: open marshland.

Suffolk grass: annual meadow grass, *poa annua*.

sull(ow): plough.

GLOSSARY 359

summer-corn, summer-grain: spring corn, especially peas, beans and oats.

summer-field: one fallowed in summer.

summer-ground: dry in summer, flooded in winter.

summerley: summer fallow, often a still one.

tail: sheep dropping.

tail-corn: refuse corn.

tash: to manure by folding or herding stock, especially sheep; manure so produced.

tath(e), teathe: to manure by herding stock, especially bullocks; manure so produced.

teg: hog.

tenantry: subject to common rights; land so subject.

theaf: yearling ewe, before shearing.

three-crop (three-year) land: sown to three successive crops between fallows.

till: lentil; two-seeded tare.

tiller: to spread by sending out horizontal shoots that take root; such a shoot.

tod: of wool—2 stone.

top-fold: to fold sheep on growing crops.

town: hamlet, village or town.

town-land: upland amidst marshes, where town stands.

treddle: tred and droppings of sheep.

tri-fallow: third successive fallow ploughing; to make same.

tucker, tucking; fuller, fulling.

turnwrest plough: having two shares and mould-boards, able to be alternately raised and lowered.

twi-fallow: second successive fallow ploughing; to make same.

twitch: couch grass.

two-crop (two-year) land: sown to two successive crops between fallows.

two-teeth: of sheep from first shearing ($1\frac{1}{4}$ years) until about 6 months later, when second pair of permanent incisors is gained.

up-and-down: alternately ploughed up for corn and laid down to grass.

urry: dark, earthy clay from near seams of coal.

vell: to pare turf with a plough.

wall: linchet, q.v.

warp: ridge, q.v.; sandy, silty loam on silt base; to pass water over land with view to gaining its sediment.

warth: estuary mud-bank.

wash: tract or basin to receive overflow of drainage works.

waterman: floater, q.v.

water-meadow: one artificially watered or floated.

weld: dyer's weed.

went: furlong.

wey: of wool—$6\frac{1}{2}$ tod, q.v.; of cheese—various: Essex 252 lb., Midland 336 lb. etc.

white corn, white crops: straw crops.

whiteland: i.q. maam, q.v.; or woodland, q.v.

whittakers: quartz crystals.

wick: dairy farm.

winter-ground: dry winter and summer.

wood-evil: disease in sheep and cattle, moor-evil or blackleg.

woodland: of soil—pale, weak, yellow, retentive clay, associated with woodland.

woodsere, woodseer, woodsheer: froth appearing on joints of plants about latter end of May, commonly called cuckoo-spit; spongy, wet, cold land.

yard: quarter of an acre.

yardland: fiscal unit of assessment for rating farms.

SELECT BIBLIOGRAPHY

OF PRINTED AND TYPESCRIPT BOOKS AND JOURNALS

(Place of publication of books, except in record society series, is London, unless otherwise stated).

Anonymous or various:

Acts of the Privy Council of England, several vols. Public Record Office, 1929, in progress (and see Dasent).

Calender of State Papers and Manuscripts relating to English affairs, existing in the archives and collections of Venice, & c., 38 vols. Public Record Office, 1864–1940.

Calendars of the Proceedings in Chancery in the reign of Queen Elizabeth, 3 vols. Record Commission, 1827–32.

'Chancery Proceedings *temp.* Elizabeth', *Collections for the History of Staffordshire*, 3rd series, 1926 (1928).

'Description of Graysbrooke, in Yorkshire', *Gentleman's Magazine*, 1763, xxxiii.

'Description of the Parish of Weston, Staffs.', *Gentleman's Magazine*, 1763, xxxiii.

Discourse of the Common Weal of this Realm of England, A, edited by E. Lamond, Cambridge, 1929.

'East Riding and the Purveyance Contracts for the Royal Household *temp.* James I, *The Transactions of the East Riding Antiquarian Society*, 1893, i.

'Elizabethan Chancery Proceedings, Series ii: 1558–79', *Collections for the History of Staffordshire*, 3rd series, 1931, (1933) and 1938.

English Reports, The, lxxii King's Bench Division, 1907, i, *lxxiv King's Bench Division*, 1907, iii, *lxxvii King's Bench Division*, 1907, vi, *cxxii, Common Pleas*, 1912, i.

'Humberstone's Survey', *Yorkshire Archaelogical Journal*, 1903, xvii.

Letters and Papers, foreign and domestic, of the reign of Henry VIII, preserved in the Public Record Office, the British Museum and elsewhere in England, Public Record Office, 23 vols., 1862–1932.

'Nathaniel Reading and the Commissioners of Sewers for the Level of Hatfield Chace', *Yorkshire Archaeological Journal*, 1905, xviii.

'Natural History of Dorking', *Gentleman's Magazine*, 1763, xxxiii.

'Proceedings of the Court of the Star Chamber: *temp.* Henry VII and Edward VI', *Collections for the History of Staffordshire*, 3rd series, 1910.

'Rowley Regis Rent Roll, 1556', *Collections for the History of Staffordshire*, 3rd series, 1936.

Shotley Parish Records, Suffolk Green Books, Bury St Edmund's, 1912, xvi.

'1614 Customs of Christian Malford', *Wiltshire Archaeological Magazine*, 1920–2, xli.

'Society's Manuscripts, The: Chiseldon and Draycot', *Wiltshire Archaeological Magazine*, 1898–9, xxx, 1900–1, xxxi.

'Star Chamber Proceedings, Henry VIII and Edward VI', *Collections for the History of Staffordshire*, 3rd series, 1912.

Victoria History of the Counties of England: Bedfordshire, Cambridgeshire, Derbyshire, Essex, Gloucestershire, Lancashire, Leicestershire, Middlesex, Rutlandshire, Suffolk, Worcestershire.

Wills and Inventories illustrative of the history, manners, language, statistics, etc., of the Northern Counties of England, from the eleventh century downwards, part i, Surtees Society, 1835.

Wills and Inventories from the Registry at Durham, pts ii, iii, iv, Surtees Society, 1860 xxxviii, 1906, cxii, 1929, clxii.

Wills and Administrations from the Knaresborough Court Rolls, i and ii, Surtees Society, 1902, civ, 1905, cx.

ADKIN, B. W. *Land Drainage in Britain*, 1933.

AIKIN, J. *Description of the Country from thirty to forty miles round Manchester*, 1795.

ALLAN, D. G. C. 'Agrarian Discontent under the Early Stuarts and during the last decade of Elizabeth', typescript thesis M.Sc. (Economics), London University, 1950.

ALLISON, K. J. 'The Wool Supply and the Worsted Cloth Industry in Norfolk in the Sixteenth and Seventeenth Centuries', typescript thesis Ph.D., Leeds University, 1955.

ALLISON, K. J. 'Flock Management in the Sixteenth and Seventeenth Centuries', *Economic History Review*, 2nd series, 1958, xi.

ANDREWS, J. H. 'The Trade of the Port of Faversham, 1650–70', *Archaelogia Cantiana*, 1956, lxix.

APPERSON, G. L. *Gleanings After Time*, 1907.

ARNOLD, R. *A Yeoman of Kent*, 1949.

ASHLEY, W. J. *The Bread of our Forefathers*, Oxford, 1928.

ASHTON, T. S. *The Eighteenth Century*, 1955.

—— *The Industrial Revolution 1760–1830*, 1948.

ASPLEY HEATH SCHOOL HISTORICAL SOCIETY, *A History of our District*, Aspley Guise, 1931.

ATKYNS, R. *A New History of Gloucestershire*, edited by Rudder, Cirencester, 1779.

ATWELL, G. *The Faithfull Surveyour*, Cambridge, 1662.

AUBREY, J. *An Essay towards the Description of the North Division of Wiltshire*, sine loco, 1838.

—— 'An Introduction to the Survey and Natural History of the North Division of the County of Wiltshire', in *Miscellanies on Several Curious Subjects*, E. Curll, 1714.

—— *The Natural History of Wiltshire*, edited by J. Britton, 1847.

—— *The Natural History and Antiquities of the County of Surrey*, (1691), 5 vols., 1719.

—— *Wiltshire. The Topographical Collections of John Aubrey, F.R.S., A.D. 1659–70*, edited by J. E. Jackson, Devizes, 1862.

AUSTIN, W. *The History of Luton*, 2 vols. Newport I. of W., 1928.

BACON, F. *Opera Omnia*, 4 vols., 1730.

BADESLADE, T. *The History of the Ancient and Present State of the Navigation of the Port of King's Lynn*, 1725.

BAIGENT, F. J. *The Crondal Records*, iii, Hampshire Record Society, 1891.

BAIGENT, F. J. and MILLARD, J. E. *A History of the Ancient Town and Manor of Basingstoke*, Basingstoke, 1889.

BAILEY, F. A. *A History of Southport*, Southport, 1955.

BAILEY, J. *A General View of the Agriculture of the County of Durham*, 1810.

BAILEY, J. and CULLEY, G. *A General View of the Agriculture of the County of Cumberland*, 1805.

—— *A General View of the Agriculture of the County of Northumberland*, 1805.

BAKER, A. R. H. 'The Field Systems of Kent', typescript thesis Ph.D., London University, 1963.

BALLARD, A. 'Notes on the Open Fields of Oxfordshire', Oxfordshire Archaeological Society's *Report*, 1908 (1909).

—— 'Tackley in the Sixteenth and Seventeenth Centuries', Oxfordshire Archaeological Society's *Report* for 1911, (1912).

BANKES, J. *The Memoranda Book of James Bankes 1586–1617*, Inverness, 1935.

BARLEY, M. W. 'East Yorkshire Manorial Bye-laws', *Yorkshire Archaeological Journal*, 1943, xxxv.

—— 'Farmhouses and Cottages 1550–1725', *Economic History Review*, 2nd series, 1955, vii.

—— *Lincolnshire and the Fens*, 1952.

BARNES, D. G. *A History of the English Corn Laws from 1660–1846*, 1930.

BARNSWELL, E. L. 'Notes on the Perrot Family', *Archaeologia Cambrensis*, 3rd series, 1866, xii.

BARRATT, D. M. *Ecclesiastical Terriers of Warwickshire Parishes*, vol. i, Dugdale Society Publications, 1955, xxii.

—— 'The Inclosure of the Manor of Wasperton in 1664', *University of Birmingham Historical Journal*, 1952, iii.

BATCHELOR, T. *A General View of the Agriculture of the County of Bedford*, 1808.

BATESON, E., *et al. A History of Northumberland*, 15 vols., 1893–1940.

BATESON, M. *Records of the Borough of Leicester*, vol. iii, Cambridge, 1905.

BATH, VAN, *see* SLICHER.

BAX, A. R. 'Notes and Extracts from the Account Book of Richard Bax, a Surrey yeoman', *The Antiquary*, 1882, vi.

BAXTER, R. 'The Poor Husbandman's Advocate', *Bulletin of the John Rylands Library*, 1926, x.

BEALE, J. *Herefordshire Orchards, A Pattern for all England*, 1657.

BELL, V. *Little Gaddesden*, 1949.

'BENEVOLUS', 'The Natural History of Eastham in Cheshire', *Gentleman's Magazine*, 1762, xxxii.

BENNETT (Canon). 'The Orders of Shrewton', *Wiltshire Archaeological Magazine*, 1887, xxiii.

BENNETT, M. K. 'British Wheat Yield Per Acre for Seven Centuries', *Economic History*, 1934–7, iii.

BENTHAM, J. *The Christian Conflict*, 1635.

BERESFORD, M. W. 'Lot Acres', *Economic History Review*, 1941–3, xiii.

(BEST, H.) *Rural Economy in Yorkshire in 1641, being the Farming and Account*

Books of Henry Best of Elmswell [edited by C. B. Robinson (Norcliffe)], Surtees Society, 1857, xxxiii.

BEVERIDGE, W. (Lord). 'A Statistical Crime of the Seventeenth Century', *Journal of Economic and Business History*, 1929, i.

—— 'The Yield and Price of Corn in the Middle Ages', *Economic History*, 1926–9, i.

—— 'Wheat Measures in the Winchester Manors', *Economic History*, 1930–3, ii.

BILLINGSLEY, J. *A General View of the Agriculture in the County of Somerset*, 1794, 1798.

BLAGG, T. M. *A Miscellany of Nottinghamshire Records*, Thoroton Society, 1945, xi.

B[LAGRAVE], J. *The Epitome of the Art of Husbandry*, 1669.

BLAND, A., BROWN, P., and TAWNEY, R. H. *English Economic History: Select Documents*, 1925.

BLENCOWE, R. W. 'Extracts from the Journal & Account Book of the Reverend Giles Moore', *Sussex Archaeological Collections* 1848 i.

BLITH, W. *The English Improver Improved* 1652.

BLOME, R. *Britannia* 1673.

—— *The Gentleman's Recreation* 1686.

BLOOM, A. *The Farm in the Fen* 1944.

BLOXSOM, M. *History of the Parish of Gilmorton* Lincoln 1918.

BLUNDELL, J. H. *Toddington: its Annals & People* Toddington 1925.

BODINGTON, E. J. 'The Church Surveys in Wilts. 1649–50', *Wiltshire Archaeological Magazine*, 1917–19, xl, 1920–2, xli.

BOND, M. F. *Manuscripts of the House of Lords*, new series, vol. xi, Addenda, 1514–1714, (H. L. 1961–2.123), HMSO, 1962.

BORLASE, W. *The Natural History of Cornwall*, Oxford, 1758.

BOSWELL, G. *A Treatise on Watering Meadows*, 4th edition, 1801.

BOUCH, C. M. L. and JONES, G. P. *A Short Economic and Social History of the Lake Counties, 1500–1830*, Manchester, 1961.

BOWDEN, P. J. *The Wool Trade in Tudor and Stuart England*, 1962.

BOWLES, W. L. *Parochial History of Bremhill*, 1828.

BOWMAN, W. M. *England in Ashton-under-Lyne*, Ashton-under-Lyne, 1960.

BOYD, A. W. *A Country Parish*, 1951.

BOYD, W. K. 'Chancery Proceedings *tempore* Elizabeth, A.D. 1560–A.D. 1570', *Collections for the History of Staffordshire*, new series, 1906, ix.

—— 'Staffordshire suits in the Court of Star Chamber, *temp*. Henry VII and Henry VIII', *Collections for the History of Staffordshire*, new series, 1907, x, pt. i.

BOYS, J. *A General View of the Agriculture of the County of Kent*, 1796.

BRACE, H. W. *History of Seed Crushing in Great Britain*, 1960.

BRADFORD, G. *Proceedings in the Court of Star Chamber in the reigns of Henry VII and Henry VIII*, Somerset Record Society, 1911, xxvii.

BRADLEY, H. *The Enclosures in England*, Columbia University Studies in History, Economics and Public Law, vol. lxxx, no. 2, Whole No. 186, New York, 1918.

BRADNEY, J. (Sir), *A History of Monmouthshire*, 4 vols. 1904–34.

BRENTNALL, H. C. 'A Longford Manuscript', *Wiltshire Archaeological Magazine*, 1947–8, lii.

—— 'A Document from Great Cheverell', *Wiltshire Archaeological Magazine*, 1950, liii.

BRETT-JAMES, N. G. 'Some Extents and Surveys of Hendon', *Transactions of the London and Middlesex Archaeological Society*, new series, 1932, vi, 1935–7, vii.

BRIERS, P. M. *The History of Nuffield*, sine loco, [1939].

BRITTEN, J. *Old Country and Farming Words*, English Dialect Society, 1880.

BROOKES, C. C. *A History of Steeple Aston and Middle Aston*, Shipston-on-Stour, 1929.

BROOKS, F. W. 'Supplementary Stiffkey Papers', in *Camden Miscellany, xvi*, Camden, 3rd series, 1936, lii.

BROWN, R. *A General View of the Agriculture of the West Riding of Yorkshire*, Edinburgh, 1799.

BROWN, T. *A General View of the Agriculture of the County of Derby*, 1794.

BROWN, W. *Yorkshire Deeds*, 3 vols. ([i], ii and iii), Yorkshire Archaeological Society Record Series, 1909, 1914, 1922, xxxix, l, lxiii.

—— *Yorkshire Star Chamber Proceedings*, Yorkshire Archaeological Society Record Series, 1909, xli.

BROWNE, J. *A Treatise on Irrigation or the Watering of Land*, 1817.

BURLEY, K. H. 'The Economic Development of Essex in the Later Seventeenth and Early Eighteenth Centuries', typescript thesis Ph.D., London University, 1957.

BURN, R. *Ecclesiastical Law*, 2nd edition, 4 vols., 1767.

BURRELL, A. *Exceptions against Sir Cornelius Virmudens Discourse for the Draining of the great Fennes &c*, 1642.

—— *A Briefe Relation Discovering Plainely the true Causes why the great Levell of Fenns . . . have been drowned . . . and briefly how they may be drained*, 1642.

BURRELL, E. D. R. 'An Historical Geography of the Sandlings of Suffolk, 1600 to 1850', typescript thesis M.Sc., London University, 1960.

BURTON, T. *The History and Antiquities of Hemingborough*, York, 1888.

BURTON, W. *The Description of Leicestershire*, [1622].

—— C. H. *A Discourse concerning the Drayninge of Fennes and Surrounded Grounds*, 1629.

CAMDEN, W. *Brittannia* edited by E. Gibson, 2 vols. 1722.

CAMPBELL, M., *The English Yeoman under Elizabeth and the early Stuarts*, New Haven, 1942.

CAMPLING, A. *The History of the Family of Drury*, no date.

'CANDIDUS', 'Description of Hanmer Parish in Flintshire', *Gentleman's Magazine*, 1762, xxxii.

CARDIGAN, Earl of, 'Domestic Expenses of a Nobleman's Household', in *Harrold Priory: a twelfth-century dispute, and other articles*, Publications Bedfordshire Historical Record Society, 1952, xxxii.

CAREW, R. *The Survey of Cornwall*, (1602), 1769.

CARRIER, L. *The Beginnings of Agriculture in America*, New York, 1923.

CAVE, T. and WILSON, R. A. *The Parliamentary Survey of the Lands and Possessions of the Dean and Chapter of Worcester*, Worcestershire Historical Society, 1924.

CHALKLIN, C. W. 'The Rural Economy of a Kentish Wealden Parish, 1650–1750', *Agricultural History Review*, 1962, x.

—— *Seventeenth-century Kent: A Social and Economic History*, 1965.

CHAMBERS, J. D. *The Vale of Trent 1670–1800*, Economic History Review, Supplement, no. 3, Cambridge, no date.

—— *Nottinghamshire in the Eighteenth Century*, 1932.

—— and MINGAY, G. E., *The Agricultural Revolution 1750–1880*, 1966.

CHAPMAN, V. 'Open Fields in West Cheshire', *Transactions of the Historic Society of Lancashire and Cheshire*, 1953, civ.

CHARLESWORTH, J. *Wakefield Manor Book 1709*, Yorkshire Archaeological Society Record Series, 1939, ci.

CHILDREY, J. *Britannia Baconica*, 1660.

CHIPPENDALL, W. H. *A Sixteenth-Century Survey and Year's Account of the Estates of Hornby Castle, Lancs*. Chetham Society, new series, 1939, cii.

CHURCHYARD, T. *The Worthines of Wales*, (1587), 1776.

CLARIDGE, J. *A General View of the Agriculture in the County of Dorset*, 1793.

CLARK, G. N. 'Enclosure by Agreement at Marston, near Oxford', *English Historial Review*, 1927, xlii.

CLARK, J. *A General View of the Agriculture of the County of Brecknock*, 1794.

—— *A General View of the Agriculture of the County of Hereford*, 1794.

—— *A General View of the Agriculture of the County of Radnor*, 1794.

CLARKE, W. G. *In Breckland Wilds*, 1926.

CLAY, C. T. *Yorkshire Deeds iv and v*, Yorkshire Archaelogical Society Record Series, 1924, lxv, 1926, lxix.

CLAY, J. W. *Yorkshire Royalist Composition Papers*, i, ii and iii, Yorkshire Archaeological Society Record Series, 1893, xv, 1895, xviii, 1896, xx.

COKER, [J]. *A Survey of Dorsetshire*, 1732.

COLEMAN, D. C. 'The Economy of Kent under the Later Stuarts', typescript thesis Ph.D., London University, 1951.

COLEMAN (Prebendary), 'The Manor of Allerton and its Tenants, 1530–1866', *Proceedings of the Somerset Archaeological and Natural History Society* for 1900, xlvi.

COLES, W. *Adam in Eden*, 1657.

COLLIER, C. V. 'Stovin's Manuscript', *Transactions of the East Riding Archaeological Society*, 1905, (1904), xii.

COLMAN, F. S. *A History of Barwick-in-Elmet*, Leeds, 1908.

COLVIN, H. M. *A History of Deddington, Oxfordshire*, 1963.

COOKE, A. H. *The Early History of Mapledurham*, Oxfordshire Record Society, 1925, vii.

COOPER, G. M. 'Berwick Parochial Records', *Sussex Archaeological Collections*, 1853, vi.

COOPER, W. *Wootton Wawen: its History and Records*, Leeds, 1936.

—— *History of Lillington*, Shipston-on-Stour, 1940.

CORBETT, W. J. 'Elizabethan Village Surveys', *Transactions of the Royal Historical Society*, new series, 1897, xi.

CORNWALL, J. C. K. 'The Agrarian History of Sussex, 1560–1640', typescript thesis M.A., London University, 1953.

—— ' Farming in Sussex, 1560–1640', *Sussex Archaeological Collections*, 1954, xcii.

CORNWALL, J. C. K. 'Agricultural Improvement, 1560–1640', *Sussex Archaeological Collections*, 1960, xcviii.

COWPER, J. M. 'Tudor Prices in Kent, chiefly in 1577', *Transactions of the Royal Historical Society*, 1875, i.

COX, D. 'The Improvement of Cornwall by Sea-sand', *Philosophical Transactions*, ii, see Hutton, *et al*.

CROFTON, H. T. 'Broughton Topography and Manor Court', in *Chetham Miscellany*, *ii*, Chetham Society, 1909, lxiii.

—— 'Relics of the Common Field System in and near Manchester', *Manchester Quarterly*, Jan. 1887.

CROSSLEY, E. W. 'A Templenewsam Inventory', *Yorkshire Archaeological Journal*, 1920, xxv.

—— 'The Testamentary Documents of Yorkshire Peculiars', in *Miscellanea*, *vol. ii*, Yorkshire Archaeological Society Record Series, 1929, lxxiv.

CRUMP, W. B. and GHORBAL, G. *History of the Huddersfield Woollen Industry*, Huddersfield 1935.

CRUTCHLEY, J. *A General View of the Agriculture of the County of Rutland*, 1794.

CULLEY, G. *Observations on Livestock*, 1786.

CULLUM, (Sir) *The History and Antiquities of Hawsted and Hardwick*, 2nd edition, 1813.

CULPEPER, T. (Sir) Senior, *A Tract Against the High Rate of Interest presented to the High Court of Parliament, A.D. 1623*, 1668.

CUNNINGHAM, W. 'Common Rights at Cottenham and Stretham in Cambridgeshire', in *Camden Miscellany xii*, Royal Historical Society, Camden, 3rd series, 1910, xviii.

—— *The Growth of English Industry and Commerce*, vol. iii, Cambridge, 1907.

CUNNINGTON, B. H. *Records of the County of Wiltshire: extracts from Quarter Sessions Great Rolls*, Devizes, 1932.

CURTIS, C. D. *Sedgemoor and the Bloody Assize*, 1930.

CURTLER, W. H. R. *The Enclosure and Redistribution of our Land*, Oxford, 1920.

DANIEL-TYSSEN, J. R. 'Parliamentary Survey of the County of Sussex 1649–53', *Sussex Archaeological Collections*, 1871, xxiii–1873, xxv.

DARBY, H. C. *An Historical Geography of England before 1800*, Cambridge, 1948.

—— *The Draining of the Fens*, Cambridge, 1940.

—— *The Medieval Fenland*, Cambridge, 1940.

DARBYSHIRE, H. S., and LUMB, G. D. *The History of Methley*, Publications Thoresby Society, xxxv, Leeds, 1937.

DASENT, J. R. *Acts of the Privy Council of England*, new series, 32 vols. 1890–1907.

DAVENPORT, F. G. *The Economic Development of a Norfolk Manor 1086–1565*, Cambridge, 1906.

DAVIES, M. 'Common Lands in South-east Monmouthshire', *Cardiff Naturalists' Society Reports and Transactions*, 1955–6, lxxxv.

—— 'Field Patterns in the Vale of Glamorgan', *Cardiff Naturalists' Society Reports and Transactions*, 1954–5, lxxxiv.

—— 'Rhosili Open Field and related South Wales Field Patterns', *Agricultural History Review*, 1956, iv.

—— 'The Open Fields of Laugharne', *Geography*, 1955, xl.

DAVIES, W. *A General View of the Agriculture and Domestic Economy of North Wales*, 1810.

—— *A General View of the Agriculture and Domestic Economy of South Wales*, 2 vols. 1814.

DAVIS, R. *A General View of the Agriculture of the County of Oxford*, 1794.

DAVIS, T. *A General View of the Agriculture of the County of Wiltshire*, 1794, 1813.

DEANE, P., and COLE, W. A. *British Economic Growth 1688–1959: Trends & Structure*, Cambridge, 1962.

DEFOE, D. *A Tour through England and Wales*, 2 vols. Everyman edition.

—— *A Plan of the English Commerce, 1728.*

D'ELBOUX, R. H. *Surveys of the Manors of Robertsbridge, Sussex, & Michelmarsh, Hampshire, and of the Demesne Lands of Halden in Rolvenden, Kent, 1567–70*, Sussex Record Society, 1944, xlvii.

DERVILLE, M. T. *The Level and Liberty of Romney Marsh*, 1936.

D'EWES, Sir Simonds, *see* HALLIWELL.

DICKSON, R. *A General View of the Agriculture of Lancashire*, edited by W. Stevenson, 1815.

DODD, A. H. *The Industrial Revolution in North Wales*, Cardiff, 1933.

—— *Studies in Stuart Wales*, Cardiff, no date.

DONALDSON, J. *A General View of the Agriculture of the County of Northampton*, Edinburgh, 1794.

DOUGHTY, H. M. *Chronicles of Theberton, A Suffolk Village*, 1910.

DOWLING, T. W. *The Records of Knowle*, sine loco, 1914.

DRIVER, A. and W. *A General View of the Agriculture of the County of Hampshire*, 1794.

DRUMMOND, J., and WILBRAHAM, A. *The Englishman's Food*, 1939.

DUGDALE, W. *The History of Imbanking and Drayning*, 1662.

DUNCUMB, J. *A General View of the Agriculture of the County of Hereford*, 1805.

DYER, J. *Poems*, 1770.

EARWAKER, J. P. *Lancashire and Cheshire Wills and Inventories at Chester*, Chetham Society new series, 1884, iii.

—— *Lancashire and Cheshire Wills and Inventories, 1572 to 1696, now preserved at Chester*, Chetham Society new series, 1893, xxviii.

EDE, J. F. *History of Wednesbury*, Wednesbury, 1962.

ELAND, G. *Purefoy Letters 1735–53*, 2 vols. 1931.

—— *Shardeloes Papers of the seventeenth and eighteenth centuries*, 1947.

ELLIOTT, G. 'The enclosure of Aspatria', *Transactions of the Cumberland and Westmorland Antiquarian and Archaeological Society*, new series, 1961, lx.

—— 'System of Cultivation . . . in Cumberland open fields', ibid., 1960, lix.

ELLIS, W. *A Compleat System of Experienced Improvements made on Sheep, Grass-lambs and House-lambs*, 1749.

—— *Chiltern and Vale Farming Explained*, [1733].

—— *The Modern Husbandman*, 8 vols. 1740.

EMERSON, W. R. 'The Economic Development of the Estates of the Petre Family in Essex in the Sixteenth and Seventeenth Centuries', typescript thesis D.Phil., Oxford University, 1951.

EMERY, F. V. 'West Glamorgan Farming, c. 1580–1620', *National Library of Wales Journal*, 1955–6, ix, 1957–8, x.

EMMISON, F. G. *Jacobean Household Inventories*, Bedfordshire Historical Record Society, 1938, xx.

—— 'Survey of the Manor of Woodham Ferrers, 1582', *Transactions of the Essex Archaeological Society*, new series, 1951, xxiv.

ERNLE, Lord, *English Farming Past and Present*, 1927, 1961.

EVANS, J. H. 'The Rochester Bridge Lands in Grain', *Archaeologia Cantiana*, 1955, (1954), lxviii.

—— 'The Upchurch Marshes in the Time of the First Elizabeth', *Archaeologia Cantiana*, 1962 (1961), lxxvi.

FAREY, J. *A General View of the Agriculture and Minerals of Derbyshire*, 3 vols. 1811–17.

FARNHAM, G. F. *Quorndon Records*, sine loco, 1912.

FARR, M. W. *Accounts and Surveys of the Wiltshire Lands of Adam de Stratton*, Wiltshire Archaeological and Natural History Society Records Branch, 1959, xiv.

FARRER, W. *The Court Rolls of the Honour of Clitheroe*, 3 vols. Manchester, 1897, Edinburgh, 1912–13.

FAY, C. R. *The Corn Laws and Social England*, Cambridge, 1932.

FIENNES, C. *Journeys*, edited by C. Morris, 1947.

FINBERG, H. P. R. *Tavistock Abbey*, Cambridge, 1951.

—— 'The Open Field in Devonshire', *Antiquity*, 1949, no. 92.

FINCH, M. E. *The Wealth of Five Northamptonshire Families 1540–1640*, Northamptonshire Record Society, 1956, xix.

FIRTH, C. H., and RAIT, R. S. *Acts and Ordinances of the Interregnum*, 3 vols. 1911, HMSO, Wt 9509.

FISHER, F. J. 'The Development of the London Food Market 1540–1640', *Economic History Review*, 1935, v, reprinted in E. M. Carus-Wilson (editor), *Essays in Economic History* [i], 1954.

FISHWICK, H. *Pleadings and Depositions in the Duchy Court of Lancaster in the Time of Henry VII and Henry VIII*. The Record Society for Lancashire and Cheshire, 1896–7, xxxii, xxxv; *ditto, Edward VI and Mary*, ibid. 1899, xl.

—— *The Survey of the Manor of Rochdale 1626*, Chetham Society, 1913, new series, lxxi.

FITZHERBERT, *The Boke of Husbandrie*, 1523.

—— *The Boke of Surveyinge and Improvementes*, 1535.

—— *The Book of Husbandry*, edited by W. W. Skeat, English Dialect Society, 1882, xxvii.

FLETCHER, W. G. *History of Loughborough*, Loughborough, 1887.

FOLKINGHAM, W. *Feudigraphia: The Synopsis or Epitome of Surveying*, 1610.

FOOT, P. *A General View of the Agriculture of the County of Middlesex*, 1794.

FORSHAW, D. M. 'Economic and Social History of Liverpool, 1540–1680', typescript dissertation B.A., Nottingham University, 1953.

FORSTER, J. *England's Happiness Increased*, 1664.

FOSTER, C. W. *Lincoln Wills*, vols. ii and iii, Lincolnshire Record Society, 1918, x, 1930, xxiv.

FOX, J. *A General View of the Agriculture of the County of Monmouth*, Brentford, 1794.

FRANKLIN, T. B. *British Grasslands*, 1953.

FRASER, R. *A General View of the Agriculture of the County of Cornwall,* 1794.

—— *A General View of the Agriculture of the County of Devon,* 1794.

FREAM, W. *Elements of Agriculture,* 10th edition, 1918.

FREEMAN, C. E. 'Elizabethan Inventories', in *Harrold Priory: a twelfth-century dispute; and other articles,* Publications Bedfordshire Historical Record Society, 1952, xxxii.

FRY, C. B. *Hannington: The Records of a Wiltshire Parish,* Gloucester, 1935.

FRY, G. S., and E. A. *Abstracts of Wiltshire Inquisitiones Post Mortem, temp. Car. I,* Index Library, British Record Society, 1901.

FULLER, T. *The History of the Worthies of England* (1662), edited by P. A. Nuttall, 3 vols., 1840.

—— *The Holy State and the Profane State,* edited by J. Nichols, 1841.

FUSSELL, G. E., 'Farming Methods in the early Stuart Period', *Journal of Modern History,* 1935, vii.

—— *Robert Loder's Farm Accounts,* Royal Historical Society, Camden 3rd series, 1936, liii.

—— 'The size of English cattle in the eighteenth century', *Agricultural History,* 1929, iii.

GARDINER, S. R. *Reports of Cases in the Courts of Star Chamber and High Commission,* Camden Society new series, 1886, xxxix.

GAUT, R. C. *A History of Worcestershire Agriculture and Rural Evolution,* Worcester, 1939.

GAY, E. F. 'The Temples of Sow and their Debts: Sir Thomas Temple and Sir Peter Temple, 1603–53', *Huntington Library Quarterly,* 1938–9, ii.

GERARD, T. *The Particular Description of the County of Somerset,* (1633), edited by E. H. Bates, Somerset Record Society, 1900, xv.

GERARDE, J. *The Herball,* 1597, 1633.

GIBSON, T. E. *Lydiate Hall and its Associations,* sine loco, 1876.

GILBERT, C. J. 'The Evolution of Romney Marsh', *Archaeologia Cantiana,* 1933, xlv.

GILL, C. *Studies in Midland History,* Oxford, 1930.

GILL, H., and GUILFORD, E. L. *The Rector's Book of Clayworth 1672–1701,* Nottingham, 1910.

GLOVER, J. H. *Kingsthorpiana,* 1883.

GODDARD, C. V. 'Customs of the Manor of Winterbourne Stoke 1574', *Wiltshire Archaeological Magazine,* 1905–6, xxxiv.

GODFREY, W. H. *The Booke of John Rowe,* Sussex Record Society, 1928, xxxiv.

GOLDNEY, F. H. *Records of Chippenham,* sine loco, 1889.

GONNER, E. C. K. *Common Land and Inclosure,* 1912.

GOOCH, W. *General View of the Agriculture of the County of Cambridge,* 1813.

GOODER, A. *Plague and Enclosure: A Warwickshire Village in the Seventeenth Century,* Coventry and North Warwickshire History Pamphlets, no. 2, 1965.

GOODMAN, F. R. *Reverend Landlords and their Tenants,* Winchester, 1930.

GOODSALL, R. H. *Whitstable, Seasalter and Swalecliffe,* 1938.

GOOGE, *see* HERESBACH.

GRAHAM, T. H. B. 'An Old Map of Hayton Manor', *Transactions of the Cumberland and Westmorland Antiquarian and Archaeological Society,* new series, 1907, vii.

GRAMOLT, D. W. 'The Coastal Marshlands of East Essex between the Seventeenth and the Mid-Nineteenth Centuries', typescript thesis, M.A., London University, 1960.

GRANGER, J. *A General View of the Agriculture of the County of Durham*, 1794.

GRAS, N. S. B. *A History of Agriculture in Europe and America*, no date.

—— *The Evolution of the English Corn Market*, Cambridge, Mass. 1926.

—— and E. C. *The Economic and Social History of an English Village*, Cambridge, Mass. 1930.

GRAY, H. L. *English Field Systems*, Cambridge, Mass., 1915.

GRAZIER, LINCOLNSHIRE, A, *see* YOUATT.

GREEN, E. 'On some Somerset Chap-books', *Proceedings of the Somerset Archaeological and Natural History Society*, 1878, xxiv, pt 2.

GREEN, R. *The History, Topography and Antiquities of Framlingham and Saxted*, 1834.

GRETTON, R. H. *The Burford Records*, Oxford, 1920.

GRIGGS, (Messrs) *A General View of the Agriculture of the County of Essex*, 1794.

GRINSELL, L. V., *et al. Studies in the History of Swindon*, Swindon, 1950.

GULLEY, J. L. M. 'The Wealden Landscape in the early seventeenth century and its Antecedents', typescript thesis Ph.D., London University, 1960.

GYNN, G. 'Thousand Gallon Herd on Watermeadows', *Farmer and Stockbreeder*, 1954, lxviii.

H., S. H. A. *Dairy of John Hervey, First Earl of Bristol*, Wells, 1894.

—— *Letter-Books of John Hervey, First Earl of Bristol*, 3 vols. Wells, 1894.

HALL, H. *Society in the Elizabethan Age*, 1887.

HALLIWELL, J. O. *Autobiography of Sir Simonds D'Ewes*, 2 vols. 1845.

—— *Ancient Inventories of Furniture, Pictures, Tapestry, Plate &c. illustrative of the Domestic Manners of the English in the Sixteenth and Seventeenth Centuries*, 1854.

HAMMOND, J. L., and B. *The Village Labourer*, Guild Book edition, 2 vols.

HAMMOND, R. J. 'Social and Economic Circumstances of Ket's Rebellion', typescript thesis M.A., London University, 1933.

HANDLEY, J. E. *Scottish Farming in the Eighteenth Century*, 1953.

HARDY, R. *Court Rolls of the Parish of Tatenhill, being 2nd volume of the History of the Parish of Tattenhill*, 1908.

HARLAND, J. *The House and Farm Accounts of the Shuttleworths of Gawthorpe Hall*, Chetham Society, 1856–8, xxxv, xli, xliii, xlvi.

HARRIS, A. *The Rural Landscape of the East Riding of Yorkshire 1700–1850*, 1961.

HARRIS, L. E. 'Sir Cornelius Vermuyden and the Great Level of the Fens. A New Judgment', *Proceedings of the Cambridge Antiquarian Society*, 1952 (1951), xlv.

—— *Vermuyden and the Fens*, 1953.

HARRISON, W. *Description of England*, (1577), edited by F. J. Furnivall, New Shakespeare Society, 1877.

HARRISON, W. 'Commons Inclosures in Lancashire and Cheshire in the Eighteenth Century', *Transactions of the Lancashire and Cheshire Antiquarian Society*, 1888, vi.

HARTLEY, M. and INGILBY, J. *Yorkshire Village*, 1953.

HASSALL, C. *A General View of the Agriculture of the County of Carmarthen*, 1794.
—— *A General View of the Agriculture of the County of Monmouth*, 1812.
—— *A General View of the Agriculture of the County of Pembroke*, 1794.
HAVINDEN, M. A. 'Agricultural Progress in Open-Field Oxfordshire', *Agricultural History Review*, 1961, ix.
—— 'The Rural Economy of Oxfordshire, 1580–1730', typescript thesis B. Litt., Oxford University, 1961.
HAVINDEN, M. A. *See also* Historical Manuscripts Commission.
HEDLEY, W. P. 'Manor of Simonburn and Warks Park', *Archaeologia Aeliana*, 4th series, 1952, xxx.
HELMSLEY AND AREA GROUP OF THE YORKSHIRE ARCHAEOLOGICAL SOCIETY, *A History of Helmsley, Rievaulx and District*, York, 1963.
HENHAM, W. N. 'Newnham Priory: a Bedford Rental 1506–7', in *Publications of the Bedfordshire Historical Record Society*, 1947, xxv.
HENNING, B. D. *The Parliamentary Diary of Sir Edward Dering 1670–3*, New Haven, 1940.
HERESBACH, C. *Foure Bookes of Husbandry*, edited by B. Googe, 1601.
[HERVEY, Lord Francis], *Ickworth Survey Booke*, sine loco, no date.
HEYWOOD, T. *The Moore Rental*, Chetham Society, 1847, xii.
HILL, J. W. F. *Medieval Lincoln*, Cambridge, 1948.
HILL, M. C. 'The Wealdmoors, 1560–1660', *Transactions of the Shropshire Archaeological Society*, 1953, (1951–3), liv.
HINE, R. *The History of Beaminster*, Taunton, 1914.
HINE, R. L. *The History of Hitchin*, 2 vols., 1927.
HINTON, R. W. K. *The Port Books of Boston 1601–40*, Lincolnshire Record Society Publications, 1956, l.
Historical Manuscripts Commission, *Household and Farm Inventories in Oxfordshire, 1550–90*, edited by M. A. Havinden, HMC Joint Publication 10, Oxford Record Society, xliv, HMSO, 1965, code no. 44-9050.*
Historical Manuscripts Commission, *Manuscripts of Lord Middleton*, HMSO, 1911, Cd. 5567.
Historical Manuscripts Commission, *Manuscripts of the Marquis of Salisbury at Hatfield House*, Pt ii, C. 5463, HMSO, 1888; Pt xiii (addenda), Cd. 7842, HMSO, 1915.
Historical Manuscripts Commission, *Manuscripts of the Duke of Buccleuch and Queensberry at Montagu House, vol. iii, The Montagu Papers, 2nd series*, vi, Wt. 18400, HMSO, 1926.
Historical Manuscripts Commission, *Report on Manuscripts in Various Collections, iii*, Cd., 1964, HMSO, 1904.
Historical Manuscripts Commission, *Manuscripts of the Duke of Rutland*, vol. iv, Cd. 2606, HMSO, 1905.
Historical Manuscripts Commission, *Report on the Manuscripts of the Duke of Portland at Welbeck Abbey*, vol. vi, Cd. 676, HMSO, 1901.
Historical Manuscripts Commission, *Fourteenth Report*, Appendix part iv, C. 7571, HMSO, 1894.
HITT, T. *A Treatise of Husbandry*, 1760.
HOARE, C. M. *The History of an East Anglian Soke*, Bedford, 1918.
HOARE, R. C. *The History of Modern Wiltshire*, 6 vols., 1822–44.

HOBSBAWM, E. J. 'The British Standard of Living, 1790–1850', *Economic History Review*, 2nd series, 1957, x.

HOELSCHER, L. 'Improvements in Fencing and Drainage in mid-nineteenth century England', *Agricultural History*, 1963, xxxvii.

HOLINSHED, R., and HARRISON, W. *Chronicles*, vols i and ii, 1586.

HOLLAND, H. *A General View of the Agriculture of Cheshire*, 1808.

HOLLOWAY, W. *The History of Romney Marsh*, 1849.

HOLT, J. *A General View of the Agriculture of the County of Lancaster*, 1794, 1795.

HONE, N. J. *The Manor and Manorial Records*, Antiquaries Books, 1912.

HOOPER, W. *Reigate*, Guildford, 1945.

HOPKINS, E. 'The Re-leasing of the Ellesmere Estates, 1637–42', *Agricultural History Review*, 1962, x.

HOSFORD, W. H. 'An Eye-witness's Account of a Seventeenth-Century Enclosure', *Economic History Review*, 2nd series, 1951, iv.

HOSKINS, W. G. 'Carts and Wagons', *Countryman*, 1950, xli.

—— *Essays in Leicestershire History*, Liverpool, 1950.

—— 'Reclamation of the Waste in Devon', *Economic History Review*, 1941–3, xiii.

—— 'The Leicestershire Farmer in the Seventeenth Century', *Agricultural History*, 1951, xxv.

—— *The Midland Peasant*, 1957.

—— and FINBERG, H. R. *Devonshire Studies*, 1952.

HOUGHTON, J. *A Collection for the Improvement of Husbandry and Trade*, edited by R. Bradley, 4 vols., 1727–8.

—— *A Collection of Letters for the Improvement of Husbandry and Trade*, 2 vols., 1681; and no. 7, Thursday, June 15, 1682.

HOWARD, H. F. *An Account of the Finances of the College of St John the Evangelist in the University of Cambridge*, Cambridge, 1935.

HOWELLS, B. E. 'Pembrokeshire Farming, *c.* 1580–1620', *National Library Wales Journal*, 1955–6, ix.

—— 'The Elizabethan Squirearchy in Pembrokeshire', *Pembrokeshire Historian*, 1959, i.

HOWSE, W. H. 'A Harley Miscellany', *Transactions of the Woolhope Naturalists' Field Club, Herefordshire*, 1958 (1955–7), xxxv.

HUDLESTON, C. R. *Naworth Estate and Household Accounts 1648–60*, Surtees Society, 1958, (1953), clxviii.

HUDSON, D., and LOCKHART, K. W. *The Royal Society of Arts 1754–1954*, 1954.

HUDSON, W. H. *A Shepherd's Life*, Everyman edition.

—— *Nature in Downland*, 1925.

HUGHES, E. *North Country Life in the Eighteenth Century* [i] *The North-East 1700–50*, 1952, ii *Cumberland and Westmorland*, 1965.

—— *Studies in Administration and Finance, 1558–1825*, Manchester, 1934.

HUGHES, P. L., and LARKIN, J. F. *Tudor Royal Proclamations: vol. i The Early Tudors (1485–1553)*, New York and London, 1964.

HULL, F. 'Agriculture and Rural Society in Essex, 1560–1640', typescript thesis Ph.D., London University, 1950.

HULME, H. 'A Probate Inventory of the goods and chattels of Sir John Eliot, late prisoner in the Tower, 1633', in *Camden Miscellany xvi*, Camden 3rd series, 1936, lii.

HURRY, J. B. *The Woad Plant and its Dye*, Oxford, 1930.

HUTTON, C., SHAW, G., and PEARSON, R. abridgement of *The Philosophical Transactions of the Royal Society of London*, 18 vols., 1809.

HYDE, F. E., and MARKHAM, S. F. *A History of Stony Stratford*, Wolverton and London, 1948.

'INCOLA', 'The Natural History of Sutton Coldfield', *Gentleman's Magazine*, 1762, xxxii.

'INGENUUS', 'A Description of the Parish of Bromborough in Cheshire', *Gentleman's Magazine*, 1762, xxxii.

INGLEBY, C. M. *Shakespeare and the Enclosure of Common Fields at Welcombe*, Birmingham, 1885.

JACKS, G. V. *Soil*, 1954.

JACKSON, C. 'Notes from the Court Rolls of the Manor of Epworth in the County of Lincoln', *The Reliquary*, 1882–3, xxiii.

JACKSON, J. E. 'Chippenham Notes', *Wiltshire Archaeological Magazine*, 1870, xii, 1872, xiii.

—— 'On the History of Chippenham', *Wiltshire Archaeological Magazine*, 1856, iii.

—— 'Selwood Forest', *Wiltshire Archaeological Magazine*, 1887, xxiii.

—— 'Vale of Warminster', *Wiltshire Archaeological Magazine*, 1878, xvii.

JAMES, M. E. *Estate Accounts of the Earls of Northumberland 1562–1637*, Surtees Society 1955 (1948), clxiii.

JAMES, W., and MALCOLM, J. *A General View of the Agriculture of the County of Buckingham*, 1794.

—— *A General View of the Agriculture of the County of Surrey*, 1794.

JEFFERY, R. W. *The Manors and Advowson of Great Rollright*, Oxfordshire Record Society, 1927, ix.

—— *Thornton-le-Dale*, Wakefield, 1931.

JOHNSON, S. A. 'Enclosure and Changing Agricultural Landscapes in Lindsey', *Agricultural History Review*, 1963, xi.

JONES, E. D. 'An Inventory of a Pembrokeshire Squire's Chattels, 1629', *National Library of Wales Journal*, 1953–4, viii.

JONES, E. G. 'Plas Cadwgan in 1586: An Inventory of the goods and chattels of Edward Jones Esquire', *Denbighshire Historical Society's Transactions*, 1957, vi.

JONES, E. J. 'The Enclosure Movement in Anglesey (1788–1866)', *Anglesey Antiquarian Society and Field Club Transactions*, 1925.

JONES, E. M. *Exchequer Proceedings (Equity) Concerning Wales: Henry VIII–Elizabeth*, Cardiff, 1939.

KALM, P. *Kalm's Account of his Visit to England*, 1892.

KAY, G. *A General View of the Agriculture of North Wales*, Edinburgh, 1794.

KEEN, R. 'Inventory of Richard Hooker, 1601', *Archaeologia Cantiana*, 1957, (1956), lxx.

KENNEDY, P. A. 'A Gentleman's Home in the Reign of Henry VIII', *Northamptonshire Past and Present*, 1954, ii, no. 1.

KENNEDY, P. A. *Nottinghamshire Household Inventories*, Thoroton Society Record Series, 1963, (1962), xxii.

KENT, N. *A General View of the Agriculture of the County of Norfolk*, Norwich, 1796.

—— *Hints to Gentlemen of Landed Property*, 1775.

KENYON, G. H. 'Kirdford Inventories, 1611 to 1776', *Sussex Archaeological Collections*, 1955, xciii.

KERRIDGE, E. 'A Reconsideration of some former Husbandry Practices', *Agricultural History Review*, 1955, iii.

—— *Surveys of the Manors of Philip Earl of Pembroke and Montgomery 1631–2*, Wiltshire Archaeological and Natural History Society Records Branch, 1953, ix.

—— 'The Agrarian Development of Wiltshire, 1540–1640', typescript thesis Ph.D., London University, 1951.

—— 'The Movement of Rent, 1540–1640', *Economic History Review*, 2nd series, 1953, vi.

—— 'The Notebook of a Wiltshire Farmer in the early seventeenth century', *Wiltshire Archaeological Magazine*, 1951–2, liv.

KERRY, Earl of, 'King's Bowood Park', *Wiltshire Archaeological Magazine*, 1920–2, xli.

KING, H., and HARRIS, A. *A Survey of the Manor of Settrington*, Yorkshire Archaeological Society Record Series, 1962, cxxvi.

KINGSTON, A. *A History of Royston*, 1906.

KIRBY, J. *The Suffolk Traveller*, 2nd edition, 1764.

KIRK, G. E. 'Wills, inventories and bonds of the manor courts of Temple Newsam, 1612–1701', in *Miscellanea*, Thoresby Society Publications, 1935, xxxiii.

KITCHIN, G. W. *The Manor of Manydown*, Hampshire Record Society, 1895, x.

KYNDER, P. 'The Historie of Darbyshire' (1663), *The Reliquary*, 1881–2, xxii.

L., E. A. 'The Goods and Chattels of a Cardiganshire Esquire in 1633', *Cardigan Antiquarian Society's Transactions*, 1936, xi.

L., J. *A Discourse concerning the great benefit of Drayning and imbanking and of transportation by Water within the Country*, sine loco, 1641.

LAMBARD, W. *A Perambulation of Kent*, 1576.

LAMBERT, H. C. M. *History of Banstead in Surrey*, Oxford, 2 vols., 1912.

LAMOND, E. *A Discourse &c*, see Anonymous or various.

LANGHAM, W. *The Garden of Health*, 1579 (1578?).

LATIMER, H. *Sermons*, Everyman edition.

LAURENCE, E. *The Duty of a Steward to his Lord*, 1727.

LAURENCE, J. *A New System of Agriculture*, 1726.

LAVROVSKY, V. M. 'Expropriation of the English Peasantry in the Eighteenth Century', *Economic History Review*, 2nd series, 1956, ix.

LAWSON-TANCRED, T. 'Three Seventeenth-century Court Rolls of the Manor of Aldborough', *Yorkshire Archaeological Journal*, 1943, xxxv.

—— *Records of a Yorkshire Manor*, 1937.

LEADAM, I. *The Domeday of Inclosures*, 2 vols., 1897.

—— 'The Inquisition of 1517. Inclosures and Evictions', *Transactions of the Royal Historical Society*, 1892, 1893, 1894, vi, vii, viii.

LEATHAM, I. *A General View of the Agriculture of the East Riding of Yorkshire*, 1794.

LEAVER, J. D. W. 'Leyland: a Lancashire Manor in the sixteenth and seventeenth centuries', typescript dissertation B.A., Nottingham University, 1952.

LECONFIELD, (Lord) *Petworth Manor in the Seventeenth Century*, 1954.

—— *Sutton and Duncton Manors*, 1956.

LEE, J. *A Vindication of a Regulated Inclosure*, 1656.

LEIGH, C. *The Natural History of Lancashire, Cheshire and the Peak in Derbyshire*, Oxford, 1700.

LEIGH, E. *England Described*, 1659.

LELAND, J. *The Itinerary*, edited by L. T. Smith, 5 vols. 1906–10.

LENNARD, R. V. *Rural Northamptonshire under the Commonwealth*, in Oxford Studies in Social and Legal History, ed. P. Vinogradoff, vol. V, Oxford, 1916.

—— 'English Agriculture under Charles II: The Evidence of the Royal Society's "Enquiries" ', *Economic History Review*, 1932–4, iv.

LENNARD, T. B. 'Extracts from the Household Account Book of Herstmonceux Castle, from August, 1643, to December, 1649', *Sussex Archaeological Collections*, 1905, xlviii.

LEONARD, E. M. *The Early History of English Poor Relief*, Cambridge, 1900.

—— 'The Inclosure of Common Fields in the Seventeenth Century', *Transactions of the Royal Historical Society*, new series, 1905, xix.

LEVY, H. *Large and Small Holdings: A Study of English Agricultural Economics*, Cambridge, 1911.

LEWIS, E. A. *The Welsh Port Books (1550–1603)*, Cymmrodorion Record Series, 1927, xii.

LINDLEY, E. S. *Wotton under Edge*, 1962.

LISLE, E. *Observations in Husbandry*, 1757.

LLOYD, T. *A General View of the Agriculture of the County of Cardigan*, 1794.

LLWYD, A. *A History of the Island of Mona*, Ruthin, 1833.

LODER, R. *The History of Framlingham*, Woodbridge, 1798.

LODGE, E. C. *The Account Book of a Kentish Estate 1616–1704*, British Academy, 1927.

LOMAS, H. A. *History of Abbotsham*, Abbotsham, 1956.

LONDON COUNTY COUNCIL, *Court Minutes of the Surrey and Kent Sewer Commission 1569–79*, 1909.

LONG, W. H. 'Regional Farming in Seventeenth-century Yorkshire', *Agricultural History Review*, 1960, viii.

LOWE, R. *A General View of the Agriculture of the County of Nottingham*, 1798.

LUCCOCK, J. *An Essay on Wool*, 1809.

LYTE, H. U. M. *A History of Dunster and the Families of Mohun and Luttrell*, 1909.

LYTHE, S. G. E. *The Economy of Scotland in its European Setting*, Edinburgh and London, 1960.

MACINNES, C. M. *The Early English Tobacco Trade*, 1926.

MACLEAN, J. 'History of the Manor and Advowson of Clifford Chambers', *Transactions of the Bristol and Gloucestershire Archaeological Society*, 1889–90, xiv.

MADDOCK, H. E. 'Court Rolls of Patrington Manors', *Transactions of the East Riding Archaeological Society*, 1900, viii.

MADGE, S. J. 'Rural Middlesex under the Commonwealth', *Transactions of the London and Middlesex Archaeological Society*, new series, 1921–2, iv.

—— *The Domesday of Crown Lands*, 1938.

MANLEY, F. H. 'Customs of the Manor of Purton', *Wiltshire Archaeological Magazine*, 1917–19, xl.

—— 'Parliamentary Surveys of the Crown Lands in Braden Forest (1651), *Wiltshire Archaeological Magazine*, 1932–4, xlvi.

MARCHAM, W. M. and F. *Court Rolls of the Bishop of London's Manor of Hornsey 1603–1701*, 1929.

MARKHAM, G. *The Inrichment of the Weald of Kent*, 1625.

—— *The English Husbandman*, 1635.

—— *A Way to get Wealth*, 1638.

MARSHALL, T. H. 'Jethro Tull and the New Husbandry', *Economic History Review*, 1929–30, ii.

MARSHALL, W. *A Review of the Reports to the Board of Agriculture from the Eastern Department of England*, 1811.

—— *A Review of the Reports to the Board of Agriculture from the Northern Department of England*, 1808.

—— *A Review of the Reports to the Board of Agriculture from the Western Department of England*, 1810.

—— *A Review (and Complete Abstract) of the Reports to the Board of Agriculture from the Midland Department of England*, 1815.

—— *A Review (and Complete Abstract) of the Reports to the Board of Agriculture from the Southern and Peninsular Departments of England*, 1817.

—— *Experiments and Observations Concerning Agriculture and the Weather*, 1779.

—— *Minutes, Experiments, Observations and General Remarks on Agriculture in the Southern Counties*, 2 vols., 1799.

—— *On the Appropriation and Inclosure of Commonable and Intermixed Lands*, 1801.

—— *On the Landed Property of England*, 1804.

—— 'On the new Leicestershire sheep', in A. Hunter, *Georgical Essays*, vol. iv, York, 1803.

—— *The Rural Economy of Glocestershire*, 2 vols., Gloucester, 1789.

—— *The Rural Economy of the Midland Counties*, 2 vols., 1790.

—— *The Rural Economy of Norfolk*, 2 vols., 1787.

—— *The Rural Economy of the Southern Counties*, 2 vols, 1798.

—— *The Rural Economy of the West of England*, 2 vols, 1796.

—— *The Rural Economy of Yorkshire*, 2 vols, 1788.

MARSHALL, W., REDHEAD, –., and LAING, –. *Observations on the Different Breeds of Sheep*, Edinburgh, 1792.

MARTIN, J. M. 'Social and Economic Trends in the Rural West Midlands, 1785–1825', typescript thesis M.Comm., Birmingham University, 1960.

MASCALL, L. *Cattell*, 1587.

MASTIN, J. *The History and Antiquities of Naseby*, Cambridge, 1792.

MAVOR, W. *A General View of the Agriculture of Berkshire*, 1808.

MAXEY, E. *A New Inst[r]uction of plowing and setting of corne*, 1601.

MAXWELL, G. *A General View of the Agriculture of the County of Huntingdon*, 1793.

MCCLURE, N. E. *The Letters of John Chamberlain*, 2 vols, Philadelphia, 1939.

MCDONALD, D. *Agricultural Writers from Sir Walter of Henley to Arthur Young, 1200–1800*, 1908.

MELLING, E. *Kentish Sources iii: Aspects of Agriculture and Industry*, Maidstone, 1961.

MELLOWS, W. T. *Peterborough Local Administration. Parochial Government before the Reformation. Churchwarden's Accounts, 1467–1573, with supplementary documents, 1107–1488*, Northamptonshire Record Society, 1939, ix.

—— *Peterborough Local Administration. Parochial Government from the Reformation to the Revolution, 1541–1689. Minutes and Accounts of the Feoffees and Governors of the City Lands, with supplementary documents*, Northamptonshire Record Society, 1937, x.

MERRICK, R. *A Booke of Glamorganshires Antiquities*, (1578), edited by J. A. Corbett, 1887.

MIDDLETON, J. *View of the Agriculture of Middlesex*, 1798.

MIDGLEY, L. M. 'A Terryar for Audley Parish for 1708 and the manner of titheing with the vicar', *Collections for the History of Staffordshire*, 3rd series, 1947, (1944).

MILLS, D. R. 'Enclosure in Kesteven', *Agricultural History Review*, 1959, vii.

MIMARDIÈRE, A. M. 'The Warwickshire Gentry, 1660–1730', typescript thesis M.A., Birmingham University, 1963.

MINGAY, G. E. 'Estate Management in Eighteenth-century Kent', *Agricultural History Review*, 1956, iv.

—— 'The Agricultural Depression, 1730–50', *Economic History Review*, 2nd series, 1956, viii.

—— 'The "Agricultural Revolution" in English History: A Reconsideration', *Agricultural History*, 1963, xxxvii.

MITCHELL, J. 'On the Preparation and Uses of various kinds of Potash', *Philosophical Transactions*, ix, see Hutton *et al.*

MOFFIT, L. W. *England on the Eve of the Industrial Revolution*, 1925.

MOIR, E. 'Benedict Webb, Clothier', *Economic History Review*, 2nd series, 1957, x.

MONEY, W. *A Purveyance of the Royal Household in the Elizabethan Age, 1575*, Newbury, 1901.

MONK, J. *A General View of the Agriculture of the County of Leicester*, 1794.

MOORE, A. *Bread for the Poor and Advancement of the English Nation*, 1653.

MOORE, J. *The Crying Sin of England of not caring for the Poor*, 1653.

—— *A Scripture-Word against Inclosures viz. such as doe Un-people Townes, and Un-corne Fields*, 1656.

MOORE, J. *The History or Narrative of the Great Level of the Fenns called the Bedford Level*, 1685.

MOORE, S. A. *A History of the Foreshore and the Law relating thereto*, 1888.

MORETON, C. O. *Waddesdon and Over Winchendon*, 1929.

MORRIS, W. *Swindon Fifty Years Ago, More or Less*, Swindon, no date.

MORTIMER, J. *The Whole Art of Husbandry*, 1707.

MORTON, J. *The Natural History of Northamptonshire*, 1712.

MOWAT, J. L. G. *16 Old Maps of Properties in Oxfordshire*, Oxford, 1888.

MUNDY, P. D. *Abstracts of Star Chamber Proceedings relating to the County of Sussex*, Sussex Record Society, 1913, xvi.

MURRAY, A. *A General View of the Agriculture of the County of Warwick*, 1813.

NAISH, M. C. 'The Agricultural Landscape of the Hampshire Chalklands, 1700–1840', typescript thesis M.A., London University, 1960.

NEF, J. U. *The Rise of the British Coal Industry*, 2 vols. 1931.

—— *The Conquest of the Material World*, Chicago and London, 1964.

NICHOLS, J. G. *The Unton Inventories relating to Wadley and Faringdon*, Berkshire Ashmolean Society, 1841.

NICHOLSON, H. H. *The Principles of Field Drainage*, Cambridge, 1944.

NORDEN, J. *The Surveiors Dialogue*, 1618.

—— *Speculi Britanniae: An Historical and Chorographical Description of Middlesex and Hartfordshire*, 1593.

—— *Speculi Britanniae Pars: The Description of Hartfordshire*, 1598.

—— *Speculi Britanniae Pars: Description of Cornwall*, 1728.

—— *Speculi Britanniae Pars: An Historical and Chorographical Description of the county of Essex* (1594), edited by H. Ellis, Camden Society, 1840 [ix].

—— *The Chorography of Norfolk*, edited by C. H. Hood, Norwich, 1938.

NOTESTEIN, W., RELF, F. H., and SIMPSON, H. *Commons Debates 1621*, New Haven, 7 vols, 1935.

NOURSE, T. *Campania Foelix*, 1700.

ORWIN, C. S., and C. S. *The Open Fields*, Oxford, 1938.

OWEN, G. *The Description of Penbrokshire*, edited by H. Owen, 4 parts, Cymmrodorion Record Series, no. 1, 1892–1936.

—— *The Taylors Cussion*, edited by E. M. Pritchard, 1906.

OWEN, G. D. *Elizabethan Wales*, Cardiff, 1962.

OWEN, T. M. 'Some Lleyn Inventories of the Seventeenth and Eighteenth Centuries', *Transactions of the Caernarvonshire Historical Society*, 1960, xxi.

PALMER, W. M. *A History of the Parish of Borough Green, Cambridgeshire*, Cambridge Antiquarian Society, Octavo Publications, 1939, liv.

PARKER, L. A. 'The Depopulation Returns for Leicestershire in 1607', *Transactions of the Leicestershire Archaeological Society*, 1947, xxiii.

PARKER, R. A. C. 'Coke of Norfolk and the Agrarian Revolution', *Economic History Review*, 2nd series, 1955, viii.

PARKES, J. *Travel in England in the Seventeenth Century*, Oxford, 1925.

PARKINSON, J. *Theatrum Botanicum*, 1640.

PARKINSON, R. *A General View of the Agriculture of the County of Huntingdon*, 1813.

—— *A General View of the Agriculture of the County of Rutland*, 1808.

PASSMORE, J. B. *The English Plough*, Oxford, 1930.

PAWSON, H. C. *Robert Bakewell: Pioneer Livestock Breeder*, 1957.

PEARCE, W. *A General View of the Agriculture in Berkshire*, 1794.

'Person of Honour, A', *Saint Foine Improved: A Discourse shewing the Utility and Benefit which England hath and may receive by the Grasse called St Foine*, 1674.

PETTIT, P. A. J. 'The Economy of the Northamptonshire Royal Forests, 1558–1714', typescript thesis D.Phil., Oxford University, 1959.

PETTY, W. *Economic Writings*, edited by C. H. Hull, 2 vols, Cambridge, 1899.

PHILLIMORE, W. P. W. and FRY, G. S. *Abstracts of Gloucestershire Inquisitiones Post Mortem in the Reign of King Charles the First*, Index Library, British Record Society, 3 parts (vols), 1893–9.

PHILLIPS, D. R. *The History of the Vale of Neath*, Swansea, 1925.

PHILLIPS, H. *History of Cultivated Vegetables*, 2 vols, 1822.

PICCOPE, G. P. *Lancashire and Cheshire Wills and Inventories from the Ecclesiastical Court, Chester*, 3 portions Chetham Society, 1857, 1860–1, xxxiii, li, liv.

PICKERING, R. 'On the Manuring of Land with Fossil Shells', *Philosophical Transactions*, ix, see Hutton *et al.*

PITT, W. *A General View of the Agriculture of the County of Stafford*, 1794 and 1796.

—— *A General View of the Agriculture of the County of Northampton*, 1806 and 1809.

—— *A General View of the Agriculture of the County of Leicester*, 1809.

—— *A General View of the Agriculture of the County of Worcester*, 1813.

PLATT(E), H. *The Jewell House of Art and Nature*, 1594.

PLOT, R. *The Natural History of Oxfordshire*, Oxford, 1676.

—— *The Natural History of Staffordshire*, Oxford, 1686.

PLUMB, J. H. 'Sir Robert Walpole and Norfolk Husbandry', *Economic History Review*, 2nd series, 1952, v.

—— *Sir Robert Walpole*, 1956.

PLYMLEY, J. *A General View of the Agriculture of Shropshire*, 1803.

POLLARD, A. F. and BLATCHER, M. 'Hayward Townshend's Journals', *Bulletin of the Institute of Historical Research*, 1934–5, (1935), xii.

POMEROY, W. *A General View of the Agriculture of the County of Worcester*, 1794.

POSTGATE, M. R. 'The Field Systems of Breckland', *Agricultural History Review*, 1962, x.

—— 'Historical Geography of Breckland, 1600–1850', typescript thesis M.A., London University, 1960.

POTTER, S. P. *A History of Wymeswold*, 1915.

POWELL, A. *John Aubrey and his Friends*, 1948.

POWELL, E. 'Pryce (Newtown Hall) Correspondence, Etc.' *Collections Historical and Archaeological relating to Montgomeryshire*, 1900, xxxi.

POWER, E. *The Wool Trade in Medieval England*, Oxford, 1941.

PRESTON, W. E. *Wills proved in the Court of the Manor of Crosley, Bingley, Cottingley, and Pudsey, in co. York, with inventories and abstracts of bonds*, Bradford Historical and Antiquarian Society, Local Record Series, 1929, (1914–29), i.

PRIEST, ST J. *A General View of the Agriculture of Buckinghamshire*, 1813.

PRINGLE, A. *A General View of the Agriculture of the County of Westmoreland*, 1805.

PUGH, R. B. *Calendar of Antrobus Deeds before 1625*, Wiltshire Natural History and Archaeological Society Records Branch, 1947, iii.

PURVIS, J. S. 'A Note on XVI Century Farming in Yorkshire', *Yorkshire Archaeological Journal*, 1944–7, xxxvi.

—— *Bridlington Charters, Court Rolls and Papers*, 1926.

—— *Select XVI Century Causes in Tithe from the York Diocesan Registry*, Yorkshire Archaeological Society Record Series, 1949 (1947), cxiv.

RADCLIFFE-COOKE, C. 'John Noble's Household and Farm Accounts 1696–1719', *Transactions of the Woolhope Naturalists' Field Club*, 1959–61, (1958–60), xxxvi.

RAINE, J. *Wills and Inventories from the Registry of the Archdeacon of Richmond*, Surtees Society, 1853, xxvi.

RAISTRICK, A. *Malham and Malham Moor*, Clapham via Lancaster, 1947.

RANDALL, H. J. *Bridgend: The Story of a Market Town*, Newport, Mon. 1955.

RATCLIFFE, S. C., and JOHNSON, H. C. *Warwick County Records ii: Quarter Sessions Order Book, 1637–50*, Warwick, 1936.

RAY, J. *Historia Plantarum*, 3 vols, 1686–1704.

REA, W. F. 'The Rental and Accounts of Sir Richard Shireburn, 1571–7', *Transactions of the Historic Society for Lancashire and Cheshire,* 1959, (1958), CX.

RECORD COMMISSION, *see* Anonymous or various, Calendars.

REDSTONE, V. B. 'The Diary of Sir Thomas Davies', *Surrey Archaeological Collections*, 1926, xxxvii, part i.

REES, W. *South Wales and the March, 1284-1415*, Oxford, 1924.

—— *A Survey of the Duchy of Lancaster Lordships in Wales, 1609–13*, Cardiff, 1953.

RENDALL, G. H. *Dedham in History*, Colchester, 1937.

REYCE, R. *The Breviary of Suffolk* (1618), edited by Lord F. Hervey, 1902.

RICE, M. A. *Abbots Bromley*, 1939.

RICHES, N. *The Agricultural Revolution in Norfolk*, Chapel Hill, 1937.

RICKARD, R. L. *The Progress Notes of Warden Woodward round the Oxfordshire Estates of New College, Oxford, 1659–75*, Oxfordshire Record Society [1949], xxvii.

—— *Progress Notes of Warden Woodward for the Wiltshire Estates of New College, Oxford, 1659–75*, Wiltshire Archaeological and Natural History Society Records Branch, 1957, xiii.

RIDER-HAGGARD, H. *Rural England*, 2 vols, 1906.

RISDON, T. *The Chorographical Description or Survey of the County of Devon*, 1723.

RITCHIE, J. *Reports of Cases decided by Francis Bacon in the Court of Chancery (1617–21)*, 1932.

RIVE, A. 'The Consumption of Tobacco since 1600', *Economic History*, 1926, i.

ROBERTS, R. A. 'Trends in semi-natural hill pastures from the eighteenth century', *Fourth International Grassland Conference Report*, Aberystwyth, 1937.

ROBINSON, T. *An Essay towards a Natural History of Westmorland and Cumberland*, 1709.

ROCHEFOUCAULD, F. DE LA, *A Frenchman in England 1784*, Cambridge, 1933.

ROSS, K. N. *A History of Malden*, New Malden, 1947.

ROWE, J. *Cornwall in the Age of the Industrial Revolution*, Liverpool, 1953.

ROWLANDS, H. *Idea Agriculturae: The Principles of Vegetation Asserted and Defended*, Dublin, 1764.

ROWLEY-MORRIS, E. 'History of the Parish of Kerry', *Collections Historical and Archaeological relating to Montgomeryshire*, 1893, xxvii.

ROWSE, A. L. *Tudor Cornwall*, 1941.

—— *The England of Elizabeth*, 1950.

RUSTON, A. G., and WITNEY, D. *Hooton Pagnell*, 1934.

RYLAND, J. W. *Records of Rowington*, Birmingham, [1896].

RYLANDS, J. P. *Lancashire Inquisitions returned into the Chancery of the Duchy of Lancaster, Stuart Period*, 3 parts, The Record Society for Lancashire and Cheshire, 1880, iii, 1887, xvi, 1888, xvii.

SACHSE, W. L. *The Diary of Roger Lowe*, 1938.

SACKVILLE-WEST, V. *Knole and the Sackvilles*, 1923.

SALAMAN, R. N. *The History and Social Influence of the Potato*, Cambridge, 1949.

SALISBURY, E. (Sir) *Downs and Dunes: their plant life and environment*, 1952.

SALMON, W. *The English Herbal*, 1710.

SALT, E. *The History of Standon*, 1888.

SALTMARSH, J. 'A College Home Farm in the Fifteenth Century', *Economic History*, 1934–7, iii.

SALTMARSH, J., and DARBY, H. C. 'The Infield-Outfield System on a Norfolk Manor', *Economic History*, 1934–7, iii.

SAUNDERS, H. W. *The Official Papers of Sir Nathaniel Bacon, 1580–1620*, Royal Historical Society, Camden, 3rd series, 1915, xxvi.

SAVINE, A. *English Monasteries on the Eve of the Dissolution*, in Oxford Studies in Social and Legal History, vol. i, Oxford, 1909.

SCOT, R. *A Perfite Platforme of a Hoppe Garden*, 1576.

SCOTT, S. H. *A Westmorland Village*, Westminster, 1904.

SCOTT, W. R. *The Constitution and Finance of English, Scottish and Irish Joint Stock Companies to 1720*, 3 vols, Cambridge, 1910–11.

SCROPE, G. P. *History of the Manor Ancient Barony of Castle Combe in the county of Wiltshire*, sine loco, 1852.

SEEBOHM, F. *The English Village Community*, 1883.

SHAW, R. C. *Kirkham in Amounderness*, Preston, 1949.

—— *The Records of a Lancashire Family from the twelfth to the twentieth century*, Preston, 1940.

—— *The Royal Forest of Lancaster*, Preston, 1956.

SHEPPARD, J. A. 'The Draining of the Marshlands of East Yorkshire', typescript thesis Ph.D., London University, 1956.

SIMPSON, A. 'The East Anglian Foldcourse: Some Queries', *Agricultural History Review*, 1958, vi.

SINCLAIR, J. *Agricultural Hints*, no date.

SKEEL, C. 'The Cattle Trade between England and Wales from the Fifteenth to the Nineteenth Centuries', *Transactions of the Royal Historical Society*, 4th series, 1926, ix.

—— 'Wales under Henry VII', in *Tudor Studies* edited by R. W. Seton-Watson, 1924.

SLACK, W. J. *The Lordship of Oswestry*, Shrewsbury, 1951.

SLATER, G. *The English Peasantry and the Enclosure of Common Fields*, 1907.

SLICHER VAN BATH, B. H. 'The Rise of Intensive Husbandry in the Low Countries', in Bromley, J. S. & Kossmann, E. H. *Britain and the Netherlands*, 1960.

—— 'Yield Ratios, 810–1820', being *Afdeling Agrarische Geschiedenis Bijdragen*, 10, 1963.

SMITH, A. *The Wealth of Nations*, edited by E. Cannan, 2 vols, 1904.

SMITH, R. 'Some Account of the Formation of Hill-side Catchmeadows in Exmoor', *Journal of the Royal Agricultural Society of England*, 1851, xii.

SMITH, W. *History of the County of Warwick*, Birmingham, 1830.

SMITH, W. *Observations on the Utility, Form and Management of Water-meadows*, Norwich, 1806.

SMITH, W., and WEBB, W. *The Vale Royall of England*, 1656.

SMITH, W. J. 'Three Salesbury Mansions in 1601', *Bulletin of the Board of Celtic Studies*, 1954, xv.

SMYTH, J. *A Description of the Hundred of Berkeley*, Berkeley MSS., iii, edited by Sir J. Maclean, Gloucester, 1885.

—— *The Lives of the Berkeleys*, Berkeley MSS, vols. i and ii, edited by Sir J. Maclean, 2 vols, London, 1883, vol. ii.

SOMERVILLE, R. *History of the Duchy of Lancaster*, vol. i, 1953.

SPEED, A. *Adam out of Eden*, 1659.

SPRATT, J. 'Agrarian Conditions in Norfolk and Suffolk, 1600–50', typescript thesis M.A., London University, 1935.

SPUFFORD, M. 'Rural Cambridgeshire 1520–1680', typescript thesis M.A., Leicester University, 1962.

STANDISH, A. *The Commons Complaint*, 1611.

STAPLEDON, G. (Sir) *The Way of the Land*, 1943.

STAPLEDON, G., and DAVIES, W. *Ley Farming*, 1948.

STEELE, R. *Tudor and Stuart Proclamations*, vol. i, Oxford, 1910.

STEER, F. W. *Farm and Cottage Inventories of Mid-Essex 1635–1749*, Chelmsford, 1950.

STEERS, J. A. *The Coastline of England and Wales*, Cambridge, 1946.

STEVENSON, W. *A General View of the Agriculture of the County of Dorset*, 1812.

—— *A General View of the Agriculture of the County of Surrey*, 1813.

STEWART-BROWN, R. (H.) *History of the Manor and Township of Allerton*, Liverpool, 1911.

—— *Lancashire and Cheshire Cases in the Court of Star Chamber*, pt i, The Record Society for Lancashire and Cheshire, 1916, lxxi.

—— 'The Townfield of Liverpool, 1207–1807', *Transactions of the Historic Society of Lancashire and Cheshire*, 1917, lxviii.

—— *Cheshire Inquisitions Post Mortem: Stuart Period, 1603–60*, The Record Society for Lancashire and Cheshire, 1934, lxxxiv, 1935, lxxxvi, 1938, xci.

STOCKS, H. *Records of the Borough of Leicester 1603–88*, Cambridge, 1923.

STOCKS, J. E. *Market Harborough Parish Records 1531–1837*, 1926.

STONE, T. *A General View of the Agriculture of the County of Bedford*, 1794.

—— *A General View of the Agriculture of the County of Huntingdon*, 1793.

—— *A General View of the Agriculture of the County of Lincoln*, 1794.

—— *A Review of the Corrected Agricultural Survey of Lincolnshire by Arthur Young Esquire*, 1800.

STOVIN, G. 'A brief account of the Drainage of the Levells of Hatfield Chase and parts adjacent . . .', *Yorkshire Archaeological Journal*, 1948–51, xxxvii.

STRAKER, E. *Wealden Iron*, 1931.

—— *The Buckhurst Terrier 1597–8*, Sussex Record Society, 1933, xxxix.

STRATON, C. R. *Survey of the Lands of William, first Earl of Pembroke*, 2 vols, Roxburghe Club, 1909.

STRICKLAND, H. E. *A General View of the Agriculture of the East Riding of Yorkshire*, York, 1812.

SUCKLING, A. *The History and Antiquities of the County of Suffolk*, 2 vols, 1846.

SUTTON, C. W. 'A Survey of the Manor of Penwortham 1570', *Chetham Miscellanies iii*, Chetham Society, new series, 1915, lxxiii.

SWITZER, S. *A Compendious Method . . . as also an Account of the La Lucerne, St Foyne, Clover and Grass Seeds*, 4th edition, 1729.
—— *A Dissertation on the True Cythisus of the Ancients*, 1731.
—— *The Practical Fruit-gardener*, 1724.
SYLVESTER, D. 'Rural Settlement in Cheshire', *Transactions of the Historic Society of Lancashire and Cheshire*, 1950, (1949), ci.
SYLVESTER, D. 'The Open Fields of Cheshire', *Transactions of the Historic Society of Lancashire and Cheshire*, 1956, cviii.
—— 'The Common Fields of the Coastland of Gwent', *Agricultural History Review*, 1958, vi.
TATE, W. *The Parish Chest*, Cambridge, 1951.
TATHAM, W. *National Irrigation or the various methods of watering meadows*, 1801.
TAVENER, L. E. *The Common Lands of Hampshire*, Hants. C.C., no date.
TAVERNER, J. *Certaine Experiments concerning Fish and Fruite*, 1600.
TAWNEY, R. H. *The Agrarian Problem in the Sixteenth Century*, 1912.
TAWNEY, R. H., and POWER, E. *Tudor Economic Documents*, 3 vols, 1924.
TEMPLE, R. C. Sir, *The Travels of Peter Mundy in Europe and Asia 1608–67*, vol. iv *Travels in Europe 1639–47*, Hakluyt Society, 1925, series II, vol. lv.
THIRSK, J. *English Peasant Farming*, 1957.
—— *Fenland Farming in the Sixteenth Century*, Leicester, 1953.
—— 'The Isle of Axholme before Vermuyden', *Agricultural History Review*, 1953, i.
THOMAS, H. R. 'The Enclosure of Open Fields and Commons in Staffordshire', *Collections for History of Staffordshire*, 3rd series, 1933 (1931).
THOMAS, W. S. K. 'A Swansea Inventory—John Moris', *Gower*, 1957, x.
THOMAS-STANFORD, C. *An Abstract of the Court Rolls of the Manor of Preston, (Preston Episcopi)*, Sussex Record Society, 1921, xxvii.
TOMLINSON, J. *The Level of Hatfield Chace*, Doncaster, 1882.
TOUGH, D. L. W. *The Last Years of a Frontier*, Oxford, 1928.
TREGELLES, J. A. *A History of Hoddesdon*, Hertford, 1908.
TROW-SMITH, R. *A History of British Livestock Husbandry to 1700*, 1957.
—— *A History of British Livestock Husbandry 1750–1900*, 1959.
TUCKER, G. S. L. *Progress and Profits in British Economic Thought 1650–1850*, Cambridge, 1960.
TUKE, –. *A General View of the Agriculture of the North Riding of Yorkshire*, 1794, 1800.
TULL, J. *The Horse-Hoeing Husbandry*, edited by W. Cobbett, 1822.
TUPLING, G. H. *The Economic History of Rossendale*, Chetham Society new series, 1927, lxxxvi.
TURNER, G. *A General View of the Agriculture of the County of Gloucester*, 1794.
TURNER, W. *The first and second partes of the Herbal*, Cologne, 1568.
—— *The Names of Herbes*, edited by J. Britten, English Dialect Society, series D, 1881.
TURTON, R. B. *The Honor and Forest of Pickering*, 2 vols, North Riding Record Society, new series, 1894, i, 1895, ii.
TUSSER, T. *A Hundreth Good Pointes of Husbandrie*, facsimile of 1571 edition, edited by D. Hartley, 1931.

TWEMLOW, F. R. *The Twemlows: their Wives and their Houses*, Wolverhampton, 1910.

—— 'The Manor of Tyrley in the County of Stafford', *Collections for the History of Staffordshire*, 3rd series, 1945–6 (1948).

TYMMS, S. *Wills and Inventories from the Registers of the Commissary of Bury St Edmunds and the Archdeaconry of Sudbury*, Camden Society, 1850, xlix.

USHER, A. P. 'Soil Fertility and Exhaustion and their Historical Significance', *Quarterly Journal of Economics*, 1923, xxvii.

VANCOUVER, C. *A General View of the Agriculture in the County of Cambridge*, 1794.

—— *A General View of the Agriculture of the County of Devon*, 1808.

—— *A General View of the Agriculture in the County of Essex*, 1795.

—— *A General View of the Agriculture of Hampshire*, 1813.

VAUGHAN, R. *His Booke* edited by E. B. Wood, 1897.

—— *Most approved and long experienced Water-workes*, 1610.

VENN, J. A. *Foundations of Agricultural Economics*, 2nd edition, Cambridge, 1933.

VERNEY, F. P. *Memoirs of the Verney Family during the Civil War*, 3 vols, 1892–4.

VIVIAN, S. P. *The Manor of Etchingham cum Salehurst*, Sussex Record Society, 1953, liii.

WAKE, J. *Quarter Sessions Records of the County of Northampton: Files for 6 Charles I and Commonwealth*, Northamptonshire Record Society Publications, 1924, i.

WALKER, D. *A General View of the Agriculture of the County of Hertford*, 1795.

WALL, J. C. *Kelmarsh*, Market Harborough, 1927.

WALLACE, R. *Farm Live Stock of Great Britain*, Edinburgh, 1907.

WANSEY, *see* Wiltshire Clothier.

WAYLEN, J. 'The Wiltshire Compounders', *Wiltshire Archaeological Magazine*, 1887, xxiii, 1889, xxiv.

WEBB, J. *Memorials of the Civil War between King Charles I and the Parliament of England, as it affected Herefordshire and the Adjacent Counties*, 2 vols, 1879.

WEBB, S. and B. *English Local Government: The Manor and the Borough*, 1924.

WEDGE, J. *A General View of the Agriculture of the County of Warwick*, 1794.

—— *A General View of the Agriculture of the County Palatine of Cheshire*, 1794.

WELD, J. *A History of Leagram*, Chetham Society, new series, 1913, lxxii.

WENTWORTH, T. *The Office and Duty of Executors*, 1641.

WEST, J. *Village Records*, 1962.

WESTCOTE, T. *A View of Devonshire in 1630*, Exeter, 1845.

WESTERFIELD, R. B. *Middlemen in English Business, 1660–1760*, Transactions of the Connecticut Academy of Arts and Sciences, New Haven, 1915, vol. xix.

WESTON, R. *An Enlargement of the Discourse of Husbandrie used in Brabant and Flanders*, edited by S. Hartlib, 1651.

—— *A Discourse of Husbandry used in Brabant and Flanders*, edited by S. Hartlib, 1652.

WHITE, G. *The Natural History of Selborne* (1788), edited by G. C. Davies, no date.

WHONE, C. *Court Rolls of the Manor of Haworth*, Bradford Historical and Antiquarian Society, 1946, iii.

WILKINSON, A. 'Observations on Middlesex Agriculture', *Annals of Agriculture*, 1794, xxii.

N

WILLAN, T. S. 'The Parliamentary Surveys for the North Riding of York-shire', *Yorkshire Archaeological Journal*, 1934, xxxi.

—— *River Navigation in England 1600–1750*, Oxford, 1936.

—— *The English Coasting Trade 1600–1750*, Manchester, 1938.

—— and CROSSLEY, E. W. *Three Seventeenth-century Yorkshire Surveys*, Yorkshire Archaeological Society Record Series, 1941, civ.

WILLCOX, W. B. *Gloucestershire. A Study in Local Government*, New Haven, 1940.

WILLIAMS, M. I. 'Some Aspects of Glamorgan Farming in Pre-Industrial Times', in Stewart William's *Glamorgan Historian*, Cowbridge, 1965, ii.

WILLIAMS, W. O. 'The Anglesey Gentry as Business Men in Tudor and Stuart Times', *Anglesey Antiquarian Society and Field Club Transactions*, 1948.

WILLIAMS-JONES, K. 'A Drover's Account', *Journal of the Merioneth Historical and Record Society*, 1953–6, ii.

WILTSHIRE CLOTHIER, A [Wansey], *Wool Encouraged without Exportation*, 1791.

WIMBLEDON COMMON COMMITTEE, *Extracts from the Court Rolls of the Manor of Wimbledon*, 1866.

WINCHESTER, B. *Tudor Family Portrait*, 1955.

WOODS, E. C. and BROWN, P. C. *The Rise and Progress of Wallasey*, Liverpool, 1929.

WOODWORTH, A. *Purveyance for the Royal Household in the Reign of Queen Elizabeth*, Transactions of the American Philosophical Society new series, xxxv, pt i, Philadelphia, 1945.

WORLIDGE, J. *Systema Agriculturae*, 1669.

WORTHY, C. *Devonshire Wills: a collection of annotated testamentary abstracts*, 1896.

WRIGHT, T. *An Account of the Advantages and Method of Watering Meadows*, Cirencester, 1789.

—— *The Formation and Management of Floated Meadows*, Northampton, 1808.

YARRANTON, A. *The Improvement Improved*, 1663.

YOUATT, W. *Sheep: their breed, management and diseases*, 1837.

—— *The Complete Grazier*, by A Lincolnshire Grazier, 1883.

YOUNG, A. (senior) 'A Five Days Tour to Woodbridge', *Annals of Agriculture*, 1793, ii.

—— *A General View of the Agriculture of the County of Essex*, 2 vols, 1807.

—— *A General View of the Agriculture of Hertfordshire*, 1804.

—— *A General View of the Agriculture of the County of Lincoln*, 1799.

—— *A General View of the Agriculture of the County of Suffolk*, 1794.

—— *The Farmer's Tour through the East of England*, 4 vols, 1771.

—— *Tours in England and Wales*, 1932.

—— *View of the Agriculture of Oxfordshire*, 1809.

YOUNG, A. (junior) *A General View of the Agriculture of the County of Sussex*, 1793.

YOUNG, E. *A History of Colston Bassett*, Thoroton Society Record Series, 1942, ix.

YOUNG, G. M. 'Some Wiltshire Cases in Star Chamber', *Wiltshire Archaeological Magazine*, 1942–4, l.

SUMMARY OF SELECT MANUSCRIPT SOURCES

PUBLIC RECORD OFFICE

CHANCERY:
Proceedings, series i, James I:
A.8/36; B.1/37, 68; B.6/57; B.12/68; B.13/47; B.14/17; B.17/19; B.27/59;
B.28/46; B.33/30; B.35/3, 23, 66; C.1/50; C.3/69; C.6/24, 35; C.7/14;
C.16/29, 59, 66; C.22/82; C.26/36; D.8/11; D.9/74; E.1/51; F.11/62;
H.8/53; H.14/34; H.36/74; K. 8/48; L.15/7; M.7/4; M.13/57; N.1/68;
R.8/36; S.9/55; S.22/71; S.29/7; S.39/53, 64; T.1/5; U.2/35; W.11/60–1;
W.26/15; Y.1/25.
Proceedings, series ii, Charles I: 260/16; 376/70.
Depositions: F.13/16.
Common Law Pleadings: bundle 24.
Close Rolls: 43 George III, 1802–3, Part 10, rotulet 10.

COURT OF REQUESTS:
Proceedings: 26/63; 39/58; 45/100; 56/18; 61/39; 65/52; 74/95; 86/61,
102/45; 105/10; 106/60; 129/45; 392/93; 393/128; 394/70.

COURT OF WARDS AND LIVERIES:
Feodaries' Surveys: bundle 30, part i, no. 425; part ii, nos 403, 702.
bundle 46, unsorted; numbered, nos 250, 268, 276.

COURT OF STAR CHAMBER:
Proceedings:
Henry VIII, volume 6.
18/2, 90; 19/11; 22/352; 23/186; 24/221; 26/431.
Philip & Mary, 3/42.
Elizabeth:
A.8/37; A.11/8; A.22/20; A.34/10.
James:
3/33; 7/6; 10/4, 23; 15/12; 16/4, 13; 17/24; 18/12; 40/22; 54/10; 55/29;
63/10; 106/20; 108/2; 111/25; 155/27; 156/4; 159/16.

COURT OF EXCHEQUER:
King's Remembrancer:
Depositions by Commission, 17 Elizabeth, Easter 1; 20 Elizabeth, Trinity
3, Easter 4; 21–2 Elizabeth, Michaelmas 8, 28; 26 Elizabeth, Trinity 8;
26–7 Elizabeth, Michaelmas 24; 29 Elizabeth, Trinity 5; 31 Elizabeth,
Hilary 25; 32 Elizabeth, Easter 10; 33–4 Elizabeth, Michaelmas 42;
35 Elizabeth, Easter 11; 38–9 Elizabeth, Michaelmas 8; 40–1 Elizabeth,
Michaelmas 19, 34; 41–2 Elizabeth, Michaelmas 4; 42–3 Elizabeth,

Michaelmas 2; 2 James, Hilary 3; 4 James, Michaelmas 25; 6 James, Easter 16, Hilary 30; 8 James, Easter 4; 10 James, Easter 10; 12 James, Hilary 11; 16 James, Hilary 18, 18 James, Easter 3; 21 James, Michaelmas 12–13; 3–4 Charles, Easter 1, Hilary 5; 4 Charles, Michaelmas 6, 24; 6 Charles, Trinity 2, Michaelmas 12, 48; 8 Charles, Easter 11, 19, Michaelmas 37; 9 Charles, Easter 10, 19, Trinity 4, Michaelmas 47; 10 Charles, Easter 19, Trinity 4, 12, Michaelmas 11, 48, 61; 11 Charles, Michaelmas 13; 12 Charles, Easter 24, 34; 13 Charles, Michaelmas 59; 14 Charles, Trinity 9, Michaelmas 25; 15 Charles, Easter 6, 19; 15–16 Charles, Hilary 8; 17 Charles Easter 16; 1650, Easter 9, Michaelmas 17; 1653, Easter 2; 1655–6, Hilary 23; 1656, Michaelmas 17; 1657, Easter 9; 1659, Easter 42; 11 Charles II, Trinity 9; 13 Charles II, Michaelmas 44; 19 Charles II, Trinity 2; 35 Charles II, Easter 3; Supplementary bundle 902, no. 42.

Special Commissions,

2395, 2409, 2418, 2424, 2450, 3047, 4577, 4684, 4697, 5021, 5553, 5554, 6057, 6507.

Inventories of goods and chattels,

file 2, nos 36–7.

Memoranda, Recorda,

Michaelmas 11 Henry VIII—Trinity 29 Henry VIII, Easter 5 James I—Hilary 8 James I.

Miscellanea of the Exchequer,

bundle 10, no. 11.

Miscellaneous Books,

37–41, 43.

Augmentation Office:

Miscellaneous Books,

358–9, 368–9, 379–80, 388, 390, 394–5, 419–22, 425.

Parliamentary Surveys, Bedfordshire, 9, 10, 14, 17, 20; Berkshire, 11–14, 16, 21–2, 28–9, 35–6, 38; Buckinghamshire, 11, 12, 14, 19; Cambridgeshire, 1; Cheshire, 11, 13A, 22; Cornwall, 5, 9, 18, 25, 35, 40, 46; Cumberland, 4, 6, 8; Derbyshire, 19, 25, 28; Devon, 6A; Dorset, 6, 8–10, 15; Essex, 12, 15, 17; Gloucestershire, 9, 20; Hampshire, 14, 15, 25; Herefordshire, 16, 19; Hertfordshire, 7, 9, 24, 27, 30; Huntingdonshire, 3, 7; Kent, 18, 26, 42, 56; Lancashire, 7, 14, 18, 30; Leicestershire, 6; Lincolnshire, 5, 6, 10A, 11, 12, 13A, 14–16, 18, 20, 26–7, 35, 42–3, 44A; Middlesex, 16; Monmouthshire, 1, 9, 10; Northamptonshire, 15, 20–1, 34; Nottinghamshire, 10A, 14A, 17, 22; Oxfordshire, 10, 12, 13; Pembrokeshire, 2; Rutlandshire, 13; Somerset, 13, 16–18, 26–7, 32–3, 36B, 37–40, 42–3, 44A, 47; Staffordshire, 44; Suffolk, 15, 17, 18; Surrey, 23–5, 31–2, 38, 44–5, 55–6, 58–60, 67; Warwickshire, 10–12, 15–17, 20–2, 24–5, 32; Westmorland, 1; Wiltshire, 24, 36, 40–1, 43–5, 47; Worcestershire, 2–4, 6, 7; Yorkshire, 15, 23, 27–8, 34–5, 39, 41–2, 50, 57, 59.

Exchequer of Receipt:

Receipt Books (Pell Books, Pellis Receptae), August 23, 1610.

Treasury of Receipt:

Books, 148, 157, 174.

Land Revenue:
Miscellaneous Books,
185–7, 189, 191–3, 195–207, 209–22, 224–6, 228–31, 238–9, 255–8, 260, 285–6.

DUCHY OF LANCASTER:
Court Rolls:
80/1101: 81/1117, 1119–20; 82/1122, 1133; 84/1155; 105/1506–7; 106/1529, 1532–5; 127/1912.
Miscellaneous Books:
108–9, 112–3, 115–7, 119, 122–7.
Rentals and Surveys:
2/11, 21; 5/12; 8/6A; 9/5, 6, 13, 15, 26, 28, 30.
Special Commissions:
313, 363, 645, 663, 679–80, 871.

SPECIAL COLLECTIONS:
Maps and Plans: MPC.11.
Court Rolls, General Series: 183/44; 194/55, 59, 77; 195/78–9, 82; 207/25, 42; 208/28, 35.
Rentals and Surveys, General Series: rolls 566, 709, 857, 909, 986; portfolios/nos, 2/46; 3/11; 4/2; 10/11; 11/1; 13/20, 87; 14/83; 20/16, 27; 25/14; 26/66.
Shaftesbury Papers: bundle 32, no. 7.
State Papers, Domestic:
volumes/nos
Mary 9/67.
Elizabeth (Addenda), 12/22.
James, 8/76; 71/107; 150/7; 191/18; 194/3.
Charles, 95/11; 152/84; 174/22; 491/94.
Interregnum, G58A/–.

BRITISH MUSEUM
ADDITIONAL
Manuscripts, 6027, 6668, 6702, 14049, 14415, 14850, 15559, 20745, 21042, 21054, 21206, 21558, 21605, 21608, 22836, 23150–1, 23949–50, 23955–6, 24741, 24782, 24787, 25079, 27403, 27534–5, 27605, 27977, 28529, 29609A, 29611, 29890, 32134, 33452–4, 33466–7, 33582, 34008, 34155, 34162, 34164, 34166, 34258, 34566, 34682–3, 36233, 36582, 36584–5, 36745, 36875, 36903–4, 36906, 36908, 36912, 36981, 37270, 37521, 37682, 38065, 38487, 38634, 40063–4, 41168.
Rolls: 5074, 9284–5, 9289, 13588, 13858, 16280, 16548–9, 16551, 17749–51, 18064, 18513, 18515, 18517, 19082–4, 26339, 26341, 26569–74, 26576, 26836, 26866, 27072, 27170, 27245, 27886, 27991, 28264, 28279, 28281, 28283, 31162, 32385, 32387, 32859–60, 32901, 32971–2, 37391, 37534, 37571, 37691, 39793–4, 39822, 44459, 44654, 49323, 49700–1, 54238, 63505, 63591, 65980.
Charters: 14054, 33101, 35524A, 53392, 54117, 54127, 54166, 55495, 59152.

COTTONIAN MANUSCRIPTS: Augustus I.i.24, 51, 78–9.

EGERTON
Manuscripts: 2559, 2789A, 2988, 2993–4, 2999, 3002–3, 3005, 3007, 3034, 3134.
Charters: 1451.

HARLEIAN:
Manuscripts: 71, 127, 368, 570, 590, 702, 779, 2039, 2192, 2239, 3696, 3749, 3961, 4606, 4781, 5827, 6006, 6288, 6697, 6721, 7017, 7180, 7369.
Rolls: T.19, Y.19.
LANSDOWNE MANUSCRIPTS: volumes/nos. 34/38; 49/54(24), 57(27), 60; 59/36 volumes 110, 615, 654, 691, 784, 1056.
SLOANE MANUSCRIPTS: 3664, 3815.
STOWE MANUSCRIPTS: 765, 775, 847, 858, 870.

BASSET DOWN HOUSE
A Booke of Accounts by Neville Maskelyne.

BEDFORDSHIRE RECORD OFFICE
ABP/W, 1605/126; 1607/98; 1611–12/144; 1612/226; 1613/185; 1614/172; 1616/54, 78; 1617/224; 1641/141, 192; AD, 1043, 1060, 1501, 2007–8; BS, 1276; C, 237; FN, 1094, 1097; G.A., 1732; H.A., 5/1: 13/6a, 11; L, 4/310, 314, 333: 26/280–1, 563; O, 190/45; OR, 804, 816; PA, 180–1; S, 19, 20; T.W., 3; 10/2/9; X, 69/6.

BEELEIGH ABBEY
Inventory of Thomas Wilson 1627 Bocking.

BERKSHIRE RECORD OFFICE
D/EAh, E2:E4/1–4:E5/1–3:T7; D/EBp, E15:M4; D/EBt, E28; D/EBy, E68, 70; D/EC, M10B, 114/1; D/EEl, E2; D/EHy, M26; D/EMt, M3, 7; D/EN, E1/2:M6, 31, 33–4; D/EPb, E42, 66A, 52/1, 2:53:M3; D/EP2, E2/2; D/ETh, M1, 10

BIRMINGHAM LIBRARY
167197, 167919, 168002, 168124–5, 168162–3, 252320, 261547, 277414, 281271, 281291–2, 324074, 335817, 344741–2, 350196–8, 350203, 350221, 350252, 350276, 350279, 351983, 370338, 373943, 378173, 382959, 394772, 422770, 437935, 468177, 477329, 478550, 499837, 501864, 505455, 508624, 572721.
Bournville Village Trust Collection: 14.
Elford Hall Collection: 294.
Fletcher Collection: 81.
Winnington Collection: 33, 45, 52, 217.

BODLEIAN LIBRARY
DEPARTMENT OF WESTERN MANUSCRIPTS:
Aubrey Manuscripts, Volume 2.
Hearne's diaries, 158–9.
Consistory and Archdeaconry Courts of Oxford: Original Wills.

BORTHWICK INSTITUTE OF HISTORICAL RESEARCH, YORK
PREROGATIVE COURT OF THE ARCHBISHOP WITH THE EXCHEQUER
COURT OF THE DEAN OF YORK:
Original Wills, Administrations, Inventories, Tuitions, etc.
COURT OF THE DEAN AND CHAPTER OF YORK:
Administrations, Inventories, Tuitions, etc.
PECULIAR COURT OF THE DEAN OF YORK:
Original Wills.
PECULIAR COURT OF SELBY:
Original Wills, Administrations and Inventories.
PECULIAR COURT OF SNAITH:
Original Wills and Administrations.
PECULIAR COURT OF BISHOP WILTON:
Original Wills and Administrations.
PREBENDARY COURT OF AMPLEFORTH, (AMPLEFORD):
Original Wills and Administrations.
PREBENDARY COURT OF MARKET WEIGHTON:
Original Wills and Administrations.
PREBENDARY COURT OF NORTH NEWBALD:
Original Wills and Administrations.
PREBENDARY COURT OF OSBALDSWICK:
Original Wills and Administrations.

BOUGHTON HOUSE
MONTAGU MANUSCRIPTS:
'*Compota Omnium et Singularum Officiariorum et Ministorum*' (Sir Edward Montagu's Account Book).

BOWOOD HOUSE:
Survey of Bremhill, 1629.

BRISTOL ARCHIVES OFFICE:
4490, 01235.
CONSISTORY COURT OF THE BISHOP OF BRISTOL IN THE DEANERY OF BRISTOL:
Inventories.

BRISTOL UNIVERSITY LIBRARY
Dauntsey Trowbridge Court Book.
Shrewton Manuscripts, 37, 67/12.
Accession, 31, Court Book of Hannington, volume A.

BUCKINGHAMSHIRE COUNTY MUSEUM:
COURT ROLLS AND FILES:
Halton Court Rolls, no. 9; Long Crendon, 10/48; Pitstone, P.24/1, 2; Quainton, rolls 1–3; Taplow, 155/21, 445/29; Weston Turvile, 38/51, 39/51; Wexham Court Rolls, bundle 1; Whitchurch, 15/51; Wing, 219/35; Wraysbury, 43/51.

BUCKINGHAMSHIRE RECORD OFFICE
Acquisition 35/39: Bye-laws and regulations for Padbury Fields 1779;
Swanbourne Field Agreement 1748; D/MH, 28/1–3, ST 1, 11.

BURY AND WEST SUFFOLK RECORD OFFICE
EPISCOPAL COMMISSARY COURT FOR BURY ST EDMUNDS (WITH
THE ARCHDEACONRY OF SUDBURY):
Inventories.

CAMBRIDGESHIRE RECORD OFFICE
L.1/8, 10, 20, 22, 50, 112, 167, 182; L.19/17, 20; L.58/5; L.64/8, 9, 14;
L.88/3, 4; L.93/139; R.51/29/1 (a) and (d).

CARTWRIGHT HALL, BRADFORD
HEATON MANUSCRIPTS, 1B, 2B, 4B, 5B, 6B, 7B, 8B, 9B.
SWINTON COLLECTION:
Court Books of Isle Abbots, Tornock and Lympsham.
Court Rolls of Newsam.
Survey of Monks Kirby, 1611.

CHESHIRE RECORD OFFICE:
NEDEHAM AND KILLMOREY COLLECTION:
Court Book of Badington Bromall.
Valuation of Badington Bromall, circa 1650.
Survey of the Hack and Bromall.
VERNON (WARREN) COLLECTION:
Court Rolls, nos. 1–15.
COURT OF THE VICAR GENERAL OF THE CHANCELLOR OF THE
DIOCESE OF CHESTER IN THE EPISCOPAL CONSISTORY OF CHESTER
AND IN THE RURAL DEANERIES OF THE ARCHDEACONRY:
Original Wills and Administrations.

CHETHAM LIBRARY, MUNIMENT ROOM:
Adlington Manuscripts.
Meredith Manuscripts: Survey of Lands of Sir William Meredith at Bowden
and Altrincham, 1726.

CORNWALL RECORD OFFICE
CONSISTORY COURT OF THE ARCHDEACONRY OF CORNWALL:
Original Wills, Administrations and Inventories.

CUMBERLAND RECORD OFFICE:
CONSISTORY COURT OF CARLISLE:
Original Wills and Administrations.

DEENE HOUSE
BRUDENELL MANUSCRIPTS:
ASR, 562.

Maps and Plans: 1, 3, 4, 6, 8, 15, 22, 29–37, 39–43; A.iv.1, A.iv.16(a), A.xii.10, A.xv.4; B.ii.15–16; E.vi.22, E.vii.1, E.10.33b; H.vii.6; I.iii.7; I.vi.61, 75; I.xi.8; J.xx.9a, 11a and b; O.viii.8, O.x.14, O.xxii.4, O.xxiv.1.

DEVIZES MUSEUM
Wiltshire Manuscripts 'C': Copy of inventory of Stoke House 1596.
Survey of Bishops Cannings Rectory and Manor of Cannings Canonicorum 1661; *Commonplace Book of Sir Henry Bayntun, Sir Edward Baynton, and Sir Edward Baynton*, 1614–79.
CATALOGUE NO. 233:
Inventories of John Sloper of Roundway, 1643, *John Filkes of Rowde*, 1629; *James Filkes of Devizes*, 1637 *and William Filkes of Devizes*, 1655.
SHELF NO. 63:
'*William Gaby His Booke, 1656*'.
SHELF NO. 64:
Imber: prosecution of Thomas Chambers.

DEVON (AND EXETER DIOCESAN) RECORD OFFICE
CONSISTORY COURT OF EXETER:
Inventories and Administrations.

DORSET RECORD OFFICE
ARCHDEACONRY COURT OF DORSET:
Inventories.
PECULIAR COURT OF CORFE CASTLE:
Wills, Administrations and Inventories.
PECULIAR COURT OF WIMBORNE MINSTER:
Administrations and Inventories.
Original Wills and Inventories.
Enclosure Award, no. 97.
Museum Collection, 1408, 7126.
D.4, Court Book of Thornhull family; D.10, E103, M91; D.12, Court Book of Holnest and Long Burton; D.16, M115–26; D.29, E65; D.37, 1, 3; D.39, H2 Puddletown Court Book; D.54, Surveys, Rentals and Terriers of Manors of Lady Margaret Arundel, widow of Sir Thomas Arundel, knight.

DURHAM, THE COLLEGE, The Prior's Kitchen.
PALATINE AND EPISCOPAL CONSISTORY COURT OF DURHAM (WITH THE PECULIAR OF CRAIKE):
Original Wills and Inventories.

EAST SUFFOLK RECORD OFFICE, *see* Ipswich and East Suffolk Record Office

ESSEX RECORD OFFICE:
D/DB, 146, M46; D/DFa, T48/22; D/DGE, 506; D/DK, E1; F2/4, 6, 9, 10; D/DKw, E2; D/DL, E61; M46, 65, 81; D/DP, A18, 22.6: E25–6: F224,

234, 240, 311: M186, 549, 777, 890; D/DPl, 9; D/DPr, 426; D/DQi, 126; D/DQs, 58/6; 90; D/DRa, C5; D/DRc, F88; D/DTh, M17; D/DYW, 17; D/SD, 1; D/SH, 7; T/B, 57/3: 65/1.

EXETER LIBRARY:
M.B.8d: Lord Dynham's Survey Book etc. 1566.

GLOUCESTER LIBRARY:
LOCAL COLLECTION: 16062, 16064, 16209; 16526, nos 11, 28, 102; 18253, Prestbury Court Book; 28899, no 4: 28917; R.24/1; RF.30/3: 274/12; RZ.152/1(38).
CONSISTORY COURT OF GLOUCESTER:
Inventories.

GLOUCESTERSHIRE RECORD OFFICE:
D.36, P26; D.114, Field Book of Bradley 1598; D.127, 608; D.129, Court rolls and files of Weston Birt; D.158, M1; D.184, M1, 7, 9, 18–20, 24; D.247, Longborough Court Rolls 18, 42, 44, 68; D.269B, M3; D.326, E1; D.444, M1, 2; D.445, M4; D.547A, M29; D.738, Colne St Dennis court files; D.745, Bisley court files; D.C1, Cowley court papers.

GUILDFORD MUNIMENT ROOM
LOSELEY MANUSCRIPTS:
674, 937, 959: 1081/41, 43: 1965: 1966/3.
97/6/13.

HAMPSHIRE RECORD OFFICE:
5M50 2531, 2536–8, 2557–8, 2561; 5M53 747–8, 768; 12M60 64; 15M50 391, 397.
CONSISTORY COURT OF WINCHESTER:
Original Wills and Inventories.
ARCHDEACONRY COURT OF WINCHESTER:
Original Wills and Inventories.
CONSISTORY AND ARCHDEACONRY COURTS OF WINCHESTER:
Original Wills and Inventories, unclassified.
PECULIAR COURTS OF BISHOPSTOKE, BRIGHSTONE, COMPTON, CRAWLEY, EAST MEON, EAST WOODHAY, MEONSTOKE, NORTH WALTHAM, TWYFORD, UPHAM, WEST MEON, AND WONSTON:
Wills; Administrations and Inventories.

HEREFORD LIBRARY
BIDDULPH COLLECTION, 966.
HOPTON COLLECTION, Deed box 2, no 57.
LOCAL COLLECTION:
Deeds 3540, 3682, 4613.
Drawer 16, no 480.

HERTFORDSHIRE RECORD OFFICE
232, 677, 1434, 6693, 6718, 7059, 7062, 7644, 8154, 8435, 8442, 8479–81, 8483–7, 8579, 8780, 9442, 10511–12, 10514, 10517–18, 10520–1, 10869, 10878, 12298, 14594, 14618, 19271, 22042, 22069–70, 22101, 41673–4, 44467, 44817–18, 46325, 65810.
BROXBORNE BURY COLLECTION: 36, 48, 58, 119.
GORHAMBURY COLLECTION: II.D.2, II.O.12a; X.B.3a; XI.2, XI.11.
WESTMILL-WAKELEY-BUNTINGFORD COLLECTION: 155.
ARCHDEACONRY OF ST ALBANS:
Inventories.
ARCHDEACONRY OF HUNTINGDON, HITCHIN DIVISION:
Original Wills, Separate Inventories.

HUNTINGTON LIBRARY, SAN MARINO, CALIFORNIA.
ST.48: *Sir Thomas Temple's Account Book of Wool Sales*, 1592–1623.

IPSWICH AND EAST SUFFOLK RECORD OFFICE:
50/1/74(1) and (12); 50/13/10.2; 50/22/3.1, 5; 50/22/12.6; 51/1/13, 14; 51/2/12, 26; 51/10/11.5; 51/10/17.2, 3; GB.1/2/14/33; HA.12/C9/9; S.1/2/6.7; S.1/10/9.12; V.5/18/10.1; V.5/22/1; V.5/23/2.1; V.11/2/1.1; V.11/3/3.
ACCESSION 519: *inventory of William Green of Cattisford* 1715.
ARCHDEACONRY COURT OF SUFFOLK:
Original Wills, Inventories.
N.B. Probate files were first renumbered thus, ——/15 and so on; then N.6/5/2.1 and so on; then FE1/1 and so on. I have eschewed all file nos in favour of citing actual years, but have retained old notation in some instances for sake of numbering individual inventories, e.g. 329/16. This notation will be found endorsed in Indian ink.

JOHN RYLANDS LIBRARY:
English Manuscripts, no 216.

KENT ARCHIVES OFFICE
U.214, E7/9, 10, 14, 21, 44, 63; E12.
U.234, A10.
U.269, A413, 415, 421, 423–4.
ARCHDEACONRY COURT OF CANTERBURY:
Inventory Papers.
CONSISTORY COURT OF CANTERBURY:
Inventory Papers.

LANCASHIRE RECORD OFFICE:
DD.Bl, 24/13; 47/45–6; 48/39–40; 54/2, 7, 8. DD.F, 52, 81, 93, 101, 112, 158, 168, 1072, 1649, 1939, 1978, 1984, 2419. DD.Fo, 13/39. DD.In, 60/26. DD.K, 1451/1; 1452/1; 1453/1, 2; 1454/1–3; 1455/1–5; 1456/1, 2; 1462/1–7; 1463/1, 2; 1464/1; 1467/1–6; 1470/1; 1471/1, 2; 1505/9, 10; 1541/5; 1542/2. DD.Pt, 1, 22, 39; DD.Sc, 19/16; 19/23. DD.To, K.35. DD.X, 33/69; 102/66; 160/3.

COURT OF THE VICAR GENERAL OF THE CHANCELLOR OF THE
DIOCESE OF CHESTER IN THE EPISCOPAL CONSISTORY OF CHESTER
AND IN THE RURAL DEANERIES OF THE ARCHDEACONRY:
Original Wills and Administrations.
CONSISTORY COURT OF THE COMMISSARY OF THE ARCHDEACONRY
OF RICHMOND, WESTERN DEANERIES:
Original Wills, Administrations and Inventories.

LEEDS LIBRARY:
CONSISTORY COURT OF THE COMMISSARY OF THE ARCHDEACONRY
OF RICHMOND, EASTERN DEANERIES:
Original Wills, Administrations and Inventories (RD/AP 1).
TEMPLE NEWSAM MANUSCRIPTS:
TN/CO/2, TN/M7/1.

LEICESTER MUSEUM:
3D42/40/71–2, 75, 85; 7D51/1; 8D39/25/1/4; 11D53/VI/1; 35/29/27–8,
32, 35, 39, 95, 272, 317–18, 340, 370, 376, 378, 397, 415, 427; 44/28/902.

LEICESTERSHIRE RECORD OFFICE:
COMMISSARY OF THE BISHOP OF LINCOLN IN THE ARCHDEACONRY
OF LEICESTER AND THE COURT OF THE ARCHDEACON:
Original Wills and Administrations, Inventories.
PREBEND OF ST MARGARET WITH THE CHAPELRY OF KNIGHTON.
Original Wills and Administrations, Inventories.
COMMISSARY COURTS OF THE MANORS OF ROTHLEY AND EVINGTON:
Original Wills and Administrations, Inventories.
CRANE AND WALTON MANUSCRIPTS:
Account no. 166.
Leire articles of agreement 1689.
DE.10:
Sir William Herrick's Account Book 1610–36.
Court book endorsed '1815 to 1829'
Court of Survey of Beaumanor 1656.
Particular of Beaumanor 1594.
Beaumanor court book endorsed 'Mr Robert Pilkington Steuarte'.
Court rolls and files of Beaumanor.
Court rolls and files of Barrow, Quorndon and Woodhouse.
DE.40/22/1, 2, 4; DE.40/37/7; DE.40/40; DE.40/46/3; DE.41/1/30/2;
DE.53 nos 64, 78, 93, 104, 350, 434.

LICHFIELD JOINT RECORD OFFICE (Staffordshire County Council and
Lichfield City Joint Record Office).
EPISCOPAL CONSISTORY COURT OF LICHFIELD:
Original Wills.
PECULIAR COURTS OF ALREWAS AND WEEFORD, COLWICH,
GNOSSALL, HANSACRE AND ARMITAGE, AND PENKRIDGE:
Original Wills.

LINCOLNSHIRE ARCHIVES OFFICE:
 MONSON DEPOSIT, NEWTON PAPERS: 7/13/232.
 MASSINGBERD-MUNDY DEPOSIT: VI/5/2, 9, 24, 30, 32.
 HENEAGE OF HAINTON COLLECTION: 3/2, 3/3.
 ANDREWS DEPOSIT: no. 1.
 MASSINGBERD COLLECTION: no. 26.
 HOLYWELL COLLECTION: 97/22/1, 2.
 CONSISTORY COURT OF LINCOLN:
 Inventories.

LIVERPOOL RECORD OFFICE
 FAMILY AND PERSONAL RECORDS: K.434 Survey Book of Sir Thomas
 Aston, 1636.
 MOORE DEEDS: 190, 511, 552, 716, 757, 923, 1212, 1296.
 NORRIS PAPERS: 552, 631, 656.

LONGLEAT HOUSE
 MISCELLANEOUS PAPERS OF SIR JOHN THYNNE SENIOR 1561–76:
 box III no L.

MANCHESTER LIBRARY
 CHESHIRE DEEDS: C.135.
 LANCASHIRE DEEDS: L.6, 7, 15, 36a, 250, 445–6.

MIDDLESEX RECORD OFFICE
 (now Greater London Record Office).
 Accession 16, nos 1, 4, 8; Accession 180, no. 2; Accession 248, no. 1a;
 Accession 249, no. 69; Accession 262, no. 16; Accession 446, EM37–8:
 44/4, 8: M102, 104–5.

NATIONAL LIBRARY OF WALES
 PITCHFORD HALL COLLECTION: 825, 901.
 PYE OF THE MYND COLLECTION: 193.
 EPISCOPAL CONSISTORY COURT OF HEREFORD:
 Original Wills, Administrations and Inventories.
 CONSISTORY COURT OF THE DEAN OF HEREFORD:
 Original Wills, Administrations and Inventories.

NORFOLK AND NORWICH RECORD OFFICE
 LIBRARY MANUSCRIPTS: 1505 (Townshend 88).
 NRS.9276 (22.B.4).
 DEAN AND CHAPTER MANUSCRIPTS: *Parliamentary Survey, 1649.*
 EPISCOPAL CONSISTORY COURT OF NORWICH:
 Inventories.
 ARCHDEACONRY COURT OF NORFOLK:
 Original Wills.

NORTHAMPTONSHIRE RECORD OFFICE
 CLAYTON COLLECTION: nos 61, 70, 100a and b, 128.

DAVENTRY COLLECTION: nos 532–3, 540–2, 549b, 573c, 585.

FINCH-HATTON COLLECTION: nos 119, 272, 296, 298, 516, 570, 574, 617, 834, 937, 982, 991, 1140, 1145, 1336, 1626, 1723, 2431–2, 2578, 2859, 3524, 3711A, 3712A, 3839, 4177.

FITZWILLIAM (MILTON) COLLECTION:

Correspondence: 176/10, 16, 26; 178/24; 179/41; 220/42–3; 221/101; 222/13, 39, 44–5, 53–4.

Miscellaneous: nos. 77, 191–2, 200, 202, 207, 211, 216, 222, 342, 453–4, 477, 792–3, 897, 900, 902–4, 907, 916–22, 1006, 1033, 1097.

Miscellaneous Volumes: 47–8, 52, 55, 71, 76–7, 86–7, 93, 99, 187, 194, 433, 437.

GRAFTON COLLECTION: nos. 3422, 3450a.

HIGHAM FERRERS COURT PAPERS:

Burgess Court Rolls, Duchy Court Rolls, Presentments.

ISHAM (LAMPORT) COLLECTION: nos 12, 21, 29, 35, 50, 110, 128, 195A, 508, 769, 811–12, 859, 865, 1491.

LEONARD BRASSEY AND OTHERS COLLECTION: nos 46, 48.

MONTAGU COLLECTION:

Buckinghamshire, old box 2, nos 1, 2.

Lancashire, old box 3, nos 6, 7; old box 4, no. 46.

Warwickshire, old box 6, no. 14.

Northamptonshire, old box 7, nos 66/4–6, 9, 10, 12: 72; old box 10, no 50; old box 13, no 12; old box 14, no 12; old box 16, nos 9, 98, 101; old box 17, no. 160; old box 18, no. 160; old box 20, no. 32; old box 24, no. 52; old box 25, nos 51–2, 55.

Huntingdonshire, old box 26, nos 22, 27–8.

Norfolk, etc, old box P, parts 1, 2.

OLD PARISH RECORDS:

Field Officers' Accounts.

ORMONDE (KILKENNY) COLLECTION: nos 289, 295, 305.

RIDER, HEATON, MEREDITH AND MILLS COLLECTION: no. 45.

SILVERMAN (GEDDINGTON) COLLECTION: no. 297.

SOTHEBY (ECTON) COLLECTION: nos 1183, 1191, 1201, 1204.

WESTMORLAND COLLECTION:

box 4, parcel xvi, no 5.; box 4, parcel xx, no. 3; box 5, found loose: Elizabethan court rolls of Farcet, Stanground, Woodnewton, and Woodstone; box 5, parcel ii, nos 2, 3; box 5, parcel iii, nos 1, 2; box 5, parcel v, no. 1; box 5, parcel vi, court roll of Duddington with Lutton 1743; inventory of Lady Mary le Despenser 1626; box 5, parcel vii, inventory of Thomas Fyssher 1586; box 5, parcel ix, surveys of Northease, Iford, Rottingdean, Rodmill, Chiltington, and Nutbourne; box 6, parcel v, nos 1, 2; box 7 parcel xv, Apethorpe tithe agreement 1700; Correspondence between earl and steward; box 7, nos 16, 16B, 71.

Miscellaneous Volume 42.

WESTMORLAND (SHARLSTON) COLLECTION: no. 11/46.

XYZ COLLECTION: nos 985, 988.

YOUNG (ORLINGBURY) COLLECTION: no 668.

MAPS: 571, 1382, 1385, 1388–9, 1392, 1493.

MISCELLANEOUS LEDGERS: 123–6, 129, 145–6.

AYNHO COURT ROLLS.

GEDDINGTON TERRIER 1687 (ex box 14).

GRETTON COURT ROLLS.

IRCHESTER COURT ROLLS.

LONG BUCKBY COURT ROLLS:

ARCHDEACONRY COURT OF NORTHAMPTON:
Original Wills, Administrations and Inventories.
Administrations and Inventories.

CONSISTORY COURT OF PETERBOROUGH:
Administrations and Inventories.

NORTH RIDING RECORD OFFICE:
ZAL, Court files of Snape and Well.
ZAX.2, Court book of West Tanfield.
ZCV.54, Court rolls of Whitwell.
ZQ.1, Survey of Marske 1655.

OXFORDSHIRE RECORD OFFICE:
Bl.I.v.2; DIL.II.w.75, 122: DIL.IV.a.2, 78/iii,v: 89; F.xiv.1; Fa.xxi.1;
J.vii.2, 6; Wi.x.34; Misc.M.I/1; Accession 477; Survey and Field Book of
Eynsham 1650 (box 110); Dashwood Collection: VIII/33–4

PETWORTH HOUSE
Survey of the Demesne of the Manor of Petworth etc. 1557.
Surveys of Sutton and Duncton 1574.

PINCHIN, *see* Vent Farm.

RYLANDS LIBRARY, *see* John Rylands Library.

SALT LIBRARY, *see* William Salt Library.

SHAKESPEARE'S BIRTHPLACE
MANORIAL DOCUMENTS AND COURT ROLLS:
Alveston and Tiddington: Court Books starting 20 April 2, James I;   Court
Rolls 11 April 18 Charles II—21 October 1761.
Great Alne: Court Rolls, 'A Declaration of all the Inclosures made'.
Henley in Arden: Court Rolls.
Park Hall in Castle Bromwich: 'Parke Hall with the Demesnes'.
Shottery: Court Rolls.
Solihull Borough and Foreign: Court Rolls.
Whitchurch: Court Files.

COUGHTON (THROCKMORTON) COLLECTION:
*Coughton Court Rolls, Oversley Court Rolls and Terriers, Sambourn Court Rolls,
Throckmorton Court Rolls, Upton in Haselor Court Rolls, Weston Underwood Court
Rolls.*

GREGORY-HOOD COLLECTION:
*Binley Court Rolls, Brinklow Court Rolls and Files, Stivichall in Coventry Court
Rolls, Wolvey Court Rolls.*

STONELEIGH (LEIGH) COLLECTION:
Adlestrop:
Sixteenth-century Court Book.

Court Rolls, October 14, 1673—April 24, 1762.
Dunton in Curdworth:
Particular of the demesnes 1687.
Kenilworth:
Court Rolls.
Langley:
Distraint inventory of Henry Chambers 1735.
Longborough:
Court Rolls 16 March 34 Elizabeth—November 16, 1716.
Maugersbury:
Court Book.
Ratley:
Court Rolls.
Sowe alias Walsgrave:
Court Files.
Stoneleigh:
Court Rolls Michaelmas 1545—October 29, 1764; Eighteenth-century Court Book; 'Customes of the Manor of Stoneley'; Pains and Orders; Survey 1597; Survey of Demesne Lands of Sir Thomas Leigh, October 18, 1623.
STRATFORD-ON-AVON COLLECTION:
Wills and Inventories: nos 22, 43, 59.
Miscellaneous Documents: volume i, nos 11, 17, 19, 26, 30–1, 42, 65, 75–7; vol. v, no. 32; vol. vii, no. 144; vol. xiii, no. 45.
Wheeler Papers: volume i.
TREVELYAN COLLECTION:
Snitterfield and Bearley Court Rolls.
WILLOUGHBY DE BROKE COLLECTION: nos 703a and b, 898, 1024a, 1080, 1194, 1253, 1386, 1393a, 1651, 1652b, 1706–11.

SHROPSHIRE RECORD OFFICE
167/43.
320/5.
BRIDGWATER COLLECTION:
Survey of Ellesmere, Middlehampton and Culmere 1602.

SOMERSET RECORD OFFICE
EPISCOPAL CONSISTORY COURT OF BATH AND WELLS:
Inventories.
CONSISTORIAL COURT OF THE ARCHDEACONRY OF TAUNTON:
Inventories.
DD/AB: Norton-sub-Hamdon Court Rolls; DD/CN: Court Book of John Francis Esq. 1573–87; DD/HK: North Perrott Court Rolls; DD/HP: Transcript of articles of agreement between Lords Farmers; and Tenants of West Buckland 1634; DD/MI: Queen Camel Court Rolls; DD/NNF: West Bagborough Court Rolls; DD/PE: South Petherton Court Book 1661–1841; DD/PO: Court Book of Farmborough Greville and Rowswell 1627–54; Survey of Compton Dando 1656; DD/S/WH: Regilbury Court

Book 1598–1639; Chew Baber Court Rolls; Survey Book of Chew Sutton, Knowle and Stone alias West Chew 1615; Court of Survey of Milton juxta Wells ,July 11, 19 James; DD/SAS: Aller custumal 1653; DD/SG: Shapwick Rectory Court Files; Particular of enclosed ground in Shapwick Rectory 1754; Survey of Shapwick *circa* 1760; DD/SH: Collected Notes of John Strachey for his proposed Natural History of Somerset; DD/TH: Inventories of Richard Draper of North Perrott 1694 and Abraham Pollard of Chard 1677; DD/WO: Surveys of Nettlecombe, Rowden and Woodadvent 1556 and 1619; Seaton Court Rolls; Survey of Farway, Sherford, Seaton and Whitewell 1682; Farway Survey 1609; Seaton Account Book 1616; Fineton Receipt Book 1599; Court Book of Trevelyan Manors. DD/X/AR: Inventory of Thomas Evans of Penselwood 1685; DD/X/GB: Combe Survey Book 1704; DD/X/GNS: Kilmersdon Court Files; DD/X/HO: Tintenhull Court Book; DD/X/MKG: Surveys of Netherham 1662, 1699 and early eighteenth century; DD/X/NW: Mendip map *circa* 1570; Taunton Deane Enclosure Award 1851.

STAFFORDSHIRE RECORD OFFICE:

D.150: 300/2: 301a.

D.260: box 3, bundle (a); box 16, bundle (b); box A, bundle (f), Otherton 'Survey' 1657; box III, bundle (b), Court of Recognition and Survey of Walsall 15 James I.

SURREY RECORD OFFICE

2/1/6: 2/5/4; 10/1–4; 18/13/1; 29/1/4; 34/1/2, 3a: 34/3–4.
Accession 137.
Accession 169, Ashtead manor plan 1638.
Accession 344, Dorking Survey 1649.

URCHFONT MANOR HOUSE

Copy of Urchfont Enclosure Act and Award 1789, 1793.

VENT FARM, FOREST HILL, OXFORDSHIRE (*penes* Mr W. Pinchin): *Field maps of Hazelbury, Ditteridge and Box* 1630.

WARWICKSHIRE RECORD OFFICE:

Deed 19/44.
Manorial Records: 5, 14, 16/9.
DRO 72a.

WEST SUFFOLK RECORD OFFICE, *see* Bury and West Suffolk Record Office.

WEST SUSSEX RECORD OFFICE:

CONSISTORY COURT OF THE BISHOP OF CHICHESTER FOR THE ARCHDEACONRY OF CHICHESTER:
Inventories.

WILLIAM SALT LIBRARY, Stafford.

D.1734/4/1/6–11.

D.1750 Madeley Holme Court Rolls.

D.1765/27 Acton Trussell Survey 16 Elizabeth.

HAND MORGAN COLLECTION:

Chetwynd Manuscripts: File O, Court Rolls of Ingestre cum membris.

Shenstone Court Rolls, Eccleshall Court Rolls.

WILTON HOUSE

Survey of Liquett, Glam. 1560; Surveys of Manors 1631; Surveys of Manors 1632–3; Survey of Burcombe 1632; Survey of Flambston 1631; Surveys of Stoke Farthing, Flambston, Fovant, and Broadchalke 1705; Survey of Stanton Barnard: eighteenth century (1705); Survey of the Manor of Alvediston 1706 and 1758; Surveys of Manors and Farms; Survey of Staunton Bernard 1792–1805; Court Rolls of Various Manors (box 25); Court Rolls 1666–89; Court Rolls of Manors 1689–1754; Papers relating to various manors:—Copies of surveys etc.: Court Rolls; Court Book of Bemerton and Quidhampton 1595–1639; Court Book of Various Parishes 1633–4; Court Books of Burcombe, Wylye, West Overton, Dinton and Teffont, Flambston and Bulbridge, Burcombe, Fugglestone, Quidhampton and Avon, Chalk, Stanton, Ditchampton, Chilmark and Rudge, Stoke Farthing, and Alvediston, beginning 1724; Court Books of Burcombe, Fugglestone, Quidhampton and Avon, Chalk, Stanton, Stoke Farthing, Alvediston, Ditchampton, Netherhampton, Ebbesbourne, Chilmark and Rudge, Foffont, and Swallowcliffe, beginning 1742–3; Court Book of Netherhampton, beginning 1742–3.

WILTSHIRE RECORD OFFICE

EPISCOPAL CONSISTORY COURT OF SALISBURY: *Original Wills, Administrations and Inventories.*

ARCHDEACONRY COURT OF SALISBURY: *Original Wills, Administrations and Inventories.*

ARCHDEACONRY COURT OF WILTSHIRE: *Original Wills, Administrations and Inventories.*

PECULIAR COURT OF THE DEAN OF SALISBURY: *Original Wills, Administrations and Inventories.*

PREBENDAL COURT OF HUSBORNE (HURSTBOURNE) AND BURBAGE: *Original Wills, Administrations and Inventories.*

EX SALISBURY DIOCESAN REGISTRY: *Miscellaneous Wills, Administrations and Inventories.*

Accession 7, Enford Court Book 1537–1723.

Accession 23, Notes on the History of Ogbourne St George.

Accession 34, Hobhouse Papers. A—Documents of Public Interest: bundle 25, no. 5 Fragment of survey of Broughton Gifford 1630.

Accession 40, Sevenhampton Court Book 1541–1624.

Accession 84, Court Book of Andrew Baynton 1545–57; Clayton Manuscripts: nos. 2, 6, 8, 9; Court Books of Ashton Keynes, Burton Marston, Down Ampney, Eisey, Latton, Leigh, Purton Wootton, and South Marston—various dates.

Accession 88, Manuscripts of the Earl of Suffolk and Berkshire:—
Charlton Estate Papers:
Box B, Ancient Books of Surveys of several manors: Survey Book of
Charlton, Brinkworth, Hankerton, and Brokenborough;
Moores Box 1, Charlton Enclosure Agreement 1631; A1/17a, Inventory of
Thomas Kebeell 15 Henry VII.
Accession 111, Surveys of the Shalbournes, the Collingbournes, Bedwyn
Prebend, Mildenhall etc. 1734.
Accession 122, Surveys of Bromham, Bremhill, Bowden, and Stanley
1612 (including court book).
Accession 132, Bishopstrow Court Books (bundle 10).
Accession 192, Thornhill Survey Book *circa* 1574.
Accession 212B, BF.14a; BH.5b; Bm.01; Sd.1a; Wr.1b.
Accession 283: Urchfont Survey *circa* 1640. *Liber Supervisus maneriorum de
Amisburie Erles et Amesbury Pryorye* (Survey of Amesbury with Baicliffe);
Amesbury Survey Book 1574; Survey of Amesbury 1635; Amesbury
Miscellaneous Papers and Documents: Billet Land *cum aliis*, Particular of
Bailcliffe; Court Book of Amesbury Erledom beginning 27 March 25
Elizabeth, Book of Extracts from Court Rolls of various Seymour Manors.
ENCLOSURE AWARDS:
Stanton St Quentin 1783; Fovant, Ebbesbourne Wake, Broadchalke,
Bowerchalke, Alvediston, Bishopstone, and Fyfield 1792; Broadchalke
and Chilmark *circa* 1860 (copy).
STOURHEAD COLLECTION:
Court Book of Lord Stourton's Manors 1644–92.
HEYTESBURY HOSPITAL COLLECTION:
Lord Pembroke's Manors (survey book).
KEEVIL AND BULKINGTON MANUSCRIPTS:
Court Book 44 Elizabeth—2 Charles I.
Court Book 1643–64.
HYDE FAMILY DOCUMENTS:
Court Baron of Sir Lawrence Hyde for Heale 1622–42.
Brigmilston and Milton: Courts Baron of the Hyde family 1606–19.
SAVERNAKE ARCHIVES:
*Surveys of Shalbourne Westcourt, Pewsey, Great Bedwyn Prebend, Chisbury,
Collingbourne Kingston, and Barton and Marlborough 1552, Surveys of Barton and
Marlborough, Shalbourne Westcourt, and the Burbages 1574–5, Survey of Colling-
bourne Kingston 1595, Survey of Chisbury 44 Elizabeth (continued until 1639),
Survey of Collingbourne Ducis 1635, Surveys of Barton and Marlborough, Manton,
Collingbourne Kingston, and Shalbourne Westcourt 1637–9, Easton Manor Survey*
circa *1760, Pewsey Notes and Particular 1614, Particular of Mildenhall* circa
*1650, Elizabethan Court Books of Collingbourne Ducis, Court Book of Shalbourne
Eastcourt 1601–14, Court Roll Book 1741–58, Court Roll of Burbage Esturmy 1598.*

WORCESTERSHIRE RECORD OFFICE
EPISCOPAL CONSISTORY COURT OF WORCESTER:
Original Wills, Administrations and Inventories.
BA.54: *Kempsey Court Rolls.*

BA.68: *Woodmanton valuation 1611; Woodmanton lease covenant memorandum 1612.*

BA.104: parcel 6: *Particular of Southend estate at Upton-on-Severn* circa 1655; parcel 37: *Inventory of Henry Bromley of Upton-on-Severn 1667.*

BA.351: bundle 8, no. 1: *Pensham terrier 1794.*

BA.385: parcel 74: *Kempsey indenture 28 April 41 Elizabeth.*

BA.494: *Particulars of Morton Underhill 1648, Lickhill 1656, Dunclent* circa *1660, Great Comberton* circa *1660, and Stoulton cum Wadborough 1653 and 1683–7.*

BA.855: *Inventory of John Sebright of Moore 1592.*

BA.950: parcel 6, no. 131: *sixteenth-century terrier of Great Comberton;* parcel 9, no. 183: *Inventory of Francis Hanford of Wollashall 1643.*

BA.1097: bundle 2, no. 2: *Inventory of Nicholas Higgins of Breedon 1669.*

BA.1176: *Inventories of Edward Hopkins of Norton Curlieu in Budbrook 1681 and Thomas More of Wootton Wawen 1686.*

BA.2358: nos 86a, 131a.

YORK, *see* Borthwick Institute of Historical Research.

INDEX LOCORUM

Damerham, 264
Danbury, 77
Darlington, 336
Dartmoor, 150, 153, 317
Dauntsey, 126
Daventry, 100, 101, 103, 276
Deal, 53, 54
Dean Forest, 147
Deben, River, 77
Deddington, 65
Dedham, 79
Dee, River, 130
Deene, 100
Deeping, 228, 229, 230, 233, 234
Delamere Forest, 129
Denge Beach, 224
Denge Marsh, 134
Deptford, 175
Derby, 209
Desford, 189
Dinton, v. Donington
Dishley, 192, 267, 320, 321, 323
Diss, 295
Ditchampton, 16
Ditteridge, 65
Doddington, 284
Dodsley, 109
Dogsthorpe, 238
Don, River, 232
Donington, 49, 218, 261
Dorchester, 69
Dorking, 54, 179, 248, 303
Dorseland Chase, 147
Dove, River, Staffs, 98, 109
Dove, River, Suffolk, 85
Dover, 53
Dovercourt, 136
Dowdyke, 213, 223, 235, 236
Down Ampney, 216
Downeham, 164
Downton, 285
Dowton Newcourt, 265
Draycott, 121
Drayton Park, 267
Duddington, 99, 101, 188
Dudley, 281
Duggleby, 60
Dunclent, 267
Duncton, 70, 71, 248, 287
Dundry, 278
Dundry Hill, 64
Dungeness, 224
Dunham, 187
Dunkenhalgh, 145, 247
Dunstable, 37
Dunster, 116, 309
Duns Tew, 66, 67
Dunton, in Curdworth, 108
Dutch River, 232

Earith, 231
Easebourne, 287, 301
East Anglia, 36, 72, 92, 301
East Anglian Heights, 56, 59
East Bedfont, 175
Eastbourne, 53
East Chelborough, 218
East Dereham, 271
East Fen, 228, 232, 234
East Grafton, 35
East Greenwich, 225
Eastham, 129
East Ham, 175
East Layton, 112
East Lilling, 186
East Meon, 50
Easton Peirce, 66
East Raynham, 274
East Sutton, 56, 185, 303, 304, 337
Eastwick, 54
East Winch, 273
East Woodhay, 82
Ebbesbourne Wake, 21
Eccleshall, 100, 112
Edge Hill, 64
Edibourne Spring, 186
Edwardstone, 283
Eisey, 216
Efford, 286
Elham, 279
Ellesmere, 130
Ellingthorpe, 112
Elm, 228, 237
Ely, 138, 230, 232
Enborne Valley, 82
Enfield Chase, 173
Enford, 46
Englefield, 265
English Channel, 222
Epping, 178
Epping Forest, 178
Epworth, 25, 213
Erith, 225, 231
Ermine Street, 91
Essex, 84
Esk Valley, 169
Etchingham, 171
Evesham, 114
Evesham Vale, 113
Evington, 94, 95
Ewshott, 285
Exeter, 282
Exeter Vale, 150, 154
Exmoor, 19, 114, 150, 153, 317
Eye, 295
Eyke, 79
Eynsham, 16, 102
Eyton, 253

INDEX PERSONARUM

INDEX RERUM